Discovering Hospitality and Tourism

The World's Greatest Industry

Second Edition

- -

Jack D. Ninemeier
The School of Hospitality Business
Michigan State University

Joe Perdue
William F. Harrah College of Hotel Administration
University of Nevada—Las Vegas

PEARSON
Prentice
Hall

Upper Saddle River, New Jersey 07458

Library of Congress Cataloging-in-Publication Data
  Ninemeier, Jack D.
  Discovering hospitality and tourism: the world's greatest industry/Jack D. Ninemeier, Joe Perdue. —2nd ed.
    p. cm.
  Rev. ed. of: Hospitality operations: careers in the world's greatest industry, © 2005.
  Includes index.
  ISBN 0-13-159199-1
  1. Hospitality industry—Vocational guidance. I. Perdue, Joe. II. Title.
  TX911.3.V62N56 2008
  647.94'023-dc22   2007000866

Editor-in-Chief: Vernon R. Anthony
Senior Editor: William Lawrensen
Managing Editor—Editorial: Judith Casillo
Managing Editor-Production: Mary Carnis
Production Liaison: Jane Bonnell
Production Editor: Linda Zuk, WordCraft, LLC
Manufacturing Manager: Ilene Sanford
Manufacturing Buyer: Cathleen Petersen
Senior Marketing Manager: Leigh Ann Sims
Marketing Coordinator: Alicia Dysert
Marketing Assistant: Les Roberts
Senior Design Coordinator: Miguel Ortiz
Interior Design: Pine Tree Composition, Inc.
Cover Designer: Geoff Cassar/Koala Bear Design
Cover Image: The Fairmont Chateau Lake Louise
Composition: Pine Tree Composition, Inc.
Media Production Project Manager: Lisa Rinaldi
Printer/Binder: Courier - Kendallville
Cover Printer: Coral Graphics

PEARSON
Education

033172

This book is not for sale or distribution in the U.S.A. or Canada

Photo Credits begin on Page 678, which constitutes a continuation of the copyright page.
Previous edition published under the title *Hospitality Operations: Careers in the World's Greatest Industry,* copyright 2005.

Pearson Education LTD.   Pearson Education Australia PTY, Limited
Pearson Education Singapore, Pte. Ltd.   Pearson Education North Asia Ltd.
Pearson Education Canada, Ltd.   Pearson Educación de Mexico, S.A. de C.V.
Pearson Education-Japan   Pearson Education Malaysia, Pte. Ltd.

PEARSON
Prentice
Hall

10 9 8 7 6 5 4 3 2

ISBN-13: 978-0-13-159199-8

ISBN-10:   0-13-159199-1

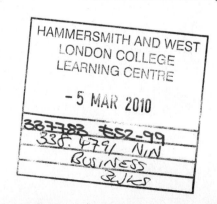

Brief Contents

Contents

PART 2 LODGING OPERATIONS   57

Chapter 4 Overview: Hotels, Hotels, Hotels!   59

Chapter 5 Full-Service Hotels   81

Chapter 6 Limited-Service Hotels   102

PART 3   COMMERCIAL FOODSERVICES OPERATIONS   173

Preface

The travel-tourism-hospitality industry is vast, and it offers seemingly endless and exciting opportunities for those who aspire to a career within it. For example, many persons enjoy the hospitality segment with its numerous types of lodging and foodservices organizations. Others find career-long challenges in recreation and leisure organizations such as private clubs, cruise lines, and amusement and theme parks. The meetings business offers services that are critical to today's organizations whose success depends on the sharing of information.

You are about to begin a fascinating journey that explores the diversity of the world's greatest industry. Along the way you will learn about many exciting professional opportunities. You will also read about persons just a few years older than the average college or university student. They will tell you about their careers and their current positions and, most importantly, they will give you suggestions based on their experience in the industry. Personal insights can be very helpful as you begin considering your own career plans and goals and the professional development activities that will help you attain them.

This book provides basic information about the travel and tourism industry. It does not provide detailed information about any segment (such as lodging) or any department (such as food production or service departments in a restaurant). Other resources and other courses can provide this information, as can the many websites included throughout this book.

Discovering Hospitality and Tourism is written for persons considering a career that involves serving people who are away from home. Perhaps you have already decided to earn a degree in travel-tourism-hospitality management. Maybe you are undecided about a major or are evaluating whether a course of study different from your current one is of interest. You may also be currently working in this industry or another, and you may or may not already have a degree from a technical school, community college, or four-year educational program. In other words, if you want to learn about many career alternatives in the travel-tourism-hospitality industry, this book will help, regardless of your education and work experience background.

FOCUS ON CAREERS

The profession you will be studying is multi-faceted. How do you start to learn about it? What are the opportunities within it? How do you match your personal interests with the alternative positions and career opportunities offered by organizations within the industry's segments? These are among the questions that this book will address. Your journey will begin with an overview of the industry. You will explore how it is organized and quickly note that quality service is a secret of any successful organization within the industry. You will also begin to see that basic management principles are applicable to and can be used by professionals working in any segment of the industry.

Then your journey will become more specific as you look in depth at many different segments of the industry. You will have a close look at careers in several types of lodging properties and commercial (for-profit) restaurants. You will learn about other segments of the industry that also provide tremendous opportunities, including foodservices in education, healthcare, and business and industry; and vending and office coffee services. Next you will study the recreation and leisure industry, including sports and recreation foodservices and private club, cruise line, casino, and amusement and theme park segments. Businesses involved in the management of meetings, conventions, and special events offer many exciting positions, and you will learn about many of them.

After you have explored the segments of the travel-tourism-hospitality industry discussed in this book, you will be better prepared to answer this question: Do I want to work in the industry? If you answer the question yes (or even maybe), you have some additional questions to address: What segment(s) is(are) of most interest? Why? How do I discover career opportunities? How do I get my first professional position in the industry? How do I plan a longer-term career? What tactics help to ensure success in my career? Do I want to work for myself (be an entrepreneur) or for someone else (be an intrapreneur)? Do I want to work domestically or in a position elsewhere in the global hospitality industry (or both)?

The last section of this book will help you to answer these and related questions. You will be on your way to taking charge of your future as you implement the information and ideas presented in this book.

CHAPTER DESIGN HELPS YOU LEARN

Appropriate and accurate chapter content is important to help you to learn. However, it alone is not sufficient. The chapters must be well organized and should have numerous features to ensure that learning is effective. Let's take a look at how the chapters in this book are organized to facilitate learning.

- **Chapter Learning Objectives.** Objectives indicate what you will be able to do after successfully studying the chapter. In other words, they specify chapter content. Objectives are stated at the beginning of each chapter to help you preview the content. Objectives are repeated in the text where information about them is discussed, and they are reviewed at the end of the chapter, where the most important information applicable to each is repeated in a section called Summary of Chapter Learning Objectives.

CHAPTER LEARNING OBJECTIVES

After studying this chapter you will be able to:

1. State features that make resorts and timeshares a special segment of the lodging industry.
2. Describe the types of guests who visit a resort or purchase a unit in a timeshare.
3. Draw an organization chart that shows departments unique to resorts and timeshares.
4. List and briefly describe the duties of selected management positions found within resorts and timeshares.
5. Identify significant current and long-term business challenges that confront managers of resorts and timeshares.
6. Provide an overview of condo-hotels and discuss the financial and marketing issues that have significantly increased their popularity.

- **Feedback from the Real World.** Each chapter begins with a situation and/or a presentation of everyday issues applicable to the topic being discussed. You are encouraged to think about these questions and issues as you read through the chapter. Then, at the conclusion of the chapter, an experienced manager or other applicable expert provides responses to the questions that were raised. This allows you to compare your responses with those of the expert. Consider these perspectives and use your analysis to expand your knowledge and to influence your thinking.

FEEDBACK FROM THE REAL WORLD

Trina and Jeffers are both about to graduate from a two-year community college program located in the suburbs of a large city. They are interested in the foodservices industry, and both think they might like to work in the noncommercial segment of the industry. Here are some of their thoughts about factors that may affect their employment decisions after graduation:

Factor	Trina	Jeffers
Preferred location	Local area	Anywhere; no preference
Additional hospitality education	No (not now)	Maybe
Good technical training	Yes	Yes
Career that will always have day to day operating responsibilities	Yes	No
Technical help when working through decisions	No (wants to be in charge)	Yes (concerned about the impact of a bad decision)
Flexibility	Probably would like to stay with the same organization and enjoy the "perks" of seniority	Yes; would consider a different position with the same or a different organization
Compensation (salary and benefits)	Better-than-average because of the belief that she is better than average	Better-than-average because of the belief that he is better than average

Based on their own personal interests, how should Trina and Jeffers assess the type of organization (self-operated or contract management

Think about your responses to this question. Then review one process of analysis in the Feedback from the Real World sec-

- **Glossary.** Every industry, including the travel-tourism-hospitality industry and the specific segments within it, uses words with meanings that may be unique and/or different from common usage. More than 600 of these terms are used and defined throughout this book, including approximately 75 that are new to this edition. Definitions are provided at the point of use in the chapter, and a glossary at the end of the book lists them in alphabetical order. You will need to learn these terms and use them correctly as you communicate in the people-intensive industry within which you will work.

Glossary

a la carte dining room (restaurant) a foodservice operation in which guests order from a menu featuring individually priced items
a la carte menu a menu in which food items are individually priced
account the contract management company's term for the organization that has retained it to operate the foodservices program; also called *client*
account location a site where a vending company's machines are located; a large account may have banks of vending machines in several (or more) places throughout its location
account retention activities undertaken to ensure

allocation the process of distributing revenues earned and/or expenses incurred between departments on a basis that approximates each department's share of the revenues and/or expenses
all-suite hotels lodging properties in which all guest rooms are suites
alternative beverages water and a wide variety of mostly noncarbonated beverages, including juices and teas and a wide range of newly popular flavored drinks
amenities hotel products and services designed to appeal to guests
American burlesque a creative mix of theatrical entertainment with sensual overtones; in base, a

- **Graphics! Graphics! Graphics!** This book contains several hundred photos that help set the context for the information being discussed. Liberal use is also made of diagrams to help show relationships among the concepts under discussion. Other information associated with the chapter topic is presented as boxed material, which allows it to stand on its own to round out the discussion.

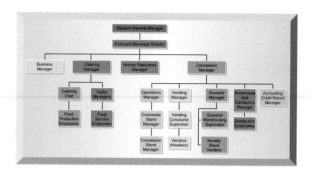

- **Challenges! Challenges!** Where appropriate, chapters conclude with a discussion of the challenges confronting those working within the industry. These discussions will be of interest because this book's readers will be among those in the next generation of decision makers and problem solvers who will address these concerns. Want to know what you will do as a manager in a particular segment? Look at the challenges, because your task on the job will be, in large measure, to resolve these issues.

> **CHALLENGES! CHALLENGES!**
> --
> Not surprisingly, two challenges are of interest or concern to employees of the amusement and theme park industry, just as they are to managers in almost all other segments of the hospitality industry: recruiting and retaining a sufficient number of employees at all organizational levels and exploiting technology to use it most cost effectively.
>
> However, these issues are a special concern of this segment because of the significant growth forecasted. As more people around the world gain additional leisure time, they will be looking for opportunities to spend it. This, in turn, will likely lead to an increase in the number of theme parks in loca-

- **Rising Star Profiles and Hospitality Leaders Profiles.** Many chapters contain a Rising Star Profile, in which a young hospitality industry professional shares his or her background and excitement about a specific industry segment. Other chapters feature a Hospitality Leader Profile, in which an executive with extensive experience provides meaningful career advice to those learning about specific industry segments.

HOSPITALITY LEADER PROFILE

Harold Skripsky

Harold Skripsky turned his entrepreneurial spirit into many successful family entertainment businesses. He is a founding father of the International Association for the Leisure and Entertainment Industry (IALEI). Today, one of his earliest ventures, the Enchanted Castle, is recognized among the premier family entertainment centers in the United States.

Skripsky started his career with McDonald's

national levels. At the national level, Skripsky and his partner became the third inductees in the SBA National Hall of Fame. Their award was based on a successful business history, efficient management of operations, and a commitment to their business community.

That same year, Skripsky became a founding member of the board of directors and charter member of the International Family Entertainment Center Association (IAFEC). He became its president in 1996/1997, has chaired numerous committees, and stays active in the association.

In 1994, Skripsky and his partner sold the Enchanted Castle to Discovery Zone. He was appointed vice-president for operations to create and develop a Family Entertainment Center Division. In 1996, Skripsky repurchased the Enchanted Castle and focused his attentions on its growth. In early November 1997, he sold the business to Ogden Corporation, and Skripsky then worked with Ogden for three years in its Entertainment Division.

In 2000, he served as the driving force and

- **Mastering Your Knowledge.** Questions posed in this section of each chapter encourage you to consider and apply information that you learned in the chapter. (Supplemental course material allows you to compare your responses to others with experience in the hospitality industry.)

MASTERING YOUR KNOWLEDGE

Discuss the following questions.

1. How do you think theme park officials assess the types of attractions, entertainment, and special events that comprise the experiences to be offered to park visitors?
2. What do you think are the primary factors that influence whether a park visitor's experience is memorable?

3. How might you defend the need to increase admission (gate) prices to visitors who complain about the alleged high charges for young family members?
4. What, if any, are the most interesting aspects of a career in amusement and theme parks that are most attractive to you?

- **Learn from the Internet.** You will be asked to check out several websites in each chapter, but you are encouraged to learn on your own, starting with the locations that are noted. Questions posed in this feature will enable you to maximize your learning as you read through and study the websites.

LEARN FROM THE INTERNET

1. Check out the websites of the following time-share exchange companies:
   - Resort Condominiums International (RCI): www.rci.com
   - Interval International (II): www.intervalworld.com
   - Disney Vacation Club: www.disneyvacation club.com

   Learn about some of the properties they represent. How does an exchange program actually work? What are some advantages to a unit owner of an exchange? What are some potential disadvantages?

the United States and Canada, Bermuda, the Caribbean, Mexico, Europe, the South Pacific, Central and South America, Africa, Asia, and the Far East. Review several sites, and answer the following questions:

- What themes (general messages) do the resorts suggest to readers?
- What strengths do they emphasize as inducements to visit?
- What role does guest service appear to play in their market positioning?

3. Check out the website for the Condo Hotel Center: www.condohotelcenter.com. What are

- Throughout the chapter, numerous special information boxes provide supportive information for the topic under discussion.

WHO STAYS IN HOTELS?

Persons staying in hotels can be classified according to the purpose of their travel:

Business or corporate (individuals)	Long-stay guests
Business or corporate (groups)	Airline-related guests
Convention or association groups	Government or military guests
Leisure travelers	Regional "getaway" guests

- Two other features are included in many chapters to provide relevant information and retain readers' interest:

  "Check It Out" references alert readers to website locations that provide supplemental information about the topic being discussed.

  "Did You Know?" anecdotes inform readers about little-known and/or interesting aspects of the chapter subject matter.

SUPPLEMENTS

The comprehensive supplement package includes the following:

- *TestGen,* featuring multiple-choice and True/False questions for each chapter, thus enabling instructors to select questions and create their own tests.
- *Companion Website,* located at www.prenhall.com/ninemeier, with the following:

  Students. Learning objectives for each chapter and PowerPoint presentation

  Instructors. PowerPoint presentation, instructor's outline with detailed content listing, teaching suggestions to accent class lectures, and suggested responses to questions and issues in the Mastering Your Knowledge section at the end of each chapter. Additional student activities and student study questions are also included.

Online instructor materials are available to qualified instructors for downloading. To access supplementary materials online, instructors need to request an instructor access code. Go to **www.prenhall.com,** click the **Instructor Resource Center** link, and then click **Register Today** for an instructor access code. Within 48 hours after registering, you will receive a confirming e-mail including an instructor access code. Once you have received your code, go to the site and log on for full instructions on downloading the materials you wish to use.

ACKNOWLEDGMENTS

The authors wish to thank many individuals whose help, beginning with the concept and continuing through the writing and review of content information, has been critical to the book's development.

First, we are indebted to the following individuals who authored selected chapters:

Duncan Dickson, Assistant Professor, Rosen College of Hospitality Management, University of Central Florida, Orlando

Vincent H. Eade, Professor and Founding Director of the UNLV International Gaming Institute, William F. Harrah College of Hotel Administration, University of Nevada, Las Vegas

Jeff Ellsworth, Assistant Professor, The School of Hospitality Business, Michigan State University, East Lansing

Bernard Fried, Associate Professor, Tourism and Convention Department, William F. Harrah College of Hotel Administration, University of Nevada, Las Vegas

Authella Collins Hawks, Director, Student Industry Resource Center, The School of Hospitality Business, Michigan State University, East Lansing

David Hayes, author and 30-year veteran of the hospitality and hospitality education industries

Curtis Lease, District Manager, ARAMARK Business Services, Houston, TX

Curtis Love, Associate Professor, Tourism and Convention Department, William F. Harrah College of Hotel Administration, University of Nevada, Las Vegas

Pat Merl, Adjunct Professor, Tourism & Convention Department, William F. Harrah College of Hotel Administration, University of Nevada, Las Vegas

Kathleen Nelson, Assistant Professor, Tourism and Convention Department, William F. Harrah College of Hotel Administration, University of Nevada, Las Vegas

Guy Procopio, Concessions Manager, MSU Concessions, Michigan State University, East Lansing

Larry Ross, Anne & Bill France Professor of Business and Coordinator of Graduate Program in Business, Department of Business and Economics, Florida Southern College, Lakeland, Florida

Robert Ross, Vice-President, Ross and Associates, Grand Rapids, MI

Theda Rudd, Visiting Instructor, The School of Hospitality Business, Michigan State University, East Lansing

John Sweeney, Chairman and CEO, Global Resorts, Las Vegas, NV

Julie Tkach, The School of Hospitality Business, Michigan State University, East Lansing

Robert Woods, Professor, Department of Hotel Management, William F. Harrah College of Hotel Administration, University of Nevada, Las Vegas

Second, special thanks to those who reviewed major components of the book: Roger Gerard, Shasta College; Carol Kizer, Columbus State Community College; Lynda Martin, Oklahoma State University; Chris Roberts, University of Massachusetts; and Nancy Swanger, Washington State University. And to the reviewers of the second edition: Geralyn Farley, Purdue University-Calumet; Samer Hassan, Johnson & Wales University-Florida; Bo Hu, San Francisco State University; Jeffrey P. Ivory, St. Louis Community College; Carol Kizer, Columbus State Community College; Paul Michael Klein, St. Thomas University; Chang Lee, New Mexico State University; Mary Nunaley, Volunteer State Community College; Gail Sammons, University of Nevada-Las Vegas; Stephen B. Shirling, Indiana University of Pennsylvania; and Sheryl A. Wittenbach, Stephen F. Austin State University.

Third, we would like to acknowledge the assistance of the following experts who contributed to chapters in this book: Ken Hisey, General Manager, Embers Restaurant, Mt. Pleasant, MI; John Rendall, General Manager, Support Services, ARAMARK Master Facility Service, Houston, TX; Robert Lippert, Chef Emeritus, Embers Restaurant, Mt. Pleasant, MI; Dr. Patti Shock, Professor and Department Chair, Tourism and Convention Department, William F. Harrah College of Hotel Administration, Las Vegas, NV; Roz Jaffer, formerly Operations Supervisor, Auxiliary Services Division, Department of Housing and Foodservices, Michigan State University, East Lansing, MI; Kathy Kane, formerly Director of Food and Nutrition Services, Fowlerville, Michigan, Community Schools; and Craig Hesch, CFO, A. H. Management Group, Chicago, IL.

Fourth, the real world was brought into this book by more than 75 hospitality industry professionals who contributed their comments and advice. There is an old saying: "If you want to get something done, ask the person who is the busiest to do it!" We found this to be true. We salute these persons who took time out from their work to make contributions that may influence those in the next generation of hospitality managers.

Fifth, several persons behind the scenes did much work to bring this project to fruition. We especially thank Leilani Ninemeier for her assistance in developing the manuscript. We also acknowledge the significant and ongoing help received from Judith Casillo, William Lawrensen, and Vernon Anthony of Prentice Hall, who have helped us in numerous ways (some of which we probably do not even know about!).

Finally, we want our family and friends to know that we really appreciate their encouragement, support, and assistance as this project evolved.

Jack D. Ninemeier
Hilo, Hawaii

Joe Perdue
Las Vegas, Nevada

Part 1

INDUSTRY OVERVIEW

Travel and Tourism and Hospitality
Services for Those Away from Home

1

The journey of many travelers begins at the airport.

CHAPTER LEARNING OBJECTIVES

After studying this chapter you will be able to:

1. Distinguish between the travel and tourism and the hospitality industries.
2. Suggest how travel patterns have evolved.
3. List and briefly describe the types of organizations in the three segments that comprise the hospitality industry:
   - Accommodations (lodging)
   - Foodservices
   - Other hospitality operations
4. Explain the difference between commercial and noncommercial foodservice operations.
5. Discuss two basic ways that noncommercial foodservice programs can be operated.
6. Review critical issues that will confront the industry in, at least, the short-term future.

FEEDBACK FROM THE REAL WORLD

In this chapter you will learn of the many professional opportunities within the diverse travel/tourism/hospitality industry. What can students do while still in school to learn as much as possible about the industry while keeping their options open about the segment in which they will begin their careers?

As you read this chapter, think about your answer to this question and then get feedback from the real world at the end of the chapter.

OBJECTIVE 1
Distinguish between the travel and tourism and the hospitality industries.

The industry that you are about to study is a challenge to define because it is large and complex. As you will learn, the numerous segments within the industry make it possible for almost anyone to enjoy a progressively responsible career within it. In this chapter we will focus our attention on this question: "What exactly is today's travel/tourism/hospitality industry?"

LET'S DEFINE TERMS

travel and tourism industry refers to all businesses that cater to the needs of the traveling public

hospitality industry refers primarily to organizations that provide lodging or accommodations and foodservices for people when they are away from their homes

Some people believe the terms **travel and tourism industry** and **hospitality industry** mean the same thing. For the purposes of this book, however, we will make an important distinction. The travel and tourism industry refers to all businesses that cater to the needs of the traveling public; the hospitality industry refers primarily to organizations that provide lodging or accommodations and foodservices for people when they are away from their homes. To clarify the distinction between the travel and tourism and the hospitality industries, look at Exhibit 1.1.

Note:

Although organizations offering some type of accommodations and/or foodservices represent the majority of those in the hospitality industry, the diversity

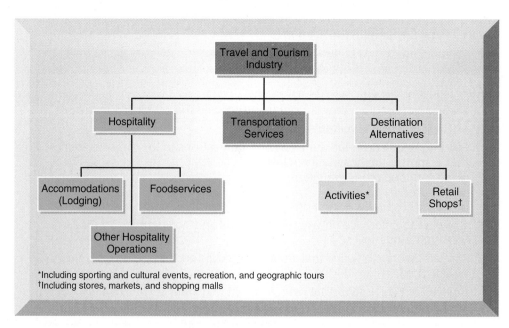

EXHIBIT 1.1
Components of the Travel and Tourism Industry

of the industry makes it difficult to develop a simple definition. For example, businesses offering conference center services and meeting, exposition (trade show), and entertainment management can also be considered part of the hospitality industry and will be discussed in this book.

People traveling away from home need accommodations and transportation services that, obviously, nontravelers do not need. However, businesses that provide foodservices and destination activities offer products and services that can be shared by the traveling and nontraveling public. As well, lodging properties offer space for foodservices, meetings, and entertainment that are utilized by nontravelers. Also, other hospitality operations, such as private clubs, casinos, cruise ships, vending, and theme parks provide hospitality (lodging and/or foodservices) options for many travelers and nontravelers.

Our study does not address the entire travel and tourism industry as pictured in Exhibit 1.1. For example, many businesses enable tourists to enjoy activities on their vacations and holidays. These include tour bus operations and companies that offer biking, hiking, fishing, climbing, diving, and numerous other recreational activities.

Travel consultants (agents) assist their clients with travel, lodging, and related arrangements. Travel wholesalers arrange trips, including numerous excursions and other activities, and sell them to individuals and/or groups. Travel coordinators work for large business and governmental organizations and may make arrangements for employees who must travel as part of their work responsibilities.

Convention and Business Bureau (CVB) personnel market their communities to those considering meeting sites and to individual travelers. They also help coordinate the needs of groups that host meetings, conferences, and conventions in their areas.

Positions in the transportation services segment, as identified in Exhibit 1.1, also provide exciting opportunities. Examples include airport terminal managers and airline flight crew, gate agents, and reservations and passenger service positions. Rental car, railroad, ferry, and cruise ship lines (discussed in Chapter 23) businesses provide additional examples of the wide array of transportation-related positions in the travel and tourism industry.

<table>
<tr><td>**OBJECTIVE 2**
Suggest how travel patterns have evolved.</td></tr>
</table>

We will look in-depth at two segments (accommodations and foodservices) that are an integral part of the hospitality industry. We will also study another segment (other hospitality operations), which includes segments such as theme parks, cruise lines, casinos, and recreation and leisure services that contain elements of both hospitality and travel and tourism. Finally, we will present an overview of the meetings business (meeting management, exhibition management, and special events management).

TRAVEL PATTERNS ARE EVOLVING

Traditionally, travelers could generally be divided into two types: those traveling for business and those traveling for pleasure. Today, however, there is often a blurring of this distinction.

Yesterday, persons frequently traveled on short business trips and relatively longer family vacations. Today, increasingly, business travelers take family members to conferences and conventions,

Many cruise ship passengers arrive in or near the port city by air and are bused to the ship.

EXHIBIT 1.2
Travel Patterns Have
Changed

	Traditional Travel Patterns		Modern Travel Patterns	
Traveler	Travel Goal	Travel Type	Travel Goal	Travel Type
Business	Business activities without family	Short trips	Business activities without family	Short trips
			Business meetings with family	Long trips
Pleasure	Family trips	Long vacations	Family holidays	Long weekends

which extends the length of many business trips. The length of pleasure trips has decreased and, for many, involves several long weekends (often prompted by low-cost **cyberfares** offered by the airlines) throughout the year. These differences are reviewed in Exhibit 1.2.

The changes in travel patterns have not lessened the need for the products and services provided by organizations in the hospitality industry. Hotels and restaurants must still meet the needs of both those who travel and those who do not. However, it has become more of a challenge to do this as consumers have become more sophisticated and as competitive hospitality organizations increasingly find more creative ways to serve their guests.

cyberfares low-cost airfares (sometimes packaged with accommodations and rental cars) offered by airlines to increase business during slow travel periods such as weekends when there is minimal business travel

SPOTLIGHT ON ORGANIZATIONS
- -

Exhibit 1.3 suggests the wide range of organizations comprising the hospitality industry as we have defined it. It identifies many of the major categories of organizations within each segment of the industry. Let's look at these briefly now; the remainder of this book will consider more specifically the many types of organizations within each of the three segments.

ACCOMMODATIONS (LODGING)
- -

amenities hotel products and services designed to appeal to guests

concierge the individual(s) within a full-service hotel responsible for providing guests with detailed information regarding local dining and attractions, as well as assisting with related guest needs

hotel a for-profit business that rents sleeping rooms and often provides other amenities such as food and beverage services, swimming pools and exercise rooms, meeting spaces, business centers, and concierge services; also referred to as motel, motor hotel, or motor inn

Where can people safely sleep when they are away from home? The answer to this question will, in part, suggest the array of opportunities that the traveling public has for rest at the end of a day. However, as you will learn later in this book, many of today's lodging properties remain competitive by offering much more than a safe night's sleep. **Amenities** can include food and beverage service alternatives, swimming pools and exercise rooms, meeting spaces, business centers, and **concierge** services to help travelers make many types of arrangements within the community. The term *amenities* can also refer to within-room giveaways such as soaps and shampoos.

Among the types of organizations in the accommodations (lodging) segment of the hospitality industry are the following:

Hotels

A **hotel** may be large or small, relatively inexpensive or more highly priced, and guests may drive up to the front door of their unit or take an elevator up many stories to their room. Hotels may or may not offer foodservices and other amenities, including those just noted. Lodging properties may be located

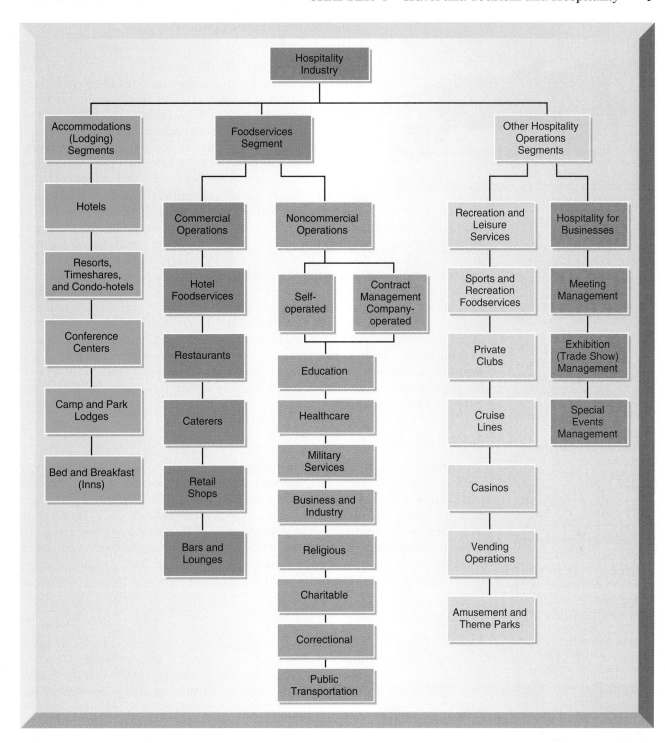

EXHIBIT 1.3
Close Look at the Hospitality Industry

along a highway, in a city or suburb, or at an airport location. They may be independently owned and operated or may be owned by an investor who has purchased a **franchise** for a popular brand and who has hired a hotel **management company** for daily operational responsibilities. While at least one type of hotel (extended-stay) markets to those desiring accommodations for several weeks or longer, most hotel properties generally rent rooms for one week or less.

franchise   an arrangement whereby one party (the brand) allows another (the hotel owners) to use its logo, name, systems, and resources in exchange for a fee

management company   an organization that operates a hotel for a fee; also sometimes called a contract company

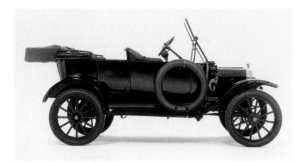

Autos like this enabled the public to begin to travel extensively.

resorts full-service hotels with additional attractions to make them a primary destination for travelers

full-service hotel a hotel is considered full-service when it provides guests with extensive food and beverage products and services

timeshare properties lodging properties selling a part ownership (for example, one week within a specified time period) in a unit within the property; also called interval ownership

condominium (or condo) a lodging property in which units are individually owned; in some condominium properties, units can be placed into a rental pool with resulting guest fees split between the owner and the company managing the units

condo-hotel a hotel with traditional public spaces and services in which some or all of the guest rooms are provided by persons who can rent their units as part of the hotel and receive a portion of the unit's rental revenues for doing so

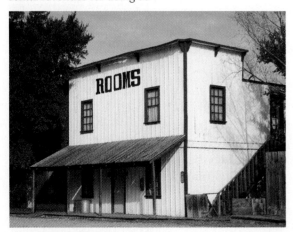

Do you think hotels have changed?

Resorts, Timeshares/Condominiums, and Condo–hotels

Most **resorts** offer all the amenities of a **full-service hotel** and enough additional attractions to make them a primary destination for travelers. For example, resorts may feature golf, spas, skiing, horseback riding, tennis, and oceanfront or other attractions sufficient to entertain guests for several days or longer. **Timeshare properties** (also called interval ownership properties) allow persons to purchase partial-year (usually in one-week intervals) ownership of a lodging property. Buyers then have access to that property for the same time period each year. Typically, purchase prices differ depending on the month or season for which the timeshare is purchased. A week's ownership during the winter months in Florida will cost more than a week's ownership in July; one week in a property in Maine during the summer is more expensive than a week in February. Once purchased, the buyer or others whom he or she desires will have access to a room in that property during that time period every year. Organizations such as Resorts Condominiums International (RCI) have established global networks that allow interval owners to trade their ownership on an annual basis with someone else in another property in another part of the world at the same or another time of the year. Point systems are also becoming popular; they allow timeshare owners to utilize traditional lodging properties for their timeshare.

Condominiums

A **condominium,** or condo is a complex in which owners can place their lodging unit on the organization's rental plan when they (the owners) are not occupying the unit. A management company markets the condominium complex, including the owner's unit on a rental plan, collects guest rental fees, and hires personnel to provide housekeeping and other services during and between guest visits. In turn, the management company is paid a fee taken from the condo rentals for these and related services. The remaining guest rental fees are paid to the unit's owner.

Condo-hotels

A **condo-hotel** is a relatively new lodging concept. As implied by its name, it is a hotel with traditional public spaces and services in which some or all of the guest rooms are purchased by persons who can rent units as part of the hotel and receive a portion of the unit's rental revenues for doing so. Rooms are sold to owners who can then use them as much (or as little) as they desire. Condo-hotels became popular in the early 2000s when traditional hotels suffered from excess capacity, and their owners and managers found a new source of revenue for the available rooms.

Conference Centers

Professionals in conference centers (also called professional development centers or executive education centers) assist organizations by planning meetings for their members. Many conference centers are operated by postsecondary institutions that work with associations and large companies to develop and offer specialized programs. These centers may also offer programs to individuals desiring to learn about a more general topic. Large corporations may have in-house conference facilities in headquarters or other offices or retreats in rural or secluded areas. Foodservices range from those necessary for coffee breaks to full sit-down meal service.

Camp and Park Lodges

Many states and the federal government offer sleeping accommodations for visitors to parks and other nature conservatories that are much more formalized than just "a tent and a campfire." Sometimes operated by management companies, these facilities offer accommodations that are frequently as nice as those offered elsewhere in the area.

Bed and Breakfast (Inns)

These units, often called B&Bs, are generally very small (one-to-several guestroom) properties owned or managed by persons living on-site. Guests sleep in a room that is part of the owners' house and generally receive a breakfast meal, the cost of which is included in the guest room's rental price. These businesses are, in fact, the modern-day equivalent of the home owner of ancient times who opened his or her home to greet travelers who needed food and a night's rest before continuing on their journey.

FOODSERVICES

Travelers must eat while on their journey. They often do so in many of the same foodservice operations that are utilized by community residents who dine out for business and/or social purposes.

A wide variety of foodservice businesses exists to generate profits from the sale of their products and services to travelers and area residents. These are referred to as **commercial foodservice operations**. By contrast, another basic type of foodservice, **noncommercial foodservices**, is not in business primarily to produce, serve, and generate profits from food and beverage products. These two basic types of organizations make up the foodservices segment of the hospitality industry. With these definitions in mind, let's review the types of for-profit and not-for-profit foodservice operations.

Commercial Foodservices

Exhibit 1.3 identifies several types of commercial foodservice businesses.

Hotel Foodservices

Dining alternatives in hotels include those offered in coffee shops, dining rooms, and banquet operations and through room service. Hotel foodservice operations are classified as commercial because their goal is to make a profit that supplements that from the rental of sleeping and meeting accommodations.

Restaurants

A **restaurant** is a for-profit foodservice operation whose primary business involves the sale of food and beverage products to individuals and small groups of guests. Restaurants may have few or many seats; they may be freestanding or located within a hotel, resort, or shopping mall. They may or

---

conference centers organizations that assist associations, businesses, and individuals to meet desired continuing education needs

camp and park lodges sleeping accommodations in parks and other nature conservatories owned by governmental agencies and often operated by for-profit management companies

bed and breakfast (inns) very small (one-to-several guest room) properties owned or managed by persons living on-site; these businesses typically offer at least one meal daily; also called B&B

OBJECTIVE 4
Explain the difference between commercial and noncommercial foodservice operations.

commercial foodservice operations foodservices offered in hotels, restaurants, and other organizations whose primary financial goal involves generation of profits from the sale of food and beverage products

noncommercial foodservices foodservice operations whose financial goal does not involve generating profits from the sale of food and beverage products; also called institutional foodservices, on-site foodservices, and managed foodservices

OBJECTIVE 3
List and briefly describe the types of organizations in the three segments that comprise the hospitality industry.

restaurant a for-profit foodservice operation whose primary business involves the sale of food and beverage products to individuals and small groups of guests

RISING STAR PROFILE

Chuck Day
Revenue Management
Marriott International
Detroit Market

Using Technology to Help Guests

Chuck began working for Marriott Corporation in 1991 after receiving his university degree in hospitality business. He has held positions in sales, reservations, front office, and telecommunications and has worked at the downtown Chicago Residence Inn, the downtown Chicago Courtyard, and the O'Hare–Rosemont Residence Inn.

When he worked as a front-office manager in a 1298-room property, his typical workday (if there is one) was made up of voice mail, e-mail and meetings! E-mail was the primary method of communication, and he spent approximately 30 to 40 percent of his time reading and sending e-mail messages. Another 40 percent of his time was spent in the hotel lobby and in front-office areas, interacting with associates and guests. Most of the rest of his time in his workday was spent in meetings.

Chuck notes that his greatest operating challenge relates to finding and retaining great staff members. His priority guest-related challenge focuses on improving the hotel's ability to satisfy guests and to increasingly build guest loyalty to his organization.

Chuck was asked about his most unforgettable moment: "Being part of the opening management team for the O'Hare–Rosemont Residence Inn. Building a hotel from scratch is one of the most rewarding experiences I have had in my work life." When asked about a negative experience, Chuck responded, "I learned much on one occasion by realizing that I was not doing a specific job task as well as I could."

Chuck has some insight into how full-service hotels will be different in the future: "First, technology will play an increasingly greater role in all aspects of the business. It will improve staff productivity in tracking and reporting guest preferences and problem resolutions. I envision a traveler staying in one Marriott property on the West Coast who requests an amenity in his room. The guest will then travel to the East Coast in the same week and that amenity will be available in his or her new room.

"Hotel guests will be able to customize the environment of their sleeping rooms by providing profile information about desired room temperature, preferred television channels, and preordered room service, among many other services. Voice and data over Internet Protocol [communication services transmitted by the Internet, rather than a public-switched telephone network] will become the norm. Guests will be able to work from any hotel room in the world and will have phone calls and e-mails routed to them. They will have access to their information network. In effect, their office will travel with them! I also think that, in the future, activities designed to build and retain guest loyalties will be the driving force behind almost all industry initiatives."

When asked what, if anything, Chuck would do differently in his career he has a quick response: "Nothing! It has been a great ride so far, and I look forward to what is around the next bend."

Chuck's advice to young people considering a hospitality career is very helpful: "Make sure that you never lose touch with your personal happiness. People in the hospitality industry spend too much of their lives at work to not be happy while they are there! Your value as a human being is not measured by the job you do or by the position you hold or by the amount of money you make. It is measured by the person you are from the perspective of the people who are around you!"

---

may not serve alcoholic beverages in addition to food and may have extensive or limited menus. They may offer fine dining at high prices (gourmet food served by highly experienced service staff to guests seated at tables covered with tablecloths and set with the finest tableware), or they may be quick-service properties with lower prices (food served at a counter by a cashier). They may offer a theme such as a spaceship, Italian villa, or jungle setting to provide a complementary dining environment or, alternatively, they may only offer down-home cooking in a dining area with modest tables and chairs and/or booths and counters. Restaurants typically serve guests on-site; however, drive-through (in quick-service) and carryout (in many table-service) restaurants offer alternative service methods.

Caterers

Some foodservice operations produce food for off-site consumption. These can range from a takeout counter in the restaurant or a food pickup area in a restaurant's parking lot for food orders called in earlier,

Sunbathers in Acapulco near a high-rise hotel

to drive-up windows in quick-service properties. These variations, however, differ from the more traditional catering businesses. **Caterers** typically produce food in their kitchen for transport off-site to a customer's location for service to hundreds (or more!) of guests. Some caterers also have dining space available for group service at the facility where the food is prepared.

Retail Shops

A wide variety of retail stores selling a wide variety of products may offer food and beverages to their shoppers. These range from large department stores offering sit-down meals, to grocery stores with significant square footage devoted to foodservice outlets, to convenience food stores and gasoline stations with counter space (or even larger areas) utilized to sell beverages, snacks, cold and hot sandwiches, and other items that were traditionally most frequently offered only by restaurants.

Bars and Lounges

Bars featuring the service of alcoholic beverages to guests seated at counters and **lounges** offering table-service alcoholic beverages generate more revenues from the sale of alcoholic beverages than they do from the sale of food products. However, some bars and lounges offer a limited menu of **short-order food items** requiring only limited production equipment, food ingredients, and cooking experience to produce.

Noncommercial Foodservices

You have learned that noncommercial foodservices are offered by organizations that, unlike their commercial foodservice counterparts, do not exist primarily to produce, serve, and generate profits from the sale of food and beverage products. Most noncommercial foodservice operations

caterers for-profit businesses that produce food for groups at off-site locations; some caterers have banquet space available for on-site use by groups desiring foodservices

bars for-profit businesses serving alcoholic beverages to guests seated at a counter (bar); limited table service may also be available

lounges for-profit businesses serving alcoholic beverages to guests seated at tables; a small counter (bar) may also be available

short-order food items food products that require only limited production equipment, food ingredients, and cooking experience to produce

Kenyatta Conference Center in Nairobi, Kenya

Interior of a restaurant

OBJECTIVE 5
Discuss two basic ways that noncommercial foodservice programs can be operated.

noncommercial foodservices (self-operated) a type of noncommercial foodservice operation in which the program is managed and operated by the organization's employees

noncommercial foodservices (contract management company-operated) a type of noncommercial foodservice operation in which the program is managed and operated by a for-profit management company

OBJECTIVE 3
List and briefly describe the types of organizations in the three segments that comprise the hospitality industry.

are not typically available to the traveling public; however, those available to travelers using public transportation such as airplanes and trains are an exception.

Noncommercial foodservices include those operated by educational institutions offering meals to, for example, primary, high school, and postsecondary students and healthcare facilities offering meals to hospital patients and those in nursing homes and retirement communities. Military services must feed their troops, business and industry organizations must provide meals to their employees while at work, and religious and charitable organizations feed their own members and those within the community who may be unable to buy food for themselves. Correctional facilities offer another example of an organization that must provide foodservices as part of their purpose, and airline and train passengers may receive meals while en route to their destinations.

There are two basic ways in which noncommercial foodservices can be operated:

- They may be **self-operated**; that is, the organization may employ a foodservice director and staff to manage and operate the program.
- They may be operated by a **contract management company**; that is, the organization may negotiate and contract with a for-profit management company to provide foodservices for the organization.

The use of contract management companies to operate noncommercial foodservices is becoming increasingly popular. Because contract management companies exist to make a profit, the distinction between commercial (for profit) and noncommercial (not for profit) foodservices is blurred.

OTHER HOSPITALITY OPERATIONS

To this point, we have discussed accommodations (lodging) and foodservice businesses. Other operations that we will also study in this book offer foodservices, so they are considered part of the traditional hospitality industry; but they also offer features that appeal to community residents and/or travelers, so they may be considered part of the travel and tourism industry.

Convenience stores increasingly compete with traditional restaurants for foodservice purchases.

Sports and Recreation Foodservices

Food and beverages served at tableside in restaurants overlooking an athletic stadium's playing field, snack bars, and products transported to fans at their seats are examples of this segment of the industry.

Private Clubs

Private membership organizations **private clubs** of numerous types exist for persons enjoying common interests. These include country (golf) clubs, city clubs, university clubs, yacht clubs, and military clubs. Clubs almost always offer some type of foodservices (ranging from very limited to very elaborate), and some also offer lodging accommodations for their members and invited guests.

Casinos

Casinos offering gaming opportunities are operated in the United States by commercial business corporations and Native American Indian organizations. Food and beverages and often lodging accommodations are part of the total entertainment package offered to casino visitors.

Cruise Lines

Cruise ships (very huge and very modern "cities on the seas") typically offer a wide range of food and beverage services, from fine dining to snack bars, fast-food outlets, and bars and lounges. Sleeping cabin accommodations are also an integral part of the experience being sold to passengers.

Vending Operations

Vending services offer food and beverage products at times when and/or in places where it is not convenient to offer **manual food and beverage services** to those being served.

Amusement and Theme Parks

Theme parks are generally very large recreational sites that are tourist destinations. Examples with which many people are familiar are Disneyland (in California) and Disney World, Epcot, and Universal Studios (in Florida). Many theme parks offer on-site hotels and numerous food and beverage outlets, ranging from sit-down restaurants with extensive menus, to quick-service outlets with limited menus, to food carts selling desserts and/or beverages and other items.

Meeting Management

Large associations and business organizations typically employ meeting planners to organize meetings, contact speakers, negotiate and select meeting sites, and attend to the seemingly endless number of details that occur as sessions are planned and conducted. Other professional

Fine dining at 30,000 feet

private clubs private membership organizations of numerous types that exist for persons enjoying common interests; examples include country (golf) clubs, city clubs, university clubs, yacht clubs, and military clubs

casinos a property that offers gaming opportunities for its guests; many casinos also offer food and beverage services and lodging accommodations for the convenience of their visitors

vending services food and beverage services that utilize equipment (vending machines) to dispense products

manual food and beverage services food and beverage operations in which food and beverages are served to consumers by foodservice employees

theme parks very large recreational sites that are tourist destinations

Sports and recreational foodservices represent big business!

meeting planners provide specialized services for a number of external clients to assure that their meetings are successful.

Exhibitions (Trade Shows)

Many associations schedule meetings and conventions for their members and invite suppliers to their industry to exhibit products and services. A significant number of hours are frequently allocated for exhibits, and a large percentage of the budget of many associations is derived from suppliers renting display booths at these trade shows. Expositions are an integral part of the meeting business, which, itself, is an integral part of the hospitality industry.

Special Events Management

Large casinos and hotels are examples of organizations within the hospitality industry that utilize popular entertainers, theatrical performances, and other talent in an effort to attract guests to their business. Events such as sporting contests, weddings, anniversaries, and holidays create opportunities

---

THERE ARE JUST TOO MANY OPPORTUNITIES!

After reading this far, you might be overwhelmed at the wide variety of organizations and the positions within them that are available to one aspiring to a career in the tourism and hospitality industries. However, numerous other positions are available for those with special interests, and many will be explored throughout this book. Whatever your interests and wherever you might like to live, there are likely to be several (or more) professional alternatives for you to consider. Also, remember that many (most?) people change jobs and organizations as their career path evolves. It is probably the rule rather than the exception that tourism and hospitality professionals work in organizations in several (or more) hospitality segments during their career.

DID YOU KNOW?

Statistics that help to describe the industry become outdated very quickly, but you can keep up by searching the web.

- Want to know the dollars generated by the travel and tourism industry in the United States? Go to Travel Industry Association of America: www.tia.org and enter "tourism revenues" in the site's search box.
- Want to know current numbers about the restaurant industry? Go to National Restaurant Association: www.restaurant.org and enter "industry profile" in the site's search box.
- Want to know statistics for the lodging industry? Go to American Hotel & Lodging Association: www.ahla.com and enter "lodging industry profile" in the site's search box.
- Want to keep up with the ever-changing industry? If so, review these online resources that are published each business day:

  www.hotel-online.com

  www.smartbrief.com/nra

  www.smartbrief.com/ahla

for celebrations requiring hospitality services. The management of these activities provides exciting career possibilities.

CHALLENGES! CHALLENGES!*

OBJECTIVE 6
Review critical issues that will confront the industry in, at least, the short-term future.

You have learned that the travel and tourism industry, including the hospitality organizations within it, is broad, diverse, and complex. As such, it is difficult to generalize about challenges that confront the entire industry. However, some concerns can be noted that are likely to face owners and managers of these businesses and those who consume their products and services. As you will note from the following list, each challenge confronts numerous organizations in many other industries.

- *Changing labor conditions.* Concerns about a shrinking labor force, some growth in employee unionization, increasing benefits costs, and "front page" news about immigration issues will likely affect "how business is done" in the industry.
- *Escalating operating costs.* Expenses for energy, insurance, labor, and the impact of increasing franchise standards imposed on franchisees may affect the bottom line.
- *Rising energy costs.* As the cost of fuel increases, for example, hotel occupancy levels may be affected, and the cost of products that must be transported to properties will also increase.
- *Increased renovation and construction costs.* Costs associated with renovating existing and building new hospitality properties are on the rise.
- *Effects of and scares about natural disasters.* Tsunamis in the Indian Ocean, hurricanes in the southern United States, and the potential of avian flu around the world are examples of concerns that can affect the industry.
- *Ongoing concerns about safety and security.* Fueled by recurring news accounts about the "hot spots" throughout the world, persons in general and travelers more specifically are increasingly concerned about their safety.
- *Increased consumer expectations.* Those using the products of and services produced by the travel and tourism industry are becoming more sophisticated. They want "more for their money," and increasingly use technology to help them when making purchase decisions.
- *Accelerating change and merging of technologies.* Technology has changed much about how businesses are organized and how work is undertaken. It is difficult (but necessary) to keep up, and to assure that technology is used when and where it is best to do so.
- *Increasing consolidation of brands and companies.* Increasingly, there are fewer companies with an increased number of **brands** for consumer choices. "Who owns what," "What is the difference between brands," are among the questions that organizations must be able to effectively address for consumers.

brand name of a hotel chain; sometimes referred to as a flag

*Adapted from Top 10 global issues and challenges in the hospitality industry for 2006. Hotel-Online Special Report. Retrieved 12/30/2005 from www.hotel -online.com.

SUMMARY OF CHAPTER LEARNING OBJECTIVES

1. **Distinguish between the travel and tourism and the hospitality industries.**
   The travel and tourism industry refers to all businesses that cater to the needs of the traveling public; the hospitality industry refers primarily to organizations that provide lodging and meeting accommodations, foodservices and other hospitality services for people when they are away from their homes.

2. **Suggest how travel patterns have evolved.**
   Yesterday, business travelers took business trips without their family and long vacations with their family. Today, business travelers frequently take their families with them for extensions of business trips, and pleasure trips are increasingly long weekends.

3. **List and briefly describe the types of organizations in the three segments that comprise the hospitality industry: accommodations (lodging), foodservices, and other hospitality operations.**
   The accommodations segment includes hotels, resorts, timeshares and condominiums, conference centers, camp and park lodges, and bed and breakfast (inns). The foodservices segment consists of commercial foodservice operations—which include hotel foodservices, restaurants, caterers, retail shops, and bars and lounges—and organizations operating noncommercial foodservices. Examples include those in education, healthcare, military services, business and industry, religious, charitable, and correctional institutions, and public transportation. Other service organizations include private clubs, casinos, cruise ships, vending services, theme parks, meeting management, expositions (trade shows), and entertainment management.

4. **Explain the difference between commercial and noncommercial foodservice operations.**
   A commercial foodservice operation exists to generate profit from the sale of food and beverage products. By contrast, a noncommercial foodservice operation is utilized by an organization such as a school or healthcare facility. These organizations do not exist primarily to offer food and beverage products and services, but must do so as an integral part of conducting their business.

5. **Discuss two basic ways that noncommercial foodservice programs can be operated.**
   Some noncommercial foodservice programs are self-operated. These organizations employ their own management staff and others to operate foodservices. By contrast, other noncommercial foodservices programs are operated by a for-profit contract management company. It, in turn, employs the managers (and often the other employees) required to operate the foodservices program.

6. **Review critical issues that will confront the industry in, at least, the short-term future.**
   Nine challenges confront most, if not all, organizations within the industry:
   - Changing labor conditions
   - Escalating operating costs
   - Impact of rising energy costs
   - Increased renovation and construction costs
   - Results of natural disasters
   - Uncertainty about safety and security
   - Evolving consumer expectations
   - Accelerating change and merging of technologies
   - Consolidation of brands and companies

FEEDBACK FROM THE REAL WORLD

Our real-world advice comes from Authella Collins Hawks, Director of the Student Industry Resource Center (SIRC), *The* School of Hospitality Business at Michigan State University.

What can students do while still in school to learn as much as possible about the entire industry while keeping their options open about the segment in which they will begin their hospitality career?

The field of hospitality is filled with limitless possibilities. It evokes images of faraway places, exotic locations, relaxation, and fun. Yet, while hospitality can encompass these settings, it is noteworthy that we can also find expressions of hospitality in providing lunches for school-children, nutritional diets in hospitals, and gourmet dinners in sky boxes at our favorite game.

So how does one choose from the myriad of options in the field of hospitality?

One begins by exploring! There are a number of entry-level or hourly jobs in all areas of hospitality. Pick a segment of the industry that attracts you and *go to work!* Exposure to the field in the form of an internship or part-time job helps you to understand yourself better in terms of what you like and what you value in a job. Finding out what you don't like is as helpful as identifying things that you do like, because it helps you in the process of eliminating choices.

Yet another way to help you to decide on what job is right for you is to *conduct a number of informational interviews* with those who are working in positions of interest. Have a prepared list of questions for these employees. Here are a few questions to ask: What do the employees do? How do they accomplish their tasks? What do they like about their jobs? How did they get started? This will add to the information you are collecting to analyze which job is right for you.

Another way to explore options for jobs that are of particular interest is to *shadow someone who works in a position that, one day, you would like to hold.* Observing a person as he or she goes about daily tasks will help you to better define the scope of responsibilities for the job. This will enable you to make choices. The advantage of shadowing someone is that, in a short time, you can get a feel for what she or he does. Employers are typically open to accommodating you since there is no pay involved.

Another key to keeping your options open is to *network.* Simply put, this means connecting with people in the field of hospitality in which you would eventually like to be employed. Those working in the field have friends, acquaintances, colleagues, and co-workers that you have yet to meet. One of these new acquaintances may be the very person who will open the door and help you to start your new job or career.

Another major factor in keeping your options open is to *continue your education* and to keep *developing your skills.* The hospitality field changes rapidly. There are new technology, enhanced training opportunities, and hundreds of articles in journals and trade magazines applicable to all areas of hospitality. Research and learn about your favorite concepts, new trends, hiring practices, and new products. Take classes to develop key skills, such as accounting, finance, and business management. Complete training in areas in which you would like to become stronger. Pursue a bachelor's or an associate college degree to make you a stronger management candidate for employment in the hospitality field. Employers also stress skills in leadership, written and verbal communication, computer basics, time management, organizational skills, and, most of all, a friendly and welcoming attitude.

If you are in an educational setting, be sure to *make the Career Service Office your second home.* It will help you to identify your strengths and gifts, to help you to determine the segment of the industry that is best for you. Career offices can also provide extensive information on employers in various hospitality segments, assist you in networking with those in the industry, and find internship and permanent job opportunities.

Last but not least, after you investigate and analyze all the information that you have collected, stop and pause to reflect, and ask yourself the following questions:

- Do I like what I am doing?
- Can I do this for more than eight hours a day and not resent it?
- Does what I do give me satisfaction in helping others?
- Do I smile often when I think about having a career in this field?

If most of your answers are yes, then perhaps you are on your way to selecting a career in hospitality.

MASTERING YOUR KNOWLEDGE

Discuss the following questions.

Part I: If you have already decided to study travel/tourism/hospitality management:

1. What factors most influenced you to learn about the industry?
2. To this point, what have you learned are among the most important ingredients for success in the industry?
3. What segment of the industry do you currently think offers you the most rewarding career? Why?
4. What are three things that you learned in this chapter that will benefit you when you become a hospitality manager?

Part II: If you are not certain about majoring in travel/tourism/hospitality management:

1. What are the pros and cons about a major in the industry?
2. What do you hope to learn from this book or course that will enable you to make an informed decision about a career in the industry?
3. In what type of organization do you think you could find a position that would be most compatible with your likes or dislikes?

Part III: For all students:

1. What is (are) your career goal(s), and what must happen for you to attain your goal(s)?
2. Have you made any decision(s) that you regret about your academic or professional career since you began your formal education? If so, what were the decision(s) and why do you regret it (them)?

LEARN FROM THE INTERNET

- Check out the following hotel and restaurant websites.

  Hotel Websites:
  - Hilton Hotels Corporation: www.hilton.com
  - Marriott Hotels, Resorts & Suites: www.marriott.com
  - Choice Hotels: www.choicehotels.com

  Restaurants
  - Houston's: www.houstons.com
  - Outback: www.outback.com
  - Ruth's Chris Steakhouse: www.ruthschris.com

  What points do these organizations make in efforts to differentiate themselves from the competition?

- Check out the following foodservice management company and hotel management company websites.

  Foodservice Management Companies Websites:
  - ARAMARK Corporation: www.aramark.com
  - Sodexho: www.sodexho.com

  - Canteen Food Service: www.canteen.com

  Hotel Management Companies
  - White Lodging Services Corporation: www.whitelodging.com
  - Tharaldson Lodging: www.tharaldson.com
  - Coakley & Williams Hotel Management Company: www.cwhotels.com

  What information would be of most interest to you if you were a business manager for a school or hospital or an independent hotel owner who was considering hiring a company to operate the foodservices and hotel?

- Check out the following Website addresses for organizations that are not in the lodging or foodservice segments.

  Non-Lodging/Foodservices Organizations:
  - Disneyland: www.disneyland.com
  - Bellagio Hotel & Casino: www.bellagio.com
  - Carnival Cruises: www.carnival.com

  What types of products and services do they offer that are similar to those offered by their hotel and foodservices counterparts? What types of products and services are different?

KEY HOSPITALITY TERMS

The following terms were explained in this chapter. Review the definitions of any words with which you are unfamiliar. Begin to utilize them as you expand your vocabulary as a hospitality professional.

travel and tourism industry
hospitality industry
cyberfares
amenities
concierge
hotel
franchise
management company
resorts
full-service hotel
timeshare properties
condominium (condo)
condo-hotel
conference centers
camp and park lodges
bed and breakfast (inns)

commercial foodservice operations
noncommercial foodservices
restaurant
caterers
bars
lounges
short-order food items
noncommercial foodservices (self-operated)
noncommercial foodservices (contract
    management company-operated)
private clubs
casinos
vending services
manual food and beverage services
theme parks
brand

2

The Secret of Quality Service

Fine dining is a great experience, and it is the service just as much as the food, beverages, and atmosphere that guests purchase with their "dining-out" dollars.

CHAPTER LEARNING OBJECTIVES

After studying this chapter you will be able to:

1. Explain the concept of quality and review its impact on the level of service provided by a travel/tourism/hospitality operation.
2. Discuss the six ingredients in a recipe to develop a quality service system.
3. Describe the concept of moments of truth in guest service.
4. Recognize the important role of employees in consistently delivering quality service.
5. Defend the concept that guest service staff are professionals.
6. Review the components of the quality service philosophy utilized by the Ritz-Carlton Hotel Company.
7. State factors that will challenge the ability of organizations to deliver quality sevice in the future.

FEEDBACK FROM THE REAL WORLD

You are the new general manager in a travel/tourism/hospitality operation that is not doing well. Previously, it was very successful. There was very low employee turnover, and staff members gave a high priority to meeting (and, almost always, exceeding!) the expectations of the guests being served. Sharon (the manager who had been there for many years) emphasized guest service as a key to success, and she was proved correct each year as business volume (and profits) increased.

Today a different organization exists. Sharon retired, and several managers have been hired and have left over the past few years. Increasingly, the emphasis on cutting costs has replaced the philosophy of providing value for the guests. Staffing patterns have changed, so each employee now has much less time for the interactions needed to learn how guests' needs can best be met.

The Big Question: What should the new manager do to reestablish a culture that focuses on quality guest service?

As you read this chapter, think about your answer to this question and then get feedback from the real world at the end of the chapter.

You have learned that there are a wide range of organizations in the industry that we are studying. Some offer lodging accommodations; others offer food and beverage products and services; still others offer opportunities in recreation and leisure and meetings organizations. What must all these organizations do to be successful? The answer is simple and basic: they must provide quality guest service.

Some persons call the industry we are studying the *hospitality services* industry. A popular name for the segment offering food and beverage is *foodservices*. Persons paying for lodging, food, and beverages in the for-profit segment of the industry consider service to be a very important part of the experience that they are buying. Those utilizing foodservices in a not-for-profit facility are equally entitled to service that addresses their needs and meets their expectations. Consumers also appreciate the services provided by organizations in recreation and leisure and meetings business.

HOSPITALITY MANAGERS SERVE GUESTS

How would you treat a special friend or a relative whom you invite into your home for a meal? The answer to this question can help to define how visitors to a hospitality operation should be treated. The earliest travelers were offered meals and a safe night's rest by families living near trade routes and were invited into the family's home for today's equivalent of lodging and foodservices.

It is true that guests in your home would not be presented with a bill of fare covering the charges at the end of their visit. By contrast, those visiting the hospitality operation must pay their bill. However, the policies and procedures, service training activities, and basic philosophies of the organization can be developed with an emphasis on serving guests.

Do the terms *customer* and *guest* mean the same thing? Perhaps they do in a dictionary; however, in the real world of hospitality, the operator who treats the visitor as a guest will likely be more successful than competitors treating the visitor as a customer.

At its most basic level, then, every travel/tourism/hospitality organization must focus on service. It is typically the service, not the product (for example, food, beverage, or sleeping room), that most influences the guests' perceptions about their experience with an organization in the travel/tourism/hospitality industry.

THE CONCEPT OF QUALITY AND ITS IMPACT ON SERVICE

quality the consistent delivery of products and services according to expected standards

The concept of **quality** is widely discussed in the world of travel/tourism/hospitality management today. Unfortunately, it is much easier to talk about quality than it is to effectively implement it and keep it going within a hospitality operation.

For our purposes, we can define quality as *the consistent delivery of products and services according to expected standards*. Note that **service** (the topic of this chapter) is specifically noted in our definition of quality. This is important: the guest renting a room at a hotel, purchasing a meal at a restaurant, or paying dues at a private club is buying and desires to receive an expected standard of service as part of the payment. Increasingly, guests are willing to pay more as they visit hospitality properties offering service that meets (or, one hopes, exceeds) their service expectations. The perceived level of service quality is an important factor in the experience that guests receive during the visit to the hospitality operation.

service the process of helping guests by addressing their wants and needs with respect and dignity in a timely manner

INGREDIENTS IN A QUALITY SERVICE SYSTEM

The hospitality industry's emphasis on quality is not just a fad that will soon go away. In fact, it requires a dramatic change in attitude about the need to focus on the guests and to use what is learned to reconsider how the operation should work. Entire books have been written about quality in the hospitality industry.[1] There are six ingredients in a recipe that should be used to develop and implement a quality service system. These are reviewed in Exhibit 2.1.

Quick-service restaurants meet the needs of a very large consumer market and, as the name implies fast service is desired by many guests.

[1]See, for example, John King and Ronald Cichy, *Managing for Quality in the Hospitality Industry*. Upper Saddle River, NJ: Pearson Prentice Hall. 2006.

Ingredient 1:   Determine who are the guests being served.

Ingredient 2:   Assess exactly what the guests desire.

Ingredient 3:   Develop practical ways that systems can be modified or developed to consistently deliver what the guests want.

Ingredient 4:   Train and empower service staff to please the guests.

Ingredient 5:   Implement revised procedures.

Ingredient 6:   Evaluate and modify service delivery systems as necessary.

EXHIBIT 2.1
Components of Quality in the Hospitality Industry

IS SERVICE IMPORTANT IN NONCOMMERCIAL OPERATIONS?

There is a popular myth that noncommercial foodservice operations, such as in hospitals, nursing homes, and military bases, have a captive market. The myth continues by reasoning that it is, therefore, unnecessary to focus on the consumers' needs because they have few, if any, alternatives.

In fact, the focus on service is just as great in the noncommercial segment of the industry as it is in commercial hospitality operations. Consider, for example, how you feel if the wait in your school's cafeteria line is lengthy. How do you think hospital patients feel if a follow-up to their dietary concerns is not made by the facility's foodservice staff within a reasonable amount of time? What do you think is among the most frequent topic of conversation between nursing home residents and their families? Answer: the food! The answers to each of these questions cause us to focus directly on the foodservice operation and the level (quality) of service that it provides. Service is important in noncommercial foodservice operations!

Let's take a look at the ingredients in the recipe for quality guest service.

Ingredient 1

Determine who are the guests being served. Some hospitality operations may serve a narrow range of guests. Consider, for example, a small rooms-only lodging property with a strategic location next to a busy interchange on an interstate highway. Most of its guests probably desire the same thing: a relatively inexpensive, safe, and clean sleeping room at a price representing a value to the travelers.

Other hospitality operations may serve a more diverse range of guests. Consider, for example, an upscale restaurant that, at the same time, is serving busy executives conducting business over dinner, a couple celebrating a wedding anniversary, a group of senior citizens enjoying their once monthly dining-out social event, and a young couple on a casual date. What exactly do these seemingly diverse groups of diners have in common? (While it is up to the restaurant manager to determine this, a possible answer is this: freshly produced food delivered by servers who are attentive to the diners' unique needs in a special environment at a price that represents a value for the products purchased and the services received.)

Let's consider two other examples of hospitality properties serving diverse guest groups. First, a downtown hotel may serve business guests during the week and other guests visiting the downtown area for shopping and social reasons during the weekend. Second, a busy restaurant in a tourist destination may serve numerous groups of guests depending on the convention and

Registration should be hospitable and flawless because it is a first step in service for many hotel guests.

group meetings in the city at that specific time. It is important for hospitality managers to assure that they know as much as possible about all the guests being served.

Ingredient 2

Assess exactly what the guests desire. A questioning process can be used to determine guests' wants and needs. Questions such as "What did you like about your visit?" and "What would make your visit more enjoyable?" can help a manager to determine guests' needs. These and related questions can be posed to guests by managers as they "manage by walking around" and/or by a simple questionnaire (comment card) given to guests at the end of a meal or in the guest room. Focus groups (in educational and business and industry settings) and member surveys about a wide range of issues (in private clubs) suggest additional ways to collect information about guest preferences in specific types of hospitality operations.

line-level employees those staff members whose jobs are considered entry-level or non-supervisory; these are typically positions for which the employee is paid an hourly (rather than salary) compensation; examples include positions such as guest service (front desk) agents, room attendants, and food and beverage servers

supervisor a staff member who directs the work of line-level employees

manager a staff member who directs the work of supervisors

benchmark the search for best practices and an understanding about how they are achieved in efforts to determine how well a hospitality organization is doing

cross-functional teams a group of employees from different departments within the hospitality operation that works together to resolve operating problems

Every hospitality manager has another way to collect information about the guests: ask employees. It is ironic but true that, many times, **line-level employees** know more about the likes and dislikes of guests than do their **supervisors** or even the unit **managers**. These staff members frequently have greater amounts of guest contact than do any other employees in the hospitality organization. Consider, for example, the guest complaining about long lines at the time of check-in to a front-desk clerk or a food server receiving compliments (or complaints!) about food in the dining room. Want to know what the guests desire: ask employees who provide the products and services to them.

Ingredient 3

Develop practical ways that systems can be modified or developed to consistently deliver what the guests want. Two of the best ways to make procedures more guest friendly are to **benchmark** and to utilize **cross-functional teams** of employees. Benchmarking is the process of understanding exactly how one's own organization does something and, additionally, determining how it is done by the competition. If, for example, guests desire fast check-in (and most guests do!), it is important to determine what the property currently does and what other properties do to minimize guest check-in times.

Wise hospitality managers know the benefit of asking employees for advice about ways to improve a work method. Cross-functional teams are comprised of staff members from several departments who meet, brainstorm, and consider ways to improve work methods. (Consider a more traditional alternative of utilizing employees from the same department to address a problem: dining room service staff addressing a slow service problem may well conclude that the problem doesn't rest with them; it is caused by the cook! Alternatively, if employees from the dining room, food production, and even housekeeping departments address the problem, creative ideas not limited to "how we have always done things" might be generated.)

Ingredient 4

Train and empower service staff to please the guests. New work methods require, at the least, changes in how work is done. New or additional tools or equipment may also be necessary. Staff members must be trained in revised work tasks, but they must also be empowered to make decisions about the unique needs, if any, of the guests being served. **Empowerment** is the act of granting authority to employees to make key decisions within the employees' areas of responsibility. For example, service employees have a primary responsibility to please the guests. Empowered staff members are allowed to make decisions about how this is to be done as they interact with guests with differing wants, needs, and expectations. Before staff members can be empowered, they must be trained and provided with the tools and other resources needed to do their jobs.

empowerment   the act of granting authority to employees to make key decisions within the employees' areas of responsibility

Ingredient 5

Implement revised procedures. Implementation does not always need to be on an all or nothing basis. Perhaps, for example, employees working on specific floors in a hotel or within specific work stations in a dining room could utilize new work methods to test and further refine, if necessary, the more guest-friendly processes before they are "rolled out" to the entire property.

CHECK IT OUT!

Enter "hospitality service training" into your favorite search engine to review websites of organizations that offer service training.

Ingredient 6

Evaluate and modify service delivery systems as necessary. Over time, guest preferences may (and are likely to) change. Technologies will evolve, as will, perhaps, new or improved work methods. These can affect what guests desire and/or how products or services can be most effectively delivered. In effect, then, the process of quality guest service is cyclical. It is driven by changes in (1) the guests being served and/or (2) guest preferences and/or (3) the work methods implemented to yield the desired quality of product or service outputs.

Today's requirement for quality service has itself evolved from a past emphasis on commodities and products and is becoming incorporated into something that guests are increasingly expecting: an experience. Exhibit 2.2 illustrates this shift using a simple component of almost every meal: bread. Long ago, bread was a simple commodity made of wheat that was likely grown by the family or someone in the community. "Yesterday" bread became a product that was purchased at a grocery store. Today, bread is considered part of a meal experience; warm, sliced bread served tableside is a featured amenity in many restaurants. In the future, bread may become part of a

A beverage operation at poolside. These guests want to have fun, and they cannot if the staff's service does not allow them to do so.

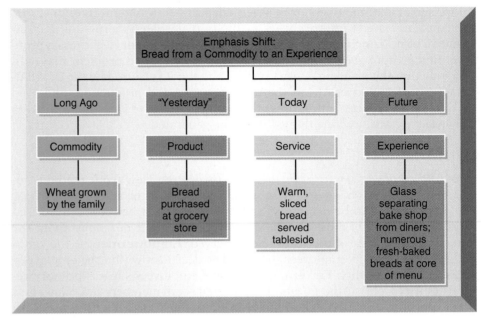

EXHIBIT 2.2
The History of Service: Bread as the Staff of Life

microbrewery a brewery that produces very small quantities of unique beers typically for consumption only on-site and/or for distribution within a small geographic area

diner's experience. Guests may consume a meal in a bakery (just as today food is served in many **microbreweries**). Diners might choose from numerous fresh-baked breads that are at the core of the menu. In fact, some specialty bakeries envision guests selecting bread for their meal in much the same way that they currently select wine to accompany their meal.

SERVICE AND MOMENTS OF TRUTH

OBJECTIVE 3
Describe the concept of moments of truth in guest service.

moments of truth any time that a guest has an opportunity to form an impression about the hospitality organization; moments of truth can be positive or negative

Moments of truth are opportunities that guests have to form an impression about a hospitality organization. While a moment of truth can involve an employee (for example, excellent or rude service), there does not need to be human interaction. (Consider, for example, negative impressions formed when guests walk through a garbage-cluttered parking lot that is downwind from a foul-smelling garbage dumpster or the positive first impression created by the

All employees require training, and procedures to deliver service that meets the property's standards must be part of that training.

MANAGING THE MOMENTS OF TRUTH

Assume that a restaurant manager determines that there is a minimum of 42 times that a guest can form an opinion of the operation. (This includes when the guest enters the restaurant, receives the initial meeting and greeting by the receptionist, is escorted to the table, is seated, is given a menu, the lapsed time until the server's first visit to the table, and so on). Assume also that the restaurant is open for lunch (200 guests are typically served) and for dinner (250 guests are served on an average shift). The number of *planned* "moments of truth" is significant:

$$\begin{pmatrix}\text{Number of moments of}\\\text{truth per lunch period}\end{pmatrix} = \begin{pmatrix}200 \text{ guests} \times 42\\\text{moments of truth}\end{pmatrix} = 8{,}400$$

$$\begin{pmatrix}\text{Number of moments of}\\\text{truth per dinner shift}\end{pmatrix} = \begin{pmatrix}250 \text{ guests} \times 42\\\text{moments of truth}\end{pmatrix} = 10{,}500$$

$$\begin{pmatrix}\text{Number of moments of}\\\text{truth per day}\end{pmatrix} = 8{,}400 + 10{,}500 = 18{,}900$$

$$\begin{pmatrix}\text{Number of moments of}\\\text{truth per week}\end{pmatrix} = \begin{pmatrix}18{,}900 \text{ moments of}\\\text{truth} \times 6 \text{ days of}\\\text{weekly operation}\end{pmatrix} = 113{,}400$$

$$\begin{pmatrix}\text{Number of moments of}\\\text{truth per year}\end{pmatrix} = \begin{pmatrix}113{,}400 \text{ moments of}\\\text{truth per week} \times\\52 \text{ weeks per year}\end{pmatrix} = 5{,}896{,}800$$

The manager in this example has 5,896,800 formal (planned) opportunities each year to make a good impression. Unfortunately, there are a seemingly infinite number of *informal* (unplanned) occasions when guest opinions can be formed. These include encounters with other employees, the perceived levels of cleanliness in the restaurant, and the guests' enjoyment of all food and beverage products served.

How can a manager effectively manage all moments of truth?

large vase of fresh, beautiful flowers on top of the receptionist's stand. Consider also the **"wow" factor** created when one of these fresh flower stems is given to lady guests as they are seated!)

Hospitality managers plan many aspects of a guest experience at their properties. For example, procedures are probably in place in a restaurant for guests to be seated, for orders to be taken, for food to be served, and for guest charges to be paid (among numerous others). Similarly, hotel managers, through an organized planning process (or by default!) have a system in place for guest registration, luggage transport to the room, guest security and safety while on-site, guest check-out, and other guest and property interactions. However, guests in these managers' restaurants and hotels will encounter (sometimes by chance alone) other moments of truth that can be favorable or unfavorable and, in the process, influence the guest's total perception of the visit.

Word-of-mouth advertising occurs when previous guests tell other persons about their experiences during a visit to the hospitality operation. Unfortunately, guests with negative impressions after a property visit are likely to tell more persons about their problems than their counterparts who have just

"wow" factor the feeling guests have when they receive or experience an unanticipated extra as they interact with the hospitality operation

word-of-mouth advertising favorable or unfavorable comments that are made as previous guests of a hospitality operation tell others about their experiences

Hotels market to persons traveling for pleasure. How are these guests' service expectations likely to differ from those of persons traveling for business?

zero defects a goal of no guest-related complaints that is established when guest service processes are implemented

OBJECTIVE 4
Recognize the important role of employees in consistently delivering quality service.

enjoyed a pleasing visit. Unfortunately as well, each time negative experiences are repeated, the extent of the problem is likely to be increased or exaggerated.

You can see, then, that our simple definition of quality at the beginning of this chapter (the consistent delivery of products and services according to expected standards) is, in fact, very difficult to attain. For example, if a hospitality operation serves 300 guests each day for several or more years, some guest-related problems will occur, regardless of the extent to which a service attitude exists and guest-friendly processes are in place. However, effective plans should be in place to minimize the number of service failures.

Managers may establish a goal of **zero defects** when quality service processes are implemented. In other words, it is their hope that there will be no guest-related complaints. However, doesn't a goal of zero defects create frustration since, even with the best intentions and most effective processes in place, mistakes (defects) will occur? Exhibit 2.3 illustrates how a decline in defects can be measured.

Service Is Delivered by Employees

After viewing a video emphasizing quality dining service, one dining room manager was heard saying to another, "I'd give anything to have service staff like those shown in the video." What the dining room manager had seen was a series of situations in which a trained dining room server (1) provided a hospitable

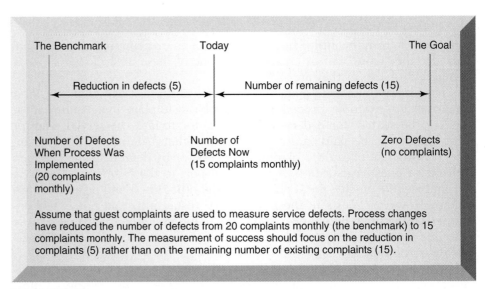

The Benchmark	Today	The Goal
← Reduction in defects (5) →	← Number of remaining defects (15) →	
Number of Defects When Process Was Implemented (20 complaints monthly)	Number of Defects Now (15 complaints monthly)	Zero Defects (no complaints)

Assume that guest complaints are used to measure service defects. Process changes have reduced the number of defects from 20 complaints monthly (the benchmark) to 15 complaints monthly. The measurement of success should focus on the reduction in complaints (5) rather than on the remaining number of existing complaints (15).

EXHIBIT 2.3
The March Toward Zero Defects

Ali Faraj
Trainer
Marriott Call Center
Santa Ana, California

Providing Effective Guest Service Looks Easy!

Ali is quick to say that he has always been interested in the world of business because he "likes to make money." He was initially interested in the landscaping business and remembers attending a convention at a Hyatt hotel. The property really impressed him, as did the staff members and the service that they provided.

Shortly thereafter, he enrolled at a community college to major in general business. At the time, he did not even know that there were postsecondary schools that offered a formal hospitality education program. He did know, however, that he liked to be around people, that he enjoyed helping people, and that he really had an interest in making people happy.

While taking courses at the college, Ali met with a career services advisor who shared information about hospitality education programs in the state; the rest is "history," and Ali transferred into a program he knew "was meant for him."

Ali's college career was very impressive, even though he has a vision impairment that would make many people think that his accomplishments would not be possible.

While receiving his university education, he was:

- President of the Hospitality Business Consultants' Club
- A member of the board of directors of the school's Hospitality Association
- A member of the school's Student Hospitality Sales Organization
- A member of Eta Sigma Delta Honors Society
- An executive board member and a corporate ambassador for the school's Career Expo
- A reception server for a large school event (Les Gourmets)

Ali is very proficient in the use of technology. For example, screen-reading software (Jaws for Windows) is very helpful in allowing him to use technology that others, increasingly, take for granted.

Ali had no difficulty succeeding in his accomplishments: "I know I can do just about anything I set my mind to do. My challenge is to prove myself by showing others that I can do it. Some day, after working my way up the corporate ladder, I would like to be the general manager of a hotel in a reputable company, and someday I would like to own my own hotel!"

While in school, Ali completed a three-month internship at the Hyatt Regency Dearborn (Michigan). He spent 45 days as a front-desk clerk, and the remainder of the time he served as a reservations agent.

How, one might ask, can a person with limited vision serve as a front-desk clerk? "Just watch me!" says Ali. "Guests completed registration cards as usual, and I placed them in a stack to be filed by another desk clerk later. I checked guest identifications by standing next to another front-desk clerk who helped with details. Money readers that can scan bills and announce their amounts were available, and I used a one-sided headphone connected to a computer to handle other aspects of guest check-ins and check-outs in a very short amount of time."

Ali notes that his fellow employees at the Hyatt were very open-minded and willing to accept him because "it was no big deal!"

Ali spent a second summer at the same property and completed an internship in the accounting department. He worked with the hotel's assistant controller, credit manager, and income audit manager. In these capacities, he performed bank statement reconciliations and did postings to the income, general, and payroll journals. He also made 30-day accounts-receivable collection calls and other calls for credit references.

Ali's accounting work was made easier by the use of a "talking" calculator. He also scanned documents into Word/Excel programs and then used the Jaws software noted previously.

During his senior year of hospitality studies, Ali completed an accounting internship at the university's Hotel and Conference Center, and he worked 15 hours weekly while taking 13 credits and serving in a leadership capacity with three hospitality student groups.

(continued)

After graduation, Ali worked for a brief time as a manager for a valet parking company with responsibility for day-to-day operations, including marketing and hiring.

Then, in 2005, he was hired as a worldwide reservations agent for the Marriott Call Center. Soon after, he was promoted to a regional agent and then became an on-the-job trainer for new staff members. In recognition of his training abilities, Ali became an assistant trainer for new classes and, at the time of this writing, he was starting to revise the training department and its resource materials.

Ali has some great advice for hospitality students: "Have a goal; try your best to fulfill it. Never say 'I can't' unless you've tried it—over and over and over again!"

He also displays his emphasis on commitment and enthusiasm when he says, "I am continuing to move forward in my career, and I will work hard so I can be successful in the hotel industry. I love proving people wrong when they think that it is impossible for me to do something because of my visual impairment. Just give me the chance, and I will show you that it can be done!"

greeting, (2) practiced the "art and science" of suggestive selling, (3) utilized product knowledge, (4) answered all guest questions about "what's on the menu," (5) helped other servers when they became especially busy during the work shift, and (6) met or exceeded the guests' service expectations.

Why couldn't (didn't) that dining room manager employ servers who consistently did these relatively simple and commonsense things? What kind of service was the manager's staff providing to guests if they did not do what was emphasized in the training video? Unfortunately, many persons considering a recent experience in a foodservice operation might also ask, "What was wrong with the staff? What was wrong with their supervisor for allowing these things to happen? If I can realize the negative impact it has on their business, why can't the supervisor?"

The quality of service provided to guests in any type of hospitality operation is affected most by the staff members providing the service and by the processes that the employees use to provide the service. If this is true and the employee is a key element in service delivery, what role, then, does the manager play?

It has been said that the vast majority of all problems in a hospitality operation are caused by the manager! This observation runs contrary to the traditional manager who thinks, "If only I could find good employees, my operating problems would be solved." In fact, it is the manager who effectively (or ineffectively) recruits, orients, trains, motivates, and empowers staff members to serve the guests. It is the manager who does (or does not) serve as a role model to emphasize the importance of guest service in the hospitality organization. As you will learn in Chapter 3, managers cannot delegate the **accountability** that they receive from their own bosses to subordinates. Instead, managers are (and should be) held responsible for the extent to which the hospitality operation is successful. As emphasized throughout this chapter, service is an essential ingredient in the success of any hospitality organization. What can managers do to best assure that employees know and consistently practice effective guest-service skills? Some helpful tactics are listed in Exhibit 2.4. Let's briefly discuss them:

accountability an obligation created when a person is delegated duties or responsibilities from higher levels of management

employer of choice the concept that the hospitality operation is a preferred place of employment within the community by those who have alternative employment opportunities

- *Maintain a vision of service priority.* Managers must understand the critical importance of service. They must recognize that what they do (and don't do) and what they say (and don't say) are the biggest factors in determining the extent to which service is emphasized in their operation.
- *Recruit and select service-minded staff.* The hospitality operation should strive to be an **employer of choice** within the community; its **turnover rate** should be relatively low, and experienced staff members

✓	Maintain a vision of service priority.
✓	Recruit and select service-minded staff.
✓	Provide effective orientation and training.
✓	Supervise with a service emphasis.
✓	Empower staff with decision-making authority for service.
✓	Emphasize continuous quality improvement.

EXHIBIT 2.4
Manager's Checklist for Effective Guest Service

should understand and consistently apply quality service principles. However, applicants will still need to be recruited and selected. They should effectively answer open-ended questions such as "What would you do if a guest pushed his way to the front of the check-in line and demanded to be registered immediately?" or "What would you do if a guest indicates the desire for food to be served immediately, and there is a backup of several large food orders in the kitchen?"

- *Provide effective orientation and training.* The manager's emphasis on quality guest service continues at the time of new-employee orientation. Staff members should be introduced to the property's **mission statement**, which should emphasize the critical importance of guest service. They must be trained in guest-friendly procedures. (There should be adequate time for new employees to gain the required knowledge and skills before they have significant guest contact.)

- *Supervise with a service emphasis.* Employees, like all other people, will normally do what they are rewarded to do. If service is important, hospitality managers should emphasize this by thanking staff members when exceptional guest service is rendered, discussing service-related problems, and noting service factors during times of performance appraisal. Employee compensation decisions should be based, in part, on the consistency of quality service delivery.

turnover rate   a measure of the proportion of a work force that is replaced during a designated time period (for example, month, quarter, year); it can be calculated as number of employees separated ÷ number of employees in the work force = turnover rate

mission statement   a planning tool that broadly identifies what a hospitality operation would like to accomplish and what it plans to do to accomplish it

DID YOU KNOW?

More than 88,000,000 websites are generated when the term "hospitality service" is entered in the Google search engine.

Hotels market to persons traveling for business. How are these guests' service expectations likely to differ from those of families staying at the hotel?

WHAT MAKES SERVICE SPECIAL?

Service is an attitude as much or more than it is a skill. Hospitality employees provide special service to their guests when they:

Acknowledge guests and thank them for visiting

Smile

Maintain eye contact

Reflect a genuine interest in providing quality service

Consider every guest to be unique

Create a warm environment of hospitality

Strive for excellence in guest service skills

Are courteous, polite, and attentive

Determine what guests *really* want and need and then provide the products and services that address these wants and needs

Pay more attention to guests than to machines and co-workers

Invite guests to return

Aren't these things easy to do? Why don't travel/tourism/hospitality employees consistently incorporate these tactics into the ways that they interact with guests?

---

continuous quality improvement (CQI) ongoing efforts within a hospitality operation to better meet (or exceed) guest expectations and to define ways to perform work with better, less costly, and faster methods

OBJECTIVE 5
Defend the concept that guest service staff are professionals.

professionals persons working in an occupation requiring extensive knowledge and skills

licensing formal authorization to practice a profession that has been granted by a governmental agency

registration acceptance for one to work within a profession that has been granted by (typically) a nongovernmental agency, such as an association

OBJECTIVE 6
Review the components of the quality service philosophy utilized by the Ritz-Carlton Hotel Company.

- *Empower staff with decision-making authority for service.* The importance of employee empowerment was noted earlier in this chapter. Hospitality managers should facilitate, not direct, the delivery of service. Staff members who are in contact with guests require the ability to make quick decisions that focus on guest needs as they arise.
- *Emphasize* **continuous quality improvement (CQI)**. Guests and the hospitality operations that serve them constantly change. Hospitality operations, then, either become better or worse; they never stay the same. Today's emphasis on "better, faster, cheaper" is important. However, the first two factors just noted (better and faster) should be developed with the guests' needs in mind. The third factor (cheaper) is also a meaningful goal as long as it involves taking error out of the products and services, rather than reducing value from the guests' point of view.

Guest Service Staff Are Professionals

Professionals are persons working in an occupation requiring extensive knowledge and skills. One often thinks about occupations such as medicine, law, accounting, and teaching to satisfy this definition. Persons in these occupations have formal education in a specialized body of knowledge and membership in their profession is controlled by, for example, **licensing** or **registration**.

Hospitality service personnel should be thought of as professionals in their own vocation because specialized knowledge and skills are required to be effective. Also, certification by professional associations, including the American Hotel and Lodging Association (www.ahla.org) and the National Restaurant Association (www.restaurant.org), is available.

Ritz-Carlton: A Case Study in Quality Service

The Ritz-Carlton Hotel Company, L.L.C., is widely known for its emphasis on quality. It has won the prestigious **Malcolm Baldrige National Quality Award**, which is administered by the federal government (National Institute of

The hotel's management team must plan service processes.

Standards and Technology, Commerce Department). The Ritz-Carlton's Employee Promise, Credo, and Service Values establish a foundation for quality excellence that is an important part of the company's corporate culture.

While very few organizations receive the Malcolm–Baldrige Award, the philosophies emphasized in the Ritz-Carlton Hotel Company Standards are useful benchmarking concepts for all service organizations, including those within the hospitality industry.

Benchmark Against the Best: Ritz-Carlton Hotels

The Employee Promise[2]

At the Ritz Carlton, our Ladies and Gentlemen are the most important resource in our service commitment to our guests.

By applying the principles of trust, honesty, respect, integrity, and commitment, we nurture and maximize talent to the benefit of each individual and the company.

The Ritz-Carlton fosters a work environment where diversity is valued, quality of life is enhanced, individual aspirations are fulfilled, and The Ritz-Carlton Mystique is strengthened.

The Ritz-Carlton Credo[3]

The Ritz-Carlton Hotel is a place where the genuine care and comfort of our guests is our highest mission.

We pledge to provide the finest personal service and facilities for our guests who will always enjoy a warm, relaxed yet refined ambiance.

The Ritz-Carlton experience enlivens the senses, instills well-being, and fulfills even the unexpressed wishes and needs of our guests.

Service Values: I Am Proud to be Ritz-Carlton

1. I build strong relationships and create Ritz-Carlton guests for life.
2. I am always responsive to the expressed and unexpressed wishes and needs of our guests.

Malcolm Baldrige National Quality Award   an award granted to relatively few U.S. businesses that demonstrate successful quality-related strategies relating to leadership, information and analysis, strategic planning, human resource development and management, process management, business results, and customer focus and satisfaction

---

The essence of hospitality: "Welcome to your home away from home."

3. I am empowered to create unique, memorable, and personal experiences for our guests.
4. I understand my role in achieving the Key Success Factors and creating The Ritz-Carlton Mystique.
5. I continuously seek opportunities to innovate and improve The Ritz-Carlton experience.
6. I own and immediately resolve guest problems.
7. I create a work environment of teamwork and lateral service so that the needs of our guests and each other are met.
8. I have the opportunity to continuously learn and grow.
9. I am involved in the planning of the work that affects me.
10. I am proud of my professional appearance, language, and behavior.
11. I protect the privacy and security of our guests, my fellow employees, and the company's confidential information and assets.
12. I am responsible for uncompromising levels of cleanliness and creating a safe and accident-free environment.

CHALLENGES! CHALLENGES!

OBJECTIVE 7
State factors that will challenge the ability of organizations to deliver quality service in the future.

The consumers' interest in service is likely to increase in the future and, as today, organizations that meet (or exceed) these guest service expectations have a competitive edge over their counterparts who do not. While the recipe for quality service discussed in this chapter is easy to read and understand, it is much more difficult to implement. Managers cannot, for example, simply determine standards, develop required procedures that address them, and train staff members to follow them.

Several factors that affect the ability of the organization to maintain its quality service standards include the following:

- **Service philosophy of top-level managers.** Contrast the manager who is a role model for effective service by constantly talking about it and helping to deliver it with another manager whose leadership style is "do what I say, not what I do."
- **Service attitude of staff members.** As suggested, line-level employees are more likely to practice the service component of their jobs when their managers do so.
- **Employee selection and training.** Staff members who have a genuine interest in providing service and who are trained to do so will more likely be successful than others who consider their employment to be "just a job."
- **Changing guest preferences.** Managers must keep current with their guests' expectations about service and the best way to provide it.

Managers must evaluate technology and consider guest service implications, along with numerous other service-related considerations. The need for "high tech" with "high touch" is important, because service in the travel/tourism and hospitality industry is delivered by people, not by machines.

SUMMARY OF CHAPTER LEARNING OBJECTIVES

1. **Explain the concept of quality and review its impact on the level of service provided by a travel/tourism/hospitality operation.**
   Quality is the consistent delivery of products and services according to expected standards. Service is an important component of our definition of quality, and guests at all types of hospitality properties are influenced by service as they form an impression of the experience that they receive from employees of the hospitality organization.

2. **Discuss the six ingredients in a recipe to develop a quality service system.**
   The six ingredients for quality guest service are the following:
   1. Determine who are the guests being served.
   2. Assess exactly what the guests desire.
   3. Develop practical ways that systems can be modified or developed to consistently deliver what the guests want.
   4. Train and empower service staff to please the guests.
   5. Implement revised procedures.
   6. Evaluate and modify service delivery systems as necessary.

3. **Describe the concept of moments of truth in guest service.**
   Moments of truth are positive or negative opportunities when guests form an impression about a hospitality organization.

4. **Recognize the important role of employees in consistently delivering quality service.**
   The majority of problems in a hospitality organization are caused by the manager, not by employees. When employees cannot consistently deliver quality service, it is most likely due to problems for which the manager has responsibility.

5. **Defend the concept that guest service staff are professionals.**
   Guest service staff are professionals in their own vocation because specialized knowledge and skills are required to be effective.

6. **Review the components of the quality service philosophy utilized by the Ritz-Carlton Hotel Company.**
   The Ritz-Carlton's Employee Promise indicates that its staff members (ladies and gentlemen) are the most important resource in its service commitment to its guests. The Ritz-Carlton's Credo pledges the finest personal service and facilities for guests.

7. **State factors that will challenge the ability of organizations to deliver quality service in the future.**
   Factors that will affect the ability of an organization to maintain quality standards include the service philosophy of top-level managers, the service attitude of staff members, and employee selection and training practices. Guest preferences will also change, and managers must keep up with and adapt to these changes.

MASTERING YOUR KNOWLEDGE

Discuss the following questions.

1. What is the definition of excellent service in the following situations?
   a. During time of check-in at a motel, on the highway, and at a Ritz-Carlton hotel
   b. During the process of taking food orders at a quick-service restaurant and at a high-check-average, sit-down restaurant
   c. In a corporate dining room of a very large and successful company and at a primary school cafeteria

FEEDBACK FROM THE REAL WORLD

Our real-world advice comes from Nancy Bacyinski, Regional Director of Operations for HDS Services in the Cincinnati, Ohio, market.

What should a new general manager of the hospitality operation do to reestablish a culture that focuses on quality guest service?

I would begin my new management position realizing that my greatest asset is my staff; they are my team. I would set up a meeting with personnel in each department and obtain feedback about the operation: What do they like? Dislike? What do our guests like? Dislike? How do they respond to our guests' needs?

An educational process would then begin. Our company team would work together to formulate a mission statement that focused on our role in serving our guests. We would define who the guests are and what they want and commit, as a team, to consistently move toward the goals expressed in our mission.

I would train the staff and empower all of them to be our ambassadors to please the guests. They would be given the authority, or power, to respond to guests to meet their expectations if we do not provide an acceptable level of satisfaction in our initial efforts.

I would realize that these changes cannot occur overnight; some time will be required for the staff to begin to respect and trust me. As well, I will need time to obtain a "big picture" overview of the best way to use resources (which are always in limited supply) to best address our mission and goals. I would understand that employees who are satisfied and happy will provide quality products and services to our guests. In turn, employee turnover will be lower, and those whom we serve will be happy with us. These results will yield the financial performance that is anticipated in our well-planned budget.

I will know we have been successful in our efforts when our levels of guests and employee satisfaction have increased and, at the same time, when our expenses have decreased.

This process, while oversimplified, provides a basic recipe that will help to reestablish the culture in the foodservice operation that had once been there but which, over time, is no longer there.

Consider the market being served, the definition of acceptable service in each alternative, and the role of value from the consumer's perspective in your analysis.

2. How do you personally define and evaluate service when you are a guest at a hotel or restaurant? Do you think other guests have the same concerns about service as you do? Review the six ingredients necessary to develop a quality service system. Assume that you are the manager of a restaurant in which the table reservation system for dinner is not working; many guests arrive on time for their reservation, but still must wait an excessively long time for an available table. Work through a potential solution to this problem utilizing the six-step method.

3. Think about the last time you visited a hotel or restaurant as a guest. What moments of truth do you recall? What impact did they have on your overall impression of the hospitality operation?

4. Discuss the following statement: "The vast majority of all problems in a hospitality operation are caused by the manager, not by the employee." Do you agree? Disagree? If you currently hold a job in the hospitality industry, what would your supervisor say about this statement?

5. Do you believe that line-level staff members in hospitality positions such as front-desk clerk and food server are professionals? Why or why not?

6. Review the components of the Ritz-Carlton Hotel Company's quality service statement

(Employee Promise and Ritz-Carlton Credo). What impact might they have on you if you were an employee of the Ritz-Carlton? Which of the concepts described in these statements would be applicable to employees working in

any other travel/tourism, food and beverage, or lodging operation?
7. What are three things that you learned in this chapter that will benefit you if you become a hospitality manager?

LEARN FROM THE INTERNET

1. Check out the website for the Ritz-Carlton Hotel Company: www.ritzcarlton.com. Carefully review it and note how it emphasizes guest service in its messages to guests.
2. Check out the websites of the following hotel and restaurant companies:

Hotels
- Red Roof Inns: www.redroof.com
- Baymont Inns & Suites: www.baymontinns.com
- Motel 6: www.motel6.com

Restaurants
- McDonald's: www.mcdonalds.com
- Kentucky Fried Chicken: www.KFC.com
- Taco Bell: www.tacobell.com

What emphasis do they place on guest service?

3. Check out the websites of the following hospitality organizations:
- Caesar's Palace Casino: www.caesarspalace.com
- Galapagos Cruises Inc.: www.galapagos-inc.com
- Gordon Food Service Distributors: www.gfs.com
- Canteen Vending Services: www.canteen.com
- Busch Gardens: www.buschgardens.com

What services do they offer? To what extent do they emphasize service?

KEY HOSPITALITY TERMS

The following terms were explained in this chapter. Review the definitions of any words with which you are unfamiliar. Begin to utilize them as you expand your vocabulary as a hospitality professional.

quality
service
line-level employees
supervisor
manager
benchmark
cross-functional teams
empowerment
microbrewery
moments of truth
"wow" factor

word-of-mouth advertising
zero defects
accountability
employer of choice
turnover rate
mission statement
continuous quality improvement (CQI)
professionals
licensing
registration
Malcolm Baldrige National Quality Award

3

Managers Must Manage

Today, technology and communication are integral to effective management.

CHAPTER LEARNING OBJECTIVES

After studying this chapter you will be able to:

1. Define the term *management,* and list seven resources that managers must manage.
2. Explain steps in the management decision-making (problem-solving) process.
3. Discuss each basic activity in the management process.
4. Review ways in which today's (modern) managers differ from yesterday's (traditional) managers.

FEEDBACK FROM THE REAL WORLD

Hospitality managers must manage. It is easy to make this statement. However, what exactly do managers do when they manage?

How would you answer the following questions?

- What management activities are the most important? Why?
- What management activities are the most difficult to learn?
- What are the most difficult challenges that confront hospitality managers?

- What, if any, role does common sense play in effective management?
- What, if any, role does experience play in effective management?

As you read this chapter, think about answers to these questions and then get feedback from the real world at the end of the chapter.

The title of this chapter may seem odd. Hospitality managers (along with managers from any other type of organization) obviously must manage. However, what do they manage, and how do they do it? These are the topics of this chapter.

OVERVIEW: THE MANAGEMENT PROCESS

There is no universally accepted definition of **management;** different authors and industry and business observers define the process differently. However, most definitions have two factors in common: a process and a goal attainment effort. These form the basis of the definition we will use: management is the process of planning, organizing, staffing, directing, controlling, and evaluating human, financial, and physical resources for the purpose of achieving organizational goals.

Unfortunately, all resources are in limited supply (Exhibit 3.1). It is doubtful that any manager in any business anywhere has all the necessary resources available in desired (ideal) quantities. The task of a manager, then, becomes one of using resources that are in limited supply to maximize (or, at least, to satisfy!) organizational objectives.

What types of goals do managers wish to attain? Among them are the following:

- *Organizational goals related to long-term viability (survival).* These goals are addressed by processes involving marketing (attracting

> **OBJECTIVE 1**
> Define the term *management,* and list seven resources that managers must manage.

management the process of planning, organizing, staffing, directing, controlling, and evaluating human, financial, and physical resources for the purpose of achieving organizational goals

Travel/tourism and hospitality managers have the following types of resources available to them that can be utilized to attain goals. All are finite (available in only a limited amount):

- Labor (employees)
- Money
- Products (food, beverages, and supplies)
- Machinery (equipment)
- Minutes (time)
- Methodology (work processes and procedures)
- Energy

EXHIBIT 3.1
Hospitality Management Resources Are in Limited Supply

guests), human resources management (facilitating the work of employees), and controlling costs (minimizing expenses without sacrificing quality).

- *Human resources goals.* For example, provision of professional development opportunities that allow staff members to learn and grow on the job and consideration of the manager's own professional goals.
- *Societal goals.* The hospitality organization must be a good citizen within the community. It wants to meet its legal obligations and should be active in community service initiatives.

OBJECTIVE 2
Explain steps in the management decision-making (problem-solving) process.

budget a financial plan that estimates the amount of revenue to be generated, the expenses to be incurred, and the amount of profit, if any, to be realized from the hospitality operation

revenue the amount of money generated from the sale of products and services to guests

expenses costs incurred by the hospitality operation to generate its revenue

bottom line a slang term relating to profit; on a budget and on an income statement, the profit line is the last line of (at the bottom of) the document

THE DECISION-MAKING (PROBLEM-SOLVING) PROCESS

How do hospitality managers best utilize resources since they are in limited supply? They must make decisions about their best use. Consider, for example, money. The manager uses a **budget** to estimate **revenue** and to consider how it should be spent on numerous types of **expenses** to yield a **bottom line** that meets financial requirements.

Exhibit 3.2 shows the steps in the basic decision-making process that many experienced hospitality managers use almost without thinking. One of the most important tasks of a manager is to solve problems. (Some managers think more positively and call them opportunities or challenges.) They must make decisions as they solve problems. In fact, then, the problem-solving process is really a decision-making process.

Let's look at the process more carefully.

Step 1: Define the Problem. A problem represents the difference between the way something is and the way it should be. For example, there is a problem when guests complain about unclean rooms or cold food. Sometimes (but not always) the problem is obvious. Declining volumes of revenue and/or increasing costs may be examples. Sometimes, however, it is much more difficult to identify the problem. Consider, for example, the view of some managers that an increasing number of job applicants are entering the work force with a lowered work ethic than their counterparts had in prior generations. (There are, probably, numerous societal, cultural, and other components of this issue that make problem identification difficult, if not impossible.) Some managers ask themselves, "What would the situation be like in the absence of the problem?" to help to define the problem.

Unfortunately, problems seldom occur on a one-at-a-time basis. Instead, managers are typically confronted with numerous problems at the same time. They must, then, set a priority (which problems are potentially most harmful to the organization and/or which solutions, after resolution, will be most helpful?) for the problem resolution process.

A group decision-making (problem-solving) approach is favored by many successful travel/tourism and hospitality managers.

Step 2: Generate Solution Alternatives. What can be done to address the

EXHIBIT 3.2
Basics of the Decision-
Making (Problem-Solving)
Process

Steps	Example
Step 1: Define the problem	Guest **check average** for food has been declining for each of the last three months
Step 2: Generate solution alternatives	Need to utilize **suggestive selling**
	Need to evaluate menu (components and design) to determine if changes can increase revenues
	Errors in equipment operation or procedures used to calculate data
	Theft of revenue by food servers
Step 3: Evaluate solution alternatives	Guest shoppers did not observe suggestive selling; training needed to implement suggestive selling program
	Menu recently redesigned; guest counts are up slightly
	An auditor has found no bookkeeping problems suggesting employee theft
Step 4: Select the best solution alternative	Implement a suggestive selling program
Step 5: Implement the solution alternative	Train service staff; implement a contest (all servers with a specified minimum guest check average win complimentary meals and sweatshirts)
Step 6: Evaluate the effectiveness of the solution	Determine the extent to which the guest check average increases after the suggestive selling training program has been implemented

check average the average amount spent by a restaurant guest: total food and beverage revenue ÷ total guests

suggestive selling tactics used by food and beverage service personnel to increase the amount spent by each guest during a visit to the restaurant

problem? The manager should have answers, but so also may the employees. The use of **cross-functional teams** can help to identify potential solutions.

Step 3: Evaluate Solution Alternatives. Perceived ability to resolve the problem, costs, ease of implementation, and impact on other work processes are some of the factors that can be used to evaluate the solution alternatives generated in step 2.

Step 4: Select the Best Solution Alternative. Often, the best solution involves utilizing aspects of several possible alternatives generated in step 2.

Step 5: Implement the Solution Alternative. Employee training, purchase of necessary equipment/tools, **process revisions**, and trial study are among the tactics that may be necessary during the implementation phase of decision making and problem solving.

Step 6: Evaluate the Effectiveness of the Solution. If one has considered what the situation would be like if the problem no longer existed (step 1), this step becomes easier. Often, solutions are not

cross-functional teams a group of employees from different departments within the hospitality operation that work together to resolve operating problems

process revisions changes to work methods in ways that reduce defects and increase opportunities to please the guests

Safety can never be compromised when decisions are made, or as problems are resolved.

A significant amount of management planning, staffing, directing, controlling, and evaluating is necessary to consistently facilitate flawless guest service.

found to be optimal; the problem may still exist but, as a result of the decision-making process, its impact on the organization will be lessened. If the problem is still significant relative to others confronting the operation, the hospitality manager may choose to repeat the problem-solving process with the hope of identifying and implementing other solution alternatives that reduce the impact of the problem still further.

CLOSE LOOK AT MANAGEMENT ACTVITIES

Hospitality managers must perform many basic activities as they go about their job. The extent to which they can successfully complete each activity affects their success. All basic management activities are important; none can be neglected. Exhibit 3.3 shows these basic management activities. Let's review each of them.

OBJECTIVE 3
Discuss each basic activity in the management process.

planning the basic management activity that involves defining goals, establishing strategies to achieve them, and designing ways to get work done

organizing the basic management activity that involves developing and grouping work tasks

coordinating the basic management activity that involves arranging group efforts in an orderly manner

staffing the basic management activity that involves finding the right people for the job

- *Planning.* Defining goals, establishing strategies to achieve them, and designing ways to get work done.
- *Organizing.* Developing and grouping work tasks.
- *Coordinating.* Arranging group efforts in an orderly manner.
- *Staffing.* Finding the right people for the job.
- *Directing.* Supervising the work of staff members.
- *Controlling.* Determining the extent to which the organization keeps on track of achieving goals.
- *Evaluating.* Assessing the extent to which plans are attained; evaluation can identify issues (problems) that should be considered by additional planning. Therefore, the management process is cyclical; over time, evaluation will likely lead to issues that can be addressed through additional planning.

It would be very convenient if a hospitality manager could manage one activity at a time. In other words, ideally, a manager could spend time **planning** how money should be spent (developing a budget) and when employees should work (developing a schedule). Then the manager in our ideal world might spend time **organizing** procedures in a specific department and **coordinating** work efforts between departments. A manager's ideal work day could continue with specific times set aside for the other management activities (**staffing**, **directing**, **controlling**, and **evaluating**). In fact, however, the manager's work is much more complicated.

In the real world, a manager must do many things simultaneously. For example, he or she might (1) plan how all organizational resources can best be utilized, (2) organize and coordinate work activities and personnel responsibilities between all departments, and (3) make staffing decisions. At the same time, the manager may be supervising ongoing work while assessing the extent to which goals are met and evaluating further work improvements. Exhibit 3.4 depicts the work of a busy hospitality manager as he or she utilizes different management activities to address different resources.

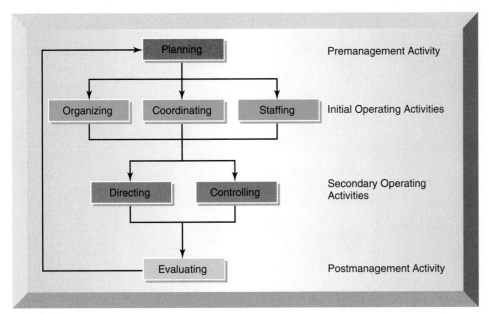

EXHIBIT 3.3
Basic Management Activities

Typically, there is not enough time in the workday for hospitality managers to do all the work that they would like to do. They must be very careful about how they spend their time. Time can best be managed by establishing priorities, by practicing **delegation**, and by doing things right the first time to reduce **rework.**

Numerous principles can be used to make the management process more effective. Let's take a look at some of these basic principles and consider how managers can use them as they undertake each management activity.

Planning

The principles of planning include the following:

- Goals and objectives must be defined, and subsequent work should focus on them.
- A formal planning process is needed. Exhibit 3.5 reviews the relationship between several planning tools.

Vision. An abstract, impossible to quantify idea about what the hospitality operation would be like if it were ideal.

Mission statement. A more focused picture of the ideal operation that indicates what it will do and how it will do it.

Long-range plan. Goal statements and the associated activities along with personnel assignments over a number of years (often 3 to 5 years in a rolling plan) that are designed to move the organization toward attainment of its mission.

Business plan. This short-term plan indicates goals and activities that will be addressed within the next year to help the organization to meet its long-range plan.

Marketing plan. A listing (typically month to month) of tactics that will be used to help the hospitality operation to meet its revenue goals.

Operating budget. A statement of estimated revenues generated from and associated expenses to be incurred as a result of the business outcomes anticipated by the business plan and implemented by the marketing plan.

directing the basic management activity that involves supervising the work of staff members

controlling the basic management activity that involves determining the extent to which the organization "keeps on track" for achieving goals

evaluating the basic management activity that involves determining the extent to which plans are attained

delegation the process of assigning authority (power) to subordinates to enable them to do work that a manager at a higher organizational level would otherwise need to do

rework doing a task a second time because of defects created the first time the task was done

vision an abstract idea about what the hospitality operation would be like if it was ideal

mission statement a planning tool that broadly identifies what a hospitality operation would like to accomplish and what it plans to do to accomplish it

long-range plan a statement of goals and the activities that will be undertaken to attain them that a hospitality operation will utilize over the next 3 to 5 years in efforts to move toward its mission

business plan a plan of goals and activities that will be addressed within the next 12 months to move the organization toward attainment of its mission

marketing plan a calendar of specific activities designed to meet the operation's revenue goals

operating budget a financial plan that estimates the amount of revenue to be generated, the expenses to be incurred, and the amount of profit, if any, to be realized

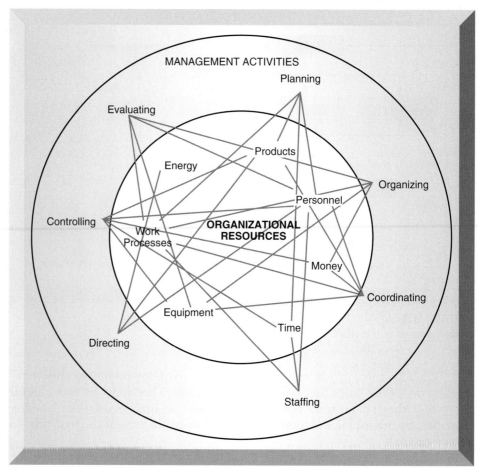

EXHIBIT 3.4
The Manager's Work Is Complicated

Numerous hospitality courses focusing on management (strategic planning), marketing, and financial management may give students the impression that planning tools are separate, with little, if any, relationship between them. In fact, planning tools should be developed sequentially, with the outcome of one driving the development of the next.

The use of other planning principles can also benefit hospitality managers. These principles include the following:

- All information required for effective planning must be available. While this appears obvious, some managers believe their position of power is best assured when access to information is controlled. This principle also suggests that planning must be done at the appropriate organizational level so that required information is more likely to be available.
- Those affected by plans should provide input to them. For example, if a new work process is being developed, input from those who do the work can be helpful. (It is more likely that the best work method will be identified.) As well, staff members are more likely to "work the plan" when it is "our" work method rather than "their" (the managers') work method.
- Adequate resources must be committed to planning, because effective planning takes time and plans must be implemented.

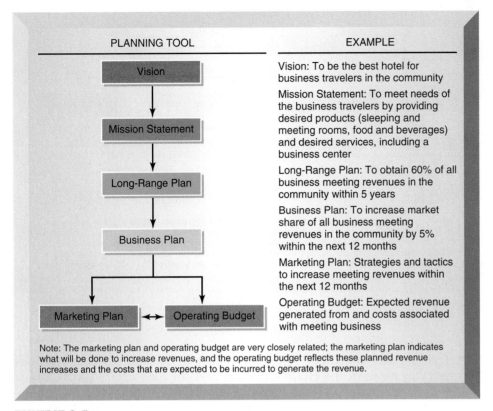

PLANNING TOOL	EXAMPLE
Vision	Vision: To be the best hotel for business travelers in the community
Mission Statement	Mission Statement: To meet needs of the business travelers by providing desired products (sleeping and meeting rooms, food and beverages) and desired services, including a business center
Long-Range Plan	Long-Range Plan: To obtain 60% of all business meeting revenues in the community within 5 years
Business Plan	Business Plan: To increase market share of all business meeting revenues in the community by 5% within the next 12 months
Marketing Plan	Marketing Plan: Strategies and tactics to increase meeting revenues within the next 12 months
Operating Budget	Operating Budget: Expected revenue generated from and costs associated with meeting business

Note: The marketing plan and operating budget are very closely related; the marketing plan indicates what will be done to increase revenues, and the operating budget reflects these planned revenue increases and the costs that are expected to be incurred to generate the revenue.

EXHIBIT 3.5
Basic Planning Tools

Organizing

Basic management principles that can help managers to organize include the following:

- **Authority** (formal power) and communication must flow through the organization. Previously, many managers believed that effective communication was one-way (down the organization); modern managers realize that communication must flow down, up, and throughout the organization.
- Relationships between different organizational levels must be specified. This is frequently done through use of an organizational chart (see a sample for a restaurant in Exhibit 3.6; numerous other organizational charts are found throughout the text).
- The organization should be designed according to the **unity of command** principle; each staff member should only have one boss.
- Similar activities should be grouped within a department; similar tasks should be grouped within a position. For example, in Exhibit 3.6 all food production and cleanup duties are centralized under the chef, and the work duties of cooks are separate from those of dishwashers.

authority the formal power that a manager has to direct the work of employees and to expect that work assignments will be completed

unity of command the organizing principle that states that each employee should report to or be accountable to only one boss for a specific activity

The hotel's executive committee at work planning goals and developing the strategies to attain them.

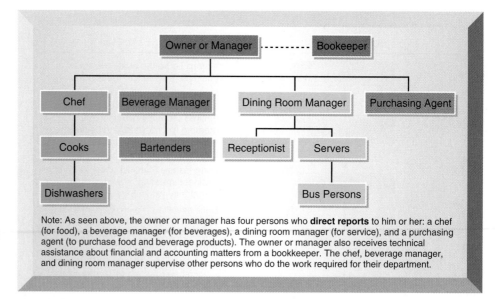

Note: As seen above, the owner or manager has four persons who **direct reports** to him or her: a chef (for food), a beverage manager (for beverages), a dining room manager (for service), and a purchasing agent (to purchase food and beverage products). The owner or manager also receives technical assistance about financial and accounting matters from a bookkeeper. The chef, beverage manager, and dining room manager supervise other persons who do the work required for their department.

EXHIBIT 3.6
Organization Chart for a Restaurant

direct reports   persons (or positions) who are supervised by the person in the next highest organizational position

line positions   those in the chain of command as authority flows from one level of management to the next

staff positions   technical, advisory specialists who provide advice to, but do not make decisions for, those in the chain of command

chain of command   the path by which authority flows from one management level to the next within the organization

- **Line positions** and **staff positions** must be considered. Line positions refer to those in the **chain of command.** In Exhibit 3.6 you will note that authority (power) flows from the owner or manager to the department head (for example, beverage manager) and down to the entry-level employee (bartender). Staff positions refer to technical, advisory specialists who provide advice to, but do not make decisions for, people in the line positions. In Exhibit 3.6, the bookkeeper is in a staff position. Many organization charts use a solid line to denote a line relationship and a broken (dotted) line to note a staff position.
- Over time, the organization's structure will change. This is necessary to keep up with the changing needs of the organization and the guests it serves.

Coordinating

Several principles help managers to assure that there is no redundancy (duplication) in work assignments. For example:

- Each employee should have specific work objectives, and these might, for example, be mutually determined at the time of performance appraisals.

E-mail enables multiunit managers to communicate with others in the organization's chain of command.

Many hotels offer business centers that allow guests to conduct small business meetings.

DID YOU KNOW?

The styles, experience, and talent of managers differ, and one can learn much from observing persons in these positions including traits that one wants and does not want to use personally.

What are some traits of successful managers?

- They accept responsibility for increasing revenue. The best general managers are the leaders of their property's sales team. They are involved in generating business even if the property has a sales department, because the manager can be a role model and can be actively involved in, at least, the larger accounts.
- They focus on success. This involves analysis of every profit center. What improvements can be made in successful programs? What should be changed in less than successful programs? Successful managers focus on the critical activities that will result in the majority of their property's success.
- They look for small successes. It is easy to criticize when something is wrong, but it is very important to compliment when things go right.
- They are great communicators, and they know how to talk and listen. Effective leadership requires understanding the needs of staff members. Much of this understanding comes from listening to staff members in efforts to find ways to help them to better perform their jobs.

Source: Neil Salerno. The best hotel general manager I ever met: How do you measure up? Retrieved on October 12, 2005, from www.hotelnewresource.com.

- There is a **span of control** that suggests the number of employees who can be supervised by one person. Typically, more persons can be supervised if the work is relatively simple and if each person in the same position performs the same work tasks. By contrast, fewer people can normally be supervised when work is more complex and relatively different from that done by peers.

span of control   the number of employees supervised by one person; also called *span of management*

responsibility the obligation that one has to do the work and to achieve the goals and objectives associated with a specific position

accountability an obligation created when a person is delegated duties or responsibilities from higher levels of management

formal work group a group of employees who work together in positions or departments as specified by the organization chart

informal work group a group of employees who are not part of a formal work group, but who still interact with each other on and/or off the job

job description a list of tasks that an incumbent in a position must be able to perform effectively

job specification a list of the personal requirements judged necessary for someone to successfully work within a position

- Authority (power) should be delegated as far down the organizational chart as possible. **Responsibility** and **accountability** cannot be delegated. These are important concepts; if, for example, a manager delegates work to someone, the power needed to perform the assigned work must be given to that staff member. By contrast, if the work is not done correctly, the supervisor cannot blame it on the employee.
- Both formal and informal employee groups must be considered. A **formal work group** is that suggested by the organizational chart. For example, the chef, cooks, and dishwashers in Exhibit 3.6 comprise a formal food production work group. An **informal work group** is comprised of persons who may be from the same or different work groups who form an unofficial group of staff members. For example, several cooks, bartenders, and food servers may take breaks together, play on a sports team, or otherwise enjoy ongoing, informal contacts. As an informal team, they may have more influence on the organization than they would as individual staff members.

Staffing

Staffing involves recruiting and selecting the job applicants who are most qualified for vacant positions. The principles involved include the following:

- Job descriptions and specifications should be developed for each position and should be kept current. Exhibit 3.7 shows part of a job description for a front-desk agent. A **job description** indicates the tasks that a person working within a position must be able to perform. By contrast, a **job specification** indicates the personal requirements judged necessary for someone to successfully work in a position. Examples include,

walk guest a guest with a reservation who is relocated from the hotel where a room reservation was made to another hotel because no room is available

guaranteed reservations an obligation (promise) incurred by a hotel that a guest room will be available on a specific date after a specified time; typically, guaranteed reservations are given upon receipt of a guest's credit card information; the guest-room rental will be charged to the card even if the guest does not use the room

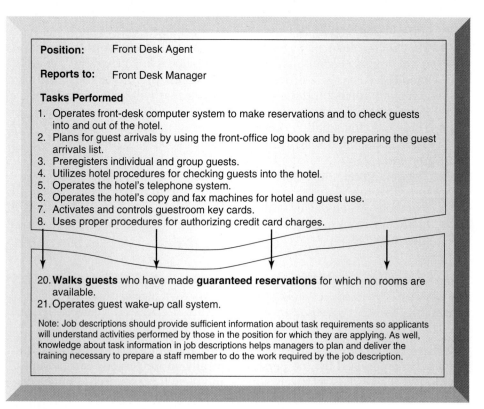

Position: Front Desk Agent

Reports to: Front Desk Manager

Tasks Performed
1. Operates front-desk computer system to make reservations and to check guests into and out of the hotel.
2. Plans for guest arrivals by using the front-office log book and by preparing the guest arrivals list.
3. Preregisters individual and group guests.
4. Utilizes hotel procedures for checking guests into the hotel.
5. Operates the hotel's telephone system.
6. Operates the hotel's copy and fax machines for hotel and guest use.
7. Activates and controls guestroom key cards.
8. Uses proper procedures for authorizing credit card charges.

20. **Walks guests** who have made **guaranteed reservations** for which no rooms are available.
21. Operates guest wake-up call system.

Note: Job descriptions should provide sufficient information about task requirements so applicants will understand activities performed by those in the position for which they are applying. As well, knowledge about task information in job descriptions helps managers to plan and deliver the training necessary to prepare a staff member to do the work required by the job description.

EXHIBIT 3.7
Job Description for a Front-Desk Agent

depending on the position, language fluency, ability to operate specific items of equipment, number of years of experience, mastery of specific skills, and certification or licensing designations.

- Job applicants should be sought from all practical sources of potential employees, and effective screening is necessary for effective recruitment.
- Properly designed job application forms (those that are legal and generate essential information) should be in use.
- Effective **orientation** and **induction** programs, training for new employees and **professional development programs** for all staff members should be in place.

Directing

Directing means essentially the same thing as supervising; managers practice effective principles of directing when they:

- Develop and implement effective training programs.
- Effectively delegate work assignments.
- Motivate employees to attain organizational goals.
- Provide **positive discipline** (to reinforce desired actions) and **negative discipline** (to discourage improper behavior).
- Effectively facilitate the work of employee teams.
- Utilize a participative management style (when appropriate) and empower their staff members.
- Vary their leadership style, when possible, based on the employees being supervised (see Exhibit 3.8).

orientation the process of providing basic information about a hospitality organization that must be known by all employees in every department

induction the process of providing basic information about the department and position that must be known only by those employees working within the department or position

professional development programs education and training given to staff members for the purpose of improving present job skills or knowledge and/or to prepare them for other positions

positive discipline supervision activities designed to reinforce desired performance

negative discipline supervision activities designed to correct undesired performance

These young persons are seeking entry-level positions in the hospitality industry. Does their appearance suggest their attitude about and interest in a position? Think about this when you apply for a job.

EXHIBIT 3.8
Alternative Leadership
Styles

Leadership Style	Example of Leadership Approach	Useful
Bureaucratic	"Do it by the book."	When standardized work (accounting, for example) must be done
Democratic	"Let's figure it out together."	For experienced and motivated employees
Laissez-faire	"You figure it out."	For consultants and subcontractors
Dictator (autocratic)	"Do it my way!"	For new employees doing relatively simple tasks

Note:

While all employees cannot be effectively managed with the same leadership style, it is relatively difficult for a supervisor to routinely modify leadership styles to meet the needs of a specific employee.

Controlling

Some persons think that the management activity of controlling involves physical action; one controls, for example, when linen storeroom doors are kept locked to prevent theft and when food is portioned to control costs. In fact, the control process requires a significant amount of planning (when performance standards are set) and evaluating (for example, to assess the extent to which standards are attained). Neither of these management tasks involves physical activity, but they are an integral part of the control process. Basic principles of control include the following:

- A formalized process of control is required (see Exhibit 3.9).
- Current and accurate operating budgets are required to establish financial performance standards. Budgets are not, then, developed "because the boss requires it"; they are an integral part of a manager's control

MANAGING THE GENERATIONS

A person's age likely affects her or his work habits. Hospitality managers should recognize basic differences when directing their staff members. There are four basic age groups:

Groups	Approximate Birth Date	Work Traits
World War II generation	1920–1945	Good work ethic; respect authority
Baby boomers	1946–1964	Team oriented; desire to do well
Generation X	1965–1975	Want balance between work and personal life; are not impressed with authority figures (such as their supervisor)
Echo boomers (also called Generation Y)	1976–1990	Ambitious; hopeful; enjoy working with their friends

Numerous procedures must be developed by managers to assure that hospitality operations of every size are kept clean.

toolbox and represent a profit plan (for the commercial operator) and an optimal cost plan (for the noncommercial operator).

Evaluating

Evaluating is the last, but very critical, step in the management process.

- It must be given a priority. (Managers cannot just evaluate "when they get around to it.")
- Managers must evaluate the extent to which goals established in basic planning documents (for example, the long-range and business plans, marketing plan, and operating budget) have been attained.
- Employee evaluation is also important and occurs when, for example, **performance appraisal** sessions are undertaken.
- Evaluation must be timely and objective and requires the ongoing collection of information to assure that data needed for evaluation are accurate and available.

performance appraisal the evaluation of a staff member's work by his or her supervisor according to preestablished factors

EXHIBIT 3.9
Steps in the Control Process

Steps	Example
Step 1: Standards must be established.	The restaurant's operating budget establishes a 35.5% food cost goal.
Step 2: Actual performance must be measured.	The income statement indicates that the actual food cost is 39.3%.
Step 3: Variance between standards and actual performance must be assessed.	The variance of 3.8% (39.3% − 35.5%) is unexplainable and excessive.
Step 4: Corrective actions to address variances between standards and actual performance must be implemented.	Decision-making (problem-solving) techniques are used to generate and select solution alternatives. Two tactics (improved purchasing and use of portion control procedures) are implemented.
Step 5: Corrective actions must be evaluated to assure success.	Food cost is reduced during the next fiscal period to 37.8%; a step toward the 35.5% goal has been taken; further corrective actions will be planned and implemented.

ALL MANAGEMENT ACTIVITIES ARE IMPORTANT

Each management activity discussed in this chapter is important; each must be done. However, some managers believe that "real" management tasks involve physical work. Therefore, they "manage by walking around." Being present as a role model and providing timely decision-making assistance are very important. So too, however, are the "mental" tasks of management, including those of planning and evaluating. These two tasks are often the management activities that are least likely to be done or the most likely to be done incorrectly.

An old saying states, "If you don't know where you are going, any road will get you there." Planning is necessary to assure that goals of the business journey are well known. With this information, other management activities can be implemented. Then the activity of evaluating becomes important to help assure that the organization is still on the best road to success.

OBJECTIVE 4
Review ways in which today's (modern) managers differ from yesterday's (traditional) managers.

MODERN MANAGERS ARE DIFFERENT FROM TRADITIONAL MANAGERS

Today's successful hospitality managers work differently from their counterparts of yesterday. Exhibit 3.10 reviews some of these differences, which represent a significant change in the philosophy of management and what is important in the process. To be successful today and certainly tomorrow, hospitality managers must recognize the importance of their guests and their employees. They will plan and deliver ways to provide value to their guests and to help their employees to find pride and joy in the workplace. They will focus on long-term success and recognize that this is done by providing the best value to their guests today.

Persons now entering the world of hospitality management have exciting opportunities. They will be successful if they recognize the importance of their guests and their employees in the success equation. They will be successful because they know the importance of quality service (see Chapter 2), because they will consistently practice basic management principles (such as

This food server is receiving training to help him do his job the correct way.

Factor	Modern Manager Says:	Traditional Manager Said:
The most important management consideration(s)	Guests, employees, quality	Money ("numbers")
Goal	Long-term success	Today's financial status
Priority employee-related concern	Help employees to find pride and joy in the workplace	Keep positions filled
How employees can help	Provide creative input to decisions	Perform physical work
How to be financially successful	Provide the greatest value to the guests	Lower quality and increase selling prices

EXHIBIT 3.10
Modern Managers Differ from Traditional Managers

reviewed in this chapter), and because they will use basic career planning practices, which are described in detail in later chapters of this book.

SUMMARY OF CHAPTER LEARNING OBJECTIVES

1. **Define the term** *management,* **and list seven resources that managers must manage.**

   Management is the process of planning, organizing, coordinating, staffing, directing, controlling, and evaluating human, financial, and physical resources for the purpose of achieving organizational goals. The resources that managers have available are labor (employees), money, products (food, beverages, and supplies), machinery (equipment), minutes (time), methodology (work processes and procedures), and energy.

2. **Explain the steps in the management decision-making (problem-solving) process.**

   The six steps in the management decision-making (problem-solving) process are to:
   - Define the problem
   - Generate solution alternatives
   - Evaluate solution alternatives
   - Select the best solution alternative
   - Implement the solution alternative
   - Evaluate the effectiveness of the solution

3. **Discuss each basic activity in the management process.**

   There are seven steps in the basic management process:
   - Planning. Defining goals, establishing strategies to achieve them, and designing ways to get work done
   - Organizing. Developing and grouping work tasks
   - Coordinating. Arranging group efforts in an orderly manner

   - Staffing. Finding the right people for the job
   - Directing. Supervising the work of staff members
   - Controlling. Determining the extent to which the organization keeps on track to achieve goals
   - Evaluating. Determining the extent to which plans are attained

   Effective hospitality managers consistently utilize principles relating to these activities in efforts to better assure the success of their organization.

4. **Review ways in which today's (modern) managers differ from yesterday's (traditional) managers.**

   The most important considerations of modern managers are guests, employees, and quality; traditional managers focus on money. The goal of modern managers is long-term success; traditional managers focus on today's financial status. The employee-related concern of modern managers is to help employees to find pride and joy in the workplace; traditional managers focus on keeping positions filled. Modern managers believe that employees can help by providing creative input to decisions; traditional managers believe that employee efforts should focus on performing physical work. Modern managers believe that providing the greatest value to guests is the way to be financially successful; traditional managers believe that lowering quality and increasing selling prices is the key to financial success.

MASTERING YOUR KNOWLEDGE

1. Think about a restaurant or hotel operation. Complete the following grid by identifying the activities necessary to manage each resource available to hospitality managers.

Note: those marked with an X are not applicable to this exercise.

Management Activity	Hospitality Resource						
	Labor	Money	Products	Machinery	Time	Method	Energy
Planning							
Organizing		X	X	X	X	X	X
Coordinating		X	X	X	X	X	X
Staffing		X	X	X	X	X	X
Directing		X	X	X	X	X	X
Controlling							
Evaluating							

FEEDBACK FROM THE REAL WORLD

Our real-world advice comes from Chef Carl Behnke, CEC, CCE.

Chef Behnke began working in restaurants in 1980. During the course of his career, he has worked for hotel companies, restaurants, and private clubs. He received his culinary training from the Culinary Institute of America (associate of science and bachelor of professional studies degrees). He later received a master's degree (major in Hospitality and Tourism Management) from Purdue University and is currently enrolled in a PhD program with an emphasis on education at Purdue. His background in food preparation, management, and education allows him to address the following questions from the viewpoint of an educator who has been out there in the real world.

What management activities are the most important? Why?

In terms of kitchen management, I believe that human resources and financial activities are the most critical. Human resources activities are a priority because even the best chefs can't do everything themselves! Selecting, training, and developing employees are activities that are crucial to running a well-balanced operation. In terms of financial activities, foodservice operations generally run on tight budgets and small cash reserves. Therefore, it is essential for managers to "keep their finger on the restaurant's financial pulse." A good chef knows exactly how much everything costs and, above all, avoids "feeding the garbage can." Following right on the heels of these two activities is sanitation. It doesn't matter how good the food is if we injure our guests because of negligence and poor sanitation practices.

What management activities are the most difficult to learn?

That really depends on the personality of the manager. An organized person will have no difficulty mastering the financial aspects of kitchen management; however, a manager who is not organized and perhaps not very mathematically oriented could have many difficulties. Sanitation is also a matter of self-discipline and organization. Human resources, on the other hand, require a manager with strong interpersonal skills.

What are the most difficult challenges that confront hospitality managers?

Currently, the most difficult challenge facing hospitality managers involves labor. The demand for foodservice operations is growing, while the labor supply is shrinking. This is forcing foodservice managers to look outside traditional labor pools and to recruit from new sources, including senior citizens, handicapped, immigrants, and others. Of course, each of these labor markets brings with it a unique set of challenges. These include working conditions and special demands needed for the elderly and handicapped and linguistic or social barriers for the immigrants. Navigating these labor challenges demands versatility and patience in today's (and tomorrow's) managers.

What, if any, role does common sense play in effective management?

Common sense is crucial in any situation, and management is no exception. Kitchens demand organization, yet the very hectic and fast-paced nature of foodservice operations often nullifies one's best efforts at organization. This is where common sense comes into play. It provides a manager with guidance in those instances where organization fails and systems break down. (Unfortunately, as one of my mentors often said, common sense is not always common practice!)

What, if any, role does experience play in effective management?

Experience (otherwise known as the "school of hard knocks") helps a manager to develop a personal foundation of common sense. Experience puts one to the test and, with effective reflection, allows a manager to imagine alternatives should the same situation recur. The more often this cycle of experience and reflection is applied, the greater the depth of common sense; consequently, the greater will be one's ability to handle abnormal situations with the wisdom and guidance of a true leader.

2. Use the decision-making (problem-solving) process to determine a solution to a problem that you currently must address.
3. List the tasks that you think would be done by persons in each position in the organization chart for the restaurant illustrated in Exhibit 3.6.
4. What are some ways that informal work groups can be beneficial and harmful to a hospitality operation.

5. Think about some managers or supervisors who have directed your work. What kind of leadership style did they practice (see Exhibit 3.8)? What are examples of their leadership traits that helped you to define their leadership style?
6. What are three things that you learned in this chapter that will benefit you when you become a hospitality manager?

LEARN FROM THE INTERNET

1. Check out the following hotel and restaurant websites:

   Hotels
   - Hilton Hotels Corporation: www.hilton.com
   - Starwood Hotels & Resorts: www.starwood.com
   - Marriott Hotels, Resort and Suites: www.marriott.com

   Restaurants
   - Hard Rock Cafe: www.hardrock.com
   - Houston's: www.houstons.com
   - McDonald's: www.macdonalds.com

   Look for "Employment Opportunities" or career information. What kinds of responsibilities are noted to be important in the positions that are cited? What, if any, differences do you note between positions in the hotel and restaurant websites?

2. Check out the following websites of organizations in the noncommercial foodservices segment:
   - Aladdin Food Management Services, Inc.: www.aladdinfood.com
   - Sodexho: www.sodexho.com
   - Morrison Management Specialists: www.iammorrison.com

   Look for "Employment" or "careers." What type of positions are discussed? How, if at all, do management positions in these organizations differ from their counterparts in commercial foodservices organizations?

3. The travel/tourism/hospitality industry has many publications that provide examples of managers in action. Review current and recent articles in the following electronic magazines:

- Restaurants and Institutions Magazine: www .rimag.com

- Hotel & Motel Management: www.hotelmotel .com

- Foodservice.com: www.foodservice.com

- Lodging Magazine: www.lodgingmagazine.com

KEY HOSPITALITY TERMS

The following terms were explained in this chapter. Review the definitions of any words with which you are unfamiliar. Begin to utilize them as you expand your vocabulary as a hospitality professional.

management
budget
revenue
expenses
bottom line
check average
suggestive selling
cross-functional teams
process revisions
planning
organizing
coordinating
staffing
directing
controlling
evaluating
delegation
rework
vision
mission statement
long-range plan
business plan
marketing plan

operating budget
authority
unity of command
direct reports
line positions
staff positions
chain of command
span of control
responsibility
accountability
formal work group
informal work group
job description
job specification
walk guests
guaranteed reservations
orientation
induction
professional development programs
positive discipline
negative discipline
performance appraisal

Part 2

LODGING OPERATIONS

Overview: Hotels, Hotels, Hotels!

4

Ciadade de Goa Beach Resort, Goa, India

CHAPTER LEARNING OBJECTIVES

After studying this chapter you will be able to:

1. Review the range of lodging property alternatives available to travelers.
2. Discuss three common ways to classify lodging properties.
3. Describe basic characteristics that all lodging properties share.
4. Explain common hotel ownership and management alternatives.
5. Describe how basic hotel functions are organized and integrated.
6. List challenges (opportunities) confronting today's hotel industry.
7. Review the wide range of positions within which one may work in the lodging industry.

FEEDBACK FROM THE REAL WORLD

Many alternatives are available to today's consumers when they select lodging accommodations. The options become obvious as one drives along the highway, flips yellow pages in the telephone book, and reads magazines marketed to travelers.

What exactly do the average travelers looking for a hotel room on a business or pleasure trip know about the hotel brands that they see and read about? How exactly do they decide where to stay on their next trip requiring overnight accommodations? How do the guests' experiences at a specific property influence their interest in staying at that property again when they return to the location or at another hotel with the same brand when they travel to another location?

As you read this chapter, think about answers to these questions and then get feedback from the real world at the end of the chapter.

When many people consider the hospitality industry, they think about hotels and restaurants. While this is not technically correct (you learned about many other types of hospitality operations in Chapter 1), it is true that hotels and restaurants are a very significant part of the industry. In this chapter you will learn basic background information about lodging properties. While there are many ways that the numerous types of hotels are different, there are also ways in which they are similar. These are the topics of this chapter.

OBJECTIVE 1
Review the range of lodging property alternatives available to travelers.

RANGE OF LODGING PROPERTIES

Today's hotels are vastly different from the private homes, hostels, and inns that were the first sanctuaries for weary travelers. Owners of lodging accommodations have likely differentiated travelers by their ability to pay since the industry's beginning: more affluent travelers are willing to pay more for the products, services, and amenities that they receive as long as they receive a value. The earliest innkeepers along travel routes likely offered their guest choices (for example, a single room or a room shared with others) based on their ability to pay.

Today's lodging industry is one of **niche marketing.** There are innumerable types of hotels appealing to widely different types of travelers. This

niche marketing the process of offering products or services that appeal to a very specific subsegment (niche) of the market; for example, hoteliers may focus on the needs of long-stay business travelers, rather than all business travelers, and may provide amenities in lodging accommodations that persons in this subsegment desire

DID YOU KNOW?

The niches (small segments) of the hotel marketplace are becoming smaller and smaller. For example, many hotels cater to female travelers. Some do so with women-only floors accessible with special key cards for security, special room-service menus, upgraded bathrooms and toiletries, extra lighting, larger closets, and makeup mirrors. Some hotels cater to tall people with oversized king-size beds, heightened shower heads, and oversized bathrobes, and many properties advertise that they are pet friendly. At least one hotel (The Doubletree Hotel Tucson) offers allergy-friendly rooms, and persons with medical concerns have increasing access to services offering physicians' house calls in guest rooms.

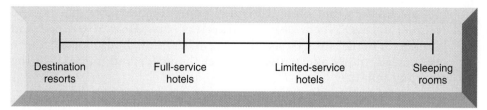

EXHIBIT 4.1
Range of Lodging Property Alternatives

> ## WHO STAYS IN HOTELS?
>
> Persons staying in hotels can be classified according to the purpose of their travel:
>
> | | |
> |---|---|
> | Business or corporate (individuals) | Long-stay guests |
> | Business or corporate (groups) | Airline-related guests |
> | Convention or association groups | Government or military guests |
> | Leisure travelers | Regional "getaway" guests |

diversity in lodging alternatives has emerged in efforts to meet the increasingly specific demands of increasingly narrow segments of the traveling public.

What is a **hotel?** In its most basic definition, a hotel is a building that offers sleeping rooms. This definition, however, is not very helpful because of the wide range of alternatives that we have already noted. Exhibit 4.1 illustrates one way to classify the range of properties that are considered hotels. Let's learn more about these basic types of lodging properties.

- Destination **resorts** typically offer lavish accommodations, several food and beverage outlets ranging from gourmet (high check average) to poolside snack bars, the highest possible service standards, and, typically, recreational alternatives, such as golf, spas, tennis, aquatic, and other activities, depending on the type of guests for whom the property is marketed. Destination resorts are frequently offered in locations with additional attractions, including snow skiing, ocean (beach) activities, and/or horseback riding.
- **Full-service hotels** have at least one thing in common (food and beverage services) and range from modest, small properties with a dining room along the nation's highways, to properties with meeting and banquet spaces near airports, to high-rise centers appealing to business travelers in the nation's cities.
- **Limited-service hotels** also have one thing in common (no or almost no food service; continental breakfasts are sometimes offered as an amenity included in the price). Most are typically found in suburban and highway locations. There are two basic types: traditional properties that rent sleeping rooms to guests for several (or fewer) days and **extended-stay** properties that market to guests desiring lodging accommodations for longer time periods (generally one week or longer).
- **Sleeping rooms** may offer barracks-style sleeping accommodations, such as youth hostels, or small, private rooms or even small sleeping compartments that serve travelers in some airport locations. These properties offer private or shared restroom facilities. There are also

hotel a for-profit business that rents sleeping rooms and often provides other amenities such as food and beverage services, swimming pools and exercise rooms, meeting spaces, business centers, and concierge services; also referred to as *motel, motor hotel,* or *motor inn*

resorts full-service hotels with additional attractions to make them a primary destination for travelers

full-service hotel a hotel that provides guests with extensive food and beverage products and services

limited-service hotel a lodging property that offers very limited food services or none at all; sometimes a complimentary breakfast is served, but there is no table-service restaurant

extended-stay hotel a midpriced, limited-service hotel marketing to guests desiring accommodations for extended time periods (generally one week or longer)

sleeping room a lodging alternative of basic sleeping accommodations with or without private rest room facilities

hostel a lodging accommodation, typically available in a dormitory style, that is generally inexpensive and frequented by youthful travelers.

upscale **hostels** that offer balconies, complimentary breakfasts, and Internet access. Where else can travelers stay? How about bed and breakfast (B&B) sites, spas, dude ranches, and houseboats? There are, indeed, many alternatives to meet the needs and interests of the traveling public.

We have still not exhausted the range of lodging alternatives. Facilities not frequently thought of as hotels may also provide sleeping rooms. Examples include private clubs, cruise ships, casinos, and privately owned and timeshare condominiums. (All these and other not so frequently thought of components of the hospitality industry will be discussed later in this book. Facilities offering sleeping accommodations for people living away from their homes, such as schools, colleges, and universities with residential services, and healthcare facilities can also be considered part of the lodging industry and will be addressed later.)

OBJECTIVE 2
Discuss three common ways to classify lodging properties.

CLASSIFICATION OF HOTELS

Lodging properties can be classified in numerous ways. As shown in Exhibit 4.2, common classifications include location, rate, and size. In 2003, most U.S. hotels were in suburban and highway locations, were low to midpriced ($30 to $59.99), and had less than 75 rooms.[1] This description of an average hotel should be of great interest to those aspiring to careers in the lodging industry. Numerous excellent positions are available in the industry. However, the number of very large properties with very high **rack rates** in large city centers and/or exotic locations is relatively small. As well, general manager positions with duties such as those glamorized in movies and television do not exist, although positions in hotels of all sizes, price ranges, and locations offer challenging and exciting professional opportunities.

rack rate the price at which a hotel sells its rooms when no discounts of any kind are offered to the guest; often shortened to *rack*

Some industry observers classify properties within the lodging industry by guest-room rental charges. Resulting classifications fall along a range such as that suggested in Exhibit 4.3. These classifications do not correlate very easily with the rate structure suggested in Exhibit 4.2. It is difficult to classify hotels strictly by rack rates because room charges vary significantly among geographic regions. For example, the most expensive hotel available in a small northern Midwest town may be one-half (or less) of the rate charged for the least expensive, safe, and clean hotel room in a major East or West Coast city.

EXHIBIT 4.2
Common Ways to Categorize Lodging Properties

By Location	By Rate ($)	By Size (rooms)
Urban	Under 30	Under 75
Suburban	30–44.99	75–149
Highway	45–59.99	150–299
Airport	60–85	300–500
Resort	More than 85	Over 500

These classifications are used by the AHLA; check out current statistics applicable to each classification on AHLA's home page (www.ahla.com). Reproduced with permission from the American Hotel & Lodging Association, 1201 New York Avenue NW, Suite 600, Washington, D.C. 20005.

---

[1] www.ahla.com; check the website for current data.

DID YOU KNOW?

- The largest hotel in the world, Asia-Asia, is scheduled for completion in 2010. Located in Dubai, it will have 6,500 rooms. Of these, 5,100 will be four-star and 1,400 will be five-star rooms.*

  * Source: Dubailand to double Dubai hotel rooms with $27bn project. Retrieved May 2, 2006, from www.ameinfo.com

- If "money were no object," how much could you spend for a one-night stay at some of the world's best hotels? Here's a sample:[†]

  The Mansion at the MGM Grand (Las Vegas): $5,000

  Fregate Island Private (Seychelles): $2,482

  Le Toiny (St. Barthelemy, French West Indies): $2,092

  Singita Private Game Reserve (Sabi Sand, South Africa): $2,200

  The Wakaya Club (Fiji): $1900

  [†] _**Source:**_ World's Most Expensive Hotels 2005. Retrieved May 21, 2006, from www.msnbc.com.

LODGING INDUSTRY CHARACTERISTICS[2]

OBJECTIVE 3
Describe basic characteristics that all lodging properties share.

As seen previously, we can classify hotels by location, by rate, and/or by size. These factors suggest differences between lodging properties. However, all properties share several common characteristics:

- _Emphasis on safety, cleanliness, and service._ Few, if any, guests consider only the room and other physical attributes of the property when making a stay or no-stay decision. For example, safety and cleanliness are very important considerations. Friendliness (hospitality) of employees is also important and, along with the property's physical aspects (size, location, quality of maintenance, furnishings, and other factors), is part of the guests' evaluation mix. By contrast to their retail store counterparts, then, there are intangible (difficult to quantify) aspects of the purchase decision that potential hotel guests consider.
- _Inseparability of manufacture and sales._ It is not possible to separate the "manufacture" (production) of a guest room with its "sale." A room exists and is sold at the same site. (Contrast this with, for example, the

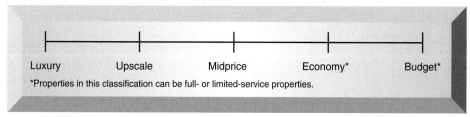

EXHIBIT 4.3
Range of Lodging Properties Classified by Guest-Room Rental Charges

---

[2]This and the next section are from David Hayes and Jack Ninemeier, _Hotel Operations Management,_ 2nd ed. Upper Saddle River, NJ: Pearson Prentice Hall, 2007.

Tropical hotel guest room. The location, view, and amenities are among the many factors that this couple considered when they selected this hotel.

manufacture and sale of an automobile, shirt, or television set. They are typically manufactured at one site and sold at another.) The hotel's general manager and his or her staff, then, must be experts at both manufacture and sales. Their counterparts in many other industries must normally be experts in only one phase of business: either manufacturing products or selling them to the consumer in the marketplace.

- *Perishability.* If a guest room is not rented on a specific date, the revenue is lost forever. By contrast, an automobile, shirt, or television can be sold tomorrow if it is not sold today.

- *Repetitiveness.* The steps involved in making guest rooms ready for sale or for preparing a specific meal or drink and then renting (selling) them are basically the same every time the guest room, meal, or drink is sold. These routines (operating procedures) allow for some standardization. At the same time, however, they create challenges. It is always important to focus on the individual needs of guests, and standardization can provide less opportunity for staff creativity in the decision-making processes used to perform required work.

labor intensive the need for people rather than for equipment (machinery or technology) to perform required work tasks

- **Labor intensive.** In many industries, including the automotive and electronics segments, technology and equipment have replaced people in some work activities. By contrast, in the lodging industry this has occurred only to a lesser degree. For example, technology is being used in the front office, sales, and accounting departments, where many tasks are highly automated. However, technology could be utilized even more in the industry: automated check-in and check-out systems are available, and convenience foods can be used to reduce on-site labor, which is otherwise needed for food production. However, the traveling public increasingly desires and is willingly to pay for services that must be delivered by employees. Staff members are (and in the near term will likely be) required to produce and deliver products and services at the quality levels desired by the guests and to the quantity standards required by the property.

Beach resort in Buzios, Brazil

It is ironic that the two hotel departments that typically require the most employees (food and beverage and housekeeping) represent the areas in the typical hotel where technology has been least able to replace employees.

POPULAR RATING SYSTEMS ALSO CLASSIFY HOTELS

Many travelers utilize the rating system of the American Automobile Association (AAA) and the Mobil Corporation when making hotel selection decisions.* Both organizations utilize detailed and objective factors to rate hotels. The Mobil rating system utilizes stars:

A one-star hotel should be clean, comfortable, and well maintained.

A two-star hotel offers the basic quality of a one-star property plus additional features, including a restaurant, swimming pool, and room service.

A three-star hotel is one offering a truly excellent lodging experience.

A four-star hotel is luxurious and characterized by attention to detail and the feeling that guest comfort and convenience are the priority concern.

A five-star property is an elite property that is ranked superior in every area of the rating system.

The AAA rating system is similar, but utilizes diamonds:

A one-diamond property offers good but modest accommodations.

A two-diamond property has room decor and furnishing enhancements superior to its one-diamond counterpart.

A three-diamond property offers a marked upgrade in amenities, service, and facilities.

A four-diamond property displays a high level of service and hospitality.

A five-diamond property offers an exceptionally high degree of service, and the facility's operations set standards in hospitality and service for the industry.

*For more information, see Mobil Corporation at www.exxonmobiltravel.com and American Automobile Association at www.aaa.com.

HOTEL OWNERSHIP AND MANAGEMENT

OBJECTIVE 4
Explain common hotel ownership and management alternatives.

A motorist is driving along the highway and sees the **flag** of a popular hotel chain. The name is easily recognizable (made so, in part, by an extensive nationwide advertising campaign). A typical reaction is, "I guess that hotel company purchased some land and built another hotel to operate in this location." In fact, this is not likely to be the case. It is very possible (and most likely) that an investor has built the property on owned (or leased) land, hired a contract management company to operate the property, and signed an agreement with a franchiser to operate the hotel **brand.**

Hotels are owned and managed in numerous ways. Here are two:

- *Single-unit property not affiliated with any chain.* Some single-unit properties have been in business for many years, are extremely successful, and may be the most preferred hotel in a community or area. This, however, is the exception. These properties (sometimes referred to as **mom and pop hotels**) are generating a smaller market share in today's lodging industry nationwide.
- *Multiunit properties.* Properties that are part of a hotel chain are the most prevalent. The brand affiliation, whether international, nationwide, regional, or located within an even smaller area, is successful because of name recognition and economy of scale in operations and

flag   the specific brand with which a hotel may affiliate; examples of currently popular flags include brands such as Comfort Inns, Holiday Inn Express, Ramada Inns, Hampton Inns, Residence Inns, Best Western, and Hawthorn Suites; hotels affiliated with a specific flag are sometimes referred to as a *chain*

brand   name of a hotel chain; sometimes referred to as a *flag*

mom and pop hotels   a slang term sometimes used to refer to an independent property (one not affiliated with a brand) that is owned and operated by a single person or family

The limited-service hotel market is growing because many guests do not require extensive food and beverage service.

because it is often easier to receive financing for business (unit or chain) growth.

Let's look at multiunit (chain) properties more closely:

franchise   an arrangement whereby one party (the brand) allows another (the hotel owners) to use its logo, name, systems, and resources in exchange for a fee

franchiser   one who manages the brand and sells the right to use the brand name

franchisee   those who own the hotel and buy the right to use the brand name for a fixed period of time at an agreed-upon price

entrepreneur   a person who assumes the risk of owning and operating a business in exchange for the financial rewards that the business may produce

investor   an individual or organization that provides money for a business such as a hospitality operation with the goal of receiving a profitable return

management company   an organization that operates a hotel(s) for a fee; also sometimes called a *contract company* or *contract management company*

- **Franchise** *hotels or nonfranchise hotels.* Franchise hotels are typically the chains with the greatest name recognition. The **franchiser,** such as Hilton Hotels, Sheraton, Hyatt, and Marriott, sells certain rights to a **franchisee,** such as to use the name (to "fly the flag"), to connect to the national reservation system, and to utilize proven operating procedures in return for numerous fees. An **entrepreneur** owning one or more hotels that are not affiliated with a franchise has the advantage of not paying numerous fees, but loses advantages such as name recognition and access to the franchiser's reservation systems.
- *Independently owned hotel or company-owned hotel.* Sometimes an **investor** (an individual or an organization) owns (or leases) land and builds the hotel. This is an example of an independently owned hotel. By contrast, a franchiser may buy land or build buildings for a company-owned hotel. (In fact, many franchisers own some properties outright, have partial ownership in others, and have no ownership in still other properties.)
- *Independent, company- or* **management company**-*operated.* Day to day operations of a hotel might be the responsibility of an independent owner, the franchiser (in a company-operated property), or a management company. When the management company is used, the owner hires a professional hotel management company for the day to day operational responsibilities for the property. Many management companies operate hotels of numerous brands that are owned by many separate owners.

Exhibit 4.4 reviews the many types of hotel ownership and management alternatives that we have discussed. When reviewing the figure, you will note that a specific hotel property can be franchise or nonfranchise affiliated. If it is a franchise operation, it can be owned by an independent investor or by a franchise company (the franchiser). Also, you will note that a franchise can be operated independently, by the franchiser, or by a management company. Exhibit 4.4 also indicates that a nonfranchise property is one that is owned by an independent investor who may operate it himself or herself or, alternatively, hire a management company for operational responsibilities.

**Daniel Pirrallo
General Manager
Millennium Harvest
House, Boulder**

A Hotel with Tennis Courts or Tennis Courts with a Hotel?

Conveniently located on 16 acres of land adjacent to the University of Colorado, the Millennium Harvest House–Boulder is a prestigious 269-room property with 18,000 square feet of function space. It is the only facility in the region with on-property tennis courts. There are 15 in total, 5 of which are contained within an all-weather "bubble." The property generates about $1 million annually in revenue from its 500 Sporting Association members who join to use the indoor and outdoor pools and the workout and tennis facilities. The Millennium Harvest House–Boulder, in effect, is the closest thing to a tennis resort in the entire region.

Dan began his hospitality career by earning an undergraduate degree in hospitality management and spent almost 20 years with ITT Sheraton Corporation. He completed management training in Minnesota and then held food and beverage positions in Atlanta, Washington, D.C., and New Orleans. After serving as resident manager at the Sheraton in Dallas, Dan moved to the ITT Sheraton World Headquarters in Boston. There he served as the director of rooms and reservations for the eastern region. He then returned to operations as the hotel manager (the number two position) for the 1200-room Sheraton Boston Hotel. He served as the general manager of the Sheraton Suites in Wilmington, Delaware, and then returned to the Sheraton Boston as its general manager.

After ITT Sheraton was purchased by Starwood, Dan chose to join Anderson Consulting in Philadelphia. However, after a short while he missed the hotel industry and returned to it by managing the Millennium Knickerbocker in Chicago. He recently moved to his present position in Boulder, Colorado.

Dan's most significant current professional challenge is the economy. Since Boulder is a regional technical center, the economic downturn that began in early 2001 hurt the corporate transient market. The leisure market is less affected, but it is also now different: "We have had to shift our marketing efforts to the weekend drive market. Guests drive in for the weekend, rather than fly in for the week."

Recruiting employees for his business is also difficult, and it is especially challenging to screen applicants to assure that only qualified candidates with valid working permits or papers are hired. Dan says it is easy to summarize a hotelier's greatest challenge: "Find new business and take care of it!"

Marketing concerns also present opportunities. "Everyone is going after the same business. There is simply more supply [rooms] than demand [guests to occupy them]." Dan also notes that it is easy to lose control of rate integrity in specific market segments due to the increasing number of reservations made over Internet booking channels.

Dan's greatest service concerns involve his employees. With high staff turnover created by seasonal employment, it is difficult to quickly train employees to meet and exceed his guests' expectations. The problem is heightened because the downturn in the economy has created the need to keep management staff to a minimum. Training, therefore, must be very focused on quickly developing the employee's skills to deliver quality service.

Dan is optimistic about the short-term future of the corporate market. "You cannot replace face to face meetings with alternatives such as teleconferencing," he reasons. "The Millennium Harvest House provides an 'oasis to escape' for business travelers looking for a secluded place to hold productive meetings and to reduce the stress created by increased business demands."

Dan begins his day between 6:30 and 7:00 A.M. by answering e-mails and voice messages and by doing administrative paper work. He then holds a daily management-briefing meeting with his management team to discuss significant events of the previous and current day. By 8:45 A.M. Dan is off to the races as he meets with department heads to address the best ways to manage the business. Every day is different.

(continued)

"Some days you just run flat out." For example, when the University of Colorado football team plays at home, the hotel staff installs a 16-foot television so that the 3,000 to 4,000 fans can view the Colorado Buffaloes taking on their latest Big 12 challenger. These events generate as much as $80,000 in beverage sales in just one afternoon!

Dan knows that to be successful a hotelier must be involved in the community. He is active with the Boulder Convention and Visitors Bureau, Boulder's cultural and arts community, and the state and local area's hotel and lodging association.

Dan offers the following advice for those considering a hospitality career: "If you think of this type of work as just a job, then this may not be the right career for you. Hotel managers are always on the job 365 days a year. You must also keep in mind that you work when everyone else plays, and vice versa. You and your family must learn to accept this. Work hours are likely to be long early in your career, and they may be long later in your career as well." Dan, for example, now works 50 to 60 hours per week, but admits that he works some of the hours simply because he likes to be there.

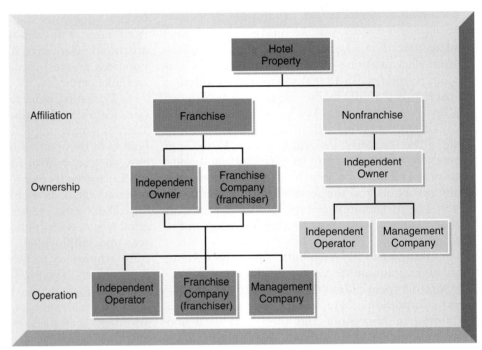

EXHIBIT 4.4
Hotel Ownership and Management Alternatives

MORE ABOUT FRANCHISE AND MANAGEMENT AGREEMENTS

Franchising is a network of business relationships that allows people to share brand identification, a successful method of doing business, and a strong marketing and distribution system.* The franchisee incurs less risk because proven operational methods developed by the franchisor are used to manage the business. However, the franchisee gives up the freedom of being completely independent and becomes part of the group committed to building a brand and increasing the groups' market share. The franchisee must also pay fees for the operating license and must comply with brand standards that have been established by the franchisor.

Today's hotel owners increasingly affiliate their hotels with other hotels under a common brand name. Most franchise companies do not own the hotels operating under their brand name. Instead, they sell the right to the brand name and determine the standards that must be followed. This arrangement can create conflict between hotel owners and franchisors. General managers of these hotels have an obvious responsibility to their employer (owner), but they also must abide by the franchise agreement signed by the property's owners.

With so many franchisors available, how is the best one for a specific hotel selected? Factors may include the quality and expertise of the brand managers, the perceived quality and service level of the brand, the amount of fees paid, and the percentage of revenue that will contributed by the brand's reservation system.

Many hotel owners do not want to manage properties. Instead, they may hire a management company to do so. Management companies often receive a predetermined monthly fee from the hotel owner in exchange for operating the property. The owner then assumes a passive position about operating decisions while, at the same time, assuming responsibility for all working capital, operating expenses, and debt-service fees, regardless of the hotel's profitability (if any).

Advantages to hotel owners may include: improved management quality may be realized, targeted expertise can be obtained, documented managerial effectiveness is available, the payment for services can be tied to performance, and partnership opportunities are enhanced. Potential disadvantages include that the owner has little or no control over the selection of the on-site general manager and other high-level managers, talented managers leave frequently, the interest of hotel owners and the management company may conflict, the cost of management company errors is borne by the owner, and transfer of ownership may be complicated.

*This discussion is loosely based on David Hayes and Jack Ninemeier. *Hotel Operations Management*, 2nd ed. Upper Saddle River, New Jersey, Pearson Prentice Hall, 2007. For a detailed discussion about franchise agreements and management contracts, see Chapter 13.

HOW HOTELS ARE ORGANIZED

OBJECTIVE 5
Describe how basic hotel functions are organized and integrated.

As you have learned, hotels are labor intensive. People, not machines, produce products and deliver service and, as consistently noted throughout this book, guests desire and are willing to pay for these "handmade" products and services when they rent a hotel room and/or purchase other accommodations at a lodging property.

Upscale hotels offer luxury guest-room accommodations.

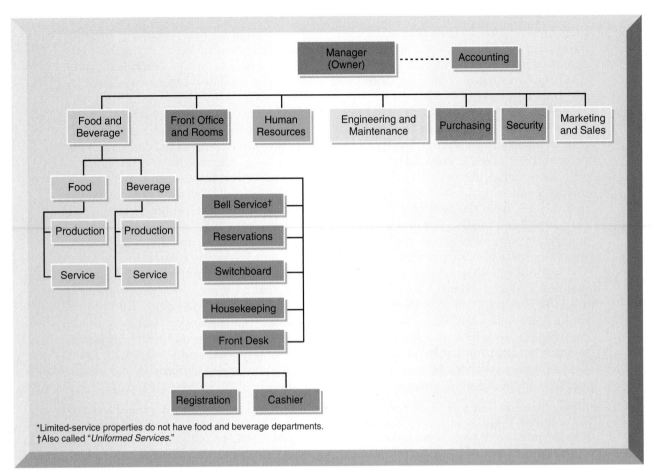

EXHIBIT 4.5
Organization of Hotel Functions

Guest rooms in limited-service hotels are comfortable.

Exhibit 4.5 identifies the minimum functions required in a lodging property of any size. (Note that some limited-service properties offer no or minimal food and beverage services.) In a very small (less than 75 rooms) limited-service property, the manager (owner) may personally perform all functions except those relating to housekeeping and engineering and maintenance. An external accountant and bookkeeper may be retained to compile operating data and for tax-reporting purposes.

By contrast, a larger (350 room) full-service property will likely have department heads who report to the manager, are responsible for each function,

NOT ALL HOTEL GROUPS ARE CHAINS

Many people think that all hotel groups belong to chains with the same company name, such as Hilton, Hyatt, and Marriott, or that all hotel groups represent a brand, such as Hilton's Doubletree, Embassy Suites, Hampton Inn, and Hilton Hotels.

While hotels that are part of the same company and brand do belong to a hotel group, there are other hotel groups that are not part of company or brand chains. These groups provide reservations and other marketing or sales services to independent hotels.

To check out some of these groups and the properties they represent, go to:

- Preferred Hotels: www.preferredhotels.com
- Leading Hotels of the World: www.lhw.com
- Relais & Chateau: www.relais&chateau.com
- Small Luxury Hotels of the World: www.slh.com

and supervise others with more specific responsibilities within that function, For example, an executive housekeeper may supervise inspectors, room attendants, public space cleaners, and laundry staff; a front-desk office manager may supervise front-desk reservation agents, bell staff, and van drivers. In a still larger (3,000 room) hotel there may be an accountant and controller who supervises the assistant controller who, in turn, supervises credit managers, payroll supervisors, and head cashiers, who then manage the work of entry-level staff within that specialty. As the size of the property increases, so do the number of positions and the more narrowly focused are the tasks within each position.

CHALLENGES CONFRONTING THE HOTEL INDUSTRY

Numerous challenges confront today's hotel industry. Most observers see these as long-term issues that will not "go away tomorrow." Persons entering the lodging industry in the near term, such as you and other students, will therefore be involved in the process leading to the way that the industry adapts to these challenges.

OBJECTIVE 6
List challenges (opportunities) confronting today's hotel industry.

REVENUE AND COST CENTERS

Hotel departments can be divided into revenue centers (if they generate revenue) and cost centers (if they exist to help revenue centers to generate sales).

Revenue Departments*	Cost Centers[†]
Rooms	Marketing
Food and beverage	Engineering
Telephone	Accounting
Fitness and recreation facilities	Human resources
	Security

*Hotels may also receive revenues from space rental (such as leasing a gift shop) and from sources such as parking garage fees, vending machines, and business center services. A relatively recent trend: hotels now sell guest-room furnishings, such as bedding (including the bed!), robes, and even desk lamps. See, for example, www.shopMarriott.com.
[†]Cost centers might be considered staff departments: hotel divisions that provide technical and supportive assistance to revenue departments.

Bed and breakfast in the Rocky Mountains

Exhibit 4.6 reviews some of the operating, marketing, technological, and economic challenges confronting today's lodging industry. Let's look at these challenges more closely.

Operating Issues

- *Labor shortages.* Labor shortages and their impact on the industry in almost every geographic location are consistently among the most difficult challenges noted by hoteliers (and by managers in all other segments of the hospitality industry as well). In many communities, hotel expansion is limited not by capital (money), but rather by human resources.
- *Cost containment.* Hoteliers are increasingly challenged to find ways to reduce costs without sacrificing the quality standards imposed to consistently meet guest expectations. The idea of "doing more with less" requires managers to think about ways to operate more effectively (in other words, to "do the right things in the right way") and to examine possibilities for cost savings that will not affect the guest's perception of value.
- *Increased competition.* Hoteliers everywhere indicate that their community is **overbuilt;** there are too many available hotel rooms relative to the guests desiring to rent them. The resulting competition, which often involves price cutting in efforts to provide greater value to guests, reduces still further the profits generated.

overbuilt   the condition that exists when too many hotel guest rooms are available for the number of travelers wanting to rent them

Marketing Issues

- **Market segmentation** *and overlapping brands.* Market segmentation is increasing as lodging chains focus on a specific niche of travelers. Additionally, brands overlap. Some industry observers are concerned that franchisers may expand their number of brands to the point that investors who purchase from the same franchiser will be in direct competition with themselves! Also, as the number of brands increases, the ability of consumers to differentiate among them decreases.

market segmentation efforts to focus on a highly defined (smaller) group of travelers

EXHIBIT 4.6
Lodging Industry Challenges

Type of Issue	Challenges
Operating	Labor shortages
	Cost containment
	Increased competition
Marketing	Market segmentation and overlapping brands
	Increased guest sophistication and amenities
Technological	Interactive reservation systems
	Guest-room innovations
	Data mining
	Yield management
Economic	Dependence on the nation's economy
	Globalization
	Terrorism and safety

- *Increased guest sophistication.* Consumers have become more sophisticated and, as a result, so have the types of products and services that they desire. Amenities, including business centers, exercise and recreational facilities, and guest-room innovations, increase costs but, if not carefully selected, may not appeal to many guests being served by a specific property.

Technological Issues

The challenge of keeping up with the fast pace of technology is difficult and expensive.

- *Interactive reservation systems.* Increasingly, guests use the Internet's interactive reservation systems, and hotel companies are sometimes criticized for the (alleged) large number of keyboard clicks required to make a reservation.
- *Guest-room innovations.* Multiple telephone lines, interactive opportunities for ordering room service, and guest-room check-out are examples of amenities that guests increasingly desire, but that are very expensive to install and implement.
- **Data mining.** This technology allows marketing and sales personnel to find new ways to use guest-related data.
- **Yield management.** This computerized process allows managers to match guest demand with room rates (high demand means higher rates because of lessened discounts; low demand results in higher discounts).

Economic Issues

- *Dependence on the nation's economy.* When the nation's economy is good, business travel generally increases. **Hotel occupancy rates** and rack rates increase, which results in higher profit levels. The reverse is also true: business travel slows when the economy slows. Then occupancy and rack rates decrease. Discounts to increase occupancy are offered, which yield lower revenues and profit decreases.
- **Globalization.** Globalization affects the lodging industry dramatically because it influences the extent to which people travel both within the country and around the world. Therefore, it is not only the economy of the nation, but also the economies of individual countries, that play an increasingly larger role in the financial success of lodging properties.
- **Terrorism** *and safety.* Fear of travel after the World Trade Center and Pentagon attacks of September 11, 2001, and

An elegant lobby in a luxury Manhattan (New York City) hotel.

data mining using technology to analyze guest- (and other) related data to make better marketing decisions

yield management demand forecasting systems designed to maximize revenue by holding rates high during times of high guest-room demand and by decreasing room rates during times of lower guest-room demand

hotel occupancy rate the ratio of guest rooms sold (including comps) to guest rooms available for sale in a given time period; always expressed as a percentage, the formula for occupancy rate is: Number of guest rooms sold ÷ number of guest rooms available

globalization the process by which countries and communities within them throughout the world are becoming increasingly interrelated

terrorism the threat of danger created and harm caused by persons for political or religious reasons

A concierge provides information to guests in upscale hotels.

worldwide concerns about terrorism have brought safety issues to the forefront of every segment of the hospitality industry, including hotels. This issue, while beyond the hoteliers' control, will be of significant concern for the foreseeable future.

RISING STAR PROFILE

Anastasia Callahan
Senior Manager
Owner and Franchise Services
Marriott International

Diversify Your Experience!

Anastasia received her bachelor of science degree in food, hotel, and tourism in 1990. She learned innkeeping while in college by rotating through numerous positions at the Sherwood in Skaneateles, New York (in the state's Finger Lakes region). While there, she worked in front desk, housekeeping, bookkeeping, hostessing, and food serving (coordinating service staff).

After graduating from college, she began working for Marriott and, over the next 13 years, she worked with properties representing all its brands. She began her career in operations by working at the front desk. Then, for the next 8 years, she worked in positions related to inside and outside multiproperty sales, generating mostly transient and extended-stay business. Her responsibilities in these sales positions included assisting potential guests who contacted the hotel

for information about group meetings. She booked the business, handled details, and communicated the guests' needs to the operations staff that delivered the services. Her outside sales responsibilities involved identifying strategic ways to find business that fit available times within the hotel. Direct sales calls, prospecting, and maintaining decision-maker relationships were her main functions.

Her next position involved revenue management. These responsibilities included yielding and managing room inventory to maximize revenue-based demand. Analysis of historical trends, current knowledge of market conditions, and awareness of competitive pricing were critical parts of her position as revenue manager.

Most recently, she has served in sales and marketing positions with Marriott's Owner and Franchise Services Division. In this position, she has done three openings for Marriott's select-service and extended-stay brands (Courtyard, Fairfield Inn, Residence Inn, SpringHill Suites, and Towneplace Suites). She has helped with preopening sales and marketing in domestic hotels across the country in major and smaller markets. For example, in 2001 she assisted with 32 hotel openings; in 2002, her work involved 23 property openings. Each opening involves two days of preopening and one day of postopening assistance for a follow-up visit. She also assists with planning and research conference calls between the pre- and postopening visits.

In Anastasia's present position, she consults with owners and franchisees about preopening sales and marketing efforts, helps them to gain access to Marriott resources, and helps with pricing and monitoring the properties' opening business from a revpar index perspective. She uses the Smith Travel Report to measure the success of a new hotel from a market share perspective in addition to topline sales. This provides a benchmark for salespersons to gauge their results against their competition.

When asked about an unforgettable moment in her career, her response is unusual: "One time we visited clients and potential customers dressed up as squirrels. We passed out bags of peanuts that said, 'We'd go nuts for your business!' I know this is silly, but people still talk about it today, 5 years after we made the site visits" (and, most importantly, we secured business as a result of our persistence, humor, and good nature).

Anastasia becomes more serious when she discusses the most significant challenges facing her segment of the industry: "The most significant challenge in hotel sales is increased competition in overbuilt markets that challenge properties to compete for business and their fair share of room nights. These issues are being addressed through an increased focus on each property's direct sales (everybody at the property sells!), shifting share away from the competition, and gaining a much sharper sense of revenue and rooms inventory management."

Anastasia was asked about what, if anything, she would do differently in her career: "I would have spent more time in operations and gained the experience of being a general manager for a property at a younger age. Successful experience in that position increases one's later credibility in the industry."

Anastasia has some great advice for young people considering a career in hospitality: "Diversify your experience! My best advice to persons considering a career in hotel sales, marketing, and revenue management is to obtain a solid understanding of the entire organization for which they work. Persons must understand their role thoroughly, be great team players, and be open to learning and experiencing areas of the hospitality industry outside of their own segment."

LODGING INDUSTRY POSITIONS

OBJECTIVE 7
Review the wide range of positions within which one may work in the lodging industry.

An increasingly wide variety of all types of positions is available in the lodging industry. Exhibit 4.7 identifies many of these positions on a by-function basis. Some require highly specialized and technical skills, for

Hotels in airport locations are popular with business travelers.

Accounting and Financial Management
Accounting Supervisor
Accounts Payable Clerk
Accounts Payable Supervisor
Accounts Receivable Clerk
Accounts Receivable Supervisor
Assistant Controller
Corporate Controller
Credit Manager
Director of Finance and Administration
Director, Purchasing Department
Hotel Controller
Night Auditor
Payroll Accountant
Payroll Assistant
Payroll Clerk
Payroll Supervisor
Purchasing Manager
Vice-president, Chief Financial Officer

Rooms Division and Facilities
Assistant Houseperson
Assistant Parking Facilities Manager
Assistant Reservations Manager
Automobile Valet
Bell Captain
Bell Staff
Cashier
Chauffeur
Coat Check Attendant
Concierge
Customer Service Representative
Electrician
Engineering Supervisor
Executive Housekeeper
Front-office Cashier
Front-office Manager
Groundskeeper
Guest Service Manager
Hotel Assistant Housekeeping Director
Hotel Front-desk Agent
Hotel Front-office Manager
Hotel General Cashier
Hotel Reservations Operator
Hotel Switchboard Operator
Inspector
Landscapers
Laundry Attendant
Laundry Manager
Linen and Uniform Attendant
Linen Distribution Attendant
Linen Room Supervisor

Lobby Attendant
Mail Information Clerk
Night Clerks
Night Manager
Night Supervisor
Package Room Personnel
Parking Facilities Attendant
Parking Facilities Manager
Receptionist
Reservations Clerk
Reservations Manager
Room Attendant
Rooms Division Manager
Seamstress
Security Director
Security Guard
Security Technician
Security and Loss Prevention Manager
Supply Clerks
Storeroom Person
Valet Parking Attendant
Vice-president, Operations

Food and Beverage
Assistant Baker
Assistant Banquet Chef
Assistant Banquet Manager
Assistant Beverage Director
Assistant Broiler and Grill Cook
Assistant Executive Steward
Assistant Food and Beverage Director
Assistant Fry Cook
Assistant Pantry Person
Assistant Pastry Chef
Assistant Restaurant Manager
Assistant Service Cook
Assistant Soup and Vegetable Cook
Baker
Banquet Assistant Cook
Banquet Bartender
Banquet Beverage Runner
Banquet Beverage Server
Banquet Busperson
Banquet Captain
Banquet Chef
Banquet Cook
Banquet Houseperson
Banquet Runner
Banquet Server
Banquet Steward
Bartenders
Beverage Manager
Beverage Runner
Broiler Cook

Busperson
Cashier
Catering Director
Catering Manager
Counter Person
Counter Server
Counter Supervisor
Dietary Aide
Dietitian
Dining Manager
Dining Room Manager
Director, Dietary Department
Dishwasher
Executive Chef
Executive Steward
Food and Beverage Controller
Food and Beverage Director
Fry and Sauté Cook
Head Broiler and Grill Cook
Head Cashier
Head Dishwasher
Head Fry Cook
Head Houseperson, Banquets
Head Pantry Person
Head Room Service Cook
Head Soup and Vegetable Cook
Head Steward
Hotel Food and Beverage Controller
Kitchen Attendant
Kitchen Manager
Kitchen Supervisor
Lounge and Bar Manager
Mâitre d'
Night Steward
Pantry Cook
Pantry Preparation Person
Pastry Chef
Pastry Cook
Receiving Clerk
Restaurant Manager
Room Service Attendant
Room Service Busperson
Room Service Manager
Service Bartender
Serving Line Attendant
Sommelier
Soup and Sauce Cook
Sous Chef
Steward
Steward's Runner
Vice-president, Food and Beverage
Waiter or Waitress

Human Resources
Manager, Equal Employment Opportunity

EXHIBIT 4.7
Lodging Industry Positions
Courtesy of the American Hotel & Lodging Association. www.ahla.com.

Personnel Assistant
Personnel and Human Resources
   Manager
Personnel Specialist
Quality Assurance Manager
Training Manager
Vice-president, Human Resources

Sales and Marketing
Assistant Vice-president, Sales
   and Marketing
Catering Sales Representative
Clerical Staff
Communications Manager
Conference Coordinator
Convention Services Coordinator
Convention Services Manager
Director of Communications
Director of Convention Sales
Director, Public Relations
Director, Sales and Marketing
Editor
Graphics Manager
Group Sales Manager
Group Sales Representative
Market Researcher
Meeting and Conference Planner

National Sales Manager
Promotion and Public Relations
   Specialist
Regional Director of Sales
   and Marketing
Research and Statistical Manager
Sales Manager
Vice-president, Sales and Marketing

Information Technology
Manager, Information Technology
Programmer and Analyst
System Programmer
Systems Analyst

Leadership
Assistant General Manager
Division President
Innkeeper Manager, Bed
   and Breakfast
Hotel General Manager
Owner and Operator
President, CEO
Vice-president, Administration
Vice-president, Business
   Development
Vice-president, Franchising

Vice-president, Hotel Development

Activities
Assistant Golf Professional
Assistant Tennis Professional
Caddie
Entertainer
Golf Professional
Golf Shop Salesperson
Lifeguard
Recreation Specialist
Ski Instructor
Social Activities Manager
Spa Director
Swimming Instructor
Swimming Pool Manager
Tennis Professional
Tour Escort

Other Positions
Administrative Secretary
Association Manager
Audiovisual Specialist
Translator

EXHIBIT 4.7
continued

example, many of the positions within the accounting and financial management areas and those within information technology. Others, such as those involving activities, require significant physical skills. Numerous positions require basic management knowledge and experience; for example, note the many management positions within food and beverage. Still other positions are entry-level (nonmanagement) positions that could represent one's first position in a career ladder "up the organization" to more responsible positions.

Lobby of Bellagio Hotel in Las Vegas, Nevada

What are your interests? The wide range of positions noted in Exhibit 4.7 suggests that there are probably many ways to match your interests with challenging and rewarding positions within the lodging industry.

SUMMARY OF CHAPTER LEARNING OBJECTIVES

1. **Review the range of lodging property alternatives available to travelers.**
   Travelers can choose from destination resorts, full-service hotels, limited-service hotels, and sleeping rooms, along with seemingly innumerable other variations within this range.

2. **Discuss three common ways to classify lodging properties.**
   Lodging properties can be classified by location, rate, and size.

3. **Describe basic characteristics that all lodging properties share.**
   Common characteristics of all lodging properties include the following:
   - Emphasis on safety, cleanliness, and service
   - Inseparability of manufacture and sales
   - Perishability
   - Repetitiveness
   - Labor intensivity

4. **Explain common hotel ownership and management alternatives.**
   A hotel property can be franchised or non-franchised. If it is affiliated with a franchise, it can be owned by an independent investor or by the franchise company (franchiser). Regardless of ownership, a franchised property can be operated by an independent owner or operator, by the franchise company (franchiser), or by a management company. If a hotel is not franchised, it will have independent ownership and can be operated by the independent owner or by a management company.

5. **Describe how basic hotel functions are organized and integrated.**
   With the exception of limited-service properties (which do not have food and beverage departments), someone in the property must be responsible for front office and rooms (including bell service, reservations, switchboard, housekeeping, and front desk), human resources, engineering and maintenance, purchasing, security, and marketing and sales. Additionally, an accounting specialist is needed. As the size of the property increases, persons in specialized positions are hired to assume responsibility for increasingly more specific tasks within each function.

6. **List challenges (opportunities) confronting today's hotel industry.**
   Hotels are confronted with four basic types of challenges:
   - *Operating.* Labor shortages, cost containment, and increased competition
   - *Marketing.* Market segmentation and overlapping brands, increased guest sophistication, and the need for increased amenities
   - *Technological.* Interactive reservation systems, guest-room innovations, data mining, and yield management
   - *Economic.* Dependence on the nation's economy, globalization, and terrorism and safety

7. **Review the wide range of positions within which one may work in the lodging industry.**
   The chapter lists more than 200 positions that are applicable to the widely diverse lodging industry.

MASTERING YOUR KNOWLEDGE

Discuss the following questions.

1. What is your definition of the term *hotel?* (Provide a general definition that will apply to each type of hotel property discussed in this chapter.)
2. Provide a basic description for each type of traveler who would select a hotel in the location and rate categories noted in Exhibit 4.2.
3. What, if any, importance does a traveler place on the number of rooms (size) in a hotel when he or she makes a selection decision?

4. What are the five most important factors that you consider when you are selecting a hotel for an overnight stay? What factors would be important to the wealthiest of travelers? To those business travelers on a modest expense account? To families traveling with small children on a visit to see relatives?
5. If you work or have worked at a hotel, describe its affiliation, ownership, and operation according to the factors described in Exhibit 4.4.

FEEDBACK FROM THE REAL WORLD

Our real-world advice comes from Liana Clark, Director of Sales and Marketing for the Comfort Inns and Suites Downtown, in Chicago, Illinois.

Liana brings many years of hands-on experience to the task of answering the following questions. She began her hotel management career as a reservations sales agent. She then held progressively more responsible positions during her 9 years of experience in the positions of sales manager, director of new hotel sales support and, currently, director of sales and marketing.

We asked Liana to respond to the questions posed at the beginning of this chapter:

What exactly do the average travelers looking for a hotel room for a business or pleasure trip know about the hotel brands that they see and read about?

They do not know which brands are operated by which companies, nor do they know how different brands operated by the same company have been segmented. To help counter this, organizations such as Marriott and Choice are increasingly advertising their brand or organization affiliation: Fairfield Inns by Marriott, Sleep Inn by Choice, and Hampton Inns by Hilton are examples. What travelers do know is whether they prefer a specific brand based on their experience with that brand. They also know that they have an incredible amount of choice as they make lodging decisions.

How exactly do they decide where to stay on their next trip requiring overnight accommodation?

Previously, a decision was often based on "location, location, location." Today it is "rate, rate, rate." Of course, safety and cleanliness are absolutely critical, and no professional hotelier will compromise standards applicable to these concerns as a tactic to reduce rates. A traveler's definition of a fair rate considers the perception of value: Is what I receive worth what I must pay for it? Increasingly, business travelers are interested in perks such as airline miles, room upgrades, and other amenities offered to frequent guests as part of their organization's frequent-traveler program.

How do the guests' experiences at a specific property influence their interest in staying at the property again when they return to that location or in another hotel with the same brand when they travel to another location?

If guests have an enjoyable stay, they are very likely to return if they are in the area and more likely to utilize the same brand when they travel to another location. (By the way, there is no such thing as a "bad hotel stay"; visits are either enjoyable or horrible!) Therefore, all staff in a hotel must be involved in the business of relationship building. All employees influence the guests and decisions about where they will stay on their next trip. Lodging organizations and the individual units that comprise them need repeat business. To do this, guests must know that they will receive the same enjoyable experience with each visit. To best assure this long-term relationship, hotel managers must do several things:

- Find out about any problems and resolve them while the guests are there; guests are very forgiving when they know that you care and will address their concerns.
- Empower staff to take care of problems. The old saying "Sales personnel get the business; everyone else keeps it!" is very correct.
- Recognize that guests want service; hiring the right employees, providing effective training, and allowing staff to utilize guest-friendly procedures are great tactics to help to ensure high-quality service.
- Recognize that a guest's perception of one unit within a brand affects his or her attitude about all units in the brand: "As the brand goes, so goes the individual property."

6. What are some of the tasks that must be performed by persons with the responsibility for the functions noted in Exhibit 4.5?
7. How do cost centers (marketing, engineering, accounting, human resources, and security) assist the hotel's revenue departments (rooms, food and beverage, telephone, and fitness and recreation facilities)?
8. What do you think the general manager and his or her staff in a well-managed property in your community can do to address the following challenges (opportunities) noted in this chapter?

- Operating
- Marketing
- Technological
- Economic

9. If possible, ask management staff in local properties about other challenges (opportunities) that confront them and their property?
10. Think about your personal interests. Consider how they might be addressed in the positions listed in Exhibit 4.7. What are some positions that might potentially be of interest to you because the tasks that they require might be among those that you enjoy doing?

LEARN FROM THE INTERNET

1. Check out the following websites:
   - Hilton Hotels Corporation: www.hilton.com
   - Marriott Hotels, Resorts & Suites: www.marriott.com
   - Choice Hotels: www.choicehotels.com

   How do these organizations differentiate the numerous brands of properties that they franchise or operate? What, if any, emphasis (information) do these organizations place on a la carte dining and conventions and banquet foodservices?
2. Check out the website for the American Hotel & Lodging Association (www.ahla.com). Review current data that describe the breadth of the U.S. lodging industry.
3. Review the following websites and learn what's happening in the lodging industry today.
   - Hotel Online: www.hotel.on-line.com
   - Hotel Business: www.hotelbusiness.com
   - AH&LA Smart Brief: www.smartbrief.com/ahla
   - Hotel News Resource: www.hotelnewsresource.com

KEY HOSPITALITY TERMS

The following terms were explained in this chapter. Review the definitions of any words with which you are unfamiliar. Begin to utilize them as you expand your vocabulary as a hospitality professional.

niche marketing
hotel
resorts
full-service hotel
limited-service hotel
extended-stay hotel
sleeping room
hostel
rack rate
labor intensive
flag
brand
mom and pop hotels

franchise
franchiser
franchisee
entrepreneur
investor
management company
overbuilt
market segmentation
data mining
yield management
hotel occupancy rate
globalization
terrorism

Full-Service Hotels

5

Hyatt Regency, Merida

FEEDBACK FROM THE REAL WORLD

The challenges of managing a full-service hotel are different from those applicable to the management of limited-service properties. The full-service hotel manager must be able to effectively supervise both the guest rooms and food and beverage services that define these hotels. Guests in full-service hotels typically pay more for their rooms than do guests selecting limited-service hotels. As a result, they expect more services, and it is the job of the hotel manager and his or her team to provide them.

When many travelers think about hotels, they think about a full-service property. We have defined a full-service hotel to be one with an on-site restaurant and lounge; many also provide large-scale (banquet) food, beverage, meetings, and other services to guests.

How would you answer the following questions?

- Which department in a full-service property typically generates the most revenue? The most profits?
- Which department in a full-service property generally creates the greatest operating challenges? Why?

- Should persons desiring a top-level management position in a full-service property begin their career in food and beverage, rooms, or another department? (Or does it make any difference?)
- Some lodging organizations offer full-service, limited-service, and other types of property alternatives for different guest markets. Is it common for managers to move between full-service and the other types of properties within the same organization? What are some advantages and disadvantages of doing so?
- What should young persons consider as they think about careers in a full-service or limited-service property?
- What is the future of full-service properties?

As you read this chapter, think about answers to these questions and then get feedback from the real world at the end of this chapter.

---

full-service hotel   a hotel that provides guests with extensive food and beverage products and services

market share   the percentage of a total market (typically in dollars spent) captured by a property

OBJECTIVE 1
State features that make full-service hotels a unique segment of the lodging industry.

midscale full-service hotels lodging properties offering three meals daily, a lounge, pool, and limited meeting and banquet spaces

FULL SERVICE: A UNIQUE HOTEL SEGMENT

Full-service hotels in the United States can trace their origins to the taverns of the pre-Revolutionary colonies. In many cases, these very small businesses were the only locations where travelers and local citizens could consume meals and/or beverages away from home. As community gathering spots, taverns played an important historical role in the development of the country. Today, in most cities, full-service hotels have assumed the tavern's original role of hosting many local public and civic events. They also enjoy a significant **market share** of housing travelers from out of town.

While the costs of staying in or using a full-service hotel vary widely from fairly inexpensive to extremely expensive, most industry observers identify full-service hotels as being in either the midscale, upscale, or luxury segments of the lodging industry.

Midscale Hotels

Midscale full-service hotels are very popular. Holiday Inns, the largest chain within this segment, is credited by most observers with founding the hotel franchise concept in the United States. In many smaller cities, one or more of these midscale full-service hotels serve as community centers to host the area's business-related meetings, local political gatherings, weddings, anniversary parties, and other significant celebratory events. Midscale properties appeal to travelers who want the services offered by a full-service hotel, but who desire room rental rates only slightly higher than their limited-service hotel alternatives.

A lighted sign for a Holiday Inn hotel, the chain that is credited with starting the mid-scale hotel segment.

Midscale hotel guests expect to find a restaurant that serves three meals per day, a lounge, a swimming pool, and designated space for meetings or meal functions. These hotels are often found on interstate highway exchanges, near airports, or in smaller cities in downtown areas. Major hotel brands in the midscale full-service market include Six Continents' Holiday Inns and Cendant's Howard Johnson and Ramada Inn brands. In addition, many Best Western hotels offer full-service amenities.

Upscale Hotels

Typically, great expense is involved in building and operating **upscale full-service hotels.** These properties are generally located in larger cities, adjacent to casinos or international airports or near significantly large tourist destinations. These properties typically offer more guest rooms and meeting space than the average midscale hotel.

Upscale full-service hotels offer all the amenities of midscale properties and, in addition, provide special services, such as an on-site gift shop, full- or part-time **concierge,** extensive workout facility, and high-speed Internet access in guest rooms. A variety of related guest services, which may include extensive room-service offerings, on-premise laundry or dry cleaning services, and recreational facilities appropriate for the location, are frequently available. These can include tennis, golf, and horseback riding or, for those properties located on the beach, motorized and nonmotorized water sports.

Upscale full-service hotel companies in the United States have been very successful in building **name recognition** and **brand loyalty.** As a result, many have expanded their properties internationally. In fact, for some of the largest U.S. hotel companies, the number of new hotels developed internationally has recently exceeded the number of their new hotels built in the United States.

The upscale full-service hotel segment is large and includes some of the best known names in the hotel business, such as Hyatt Hotels, Sheraton, Hilton, Radisson, Westin, and full-service Marriott properties. These hotels range in size from smaller properties with 200 to 500 rooms to 1000 plus room properties in downtown areas such as New York, Chicago, and Atlanta.

upscale full-service hotels lodging properties offering the amenities of midscale hotels and additional services, such as a gift shop, concierge, exercise facility, high-speed Internet access, and numerous guest services

concierge the individual(s) within a full-service hotel responsible for providing guests with detailed information regarding local dining and attractions, as well as assisting with related guest needs

name recognition the ability of guests or potential guests to remember and associate with a hotel (or restaurant) name

brand loyalty the interest of guests or potential guests to revisit and/or recommend a hotel or restaurant

RISING STAR PROFILE

Sharon Larkins
Sales Manager
Hyatt on Capitol Square
Columbus, Ohio

Try to "Book Smart," Don't Just "Book Anything"

Sharon's position as a sales manager for her hotel involves several different markets. She is responsible for all entertainment and religious groups of any size and location, and she also handles all groups with 50 or fewer sleeping rooms originating in specific U.S. locations. **What does this mean?** Her hotel is a four-diamond property, and she has been with the Hyatt on Capitol Square since 2004.

What is your professional experience?

I received an associate's degree in Hospitality Management from Columbus State Community College. I really began my career in the industry when I was 14 years old working as a "coffee girl" at a private restaurant. I then worked at a Wendy's quick-service restaurant while I was in high school.

I began working in the front office at another hotel in Columbus in 1994, and then I was promoted to reservations and catering coordinator. I left the hotel business for a while, but remained in the hospitality industry working as a bartender for 7 years. My current position with the Hyatt on Capitol Square is my first sales position.

What is the accomplishment of which you are most proud?

This occurred when I booked a large convention for our hotel. I worked very hard for a long time to close the deal and went through a lot of ups and downs, but finally got it! Was it the biggest convention for our hotel? No, but it was something I accomplished myself, and I was ecstatic! Another unforgettable moment occurred when I was assigned the entertainment market, because I really wanted it, and I enjoy working with persons who book these meetings.

What challenges confront you in your position?

Most of my challenges relate to trends in the business. When I first began, my hotel and all others were struggling in a slow economy. It was a meeting planner's market, and we were offering unbelievable deals to build business. Today, by comparison, hotels can be a little more selective, and we "book smart" as opposed to "book anything."

To address this challenge you have to pay attention to the booking trends at your property and at your competitors' properties, as well as all other meeting venue sites in the city. It is important to focus on your booking pace for the previous and upcoming years to assure you know everyone with definite and potential interest in booking a meeting. You must know your competition and your Convention and Visitors' Bureau personnel as well.

What, if anything, would you do differently in your career?

I would have worked as a sales assistant before becoming a sales manager. I struggled through my first 18 months in my position just learning about all the internal programs and policies. It was, therefore, difficult to learn about the actual sales process. Had I first worked as a sales assistant, I would have had a much better understanding of all the support staff needed, and I would have been able to watch and learn from other managers.

What is your advice for those considering a hospitality career?

Take your time and carefully consider what you do well and what you enjoy doing. Get to know as much as possible about the business. Appreciate and never take for granted each person's role in your company's success. You will encounter hard to handle people, including some who work for your organization, and clients, guests, and others who do not. Keep in mind that you do not know what these individuals went through before you began to interact with them. I don't take anything personally, and I always do my very best to create a positive and productive experience whenever I have the opportunity.

Luxury Hotels

When persons discuss the very best hotels in the world, these are the properties they are talking about. A **luxury full-service hotel** can be located in a resort area if it targets the vacation traveler, in the heart of a major city if it seeks to serve the upscale business traveler, or in locations that appeal to both leisure and business travelers. In all cases, these hotels cater to clientele who demand the very highest levels of products and services and are willing to pay the premium prices that such products and services justify.

luxury full-service hotels lodging properties offering the amenities of upscale full-service hotels and numerous additional features that appeal to discriminating clientele who desire the very best and who are willing to pay premium prices for it

Hotel Bellagio, The Strip, Las Vegas, Nevada, is a premier luxury property in a city with many luxury hotels.

In this hotel segment, typical room rates range from several hundred to several thousand dollars per night. While heavily dominated by independent hotels, brands include world-famous names such as the Four Seasons, Marriott's Ritz-Carlton, Starwood's St. Regis, and the Hong Kong-based Regal Hotels group.

What do guests expect at luxury full-service properties? Quite simply, "the very best." Luxury hotel guests desire and are willing to pay for superlative accommodations, food, beverages, banquets, meetings, and activities. Depending on the location and the clientele they serve, luxury full-service properties offer a wide range of products and services. Typically, the luxury full-service hotel will offer all the amenities found at the best upscale properties and additional features that may include the following:

- 24-hour concierge services
- Extensive in-room amenities, including monogrammed terrycloth bathrobes and other products for complimentary use in the rooms
- Personalized shopping services to replace lost or forgotten travel necessities, such as clothing, luggage, or personal care items
- Complimentary towels and drinks at poolside or on the beach
- Personal chefs available to prepare guest-selected (rather than property-selected) menu items
- Private and confidential check-in services
- In-suite offices complete with in-room fax and 24-hour clerical personnel
- Complimentary child-care services
- Outstanding gourmet restaurants offering a variety of regional and international cuisines, with extensive and exceptional wine lists
- Complimentary international newspapers
- Multiline telephones near the bed, on work desks, and in bathrooms
- 24-hour laundry and tailoring services
- Health and recreation facilities that include extensive health spa services
- Twice (or more) daily housekeeping services
- Complimentary use of luxury autos with unlimited mileage

THE FULL-SERVICE HOTEL TRAVELER

OBJECTIVE 2
Describe the types of guests who most frequently select full-service hotels.

Who are the guests in full-service hotels? One important type of guest that does not typically represent a large client base for limited-service, resort, or convention hotels is the local resident using the property's restaurants and

Fine dining restaurant in the Grand Hotel Krasnapolsky, Amsterdam

room night a single night's use of a guest room; a group using 10 rooms for 5 nights generates 50 room nights; the number is used as an indicator of group size and quantifies the group's importance to the hotel

business travelers those who travel primarily for business reasons (often on an expense account to defray the reasonable travel costs incurred)

price sensitive (guest) a person with a great concern about the costs of products and services who makes purchase decisions on the basis of minimizing costs.

leisure travelers those who travel primarily for personal reasons; these guests use private funds for travel expenses and are often sensitive to the prices charged

meeting facilities. These individuals live in the area and visit it because of the important community activities that are held there. Since full-service hotels have meeting space, local business associations, service clubs, and social groups, including Chambers of Commerce, Rotary clubs, Kiwanis, Lions clubs, and others, may use the hotel's meeting space on a regular basis. Weddings, anniversary parties, company holiday parties, and political gatherings are additional community uses of full-service hotels.

While local residents rarely rent guest rooms from the full-service hotel, their use of the hotel's meeting and dining spaces can be significant and typically represents a large portion of a hotel's annual food and beverage meeting room rental revenues.

Guests who rent guest rooms at full-service hotels typically are either part of a group meeting or are transients who seek their unique services. Groups at a full-service hotel include those attending sales meetings, conferences, technical seminars, training sessions, educational meetings, and business planning sessions. In a successful full-service hotel, group business often accounts for one-third (or more) of the total number of guest **room nights** each year. In hotels with large convention and meeting room space, the percentage is a great deal higher.

While groups often utilize full-service hotels, these properties are also popular with corporate and leisure travelers. **Business travelers** like the fact that many full-service hotels are in excellent locations, and they like the convenience of informal and formal meetings that can be held in the restaurant or lounge areas. In addition, these guests may be less **price sensitive** than some other travelers because some (or all) of their travel costs are reimbursed. As a result, the slightly higher prices charged by full-service hotels can be justified by the additional services and amenities offered.

Many **leisure travelers** also enjoy the added elegance of full-service hotels. This is especially true of upscale and luxury vacation travelers. For many of these individuals, a night, a week, or even longer in a quality full-service hotel is an experience to be remembered for a lifetime.

DID YOU KNOW?

- The total food and beverage departmental profit in full-service hotels grew at a compound annual growth rate of 5.4% in the 10 years from 1994 to 2004. By contrast, the operating profit in these hotels grew at a 3.0% rate. The conclusion: F&B profits grew at a faster rate than operating profit.

Source: Miller, G. Let them eat cake: the growing contribution of hotel food and beverage to the bottom line. Retrieved April 21, 2006, from www.hotel-online.com.

- **Mini-bars** are losing popularity. These small, in-guest room refrigerators or unrefrigerated cabinets are used to store beverages, snacks, and other items the hotel offers for sale to guests. They are being removed in many hotels because of a lack of demand and the high labor cost required to restock them.

- The "bedding wars" undertaken by several hotel chains in the mid-2000s attempted to provide guests with the most comfortable beds and bed linens as a competitive advantage over other properties that did not offer them. One result: guests really liked them, and some properties began to sell them. Another result: it took housekeeping personnel longer to clean guest rooms, and this might be a future negotiating concern in hotels with employee unions.

- While many hotels have long offered no-smoking guest rooms, some properties and even hotel chains have banned smoking entirely. Case in point: Western Hotels & Resorts implemented a smoke-free policy in its United States, Caribbean, and Canadian properties in January 2006. Marriott followed with its announcement in July 2006.

- High-tech hotel rooms are here. New computer systems enable regular guests to have their rooms set to a specific temperature, entertainment systems to be playing a specific type of music, and curtains to be opened or closed when they first enter their guest rooms, for example. Networks can also connect guest profiles between chain hotels. Universal remote controllers allow guests to control room temperature, adjust lighting, and operate multimedia equipment.

- Some hotels provide specific scents, such as lemongrass in hotel lobbies, and pay more attention to the background music in public areas to help assure that the senses of smell and sound are positively affected as a guest forms a first opinion of the property.

- Boston's Fairmont Copley Plaza Hotel has adopted resident dog (Catie) that guests can walk and play with while staying at the property. Guests make appointments (up to three months in advance) to ensure a visit with Catie.

Source: Wangsness, L. At Copley, at A Tail of Hospitality. Retrieved November 29, 2005, from www.hotel-online.com.

mini-bar a small, in-guest room refrigerator or unrefrigerated cabinet used to store beverages, snacks, and other items the hotel offers for sale to guests

ORGANIZATIONAL STRUCTURE OF FULL-SERVICE HOTELS

OBJECTIVE 3
Draw an organization chart for a full-service hotel that shows hospitality management positions unique to this segment.

Full-service hotels offer unique opportunities for food and beverage-oriented hospitality managers. Exhibit 5.1 details the food and beverage portion of an organizational chart for a mid-sized full-service hotel.

You will learn later that food and beverage position titles and job responsibilities are the same in hotels and in their commercial counterpart: restaurants. We will review some of the basics in these positions now and will discuss other aspects in later chapters that provide details about restaurant segments.

In all but the very smallest of full-service hotels, foodservice operations are managed by a department head titled food and beverage (F&B) director. This member of the **executive committee** is critical to a full-service hotel's

executive committee
short for *executive operating committee;* it consists of members of the hotel's management team (generally department heads) responsible for departmental leadership and overall property administration

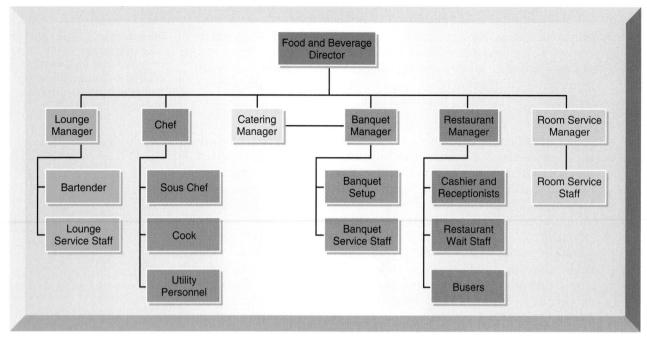

EXHIBIT 5.1
Organization Chart for Food and Beverage Department in a Full-Service Hotel

chef the person responsible for food production

banquet department the unit within a hotel responsible for producing and serving food and beverages at large meal functions

kiosk a very small refreshment (concession) stand offering just one or a very few food or beverage products

success because of the importance of providing excellent foodservices. Also, a strong and creative food and beverage department is a competitive marketing advantage to be aggressively promoted by the hotel's sales staff.

In nearly all cases, a full-service hotel operates one or more cocktail lounges. In addition to alcoholic beverages, these lounge areas may provide entertainment, light snacks, and appetizers or even full meal service. These outlets are managed by the lounge manager.

The **chef** is in charge of all food production. In a very large property, there is a large culinary staff. In most cases, the chef is also responsible for staff members who clean the kitchen and wash the pots, pans, and dishes required for food production and service.

In many full-service hotels, the **banquet department** accounts for 50 percent or more of all food and beverage revenues. This department is responsible for producing and serving the food and providing other guest services at the banquets and special events held in the hotel's meeting rooms and ballrooms.

Full-service hotels may offer their guests the use of one or more on-site restaurants, coffee shops, snack bars, food service **kiosks** and/or other outlets. These outlets have their own restaurant management staff. Cashiers, servers, and busers will be needed and, depending on the size of the restaurant, a staff of several dozen employees may be required in **front-of-house** positions.

Front desk of the Palace of the Lost City, Sun City, South Africa

Finally, many full-service hotels offer room service, which involves the delivery of meals and/or beverage products to the guests' rooms. A room-service manager supervises this process.

In an effort to best meet their guests' needs, some hotels have only one restaurant and therefore fall in between their full-service counterparts and properties with no or only very limited food and beverage services. Some industry observers refer to these as **select-service hotels** and, for example, they may have only one restaurant that serves guests during one or two meal periods, or perhaps the property only offers food service on selected days.

UNIQUE MANAGERIAL POSITIONS IN FULL-SERVICE HOTELS

The products and services offered by full-service hotels vary widely based on the size and segment level (midscale, upscale, or luxury) of the property. However, a common element in all properties is food and beverage service. Therefore, this chapter examines some important managerial positions in this department.

Food and Beverage Director

The food and beverage **(F&B)** director is responsible for the overall profitability of the department. Many general managers believe that it is not possible for a hotel's food and beverage department to be profitable. The definition of profitability, however, varies widely, and broad statements about a hotel's ability to make money in food and beverage departments are not of great value.

The profitability of a F&B department varies based on the quality of its management and the unique products and services that it offers. In all cases, F&B directors must maximize the quality of food, beverages, and services while maintaining excellent cost-control procedures. To do so, especially in a large hotel, requires the assistance and talents of many managers who report directly to the F&B director.

Lounge Manager

Lounge managers supervise the production and service of alcoholic beverages in the hotel's bars and lounges. They hire, train, and supervise bartenders and the wait staff needed to service guests. In large hotels, beverage service may involve several outlets in different areas with unique theme and ambiance environments. Snacks, appetizers, and/or meals are often served in these areas, but beverage service is clearly most important. Decor can range from comfortably casual to extremely upscale. Entertainment, when provided, may consist of television, recorded music, or live entertainment.

Lounge managers must have excellent knowledge about alcoholic beverage products and must be capable of implementing the

Dining room table set for elegant meal

---

front-of-house pertaining to guest-contact employees, positions, and/or departments

select-service hotel a hotel with one restaurant that is open for service on some basis, less than three meals daily for seven days weekly.

OBJECTIVE 4
List and briefly describe the duties of the unique managerial positions found within full-service hotels.

F&B abbreviation for food and beverage

lounge managers persons responsible for the production and service of alcoholic beverages in the hotel's bars and lounges; they hire, train, and supervise bartenders and the wait staff needed to service guests

HOSPITALITY LEADER PROFILE

Bill Taylor
Hotel Manager
Four Seasons Hotel, Chicago
Chicago, Illinois

An Education Is No Guarantee of Success

Bill is originally from northern England and received an undergraduate degree in hospitality management from the University of Surrey. While studying for his degree, he participated in a one-year educational exchange program with a hospitality management school in the United States.

After graduation, Bill completed a management training program at the Boca Raton Hotel and Club in Florida and then joined Rockresorts. He spent two years at that organization's Caneel Bay (U.S. Virgin Islands) property before transferring to England to open the Hanbury Manor Hotel. He remained there for two years.

Bill's experience to that point had involved only food and beverage responsibilities. He realized the need to broaden his background to become eligible for a general manager position. Since he wanted to be associated with the luxury market, he joined Four Seasons. "Actually, joining that organization was difficult because it was in the middle of the Gulf War crisis, and the economic recession meant that no one was hiring. After a great deal of persistence and a lot of rejections, I finally landed a job at the Ritz-Carlton Hotel, Chicago (a Four Seasons Hotel), as a front-desk receptionist. While it meant financial sacrifices and several steps back down the career ladder, I got exactly what I wanted: rooms exposure, luxury experience, and an environment in which I could learn." Over the next six years, Bill held numerous positions in the front desk, guest services, and housekeeping departments.

Bill's next position was with the Four Seasons Hotel in Atlanta, first as director of rooms and then as its hotel manager. After three years at the Atlanta location, he became hotel manager of the Four Seasons Chicago in September 2001.

Bill was asked about the most unforgettable moment in his career: "It was not so much a moment as it was a six-month period. In April 2002, we acted as the host hotel for the Mobil Five Star Awards ceremony where the thirty-five recipients of this coveted award enjoyed a weekend of memorable activities. This group of persons is not easily impressed because they run the finest establishments in North America. The successful execution of the event and weekend involved months of planning and commitment from all of our hotel's 550 employees. What was particularly gratifying was the incredible enthusiasm, involvement, and esprit de corps throughout the hotel and the enormous sense of pride that everyone demonstrated as we achieved our objective."

Bill was asked about the most significant challenges confronting the luxury segment of the lodging industry: "It is our ability to effectively respond to the current market downturn and to remain successful despite the decrease in business travel. Hoteliers must be creative in not only focusing their efforts on those markets that have been relatively resilient, but also in aggressively looking at new opportunities. While we must demonstrate fiscal prudence in our operating expenses, we cannot, at the same time, permit our standards of service to suffer. If we continue to focus on providing the highest level of quality, when the economy does rebound we will be well placed to take advantage of the increased consumer spending because our reputation will have remained intact."

Bill was asked about what, if anything, he would have done differently in his career: "I thought, until recently, my only regret was not joining Four Seasons Hotels earlier in my career. However, someone recently pointed out that, if I had joined the organization earlier, I would not be able to compare and to appreciate the inherent differences in culture and values that makes Four Seasons not only the world's premier operator of luxury hotels, but also a world-class employer. We again this year made *Fortune* magazine's top 100 companies to work for and received the highest ranking of any hotel company."

Bill has several suggestions for young people considering a career in lodging: "First, be realistic; an education will help you to get in the door, but it is no guarantee of success. I can't tell you how many young graduates I interview who see themselves immediately moving into a sales and marketing or a human resources position. If you wish to specialize in these disciplines, that is fine. However, first you must understand what you are selling or what people issues you will be facing. You can only do this by spending time in the trenches. The upside is that, when your time comes, you will be far more effective in your specialty.

"If you want to be successful, you have to work hard. This involves sacrifices in the early years. The hours you work will often be unsociable, the pay will be less than your friends may earn in other fields, and the work may seem repetitive. However, it is all part of building a solid foundation for yourself based on experience and practical knowledge.

"If you want to get a job in a luxury property, you must demonstrate that you fit with the image. This includes how you present yourself. For example, you don't see employees in a luxury hotel that are anything less than immaculate.

They cut their hair above the collar, they don't have long sideburns, and they certainly don't have studs in their tongues!

"When I consider candidates, I am first and foremost interested in their personality: are they outgoing, confident, mature, and caring? If they are, then I am interested. Next, I want to know about their motivation. Also, do they have practical experience to demonstrate that they clearly understand the career in which they want to work? If their experience involves rolling up their sleeves, front-line, in-the-trenches work, then I am even more interested. If they have demonstrated initiative by working during their vacations in top-notch properties (instead of being a lifeguard), then I don't want them going to work for the competition; I want them to work for me!"

---

cost-control policies and procedures required in a modern beverage operation. Properly managed, hotel bars can be very profitable, with **product cost percentages** averaging as low as 25 percent and gross profits in the range of 50 percent of revenue. As a result, lounge managers play an important part in the profitability of the entire F&B department.

product cost percentages the percentage of revenue generated from the sale of a food or beverage product that is required for its purchase

Chef

A knowledgeable and skilled chef is a tremendous asset to a full-service hotel. The chef is responsible for developing and ultimately supervising the production of the items on the hotel's restaurant and banquet menus. Another responsibility is to ensure that the food produced meets (or exceeds) the expectations of the hotel's guests. The chef has a difficult job that requires great creativity and administrative skill.

In a larger hotel, a **sous chef** is chosen to be the chef's first-level assistant. The term *sous* is a French word meaning *under* and, as the individual reporting to (under) the chef, this person is often the one who actually makes the kitchen run smoothly. The sous chef supervises the cooks who prepare the

sous chef the first assistant to the chef

The banquet captain gives instructions to service staff before the event begins.

food and the individuals responsible for the cleanliness of the kitchen and all that is in it.

Catering Manager

In many full-service hotels, banquet functions generate the most revenue for the F&B department. In fact, profits from banquet operations help to offset losses in restaurant and room-service operations. Remember our definitions:

- *Catering.* The task of selling group (banquet) functions
- *Banquets.* Group functions involving the production and service of food and/or beverage products

Catering personnel may be in the marketing or F&B departments; banquets are administered from the F&B department. When catering responsibilities are part of the marketing department, there is an obvious need for very close coordination and cooperation with the banquet personnel who will "deliver" what the catering staff sell.

F&B directors require talented catering managers because they can make or break departmental profitability. Banquet events can generate significant profits because of the following:

- Banquet meals are often priced higher than regular restaurant meals that include the same items.
- All guests at banquet events select from a relatively limited number of menu items; this eases food production requirements and reduces waste.
- The number of attendees at the meal event is guaranteed, so the number of service staff required will be known in advance.
- There are often additional guest charges for setting up the room and, perhaps, for valet parking, bar personnel, and other related expenses.
- Mandatory **service charges** help to ensure that the best of the hotel's servers work banquet events, and these workers are scheduled only for as long as needed.

Hotel banquet functions may include both on- and off-site events; however, for most hotels the majority of these events are held at the hotel. A catering manager works with the client to develop a **banquet event order (BEO).** Exhibit 5.2 illustrates the flow of information on a BEO from the catering manager to those who must use it. Note the significant amount of behind the scenes coordination and communication required to assure that banquet events function smoothly.

The **banquet manager's** main tasks include pre-event planning with the catering manager to ensure that special event rooms are set to the client's specifications. As well, **head tables,** if any, must be identified and planned for, proper service personnel must be available to service the function, and all special requests for the event must be handled properly. During the event, the catering manager and banquet manager may be available to ensure that all goes smoothly. This is a significant task when you realize that on a busy night a large full-service hotel may be serving several hundred (or more) guests who consume different meals in several (or more) different meeting room locations within the hotel.

Restaurant Manager

Hotel restaurant managers may have one of the most difficult jobs in foodservice management. As a condition of maintaining their franchise, a full-service

service charge a mandatory amount added to a guest's bill for services performed by a staff member of the hospitality organization

banquet event order (BEO) a form used by the sales, catering, and food production areas to detail all requirements for a banquet; information provided by the banquet client is summarized on the form and it becomes the basis for the formal contract between the client and the hotel

banquet manager the person responsible for service of food and beverage products at a group function

head table special seating at a banquet reserved for guests of honor

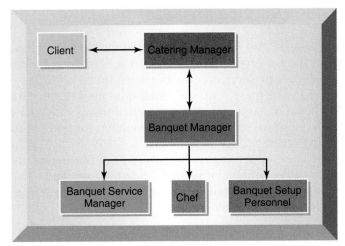

EXHIBIT 5.2
Who Receives a Copy of the BEO?

hotel will, in nearly all cases, be required to operate at least one restaurant open seven days a week serving three meals daily. In larger properties, additional restaurants are operated as needed. Restaurant revenue in a full-service hotel often depends in large measure on the occupancy level of the hotel. Therefore, guest demand and daily restaurant revenues vary tremendously. Restaurant managers must be prepared to operate a restaurant that may be nearly empty several nights per week and then so busy on the remaining days that guests are accepted on a reservations-only basis. The challenges of maintaining a sufficient staff of well-trained and motivated servers in these situations are obvious, and it is the responsibility of the restaurant manager to address them.

Since hotel restaurant profitability is often very low, some hotel owners or operators lease their restaurant space to external foodservice organizations. There are at least two concerns here: first, hotel managers must still understand the unique challenges of managing a restaurant that serves their guests and, second, managers should recognize that their guests' opinions of the hotel are influenced by the foodservices that they receive (and guests typically do not know nor care who has operational responsibility for it).

DID YOU KNOW?

Which do you think is most profitable: a food and beverage department in a full-service hotel or a free-standing restaurant? The answer is somewhat difficult to determine because all the revenue and costs for the latter can be easily identified. By contrast, some costs required to operate a hotel's food and beverage department are shared by an **allocation** process between departments.

If all costs were allocated accurately and if room rental and other income were deducted from total hotel food and beverage revenue, because these sources are not available to restaurants, it is likely that a hotel's bottom-line profit from food and beverage sales would be much less than that generated by a restaurant.

If you are interested in a detailed discussion of hotel food and beverage department and restaurant profitability see David Hayes and Jack Ninemeier, *Hotel Operations Management*, 2nd ed. Upper Saddle River, NJ: Pearson Prentice Hall, 2007, (pp. 352–354).

allocation the process of distributing revenues earned and/or expenses incurred between departments on a basis that approximates each department's share of the revenues and/or expenses

Room-Service Manager

All upscale and luxury and most midscale full-service hotels offer room service: the delivery of food and beverages to an individual guest room. In many hotels, room service contributes as much as 15 percent of total food and beverage revenue, but still does not break even. Historically, breakfast has been the most popular room-service meal. The room-service manager must plan, organize, and staff this department for quality, speed, and accuracy. Providing room service is generally a costly service, yet one that guests consistently find appealing for a variety of convenience and/or privacy reasons. A room-service manager who can control costs and who possesses the organizational skills to effectively manage the department is a hotel professional who is always in great demand.

OBJECTIVE 5
Identify significant current and long-term business challenges that confront managers of full-service hotels.

CHALLENGES CONFRONTING FULL-SERVICE HOTEL MANAGERS

Full-service hotels represent the most mature segment of the hotel industry. This maturity yields the advantages of highly preferred property locations, long-established operating procedures, and significant consumer brand recognition. However, the segment faces considerable challenges that threaten its long-term continued growth and profitability, such as the following:

- Increased competition from limited-service hotels
- Increased costs required to operate on-site food services
- Rising construction costs
- Difficulties in developing a unified Internet marketing strategy

Let's look at each of these challenges.

Increased Competition from Limited-Service Hotels

The limited-service hotel segment is expanding rapidly. As a result, full-service hotels increasingly must compete with other full-service hotels and with newer (and often more modern) limited-service properties.

Complimentary (but limited) breakfast programs, larger guest bathrooms, and the availability of suites and locations near emerging business areas are features that make newly constructed limited-service hotels a strong challenge to the popularity of full-service properties. Also, many limited-service hotels are designed with one or more small meeting rooms, and they can successfully compete with their full-service hotel counterparts for business.

The lobby in a high-rise full-service hotel can be spectacular.

Increased Costs Required to Operate On-Site Foodservices

It has always been difficult (some would say nearly impossible!) for a full-service hotel to make a significant profit from its food and beverage operations. This is especially true today as one recognizes that labor costs often increase more quickly than do food costs. Unfortunately, hoteliers are often unable to pass these costs on to guests in the form of increased food and beverage charges.

Some hotel managers elect to address rising operating costs by leasing foodservices, increasing menu selling prices, reducing service levels, and/or curtailing operating hours. Remember, however, that it is the presence of foodservice that makes this segment of the hotel industry distinctive. Providing quality food and beverage services at prices that guests will readily accept is a critical challenge confronting full-service hotel general managers and the food and beverage professionals with whom they work.

Rising Construction Costs

Hotel construction costs, like most building costs, rise each year. The costs to furnish a quality full-service hotel guest room are generally no higher than those required to furnish a room at an extended-stay or limited-service property seeking to achieve an **average daily rate (ADR)** in the same range as the full-service hotel. It is, however, more expensive to build a full-service hotel of any size than to construct an equal number of rooms in another type of hotel. Construction costs for full-service hotels rise faster than those in other segments because of real estate, parking, and food and beverage services.

Real estate costs are generally higher for full-service hotels because more land (and, therefore, higher acquisition cost) is needed for the foodservice facilities, meeting space, and other amenities typically found at a full-service property. Also, the amount of land required for parking is much higher. Consider a 300-room full-service hotel that must provide parking for its sleeping room guests and also for those attending events in the hotel's

average daily rate (ADR) the average selling price of all guest rooms for a given time period; the formula for ADR is

Total room revenue ÷ total number of rooms sold = ADR

Constructing a new hotel is expensive. Costs begin with land acquisition and continue with the large number of square feet needed to provide foodservices, meetings, and other services.

function spaces. With additional parking space comes the increased costs of maintaining the parking areas.

Full-service hotels incur ever-increasing costs for foodservice storage, production, and dining areas that are not incurred in other properties. As a result, hotel owners, developers, designers, and managers are continuously attempting to maximize the guest services provided by food and beverage departments while minimizing related building and operating costs.

Difficulties in Developing a Unified Internet Marketing Strategy

Full-service hoteliers, with the possible exception of those managing hotels located in the downtown areas of major cities, face a unique challenge as they manage the Internet. This technology offers travelers who use it the lowest-cost hotel selections, and limited-service hotels have been major beneficiaries of the increased use of the Internet to book room reservations. Travelers seeking, for example, the lowest-cost room rate in an area may simply log onto one of the many booking sites available (or even the website of a hotel brand) to find the property that offers the lowest rate for the desired dates. The result has been a downward pressure on ADR as hotels seek to secure their fair share of the available market.

Since limited-service hotels appeal to cost-conscious travelers, these properties benefit most from comparison shopping. In other segments, such as resort and convention hotels that serve less price-conscious clientele, the Internet's impact in reducing room rates has been less pronounced.

There is little doubt that travelers will continue to utilize the Internet in larger numbers each year. How full-service hotels market their rates on the Internet will be very important, and their tactics will be interesting to watch in the coming years.

DID YOU KNOW?

If this book was written six or seven years ago, little or no space would need to be spent on Internet marketing. Today, travel is the most popular item sold on the Internet, and it is estimated that by 2008 more than 50 percent of all room reservations will be made via the Internet.

Internet sales can be good or very bad. When a room is sold to a guest through an online intermediary, the room will have been sold to that source at a heavy discount. When Internet usage fees, franchise fees (if applicable), and other incurred expenses are considered, a room normally sold for $100 per night may generate hotel revenues of $50 per night or much less. This may be "good" if the room would otherwise be vacant and "bad" if the hotel could have made more money selling it on its own website or to a **walk-in guest**.

walk-in guest a guest desiring a room who arrives at the hotel without a reservation

---

DID YOU KNOW?

Technology has yielded one significant reduction in construction costs: wireless Internet access. Before the early 2000s, hotels had to hardwire Internet connectivity, and this was most typically done only for guest rooms. To compete, hotels constructed before this time had to retrofit for this amenity at a cost that could approach $1,000 per room. Since the early 2000s, wireless Internet connectivity has been available and is used for almost all new hotel constructions and, probably, in all hotel remodeling purposes. New properties all offer the duel option (both plug-in and wireless access), and there is now a trend toward offering Internet access as a complimentary amenity.

Wireless Internet access is relatively inexpensive. For example, a 150-room hotel with a restaurant, lounge, and meeting spaces that can accommodate several hundred guests could provide service throughout the entire building (guest rooms, public spaces, and back-of-house areas) for less than $1,000 per month.

PRESSURE ON ROOM RATES

Hoteliers operating upscale and midscale hotels have attempted to increase occupancy levels in the face of terrorism concerns and the slowing of the economy by reducing room rates. However, many observers believe that discounting is actually counterproductive to the long-term financial health of the full-service segment. As these properties help to condition travelers to look for low rates rather than for exceptional service, the segment may find it difficult to raise rates when economic times improve.

SUMMARY OF CHAPTER LEARNING OBJECTIVES

1. **State features that make full-service hotels a unique segment of the lodging industry.**
   The most distinguishing feature of a full-service hotel is its provision of food and beverage services to guests and groups. As a result, these properties include on-site restaurants, lounges, and group meeting spaces.

2. **Describe the types of guests who most frequently select a full-service hotel.**
   Full-service hotels, unlike hotels in other segments, typically play a significant role in servicing their community's meetings and special events needs. Groups requiring meeting space are a significant source of business for full-service properties, as are business travelers willing to pay the higher room rates generally charged at these hotels. Leisure and vacation travelers, especially at the upscale and luxury levels, are also a significant market for many full-service hotels. In all cases, full-service hotel guests seek the extra amenities and service levels found only at these properties.

3. **Draw an organization chart for a full-service hotel that shows hospitality management positions unique to this segment.**
   Unique managerial positions in full-service hotels include those related to the F&B department. These consist of the food and beverage director, lounge manager, chef and sous chef, catering manager, restaurant manager, and room-service manager.

4. **List and briefly describe the duties of the unique managerial positions found within full-service hotels.**
   The F&B director is responsible for the overall quality of food, beverages, and services provided by the F&B department, as well as for its profitability. Lounge managers supervise the production and service of alcoholic beverages in the hotel's bars and lounges. They are responsible for hiring, training, and supervising bartenders and the staff needed to service guests. The chef is responsible for developing and producing the items on the hotel's restaurant and

banquet menus and receives direct assistance from the sous chef. The catering manager sells and the banquet manager services the hotel's banquet functions. The restaurant manager supervises service in the hotel's public dining rooms. Room-service managers ensure speedy, high-quality, and cost-effective delivery of food and beverages to guest rooms.

5. **Identify significant current and long-term business challenges that confront managers of full-service hotels.**

Significant business challenges in the full-service hotel segment include increased competition from limited-service properties and the increasing cost of providing on-site food services. Additional challenges include rising costs of hotel construction and the difficulties inherent in harnessing the booking power of the Internet for the long-term benefit of the segment.

MASTERING YOUR KNOWLEDGE

Discuss the following questions.

1. If you were traveling to a specific community with alternative full-service hotels, how would you decide whether to stay at a midscale, upscale, or luxury alternative?
2. What do you think would be some of the biggest differences in the responsibilities of and the work involving the management of a midscale, upscale, and luxury full-service property?
3. What, if any, are differences in the work undertaken by a chef and a restaurant (dining room) manager in a full-service hotel and a restaurant?

4. What are examples of ways in which a hotel's catering manager and banquet manager must interact as a special event is being planned and implemented?
5. If you were the general manager of a full-service hotel, what are some tactics you might utilize to deal with increased competition from limited-service hotels in your area? To better manage the increased costs that are required to operate on-site foodservices in your hotel?

FEEDBACK FROM THE REAL WORLD

Our real-world advice comes from Jim Harvey. Jim received a four-year hospitality degree and has managed full-service properties in Florida, Pennsylvania, Michigan, Ohio, Illinois, Connecticut, and Massachusetts.

Which department in a full-service property typically generates the most revenue? the most profits?

This is an easy question to answer, and my response is the same to both questions. The rooms department typically generates the most revenue and profits.

Which department in a full-service property generally creates the greatest operating challenges? Why?

The housekeeping department generally creates the greatest operating challenges. First, it is labor intensive. Staffing (recruiting, training, and retaining) is an ongoing challenge. However, in today's economy in my part of the country (northeastern United States), staffing is less of a problem than it has been because of the relatively high unemployment rate. This means that more persons are looking for jobs and are not as likely to leave them once they are employed.

Another operating challenge: it is not unusual for hotels to have a very diverse housekeeping work force. There might be, for example, persons from five or six different countries speaking as many different languages in the same department. The ability of the management team to effectively communicate with all these persons is difficult. As well, language problems cause difficulty for our guests when, for example, they make simple requests or ask for simple directions within the property and our staff member, who really wants to be helpful, is not able to communicate with the guest.

Should persons desiring a top-level management position in a full-service property begin their career in food and beverage, rooms, or another department? Or does it make any difference?

Theoretically, it doesn't make much difference. A general manager must have some experience in and a great deal of knowledge about several areas, including front office, food and beverage, and sales.

Some organizations offer training programs for recent graduates that allow them to gain initial experience in each department before focusing on a specific functional area and gaining more extensive experience within it. However, the amount of experience gained in a rotational training program is not likely to provide sufficient knowledge or skills to become a manager within a specific department or to supervise someone who is. Persons desiring a top-level management position will, then, likely need to move between departments on their way up the organizational ladder.

Suggestion: When considering employment with a specific lodging organization, ask about the career tracks of general managers. Find out whether, for example, GMs typically have more experience in a specific department. If so, consider this as you make your employment decision.

Some lodging organizations offer full-service, limited-service, and other types of property alternatives for different guest markets. Is it common for managers to move between full-service and the other types of properties within the same

organization? What are some advantages and disadvantages of doing so?

The movement of managers between properties in different tiers of the industry (for example, from a full-service property to a limited-service property) is relatively uncommon. First, managers of limited-service properties do not typically have the more extensive knowledge and experience of all operating departments in a full-service property and may not, therefore, be fully qualified for the top management position in a full-service property. By contrast, managers of full-service properties are less likely to move to limited-service hotels because they will be required to do much more hands-on work because of the smaller management staff in the limited-service property.

General managers of limited-service hotels sometimes move to full-service properties. However, they typically begin in a middle-level management position (for example, sales manager or front office) and then, after sufficient experience, may be promoted to general management positions at that or another property in a multichain.

It is very common for general managers to move between full-service properties within an organization and even between organizations. Consider, for example, managers employed by contract management companies who may operate several (or more) brands for individual owners. Consider also a qualified general manager working for a franchiser or a company-owned property who receives employment opportunities elsewhere. It is, then, a fact of life in our industry that turnover occurs at the top level as well as throughout the organization.

What advice should young persons consider as they think about careers in a full-service or limited-service property?

I suggest that they consider the type of environment in which they wish to work. In a small, limited-service hotel, they are likely to do a wide variety of work in different functional areas. By contrast, in a larger, full-service property they will, at some point, become more specialized as they work their way through the management layers within a specific department. Since responsibilities are typically fewer, one can become general manager of a limited-service

(continued)

property more quickly than in a full-service property. It all depends on the individual; the important thing is to find a career and a position within it that you enjoy.

What is the future of full-service properties?

The lodging business is cyclical. During times of a weak economy, the business suffers; there is little construction because lenders will not finance it. In time, the economy improves, and the hotel business goes along with it. Higher occupancy and room rates yield increased profitability, which makes renewed construction possible (because lenders see opportunities in the business). In effect, the hotel business is clearly one of supply and demand; after several years of economic downturns, the next cycle of prosperity for hoteliers begins.

LEARN FROM THE INTERNET

1. Check out the three different levels of full-service hotels by visiting the website of a midscale, upscale, and luxury brand.

   Midscale Full-Service Hotel

   Holiday Inns: www.holidayinn.com

   Upscale Full-Service Hotel

   Hyatt Hotels: www.hyatt.com

   Luxury Full-Service Hotel

   Four Seasons Hotels: www.fourseasons.com

   What guest amenities are offered in the higher-priced brands that are not offered in lower-cost brands? Which segment, if any, do you think would provide the most rewarding employment opportunities for you? Why?

2. Check out a website for a full-service hotel in your own area. Who do you think are its target customer(s)? What hotels are directly competitive to it? If you were the manager of the full-service property, what features of the hotel would you emphasize to capture your fair share of business in a competitive market? How would you emphasize these features?

3. Check out the websites for the following three companies that allow you to book your own hotel reservations online:
   - Expedia: www.expedia.com
   - Orbitz: www.orbitz.com
   - Travelweb: www.travelweb.com

   Select a luxury-level hotel in a location that you might want to visit. Second, compare the rates offered to you (remember to select the same arrival and departure dates as well as the same room type each time) at each of the three websites. Third, go to the home website of a luxury hotel company and find the rate that you would be charged if you booked online at that website. Were the rates the same at all four sites? Which was lowest? What do you think of the rate strategy in place for that specific hotel on the dates you selected?

KEY HOSPITALITY TERMS

The following terms were explained in this chapter. Review the definitions of any words with which you are unfamiliar. Begin to utilize them as you expand your vocabulary as a hospitality professional.

full-service hotel	banquet department
market share	kiosks
midscale full-service hotels	front-of-house
upscale full-service hotels	select-service hotels
concierge	F&B
name recognition	lounge managers
brand loyalty	product cost percentages
luxury full-service hotels	sous chef
room night	service charge
business travelers	banquet event order (BEO)
price sensitive	banquet manager
leisure travelers	head tables
mini-bar	allocation
executive committee	average daily rate (ADR)
chef	walk-in guest

6

Limited-Service Hotels

Sleep Inn, Salisbury, North Carolina

CHAPTER LEARNING OBJECTIVES

After studying this chapter you will be able to:

1. State features that make limited-service hotels a unique segment of the hotel industry.
2. Describe the type of guests who most frequently visit limited-service hotels.
3. Outline an organization chart for a limited-service hotel and briefly describe the duties of managerial positions found within this segment.
4. Identify short- and long-term business challenges that confront those who manage limited-service hotels.

This chapter is authored by David Hayes, PhD. Dr. Hayes is an author and a 30-year veteran of the hospitality and hospitality education industries.

FEEDBACK FROM THE REAL WORLD

For many travelers, the best hotel is one that offers safe, clean, and moderately priced guest rooms in a convenient location. For these guests, on-site restaurants and lounges, extensive meeting space, and other amenities offered by full-service hotels are thought to drive up costs for guest-room rentals and to make them less desirable. The limited-service segment of the hotel industry was developed to meet the lodging needs of these persons. Managers who work in this segment must be very guest focused. They must find ways to provide excellent service with a limited staff and, because there are relatively few employees, these managers encounter guests directly and frequently.

If you enjoy direct guest contact and the excitement of possible multiple property management or ownership, a career in the fast-paced limited-service segment of the hotel industry may be ideal. If you had a choice between taking an early-career management position in a limited- or full-service hotel, which might be best for you? Why? To what extent do potential guests want to bargain on the room rental rate at a limited-service property?

As you read this chapter, think about answers to these questions and then get feedback from the real world at the end of the chapter.

LIMITED-SERVICE HOTELS ARE A UNIQUE LODGING SEGMENT

Limited-service hotels developed as a direct result of consumer demand and, at the beginning of the twenty-first century, they were the largest and fastest growing segment of the lodging industry. For many travelers, a simple, clean and safe hotel room located near their desired destination (or on the way to it) is all that is required. Consider, for example, a couple that has accepted an invitation to an out-of-town wedding. They will fly or drive to the wedding location, attend the ceremony and reception, and then, after spending the night, return home the next day. For this couple, features offered by a full-service property are not required. Their lodging choice will be primarily determined by the convenience of the hotel's location and the price charged for the room.

Four features that make limited-service properties a unique segment of the hotel industry include their size, the large proportion that is affiliated with a franchise brand, and, most significantly, the room rental charges and guest services that are offered.

Most limited-service properties are small, with an average size of less than 150 rooms. In addition, nearly all limited-service hotels are affiliated with a franchise brand. The most distinguishing feature of the limited-service hotel segment, however, is its price and service segmentation.

The number of travelers using limited-service hotels is large, and the segment consists of several price levels to satisfy the needs of these many travelers. While there is no industry standard, some observers group limited-service hotels into the following three categories.

Budget (Economy) Limited-Service Hotels

Budget (or economy) limited-service hotels were among the first to be developed in the United States. Popular brands include Accor Hotels' Motel 6, Choice Hotel International's Econolodge, and Cendant Corporation's Super 8.

> **OBJECTIVE 1**
> State features that make limited-service hotels a unique segment of the hotel industry.

limited-service hotel a lodging property that offers very limited food services or none at all; sometimes a complimentary breakfast is served, but there is no table-service restaurant

> **CHECK IT OUT!**
>
> • *Hotel and Motel Management* conducts a Limited-Service Hotel Chain Survey each year. This survey ranks chains in the segment by size. To view the latest survey, go to www.hotelmotel.com. Enter "limited service hotel chain survey" in the site's search box. This electronic magazine is also an excellent source of news activities about limited-service properties. Enter "limited service hotels" in the search box.
>
> • You can find numerous news articles about limited-service hotels at the Hotel-online website. Go to www.hotel-online.com. Enter "limited service hotel trends" in the site's search box.

budget (or economy) limited-service hotels hotels within the limited-service segment that offer low-priced guest rooms and few, if any, amenities other than a complimentary continental breakfast or coffee service

continental breakfast a morning meal that includes coffee, juices, and pastries. An upscale continental breakfast may include additional items such as fruit and hot and cold cereals with milk and yogurt. Most limited-service hotels offer a complimentary continental breakfast as a guest amenity

lobby foodservices food and beverage service offered by limited-service hotels

midpriced limited-service hotels hotels within the limited-service segment that offer selected property and within-room upgrade amenities for room rates that are higher than budget (economy) hotels within the segment

frequent-traveler program a program developed to reward a hotel company's guests with free room nights, frequent-flyer airline miles, and/or other awards as an incentive to book rooms at a property within the brand

upscale limited-service hotels hotels within the limited-service segment that offer a wide range of property and within-room amenities designed to provide high levels of comfort, convenience, and elegance to their guests

These brands are attractive to owners and investors because they are relatively inexpensive to build and very simple to operate. Travelers are attracted by low room rates and, in many cases, convenient locations.

Traveler amenities offered by these hotels are few. Properties in this segment are not likely to have swimming pools, meeting space, or food and beverage facilities (although many do offer some type of complimentary morning coffee service or limited **continental breakfast**). Since foodservice amenities are typically offered in the lobby or a small room near the lobby, a relatively new term, **lobby foodservices**, has been coined to describe this type of food and beverage option. As well, almost all franchised hotels offer Internet access to their guests. Successful budget hotels in this segment offer clean and safe rooms, low prices, and few frills.

Midpriced Limited-Service Hotels

For many travelers, **midpriced limited-service hotels** offer the amenities they want at prices that are below those offered by most full-service hotels. These hotels typically offer, in addition to the features found at budget hotels, amenities such as these:

- **Frequent-traveler programs**
- Swimming pools
- Larger bathroom areas
- In-room coffee makers
- In-room irons, ironing boards, and hair dryers
- Upgraded complimentary continental breakfasts
- Complimentary morning newspapers
- Complimentary local telephone calls

Popular midpriced brands include Marriott's Fairfield Inn, Hilton's Hampton Inn, Six Continent Hotels' Holiday Inn Express, Carlson Hospitality's Country Inn and Suites, and Choice Hotels' Comfort Inn. Midpriced hotels make up the largest portion of the limited-service market, and each brand has developed its own loyal clientele.

Upscale Limited-Service Hotels

Some travelers do not need or want to pay for the restaurants, lounges, gift shops, and meeting spaces found at full-service hotels, but do, however, desire the comfort and amenities offered at the finest full-service properties. For these guests, **upscale limited-service hotels** provide the comfort, convenience, and in many cases the elegance that these travelers desire.

Popular up-scale brands include Marriott's TownePlace Suites, U.S. Franchise System's Hawthorn Hotels and Suites, and Candlewood Hotels' Candlewood Suites. In many markets, these properties target their

Front desk of an upscale limited-service hotel

Guest room in a budget (economy) limited-service hotel

sales efforts on the extended-stay guest, the transient corporate market, or both.

Upscale limited-service hotels typically offer all the guest services and amenities offered at midpriced properties, as well as one or more of the following:

- Substantially upgraded room furnishings and decor
- Multipurpose suites
- Hot breakfasts in addition to continental breakfasts
- Upgraded in-room amenities (soaps, shampoos, and other toiletries)
- Personal shopping and laundry services
- In-room safes
- On-premise laundry facilities
- On-premise convenience stores

GUESTS OF LIMITED-SERVICE HOTELS

OBJECTIVE 2
Describe the type of guests who most frequently visit limited-service hotels.

Limited-service hotel guests include diverse travelers, such as families traveling by auto, businesspersons arriving by plane or auto, and senior citizen groups traveling by bus. Traditionally, hotel guests have been classified as either with a **group** (often defined as 10 or more rooms reserved per night) or as a **transient** (traveling alone). These classifications are useful when examining the characteristics of the limited-service hotel guest.

Limited-Service Group Guests

Many group travelers enjoy the convenience and generally lower costs offered by limited-service hotels. For example, tour bus operators often find that their clients want to eat in well-known, popular, local restaurants when traveling through an area. They do not want to pay the price required to stay at a hotel with an on-site restaurant. They also wish to visit local attractions, rather than spend time in elaborate hotel facilities. For groups such as these, limited-service hotels offer great value.

Other groups that routinely prefer limited-service hotels include visiting sports teams, religious and fraternal organizations, and social groups.

group (type of guest) a large number of guests sharing a common characteristic who are staying at a property at the same time; groups may receive special rates, amenities, and/or privileges because of the increased revenue that they generate; also called *tour group*

transient (type of guest) a guest who is not part of a group; transient guests can be further subdivided by traveler demographic to gain more detailed information about the type of guests staying at a property

Many businesspersons stay at limited-service properties.

In addition, an important source of business for many limited-service properties is the overflow from large groups staying in full-service convention hotels. For example, a 350-room full-service hotel with extensive meeting space may be asked by a military veterans' group to host its annual meeting. The group requires 400 guest rooms per night to house its attendees. In this case, the full-service hotel cannot accommodate all the group's guest-room needs, but may be able to satisfy its meeting needs. A nearby limited-service hotel may be asked to house the group's **overflow** and would likely find it advantageous to do so.

Some individuals not familiar with the hotel industry believe that limited-service hotels cater only to transient travelers. In fact, groups of all types make up an important part of the client base for many limited-service properties. Group sales can, depending on the hotel's location, represent 10 to 30 percent of the total number of rooms sold.

Limited-Service Transient Guests

Transient guests rent the largest number of guest rooms offered by limited-service hotels. Traditionally, these guests are classified into corporate and leisure traveler segments. Nearly all the limited-service hotel brands market to both types of guests. The hotel's location, amenities offered, and pricing structure significantly affect the ability of a specific hotel to attract these guests.

Corporate Travelers

overflow guest rooms that are part of a larger group booking that cannot be accommodated by a single hotel; the room rates for overflow rooms are often established at a rate similar to that of the hosting hotel

Corporate travelers are guests who are traveling on business or because of their jobs. While all hotel segments routinely target these guests, limited-service properties have been extremely successful in attracting corporate travelers, including those who:

corporate travelers guests who are traveling on business or because of their jobs

- Are self-employed and are seeking to control their travel costs
- Work for the government, military, or a nonprofit organization that limits hotel expenditures to **per diem** levels
- Must stay in one location for several days
- Want to stay at or near the specific location of a limited-service hotel
- Are traveling salespersons attracted by the highway locations of many limited-service hotels

per diem a fixed dollar amount per day that a traveler will be reimbursed for a hotel room and/or meals; the amount is determined by the traveler's employer and may differ by travel destination

Leisure Travelers

leisure travelers those who travel primarily for personal reasons; these guests use private funds for travel expenses and are often sensitive to the prices charged

Leisure travelers are guests who are traveling for pleasure or for other nonwork-related activities. Examples include vacationers, those attending weddings, family reunions, or funerals; highway travelers en route to and from their destinations; and local residents who want to enjoy a night out in a hotel for a special occasion.

Leisure travelers are an important part of the customer base of most limited-service hotels. Increasingly, these guests are loyal to a specific brand because of its frequent-traveler program. Also, now that the Internet is increasingly used by travelers to book their own hotel room reservations this hotel segment will continue to grow. Price plays an important part in these guests' decisions about where to stay, as does location and the guests' perception of brand quality.

Not all limited-service hotels are chain affiliated.

ORGANIZATIONAL STRUCTURE AND MANAGEMENT OF LIMITED-SERVICE HOTELS

Limited-service hotels sometimes exceed 150 rooms; however, more typically, they contain 50 to 100 guest rooms. Since the properties are small, their organizational structure varies substantially from a larger, full-service property. Exhibit 6.1 shows a simplified organizational chart for a small limited-service property.

> **OBJECTIVE 3**
> Outline an organization chart for a limited-service hotel, and briefly describe the duties of managerial positions found within this segment.

Focus on General Manager

The general manager (GM) has a most important responsibility in the operation of a limited-service hotel. As already noted, the typical property is small, and the GM will likely be responsible for supervising many tasks that would otherwise be assigned to a department head in a larger property. While the position of GM is not unique to the limited-service hotel segment, the role played by the GM in these properties requires close examination, because it is different from a GM counterpart in a larger full-service property.

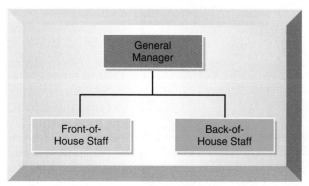

EXHIBIT 6.1
Simplified Organization Chart for a Limited-Service Hotel

The responsibilities of the GM of limited-service hotels are numerous, but can be divided into four major areas:

- Investor (owner) relations
- Brand affiliation management
- Community relations
- Property operations

Investor (Owner) Relations

Regardless of whether the GM is the hotel's owner or an employee of the owner, his or her role in investor relations is important. Investor relations include all communications between the GM and those who own the property and/or who have helped to finance it. Hotel ownership can take many forms. In addition to hotel ownership and operation by the GM, he or she may be employed either by the hotel's owners or by a management company that has been selected to operate the hotel for the owner. In all cases, those who own or invest in the hotel property will hold the GM responsible to operate it profitably and to maintain its proper physical condition. Investors and owners must know about their property's performance. The ability of a GM to effectively communicate with these interested parties is critical to a limited-service hotel's long-term success.

Brand Affiliation Management

Nearly all limited-service hotels are affiliated with a franchise brand. As a result, an important part of a GM's role in a limited-service property relates to continually monitoring operational standards set by the brand. This activity is necessary to ensure property conformance with the requirements that these standards impose. In addition, the GM must effectively communicate with franchise brand managers about marketing and sales programs and the other operational services offered in efforts to improve the hotel's profitable operation. The skills required for a GM to effectively manage brand relationships include persuasive ability, listening skills, and the ability to communicate successfully in writing.

This is the entire management team at a limited-service hotel making plans to resolve an operating problem.

Community Relations

In many communities (especially smaller ones), a hotel is an important factor in attracting more business to the area. Local governmental and community leaders often look to hotel GMs to lead efforts to attract new businesses, expand tourism opportunities, and provide input about the needs of the local business community. The talents required to successfully perform the community relations segment of the GM's job include an outgoing personality, well-developed social skills, and, very often, effective public speaking and presentation skills.

Functional Area	Responsibilities
Human resource manager	Hotel staffing needs
Controller	Accounting for hotel assets and liabilities
Front-office manager	Guest services and sales
Executive housekeeper	Property cleanliness
Food and beverage director	Food and beverage production and service
Director of sales and marketing	Revenue production and promotions
Chief engineer	Upkeep of the hotel's physical facility

EXHIBIT 6.2
General Manager's Responsibilities in a Limited-Service Hotel

Property Operations

While GMs are leaders in the community, it is on the hotel property itself where their skills must be broadest. In limited-service hotels, the GM must be knowledgeable about all the property's functional areas. He or she must work very closely with individual staff members, because there are so few other managers on the property. In some smaller hotels, the GM may be the only salaried manager on the property and, therefore, will be the lead manager for many functional areas. (See Exhibit 6.2.) Since GMs must know much about how each of the hotel's functional areas operate, they must be multitalented and multitasked.

SHORT- AND LONG-TERM BUSINESS CHALLENGES

That GMs of limited-service hotels must confront several challenges now and in the future to remain competitive:

- Increased consumer expectations for budget and midpriced properties
- Declining number of affordable operating sites
- **Brand proliferation**
- Franchiser–franchisee conflicts

OBJECTIVE 4
Identify short- and long-term business challenges that confront those who manage limited-service hotels.

brand proliferation the oversaturation of the market with different brands

Increased Consumer Expectations for Budget and Midpriced Properties

The first limited-service hotels were readily accepted by consumers because of their good locations and moderate room rates. As this segment became more mature, some brand managers upgraded their organization's services and amenities and, in many cases, these upgrades have been substantial. In today's limited-service market, the guests' expectations are high. This is true even in the budget segment. As a result, some limited-service brand operators struggle to meet increasing guest expectations and brand requirements while maintaining profitable operations. In the future, the guests' wants and expectations will likely increase still further. This will result in even greater managerial challenges and pressures on profit levels for those who own and operate limited-service hotels.

Declining Number of Affordable Building Sites

Most hoteliers agree that the best real estate location for a limited-service hotel is near one of the following:

- An interstate highway entrance or exit
- A highly developed shopping or office complex
- A popular recreational area
- A high-density population center
- A significant local tourist attraction or other **demand generator**

demand generator an organization, entity, or location that creates a significant need for hotel services; examples include large businesses, tourist sites, sports stadiums, educational facilities, and manufacturing plants

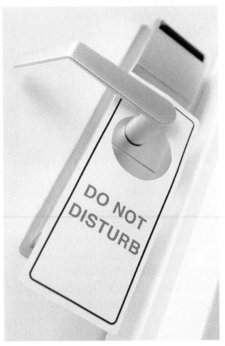

All guests are concerned about security and want to feel safe, regardless of the type of hotel in which they stay.

The problem is that each hotel operator's competitors also look for the same locations. Therefore, the demand for choice building sites has, in many areas, exceeded their availability. The result is often inflated real estate costs and associated property taxes and, consequently, excessive building and operating costs.

Small limited-service hotels must control all their costs carefully, including those related to land acquisition and taxes. A decline in the number of affordable building sites makes it more difficult for hotel developers to build cost-effective properties and for hotel managers to operate them profitably.

Brand Proliferation

Marketing professionals know that, when consumers clearly understand the defining characteristics of a brand name and when the demand for that brand's products is good, it is a win–win situation for consumers and for the brand. If, however, consumers are not clear about what a brand stands for (or, even worse, are not familiar with a brand's defining attributes), neither the consumer nor the brand is well served.

In the limited-service hotel business, brand proliferation (the oversaturation of the market with different brands) has reached the point that some observers believe consumer confusion will negatively affect the segment. Unless consumers are certain about what they will receive when they select one brand over another, they will likely hesitate to try the brand. As a result, brand managers have little choice but to attempt to influence consumers by reducing room rates, spending large numbers of advertising and marketing dollars, and/or creating highly discounted introductory rates. When organizations create, market, and promote additional brands that are similar to others, consumers can become confused about brand differences. As this occurs, hotel owners, consumers, and the brands themselves will suffer.

Franchiser–Franchisee Conflicts

Franchise brand managers (franchisers) must ensure that all franchisees uphold the organization's standards of operation. Hotel owners and operators (franchisees) desire to affiliate with strong brands that will help them to sell more rooms to maximize the value of their hotel asset. As hotel operators, they are keenly concerned about how their franchiser will manage their brand's image and operations.

Since most brand managers are not directly responsible for hotel operations (remember that they manage brand images, not hotel properties), conflicts can arise about how to best position the brand in the marketplace and about what each operating hotel within the brand should do to assist in the effort. For example, assume that the managers of a limited-service brand believe that their guests want irons and ironing boards available in each guest room. Assume also that no such standard (requirement) currently exists.

*Many European hotels offer a room with breakfast as part of the guest room price. Surprisingly, this is called the **American Plan**, even though, in the United States, a room and a meal are typically offered at an inclusive price only at some resorts and at many limited-service hotels.*

American Plan   the hotel pricing structure in which some (or all) of a guest's meals are included in the basic room rate.

The brand manager may genuinely believe that this upgrade in the standards is highly desirable. Hotel owners and operators who must bear the substantial cost of buying and installing the irons and ironing boards may, however, disagree. There is little doubt that guests would benefit from the iron and ironing board upgrade. The question of who pays for brand-mandated programs and amenities is one that is common to all hotel segments. However, these concerns are stronger in limited-service properties because of the historic strength of franchisers in setting and enforcing brand standards.

As talented professionals in the hospitality industry address these and other important issues, the future of the limited-service segment is indeed bright. Lower construction costs, ease of operation, and perceived value on the part of the consumer are among the driving forces that will continue the rapid development of this popular segment of the lodging industry.

Businessperson working in guest room of a limited-service property

RISING STAR PROFILE

Mike Rice
General Manager
Quality Suites Hotel
Lansing, Michigan

Managing the Accounts Receivables!

Mike's property is a 117-room all-suite hotel. It has limited food service (hot made-to-order breakfasts and a daily welcome reception). Approximately 10 percent of the property's guests stay more than two weeks.

Mike graduated from a hospitality business school in 1991. His first hospitality position was at the Stouffer Renaissance Hotel in Chicago (565 rooms), where he learned much about the hospitality business by working in numerous positions: room service, stewarding (kitchen and banquet), restaurant manager, laundry manager, and director of housekeeping. He enjoyed the food side of hotel operations and opened his own catering business. After about two years he recognized that "you must leave to know you must come back." He returned to the hotel industry as director of guest services at the Allerton Crown Plaza Hotel (Chicago) and then moved to the Courtyard by Marriott (Detroit) as director of room operations.

Mike's most significant marketing challenge relates to gaining access to government- and company-preferred listings for their traveling employees. These employers only reimburse travelers who stay at *preferred* properties where special rates have been negotiated. Often the contract of a preferred property specifies that the employer must be "direct billed" for their staff members' lodging costs. For example, approximately 50 percent of hotel guests during the work week at Mike's property are state government employees who are only permitted to stay at preferred hotels while on business. Lodging expenses are not paid by these guests upon checkout; instead the hotel must submit a bill for later payment. This can create cash flow problems. Mike must be able to close his accounts receivables to meet the hotel's expense obligations.

A related challenge concerns contract negotiations with major employers. For example, a major airline might agree to house several flight crews in the property each night in return for a relatively low room rate. However, a hotel must consider not only its occupancy rate, but also revenue per available room (rev par). Occupied rooms that generate low revenue levels are not available for other guests who will pay higher rates.

Mike has had many memorable experiences during his career. He has made drinks for movie stars and has been through the excitement of opening a new hotel. "On the day the property opened, we had 20 guests arrive at 4 P.M. We could not register them until 6 P.M. when the city formally gave us our Certificate of Occupancy license."

What does the general manager of All Suites property do on an "average day"? First, according to Mike, "There is no 'average' day! From 6:30 to 7:00 A.M. I walk the property and make notes. From 8:00 A.M. to 12:00 noon I have rally meetings with department heads. I also review reports, send e-mails, make and take telephone calls, and address problems. At noon I try to learn more about the city's market. I lunch with clients and visit other hotels to see who they are hosting. Between 1:00 and 4:00 P.M. there are additional meetings with staff members. I also talk with building owners and work on seemingly innumerable projects. After 4:00 P.M. I often attend Convention and Visitors Bureau, Chamber of Commerce, or other civic and community service group meetings."

Mike has some advice for young people considering a career in the hospitality industry:

- "If you want to move around, do so while you are younger; you may have less interest in frequent moves as you get older, so take advantage of your youth.
- "Work in different positions; be flexible. Your future employers will want to hear about your employment history in multiple departments and on different work shifts.
- "You will likely need an operations background for almost anything you want to do in the hospitality industry later in your career; get that experience.

- "Work on the firing line; you need to be in front of guests when it is necessary to tell them that the property is sold out, and you can't sell banquet functions unless you know all about them.

- "Don't look for nine o'clock to five o'clock positions early in your career. You have to work your way to them, if they are ever available."

ASIAN AMERICAN HOTEL OWNERS ASSOCIATION (AAHOA)

The Asian American Hotel Owners Association (AAHOA) has more than 8,300 members who own more than 20,000 hotels, which have more than 1 million rooms. This represents more than 50 percent of the economy lodging properties and nearly 37 percent of all hotel properties in the United States.

The hospitality industry was a popular career choice for Asian Indians migrating to the United States during the last 50 years because it offered immediate housing and cash flow. Soon the name Patel became synonymous with the limited-service hotel business. In ancient India, rulers appointed a record keeper to track annual crops on each parcel of land (called a "pot"). That person became known as a Patel.

Source: Home page of Asian American Hotel Owners Association: www.aahoa.com.

SUMMARY OF CHAPTER LEARNING OBJECTIVES

1. **State features that make limited-service hotels a unique segment of the hotel industry.**
   Originally defined as a hotel without foodservice facilities, the services and amenities offered to guests by limited-service hotels vary. Budget (economy) limited-service hotels offer no-frills rooms at modest prices; midpriced limited-service hotels offer increased services and amenities; upscale limited-service hotels offer guests many of the same high-quality amenities that these guests would expect to find in full-service hotels. Nearly all limited-service hotels are franchise branded and, in most cases, they are small properties with 150 or fewer rooms or suites.

2. **Describe the type of guests who most frequently visit limited-service hotels.**
   Limited-service hotel guests travel for a wide variety of reasons. They include both group and individual transient guests. Transient guests are an important segment of most limited-service

hotels' client base and include corporate and leisure travelers. These travelers look for hotels in specific locations, are generally loyal to a specific brand, and are usually price conscious. Increasingly, these travelers use the Web to compare room prices across brands and to book their own hotel reservations.

3. **Outline an organization chart for a limited-service hotel, and briefly describe the duties of managerial positions found within this segment.**
   The organization chart in a limited-service hotel can be evaluated by examining the three key functional areas (general manager, front-of-house staff, and back-of-house staff). The general manager's position is unique. He or she is responsible for (a) communicating the property's physical and financial condition to its investors or owners, (b) representing the property to the brand with which the hotel is affiliated, (c) playing an active role in the local

business community, and, most importantly, (d) managing the day-to-day operations of the hotel. Often the GM is the only or one of the few full-time managers on the property.

4. **Identify short- and long-term business challenges that confront those who manage limited-service hotels.**

Rising guest expectations and the increase in brand standards that results have created (and will continue to create) profitability challenges for those who own and manage limited-service hotels. Developing hotels in the face of a declining number of affordable building sites is an additional challenge. Also, as franchisers create new brands, consumers may lose the ability to clearly distinguish among these brands. Consumer confusion can result, which will lessen profitability for hotel owners. Finally, conflicts between franchisers and franchisees over brand standards will, unless both groups work together, pose a significant problem in the future development of strong and profitable limited-service hotels.

FEEDBACK FROM THE REAL WORLD

Our real-world advice comes from Sheila Patel, Vice-President, Sheldon Management, Inc., Lutz, Florida. Sheila is the owner and operator of three limited-service hotels in Florida, including one that was a "new build" (new construction). Her company is considering growth by building new properties in central Florida. She has approximately 15 years of experience in the industry and believes that an owner's active participation in the day-to-day operations of a hotel is essential to its success.

If you had a choice between taking an early-career management position in a limited- or full-service hotel, which might be best? Why?

Full-service properties typically provide expanded opportunities for young persons to learn more about the lodging industry. Unlike a limited-service property, which often has a general manager and probably no other department heads, full-service properties typically have middle-management (department head) positions in different functional areas. All general managers in full-service properties must know something about all these areas. If full-service property management is a long-term career goal, it is probably best to obtain this experience in the beginning of one's hospitality career.

Let's assume that one is currently managing a hotel. I think it is much more likely that a limited-service manager would move to a full-service property than the reverse, even though there would likely be fewer transitional problems moving from a full-service to a limited-service property. Why? Persons with a full-service management background have dealt with all or most of the things that his or her limited-service counterpart has. However, the reverse is not true: a limited-service manager will not likely have had experience with, for example, food and beverage, catering, and conventions. Also, management salaries in a limited-service property are likely to be less than those in a full-service operation.

To what extent do potential guests want to bargain on the room rental rate at a limited-service property?

Some prospective guests arrive at the hotel without a reservation and other persons "call around" before they take a trip to make a hotel reservation. Most persons are looking for a "good" price; however, I think this means that they want value for the money they spend. Some persons base their decision on price alone without seeing a property and without learning about the amenities and services it offers. It is a little easier to sell a guest room to walk-ins because they have seen at least a little bit of the property (for example, the exterior and front-office lobby and registration areas).

In either instance, it is important to have trained front-desk clerks who can back up quoted room prices with intelligent product information. We train our staff, for example, to describe the hotel before quoting a price. Also, information about dates, number of people, and room type must be known to quote a correct rental rate.

Potential guests who have experience at another property in the franchise have a stereotype of the brand. This helps them to understand what to expect. When quoting rates, however, this gives the desk clerk the opportunity to review and expand on the unique amenities that the property offers. When selling a room, it is important to acknowledge your guests' needs (for example, two queens or a king or a nonsmoking room). When there are differences in room rates, one should start at the highest rate and then go down to a more moderately priced rate. At each step, it is important to tell the guests exactly what they will be getting for the rate being charged.

MASTERING YOUR KNOWLEDGE

Discuss the following questions.

1. What are examples of times when a group traveler would choose a limited-service property? A full-service property?
2. What are some times when a transient traveler would select a limited-service property? A full-service property?
3. What factors would be important to a corporate traveler when considering a budget (economy), midpriced, or upscale limited-service property?
4. What factors would influence a leisure traveler as he or she considers staying at a budget (economy), midpriced, or upscale limited-service property?
5. How do brand managers determine the types of property-level and within-guest room amenities that should be offered?
6. How would a general manager of a limited-service property learn all that is necessary within each functional area to be an effective manager of the property?
7. Which of the four responsibilities of a limited-service hotel general manager would you feel the most comfortable performing? The least comfortable? (What can you do to become more effective in performing the work required by this responsibility?)
8. What would you do if you were the owner or general manager of a limited-service property who was confronted with the need to meet an expensive new standard required by the brand?

LEARN FROM THE INTERNET

1. Check out the following three websites operated by limited-service hotel companies:
   - Budget (Economy) Limited–Service Hotel Motel 6: www.motel6.com
   - Midpriced Limited-Service Hotel Hampton Inn (Hilton): www.hamptoninn.com
   - Upscale Limited-Service Hotel TownPlace Suites (Marriott): www.townplacesuites.com

   What marketing similarities do you notice? How do the upscale brands attempt to attract their clientele? Which segment(s) do you feel will grow the fastest in the near future? Why?

2. Check out these websites:
   - Country Inn and Suites (Carlson Hospitality): www.countryinns.com
   - Comfort Inn (Choice): www.comfortinn.com
   - Econolodge (Choice Hotels International): www.econolodge.com
   - Super 8 (Cendant Corporation): www.super8.com

   Examine their amenity features and marketing approaches. Do you believe these brands are attempting to target the corporate or the leisure traveler? What amenities offered and advertising orientation, in each case, led you to your conclusion? Use specific examples.

3. Check out these websites of companies that allow you to book your own hotel reservations online:

   • Hotels.com: www.hotels.com

   • Hotel Supermarket: www.hotelsupermarket.com

   • Expedia.com: www.expedia.com

Select a city you might like to visit and then review the display ads for two limited-service hotels and two full-service hotels located in that area. Based on the ads, do you think you would want to stay at the full-service property? What factors might influence your decision? How could the display ads you saw for the limited-service hotels be modified to address your decision-influencing factors?

KEY HOSPITALITY TERMS

The following terms were explained in this chapter. Review the definitions of any words with which you are unfamiliar. Begin to utilize them as you expand your vocabulary as a hospitality professional.

limited-service hotel
budget (or economy) limited-service hotels
continental breakfast
lobby foodservices
midpriced limited-service hotels
frequent-traveler program
upscale limited-service hotels
group (type of guest)

transient (type of guest)
overflow
corporate travelers
per diem
leisure travelers
brand proliferation
demand generator
American Plan

Extended-Stay Hotels

7

Lobbies of extended-stay hotels may offer a den or family room that long-term guests miss when away from home.

CHAPTER LEARNING OBJECTIVES

After studying this chapter you will be able to:

1. State why extended-stay hotels are a unique segment of the lodging industry.
2. Describe the type of guests who most frequently utilize extended-stay properties.
3. Sketch an organizational chart showing common positions in an extended-stay property.
4. Describe unique duties of management positions within extended-stay hotels.
5. Explain significant challenges confronting hospitality managers in the extended-stay segment.

This chapter is authored by David Hayes, PhD. Dr. Hayes is an author and a 30-year veteran of both the hospitality and hospitality education industries.

FEEDBACK FROM THE REAL WORLD

The extended-stay segment of the hotel industry is designed to appeal to a specific type of traveler. Typical extended-stay guests stay at their hotel for long periods of time (from one week to one or more years).

As you read this chapter, consider the following: What type of hospitality manager is best suited for operating an extended-stay hotel? What guest-room features are of greatest interest to extended-stay visitors in their "home away from home"? What tactics can a chain of extended-stay properties utilize to differentiate itself from its competitors? What is the best way to handle concerns raised by guests during their stay? What are important factors to consider when thinking about a career in the extended-stay segment?

As you read this chapter, think about answers to these questions and then get feedback from the real world at the end of the chapter.

OBJECTIVE 1
State why extended stay hotels are a unique segment of the lodging industry.

Extended-stay hotels are a relatively recent entry into the ever-evolving lodging property marketplace. They are the perfect accommodation for travelers whose needs are a little different from others who purchase lodging products and services. Who are these people and what do they want? This chapter will address these and related questions.

extended-stay guest a hotel guest seeking lodging accommodations in the same property for a period of seven or more days

EXTENDED STAY: A UNIQUE HOTEL SEGMENT

A small, but very important segment of the hotel industry is designed for **extended-stay guests.** Industry observers note that the extended-stay market

---

EXTENDED-STAY HOTEL GUEST-ROOM AMENITIES

Typical extended-stay properties offer numerous features to their guests:

Larger rooms
Free local telephone calls
Complimentary grocery shopping service
VCRs and videos to rent (or complimentary)
In-room refrigerators, microwave ovens, full kitchens (or at least kitchenettes), coffee makers, fireplaces, cooking utensils and serviceware
Complimentary breakfasts
Fitness centers
On-site coin-operated laundry facilities
Travel store or on-site vending machines with essential travel items
Outdoor sports areas
Outdoor barbeque and picnic areas
Complimentary newspapers
Manager's reception
Pool and spa
Frequent-traveler rewards

was first developed by hotelier Jack DeBoer and the Marriott Corporation when the Residence Inn brand was established in the United States in the 1980s. The segment is growing very quickly, having expanded nearly fivefold between 1995 and 2002. Sometimes **all-suite hotels** are classified as extended-stay properties; with these properties included, the extended-stay segment represents approximately 10 percent of the entire hotel market.

The typical extended-stay hotel consists of rooms or **suites** that have been specially designed to appeal to guests staying for a long period of time. As a result, the rooms or suites offer a wide range of amenities, some of which are not found in other properties.

manager's reception time (typically during early evening) in which registered guests are offered complimentary food and beverages in a central hotel location or dining area

all-suite hotels lodging properties in which all guest rooms are suites

suite a hotel guest room in which the living area is separated from the sleeping area

Many extended-stay hotels feature exercise rooms for their guests.

A typical extended-stay hotel consists of 80 to 100 medium to very large suites. Many offer a fitness center and a pool or spa. The suites are usually 350 (or more) square feet in size and typically include a living area, recliner-type chair, coffee table, TV with remote control and cable, voice mail with free local calls, and a computer data port. Foodservice amenities include a separate kitchen with a coffee maker, refrigerator, microwave, cooking and dining utensils, a stove, and a dining table with chairs. The sleeping area generally has a king- or queen-sized bed and a dresser and may include an additional pull-out sleeper sofa.

The significant and distinguishing features of extended-stay hotels, then, are larger rooms and more amenities than those typically found in other hotels. The objective of an extended-stay facility is to make guests feel as at home as possible during their (extended) stay. This is accomplished by the exterior and interior architecture of the hotel facility itself, by the design of guest rooms and suites, and by the service levels provided by the hotel's staff.

THE EXTENDED-STAY TRAVELER

OBJECTIVE 2
Describe the type of guests who most frequently utilize extended-stay properties.

When individuals or families must reside in a community for a temporary but extended time period, many have traditionally chosen to lease an apartment because the per night cost to stay in an apartment is much less than that of renting a hotel room. Sometimes, however, this cost advantage is offset by an apartment lease that must be signed for many months at a time.

The advantages of staying in an extended-stay hotel instead of an apartment include regular housekeeping services, complimentary breakfasts (in many properties), and the free use of amenities, such as a swimming pool and exercise facilities. In addition, an extended-stay hotel guest does not incur the cost of utility deposits (telephone, electricity, gas, water, cable)

These guests are enjoying the manager's reception at an extended-stay property.

CHECK IT OUT!

- To view annual reports about the extended-stay hotel segment, go to www.highland-group.net. When you reach the site, click on "extended stay."

- Want to learn what *corporate apartments* are like, and consider how they might compete with extended-stay hotels? If so, go to www.tempstay.com.

- Organizations seeking corporate housing for personnel on long assignments away from home can use the services of organizations that provide directories of extended-stay hotels, apartments, and homes that compete with each other for this business in specific locations. To review one of these businesses, go to www.corporatehousing.com.

normally incurred by an apartment dweller. Extended-stay guests, especially those who are not sure how long they will be in the community, also appreciate the fact that no long-term leases need be signed. For many guests, then, the advantages of staying in a hotel outweigh a cost per night that may be somewhat higher than an apartment.

There are a variety of reasons why a guest may need or want to stay at a hotel for a long period of time. A few examples of typical extended-stay hotel guests will explain the popularity of this segment. Consider, for instance, persons whose homes have been damaged by fire or flood. While these guests did not originally intend to become long-term guests, it is likely to be several weeks (or more) before their home is repaired so that they can return. The needs of these guests are different from those of a highway traveler staying one night at a traditional hotel.

Alternatively, consider the retired couple from the midwestern United States who elect to spend the winter months in a warm southern climate. They may stay for several months in the same hotel while enjoying the available local shopping, restaurants, and recreational activities. Finally, consider the case of a professional trainer hired by a large manufacturer to do safety training in a manufacturing facility located within a specific community. If the safety training is to be done on-site and if many employees are involved, the trainer may need to stay in a hotel for several months or longer. Other typical guests include privately employed subcontractors, corporate employees on extended assignments, people relocating or building a home, participants in training programs, retirees visiting family, vacation travelers on long-term vacations, skilled laborers, and people whose homes are being remodeled or repaired.

The extended-stay guest market represents a wide spectrum of business and personal travelers searching for high quality and affordable lodging. Whether they stay because of circumstances, choice, or work, long-term-stay travelers look for the specific features offered by hotels in the extended-stay segment.

OBJECTIVE 3
Sketch an organizational chart showing common positions in an extended-stay property.

ORGANIZATIONAL STRUCTURE OF EXTENDED-STAY HOTELS

Not surprisingly, the general manager plays a very important role in the typical extended-stay hotel. In an independently owned and operated hotel, the

GM may be the hotel's owner. If this is not the case, he or she will be the primary contact with the owner. If a management company operates the hotel, the GM will likely report to an area or regional manager, who, in turn, is also in contact with the hotel's owners.

As indicated in Exhibit 7.1, the on-site general manager is typically assisted by persons in three management positions:

- *Director of sales.* Responsible for the property's sales and marketing efforts
- *Chief engineer.* Responsible for the repair and maintenance of the hotel's physical facilities
- *Assistant general manager* **(AGM).** Responsible for operation of the front desk, housekeeping, and, if offered, the limited food and beverage services

AGM   abbreviation for assistant general manager

The organizational structure of an extended-stay hotel varies based largely on the property's size. In a very small hotel (less than 50 rentable units), the general manager may play multiple roles, including those assigned to the director of sales and/or the assistant general manager. In a large extended-stay property, the front desk, housekeeping, and food and beverage areas may be large enough to warrant a full-time department head. When this is the case, these department heads may report to an AGM or directly to the general manager.

Franchise Organization

Most extended-stay hotels are part of a franchise organization. Therefore, the general manager must understand and implement the standards of the brand under which the hotel operates. In most cases, the on-site manager works with the brand managers to uphold the brand's standards.

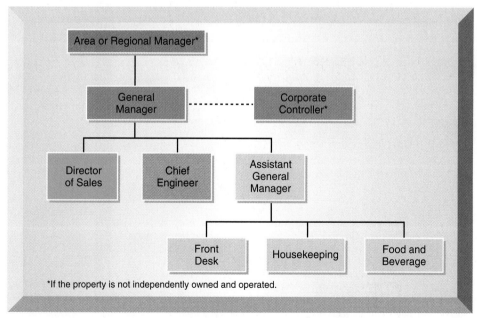

EXHIBIT 7.1
Organization Chart for an Extended-Stay Hotel

average daily rate (ADR)
the average selling price of all guest rooms for a given time period; the formula for ADR is Total room revenue ÷ total number of rooms sold = ADR

Extended-stay hotels that achieve a relatively high **average daily rate (ADR)** offer the quality of amenities and many of the services found in traditional upscale hotels. Extended-stay hotels that appeal to more budget-conscious travelers likely have fewer amenities, and those offered will be of a more modest nature. Regardless of the rate charged, however, every extended-stay hotel seeks to offer guests a comfortable home away from home. It is up to the management team at the property to create the "at-home" environment sought by long-term guests.

OBJECTIVE 4
Describe unique duties of management positions within extended-stay hotels.

UNIQUE DUTIES OF MANAGEMENT POSITIONS IN EXTENDED-STAY HOTELS

An extended-stay hotel provides many challenges to its on-site managers. These include the need to perform a wide range of tasks, because the smaller property size means that there are fewer specialized positions. Also, hosting skills exceed traditional levels, and a strong orientation toward hotel sales is a must.

In small- to midsized extended-stay hotels, managers must often assume the duties fulfilled by several different hospitality managers in their larger counterparts. For example, in smaller properties, the GM and/or AGM will likely be responsible for the financial management of the property (the role typically filled by an on-site controller), as well as the human resource function (the role typically filled by an on-site human resources director). In extended-stay hotels that provide guests with complimentary breakfasts, the manager will also assume the role of food and beverage director.

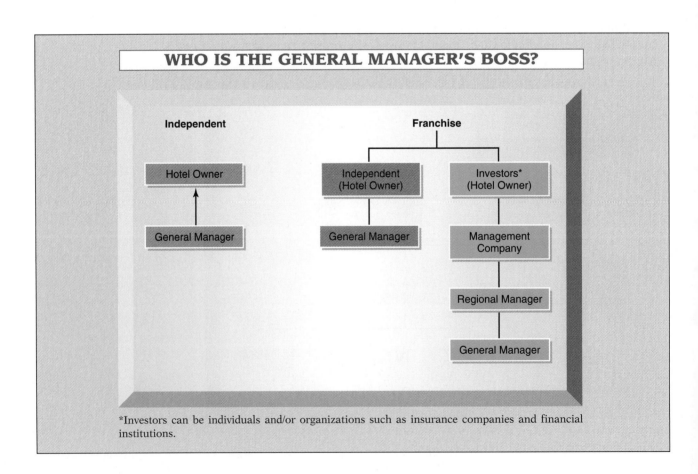

WHO IS THE GENERAL MANAGER'S BOSS?

*Investors can be individuals and/or organizations such as insurance companies and financial institutions.

Jennifer Waite Connell
Senior Manager
Development Planning and Feasibility
Marriott International
Washington, D.C.

Good Advice: Find a Mentor!

Jennifer's personal interest in hospitality goes back to when she was a child: "I grew up in Jackson, Mississippi, where my parents owned a business. We frequently traveled to conventions around the country and stayed in large hotels close to convention centers. While my parents were in meetings, I had a chance to wander around the hotels and marvel at the staff members dressed in their starched uniforms. The grandeur of the atrium lobbies with glass elevators is another memory, and I remember thinking about how wonderful it would be to manage the Atlanta Marriott Marquis." However, in spite of her personal interests, she studied political science in college and, while in school, did part-time work in state government and at a Washington, D.C., think tank.

Realizing that she did not want to pursue a political career, she began working at the headquarters of StudioPLUS Hotels in Lexington, Kentucky, as its preopening sales and marketing coordinator.

"From the beginning of my hospitality career, I have been working around the hotel-opening process. StudioPLUS opened close to 35 hotels in 1997. I was responsible for conducting marketing research in the cities where the hotels were opening. I studied the top extended-stay-demand generators and competitors in each market, set opening rates for our hotels based on this information, and conducted numerous marketing activities, including direct mail and advertising campaigns."

Jennifer's next career move was to Austin, Texas, where she was a director of sales for a 150-room extended-stay at Homegate Studios Suites. While there, she helped the regional team open three additional properties in the Austin area within one year.

Jennifer's next job took her to Wichita, Kansas, with Candlewood Hotel Company. She was able to work closely with Jack DeBoer (the "Father of Extended Stay"). She was a market research manager responsible for conducting revenue feasibility studies for potential hotel sites. "After money for new buildings dwindled, I moved to the Washington, D.C., area to become a sales manager for a 185-room independent hotel owned by three former StudioPLUS and Marriott executives. That's how I began my career with Marriott."

Jennifer started in Marriott's Extended Stay Franchising Division working with TownePlace Suites openings. "Two of us trained the staff, owners, and management company personnel in new properties about the important role of direct sales in their revenue strategies. We also helped to organize their sales efforts and provided direct sales training to the GM and his or her sales staff. We also worked with the vice-president of extended stay brands on a six-month project to increase the revenue performance of the existing TownePlace Suites, which were managed by Marriott International."

In Jennifer's current position, she educates owners, franchisees, and general managers about effective tools, resources, and processes for preopening sales and marketing and revenue management. Typically, she works at each hotel for four to six months before opening and four to six months after opening. Her role is to keep them accountable for carrying out sales strategies and for utilizing all tools to effect positive revenue performance. "When franchisees open multiple hotels, I act as an account manager and liaison between that franchise company and Marriott regarding sales and marketing issues."

Jennifer has lots of unforgettable moments: "I'm not sure I can pick only one. The day I began working for Marriott was one of my proudest moments, because Marriott has always been known as the best hospitality company. Other unforgettable moments occur when I am teaching someone. The best feeling that I've had is after I see someone take the information that I give them, put it into action, and realize success. I love to see the light in someone's eyes when an idea that they have struggled to understand becomes clear."

(continued)

Jennifer has identified special challenges for the extended-stay segment and for persons working in sales and marketing and franchising and openings:

- Extended-stay segment. "The biggest challenge of this segment is the overwhelming number of properties built specifically for extended stay. The original Residence Inn and StudioPlus Properties of yesterday had a different challenge: educating the customer about extended stay. Now that customers are educated, they have a wide range of alternatives from which to choose. It used to be easy to steal share from the competition because existing hotels chains were not built to house extended-stay travelers. For example, they had smaller guest rooms without kitchens. Now that there are so many properties built specifically for this purpose, how do we distinguish ourselves from the competition? All brands require that their franchisees and owners install the latest and greatest amenities: free Internet access, bigger and better breakfasts, and so forth. This helps to distinguish the quality tier brands from their moderate counterparts (which have had the greatest increase in supply).
- Sales and marketing. "Direct sales is the latest and greatest marketing tactic now that the economy is on a downswing. Marriott hires proactive salespersons for brands that never needed them before. As a result, there are more salespersons on the street calling on the same customers. To address this problem within Marriott, we have created cluster sales efforts, where a few salespersons are deployed as a team against other customers or territories. They sell multiple brands, but, while efforts are not duplicated, cluster sales is not a perfect strategy. Each salesperson must have a broader focus and does not necessarily focus on achieving the strategy of a specific property."
- Franchising and openings. "Today, hotel companies realize that they cannot increase revenue steadily and significantly with their existing product alone. The way to make more money is to increase the number of hotels from which they receive revenues. The way to grow a hotel company is to franchise. However, it is necessary to balance quantity with quality. We cannot grow our brands at the expense of their integrity. We must choose franchisees and hotels that are committed to the brand, to its standards, and to the goal of meeting customer expectations. A franchiser must also keep a relationship with new and existing franchisees in check. No one who owns or operates an existing hotel wants another hotel to be built nearby, especially if it is of the same brand. A franchiser must have a process in place to notify existing hotel owners when a new hotel is up for approval by the development committee."

Jennifer was asked what she might do differently in her career. "I would have spent more time working in an individual hotel before moving into positions with multiunit responsibility. I would also like to have more full-service and group sales experience. It is hard to go back and get that type of experience when you move into higher-salaried positions."

Jennifer has some excellent advice for young people considering a career in the hospitality industry: "One's most valuable asset is understanding how to deal with people. And, unfortunately, this is a skill that is more difficult to learn than accounting, maintenance, food and beverage, and other important aspects of hotel management. While college classes can help, it takes more than classroom training to learn how to deal with people. Work in an internship where you interact with the public. Observe how your superiors work with customers and employees, and read Dale Carnegie's *How to Win Friends and Influence People*.

"Find a mentor: someone that you respect and who holds a position you would like to have one day. Ask as many questions as you can. Be willing to learn. A person can learn more quickly from someone else's mistakes than they can from their own.

"Be flexible; your career may not progress exactly the way you plan. You may have to move to a different state or country to take the job you have always wanted. You may end up in a position that you didn't even know existed! You may get laid off from a great job because of downturn in the economy. That happened to me twice, and I landed in a much better position because of it! There is no such thing as a master plan that never changes.

"Learn as many facets of the business as you can. Work in all areas of a hotel, especially sales, before you begin to move up. There is no such thing as a job that is completely operations or completely sales and marketing, even though some people mentally or organizationally separate the two disciplines. Every job is about sales, and every hotel job is about operations and serving the guests.

"Respect persons with differences. This is an industry with people of many different creeds and colors. There is no room for intolerance. Tip: you may want to pay attention in your foreign language classes."

Managers with strong backgrounds in housekeeping, maintenance, and sales typically do well as extended-stay managers because, in many cases, the hotel's manager will be the on-site "expert" in these areas. For example, a 75-unit extended-stay property will not be able to afford a chief engineer with extremely strong skills or many years of experience. Then the hotel's general manager will make decisions that, in a larger property, would normally be made by the chief engineer.

In addition to possessing a wide range of operational-specific skills, the best extended-stay managers understand that an important part of their job is to create a home-like atmosphere for their guests. As a result, individuals who enjoy significant amounts of guest contact are likely to be excellent extended-stay managers. Opportunities for guest contact in an extended-stay hotel include breakfast serving times, hospitality hours or manager's receptions, and the inevitability of meeting guests within the hotel due simply to the long-term nature of the guest's stay. Extended-stay hotel managers often know each of their guests by name, are aware of the circumstances

Reception desk at extended-stay property

WHO'S WHO IN THE EXTENDED-STAY INDUSTRY

Many hotel companies offer extended-stay products as part of their hotel portfolio. The Marriott Corporation has had great success with its Residence Inn brand, the Hilton Corporation offers the Embassy Suites brand, and U.S. Franchise Systems has quickly grown its Hawthorn Suites brand. Other significant extended-stay brands include Candlewood Suites, Staybridge Suites, Extended Stay America, and TownePlace Suites.

Business can be conducted in the lobby of an extended-stay hotel.

that brought them to the property, and quickly learn each guest's individual preferences. Use of this information allows managers to make each long-term guest's stay even more enjoyable.

The extended-stay hotel market is very competitive. As a result, managers often find that, regardless of their job title, they assume the role of salesperson for their respective properties and brand. Much of the extended-stay hotel's business relates to corporate travel. Managers who are active in their local Chambers of Commerce and other business-related organizations normally make personal contacts that are helpful in securing a share of the area's extended-stay travel business. Even when properties have a designated salesperson, the general manager and his or her assistant will, inevitably, play a critical role in the hotel's sales efforts.

> Who helps with the property's sales and guest-relation efforts?
>
> Answer: All Employees!

<table>
<tr><td>

OBJECTIVE 5
Explain significant challenges confronting hospitality managers in the extended-stay segment.

</td></tr>
</table>

CHALLENGES CONFRONTING THE EXTENDED-STAY SEGMENT

You have learned that hotels built specifically for extended-stay guests represent a relatively recent trend in the hotel industry. As a result, many challenges confronted by those who own and manage extended-stay properties relate to the relative newness of the concept. Of course, extended-stay hotels must cope with many of the same challenges faced by any commercial hotel. There are, however, specific concerns within this segment of the industry that are unique (or, at least, must be uniquely addressed). These include the following:

- Extensive growth
- Overreliance on corporate travel
- Competing in a multicompetitor environment

Let's look at each of these concerns.

Extensive Growth

When the first extended-stay hotels were developed in the mid 1980s, they met with immediate success. As a result, the next 15 years saw tremendous building and development within the segment. In many areas of the country, the segment became **overbuilt.** The number of rooms added in the extended-stay market was nearly three times the industry average during this time period. Absorbing that level of room growth can be difficult in the most robust economic environment but, in a struggling economy, it is very difficult.

The tragedy of September 11, 2001, and its resulting impact on travel, as well as the development of so many brands that consumers had difficulty recognizing which truly represented an extended-stay alternative, caused a virtual halt to the segment's **revpar** growth in the early 2000s. Fortunately, by late 2005 the growth of the extended-stay hotel market had rebounded significantly. In fact, extended-stay properties had occupancy rates much greater than the overall hotel industry, and hoteliers generated double-digit growth of revenue per available room.[*] As well, growth in the extended-stay market at that time (2005) was more than double overall hotel demand. While this is good news for investors and owners, significant market growth traditionally leads to the building of additional units that, in turn, leads to competitive pressures to reduce room rates.

overbuilt the condition that exists when too many guest rooms are available for the number of travelers wanting to rent them

revpar short for revenue per available room; the average revenue generated by each guest room available during a given time period; the formula for revpar is Occupancy % × ADR = revpar

Overreliance on Corporate Travel

Many extended-stay guests travel because of their work. When business is good, there are many travelers. When the economy slows, however, so does business travel. When the economy faces significant slumps (as it did in the early 2000s), business travel is severely curtailed. During these periods, the extended-stay segment, because it is so dependent on business travel, suffers more than other segments of the hotel industry. In a depressed economy, it is common for all segments of the hotel industry to experience some decline in occupancy and ADR. During the weak economy of 2000–2002, the extended-stay segment experienced a larger occupancy decrease than did other hotel segments. This put pressure on (lowered) the average daily rate, which resulted in larger than industry average declines in both of these critical measurements of hotel success (occupancy and ADR).

The challenge for extended-stay owners and managers is to find ways to maintain occupancy levels and rates during the swings in economic activity that are normally experienced over the life of an extended-stay hotel property.

Competing in a Multicompetitor Environment

Nearly every hotel must compete with other hotels for its guests. Economy hotels, for example, compete with other economy hotels for the budget-conscious traveler. Extended-stay hotels are unique, however, because they face more than the normal number of competitors as they seek business from potential guests. First, the extended-stay hotel must compete with other extended-stay properties and, as we have seen, as the number of these properties increases, so does the competition among them.

---

[*]Halstead, Larry. Front desks keep busy at extended stay hotels as concept turns the corner. Retrieved December 28, 2005, from www.bizjournals.com.

Some extended-stay properties have saunas.

Traditional hotels, including all-suite brands or those that contain suites, are finding that the extended-stay market is lucrative for them also. For example, a traditional full-service hotel that contains, as part of its room inventory, some multiroom suites, may decide to seek extended-stay guests in addition to its traditional shorter-term-stay guest business. As well, all-suite hotels that offer many of the same amenities as do extended-stay hotels can also effectively compete for the long-term-stay traveler's business and loyalty.

The extended-stay market may face its most serious challenge, however, from the apartment industry. Apartment complexes have traditionally required long-term leases and deposits that have made apartment living less attractive to extended-stay travelers. However, this industry has the facilities to compete for the long-term traveler's business should it wish to. In markets where their units are in great supply and where demand is less than supply, apartment owners electing to target the extended-stay traveler can create significant challenges for the extended-stay hotelier.

Extended-stay guests appreciate nearby shopping outlets and, like their counterparts in the lodging industry, the location of these properties is of great interest to the guests.

SUMMARY OF CHAPTER LEARNING OBJECTIVES

1. **State why extended stay hotels are a unique segment of the lodging industry.**
   The extended-stay segment is characterized by specially designed lodging facilities that offer guests larger rooms and more amenities than can be found at a traditional hotel that does not target this market. Extended-stay hotels seek to create a home away from home for guests.

2. **Describe the type of guests who most frequently utilize extended-stay properties.**
   Extended-stay guests stay in hotels for business or pleasure or by necessity. The typical extended-stay traveler remains in the same hotel for one week or more and seeks specific amenities offered by hotels in this market.

3. **Sketch an organizational chart showing common positions in an extended-stay property.**
   The organizational chart for an extended-stay hotel features the general manager and assistant general manager. These positions, depending on the size of the property, may require managers to perform multiple tasks

that, in larger hotels, would be the responsibility of different department heads.

4. **Describe unique duties of management positions within extended-stay hotels.**
   Because of their property's smaller size, extended-stay hotel managers must have a wider range of managerial skills than does a typical manager in a larger, full-service hotel. In addition, successful extended-stay hotel managers must have well-developed social skills and display a strong interest in sales and personal selling.

5. **Explain significant challenges confronting hospitality managers in the extended-stay segment.**
   Challenges faced by this market segment include potential overbuilding, an overreliance on corporate travel that has negative consequences during economically difficult times, and the fact that the segment must compete for its clientele against traditional and all-suite hotels and the apartment industry.

FEEDBACK FROM THE REAL WORLD

Our real-world advice comes from Adam Dougherty. Adam has been the general manager of the 276-room Candlewood Suites in Las Vegas, the largest property in the chain. He also served as the general manager of the Candlewood Suites property in Albuquerque, New Mexico, for two years and, during his first year with the organization, was a member of the opening team that oversaw the start-up of twenty-five new properties.

What type of hospitality manager is best suited for operating an extended-stay hotel?

The successful manager of an extended-stay property will have a well-rounded background in management and hands-on skills. While an extended-stay property is relatively large [number of rooms], it is also relatively short of management positions. A full-service property of similar size may have a general manager and directors of

sales, front office, and housekeeping. In our property, all these positions are basically collapsed into one: the general manager. You need, then, to be able to think on your feet, because you spend lots of time around the property making decisions about a diverse range of issues and concerns.

A manager in this segment must have great people skills. You can learn a lot about your guests when they stay with you for 30 to 90 days. One of the things guests typically like

(continued)

is a hotel staff that is genuinely hospitable. Our staff and I know our guests by name, we know about their jobs and their families, and about anything else they wish to share with us. We enjoy, as they do, the opportunities to keep up with part of their lives as they become a member of our guest family.

The general manager's people skills are important for another reason: much of our business comes from referrals from other guests. For example, people working in different trades on a big construction project talk about where they are staying. If they are having a great experience, we get additional business. As a second example, we have movie crews stay with us. They tell others about our hotel and, again, this positive word of mouth generates additional business. Also, when the trade persons and movie crew return to the city for additional work, they will stay with us.

What guest-room features are of greatest interest to extended-stay visitors in their home away from home?

The question is well phrased because our guests truly are searching for a home away from home. The home we provide them may not be as spacious and is not likely to be designed or decorated exactly the way that their real home is. This said, we can still provide a very comfortable and enjoyable living place for our guests. For example, we provide voice mail and a dual phone line to meet our guests' communication needs. Almost no one likes to eat all meals in restaurants (even though we have lots of good ones in Las Vegas!). Therefore, we provide all the basic kitchen appliances so that our guests can eat in or out as they wish. We have a convenience store on-site where we sell food and beverage items at the price we pay for them; there is no markup. If our guests want more than just basic food items, we have several grocery stores nearby.

We offer laundry services free of charge and even laundry baskets in every room. Our rooms are divided into working, relaxing, and sleeping areas, and we provide very appropriate and comfortable furniture along with a pleasantly decorated environment.

What tactics can a chain of extended-stay properties utilize to differentiate itself from its competitors?

We began to answer this question when we talked about providing what our guests want. As in other segments of the lodging industry,

one can rent an extended-stay room for $90 or more or for a midrange price of $40 to $80, or one can even select a very budget-conscious room for $30 or less.

Candlewood Suites is in the midrange market, and we think we know what our guests want. Since we know this, we provide it for them. Free in-room telephone, the gazebo where our guests can barbecue (even in 100°F weather!), and an exercise room that meets almost everyone's needs are further examples of how we provide what our guests want so that they will be happy, stay with us, and refer others as well.

What is the best way to handle concerns raised by guests during their stay?

You have got to take responsibility for a guest's problem. I call this "falling on your sword"! In my years of experience, I found that it typically does not take much to make a guest happy. The vast majority (90 plus percent) of complaining guests are not looking for something free. All they want is for someone to take care of their problem and, most typically, the problems are reasonable and often caused by our oversight.

Many problems can be resolved quickly, and they should be. I recall, for an example, a guest that was having problems with the in-room phone while trying to arrange an important conference call. I happened to be at the front desk when the guest stopped by to complain. "No problem," I said, "please come in and use my office." During the conference call, I brought in a cup of coffee for the guest and, during the call, I was able to replace the in-room phone. The guest was very happy, and I had a surprise: our visitor was a sales representative for a very high quality crystal tableware company; the beautiful etched bowl I received as a thank you is now on display in my office!

What are important factors to consider when thinking about a career in the extended-stay segment?

Extended-stay properties require personnel who are very service conscious. I know that this is true in all other segments of the hospitality industry as well. However, the amount of time that our guests remain with us makes an emphasis on service absolutely critical.

We need to remember that our guests are not just numbers. You need to know your guests and recognize the impact they have on the success of your hotel. The relationship you create with them is just not possible in lodging segments serving short-term guests.

General managers who can find and motivate great service staff will have a successful property. At the same time, they will be able to have a personal life, because a great staff will be available to take care of business when the general manager is not there.

MASTERING YOUR KNOWLEDGE

Discuss the following questions.

1. How easy (or difficult) would it be to retrofit (bring up to date) an existing traditional hotel to accommodate the extended-stay market?
2. If you were an extended-stay traveler, how would you learn about and differentiate between alternative brands? How would you decide on the brand that you prefer? What would need to happen for you to continue to favor this brand?
3. What amenities would need to be available, because they are absolutely necessary, for you to consider staying at an all-suite property of a specific brand?
4. What are things that you could do as a general manager of an all-suite property to make the guests feel at home? What, if anything, would you do differently in your interaction with guests who have been staying at your property for several months as opposed to several weeks?
5. What, if any, kinds of cross-training or job rotation would you do as a general manager of an extended-stay property to train subordinate managers to be generalists?
6. One challenge confronting the extended-stay market was noted to be an overreliance on corporate travel. If you were a general manager of this type of property, what are tactics you could utilize to expand your market base?

LEARN FROM THE INTERNET

1. Check out the following websites for extended-stay hotels:
   - Residence Inn (Marriott): www.marriott.com/residenceinn).
   - Hawthorne Suites (U.S. Franchise Systems): www.hawthornesuites.com.
   - Extended Stay America: www.extendedstayamerica.com.

   Make a comprehensive list of the amenities that these hotel brands offer to extended-stay travelers.

2. Check out the following websites for all-suite properties:
   - Candlewood Suites (Intercontinental Hotels Group): www.candlewoodsuites.com.
   - Staybridge Suites (Intercontinental Hotels Group): www.staybridge.com.
   - Embassy Suites (Hilton): www.embassysuites.hilton.com

   How do these brands seek to extend their markets beyond those of traditional extended-stay properties? Why do you think all-suite hotels are so popular?

3. Check out the rates you would be charged for a seven-night stay in a major city near you. Use travelocity.com or one of the other hotel reservation search engines to see how the price per night varies for an extended-stay, all-suite, and traditional hotel. Which do you think the typical traveler would choose? Why?

KEY HOSPITALITY TERMS

The following terms were explained in this chapter. Review the definitions of any words with which you are unfamiliar. Begin to utilize them as you expand your vocabulary as a hospitality professional.

extended-stay guest	AGM
manager's reception	average daily rate (ADR)
all-suite hotels	overbuilt
suite	revpar

8

Convention Hotels and Conference Centers

Las Vegas Convention Center

CHAPTER LEARNING OBJECTIVES

After studying this chapter you will be able to:

1. State the features that make convention hotels and conference centers a unique segment of the lodging industry.

2. Describe the types of organizations that most frequently utilize space at a convention hotel or conference center.

3. Draw an organizational chart for a convention hotel or conference center that shows hospitality management positions unique to these properties.

4. Describe how a Convention and Visitors Bureau (CVB) works with convention hotels and conference centers to promote group travel to their market area.

5. Identify current and long-term challenges confronted by managers of convention hotels and conference centers.

This chapter was authored by Curtis Love, PhD, Associate Professor, Tourism and Convention Department, William F. Harrah College of Hotel Administration, University of Nevada, Las Vegas.

FEEDBACK FROM THE REAL WORLD

Many groups of people, for numerous reasons, meet together regularly. Often these groups choose to meet at a convention hotel or conference center. Convention hotels offer an array of meeting services and amenities that make this a unique segment of the hotel industry. Conference centers, which may or may not offer sleeping rooms or be attached to a lodging facility, typically offer meeting spaces specifically geared toward groups gathering for education, training, or professional development purposes.

Assume that you are on the management team for a conference center and that you are competing for group business from a convention hotel. What services can your conference center provide that might differentiate it from its convention hotel competition? If the center does not include sleeping rooms, but these are available at a nearby hotel, how do you address the potential inconvenience that might be a problem for meeting attendees if sessions are held at the convention hotel? How, if at all, is the work of a top-level manager in a conference center different from that of his or her counterpart in a convention hotel? How is the work similar?

As you read this chapter, think about the answers to these questions and then get feedback from the real world at the end of the chapter.

A CLOSE LOOK AT A UNIQUE LODGING SEGMENT

Virtually all hotels have the ability to host both individuals and groups of travelers. **Convention hotels,** however, are specifically designed to meet the lodging and meeting needs of large groups. **Conference centers** are designed for the meeting-related needs primarily of small groups, and many also offer or have easy access to guest rooms. This singular focus on group activities most distinguishes these two types of facilities from other segments in the lodging industry.

While there is no universally accepted definition of the term **group,** many hotels define a group as a lodging reservation exceeding 10 rooms per night. For example, if someone planning a high school class reunion contacted a convention hotel to plan the dinner and other activities and reserved more than 10 sleeping rooms, he or she represents a piece of group business.

Three characteristics differentiate group-oriented convention hotels and conference centers from other segments of the lodging industry:

- Facilities oriented to groups
- Services designed to meet the needs of groups
- Marketing efforts targeted to group sales

Facilities for Groups

The needs of group travelers visiting a hotel or conference center differ markedly from those of individual travelers. For example, they require the following:

- Adequate function space
- Breakout rooms
- Larger dining areas
- Group entertainment and/or activity areas

The most common facility requirement for group gatherings relates to an adequate number of appropriately sized **function rooms.** Large hotels and

> **OBJECTIVE 1**
> State the features that make convention hotels and conference centers a unique segment of the lodging industry.

convention hotel a lodging property with extensive and flexible meeting and exhibition spaces that markets to associations, corporations, and other groups bringing persons together for meetings

conference center a specialized hospitality operation specifically designed for and dedicated to the needs of small- and medium-size meetings of 25 to 75 people

group a lodging reservation that exceeds 10 rooms per night

function room public space, including meeting rooms, conference areas, and ballrooms (which can frequently be subdivided into smaller spaces), available for banquet, meeting, or other group rental purposes

hospitality suite   a private guest room of sufficient size to provide meeting space, food, and/or beverages for a small group of guests

breakout room   a room used when a large group wishes to temporarily break into smaller groups

Marriott Marquis Hotel in New York City is one of the country's greatest convention hotels.

conference centers contain thousands (and sometimes hundreds of thousands!) of square feet of function space that can easily be separated into function rooms of almost any size needed by any group. The function space may consist, for example, of a large ballroom capable of holding several thousand persons seated for an opening session of a convention or hundreds or thousands of guests seated for a meal function. At the other extreme, space will also be available for a small **hospitality suite** to provide selected group members with a quiet getaway following a busy day of meetings. The function spaces of the property must be sufficiently flexible to match the needs of the numerous groups who hold meetings at the site.

In addition to an adequate amount of square footage, a convention hotel or conference center must be capable of providing the number of **breakout rooms** needed by the group. Consider, for example, a group of 1,000 meeting attendees, all of whom must meet at 8:00 A.M. for a general group session. At 10:00 A.M. they need to break into 10 groups of 100 delegates for special topic sessions. The convention hotel or conference center hosting this group must have the facilities available to seat the 1,000 attendees in one area, as well as 10 additional breakout rooms with a capacity of at least 100 persons in each room. The dining needs of this group will also likely be extensive. It takes a special hotel with special facilities and hotel staff to serve 1,000 or more quality meals at the same time. For the large convention hotel or conference center, this type of meal service is routine.

Convention hotels and conference centers typically have significant space for exhibitions (trade shows). Exhibit spaces, food outlets to accommodate visitors to these events, rest rooms, registration, and other public spaces are needed. (Details about exhibitions and trade shows are presented in Chapter 29.)

In addition to adequate function space, appropriate breakout rooms, dining areas, and exposition (trade show) areas, the best convention hotels and conference centers also offer entertainment and activities for meeting attendees to enjoy after daily meetings have ended. Some of these activities, including swimming, golf, tennis, casinos, and entertainment lounges, may be housed within the property. In other cases, entertainment possibilities consist of nearby areas, such as beaches, shopping areas, and historical sites.

Group Services

As you have seen, groups need special facilities. Groups also require special services, which are often provided only by convention hotels and conference centers. These include activities involving the property before, during, and after a meeting is held.

Before a meeting begins, staff at a convention hotel or conference center assist a group by arranging guest-room reservations, scheduling function

This small breakout room in a conference center is perfect for case-study work or for a small meeting.

spaces, planning meals and related functions, and coordinating numerous activities. Often, premeeting services include help in planning for transportation to and from the facility during the meeting. Property representatives may also arrange local entertainment activities or sight-seeing excursions for the group. In some cases, activities are planned for the spouses and guests of the attendees and, in others, all meeting attendees participate.

During the meeting, convention hotel or conference center professionals may assist the group with welcoming and registering meeting attendees. Staff may also perform many tasks to properly service the meeting. These may include initial setup of and **refreshing** the function rooms and provision of audiovisual, sound, or lighting needs. Added services provided before and during the meetings may include scheduling and coordinating speakers, handling **VIPs,** and managing recognition or certification procedures applicable to meeting attendance. Food and beverage services and dining area decorations are always important to meeting attendees, and the hotel or conference center's food and beverage department helps to plan and provide them. (The quality of food and beverage service is often a deciding factor when a meeting planner selects a facility.)

After the group has concluded its meetings, convention hotel or conference center staff properly total and document the charges incurred by the group. Timely and professional billing and collection activities are critical to a meeting's financial success and to the chance to host the group's future meetings.

refresh to clean and restock a meeting room with water, beverages, or other meeting room supplies; this activity often takes place during the meeting's scheduled breaks or meal periods

VIP short for *very important person* (guest); used to identify guests who should receive special treatment or attention during their visit

Group Marketing and Sales Activities

A significant difference between convention hotels and conference centers and their counterparts in the lodging industry relates to marketing and sales efforts. You have learned that traditional hotels attract transient business and leisure travelers, while convention hotels and conference centers pursue the meetings market. To do this requires an understanding of how to best address the needs of travelers who attend meetings. The marketing personnel in convention hotels and conference centers are concerned about the following:

- *Who* are the potential guests most likely to use the property?
- *Why* does the targeted group hold its meetings (for example, training, social, recreation, sight-seeing, or other events)?
- *What* are the group's facility needs? Can these needs be met by the property at a mutually acceptable price?
- *From where* will these guests be coming and *how* will they arrive at the property?

> • *When* are the group's meetings held? *Does* the property have adequate space available when the group needs it?

An analysis of the above and related group guest information and an assessment of competitive facilities and locations help convention hotels and conference centers to best meet the needs of the groups they serve.

CLIENTS FOR BUSINESS MEETINGS

Organizations and groups using the facilities and services of a convention hotel or conference center have goals related to the meetings they schedule. A corporation's short-term goal may be training sales staff about how to best sell a new product. The meeting goal of a nonprofit organization may be to discuss the best ways to design and implement an annual fund-raising campaign. For groups meeting primarily for social reasons, the goal may simply be to network with others sharing the same interests.

Three of the largest group meeting markets include associations, government and nonprofit organizations, and corporations. Let's see why these groups require meetings.

Associations

Buffets can serve a wide variety and quantity of food items to a large number of convention delegates quickly.

professional association a group of persons who affiliate to promote common interests (which may or may not include business)

Professional associations are groups who meet because of their common interests. For example, the American Culinary Federation is the association for professional chefs and culinarians, and the Hospitality Sales and Marketing Association International is the professional association for those involved in the industry's sales and marketing efforts. Examples of other professional associations include the American Medical Association for physicians and the American Bar Association for attorneys. Nearly every profession has formed a group for its members. Professional associations typically hold annual conventions, quarterly or monthly meetings, professional development and awards meetings, and training sessions.

trade association a group of persons who affiliate because of common business and/or industry concerns

There are thousands of business groups whose members have formed a **trade association** for the purpose of advancing their own business and industry goals. Examples in the hospitality industry include the National Restaurant Association and the American Hotel & Lodging Association. Examples in other industries include the Hardwood Manufacturers Association (serving U.S. hardwood sawmill owners and operators) and the American Society of Association Executives (serving professionals in the trade association management field). Groups such as these may have national, regional, and state **chapters,** all of which may convene meetings.

chapter a group that is a subset of an association; chapters are often formed on the basis of geography (a state association chapter is a subset of a national association)

There are numerous other categories of professional associations. For example, military associations are joined by those currently in the armed forces and by those discharged from the armed services. Examples include the Veterans of Foreign Wars and the American Legion. Education associations

> ## ASSOCIATIONS FOR EVERY PURPOSE
>
> *Gale's Encyclopedia of Associations* lists more than 114,000 associations operating in the United States. It is accessible by print or online through many libraries. A common characteristic of associations is that they meet to advance the goals of their group. It is a requirement of the federal government that nonprofit associations hold an annual meeting as a condition of their nonprofit status. Often it is the convention hotel and conference center segment of the hotel industry that provides the venue for their meetings.

include members working in elementary, high, and postsecondary schools and those who work in related fields, including textbook publishing, school administration, and facility operations. Examples include the American Association of School Administrators and the American Federation of Teachers. Religious associations include members employed by or who volunteer for churches, church organizations, and religious orders. Examples include various church denominations and special-interest groups, such as the National Association of Church Food Services. Thousands of other associations relate to specific interests, such as hunting, gardening, softball, and stamp collecting. Examples include the American Astronomical Society and the U.S. Chess Federation.

Government and Nonprofit Organizations

The government meetings market is very large. Government agencies and employees at the federal, state, and local levels meet for training, policy development, and planning purposes. A wide variety of nonprofit organizations have been formed to advance a cause of interest to the membership. Examples include the United Auto Workers (a labor union), the National Organization for Women, and the Sierra Club (which advances environmental causes).

Corporations

Businesses are a large user of convention hotels and conference centers. They meet to provide training, to introduce new products to sales personnel, to plan strategies, and to reward employees or customers. Transportation, lodging, and dining expenses related to meetings for business purposes may be tax deductible. Many companies plan the meetings to allow attendees to mix business with pleasure. They select meeting sites based on their ability to service meetings and to provide mini-vacations for the employees and customers.

ORGANIZATIONAL STRUCTURE

OBJECTIVE 3
Draw an organizational chart for a convention hotel or conference center that shows hospitality management positions unique to these properties.

The organizational charts for a large convention hotel and a conference center are similar to that of any large hotel with one important difference: a specialized sales and marketing department. Exhibit 8.1 shows that the director of sales and marketing supervises two important positions that exist in facilities serving the meetings market. What do the convention sales manager and the convention services manager do?

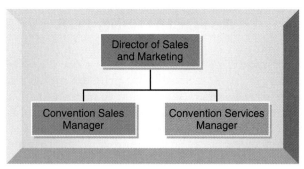

EXHIBIT 8.1
Organization Chart: Specialized Sales and Marketing Department for a Large Convention Hotel or Conference Center

The Convention Sales Manager

convention sales manager
the professional in a convention hotel and conference center who is responsible for booking a continuous flow of desirable group-business

booking   (verb) concluding a sale that results in a contract between the hotel and the guests(s)

classroom style   a seating arrangement in which tables and chairs are in rows on each side of a function room; all chairs face the head table, and a center aisle separates the rows

breakdown time   the time required to return a function room to its original condition after an event; this involves removing tables, chairs, and other fixtures and cleaning the area

setup time   the time required to modify a function room as required by a client; this involves setting tables and chairs and installing audiovisual equipment and other fixtures

convention services manager   the professional in a convention hotel and conference center who helps assure that all groups receive the contracted service negotiated by the convention sales manager

The **convention sales manager** is directly responsible for **booking** a continuous flow of desirable group business. In a smaller convention hotel or conference facility, sales managers may sell to any group wishing to utilize the property. In a larger property, a convention sales manager may have responsibility for a specific group segment. For example, there may be one (or more) convention sales manager(s) assigned to the corporate meetings market, specific association markets, the governmental market, the social market, or any other meetings subgroup considered important by the director of sales and marketing.

Convention sales managers must be able to sell sleeping rooms and food and beverage services. Additionally, they must know about and be able to offer all the facility's capabilities that can help to meet each group's needs. For example, assume that a group wants to hold a **classroom-style** meeting in the ballroom in the afternoon. It then wants to have dinner in the same ballroom that evening. The convention sales manager must know the **breakdown time** and **setup time** needed to prepare the ballroom for dinner service.

The convention sales manager must understand the facilities and service capabilities of the property so that guests are not promised something that the staff cannot deliver. The best convention sales managers are very thorough, creative, and honest. They determine all of a group's meeting needs and objectively inform prospective clients about the property's physical characteristics and service capabilities.

Convention sales managers book meetings from only a few weeks to many months or even years into the future. Booking far in advance can cause problems for both the convention sales manager and the meeting planner. Costs for food and beverage, labor, and utilities are variable costs that can change over time. Whatever is agreed on in the contract between the meeting planner and the property is legally binding. Likewise, the meeting planner may not know how many people will actually attend the event. If she or he contracts for a specified amount of food and beverage, sleeping rooms, and meeting space, this commitment will also be legally binding. If fewer people attend the event, the planner may still owe for what was ordered in the contract, regardless of whether it was needed.

Convention Services Manager

While the convention sales manager works with meeting planners to secure business for the hotel or conference center, the **convention services manager** (or, in a very large property, the convention services department) provides the guests with the contracted services negotiated by the convention sales manager. For example, a meeting planner may request that a special area be set up to register attendees. This request would be specifically noted in the contract that the convention sales manager negotiates with the group. The responsibility for ensuring that the property fulfills its contract (sets up the registration area) rests with the convention services manager.

A key difference between the convention sales manager and the convention services manager is the difference in the amount of time that the managers interface with the meeting planner. Corporate meetings are typically planned over a much shorter time period than are major association meetings. A few weeks or months in advance are typical for small- to medium-sized meetings. Both the sales and convention services managers may be on hand to work with the planner. By contrast, contracts for large association meetings may be signed years (two to five is typical) in advance of the actual meeting. Therefore, the convention sales manager who negotiated the contract may not even be employed by the hotel or conference center at the time of the meeting. An adage (the convention sales manager promises the dream; the convention services manager services the nightmare) is unfortunately sometimes true. This highlights the importance of having thorough contracts that will protect the interests of both the facility and the meeting planner.

A full-service convention hotel or conference center offers guests many services. You have learned about guest-room reservations (made by the front office or reservations department), sleeping rooms (maintained by the housekeeping and maintenance departments), and food and beverage services (provided by the food and beverage department). Every department of the hotel or conference center helps to provide excellent guest service. However, the convention services manager assures that the services directly linked to a group's meeting-related needs are met. This is done, in part, by coordinating the efforts of all the property's departments.

The work of the convention services manager begins when the convention sales manager has made a group sale. (Until then, the convention sales manager may advise the convention services manager about the plans being proposed.) After the sale has been made, the convention services manager ensures that the group receives everything promised by following the six-step process outlined in Exhibit 8.2.

All correspondence between the group and property personnel is very important. To understand the history of and the final agreement about the expectations of both parties, ongoing communication, which increases as the time of the event nears, is important. Pre-event meetings (precons) between the property and group representatives are critical; the property's promises outlined before the meeting and spelled out in the contract must be fulfilled. A postevent (postcon) meeting can assess the extent to

Miami Beach hosts many conventions.

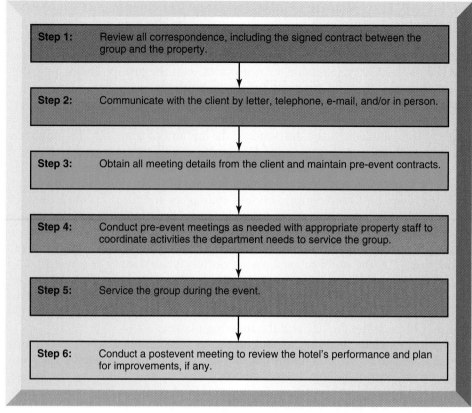

EXHIBIT 8.2
Six Steps Necessary to Effectively Deliver a Meeting

which the property met its responsibilities, yield improvements for the same (or similar) future events, and help to further improve the relationship between the property and the sponsoring group. Computer software is often used to record, track, and manage information flow between the property and planner. This is useful as a permanent record should there be unforeseen problems before, during, or after the event. It also allows a group's history to be stored electronically should the group want to repeat the event at that property or at an affiliated property in another location.

A successful convention services manager has a strong orientation to details, is a good listener, is able to react quickly to guest needs, and can effectively coordinate efforts among diverse departments within the property.

ROLE OF A CONVENTION AND VISITORS BUREAU

OBJECTIVE 4
Describe how a Convention and Visitors Bureau (CVB) works with convention hotels and conference centers to promote group travel to their market area.

Convention and Visitors Bureau (CVB) an organization generally funded by taxes levied on overnight hotel guests and/or from membership fees paid by members; the purpose is to increase the number of visitors to the area it represents

When a convention hotel or conference center is located in the same market as other properties, they compete against each other for business. Savvy hotel and conference center managers, however, know that they are also competing with properties in alternative locations. For example, a corporate meeting planner who has determined that the next meeting will be held in a skiing area can consider several states and numerous areas that offer skiing. It is in the best interests of all properties within a specific ski area to make the activities of that area known to meeting planners.

Convention and Visitors Bureaus (CVBs; also known as conference and/or tourism boards) are not-for-profit organizations that represent, for marketing purposes, a specific destination, such as a city or other geographic region. They serve as the official contact point for their destination for meeting planners, tour operators, and individual visitors.

Auditorium with fixed seating in Pulkovskaya Hotel, St. Petersburg, Russia

Convention hotels and conference centers help CVBs do their jobs in two important ways. First, they collect the **occupancy taxes** that provide funding for a CVB's efforts. Second, when the CVB needs help hosting potential guests, attending events designed to showcase the area, and/or making sales calls on potential visitors, convention hotel and conference center staff are eager to help: bringing more visitors to an area will generate increased business for the properties in the area.

occupancy taxes money paid by a lodging property to a local taxing authority; the guest-room revenue generated determines the amount paid; also known as *bed tax*

On the other hand, CVBs often provide assistance to lodging properties and meeting planners in the form of employees and/or volunteers. CVBs have their own professional association, the **Destination Marketing Association International (DMAI).** A major function is to encourage its many members to meet with planning professionals. Most major cities in the United States are members, as are cities and countries abroad. The DMAI hosts an extensive website at www.officialtravelinfo.com that provides links to its members worldwide. DMAI has created a student membership category for those seeking internships or positions after graduation.

Destination Marketing Association International (DMAI) a professional association that promotes its member Convention and Visitor Bureaus to those who plan meetings

CHALLENGES! CHALLENGES!

Convention hotels and conference center managers face many challenges. Three of the most significant are

- High construction costs
- Competition from nontraditional sources
- Rapidly increasing technology to assist meeting service personnel

Let's look at each of these challenges.

OBJECTIVE 5
Identify current and long-term challenges confronted by managers of convention hotels and conference centers.

High Construction Costs

Convention hotels are usually much larger than an average-sized hotel. They are built to service a very large group of meeting attendees or several smaller meetings groups at the same time. They are therefore expensive to construct. They require more land, more sleeping and function rooms, larger dining and food production areas, and, in many cases, extensive guest-service areas such as swimming pools and fitness areas. In addition, if a convention hotel

Multipurpose meeting space maximizes flexibility, which benefits those who sell, as well as those who use the space.

or conference center is located in a very popular geographic area (such as a ski or beach location), the cost of property and its taxes are likely to be especially high. Those who design, build, finance, and operate convention hotels and conference centers must continually strive to construct and manage these facilities in a way that maximizes efficiency and the owners' return on investment.

Competition from Nontraditional Sources

Convention hotels and conference centers compete for business with similar properties and, in some cases, with other facilities. In the United States, the large number of limited-service hotels built in the past few decades has hindered the ability of large properties to do business with small groups. Limited-service hotels may have only one or two small function rooms; however, that may be all that is necessary for a small group that generates function room rental and sleeping rooms. As this occurs, larger hotels and conference centers book a reduced number of clients. It becomes more difficult to generate revenues when no large group has booked all (or most) of the facility's function space and sleeping rooms.

Many convention hotels face competition from cities and counties who build conference centers to attract meeting groups to their areas. For example, a city may build a taxpayer-funded convention center that offers many of the facilities and services found within the area's convention hotels. A modern convention center will generally increase the area's ability to attract groups. While an increased number of visitors improves business for restaurants, shopping centers, transportation providers, and other local businesses, which results in greater revenues for taxing authorities, traditional convention hotels and conference centers in the area may see a decline in their business.

Rapidly Increasing Technology

When the telephone became commonly available in hotels, some observers believed its use would replace the need for face-to-face meetings and negatively affect the group meeting business. The same was said when videoconferencing became popular in the early 1990s. In fact, however, both of these

Many conventions offer entertainment for the delegates during evening hours.

technological advancements served to increase, not decrease, business for convention hotels and conference centers.

Today, advances in meeting technology offer tremendous opportunities to improve meeting services. In fact, one of the greatest challenges facing this segment of the industry relates to keeping up with the rapidly changing technology that has occurred in the areas of required facilities and required services.

One facilities-related example is the availability of high-speed Internet access. Increasingly, meetings groups request this service, and it must be supplied by the modern meeting property to attract and retain business. The cost, however, of supplying the service to all areas of an older hotel or conference center can be high.

Technological advances related to services are also significant. In the past, for example, a hotel employee may have been called on to change a bulb in an overhead projector. Today that same employee may be called on to connect multiple computers to a digital display board that allows multi-screen projection of a presenter's Power Point presentation. Clearly, technology has increased in the meetings area. Those that manage and train employees to service the meetings business must also continually increase their skill levels.

DID YOU KNOW?

Executives of multiunit hotel organizations can likely note numerous trends affecting their segment of the industry. One, Benchmark Hospitality International, manages resorts, hotels, and conference centers throughout the United States and has listed several trends applicable to meetings and conferences:

- Spending levels for corporate meetings is increasing. More companies are investing in meetings, and the amount spent per attendee is also increasing. More meetings are being held in higher-priced

(continued)

properties where comfort and the correct statement ("We care about the attendees") are possible.
- The most popular meeting sites are those that offer the most efficient and productive conference environments.
- Training and strategic planning are popular meeting purposes. High- and lower-level managers participate in the former; executives are involved in the latter.
- While **e-commerce** is becoming more prominent, print advertising, especially direct mail, is a popular advertising media.

Source: Benchmark's Top Ten Hospitality Trends. Retrieved May 23, 2005, from www.hotelmotel.com

e-commerce (electronic commerce) the buying and selling of products and services on the Internet; also called *e-business.*

Convention Hotels and Conference Centers Are Different

Much of this chapter has focused on ways that convention hotels and conference centers are similar. They are, however, different in some other ways. One that is significant relates to the use of space. For example, convention hotels require space that is adaptable for numerous uses. A large function room with significant open spaces may be utilized for a banquet on one day, a lecture presentation on the second day, and trade show exhibits on the third day. By contrast, conference centers frequently have dedicated space that can be best (or only) utilized for group training and education programs. For example, there may be special meeting rooms including multitiered, high-tech amphitheaters featuring built-in fully wired desks. These rooms are designed for conference sessions, discussions, facilitated meetings, interactive computer-based learning, lectures and seminars, and similar purposes. They are not designed for other uses, and conference center administrators and meeting planners may be confronted with significant challenges when they attempt to use them for other purposes.

International Association of Conference Centers (IACC) a professional association of conference centers that focuses on the physical structure of and ability of member facilities to provide specific services

universal criteria guidelines that conference center facilities must meet to receive IACC membership

While many facilities advertise themselves as conference centers, the gold-bar standard is to achieve membership in **the International Association of Conference Centers (IACC).** IACC considers very specific membership factors for membership eligibility. For example, rather than focusing on the qualifications of a person to be a member, IACC members are represented by the physical structure of their facility and their ability to provide specific services. IACC members must meet stringent guidelines known as **universal criteria.** To date, 31 criteria are required for membership (www.iacconline.com). A sample of these includes the following:

Convention hotels host trade shows.

- A minimum of 60 percent of meeting space in the conference area must be dedicated, single-purpose conference space.
- Conference rooms must be available on a 24-hour basis.
- Climate-controlled conference rooms built after 1993 must have individual climate controls.
- Ergonomically designed chairs must be available to maximize attendees' comfort.
- A designated conference planner must be assigned to each group.
- The conference center must offer continuous refreshment service outside meeting rooms unless requested otherwise by the client.
- Guest rooms (if provided) must include adequate work station(s) for the occupant(s), adequate reading and work lighting, and comfortable seating.

Unlike convention center hotels, most conference centers charge for services based on a predetermined package rate. The **complete meeting package (CMP)** incorporates all elements needed to support a successful meeting: guest rooms (if applicable), conference rooms, meals, refreshment breaks, basic audiovisual requirements, and technical and conference staff support. (Most hotels also offer all these services, but they are typically negotiated for independently.)

complete meeting package (CMP)   all elements needed to support a successful meeting

Conference rooms may be equipped with state-of-the-art audiovisual equipment, such as the following:[1]

A technology podium with computer (DVD-enabled), VHS player, environmental controls, laptop hookups, and amplifiers

Stereo sound systems and cable TV connections

Triple-wide recessed (powered) projection screens

Projection booth for 35mm slide or other media and controls

Retractable, ceiling-mounted, high-power LCD (digital) projector for computer and video or DVD images

White boards and grip strips on walls

Cordless presenter lapel and hand-held microphones with additional participant microphones at each (or every other) seat

wireless internet connections

Sessions in well-equipped conference rooms may be simultaneously linked or recorded and broadcast on the Internet or on a cable TV network. Lighting control systems are built to ensure optimal conditions for audiovisual presentations.

For smaller meetings, conference tables may incorporate concealed connections for power and Ethernet (100 mV) link to connect laptop computers. These executive rooms may also feature the following:

Personal computers with DVD/CD-ROM, Zip, and floppy drives

Remote controls for all audiovisual and environmental features

VCR and cable TV

Retractable, concealed, ceiling-mounted LCD (digital) computer projector

Recessed projection screen

Full videoconferencing facilities

---

[1]This information is adapted from the homepage for the James B. Henry Center for Executive Development at Michigan State University.

They may also feature blackout blinds (window coverings) that can be used in conjunction with a sophisticated lighting control system.

Costs to wire and equip modern conference center facilities are several million dollars (or more). One center, for example, has 310 Ethernet jacks in just four conference rooms! (The wiring was included with new construction, because planners recognized the principle that "it is astronomical to retrofit" but "only incremental to build as a new installation.")

The availability and affordability of wireless local area networks (WLAN) have prompted many conference facilities to invest in this technology. Planners are increasingly adding wireless Internet connections to their list of factors for site selection. Attendees are increasingly "plugged in" with laptops, Blackberries, and numerous other electronic devices. Managers in some conference centers that, just a few years earlier had retrofitted their facilities with cable, are now wishing they had waited a short time before investing so much effort and money. As technology changes, meeting facilities must adapt to meet the needs of their customers.

SUMMARY OF CHAPTER LEARNING OBJECTIVES

1. **State the features that make convention hotels and conference centers a unique segment of the lodging industry.**
Convention hotels and conference centers are a distinctive segment because of the facilities they offer, the services they provide, and their group-oriented approach to marketing.

2. **Describe the types of organizations that most frequently utilize space at a convention hotel or conference center.**
The major types of groups using convention hotels or conference centers are associations, government agencies, nonprofit organizations, and corporations.

3. **Draw an organizational chart for a convention center hotel or conference center that shows hospitality management positions unique to these properties.**
An organizational chart for a convention hotel or conference center highlights the unique positions of convention sales manager and, depending on the size of the facility, convention services manager(s) or a convention services department. Convention sales managers must know how to price and sell the facilities and services of the hotel and conference center. They must have an excellent understanding of their property's operational capabilities regarding its facilities and services. When servicing an event, a convention services manager follows a six-step process; he or she must (1) review applicable correspondence, (2)

communicate with the client, (3) meet with the client, (4) conduct pre-event meetings, (5) service the client's event, and (6) hold a postevent meeting to assess ways to improve future service levels.

4. **Describe how a Convention and Visitors Bureau (CVB) works with convention hotels and conference centers to promote group travel to their market area.**
Hotels assist in funding CVBs through the collection of occupancy taxes. CVBs use these funds (and, in many cases, hotel and conference center staff members) to promote the facilities and services of the hotels and the attractions within the area that the CVB represents. In turn, CVBs generate business for the properties and, in the case of large meetings, many also assist with on-site meeting-related activities.

5. **Identify current and long-term challenges confronted by managers of convention hotels and conference centers.**
Important challenges faced by those in the convention hotel and conference center business include managing the high cost of facility construction and operation, dealing with increased competition from limited-service hotels and governmentally funded convention centers, and keeping up with the rapid advance of meeting technology in the areas of facilities and services.

FEEDBACK FROM THE REAL WORLD

Our real-world advice comes from Susan Pritchett, Conference Center Director, Willis Conference Center, Nashville, Tennessee.

Susan has been at Willis Conference Center for more than 12 years. She served five years as sales manager and two years as director of sales before being promoted to director of the center. The property has 17 meeting rooms, including an amphitheater seating 200 persons.

What services can your conference center provide that might differentiate it from its convention hotel competition?

We offer rooms that are specially designed and constructed for meetings. They are not typically used for the multipurposes that a convention or other hotel would require of its public spaces. For example, our rooms are soundproof and feature fluorescent and incandescent lighting, tackable wall surfaces, and ergonomic furniture (in all rooms, not just some). No rooms are divided by airwalls; meeting attendees will not be disturbed by activities in adjacent or nearby rooms.

Due to the size of my facility (11,500 square feet of meeting space), one large group usually has most if not all of the available meeting space and would probably be the only group meeting here. Therefore, the group has the undivided attention of all our staff, who are readily available to help them. However, we can also accommodate multiple groups of 5 to 60 people on the same day. Our offices are located in the same general area as is the meeting space; it is not in a remote area, as is generally true with many hotels. We offer a 24-hour hold on all meeting rooms without charge. For example, as long as there is not another group who has scheduled the space, meeting planners can set up the day prior to their meeting at no additional charge. We offer a central refreshment center available throughout the day. Groups can select from our list of food and beverage items, or they can allow us to plan the daily menu; we always offer a great variety. (Meeting planners are charged a complete meeting package for each attendee for each day of the meeting, which includes this refreshment service.)

There are some other basic ways that our conference center differs from a convention hotel. For example, audiovisual equipment is included in the pricing package. (Last minute additions will not affect the planners' budget.) Our facility offers complimentary parking. Finally, our professional staff is committed to serving meetings, not to selling sleeping rooms, catering, and other more traditional hotel services.

If the center does not include sleeping rooms, but these are available at a nearby hotel, how do you address the potential inconvenience that would not be a problem for meeting attendees if sessions are held at the convention hotel?

We provide complimentary shuttle service, and the affected hotels also assist with this. We provide referrals of clients with whom we have worked who have been pleased with the more remote location of rooms. We stress that being away from the sleeping rooms benefits the programs. (People are more likely to stay and attend their sessions, rather than go back to their rooms during the meeting.)

How, if at all, is the work of a top-level manager in a conference center different from his or her counterpart in a convention hotel? How is the work similar?

A top-level manager at a convention hotel has many more areas of management, including responsibility for sleeping rooms and front-desk operations and related staff and, overall, a much larger operation. Nonhotel conference centers are usually much smaller. I outsource several areas, such as housekeeping, security, and catering. I don't have front-desk staff, and my sales staff is smaller.

(continued)

I manage a corporate conference center; therefore, we are all employees of a large corporation. I report to corporate officials who may not be as familiar with the hospitality industry as are hotel owners. I have a primary responsibility to service my corporation and to sell our facilities to other companies. My day to day responsibilities are varied, and I can be very hands-on with our clients (assisting with last minute setup changes, overseeing catered events, assisting clients with business services needs, or taking sales calls).

My role is similar to a hotel general manager in the ways that we manage our sales and catering staff, how we manage our space, in our desire to effectively service our clients, and in efforts to foster long-term relationships with them. Also, our ultimate desired outcome (a successful and long-lasting relationship with our clients to yield long-term success for our business) is the same.

MASTERING YOUR KNOWLEDGE

Discuss the following questions.

1. What tactics can large convention hotels utilize to more quickly check in and check out large numbers of meeting attendees arriving and departing at approximately the same times?
2. Do you think food and beverage services in a hotel's hospitality suite should be managed by that property's room service or banquet department? Why?
3. What are basic activities that you as a convention sales manager would utilize to generate an increased volume of meetings business?
4. What are special tactics that convention sales managers and convention services managers can utilize to communicate details about meetings they are coordinating?
5. What can a hotel or conference center manager do to help to assure that his or her property has a very effective working relationship with the area's Convention and Visitors Bureau?
6. If you were the convention sales manager for a relatively large hotel, what would you offer to small groups that were considering the use of a limited-service property? What would determine whether you wanted this small meeting business?

LEARN FROM THE INTERNET

1. Check out the following convention hotel websites:
   - Gaylord Opryland Nashville: www.gaylordhotels.com
   - Las Vegas Hilton: www.lvhilton.com
   - Atlanta Marriott Marquis: www.marriott.com/atlantamarriottmarquis

   Evaluate whether each hotel's emphasis is on its location, facilities, and/or services. Which do you think would be most important to a meeting planner? What, if any, types of assistance do the websites provide for meeting planners? What suggestions do you have to improve the websites?
2. Check out the websites of the regional and/or local Convention and Visitors Bureaus that represents your area. How do they promote the area? How would you improve the site(s)? Do

you think the information is helpful to meeting planners? Why or why not? What are some unique ways that they promote their areas?

3. Check out three websites for convention-type hotels in large cities or convention areas near you. (You can locate these hotels on their respective city or area CVB sites.) Look specifically for group entertainment and/or activities that are offered. Do you think most convention hotels compete against other convention hotels in their own geographic area (or city) or against convention hotels in other areas? What are the marketing implications of your answer?
4. Check out the website for the International Association of Conference Centers: www.iacconline.com. Use the "IACC Planner Express" to learn about conference centers in the cities of your choice. What are the similarities

in the type of information provided for each conference center? Do they provide the assistance that meeting planners require? How would a meeting planner use this feature of the IACC website?

5. Want to view websites of some companies that develop, own, and/or manage conference centers? If so, check out

- ARAMARK Harrison Lodging: www.aramarkharrisonlodging.com
- Dolce International: www.dolce.com
- Benchmark Hospitality: www.benchmarkhospitality.com

KEY HOSPITALITY TERMS

The following terms were explained in this chapter. Review the definitions of any words with which you are unfamiliar. Begin to utilize them as you expand your vocabulary as a hospitality professional.

convention hotel
conference center
group
function room
hospitality suite
breakout room
refresh
VIP
professional association
trade association
chapter
convention sales manager
booking

classroom style
breakdown time
setup time
convention services manager
Convention and Visitors Bureau (CVB)
occupancy taxes
Destination Marketing Association International (DMAI)
e-commerce
International Association of Conference Centers (IACC)
universal criteria
complete meeting package (CMP)

9 Resorts, Timeshares, and Condo-Hotels

Are any of these buildings condo-hotels? We can't tell just by looking at them.

CHAPTER LEARNING OBJECTIVES

After studying this chapter you will be able to:

1. State features that make resorts and timeshares a special segment of the lodging industry.
2. Describe the types of guests who visit a resort or purchase a unit in a timeshare.
3. Draw an organization chart that shows departments unique to resorts and timeshares.
4. List and briefly describe the duties of selected management positions found within resorts and timeshares.
5. Identify significant current and long-term business challenges that confront managers of resorts and timeshares.
6. Provide an overview of condo-hotels and discuss the financial and marketing issues that have significantly increased their popularity.

This chapter is authored by John F. Sweeney, RRP, ISHC, former opera singer, concert pianist, Korean War code breaker, National Security Administration officer, and currently chairman and

FEEDBACK FROM THE REAL WORLD

Most people enjoy taking time off from their work and daily responsibilities to relax and enjoy their favorite leisure activities. In many cases, they vacation at hotels built in desirable locations that offer unique recreational opportunities, upscale foodservices, excellent personal services, and numerous amenities. Hotels of this type are commonly called *resorts*.

Many resort hotels cater to guests that rent their rooms on a one-time temporary basis. By contrast, a timeshare sells units to guests for their use during a specified time period. As a result, guests who purchase a timeshare actually own, for the period purchased, their own space at the property. They can stay at their timeshare unit during their period of ownership or, alternatively, each year they may trade their period of ownership for another time and/or for another property virtually anywhere in the world.

Those desiring partial ownership in a lodging property have another and increasingly popular alternative: condo-hotels. A specific unit in a resort or hotel can be purchased and, depending on the applicable agreement, the owner can permanently reside in the unit, place the unit in the property's rental pool, and/or do both: live in the unit for part of the year and make it available for rent during the remainder of the year.

As you consider whether you want to make a career in the resort or timeshare (vacation ownership) industries, consider the following questions:

- How is managing a timeshare property similar to managing other types of hotels and resorts? How is it different?
- What advice would a seasoned professional in timeshare management give to someone considering this career alternative?
- What are the professional and personal implications of working and living in an exotic location that may be very different from that in everyday America?

As you read this chapter, think about answers to these questions and then get feedback from the real world at the end of the chapter.

RESORTS AND TIMESHARES: AN IMPORTANT SEGMENT

OBJECTIVE 1
State features that make resorts and timeshares a unique segment of the lodging industry.

Resorts

Resorts exist in nearly every part of the world in cold, moderate, and very warm climates. Resorts are, in many instances, open year round. In other cases, a resort is operated as a **seasonal hotel**.

Many travelers like to visit exciting places and to engage in enjoyable recreational or leisure activities that are not possible in their everyday lives. Typically, resorts are built in popular tourist locations. Many of these sites offer leisure activities related to water, such as swimming or other water sports, or other leisure activities, such as snow skiing, tennis, golf, sightseeing, shopping, or hunting. Unlike their hotel counterparts, resorts are often a traveler's destination, rather than (in the case of many hotels) a resting place on the way to a destination.

Nearly every state in the United States has a popular tourist resort area. The most popular tourism states include Florida, California, Hawaii, Arizona, and Nevada, and there are numerous other locations in many countries throughout the world.

resort a full-service hotel with additional attractions (recreational opportunities, upscale foodservices, excellent personal services and/or numerous amenities) that make it a primary destination for travelers

seasonal hotel a hotel whose revenues and expenditures vary greatly depending on the time (season) of the year; examples include ski resorts, which are busy in winter months, and northern lake resorts, which are busy in summer months; many seasonal resorts are open for only part of the year

CEO of Global Resorts, Las Vegas, Nevada, and Robert H. Woods, PhD, ISHC, Professor, Department of Hotel Management, William F. Harrah College of Hotel Administration, University of Nevada, Las Vegas.

While tourists represent a large percentage of guests visiting resorts, they are joined by others attending corporate meetings and conventions. Groups often hold their meetings in resort locations, and this allows participants (and often their families who travel with them) to mix business with pleasure during their stay.

Resorts are an interesting segment within the hotel industry because of the seasonality of their business (in many locations), a dependence on location, and the availability of leisure activities beyond those normally provided by a hotel.

Timeshares (Vacation Ownership Properties)

timeshare a lodging property that sells its rooms to guests for use during a specific time period each year; also called *vacation ownership property*

interval ownership a phrase meaning timeshare; also called *vacation ownership*

high season period of time when the purchase of a timeshare unit is most costly

low season period of time when the purchase of a timeshare unit is least costly

shoulder season period of time (season) between high and low seasons

deeded interest (timeshare) ownership in perpetuity that can be sold or passed on to the owner's heirs

leased interest (timeshare) a right that is limited to a length of time (for example, 10 years); when the lease expires, ownership (access) expires

One way that vacationers can visit tourist locations involves the purchase of a **timeshare**. Located primarily in popular tourist locations, timeshares (also called **interval ownerships**) provide owners with the opportunity either to go to the same location each year (this is usually not done) or to trade their timeshare for one at another location. Some timeshare resorts are newly built properties, while others are conversions of hotels, resorts, apartments, or condominiums. Even if they stay at their home resort, timeshare buyers do not typically occupy the same room during each visit. Prices for timeshares vary depending on the quality of the resort, its location, and the time of year guests purchase units. Owners typically purchase units in high, low, or shoulder seasons. **High-season** purchases give the owner the opportunity to visit during that period and to trade for better properties. **Low-season** purchases have less trading value and, as well, are more limiting at the home resort. Most timeshares have been built on oceanfront property, near mountains (for skiing), or around lakes (for water-related sports). **Shoulder seasons** fall between high and low seasons.

As you have learned, timesharing involves the right to use resorts during a specific time period. Essentially, then, it is the prepurchase of future vacation weeks. Most vacation ownerships in the United States are **deeded interests**; buyers purchase access to real estate that is owned outright forever. A few U.S. timeshares and some properties around the world are **leased interests** for long terms, rather than deeded. Timeshare ownership is an absolute right that can be sold or passed on to the owner's heirs. Therefore, a timeshare owner may legally use, sell, rent, give away, donate, or will a timeshare, much like the owner of a private home or other real estate property might do. By contrast, a leased interest in a timeshare is for a specific number of years. When the lease expires, the right to control the space reverts to the resort's

Fine dining restaurant in a resort

owners, and the space is sold again. Leases of timeshares are most common in Mexico and other international locations.

People can buy timeshares on a fixed, floating, or points basis. **Fixed basis** refers to a specific week during the year. A timeshare week usually begins on a Friday, Saturday, or Sunday and is given a number starting with the first week in January and continuing through the end of December. For instance, an owner might own the 42nd week of a unit each year. While this use plan was most common when the industry began, today it is the least common. A **floating basis** (floating weeks) for timeshare access allows the owner to select any available week within a certain season. If, for example, you own a winter season week at a ski resort, you can pick any available week that falls within the resort's defined winter months. Today, most timeshares are sold on a **points basis**. Points are similar to credit and can be used when and how the owner prefers. Purchases of timeshares in high season offer more points (and cost more) than purchases of timeshares in low or shoulder seasons. The industry has no common points value. While 100 points may equal a week's vacation in high season in one company, the same week in another company may require 20,000 points.

In some cases, owners want to exchange their time to visit another resort. For example, the owners of a January timeshare week at a Colorado ski resort may wish to exchange their week with someone who owns a week at a Vermont ski resort. Alternatively, they may want to visit a property at a beach location in the summer or another location where summer activities are available year round.

Exchanging ownership on an occasional or more frequent basis can bring variety and flexibility to one's vacation experience. In addition, since well-known hotel operators, including Disney, Hilton, Starwood, Wyndham, and

fixed basis (for timeshares) access to owned or leased space during one or more specific weeks during the year

floating basis (for timeshares) access to owned or leased space during any available week within a certain season of the year

points basis (for timeshares) access to owned or leased space based on points determined by factors such as unit size, location, season, and resort demands

MORE ABOUT TIMESHARES

The concept we know as timeshare began in Europe during the 1960s and spread to the United States in the early 1970s. While the concept of purchasing a unit at a resort condominium for only specific weeks was a good one, it had one flaw: many buyers did not want to commit themselves to taking a vacation at a specific location during a specific week each year. The alternative: place ownership of the unit into a pool and exchange it for a similar unit elsewhere.

There are two large and several smaller vacation ownership exchange companies. Resort Condominiums International (RCI) is larger than Interval International (II). In 2006, RCI had affiliations with about 3,700 resorts in 100 countries, while II had affiliations with about 2,000 resorts worldwide. Together, these two companies provide services to owners in more than 200 countries.

RCI utilizes a system called RCI Weeks to allow members to exchange their vacation unit at one timeshare property for a comparable unit at another property. Both large timeshare exchange companies use systems that allow members to have their ownership interests converted to points (determined by factors such as unit size, location, season, and resort demand), which can then be exchanged for other timeshare accommodations that are available in the points system. (Points are a commodity that can also be used to purchase hotel rooms, airline tickets, rental cars, and activities such as rafting, skiing, and snorkeling.) Exchange companies charge a fee to the owner who initiates the vacation exchange. For more information, look up www.rci.com or www.intervalworld.com on the Worldwide Web. Most U.S. hotel companies that enter the timeshare business, including Marriott, Hyatt, Starwood, Carlson, Four Seasons, and Ritz-Carlton, affiliate with Interval International.

(continued)

Many resorts offer golf.

Marriott, offer timeshare alternatives, the option to exchange units is a major reason that many people consider purchasing a timeshare. Each year the American Resort Development Association (ARDA) conducts surveys to determine why customers buy timeshares. Currently, about 87 percent of the customers indicate that they buy to exchange and go to many different vacation locations.

CONDOMINIUM RESORTS ARE DIFFERENT FROM TIMESHARE CONDOMINIUM RESORTS

In this chapter we are discussing timeshares: an owner or leasee has access to a unit each year. Persons who like to visit a location for extended time periods (such as retired snowbirds who live in the North during the summer and in the South during the winter) have another option: purchase a unit (space) in a condo-hotel or resort for year-round use. With this plan, owners purchase a specific unit, furnish it, and have continual access to that specific unit throughout the year. These properties are frequently operated by a management company, which charges owners a fee for its services. Many resort condominiums have a rental pool plan that allows owners to make their unit available for rent when they are not occupying it. The management company markets the resort, rents available units, and provides the rental fees that have been generated to the owners after deducting housekeeping and other charges applicable to the rental. **Fractionals,** a timeshare product in which no more than 13 owners own a unit, are similar to wholly owned condominiums, except for the fact that owners own only a portion of the year. Fractionals vary in quality from very high to low. In either case, ownership of a fractional is less costly than whole ownership of a condominium.

fractional (timeshare) a timeshare product in which no more than 13 owners can own a unit. In other words, on average, each owner has access to the unit for 4 weeks (52 weeks per year /13 possible owners)

The many potential advantages to timeshare ownership include the following:

- Savings that result from not having to pay high guest-room rental rates for the days that the timeshare unit is used. (Timeshare owners "own" their units, while guest-room rental customers rent their units).

- Lower costs over time. Those who rent resort units will see increases in prices annually; timeshare owners do not experience this inflation in vacation costs.
- The ability of timeshare owners to stay at a resort that may be of a higher quality than possible for a typical resort stay.
- The opportunity to trade time intervals with others through exchange programs.
- The potential for financial gain that results from the appreciation of real estate values (recall that timeshare ownerships can be sold).

DID YOU KNOW?

Some relatively new types of housing alternatives are available for those wanting to live in a deluxe hotel. Their choice depends, in part, on the amount of time they want to live there. Each of the concepts is defined next.

- *Condo-hotels*. You have learned that a condo-hotel is a hotel with traditional public spaces and services in which some or all of the guest rooms are purchased by persons who can rent their units as part of the hotel and receive a portion of the unit's rental revenues for doing so.
- *Fractional ownership*. Persons purchase up to three months of home ownership at a deluxe hotel or resort; also called a private residence club.
- *Hotel residences*. Persons own their own home in a mixed-use hotel building.

RESORT AND TIMESHARE GUESTS

OBJECTIVE 2
Describe the types of guests who visit a resort or purchase a unit in a timeshare.

There are as many types of guests visiting resorts or purchasing a timeshare as there are activities that these properties offer. In addition to food and lodging services, popular facilities attract guests interested in varied recreational activities, sightseeing, and shopping and those who enjoy relaxing on the beach, near a swimming pool, or around the ski lodge fireplace.

Guests who utilize resorts and timeshares do so primarily for pleasure. They are typically attracted to a specific property for one or more of four reasons:

- Location
- Reputation
- Property activities
- Local activities

Location

While resorts and timeshares are located about everywhere in the world, some are in remote locations. They offer visitors a chance to get away from the traffic congestion, noise, and fast pace of the modern world. As a result, island properties and their counterparts located on the beach or in the mountains provide vacationers with the change of scenery visitors often desire and the chance to relax or enjoy leisure activities in an exotic setting. Other timeshares are located in major cities that are tourist attractions, including New York, Washington, San Francisco, Paris, and London.

GUESTS' QUESTIONS ABOUT TIMESHARE EXPERIENCES

What are some common concerns of guests in timeshare properties? Here are common questions (and their answers) that help identify guests' responsibilities and opportunities as they become comfortable with their timeshare experience.

	Question	Typical Timeshare Answer
1.	How often do I receive housekeeping?	Every other day.
2.	Do housekeepers clean refrigerators, microwaves, ovens, and other kitchen appliances, or must I do so?	Refrigerators are cleaned on request; other appliances are cleaned without asking.
3.	Do you provide shuttle service to nearby points of interest?	Yes, virtually all timeshares provide shuttle service.
4.	Can I invite guests to stay in my unit, since it has a sleeper sofa?	Yes, two bedroom–two bath units accommodate six, and that number of guests can be accommodated at no extra charge.
5.	How far in advance can I make reservations?	This varies by company, but reservations can typically be made one year or longer in advance of the preferred lodging dates.
6.	Can you help me trade my timeshare and vacation somewhere else?	GMs and staff can refer customers to an exchange company, but that is all the assistance they can typically provide.
7.	Do you have a restaurant?	Most timeshares do not have restaurants. However, most have small grocery stores inside the property where guests can purchase basic items.
8.	Does the property have on-floor vending machines?	In most cases "no," but they do offer common grocery selections.
9.	I see that the property has outdoor grills. Can I use them?	Yes, these are for guests' use and are available at no charge.
10.	Can I have food delivered to my unit?	Yes.
11.	Do you offer any deals on activities in the area (shows, golf, and the like)?	Most do; many properties have concierge staff to handle this; others use front-desk personnel.
12.	Are in-room amenities, such as soap, iron, hair dryers, and shampoo, offered as they are in hotels?	Yes, in every room.
13.	How do you charge for phone calls?	Local calls are usually free. Long-distance calls are at cost (without up-charges as in many hotels).
14.	Do you offer Internet connection, and is it free?	Most timeshares now offer Internet, and usually (not always) it is free.
15.	What are the check-out and check-in times?	Noon check-out. Check-in is around 3:00 P.M.
16.	Do I have to stay a week (use my whole week all at the same time)?	No. Most timeshare companies and both exchange companies allow guests to break up weeks and use one, two, or three or more days at a time.
17.	I bought a two-bedroom and two-bath unit, but only my wife and I are vacationing this time. Can we just use and pay for part of the unit?	Yes, owners can use either the large part or small part and save vacation time accordingly for later use. Most guests do this.
18.	Can I rent my timeshare out to someone?	Yes.
19.	Can I let friends and relatives use my timeshare?	Yes.
20.	Do you offer television and premium channel programs?	Yes, timeshares have TVs, and most offer premium channels.

Reputation

Some resorts are world renowned for their specific location, the guest amenities offered, and/or the service levels provided. Resorts and timeshares perceived to be exclusive because of their cost and/or the difficulty of securing reservations generally allow the owners to demand and receive high room rates or purchase prices. Managers operating these properties are keenly aware of the importance that service levels play in maintaining an image as an exclusive and highly desirable destination.

Property Activities

Many guests enjoy a resort for seclusion and relaxation. Other guests, however, desire the varied activities offered on-site or nearby. Most timeshares are sold to owners who plan to use them for family vacations, and families enjoy properties that offer "something for everyone" activities that appeal to a wide range of ages and physical abilities. Some of the most popular resort activities include the following:

Basketball	Beach water sports
Biking	Boating
Casinos (gambling)	Children's activities
Fishing	Fitness activities
Glider rides	Golfing
Health and wellness	Historic sites
Hiking	Hot-air ballooning
Horseback riding	Ice skating
Jet skiing	Kayaking
Museums	Sailing

Some resorts offer casino entertainment.

Scuba diving	Snorkeling
Snowboarding	Snow skiing
Snowmobiling	Spas
Tennis	Theme parks
Water skiing	Whale watching
Whitewater rafting	Windsurfing

DID YOU KNOW?

- Resorts are implementing creative ways to keep their guests on the property. Advantages include increased revenues for the resort and convenience for the guests. Examples include wine tasting, cooking classes, yoga, incredible spa and fitness centers, and off-road driving schools. Programs for children include hermit-crab races, sand castle building contests, scavenger hunts, and sand-dollar painting.

Source: Matthew Benson. Have a Great Vacation Right At Your Hotel. Retrieved October 3, 2005, from usatoday.com

- Have you heard about private clubs at destination resorts? Private member clubs in resorts can have a special appeal. However, they are a challenge to develop in a way that will provide value to members beyond what a guest at the resort receives while staying at the property. For payment of a membership fee and annual dues, resort club members can receive special pricing on lodging, golf, spa services, and recreational and sporting activities. Also included may be private members-only areas and VIP receptions.

Source: Resorts as Private Clubs Business Trend. Retrieved January 5, 2006, from www.hotel-online.com

Local Activities

Not all activities "offered" by some resorts and timeshares are found on-site. For example, many tourists visit Hawaii for its excellent weather and famous beaches; others, however, go to see an active volcano. Resorts and timeshares in Hawaii market this unique experience as one of many to encourage visitors. In a similar manner, a ski property in Vail, Colorado, may promote the excellent skiing in the Rocky Mountains, while timeshares in Las Vegas offer that city's unique blend of gaming and entertainment options.

Other examples of attractive local activities include visiting historic sites and museums, attending concerts and live theater productions, or simply enjoying the natural beauty of the geographic setting. Natural attractions and other alternatives allow developers and managers to market to additional types of guests in the hope that their property will be selected over another.

Whether traditional or timeshared, resorts are increasingly popular. In the United States, reasons for this popularity include a trend to smaller families (which makes family-oriented resorts more affordable), an increase in two-income families (which results in more disposable income), and the availability of air travel (which increases the desire for more vacations).

Four Seasons Resort, Wailea, Maui, Hawaii

Some factors that interest resort visitors also have affected the time-share industry. Those who buy timeshares may want to return to a specific resort on a frequent basis or trade their unit for another each year. In the past, many thought that only the very wealthy could own a "home" on the beach or near a ski resort. Today, because of timeshares, owning property in a desirable resort location is well within the reach of many individuals and families. In fact, most timeshare companies market to couples with annual incomes as low as $50,000.

UNIQUE ORGANIZATIONAL STRUCTURE

Depending on the type of resort, many managers with very specific skills may be needed. Nearly all resorts offer food and lodging, and the procedures to manage these products and services at a resort are similar to those utilized at a full-service or convention hotel. A resort that features its own golf course, however, will additionally require individuals skilled in the management and operations of golf facilities and grounds. Similarly, resorts offering skiing, water sports, or other leisure activities will require specialized staff to manage these functions.

Traditional full-service hotels divide their organization into **front-of-house** and **back-of-house** departments. Resort hotels add a third major department, activities or recreation (see Exhibit 9.1), and timeshares offer a fourth department, sales, which is responsible for selling timeshares to potential buyers. Persons working in nonsales departments are directly involved with managing the guest-related activities offered by the resort.

In addition to differences in the organizational structure related to guest activities, timeshares staff their sales offices differently than do properties that do not offer this alternative. In cases where the entire property is available for timeshare, entire sales efforts are essentially directed to timeshare sales (see Exhibit 9.2). In properties where timeshare sales utilize a relatively small portion of available units, the manager of this function (timeshare sales) may report to the resort's director of sales and marketing (see Exhibit 9.3). In all cases, however, the duties of timeshare sales personnel differ markedly from those of their nontimeshare sales counterparts.

OBJECTIVE 3
Draw an organization chart that shows departments unique to resorts and time-shares.

front-of-house pertaining to guest-contact employees, positions, and/or departments

back-of-house pertaining to employees, positions, and/or departments that have little direct contact with guests

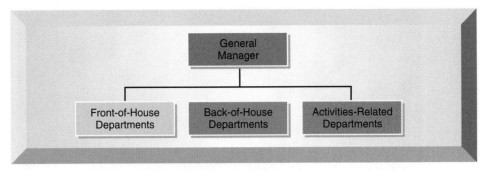

EXHIBIT 9.1
Resort Hotels Have Three Types of Departments

OBJECTIVE 4
List and briefly
describe the duties
of selected manage-
ment positions found
within resorts and
timeshares.

resort activities director
the property manager with responsibility for revenue-
generating recreational
activities

timeshare sales manager
the condominium manager
with responsibility for selling
timeshare ownership in the
property

UNIQUE MANAGEMENT POSITIONS

At least two management positions are unique to the resorts and timeshare segment: **resort activities director** and **timeshare sales manager**.

Resort Activities Director

Nearly every resort offers guests a selection of activities that are either in-cluded as part of the room rate or are available for an additional fee. (If activ-ities are included, a process to allocate revenue between the rooms and activities departments is usually in place.) In timeshares, because the guests actually own their units (or have traded into them), costs for amenities are typically much less than in hotels. It is important that the available activities be of the appropriate quality and that the guest's safety while engaging in the activity is ensured. These are among the duties of the resort activities director.

In a large resort with multiple guest activity offerings, the activities de-partment employs many persons. For example, if a resort offers golf in the summer and cross-country skiing in the winter, the staff required to offer these activities will be substantial. By contrast, a resort offering less extensive activities will require fewer individuals.

The duties of a resort activities director vary. A large resort with many activities may require, for example, managers of golf, swimming, tennis, and skiing who report to the activities director. These activity-specific managers will, in turn, require the assistance of instructors and entry-level staff mem-bers in numerous positions.

The specific responsibilities of the resort activities director mirror those of counterparts in other departments. Duties include those related to

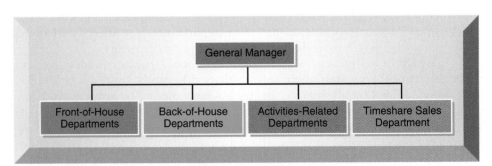

EXHIBIT 9.2
Types of Departments in a Timeshare Condominium

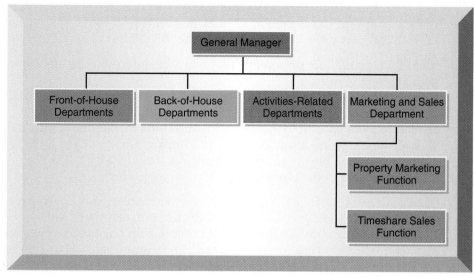

EXHIBIT 9.3
Types of Departments in Resorts with Some Timeshare Sales

personnel matters (selection, supervision, and performance appraisal, for example), budgeting and financial management, and interactions with **superordinates** and other departmental managers. Resort activities directors are likely to spend much time working with **subordinate** managers to continually upgrade the methods used to inform guests about available leisure activities and to assist guests in scheduling these activities. Determining the costs related to each activity and assuring that these costs with appropriate markups are incorporated into guest charges are also important additional responsibilities.

superordinate   a person who directs the work of others; one's superordinate is his or her boss

subordinate   a person whom one supervises

Timeshare Sales Manager

In many ways, selling timeshares in a resort is more similar to selling residential real estate than it is to selling (or renting) hotel rooms. Therefore, timeshare sales personnel must bring specific skills to their jobs. Sales departments in timeshares are heavily supported by marketing departments. Timeshare sales are conducted both at the property and at off-site locations. Typically, the sales staff is the largest in the property. Timeshares average

At your service

about one salesperson for every two units at the resort, depending on how much of the property has been sold. Duties performed by those in the sales and marketing departments typically include the following:

prospects (timeshares) potential purchasers of time-shares

- Identifying qualified **prospects** that may be interested in timeshare ownership (marketing)
- Communicating (by direct mail, telephone, e-mail, or fax or, in many cases, in person) with large numbers of potential buyers (marketing)
- Explaining the specific benefits and restrictions of purchasing a time-share from a specific resort property or company (sales)
- Helping qualified buyers to secure financing, if necessary (sales)
- Assisting buyers in the **closing** of their purchase (sales)

closing (timeshare sale) the final meeting in which the buyer and seller (or their rep-resentatives) exchange docu-ments, money, and property rights; in most cases, the transfer of title to the property is also registered with the proper state or local authori-ties at the meeting

These duties typically are conducted by different people. For example, some staff members identify and communicate with prospects, others at-tempt to sell timeshares to prospects, while others help customers complete the transactions by offering financing, deed preparation, and related assis-tance. Different skills are needed for these functions: the first requires strong marketing skills, the second requires strong sales skills, and the third requires financial and legal skills.

Timeshare sales managers face many challenges. Historically, these have included the need to overcome a negative reputation resulting from overly aggressive sales techniques and, sometimes, questionable high-pressure marketing tactics utilized by some developers when the segment developed. Older Americans may remember timeshares operated by unscrupulous de-velopers who often disappeared once the units were sold. Today, the industry is dominated by public stock corporations and hotel companies who must comply with rigorous legal and other requirements designed to protect the public. They must also confront problems relative to the disinterest of many persons to vacation in the same location year after year. (The advent of inter-val exchange programs noted earlier has eased this task.) Timeshare sales managers often compete for sales in markets with the most highly desirable locations. The best timeshare sales personnel and managers are successful because they can offer, at a fair price, quality resort units to those who are interested in the advantages offered by timeshare ownership.

CHALLENGES! CHALLENGES!

OBJECTIVE 5
Identify significant current and long-term business challenges that confront man-agers of resorts and timeshares.

Numerous challenges confront managers in the resort and timeshare market-place. Four are discussed here:

- Lagging productivity gains
- Increased expectations about social and local economic responsibilities
- **Transnational** competition for leisure dollars
- Developing creative timeshare marketing and exchange programs

transnational a company with its headquarters in one country but with company op-erations in several (or more) other countries

Lagging Productivity Gains in a Labor-Intensive Lodging Segment

All segments of the lodging industry require labor to supply guest services. Un-fortunately, the industry has not enjoyed the productivity gains achieved by other industries. This especially affects resort hotels, because they depend on a vast number of skilled and unskilled persons in many different positions. Also, properties that hire many staff members at the beginning of a season and then dismiss them at the end of the season have special problems to address.

Some observers point out that labor shortages result when there is a growing consumer demand, but relatively constant productivity outputs. This is true in some areas where the labor supply is small and the demand for resort services grows. In other geographic areas, however, it is the cost of recruiting and developing highly trained staff members, rather than a shortage of potential workers, that creates the productivity problem.

If the resort and timeshare segment (and the entire lodging industry) is to meet its potential, managers must devote more attention to finding ways to improve employee productivity. This will enable them to better utilize existing staff and to create opportunities to employ more individuals at wages that benefit both the employer and employees.

Increased Expectations About Social and Economic Responsibilities

While not all resorts and timeshares are in areas that can benefit from projects to yield an additional resort or timeshare property, some are. Many tourists, however, want to visit pristine and, in many cases, exclusive areas that are remote or exotic, where little if any development has occurred. While the intentions of these travelers is not to harm these areas, the influx of large numbers of tourists and their subsequent demands on local labor, food supplies, and natural resources can significantly change the area. Costa Rica is famous for its ecology-focused tourism, for instance. In some cases, these changes can potentially spoil the very local attributes that attracted the tourists initially. In others, increased demand for scarce natural resources can cause the prices for these resources to exceed the abilities of local residents to afford them.

Increasingly, those who build and manage resorts and timeshares are being held responsible for the potentially negative impacts that development can have on the lives of local residents and on the natural environment. Responsible hospitality managers welcome the opportunity to work with local officials to ensure that the quality of life enjoyed by local residents is improved by, and not diminished as a result of, area development. These challenges, however, require that managers carefully balance the best interests of their guests, their companies, and the local environment and residents when making decisions that can positively or negatively affect all of them.

Transnational Competition for Leisure Dollars

Resort and timeshare condominium guests come from all over the world and from a wide variety of cultural backgrounds and income levels. Increasingly, these consumers can choose between more and more world-class properties that are operated by fewer and fewer management organizations. In fact, the high costs of building facilities and the complexities of operating them have resulted in management being concentrated in the hands of fewer and fewer transnational companies.

Beginning in the late 1970s and continuing to the present, governments across the globe have increasingly decentralized their operation of tourism-related sites. They have, instead, turned the management of resort and tourism components over to private companies. In many cases, governments have helped to fund tourism development as a means of boosting their own local economies. As a result, the number of countries hosting resort development or operations companies has increased. At the same time, the number of these companies capable of competing on a worldwide scale has dwindled.

The challenge for managers working with these companies is to keep focused on guest satisfaction in the context of the cultures and desires they will encounter when managing properties in countries that are very different from their own.

Developing Creative Timeshare Marketing and Exchange Programs

recession a period of downturn in the nation's economy

Since the September 11, 2001, terrorist attacks, the timeshare industry has learned that it is relatively **recession** and terrorist proof. While hotel occupancies dwindled to virtually nothing and airlines canceled many flights after the attack on New York's World Trade Center, timeshares barely missed a beat. People who already owned timeshares continued to use them for vacations. In the aftermath of the terrorist attacks and the recession that followed, timeshare owners exchanged their access to units closer to home (someplace to which they could drive their car). With this exception, the industry has not been hurt by recent national and international events. Overall, timeshares are viewed as safer places to vacation by many people because everyone in the property is an owner.

As talented hospitality managers address and solve the concerns noted here, the timeshare segment will remain a viable and exciting part of the lodging industry and, in all likelihood, will continue its rapid growth.

CONDO-HOTELS

OBJECTIVE 6
Provide an overview of condo-hotels and discuss the financial and marketing issues that have significantly increased their popularity.

condo-hotel a hotel with traditional public spaces and services in which some or all of the guest rooms are purchased by persons who can rent their units as part of the hotel and receive a portion of the unit's rental revenues for doing so

The term **condo-hotel** describes a wide array of properties that have residential (condo) and hotel components. Some condo-hotels offer units purchased for primary residences that share property and, possibly, amenities with a hotel. Others involve an operation where some or all of the rooms are condos that are made available to condo-hotel guests through a condo-hotel rental management agreement. Rules for condo-hotel owners also vary. Some owners have unrestricted use of their properties, while other owners may not have access to their unit except at specified times or on a space-available basis.

Condo unit owners may have access to hotel amenities such as housekeeping, room service, spa privileges, and parking. In the United States, the income generated from renting a unit as a condo-hotel room is typically accounted for on a by-unit basis because of securities laws. A strong hotel brand will add sales value to the project, but some condo-hotel properties are not branded.

Why Are Condo-Hotels Popular?

Condo-hotels may be the hottest entity in the hospitality industry in the last decade. Approximately 65 percent of all hotel projects now have a condo-hotel component. Why are condo-hotels so popular? We will answer this question from several perspectives: consumers, developers, hotel operators, and lenders.

Popularity With Consumers

Consumers, particularly those nearing retirement, want to own real estate for personal reasons and investment purposes. Real estate in a resort location, with hotel-style amenities and conveniences provided by a condo-hotel, can be an attractive option. Likewise, an increased number of condo-hotels in urban areas speaks to buyers' interests in these locations. Many consumers also like

Luxurious swimming pool in Cancun, Mexico

the investment potential, particularly through **appreciation,** and the possibility of defraying some ownership costs by renting out the unit. The widely held belief that real estate is an attractive investment compared to alternatives such as the stock market also helps to drive consumers to condo-hotel purchases. Finally, and perhaps most unexpectedly, these purchases represent a prestige factor identified with a highly exclusive life-style.

appreciation (accounting) an increase in the value of an asset such as real estate

Popularity with Developers

In a hotel financing environment in which 50 percent **loan-to-cost construction loans** are normal, condo-hotels allow a developer to gain the **equity credits** for presold units that traditional condominium developers have used for years to obtain construction loans that approach 90 percent of expected construction costs.

Premium pricing and preferred financing options have helped build condo-hotels from South Beach (Miami) to Boston and from Manhattan to Hawaii, and now this same strategy is being used in destination ski and golf areas.

loan-to-cost (construction loans) the percentage of the expected cost of construction that a lender will fund

equity credits (construction loans) the amount of a developer's equity that a lender will consider as cash calculated as a percentage of expected construction costs

Popularity with Hotel Operators

Most hotel operators want a new supply of properties to expand their brands in efforts to provide system product balance and to generate fees from the management and franchising of condo-hotels. They may also earn additional fees from renting out units placed in the rental management program and for managing condominium homeowner associations (HOAs). They may even receive royalty fees from licensing their names to the development project and collect a percentage of the sales price of units sold.

Popularity with Lenders

Lenders find the financing of condo-hotel conversion and development projects attractive because the pre-sale of units eliminates substantial financial risk during the construction phase. Typically, such projects have a fast payoff: as condo units are sold, the lending risk is transferred to the buyers of individual units.

More About Condo-Hotels

securities laws laws that regulate investments of all types in an organization when there is an expectation that profits will be made through the efforts of other persons

Condo-hotel developers and their lenders must be familiar with special regulatory and legal concerns, details about condo-hotel management agreements and operations, and the impact each has on the other. Additionally, developers must know how to market (sell) units. If sales representatives are not properly trained and monitored, they can trigger liability under **securities laws** that could wipe out a developer's profits or trigger mass purchase contract terminations from investors. For example, about the only statement that can be made to a potential purchaser in literature or discussions is acknowledgement that "ownership may include the opportunity to place your condominium in a rental arrangement." Any further inquiry by a potential purchaser must be referred to rental management personnel who must maintain physically separate offices and staff, and they are also limited in what can be said because of securities laws.

Stormy's Grill, Marriott Bay Point Resort, Panama City Beach, Florida

Condo-hotels must be able to operate as a financially successful hotel. Developers are challenged because these properties must include less profitable (and even non-revenue-producing) elements including public and back-of-house areas, food and beverage outlets, and meeting spaces. How can sufficient revenues from consumer sales and/or expense allocations to unit owners be generated to offset the costs of operating and maintaining those business elements? Finally, developers must consider the long-term capital requirements of the project to establish reserves for renovations to guest rooms and public areas of the project.

Adding a condo-hotel to a condominium development can increase a unit's selling price by as much as 40 percent, and a luxury brand can raise that spread even higher. This has created a sharp increase in demand for luxury brand affiliations in the key condo-hotel markets which, in turn, has caused a bidding war between developers and luxury brands they wish to secure.

CONDO-HOTEL ALTERNATIVES

Various types of condo-hotels exist. One arrangement combines residential condo units in the same building as a condo-hotel. These units are full apartments for people who want a primary residence, and who may use the condo-hotel services. These condos are accessed by an entrance lobby and elevators that are separate from those for the condo-hotel. Combining traditional condos with condo-hotels and their amenities typically enables developers to charge premiums of 10 to 30 percent over residential projects that do not have a condo-hotel component.

Some condo-hotels have no residential component. Each condo-hotel room is a separate condo unit that has been sold to an investor looking for a return on their investment. To the guests the property appears to be a traditional hotel. Unit rental in these developments may be split 50-50 or some other predetermined percentage between the investor and management entity or operator after agreed-to fixed and/or operating costs specified in the applicable Hotel Use/Management Agreement are deducted.

Challenges For Condo-Hotels

Condo-hotel challenges can be discussed from the perspectives of developers and owners. The physical components of the property must be designed to address the needs of a specific market segment in a given location, and there must be an adequate supply of rooms available on a predictable basis. Accordingly, operators must know about the following:

- Number of condo units available for rental and the time of their availability.
- Number of rooms available for large group meetings (usually booked 12 to 24 months in advance, and the amount of meeting space needed.
- Seating capacity of restaurants and lounges.
- Whether occupancy rates will support the employees required to maintain desired service levels.
- If room rental revenues will support the traditionally unprofitable or less profitable hotel operations that condo owners expect or demand.
- How cost allocations can be undertaken while protecting the reasonable expectations of condo owners.
- How capital can be generated to provide the maintenance needed to provide uniform and required room quality to satisfy condo-hotel guests.
- How to interact with condo unit owners on issues requiring owner consent.
- How room rental allocations should be distributed among condo owners and how to satisfy unit owners who receive less income than hoped for.
- Managing and satisfying the expectations of condo unit owners will be a challenge, particularly given securities laws restrictions about information that can be provided. A buyer of a condo-hotel unit at five times the price of a comparable "ordinary" condominium may be disappointed about the unit's resale value or when proceeds from rental revenues are insufficient to cover debt service, insurance, and other costs of ownership, much less provide a reasonable return on investment.

A polluted beach is not inviting to tourists.

Sophisticated condominium buyers must know the following:

- Reasonable cash flow and profit expectations from placement of units in the rental management program.
- Whether unit owners (Home Owners' Association) can effectively work with operators in the cooperative effort required for project success.
- That the condo unit may need to be thought of as a real estate investment that may appreciate over time, but that may not provide the desired near-term return.
- Cash flow possibilities and required capital expenses when units are rented.
- Likely **FF&E** and capital costs. FF&E reserves of 4 to 5 percent of gross income may cover routine costs of maintaining a typical new condo-hotel property. However, over the long term, the capital required is substantially greater, and comes in spikes at certain stages in the property's life cycle.
- How to control an inefficient operator or one who does not maintain the property.
- Procedures to ensure fair rotation of available condominiums rented to condo-hotel guests.
- How the operator will manage assets in the absence of a single owner and the presence of individual unit owners and a home owners' association that may lack hotel expertise.

FF&E abbreviation for furniture, fixtures, and equipment

SOME FINAL THOUGHTS

The condo-hotel trend is evolving as the management systems, structures, and operations become more finely tuned. There are a few spectacular projects with condo units selling quickly at a multiple of the "normal" condo price. However, the preferable model is realistic and conservative, and a well-designed and executed condo-hotel project is still fairly unique. The condo units in an excellent property can sell for a premium of 15 to 40 percent per square foot over "regular" condos because of the availability of services such as housekeeping and room service that are inherent in being part of a hotel operation. This premium may also be justified by unique design, sophistication, and overall product offering that is part of a well designed and managed condo-hotel.

Many resorts offer extravagant buffets.

The condo-hotel business also presents entirely new areas of business and legal risks not present in the traditional hotel development. Condo-hotels are part of a condominium environment that will ultimately vest considerable legal and business authority in an association comprised of unit owners. Legal actions taken by homeowner associations, and significant increases in premiums for completed operations and project protective liability insurance coverage are examples of the "downside" of condo-hotel projects. However, strong demand by consumers often makes condo-hotel development the highest and best use for many of the locations where developers want to build.

Condo-hotels share many things in common with more traditional hotels including the need to be planned, managed, and operated in a manner that satisfies owners, guests, and employees, among other constituencies. However, they are also very different. Those aspiring to the most responsible positions in condo-hotels should have multi-disciplined backgrounds in real estate, hotel development and management, and in the mechanics of condo-hotel financing.

SUMMARY OF CHAPTER LEARNING OBJECTIVES

1. **State features that make resorts and timeshares a special segment of the lodging industry.**

   Resorts are a special segment within the hotel industry because of seasonality, a dependence on geographic location, and leisure activities beyond that normally found in a traditional hotel. Timeshares allow persons to own or lease space within a property for some specified time each year. Exchange programs are available that enable owners or leasees to trade time with other owners or leasees in other properties throughout the world.

2. **Describe the types of guests who visit a resort or purchase a unit in a timeshare.**

   Resort guests come from all over the world and from a wide variety of backgrounds and income levels. Some may attend conventions or business meetings, but most are drawn to the resort primarily for leisure and recreation activities. Those who buy timeshares are often attracted by a desire to return to the resort and/or to utilize other properties on a frequent basis.

3. **Draw an organization chart that shows departments unique to this segment.**

   Organization charts that indicate areas of responsibility in a resort hotel typically include special activities-related departments featured by the resort. Timeshare properties utilize timeshare sales staff as an integral part of their organization's team.

4. **List and briefly describe the duties of selected management positions found within resorts and timeshares.**

   Resorts and timeshare resorts have two specific hospitality management job titles that relate specifically to this lodging segment. These are the resort activities director and timeshare sales manager. The duties of a resort activities director vary depending on the activities offered by the resort. However, most individuals holding these positions have personnel and financial management responsibilities. Also, they or a subordinate manager must inform guests about leisure activities available during the guests' stay at the resort, assist guests in scheduling leisure activities, and arrange required transportation. They must also ensure that the costs required to offer leisure activities are recovered through guest charges. Timeshare sales managers are responsible for the sales of timeshare units. They identify potential buyers, explain the benefits of timeshare ownership, and assist interested buyers in selecting and purchasing the resort unit that best meets the buyer's needs.

5. **Identify significant current and long-term business challenges that confront managers of resorts and timeshares.**

   Those who manage resorts and sell timeshares face a variety of operational, marketing, and investment challenges. Among the greatest of these are lagging labor productivity gains, increased expectations about social responsibilities and a resort's impact on the local economy and environment, transnational competition for leisure dollars, and, for timeshares, the challenges of developing marketing and exchange programs that ensure continued interest in this specialized resort segment.

6. **Provide an overview of condo-hotels, and discuss the marketing and financial issues that have significantly increased their popularity.** Condo-hotels offer rental rooms to guests that are owned by individual investors under numerous arrangements. Units are marketed to potential buyers interested in a year-round or partial year residence with access to hotel amenities, investment potential, use of rental income to defray lodging expenses, and for ownership prestige. Developers can typically borrow a larger percentage of construction costs, and hotel operators can expand brands and earn additional fees from renting units, managing home owner associations, licensing their names, and selling units. Finally, lenders are often interested in condo-hotel projects because of reduced financial risk. This very new segment of the lodging industry does offer many potential advantages, but there are also many risks, especially for unit owners and hotel operators, that must be considered.

MASTERING YOUR KNOWLEDGE

Discuss the following questions:

1. What are the most popular types of activities offered by resorts?
2. What are the pros and cons of having a deeded and a leased interest in a timeshare?
3. What are some unique concerns that the director of marketing and sales in a resort with some timeshare sales must assume?
4. What are some things that you as a resort and timeshare manager could do if your property was located in an area where there is special concern about the environment?
5. If you were the timeshare sales manager of a property, what advantages might you cite to a prospective buyer?
6. What advantages can accrue to the owner of a condo-hotel unit? What are potential disadvantages?

FEEDBACK FROM THE REAL WORLD

Our real-world advice comes from Jeffrey E. Powles, District Vice President – Florida Region, Wyndham Vacation Ownership.

Jeffrey graduated from Mount Union College in Alliance, Ohio, with a degree in sports management (business minor). He has been in the timeshare industry for approximately 15 years, starting as a recreation intern. While consulting and/or managing, he has personally visited more than 200 timeshare resorts throughout the United States and Mexico.

How is managing a timeshare property similar to managing other types of hotels and resorts? How is it different?

First, the facilities themselves will be similar. There will, for example, be guest sleeping rooms (units), common public areas such as a lobby and reception space, and a dining area. Exterior amenities, including landscaping, athletic facilities such as a swimming pool and tennis courts, and parking areas, often make it difficult to determine whether a property is a hotel and resort, which is marketed to guests, or a timeshare facility selling units to prospective owners. By contrast, there are many differences between timeshare properties and their counterparts in the lodging industry.

- Timeshare units are frequently much larger. They are sometimes as large as a home (2,500 square feet) and are, essentially, small condominiums. It takes approximately one to two hours to clean each unit instead of, perhaps, two or more rooms per hour in a hotel.
- If timeshare units are self-contained, the maintenance staff must know just as much about caring for them as it would to take care of a private home.
- On the management side, my biggest concern focuses on expense management. Timeshares must be sold, but, in my position, we do not have the pressure to generate revenue every day by renting guestrooms as occurs in more traditional lodging operations.

What advice would a seasoned professional in timeshare management give to someone considering this career alternative?

My advice is simple: Learn all aspects of operations as much as possible. Develop an understanding for each department, as well as for the sales and marketing team and the pressures that confront them. Revenue generation (sales and marketing) and operations (expense management) personnel have different concerns, but common objectives (the success of the timeshare property). They must work closely together everyday.

My other suggestion is equally important: Always keep the customers in mind. You are in business for them; you must consistently work to meet and, if possible, exceed their expectations as they are ultimately your boss.

What are the professional and personal implications of working and living in an exotic location that may be very different from that in everyday America?

The professional implications are straightforward. If you want to work within the timeshare industry, then it is unlikely that you will live in middle America. The vast majority of all timeshare locations are located in areas that are very desirable locations for persons desiring to get away from their work and daily routines for a vacation or holiday. As such, many of these properties are located in areas with expensive real estate and a relatively high cost of living that is beyond the reach of many persons except during their visit. Many timeshare professionals find the opportunity to live and work in these locations to be a significant benefit; there is always something to do on your days off. A potential downside: It is often more difficult to recruit, manage, and retain staff members in these areas. "When the surf is up, the employees don't always show up!"

LEARN FROM THE INTERNET

1. Check out the websites of the following timeshare exchange companies:

   - Resort Condominiums International (RCI): www.rci.com
   - Interval International (II): www.intervalworld.com
   - Disney Vacation Club: www.disneyvacation club.com

   Learn about some of the properties they represent. How does an exchange program actually work? What are some advantages to a unit owner of an exchange? What are some potential disadvantages?

2. Want to learn about the features, services, and activities of some of the best resorts in the world? If so, go to: www.besthotelsresorts.com. When you arrive at the site, you can read about and view photos of resorts throughout the United States and Canada, Bermuda, the Caribbean, Mexico, Europe, the South Pacific, Central and South America, Africa, Asia, and the Far East. Review several sites, and answer the following questions:

   - What themes (general messages) do the resorts suggest to readers?
   - What strengths do they emphasize as inducements to visit?
   - What role does guest service appear to play in their market positioning?

3. Check out the website for the Condo Hotel Center: www.condohotelcenter.com. What are the differences between condo-hotels, fractional ownership properties, and hotel residences? What are the advantages and disadvantages of each from the perspective of unit purchasers?

4. Much information about condo-hotels is available. To view current news and reports available from Hotel-Online, go to its website: www .hotel-online.com. Enter "condo-hotels" in the site's search box ("Search Hotel Online").

KEY HOSPITALITY TERMS

The following terms were explained in this chapter. Review the definitions of any words with which you are unfamiliar. Begin to utilize them as you expand your vocabulary as a hospitality professional.

resorts
seasonal hotel
timeshare
interval ownership
high season
low season
shoulder season
 deeded interest (timeshare)
leased interest
fixed basis (for timeshares)
floating basis (for timeshares)
points basis (for timeshares)
fractional (timeshare)
front-of-house
back-of-house

resort activities director
timeshare sales manager
superordinate
subordinate
prospects (timeshares)
closing (timeshare sale)
transnational
recession
condo-hotel
appreciation (accounting)
loan-to-cost (construction loan)
equity credits (construction loans)
securities laws
FF&E

Part 3

COMMERCIAL FOODSERVICES OPERATIONS

Overview: Profit-Making (Commercial) Foodservices

10

A common dining area in a shopping mall

CHAPTER LEARNING OBJECTIVES

After studying this chapter you will be able to:

1. Describe the basic types of commercial foodservices.

2. Discuss the marketing- and operations-related concerns that must be addressed as a menu is planned.

3. Review each process that must be managed in a comprehensive foodservices system after the menu has been planned: procurement, receiving, storing, issuing, production (preparing, cooking, holding), and delivery to guest (serving, service).

4. List traits of professional food and beverage servers.

5. Explain challenges (opportunities) that must be addressed by commercial foodservice operations.

FEEDBACK FROM THE REAL WORLD

There is a saying that "It all starts with the menu!" Many experts in all segments of the foodservices industry believe this to be true.

- Why do some experts say that the financial success of a foodservice operation begins with the menu?
- What are some tactics of effective menu planning that can be most helpful?
- Who should be part of a restaurant's menu planning team? What role does each member play?

- What are the most difficult challenges confronting menu planners as they implement changes in an existing menu?

As you read this chapter, think about the answers to these questions and then get some feedback from the real world at the end of the chapter.

OBJECTIVE 1
Describe the basic types of commercial foodservices.

commercial foodservices foodservices offered in hotels, restaurants, and other organizations whose primary purpose for existence involves generation of profits from the sale of food and beverage products

noncommercial foodservices (contract management company-operated) a type of noncommercial foodservice operation in which the program is managed and operated by a for-profit management company

restaurant a foodservice business that generates all (or most) of its revenues from the sale of food and beverage products

freestanding (restaurant) a restaurant that is the sole occupant of a building; freestanding restaurants typically have dedicated parking spaces for their guests

upscale (high check average) restaurants foodservice operations that offer the highest quality of food and beverage products and services; also called *luxury* or *gourmet restaurants*

You have learned that there are two basic types of foodservice operations. One type, **commercial foodservices,** is offered by those who wish to generate a profit from the sale of food and/or beverage items. The second type, **noncommercial foodservices,** is provided by organizations that exist for another reason (such as education or healthcare) but, as part of what they do, must provide foodservices to their constituencies and/or employees. In this and the next six chapters we will examine commercial foodservice operations. The business of managing noncommercial foodservices will be presented in Part 4.

OVERVIEW OF COMMERCIAL FOODSERVICES

Exhibit 10.1 shows the four basic types of foodservice operations in the commercial foodservices segment of the hospitality industry.

Restaurants

Restaurants are individual foodservice businesses that generate all or most of their revenues from the sale of food and beverage products. Some restaurants are **freestanding;** others occupy (share) space with other businesses.

There are four basic types of restaurants:

- **Upscale (high check average) restaurants.** Also called luxury or, sometimes, gourmet, these restaurants offer the highest quality of food and beverage products and service. Most serve alcoholic beverages and many offer extensive wine lists. They are typically relatively small and frequently are owned or managed by entrepreneurs. The number of **guests per labor hour** is typically lower than for other types of restaurants.
- **Casual-service (midscale) restaurants.** These moderately priced properties generally offer a fuller (wide range) but less formal menu than do their upscale counterparts. These properties also offer a less formal atmosphere and, often, an ethnic or theme environment. Many restaurants in this category serve alcoholic beverages. The number of guests per labor hour is typically more than in upscale (high check average) properties, but much less than for quick-service properties.

GOOD NEWS! GOOD NEWS! GOOD NEWS!

At their most basic levels, the principles of managing commercial and noncommercial foodservices operations are much more similar than they are dissimilar. While language may differ (for example, managers are responsible for commercial operations, and administrators are in charge of their noncommercial counterparts), the basic principles of managing the resources of the food and beverage operation are almost identical. For example, employees must be managed. Principles of recruitment, selection, orientation, and training, along with ongoing supervisory tactics involving motivation, performance appraisal, facilitating teams, and the consistent reinforcement of quality standards, are the same. As a second example, managers in operations of all types must, first, plan menus that focus on those being served. Then products that are required by the menu must be purchased, received, stored, issued, produced, and served and, as well, principles involving sanitation, safety, and cleanup are the same.

Why is the similarity between the two basic types of foodservice operations good news? Students studying the basics of foodservices may not know the industry segment in which they will be initially employed. However, this is not a problem, because the knowledge they learn and skills they acquire can be applied in any segment. Second, foodservice managers have increased freedom to move between industry segments as their careers evolve. As they do so, they will bring with them the knowledge and experience learned in earlier positions, regardless of whether previous work was in the commercial or noncommercial sector.

It is, indeed, good news that there are universal practices of management that apply throughout the world of foodservices. These are among the topics discussed in this chapter.

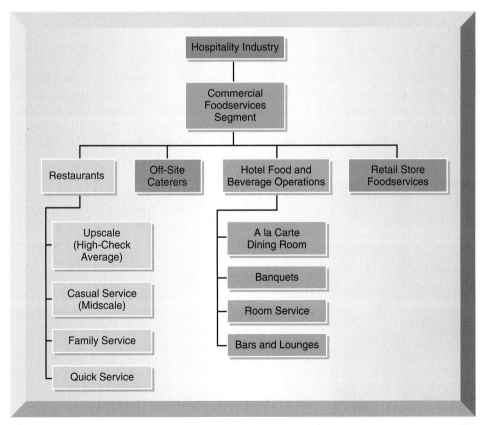

guests per labor hour the number of guests served per each hour of labor incurred by the property; if 10 hours of labor are incurred on a day when 50 guests are served, there are 5 guests per labor hour (50 guests ÷ 10 hours)

casual-service (midscale) restaurant a moderately priced restaurant offering a full, informal menu often with an ethnic theme or environment; alcoholic beverages are frequently served

EXHIBIT 10.1
Types of Commercial Foodservices

family-service restaurant a restaurant featuring table (and frequently counter) service and offering a wide range of value-priced menu items that generally does not offer alcoholic beverages

comfort foods familiar menu item prepared in a way that is reminiscent of how it was served during the customer's childhood or how the customer would prepare it at home; also called *homestyle*

California-style menu a menu featuring items traditionally available for breakfast, lunch, and dinner that are offered throughout the time the property is open for business

quick-service restaurant an operation that provides a limited menu and limited service (generally self-serve at counters or through vehicle drive-throughs) with low prices; also called *limited menu* or *fast-food restaurant*

off-site caterer a foodservice business that produces food items at a commissary (central kitchen) for transport to remote locations for service; some caterers also offer on-site banquet (dining) areas

commissary a kitchen that produces food for at least some off-site consumption; also called *central kitchen*

a la carte dining room (restaurant) a foodservice operation in which guests order from a menu featuring individually priced items

- **Family-service restaurants.** These restaurants appeal to families and others desiring familiar or **comfort foods.** Many feature a **California-style menu** in which items traditionally offered for breakfast, lunch, and dinner are available throughout the time the property is open for business. Most family-service restaurants do not serve alcoholic beverages.
- **Quick-service restaurants.** Often called limited-menu or fast-food operations, these operations typically provide a limited menu and service (often self-service at counters or drive through without entering the building) with low check averages. The number of guests per labor hour is typically much higher than in upscale, casual-service, or family-service restaurant properties.

Off-Site Caterers

Off-site caterers are businesses that produce food items at a **commissary** (central kitchen) for transport to remote locations for service. In practice, this description is less clear. Some caterers also offer on-site banquet (dining) areas. A distinguishing characteristic is that the majority of an off-site caterer's business comes from the sale of a preselected menu to relatively large groups of people in a banquet-type setting.

Hotel Food and Beverage Operations

You have learned that hotels offering food and beverage services are called full-service properties. The following are the four basic types of foodservices offered by these properties, which will be discussed more fully in Chapter 11.

- **A la carte dining room (restaurant).** Guests order from a menu offering food items priced individually. Hotel a la carte dining is, essentially, organized, managed, and staffed in the same way as upscale (high check average) and casual-service (midscale) restaurants. Remember the good news we learned earlier: there are many similarities in the principles and practices of managing commercial foodservice operations. A food and beverage operation within a hotel is, basically, a restaurant that has the basic requirements for meeting the guests' expectations at a profit.

- **Banquets.** These are meal functions served to large groups of people in which the same menu is served to all or most persons. (Hotel banquet operations are managed much like those of off-site caterers when they have on-site dining facilities available.)
- **Room service.** Food and beverage products served to guests in their sleeping rooms.
- **Bars and lounges.** Full-service hotels often have bar or lounge areas available. These can be adjacent to or in areas different from a la carte dining rooms.

Tourists spend a significant amount of money on food and beverage purchases.

Retail Store Foodservices

Businesses such as convenience stores, grocery and food markets, and gasoline stations sometimes generate some (a relatively small percentage) of

KNOW COMMON MENU TERMS

The word *menu* is French and means a *detailed list*. The menu, then, provides readers with a list of available food items. There are several common types of menus:

A la carte menu. The phrase *a la carte* implies individually priced; an a la carte menu lists food items that are separately priced. The charge is then based on the prices of the items that the guest orders.

Table d'hôte menu. This term basically implies *all at one price*. The guest charge does not vary based on what is selected. Some hotels and restaurants offer, for example, a Sunday or holiday buffet for a specified (fixed) price. The items offered on this buffet are a table d'hôte menu because the guest is charged a fixed price that is unrelated to the specific buffet items selected.

Cyclical menu. The word *cyclical* refers to a cycle; the foodservice operation may, for example, plan a 28-day menu, which is then repeated. (Cycle menus are most typically offered by noncommercial foodservices, but may also be used by commercial buffets.)

Du jour menu. Also called *daily specials*, the phrase *du jour* means *of the day*. Many foodservice operations offer daily specials (du jour items) in addition to their regular menu items.

---

their revenues from the sale of food and beverage products intended for immediate consumption.

Note: While technically not considered retail stores, licensed street vendors and persons operating unlicensed store-front or street-corner businesses also sell food and beverage products to the public with the hope of making a profit.

CHECK IT OUT

A central theme of this book is that the travel and tourism industry and the numerous segments of hospitality that are part of it are changing at an increasingly fast pace. Here's another example: Entrepreneurs in an ever-increasing number of locations around the country have introduced a new concept in which customers electronically order a specified number of different meals. They then visit a *food assembly center* (commercial kitchen) and follow recipes at work stations that have been supplied with the ingredients needed for the meals they have ordered. For example, frozen chicken breasts, chopped onions, and seasonings may be required for a chicken entrée they have prechosen. The customers can assemble these ingredients to prepare a meal that will just need to be transported home for the oven or freezer. All applicable ingredients will have been peeled and chopped, so the customer does not need to have a knife, cook an item, or wash dishes or pots and pans.

Want to learn more? Go to www.supersuppers.com.

MENU PLANNING: A CRITICAL FOODSERVICE PROCESS

We noted at the beginning of this chapter that the management of any type of foodservice operation involves similar processes. These are reviewed in Exhibit 10.2. Each process is important, and basic management principles must consistently be utilized to assure that the foodservices operation is successful.

We will begin our study of foodservice processes where they begin: with the menu. Industry experts agree that "it all starts with the menu!" Menus must offer items desired by those being served (*guests* in commercial

banquet a food and beverage event in which all or most guests are served items on a preselected menu

room service food and beverage products served to guests in their sleeping rooms

retail store foodservices businesses such as convenience stores, grocery and food markets, and gasoline stations that generate some (a relatively small percentage) of their revenues from the sale of food and beverage products intended for immediate consumption

a la carte menu a menu in which food items making up the entire meal are sold at a fixed price

table d'hôte (menu selections) a menu in which food items are sold at a fixed price

cyclical menu a menu in which food items rotate according to a planned schedule

du jour menu a menu in which some or all food items are changed daily

This person is enjoying his breakfast at a family service restaurant before beginning work.

marketing the business from the perspectives of those who consume the products or services provided by the operation

competitor any business attempting to attract the same guests as one's own business

foodservices). Foodservice managers must use **marketing** principles to learn what guests will buy and at what price to effectively differentiate their business from that of their **competitors.**

Menu Planning

Our study of commercial foodservice management begins with the menu. While being planned, it must focus on the guests and address operating concerns.

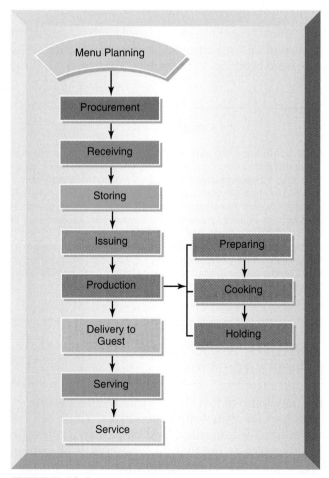

EXHIBIT 10.2
Overview of Foodservice Processes

Entire books have been written on the topic of **menu planning.**[1] However, two of the most important considerations relate to the guests (what they want and will pay for) and to the resources available to the foodservices manager to provide menu items that meet the operation's required quality standards.

menu planning the process of determining the food and beverage items to be offered by the foodservice operation that will most please the guests while generating acceptable revenue and/or cost objectives

Menu Planning: Focus on the Guests

The guests are the most important consideration when planning the menu. It is critical to determine, first, the menu items that will be of interest to guests. What guest-related factors should be considered as the menu is planned? Exhibit 10.3 helps to answer this question. You will note that there are many factors, including these:

Businesspersons check out their menu in the a la carte dining room of a hotel.

- *Purpose of visit.* Guests dining in a commercial foodservice operation are there for a reason. They want an experience that is in concert with the purpose of their visit. They may just be hungry (for example, when travelers on an interstate highway stop at a roadside family-service restaurant), or they may be celebrating a special occasion (such as hotel guests who have successfully negotiated business arrangements), or a

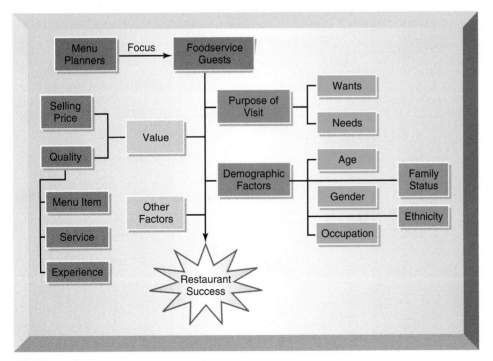

EXHIBIT 10.3
Menu Planning: Focus on the Guests

---

[1]See, for example, Jack Ninemeier and David Hayes. *Menu Planning, Design, and Evaluation.* Richmond, CA: McCutchan Publishing Corporation, 2003.

couple or a family may visit an upscale restaurant for a birthday event. Some commercial menu planners also consider their guests' nutritional needs (although these are more likely a concern of noncommercial menu planners, who must consider nutritional requirements for those receiving all or most meals from the foodservice operation).

value (menu item) the guest's perception of the selling price of a menu item relative to the quality of the menu item, service, and dining experience

- **Value** is the concept that relates to a guest's perception of the selling price of an item relative to the quality of the menu item, service, and dining experience. Guests desire to "receive what they pay for"; they do not want to feel cheated and, increasingly, many guests will pay more for a higher perceived quality of dining experience.

demographic factors factors such as age, marital status, gender, ethnicity, and occupation that can help to describe a person

- **Demographic factors** are concerns, such as the potential guests' age, marital status, gender, ethnicity, and occupation, that are likely to influence menu item preferences. Efforts to answer the question "Who will be visiting the restaurant?" will be of significant help in the menu planning task.
- *Other factors.* Social factors such as income, education, and wealth may influence what a potential guest desires in a commercial foodservices experience. Other factors such as life-style and even personality (for example, the extent to which one desires to try new foods) can also be relevant to restaurant selection decisions.

repeat business revenues generated from guests returning to a commercial hospitality operation as a result of positive experiences on previous visits

The goal of every menu planner is to offer items that please the guests. When this is done, guests are more likely to provide **repeat business.** At the same time, they will tell their friends, and **word-of-mouth advertising** helps the restaurant to remain successful.

word-of-mouth advertising informal conversations between persons as they discuss their positive or negative experiences when visiting a hospitality operation

Menu Planning: Focus on Operational Concerns

Exhibit 10.4 highlights some of the ways that the menu, once planned, affects the foodservice operation. Let's review these operational aspects of menu planning more closely.

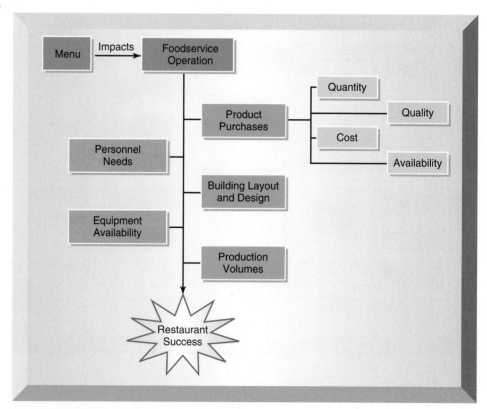

EXHIBIT 10.4
Operational Aspects of Menu Planning

- *Product purchases.* All ingredients required to produce all menu items must be consistently available in the required quantity and quality and at the right cost. If this does not occur, guests may be disappointed because desired items are not available. There will also likely be significant operational disruptions as alternative menu items will need to be produced.

- *Personnel needs.* Staff members must be available to produce and serve the items required by the menu. Consider differences in the experience and skill levels necessary, for example, for an effective order taker at a quick-service counter and a server performing tableside flaming activities in an upscale (high check average) restaurant.

- *Building layout and design.* If, for example, the menu specifies a help-yourself salad bar, the space must be available for the serving counters and to accommodate guest **traffic** in the salad bar area. As a second example, a menu featuring fresh-baked breads requires the property to have the allowable square feet necessary for an on-site bake shop (or, at least, bake ovens).

  > traffic   guests and/or employees who occupy or move within a specified area

- *Equipment availability.* If the menu requires fried foods and grilled items, for example, the proper number of deep-fat fryers and grills will be necessary based on anticipated business volume. The space needed to place the equipment and obtain adequate ventilation as dictated by local or other fire safety codes must also be considered.

- *Production volumes.* A properly planned menu anticipates business volume. For example, it is difficult (impossible?) for a kitchen to have one oven and to produce baked appetizers, entrées, desserts, and breads in any significant volume. The menu planner in this operation must be careful about the potential to **overload** the oven.

  > overload (equipment)   the act of requiring equipment to produce more than it is reasonably capable of producing

DID YOU KNOW?

Traditionally, nutritional concerns have been considered to be most important in the noncommercial segment of the food service industry. Today, however, nutrition is becoming more of a concern for the dining-out public.

There is evidence that oversized portions contribute to obesity. Simply stated, when many persons are offered larger-sized portions than they might desire, they will consume them. Unfortunately, when larger-than-necessary meals are routinely consumed, weight gain can be significant.

A study directed by ARAMARK Corporation of approximately 5,300 adults found that:

- Americans eat away from home an average of 5.6 times weekly.
- More than 50 percent of restaurant guests desire half-portion entrées, and they would be more likely to order healthy items if they were part of a value-priced combo meal.
- More than 80 percent of restaurant guests believe restaurants should make nutrition information available for menu items, and they would like to have healthy items highlighted separately on the menu.

It appears, than, that commercial operators are likely to become more concerned about nutrition as their guests become more interested in it.

Source: Nanci Hellmich. "Bigger Portions Will Be Eaten" and "Diners Want More Info and Smaller Entrées." *USA Today*, October 20, 2005.

OTHER FOODSERVICE PROCESSES

After the menu is planned, other processes must be effectively managed to assure that the foodservice operation will be successful. Exhibit 10.2 indicates, in sequence, the processes that must occur after the menu is planned. We will review these here.

Product Procurement

food (menu) items the food selections that the menu specifies will be available for sale to guests

ingredients the individual components of a food (menu) item; for example, flour and sugar are two ingredients in bread

procurement the process of determining the right quality and quantity of all food products and ingredients that should be purchased and of selecting the supplier who can provide these items at the right price and at the right time

quality (of a food item) suitability for intended use; the closer an item comes to being suitable for its intended use, the more appropriate the product's quality

theft to steal all of something at one time

pilferage to steal small quantities of some item over a period of time

stockout the condition that arises when a food or beverage item needed for production is not available on-site because it is not in inventory

value (procurement) the relationship between price paid to a supplier and the quality of product, supplier information, and service received

After the menu is planned, the **food items** and **ingredients** needed to produce it will be known. These, then, are the items that must be purchased. Exhibit 10.5 identifies five special concerns in **procurement.**

Quality is, perhaps, the single most important concern when purchasing food and beverage items. The term *quality* requires the purchaser to consider the intended use of the items; the closer an item comes to being suitable for the intended use, the more appropriate the product's quality. Consider, for example, maraschino cherries, which might be required both at the bar for a drink garnish and in the kitchen as an ingredient in a fruit gelatin salad. A whole cherry with stem (at a relatively higher cost) might be required at the bar because it is most attractive; chopped cherry pieces (at a relatively lower cost) might be used in a fruit gelatin salad. It is not possible to think about quality without, first, considering how the product will be used.

A second very important procurement factor relates to the quantity of items needed. If too much product is available, money that could be utilized for other purposes is tied up in inventory. Also, the quality of some products can deteriorate in storage, space must be available to house excess inventory, and there is increased chance of **theft** and **pilferage.** By contrast, when an inadequate quantity of product is available, **stockouts** occur. Guests can be disappointed because a desired item is not available, and production (operating) concerns can arise if substitute items must be produced.

The *right* price refers to the cost of a food item or ingredient that provides a good **value** for the foodservice operation. Wise purchasers realize that more than just a product is purchased from a supplier. They also receive product information and service from the supplier. It is the perceived value of these three factors (product quality, information, and service) that should most influence the purchase decision.

The right time for product delivery must also be considered. The supplier offering a good deal on an item needed for tomorrow's banquet that is not delivered until next week is obviously not providing value to the

This happy couple is celebrating a special occasion in a restaurant.

MENU PLANNING: FOCUS ON MENU DESIGN

After the menu is planned, it must be designed. In a quick-service restaurant, a menu board or other signage may announce available items. In a banquet provided by a restaurant, hotel, or commercial caterer, there may be a simple menu card at the guest table (if the meal is served to seated guests) or, alternatively, name cards identifying items may be available by each help-yourself serving dish on a buffet line.

In most upscale and casual-service restaurants and in hotel room-service operations, a menu is made available to guests. Traditionally, the purpose of providing a menu was to simply inform guests about available items. Today, however, menus are seen as powerful in-house selling tools. They are designed to influence and encourage guests to select items that are popular (the guests like them) and profitable (the foodservice operation desires to sell them). A process called **menu engineering** can be utilized with almost any type of menu, including menu boards and even those utilized by noncommercial foodservices without selling prices, to take advantage of the selling opportunities that an effectively designed menu can provide.

---

purchaser. Purchasers who must frequently **expedite** orders should look first at their operation to determine if there is a problem with the flow of information between production, storeroom, and purchasing personnel. In the absence of these problems, they may be wise to select suppliers who can consistently deliver required products on a timely basis.

As noted in Exhibit 10.5, the right supplier is, then, the one who can consistently deliver the right quality and quantities of product at the right price and at the right time. Some foodservice operations desire to have as few suppliers as possible to eliminate paperwork and to enhance their relationship with suppliers. Other foodservice managers, by contrast, are concerned about making product selection decisions on a by-supplier basis. Whichever of these (or intermediate) approaches is used, the importance of procurement to food-service success cannot be overlooked.

menu engineering the process of menu evaluation that allows menu planners to determine items that are most popular and profitable and to use this information to design menus that emphasize selected items to be sold

expedite (purchasing) the act of facilitating a delivery of food and beverage products previously ordered from suppliers

Receiving, Storing, and Issuing

After products are purchased, they must be received, stored, and issued to production areas. **Receiving** involves the transfer of ownership from the supplier

OBJECTIVE 3
Review each process that must be managed in a comprehensive foodservices system after the menu has been planned: receiving, storing, and issuing.

receiving the transfer of ownership from a supplier to the foodservice operation that occurs when products are delivered to the operation

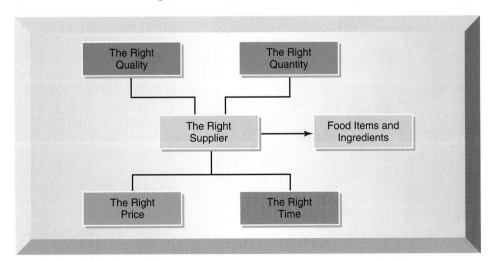

EXHIBIT 10.5
Five Special Concerns in Procurement

storing the process of holding products under optimal storage conditions until they are needed for production

issuing the process of moving products from storage areas to the point of use (place of production)

OBJECTIVE 3
Review each process that must be managed in a comprehensive foodservices system after the menu has been planned: production.

production the process of readying products for consumption

standard recipes a written explanation specifying exactly how a food or beverage item should be prepared; a standard recipe lists the quantity of each required ingredient, preparation techniques, portion size and portion tools, and other information required to assure that the item is always prepared the same way

"scratch" (food preparation) the use of individual ingredients to make items available for sale; for example, a stew may be made on-site with vegetables, meat, and other ingredients, and a Bloody Mary mix can be made on-site with tomato juice and seasonings

convenience food food or beverage products that have some labor built into them that otherwise would need to be added on-site; for example, beef stew can be purchased in a ready-to-serve form (just heat it), and a Bloody Mary mix can be purchased ready to pour

make or buy analysis the process of considering quality, costs, and other factors in "scratch" and convenience food alternatives to determine how products should be purchased for the operation

Foodservice operations purchase many items, such as this dishwasher and the dishes being washed, in addition to food and beverage products.

Formal platter service in an outdoor dining area

to the foodservice operation. It occurs when the products are physically delivered. **Storing** is the process of holding products in optimal storage conditions (in a secure space with proper temperature, humidity, and product rotation, for example) until they are needed for production. **Issuing** involves moving products from the storage area to the point of use (the place of production). Basic receiving, storing, and issuing procedures are similar for food products and their beverage counterparts. An overriding concern is that purchased products obviously cost money. These products must be protected until the time of production so that they can be utilized in menu items that are produced at the lowest possible cost.

Production

Production is the process of readying products for consumption. Many people think first about cooks working in the kitchen when they think about production. However, it is also important for systems to be in place for bartenders in bars (beverage production units) as drinks are prepared. In fact, concerns about beverage product and revenue theft at the bar provide great incentives for management staff to implement control procedures that address these concerns.

Effective food or beverage production requires the use of **standard recipes.** These indicate the type and quantity of ingredients, preparation methods, and portion tools, along with production instructions such as cooking times and temperatures (for food items) and glassware and garnishes (for beverage items). Some items may be produced from **"scratch"**; others can be purchased in a **convenience food** form. Chefs, foodservice managers, and/or purchasers should undertake a **make or buy analysis** to determine which items should be made from scratch and/or purchased as a convenience food.

Conversation at a busy restaurant bar
Source: Nigel Hicks © Dorling Kindersley, courtesy of John Riley Silver Burdett Ginn

The production of food items generally requires more elaborate and more extensive preparation skills than those for beverages. On a typical menu, the range of food items may require different levels of preparation skills. For example:

- Hamburger patties that must only be grilled or oven baked
- Casserole-type dishes that require cleaning, prepreparing (cutting and chopping), and cooking of numerous ingredients
- Elaborate sauces that may require experience in stock reduction and preparation for a sauce that is itself an ingredient (**chained recipe**) in another menu item

The items produced can be made individually (**per portion**) or in batches. The term *per portion* relates to preparing one portion of a menu item for service. By contrast, **batch cooking** refers to preparing a number of portions of a menu item at the same time. Some ingredients require **preparing** as a first step in production to get them ready for **cooking** (the application of heat). For example, fresh celery will need to be cleaned and chopped if it is an ingredient in a stew. When food items are batch cooked, a final step, **holding,** may be necessary until menu items are served.

Product Delivery to Guests

In a table-service operation, food items that have been prepared by cooks are transferred to foodservice personnel, who then serve them to the guests. Bartenders

Guests at a casual-dining restaurant

chained recipe a recipe for an item (such as a sauce) that is, itself, an ingredient in another recipe (such as a casserole)

per portion a single serving of food; for example, a portioned hamburger patty

batch cooking the process of preparing smaller quantities of food several times during a serving period, rather than the total number of portions required at the same time

preparing steps involved in getting an ingredient ready for cooking or serving; for example, celery must be cleaned and chopped before being cooked in a stew or cleaned and sliced before use on an appetizer tray

cooking applying heat to a food item

holding the task of maintaining food items at proper serving temperature after they are prepared; holding involves keeping hot foods hot and cold foods cold

OBJECTIVE 3
Review each process that must be managed in a comprehensive foodservices system after the menu has been planned: delivery to guest.

COMMON TYPES OF RESTAURANT SERVICE

Prepared food can be presented to guests in several ways:

American (plated) service. Food is preportioned onto plates or other serviceware in the kitchen and is served to guests seated at the table.

Traditional French service. Foods, such as a classic Caesar salad or a flaming steak Diane are, respectively, prepared and cooked in front of the guests at their table.

Russian (platter) service. Food is placed on serviceware in the kitchen and is brought to the guests' table by the server. Individual portions are then placed by the server onto the guests' plates.

English (family) service. Food is placed in serving dishes, brought to the table by the server, and placed on the table so that guests can pass the food items around the table.

Buffet (self-service). Guests help themselves to a variety of food that has been placed on a serving counter.

Counter service. Guests indicate orders to service personnel stationed behind an order counter, who then retrieve food for the guests.

Service styles can be combined in the same meal. For example, a Caesar salad may be prepared tableside (French service), and the entrée may be preplated in the kitchen (American service).

service bar a bar in which drinks prepared by bartenders are given to personnel who serve them to guests

serving the process of moving the food or beverage items that have been prepared from production staff to service personnel

service the process of transferring food and beverage products from service staff to guests

preparing drinks in a **service bar** also produce items for transfer to personnel who serve them to guests. The process of moving products from production to service personnel is called **serving.** Service personnel then deliver food and beverage products to guests in a process called **service.**

Systems for food and beverage serving must be effectively designed to minimize bottlenecks in service that can cause lowered food quality (such as cold food) and longer guest waits (for example, when a large volume of slow-to-prepare ice cream drinks hinders the production of other drinks). The speed and manner in which products are delivered to guests is very important: the perceived quality of service is an important factor considered by guests as they evaluate their foodservice experience.

OBJECTIVE 4
List traits of professional food and beverage servers.

TRAITS OF PROFESSIONAL FOOD AND BEVERAGE SERVERS

Professional food and beverage servers must be knowledgeable (for example, about the available food or beverage products and about work tasks required to serve their guests). They must also be skilled (to deliver service meeting the foodservice operation's quality standards). As importantly, professional servers must have an attitude that emphasizes pleasing the guests.

Exhibit 10.6 describes some of the traits required for professional food and beverage servers. These are important for servers in all operations, including sit-down (table service), cafeteria and buffet operations, walk-up counters and drive-up windows, or any other venue in which food and beverage products can be delivered to guests.

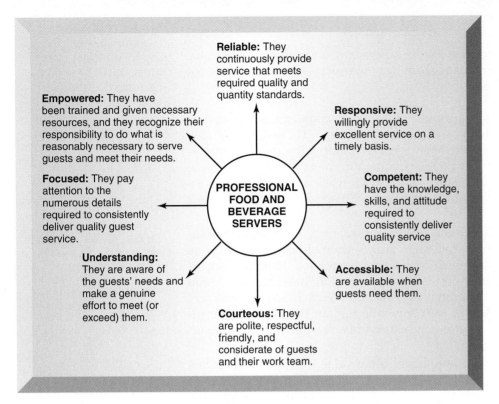

Reliable: They continuously provide service that meets required quality and quantity standards.

Responsive: They willingly provide excellent service on a timely basis.

Empowered: They have been trained and given necessary resources, and they recognize their responsibility to do what is reasonably necessary to serve guests and meet their needs.

Focused: They pay attention to the numerous details required to consistently deliver quality guest service.

PROFESSIONAL FOOD AND BEVERAGE SERVERS

Competent: They have the knowledge, skills, and attitude required to consistently deliver quality service

Understanding: They are aware of the guests' needs and make a genuine effort to meet (or exceed) them.

Accessible: They are available when guests need them.

Courteous: They are polite, respectful, friendly, and considerate of guests and their work team.

EXHIBIT 10.6
Traits of Professional Food and Beverage Servers

When reviewing the traits of professional food and beverage servers, you should begin to see that service is more than just taking an order and physically delivering it. Guests in all types of food and beverage operations want service that meets or exceeds their expectations. The proper attitude that precedes one's ability to deliver this service is absolutely critical to the success of the food server and his or her employer (the foodservice operation).

Open kitchen of Coyote Cafe, Santa Fe, New Mexico

CHALLENGES! CHALLENGES!

Managers in commercial food service operations are, and will continue to be, confronted with several significant challenges that present opportunities for creativity as they are resolved:

OBJECTIVE 5
Explain challenges (opportunities) that must be addressed by commercial foodservice operations.

- **Addressing the labor shortage.** Like their counterparts in almost every segment of the travel and tourism industry, "There aren't enough staff members to go around." Managers are addressing this concern by keeping the employees they have (reducing turnover), finding ways to increase productivity (use of convenience foods when appropriate is an example), and recruiting from nontraditional labor markets such as senior citizens for selected positions.

- **Changing guest preferences.** Managers cannot meet their guests' needs unless they know what their guests want. **Food fads,** such as low-carbohydrate (carb) diets, and longer-term **food trends,** such as evolving concerns for nutritious food consumption, must be understood and, if applicable, incorporated into menus. Many industry observers believe that diet and health concerns will play an increasingly significant role in the process by which restaurants plan menus and develop recipes.

- **Financial concerns.** As guests desire more value for the dining dollars they spend, it becomes difficult to increase selling prices to yield greater revenues. At the same time, operating costs are increasing. Managers are, then, challenged to find ways to achieve financial goals.

- **Maintaining standards.** Successful food service managers must do everything they can everyday to earn the repeat business of their guests. It is very difficult, but important, to consistently meet the operation's quality goals.

- **Ever-present sanitation concerns.** Unfortunately, sanitation problems can cause foodborne illness in any type of operation regardless of whether it is an unknown independent or a well-known brand-name operation. The impact on the health and wellness of victims and on the financial stability of the operation can be almost immeasurable and very difficult to overcome.

- **Increasing government regulations.** Compliance with numerous government regulations and local laws and ordinances are a must! However, it is sometimes difficult for independent business persons to keep up with and even know about these obligations. As well, significant additional time is often required by human resources or other staff specialists in larger operations.

food fad a relatively short-lived interest in or preference for specific food items

food trend a longer-lived change in the preference for or interest in specific food items

SUMMARY OF CHAPTER LEARNING OBJECTIVES

1. **Describe the basic types of commercial foodservices.**
Commercial foodservice operations are those that exist to generate profits from the sale of food and beverage products. Restaurants can be classified as upscale (high check average), casual service (midscale), family service, and quick service. Off-site caterers, hotel food and beverage operations (which offer a la carte dining, banquets, room service, and bars and lounges), and retail store foodservices are also commercial foodservice operations.

2. **Discuss the marketing- and operations-related concerns that must be addressed as a menu is planned.**
   Marketing aspects of menu planning focus on the guests. Issues such as the purpose of their visit (in other words, the guests' wants and needs), value (the perceived relationship between selling price and quality), demographic factors, including age, family status, gender, ethnicity, and occupation, along with other factors specific to the individual guests, must all be considered by the menu planner. Operating concerns to be addressed as menus are planned include the consideration of the menu's impact on product purchases (quantity, quality, cost, and availability), personnel needs, property layout and design, equipment availability, and production volumes.

3. **Review each process that must be managed in a comprehensive foodservices system after the menu has been planned.**
   Food and beverage products that are required by the menu must be purchased, received, stored, issued, and produced. (Production may require preparing, cooking, and/or holding.)

Products must also be delivered to the guests by procedures involving serving (moving products from production to service personnel) and service (moving products from service personnel to the guests).

4. **List traits of professional food and beverage servers.**
   Professional food and beverage servers must have a significant amount of knowledge and skill and the proper service attitude. To be professionals, servers must be reliable, responsive, competent, accessible, courteous, understanding, focused, and empowered.

5. **Explain challenges (opportunities) that must be addressed by commercial foodservice operations.**
   Managers in commercial foodservice operations are concerned about addressing the labor shortage, meeting the needs of ever-changing guests' preferences, and attaining financial goals. Other challenges include maintaining standards, successfully confronting sanitation and food safety issues, and maintaining compliance with increasing governmental regulations.

MASTERING YOUR KNOWLEDGE

The chapter makes the point that menu planning is a very important first step in the management of a food and beverage operation. Discuss the following questions.

1. What are some ways that a competitor's menu may affect planning the menu in your operation?
2. How would you describe the types of guests who are most likely to visit the four types of restaurants (upscale, casual service, family service, and quick service) discussed in the chapter?
3. What are some factors you would consider if you were planning a relatively large group function? How would each factor influence your choice of a restaurant, caterer, or hotel?
4. How would the food items planned for the menu be different if that menu was planned for:
   a. Persons dining in an upscale restaurant?
   b. A family including children at a family-service restaurant?
   c. A young couple (mid-twenties) at a mid-scale property?
   d. Customers at a quick-service restaurant?
5. Give several examples of how the menu influences the following:
   a. Product purchases
   b. Personnel (production and serving) needs
   c. Building layout and design concerns
   d. Equipment availability
6. How would you determine the quality of menu items that are most suitable for your operation?
7. What are some ways that food costs can increase unnecessarily at the time of product receiving, storing, and issuing?
8. Think of a recent time when you were a guest in any type of foodservice operation. Describe the positive and negative instances in your interaction with food servers. What were some professional and unprofessional aspects of this interaction? How did the interaction with the server affect your total foodservice experience?

FEEDBACK FROM THE REAL WORLD

Our real-world advice comes from Jim Nuetzl who has served as corporate executive chef, The Capitol Grille, Decatur, Georgia.

Why do some experts say that the financial success of a foodservice operation begins with the menu?

The restaurant's menu is the primary tool that influences guests to dine in your establishment. The most cost-effective menu does no good if it does not appeal to your guests. The menu is also the building block that affects all resources, including labor and food products. Cost control is, then, influenced by what the menu requires you to do and by what it does not allow you to do.

What are some tactics of effective menu planning that can be most helpful?

I have found that the best way to drive menu planning is to meet with and talk to our guests. They know what they want, and they are often anxious to talk to me about what they are looking for in a dining experience in our restaurants. Guests are the reason we are in business, the menu is what brings them into our restaurant, and we want and need their input.

Who should be part of a restaurant's menu-planning team? What role does each member play?

After gathering ideas from our guests, I begin testing ideas on our service teams and managers.

These individuals serve our guests daily, and they have great insights about how we can take a good idea and turn it into a great one. Once they are satisfied, I present the ideas to our regional directors, vice-president of operations, and corporate-level officials. By the time we put an idea in front of them, it has been extensively tested with our guests and staff, and we have objective data about its appeal and profitability. The "numbers" can then speak in support of our proposed menu changes.

What are the most difficult challenges confronting menu planners as they implement changes in an existing menu?

Once the decision is made to implement a menu change, the greatest challenge becomes effective training. With 15 restaurants that are spread throughout the country, a solid method of training is integral to ensure consistency. Training obviously is needed and involves the production staff, who must prepare the new items. However, it also involves the service staff, who must know about the products. Sometimes, as well (especially when new and different ingredients are involved), purchasers must also learn about the new product specifications.

LEARN FROM THE INTERNET

1. Check out the home pages of the following restaurants:
    *   Damon's Grill: www.damons.com
    *   Johnny Rockets: www.johnnyrockets.com
    *   Emeril's New Orleans Fish House: www.emerils.com
    *   Olive Garden: www.olivegarden.com
    *   Denny's: www.dennys.com

    Looking just at the menu, what are your thoughts about the type of guests whom the restaurant is trying to attract? In what ways is the presentation of menu items attractive and distracting?

2. Check out the home pages of the following foodservice software companies:
    *   Cost Guard: www.costguard.com
    *   Eatec Corporation: www.eatec.com
    *   Micros Systems, Inc.: www.micros.com
    *   Food Trak: www.foodtrak.com

How do their products help foodservice managers to control products at the time of purchasing, receiving, storing, issuing, producing, and delivering to guests (serving and service)? Based on its description, which software appears to provide the best overall control of products from procurement to service?

3. Check out the home pages of restaurants in each segment discussed in this chapter:

Upscale

Lettuce Entertain You Enterprises: www.leye.com

Casual Service

Applebee's Neighborhood Grill and Bar: www.applebees.com

Family Service

Pizza Hut: www.pizzahut.com

Quick Service

Hardee's: www.hardees.com

What points do they make about food service and environment as part of their guests' dining experience?

KEY HOSPITALITY TERMS

The following terms were explained in this chapter. Review the definitions of any words with which you are unfamiliar. Begin to utilize them as you expand your vocabulary as a hospitality professional.

commercial foodservices
noncommercial foodservices
restaurant
freestanding (restaurant)
upscale (high check average) restaurants
guests per labor hour
casual-service (midscale) restaurant
family-service restaurant
comfort foods
California-style menu
quick-service restaurant
off-site caterer
commissary
a la carte dining room (restaurant)
banquet
room service
retail store foodservices
a la carte menu
table d'hôte menu
cyclical menu
du jour menu
marketing
competitor
menu planning
value (menu item)
demographic factors
repeat business
word-of-mouth advertising
traffic
overload (equipment)

food (menu) items
ingredients
procurement
quality (of a food item)
theft
pilferage
stockout
value (procurement)
menu engineering
expedite (purchasing)
receiving
storing
issuing
production
standard recipes
"scratch" (food preparation)
convenience food
make or buy analysis
chained recipe
per portion
batch cooking
preparing
cooking
holding
service bar
serving
service
food fads
food trends

11

Food and Beverage Operations in Hotels

A hotel food and beverage director and cook check on food quality.

CHAPTER LEARNING OBJECTIVES

After studying this chapter you will be able to:

1. Describe the guests served by hotel food and beverage operations.
2. Provide an overview of the way in which large and small hotel food and beverage operations are organized.
3. Discuss common room-service challenges and operating concerns.
4. Explain planning and operating challenges that confront hotel banquet departments.
5. Review special concerns about the service of alcoholic beverages in hotels.

FEEDBACK FROM THE REAL WORLD

You have learned about numerous ways in which commercial and noncommercial food-services are similar. By contrast, there are also some ways that specific segments within each of these two basic types of foodservices differ. Here are some questions that address some of the unique features of food and beverage operations in hotels:

- What factors make it most difficult for a hotel's food and beverage department to generate optimal levels of profit?
- What are the most significant challenges confronting room service that affect its profitability? Its level of acceptance by guests?

- What should a hotel catering salesperson do when a potential client desires a menu that is very difficult, if not impossible, to deliver in a manner meeting the hotel's standards for quality products and services?
- What, if anything, do hotel employees in nonfood and beverage positions need to know about responsible alcoholic beverage service?

As you read this chapter, think about the answers to these questions and then get feedback from the real world at the end of the chapter.

All commercial foodservice operations have one thing in common: a financial objective to generate a profit from the sale of their food and beverage products. There are also some ways in which they are different; this chapter focuses on the unique characteristics of food and beverage operations in hotels.

OBJECTIVE 1
Describe the guests served by hotel food and beverage operations.

HOTEL FOODSERVICES: WHO ARE THE GUESTS?

Full-service lodging properties offer foodservices for travelers who stay at the property and for others, including those living in the community. Let's consider travelers first: Is the hotel attempting to attract motorists on a nearby roadway who are traveling for pleasure and/or business? Is the hotel located in a city's busy business district? Does the property do a large volume in convention business, and/or is it a resort (destination) property? Foodservices offered within a property must be planned to meet the dining needs of the travelers to whom the property is marketed.

Most hotel foodservices also generate additional revenues from persons living in the community who enjoy the same types of dining options as do the hotel's guests. For example, residents of a rural community may enjoy the no-nonsense, value-priced meals offered by a lodging property on an interstate near the community that also appeals to the motorists passing by. Residents in a large city may like to celebrate special occasions in a dining outlet of a hotel that is marketed to upscale business and pleasure travelers. It is a challenge for managers in every segment of the hospitality industry, including hotel foodservices, to identify their guests and to understand and consistently provide what their guests need. If they do not do this, others (their **competitors** who are attempting to provide products and services to the same market of guests) will.

Exhibit 11.1 reproduces part of a figure first shown in Chapter 10 because it illustrates the types of food and beverage products and services that guests might want in a specific property.

competitors operations that attempt to provide products and services to the same market of guests

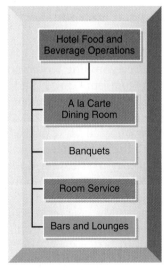

EXHIBIT 11.1
Food and Beverage Services Offered by Full-Service Hotels

RISING STAR PROFILE

Caroline Park
Director of Diplomacy
Lotte Hotel
Seoul, Korea

The Guests' Perceptions are Reality!

Caroline received her undergraduate and master's degrees in hospitality management in the United States. After receiving her graduate degree, she worked as an assistant banquet manager at the Chicago Marriott Downtown. She then transferred to Korea to help to support the opening of the new JW Marriott Seoul in 2000. She was promoted to restaurant manager for the Marriott Café in that property and then served as a consultant, catering manager for the Marriott Corporation to the Korea World Cup Organization in 10 cities.

The Lotte Hotel is the largest hotel in Seoul (1,486 rooms), Caroline has served as Special Events Manager with responsibility for 14 restaurants and bars within the hotel.

In her present position, Caroline is a member of the hotel's sales department. Her primary duties include all of the planning and preparation for visits to the hotel by embassy members and top delegations, such as the president, prime minister, princess, prince, and other dignitaries. Caroline's responses to the following questions illustrate the high energy and enthusiasm that have served her well in her work experience to date.

What are your short- and long-term career goals?

My short-term goal is to move to Asia Pacific areas outside Korea so that I can have more international food and beverage experiences in different environments. I plan to be an F&B director within five to six years: this is my short-term goal. I want to build a solid foundation with more international experiences in addition to my past career both in the United States and Korea that will help me to achieve my long-term goal.

My long-term goal is to become a hotel general manager while still in my thirties. In Asia, we don't usually have female general managers because, in great part, most Asian countries have male-dominated societies. Also, many women face special challenges with international experiences, such as relocation and family, that create fewer problems for most men. If I do become a GM, I will be the first female GM in Korea, and I want to be the one!

What is your advice for young people considering a career in the hospitality industry?

The first thing is to gain experience, experience, experience. Before you decide that a career in the hospitality industry is for you, work at a hotel or restaurant and find out what it is like. I've seen many hotel employees who graduated from hotel school and just dreamed of becoming a hotelier or restaurant manager without actually knowing what their life will be like. Needless to say, a few years later, many quit and seek another career. Long work shifts shouldn't bother you. Cleaning glasses and flatware and carrying heavy trays will be part of the job. What about guest complaints that do not make sense; are you ready for that?

Second, as a professional in the hotel and restaurant industry, the more food and beverage knowledge you have, the further you can go, and the more you will enjoy your work. So learn about different kinds of food and beverages to become a real professional in this industry.

Finally, visit other properties as a guest; you'll learn a lot. If you have an unenjoyable experience, that will be beneficial because you won't let it happen in your own properties. If you have positive experiences, you can always learn from them as well, and you can later use good ideas when you are manager.

The world is changing everyday, and you can't get stuck in an old-fashioned daily routine. Endless interests and efforts will make a huge difference as time goes by. Unfortunately, many people do not "go the extra miles" needed to learn all they can and to keep up with changes.

To make a long story short, hospitality is a fun, exciting, and dynamic business you can enjoy, even though you will likely need to overcome many challenges. Also, many available positions are needed to keep hospitality operations profitable; you won't be bored if you keep moving. Can you name any other job that gives you these kinds of options?

Always remember: the guests' perceptions are reality. Therefore, one more time, ask yourself if you truly have the service-oriented mindset that will be needed to be successful.

SPECIAL HOTEL FOODSERVICES

Restaurants typically offer a la carte dining, and many are able to serve banquets to relatively small groups of guests. Hotels, however, offer three types of foodservices that are not seen in most other types of hospitality organizations:

Banquets for very large groups of people. Some hotels have ballrooms and meeting spaces that can serve several thousand or more guests at the same function and/or at several events simultaneously.

Room service. While sleeping rooms are not unique to hotels (for example, some private clubs offer this amenity), the service of food and beverages within a guest room is uncommon in any other segment of the hospitality industry. (Hospitals and nursing home foodservices provide meals to, respectively, patients and residents who are confined to beds, but the service techniques are very different. See Chapter 19 for more about healthcare foodservices.)

Employee foodservices. Large hotels may employ hundreds or thousands of staff members. Employee cafeterias are sometimes available for their exclusive use, and a subsidized meal is considered a fringe benefit. By contrast, many noncommercial foodservices exist to feed employees of an organization, and most do so in cash cafeteria operations. Some (including hospitals) allow nonemployees such as visitors to utilize the same cafeteria.

- *A la carte dining.* A lodging property might have one or more dining alternatives depending on its size. A small property might have one coffee shop or dining room. A very large property may have several theme restaurants and a coffee shop. It may also offer one or more quick-service outlets in lobbies and/or at a swimming pool or other locations around the property.
- *Banquets.* Many hotels offer banquet functions for groups of guests meeting at the property and for others celebrating special occasions within the hotel.
- *Room service.* Some hotels deliver food and beverage products to guest rooms. This type of food and beverage service is unique to lodging properties and will be discussed in depth later in this chapter.
- *Bars and lounges.* Some hotels offer bar or lounge service in conjunction with their a la carte dining room. In some properties, guests may order food items with their beverages that are available on the a la carte dining menu. Sometimes all items available on the menu are served in the bar or

Pastry chef puts the finishing touches on desserts.

DID YOU KNOW?

- With the advent of "no frills" airline services that provide no food during flights or, alternatively, offer snacks and/or sandwiches that can be purchased during the flight, some hotels have discovered a new revenue source: takeout bags or boxes for airline travelers.
- Guests at some properties such as the Ritz-Carlton, Peninsula Beverly Hills, and Hotel Plaza Athene (New York) can order gourmet food items that may be packed in a cardboard box with a suitcase-like handle. In addition to the finest takeout food available, cloth napkins and/or reusable thermos bottles may be provided. In addition to generating revenue, hoteliers offering the service believe it enhances guest loyalty.[1]

[1]*Source:* Luxury hotels take dining sky high. Retrieved March 22, 2006, from cnn.worldnews.printthis.clickability.com

- It's interesting to note that the majority of new hotel properties being built today (limited service) are being constructed with little or no foodservice facilities and space. At the other extreme, one of the biggest trends in full-service hotels is an expansion in the space, facilities, and variety of food and beverage services offered in these properties.
- Some full-service hotels are building limited-service motels nearby in the hope of attracting guests who want either a lot (full-service) or fewer (limited-service) products and services. Some of these properties even share staff from the housekeeping and maintenance departments. Advantages include the full-service property potentially increasing its food and beverage business to limited-service property guests, and the limited-service property gaining extra room sales when there is a large meeting at its full-service counterpart.[2]

[2]*Source:* Don Dodson. Holiday Inn Hotel and Conference Center, Urbana, Ill., expands with an adjacent 74 room Holiday Inn Express. Retrieved May 24, 2006, from hotel-online.com

lounge and, in still other properties, a separate bar menu may be offered. Bars and lounges may also be located in more distant locations from food outlets with beverage-only services for guests. Sometimes bars are designed so that (1) bartenders serve guests seated at the bar, (2) beverage servers deliver beverages and food to guests seated in the bar area, and (3) food servers provide beverages to guests in the dining room.

OBJECTIVE 2
Provide an overview of the way in which large and small hotel food and beverage operations are organized.

ORGANIZATION OF HOTEL FOODSERVICES

The organization of a food and beverage operation in a full-service hotel typically depends on the hotel's size. Small hotels tend to operate lower-volume foodservices, and vice versa. The average full-service hotel generates approximately 26 percent of its total revenue from food and beverage sales.[1] However, some properties, especially those with significant convention, meeting,

[1]Gregory Miller. Let them eat cake: The growing contribution of hotel food and beverage to the bottom line. Retrieved April 21, 2006, from hotel-online.com

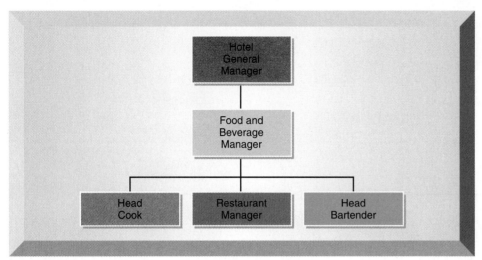

EXHIBIT 11.2
Organization of Food and Beverage Services in a Small Hotel: Management Positions

and banquet business, generate much larger volumes of food and beverage service revenues. Other properties that de-emphasize foodservices may generate the majority of such revenue from relatively low priced breakfasts, with a resulting low volume of food and beverage service revenue.

Exhibit 11.2 shows one way that a foodservice operation might be organized in a small hotel. The hotel's general manager supervises a food and beverage manager who, in turn, manages the work of someone responsible for food production (head cook), dining room service (restaurant manager), and beverage production and service (head bartender). In a small operation, management functions are combined into just a few positions. For example, the food and beverage manager may be responsible for food, beverage, and supply purchasing, for applicable accounting and control activities, and for banquet operations, among many other duties. By contrast, larger operations generally have specialized positions for these tasks.

As the foodservice operation within the hotel becomes larger, additional management positions will be needed. Exhibit 11.3 illustrates some of these. The food and beverage manager in Exhibit 11.2 is now the director of food and beverage operations. He or she supervises the work of an executive chef who, in turn, supervises a sous chef (with responsibility for food production for a la carte dining and room service) and a banquet chef (with responsibility for food produced for group functions). The director of food and beverage operations may also direct the work of a catering manager (who interacts with clients and sells group functions) and a banquet manager (who is responsible for banquet setups and teardowns and banquet foodservice). Other positions managed by the director of food and

Part of a work station in a hotel's kitchen

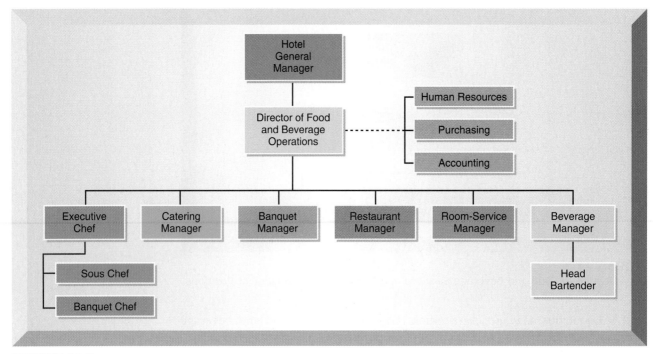

EXHIBIT 11.3
Organization of Food and Beverage Services in a Large Hotel: Management Positions

direct report one's immediate supervisor; also called *superordinate*

captain a foodservice management position with responsibility for guest service; for example, the banquet captain is responsible for service to all or some guests in banquets

Chef preparing a buffet at the Sheraton Auckland Hotel in New Zealand

beverage operations are the restaurant manager (responsible for service in a la carte dining rooms), the room-service manager, and the beverage manager (who is responsible for head bartenders at each beverage outlet.)

The director of food and beverage operations also has the benefit of technical assistance from personnel whose specialties involve human resources (including recruitment, selection, orientation, compensation and benefits administration, and interpretation and implementation of the ever-expanding body of legal issues relating to employment), centralized purchasing, and accounting and financial management.

As the hotel food and beverage operation becomes still larger, an increased number of specialized management positions are needed. Exhibit 11.4 illustrates these. The director of food and beverage operations now reports to a resident (assistant) manager. (He or she is no longer a **direct report** to the hotel's general manager.) A banquet director has been added to supervise several banquet managers who, in turn, supervise banquet supervisors (for function setups and teardowns) and banquet **captains** (for banquet service).

The executive chef may now manage a pastry chef in addition

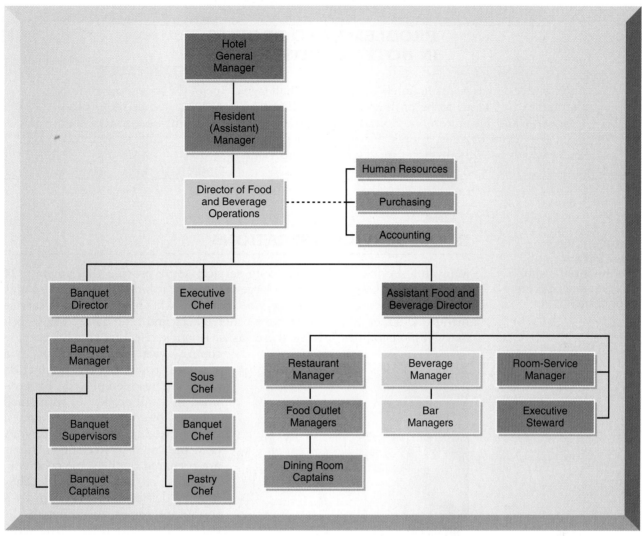

EXHIBIT 11.4
Organization of Food and Beverage Services in a Very Large Hotel: Management Positions

to the sous chef and banquet chef. Food and beverage service is now the responsibility of an assistant food and beverage director who supervises a restaurant manager, with responsibility for persons who manage each food outlet; a beverage manager, who supervises persons with responsibility for each bar; a room-service manager, and an executive steward who supervises the work of dish and pot washers, who are called **stewards** in many operations. The director of food and beverage operations also has access to specialized human resources, purchasing, and accounting personnel who, in a large organization, may be involved primarily with duties in the food and beverage areas. In operations of this size, banquet-selling responsibilities often rest with a director of catering, who may be part of the hotel's sales and marketing department.

The remainder of this chapter addresses special room service, banquet operations, and alcoholic beverage service issues applicable to hotels. Many of the challenges confronting restaurant a la carte dining operations are applicable to hotel foodservices operations. These are addressed in Chapters 10 and 12 through 14.

steward employee responsible for washing pots, pans, and dishes and for cleaning the facility in a food and beverage operation

PROBLEMS AND PROFITS IN HOTEL FOODSERVICES

Foodservice departments in hotels have unique challenges. One of the most important is the inability of many to be profitable. Many full-service hotels experience more problems with and fewer revenue dollars and bottom-line profits from foodservices than from the rental of guest rooms. Financial management concerns create an umbrella under which hotel foodservices must constantly operate.

OBJECTIVE 3
Discuss common room-service challenges and operating concerns.

ROOM-SERVICE OPERATIONS[2]

Many full-service hotels offer room service; some provide this amenity 24 hours per day. Large hotels with large volumes of room-service business may utilize the services of a room-service manager, who plans the room-service menu and supervises room-service order takers and attendants, whose primary responsibilities involve these tasks. Room-service cooks who prepare room-service orders (perhaps in a separate room-service production area) are also employed. By contrast, in small properties with small volumes of room-service revenues, the food and beverage manager may plan the room-service menu. Items are prepared by the same cook who prepares restaurant meals. They may be delivered to the room by a restaurant server according to the guest order written by a front-desk clerk or dining room receptionist (who serves as the order taker).

Even though the menus of many room-service departments have relatively high selling prices, many of these operations do not generate profits. Rather, room service is offered as a guest amenity, because some guests select properties on the basis of room-service availability. Other guests select properties based on rating services such as those offered by the American Automobile Association (AAA) and Mobil. (These services assign their highest ratings to properties with room service.)

At your service in a hotel's dining room

---

[2]The remainder of this chapter is loosely based on The Food and Beverage Department, Chapter 10 in David Hayes and Jack Ninemeier, *Hotel Operations Management,* 2nd ed. Upper Saddle River, NJ: Pearson Prentice Hall, 2007.

Room service frequently operates at a loss for several reasons, including:

- Labor costs are high and it takes a significant amount of time to transport food from the kitchen to often remote guest-room areas and back to the kitchen.
- Expenses for equipment such as delivery carts and warming devices can be significant.
- Cost for items such as glasses, cups, flatware, and serviceware increase room-service costs. These items are frequently stolen since they are out of the direct control of hotel staff members for long periods of time.

Hotel function room set for banquet

Room-service menus must be carefully planned. Quality is always important, and the menus should only offer products that can be transported relatively long distances from food-preparation areas without decreases in quality. Unfortunately, some popular foods (omelets and french fries, for example) are typically not ideal room-service menu items because of quality deterioration that occurs as these items are held at serving temperatures for long periods of time while being transported to guest rooms.

Room-service menus have the opportunity for **cross-selling,** but properties housing international guests have a unique challenge: language barriers. For example, a guest in the United States who does not read English and who is alone in a guest room with a menu written in English will have difficulty ordering from the menu.

Special room-service operating concerns include the following:

cross-selling messages designed to advertise the availability of other hotel services; for example, a dinner menu may provide information about the hotel's Sunday brunch

- *Communication problems.* These can arise when incomplete order information is received from the guests. (The same questions asked of guests by a server in an à la carte restaurant should be asked by the room-service order taker. Problems are less likely to occur when the cook or server knows how the steak is to be prepared, whether

Conducting business over a room-service meal

upselling (food server)
information suggested by an
order taker (in a room-service
operation) or by a server (in
an a la carte dining operation)
designed to encourage guests
to purchase items they might
otherwise not have ordered

OBJECTIVE 4
**Explain planning and
operating challenges
that confront hotel
banquet departments.**

banquet   a food and/or beverage event held in a function
room

finish kitchen   a food preparation area used to cook or
hold menu items preprepared
in another food production
area; for example, a finish
kitchen may be used to cook
spaghetti noodles to which a
spaghetti sauce prepared in
another kitchen is added

catering (hotel)   the process
of selling a banquet event and
interacting with the banquet
client

hosted bar   a beverage service alternative in which the
host of the function pays for
beverages during all or part of
the banquet; also called an
open bar

cash bar   a beverage service
alternative where guests desiring beverages during a banquet function pay for them
personally

contribution margin   the
amount that remains after the
product (food) cost of a menu
item is subtracted from its
selling price

sour cream is desired with the baked potato, if tartar sauce is to be served with the fish fillet, and whether the guest desires a glass of wine—and, if so, the type.

- *Lost opportunities for* **upselling** *by the order taker*. Guests will often order items such as appetizers, alcoholic beverages, and desserts, for example, if they are asked.
- *Within-guest-room service challenges*. Room-service attendants must know how to (1) set up the room-service meal when it is delivered, (2) explain procedures to retrieve room-service items, (3) present the guest check and secure payment, (4) open bottles of wine, and (5) provide an attitude of genuine hospitality (as opposed to being rushed to return to the kitchen for another room-service delivery).

HOTEL BANQUET OPERATIONS

Many hotels routinely sell and service **banquets** of sizes ranging from very small to very large. In some properties, the food production is done in the same kitchen as is the production of meals for a la carte dining outlets. Other hotels have specialized banquet kitchens; still other properties produce some banquet meal items in the kitchen used for a la carte food preparation and have other **finish kitchens** conveniently located in banquet service areas. Banquet events are typically sold by a **catering** salesperson, who may be located within the food and beverage or the marketing department.

Banquet events are often more profitable than a la carte dining operations in hotels for several reasons:

- Banquets are frequently used to celebrate special events, which create an opportunity for the sale of more expensive and therefore more profitable menu items.
- The number of meals to be served is known in advance, and it becomes easier to schedule production and labor requirements. There is also less likelihood of overproduction of food with subsequent waste.
- Banquet planners can frequently sell **hosted bars** or **cash bars** that enable increased sales of alcoholic beverages.

Seemingly innumerable details are required to successfully execute a banquet event of any size. Exhibit 11.5 shows a **banquet event order (BEO)**.

BANQUET MENU PLANNING

Most of the factors involved in planning a menu for a hotel's a la carte dining operation apply to planning banquet menus. However, special concerns apply to planning banquet menus:

The menu planner must be confident that the items to be offered can be produced in the appropriate quantity at the appropriate level of quality and within the required time schedule.

Preestablished banquet menus are helpful in considering production limitations and in suggesting items that emphasize **contribution margins**.

For many convention attendees, it is business during the day and an enjoyable banquet event in the evening.

banquet event order (BEO) a form used by the sales, catering, and food production areas to detail all requirements for a banquet; information provided by the banquet client is summarized on the form, and it becomes the basis for the formal contract between the client and the hotel

It identifies the information that a banquet planner must obtain to meet the banquet host's expectations.

The cost for labor needed to produce and serve banquet food is normally included in the banquet selling price. However, sometimes, when the estimated number of guests is small, additional charges for several types of labor are assessed:

- Bartenders
- Beverage servers
- Beverage cashiers
- Security personnel
- Valet (parking) staff
- Coatroom employees

Hotels may also charge for meeting space and/or **function room space** if the number of guests to be served (and, therefore, the amount of revenue to be generated) is small. These charges are normally waived when a specified minimum amount of revenue will be generated by a banquet.

function room space public space such as meeting rooms, conference space, and ballrooms (which can frequently be subdivided into smaller spaces) available in the hotel for banquet, meeting, or other group rental purposes

guarantee a contractual agreement about the number of meals to be provided at a banquet event; typically, a guarantee must be made several days in advance of the event; at that time, the entity contracting with the hotel for the event agrees to pay for the larger of the actual number of guests served or the number of guests guaranteed

BANQUET CONTRACTS AND BILLING POLICIES

A banquet contract helps to assure that there are no surprises as banquets are planned and served. Topics to be addressed include these:

- Last day a banquet space will be held without a signed contract
- Time by when an attendance **guarantee** must be received
- *Cancellation policy.* An explanation of fees to be assessed if the banquet contract is canceled
- *Guarantee reduction policy.* If, for example, the final guarantee is less than the specified percentage of the initial guarantee, an additional charge may be assessed
- *Billing.* Information about the amount and schedule for guest payment. (Typically, the full remaining payment is due at the end of the event.)
- Information about the service of alcoholic beverages
- Other information applicable to the specific event

EXHIBIT 11.5
Sample Banquet Event
Order (BEO)

EVENT DATE:	BANQUET EVENT ORDER (BEO) #:
Organization:	
Billing Address:	Business Phone #:
	Business Fax #:
Contact Name:	Business E-Mail:
Account Executive:	Room Rental: $
Guaranteed: ( ) persons	

BEVERAGES

❏ Full   ❏ Limited   ❏ Hosted bar
❏ Nonhosted bar

With bartender   ( ) bars
Cash bar   ( ) cashiers
❏ Premium ❏ Call   ❏ House
( ) per drink   ( ) bar package
( ) hours of operation
Time: Room:

Bar Opening/Closing Instructions:
Bar to close at: _____ AM/PM
Bar to reopen at: _____ AM/PM
Wine with Lunch/Dinner
_____ with entrée, _____ servers

Time: Location:

Additional Instructions:

FOOD MENU
_____ baseplates _____ waterglasses
_____ butter rosettes on lemon leaves

❏ Introduction   ❏ Invocation
❏ Nothing before meal
First course served at: _____ AM/PM
Meal served at: _____ AM/PM

BEVERAGE MENU

ROOM SETUP
❏ Classroom   ❏ Theater
❏ Other: _____
❏ Diagram below

Need:
❏ Registration table/chairs: _____
❏ Wastebasket
❏ Easels
❏ Podium: ❏ standing ❏ tabletop
❏ Pads / pencils / pens / mints
❏ Water / glasses

Diagram:

Linen:
❏ White ❏ Other: _____

Skirting:

Napkin:
❏ White ❏ Other: _____

Music:

AUDIOVISUAL
❏ Microphone: _____
❏ Slide projector - package: _____
❏ Overhead projector - package: _____
❏ VHS / monitor / package: _____
❏ Mixer, ____ channel   ❏ AV - cart
❏ White board/markers   ❏ Screen
❏ Flipcharts/pads/tape/   ❏ LCD
___ pens   projector

COAT CHECK
❏ Hosted   ❏ Cash: ____
( ) Attendant(s) ( ) Coat Racks

PARKING
❏ Hosted   ❏ Cash $ _____
Fee per car: $ _____

BILLING (METHOD OF PAYMENT)

Deposit received: $ _____

Getting ready for a busy bar shift

ALCOHOLIC BEVERAGE SERVICE IN HOTELS

All organizations selling alcoholic beverages must comply with applicable state and/or local laws and regulations. Several unique aspects of responsible alcoholic beverage service apply to hoteliers and to all their staff:

> **OBJECTIVE 5**
> Review special concerns about the service of alcoholic beverages in hotels.

- Hotel personnel in nonfood and beverage positions must be trained to recognize and respond to obvious and visible signs of guest (and non-guest) **intoxication.** For example, a guest in a hotel restaurant or bar may leave the area to return to the guest room. The hotel will likely be responsible for that guest as he or she walks through the lobby, enters an elevator, and passes through hallways on the way to the guest room. Alcoholic-related injuries in the guest room itself will also be a concern to the hotel.

intoxication legally, the point at which a person's blood alcohol concentration (BAC) rises to a pre-determined level; for example, 0.08 in many jurisdictions

- Hotel visitors using the property's bars and lounges may need to walk long distances within the property and may use the hotel's parking or valet services.
- Issues arise when, for example, front-desk, house-keeping, maintenance and/ or security staff observe guests who appear to be underage bringing alcoholic beverages onto the property and into guest rooms. Signs of alcoholic beverage consumption by underage guests may also be evident as guest rooms are cleaned.

Cigar bar at an upscale hotel

Hotel food and beverage management staff must work with human resources, security, and other personnel within the property to develop and implement ongoing training for all employees about responsible alcoholic beverage service. Tragedies can occur when these policies and procedures are not consistently utilized, and hospitality managers, as professionals and responsible citizens of their community, must do their part to assure that alcoholic beverages are responsibly enjoyed and not abused.

SUMMARY OF CHAPTER LEARNING OBJECTIVES

1. **Describe the guests served by hotel food and beverage operations.**
   Full-service hotels must meet the food and beverage needs of their guests. Therefore, those to whom a hotel is marketed are potential guests of its food and beverage operation. Community residents and others are also likely to consider a hotel along with its restaurant alternative(s) when evaluating dining options that are most appropriate for a specific dining experience.

2. **Provide an overview of the way in which large and small hotel food and beverage operations are organized.**
   As the volume of food and beverage operations increases, the number of more specialized management positions also increases. For example, in a very small hotel, the food and beverage manager may be responsible for service in a banquet. By contrast, in a very large property, the responsibility for a banquet function may rest with someone who is four organizational levels removed from (below) the F&B manager (banquet director, banquet manager, banquet supervisor, banquet captain).

3. **Discuss common room-service challenges and operating concerns.**
   Room-service departments frequently operate at a loss because high selling prices are not offset by associated costs for labor, equipment, and supply expenses. Special concerns must be addressed when room-service menus are planned to assure that quality standards can be met for items held for long time periods during transport. The order taker's job is important to assure that communication problems do not occur and that opportunities for upselling are consistently taken.

4. **Explain planning and operating challenges that confront hotel banquet departments.**
   Banquet events are typically more profitable than a la carte dining. The numerous details involved require the use of a banquet event order, and contracts must spell out the obligations of both the hotel and the banquet host (client).

5. **Review special concerns about the service of alcoholic beverages in hotels.**
   Hotel guests and others, including those who may have consumed alcoholic beverages, have access to much of the hotel's property. Therefore, staff members, including front-desk, housekeeping, maintenance, and/or security personnel, must be able to recognize signs of obvious and visible intoxication. They must also be aware of the potential for underage drinking and know the procedures to follow when these issues arise.

MASTERING YOUR KNOWLEDGE

Discuss the following questions.

1. What, if anything, can a hotel manager do in efforts to maximize food and beverage revenues from hotel guests? From those living within the community?

2. The chapter indicates that very large hotels may have several a la carte dining outlets. Are separate kitchens (which are expensive to build and equip and which occupy nonrevenue-producing space) necessary for each dining outlet? What, if anything, can be done to minimize capital costs associated with kitchens for multiple dining outlets?

3. Tasks involved with managing a food and beverage operation are very specialized. What are some basics that a general manager with overall property responsibilities must know as he or she manages the work of the director of food and beverage operations?

FEEDBACK FROM THE REAL WORLD

Our real-world advice comes from Steve Yannarell. Steve has almost 20 years of food and beverage management experience with hotel organizations, including Hyatt Hotels, Hilton Hotels, Wyndham Hotels, and Outrigger Hotels and Resorts.

What factors make it most difficult for a hotel's food and beverage department to generate optimal levels of profit?

The profitability of any hotel's food and beverage department is affected by its level of revenues and the amount of its expenses. Both, to some extent, can be managed. At our property, the most important factor relates to the hotel's occupancy, because a significant percentage of the department's revenue is generated from our guests. Our resort cannot rely on significant business volumes from the local market [community]. Therefore, when our occupancy rates decrease, food and beverage revenues are affected accordingly. We must, therefore, first attract guests to our property and then use tactics to increase revenues and decrease costs without sacrificing quality. For example, we can increase revenues per check averages from our hotel guests by suggestive selling. We can also provide a menu that encourages guests to return to our food and beverage outlets often during their visit. We also work hard to manage our variable costs (those that we can control). These tactics of managing revenues and reducing expenses help us to meet budget goals, which are, in large measure, driven by forecasted occupancy rates.

What are the most significant challenges confronting room service that affect its profitability? Its level of acceptance by guests?

Guests staying at a resort want to enjoy the property and all its amenities. They have less interest in staying in or dining within their rooms. Therefore, opportunities to provide room service are less than in our counterparts in other sectors of the full-service lodging industry. Our property also does not do a significant amount of conference business during which, for example, hospitality suite service can have a significant impact on revenues. The most significant challenges, then, are to provide the quality of room-service products and the in-room dining experience that guests who desire them will expect. Since room service is traditionally a less than profitable amenity that the hotel must provide, we are pleased when guests choose to dine in one of our property outlets where our services can be more profitably offered.

What should a hotel catering salesperson do when a potential client desires a menu that is very difficult, if not impossible, to deliver in a manner meeting the hotel's standards for quality products and services?

First, our goal is always to meet the guest's needs. If we can provide what the guest wants, we will do so. However, if this cannot be done because of logistical or other reasons, it becomes the responsibility of the salesperson to steer the guest toward a menu that we can deliver. Our property, like most others, offers preplanned menus for banquet operations. These are, however, just a guide for guests, and we are pleased to start from scratch and/or to modify an existing menu if the guest prefers that we do so. Agreeing to provide a menu that is impossible to deliver may generate some revenue in the very short term. However, over the longer term, that decision will likely be detrimental to the property. After all, guests who experience a banquet plagued with problems will, justifiably, be frustrated with the property (it will be our fault), not with the event's sponsor who is paying for it. This is, by the way, understandable because the property representative should know when to say yes and when to say here are some suggestions, as well as, when necessary, to say "no, we cannot do it."

What, if anything, do hotel employees in nonfood and beverage positions need to know about responsible alcoholic beverage service?

This answer is simple: they must know just about everything that staff members in food and beverage service positions must know. We are

(continued)

very concerned about guest injury and the resulting potential for liability when alcoholic beverages are served irresponsibly. Therefore, all our employees in all positions in the hotel receive training in the responsible service of alcoholic beverages. Our front-desk clerks, bell staff, housekeepers, and numerous other employees may come in contact with guests in situations where prior training and knowledge will be helpful. What are signs that guests may be obviously and visibly intoxicated? What are the hotel's responsibilities? What should be done? We have a responsibility to provide our employees with this information, and we do so.

4. What are some basic strategies that a food and beverage manager can utilize to increase revenues and profits from room-service sales?

5. What are some things you could do when planning a room-service menu to minimize the impact on quality that occurs when food must be held or transported long distances from the preparation area to the guest room?

6. Banquet sales are generally profitable. What are some things that you as a manager would want to have done to maximize the sale of banquet events for (a) groups meeting at the hotel and (b) groups living within the community?

7. How would you determine the rental charge for meeting space if the number of guests to be served is small and therefore revenue levels will be low?

8. What are some common problems that can arise in a hotel when hotel guests or others become obviously and visibly intoxicated? What should you as a manager do to alert all hotel staff about these potential problems?

LEARN FROM THE INTERNET

1. Check out the following websites:
   - Hotel Del Coronado: www.del.com
   - Hilton Hawaiian Village: www.hiltonhawaiianvillage.com
   - Opryland Hotel: www.gaylordhotels.com
   - Bellagio Hotel & Casino: www.bellagio.com
   - Waldorf-Astoria Hotel: www.waldorfastoria.com

   What information do they provide about their food and beverage operation? Does it appear that the hotels are emphasizing food and beverage as an incentive for guests to book rooms or, alternatively, is food and beverage de-emphasized?

2. Check out the following hospitality industry publications:
   - *Hotel On-Line:* www.hotel-online.com
   - *Hotel & Motel Management:* www.hotelmotel .com
   - *Hotel Food & Beverage Executive:* www.hfexecutive.com

Look for articles whose titles suggest that the topic specifically addresses hotel food and beverage operations. What is the issue being addressed? How, if at all, are the articles' topics applicable to restaurant operations?

3. Check out the following websites. Find "room service" in the dining or food and beverage section of the site.
   - Covent Garden Hotel (London, England): www.firmdale.com
   - Hotel Cipriani (Venice, Italy): www.hotelcipriani.com
   - Gleneagles Hotel (Perthshire, Scotland): www.gleneagles.com

How important is the offering of room service in these properties? Why would these hotels devote significant space on their website to this amenity? Why do other properties choose not to emphasize room service?

KEY HOSPITALITY TERMS

The following terms were explained in this chapter. Review the definitions of any words with which you are unfamiliar. Begin to utilize them as you expand your vocabulary as a hospitality professional.

competitors

direct report

captain

steward

cross-selling

upselling (food server)

banquet

finish kitchen

catering (hotel)

hosted bar

cash bar

contribution margin

banquet event order (BEO)

function room space

guarantee

intoxication

12 Upscale Restaurants

Dining room in E1 Tovar Hotel in the Grand Canyon National Park

CHAPTER LEARNING OBJECTIVES

After studying this chapter you will be able to:

1. Define the term *upscale restaurant.*
2. Describe the types of guests who visit upscale restaurants.
3. Describe how an upscale restaurant is organized for food preparation and foodservice activities.
4. Describe positions unique to upscale restaurants.
5. Describe unique challenges that confront upscale restaurants.

FEEDBACK FROM THE REAL WORLD

In this chapter you will learn that there are many people who, for different reasons, enjoy and will pay for the highest possible quality of food and beverage products, guest service, tabletop appointments, and a dining environment perceived to be among the best that there can be.

What are examples of operating procedures (food production and food service) that your organization uses to assure that your high-quality standards are most consistently attained? What, if any, changes in marketing tactics are used by upscale properties during times of economy downturns to attract guests with reduced discretionary dollars for dining away from home? What are the most important things a multiunit official can do to assure that the proper corporate culture permeates throughout the organization?

As you read this chapter, think about answers to these questions and then get feedback from the real world at the end of the chapter.

In this chapter we will learn about upscale restaurants (also called fine dining and/or white tablecloth properties). You will learn about management positions that are unique to this segment of the restaurant industry and also discover some features that make the segment different from its foodservice counterparts.

upscale restaurant   a food-service operation that provides a very high quality of food and beverage products served at a very high standard of service with appropriate tabletop appointments in a tasteful environment; also called *fine dining* or *white tablecloth* restaurants

A CLOSE LOOK AT UPSCALE RESTAURANTS

An **upscale restaurant** is a foodservice operation that provides a very high (if not the highest!) quality of food and beverage products served at a very high (if not the highest!) standard of service with appropriate tabletop appointments in a tasteful (if not elegant!) environment. To accomplish these goals,

UPSCALE RESTAURANTS OFFER MANY CUISINES

Many observers note that French chefs are most responsible for the evolution of fine dining as we know it today. Changes in food preparation procedures, recipe innovations, sequence of courses within a meal, and emphasis on **food and wine affinities** are examples of contributions that affect modern foodservice operations. In fact, the French chefs developed a **haute cuisine** that addressed their standards about how a meal should be produced and served.

Today, some persons equate upscale restaurants with French menus. They envision, for example, difficult to prepare items written on menus in French and, when ordered, prepared at tableside by servers wearing tuxedos and white gloves in a very formal dining environment.

There are, of course, many successful upscale restaurants that offer menu items prepared and served by traditional methods. However, many other properties meeting our definition offer cuisines of all types. These properties feature menu items prepared with numerous (and sometimes very creative) preparation methods and served by staff in environments far different from the French style described above.

The characteristic that sets upscale properties apart from others is *not* the cuisine, service, or environment, but rather an emphasis on providing the very highest quality dining experience to its guests.

food and wine affinity the recognition that wine, if properly chosen, can complement the foods with which it is served; one should select, for example, the entrée and then consider wines to accompany it

haute cuisine high (fine) food preparation

a la carte (menu selections) a menu in which food items are individually priced

table d'hôte (menu selections) a menu in which food items comprising the entire meal are sold at a fixed price

owners and managers must typically spend more money than their peers in other restaurant segments. This, in turn, means that guests will be charged more; the per person check average is higher than that in other types of properties. How much does a meal (with or without wine) cost in an upscale property? Check averages vary across the country. For example, a meal in an upscale restaurant can cost several hundred dollars or more in a large metropolitan area and 75 dollars or less in a less urbanized area.

Many upscale restaurants offer limited menu selections, which may be **a la carte** (individually priced) or **table d'hôte** (the entire meal is sold at a fixed price). The items on the menu may be available for long periods of time (for example, they may change seasonally) or, alternatively, they may change daily. Very frequent menu changes are often required when the desired quality of necessary ingredients is inconsistently available. In some upscale operations, for example, the chef may visit a local market daily to determine what will be prepared for guests that day. (This tactic is used less frequently in today's marketplace because modern transportation and storage systems make many food items available year round, although quality and costs can vary significantly.) However, daily market visits were commonly used in the past by world-famous chefs, who helped the world of the culinary evolve into what it is today.)

OBJECTIVE 2
Describe the types of guests who visit upscale restaurants.

WHO VISITS UPSCALE RESTAURANTS?

This question is just as difficult to answer as questions about guests at other types of restaurants. Some guests, for example, visit upscale properties infrequently. Examples include persons celebrating special occasions such as birthdays and job promotions. They may be of all ages, from senior citizens celebrating a wedding anniversary to middle-age persons enjoying a holiday, and even to teenagers having dinner before their senior high school prom. Other guests visit an upscale restaurant to conduct business, to impress someone (because it is high check average!), or because of its reputation. (Upscale restaurants are often featured in local, regional, and even national publications.)

Another type of guest who visits upscale properties might be unique: those who enjoy food and beverages as a hobby and who want to learn more about **gastronomy.** They may, for example, belong to a local gourmet food club, subscribe to fine dining magazines, visit areas known for

gastronomy the art of fine dining as enjoyed by a connoisseur (a knowledgeable person) of good food and drink (wines)

Elegant place setting with the finest crystal and china in an upscale restaurant

regional food specialties, and be regular guests of reputable upscale restaurants. They likely enroll in cooking classes and demonstrations by chefs, attend wine tastings offered by restaurants and/or wineries, and enjoy learning from food preparation and service personnel during their restaurant visit.

ORGANIZATION OF UPSCALE RESTAURANTS

An upscale restaurant is organized into front-of-house and back-of-house (or heart-of-house) positions in much the same way that a hotel foodservice, midscale, or family-service restaurant featuring table service is organized. A major factor is the size (volume of food preparation and service). Some upscale restaurants still feature many of the positions (or, at least, position titles) as dictated by the traditional **classical brigade.** Exhibit 12.1 illustrates many of these positions. Increasingly, however, contemporary kitchens have modified the classical brigade organization by reducing (combining) positions and by modernizing titles. A sample organization chart for a modernized *kitchen brigade* is shown in Exhibit 12.2.

Professional development of food preparation personnel working in upscale restaurants has traditionally also been structured. **Apprenticeships** lasting many years and involving increasingly more responsible culinary positions have historically been utilized to expand one's culinary knowledge and experience in a very structured manner. Even today, for example, many students in postsecondary culinary education programs seek apprenticeship (internship) positions in upscale restaurants. More experienced chefs with upscale dining capabilities seek positions in other upscale properties and in similar outlets in hotels and private clubs. Many aspire to be the proprietor of their own restaurant.

Upscale restaurants often require more dining room service positions and personnel than do their counterparts in other foodservices segments. The reason: timely service consistently meeting the highest standards of excellence are necessary, and service must be delivered by an adequate number of staff with appropriate knowledge and skills.

Exhibit 12.3 illustrates the classical (French) organization for dining room service still used by some upscale restaurants today. (Only one section

> **OBJECTIVE 3**
> Describe how an upscale restaurant is organized for food preparation and food-service activities.

classical brigade a system of kitchen organization established by Auguste Escoffier that was designed for large-volume preparation of complex and extensive menus

apprenticeship a structured process used to train persons in the skills necessary to be proficient in a trade or profession

ARE FOOD AND SERVICE THE PRIME ATTRACTIONS OF UPSCALE RESTAURANTS?

This chapter emphasizes that high-quality food, beverage, service, environment, and other amenities are integral to the fine dining experience offered by upscale restaurants. However, to the extent that "upscale" refers to "high-check average," features offered by other restaurants could place them in this category. Consider, for example, restaurants owned all or in part by celebrities and those in unique locations, such as revolving restaurants on top floors of skyscrapers and others with commanding views of scenic attractions. Consider also restaurant operations that are "trendy," those featuring chefs with a large following of admirers, and properties that, because of their many decades (or longer!) of operation, have become local institutions. These are examples of an observation made throughout our study of foodservices: it is not just the product and service that attracts guests and generates repeat business; rather, it is the sum of all the physical and psychological components of the experience that affects the guests.

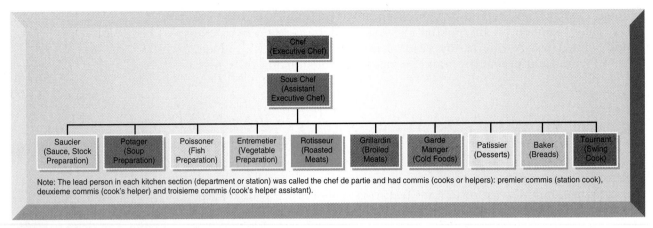

Note: The lead person in each kitchen section (department or station) was called the chef de partie and had commis (cooks or helpers): premier commis (station cook), deuxieme commis (cook's helper) and troisieme commis (cook's helper assistant).

EXHIBIT 12.1
Classical (French) Organization of a Kitchen (Kitchen Brigade)

maitre d'hotel the manager in charge of the dining room; sometimes called *head waiter*

of the dining room is illustrated by the captain and supportive staff in this figure.) The **maitre d'hotel** was in charge of the dining room and was responsible for other tasks, including supervising other dining personnel, accepting guest reservations, seating guests, and perhaps presenting the menu. This manager was also responsible for assuring the smooth and efficient operation of the dining room when it was open.

captain (dining room) the person in charge of a section in a dining room

The maitre d'hotel typically supervised the work of dining room **captains** (who, in turn, were responsible for service at several tables). Each guest table was served by a chef du rang who had an assistant (commis du rang). Traditional French cuisine typically featured menu items that were

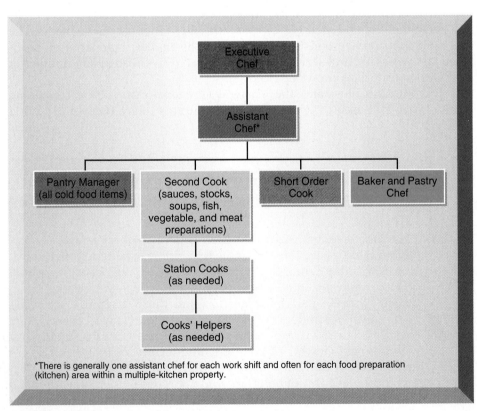

*There is generally one assistant chef for each work shift and often for each food preparation (kitchen) area within a multiple-kitchen property.

EXHIBIT 12.2
Contemporary Version of Classical Kitchen Organization

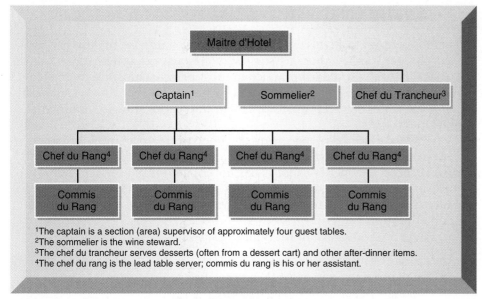

```
                    ┌─────────────────┐
                    │ Maitre d'Hotel  │
                    └────────┬────────┘
          ┌──────────────────┼──────────────────┐
   ┌──────────────┐  ┌──────────────┐  ┌────────────────────┐
   │  Captain¹    │  │ Sommelier²   │  │ Chef du Trancheur³  │
   └──────┬───────┘  └──────────────┘  └────────────────────┘
   ┌──────┴───────┬──────────────┬──────────────┐
┌──────────┐ ┌──────────┐ ┌──────────┐ ┌──────────┐
│Chef du   │ │Chef du   │ │Chef du   │ │Chef du   │
│Rang⁴     │ │Rang⁴     │ │Rang⁴     │ │Rang⁴     │
└────┬─────┘ └────┬─────┘ └────┬─────┘ └────┬─────┘
┌──────────┐ ┌──────────┐ ┌──────────┐ ┌──────────┐
│ Commis   │ │ Commis   │ │ Commis   │ │ Commis   │
│ du Rang  │ │ du Rang  │ │ du Rang  │ │ du Rang  │
└──────────┘ └──────────┘ └──────────┘ └──────────┘
```

¹The captain is a section (area) supervisor of approximately four guest tables.
²The sommelier is the wine steward.
³The chef du trancheur serves desserts (often from a dessert cart) and other after-dinner items.
⁴The chef du rang is the lead table server; commis du rang is his or her assistant.

EXHIBIT 12.3
Classical (French) Organization for Dining Room Service

prepared all or in part at tableside. Service responsibilities, then, also included some tableside cooking or menu item **finishing.**

Orders were taken by the chef du rang, who gave them to the commis du rang, for transport to the kitchen. Their orders were given to the aboyeur (announcer), who then served as the liaison between the service and food preparation staff. The aboyeur position remains today in some properties of all sizes in the form of an **expediter.** A person in this position may be an assistant manager who coordinates food **serving** activities between production and service staff during busy dining times.

A **sommelier** (wine steward) and a chef du trancheur (dessert server) are examples of other specialized positions that were available to assure that the highest-quality guest service standards were attained. (The sommelier is discussed in the next section.)

Just as for kitchen organization, positions in contemporary dining room organizations have been collapsed and combined. Exhibit 12.4 shows an example. With the exception of one position (wine steward), the dining room organization is not unlike that of the upscale restaurant's counterparts in other segments of the industry. One difference, however, is that the number of guests served by a food server is likely to be much less than in other segments.

Upscale restaurants feature a beautiful array of foods.

finishing completion of the last step(s) in the recipe for a food or beverage item; for example, preportioned ingredients for a salad (such as Caesar) could be mixed or a preportioned meat item may be cooked with preassembled herbs and spices (steak Diane)

expediter a person serving as liaison between food production and serving staff during busy shifts

serving the task of moving food products from production to service staff

sommelier a service staff member with extensive knowledge about wine, including its storage and wine–food affinities, who advises guests about wine selection, takes wine orders, and presents and serves selected wines to guests; also called *wine steward*

DID YOU KNOW?

There is a trend in many upscale restaurants to impose mandatory service charges, rather than to suggest voluntary gratuities (tips) from guests. (This is a standard practice in most private clubs.) Many restaurants levy this charge for large guest parties, it has become a standard for hotel room service, and U.S Cruise lines also impose "automatic" gratuities.

The word *tip* has long meant "to improve performance" or "to ensure promptness." Most persons prefer to determine their own level of tips, because they believe that it has an impact on the service they will receive. Another irritation: properties that add a mandatory service charge and then leave the credit card slip open to allow guests to provide another gratuity.

Here are some restaurant tipping guidelines around the world:

- China. – Three percent in major cities
- England. – Ten percent if no service charge
- Japan. – Tips are viewed as insulting
- New Zealand, Thailand, and Fiji. None

Source: Laura Bly. The tipping point: Will mandatory service charges replace voluntary gratuities. *USA Today*, August 26, 2005.

OBJECTIVE 4
Describe positions unique to upscale restaurants.

from scratch the preparation of food on-site with the use of (generally) fresh ingredients; the opposite of convenience foods

POSITIONS IN UPSCALE RESTAURANTS

Most positions used by upscale foodservice operations may be required by other table-service properties. However, the knowledge and skills required for many positions exceed those required for similar positions in other segments. Consider, for example, the knowledge that chefs must have to prepare sauces, stocks, and soups **from "scratch"** for the numerous recipes that require these as an ingredient. Consider also the skills required by service staff. They may need to prepare some food items tableside (French service) or serve single portions from trays assembled with many portions (Russian service).

Exhibits 12.1 through 12.4 reviewed positions in classical and more contemporary upscale restaurant organizations. We noted that, in addition to obvious name changes, more specialized positions in the classical organization

Sommelier presenting wine to a couple in an upscale restaurant

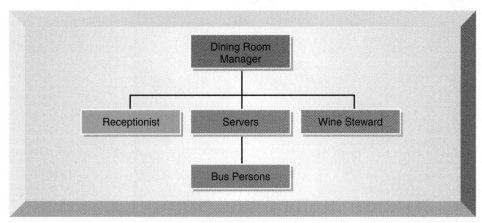

EXHIBIT 12.4
Contemporary Version of Dining Room Service Organization

have become collapsed in many of today's more contemporary organizations. One exception is the position of sommelier (wine steward), which has remained important in the upscale segment because of the role that fine wine plays in the enjoyment of food.

Let's look at some of the many tasks that a sommelier might be expected to do:

- Develop (or assist in development of) the wine list
- Purchase (or assist in the purchase of) wines
- Manage the proper storage and issuing of wines
- Present the wine list to guests and suggest appropriate wines, if requested, based on the menu items that have been ordered
- Take wine order from guests and determine when it should be served
- Obtain proper wine glasses and place them on the guest's dining table
- Bring wine to table and present it to guests
- Open and serve wines according to specified procedures
- Replace wine if it has been rejected
- Refill glasses and serve additional bottles, if requested
- Obtain and serve wines ordered by the **carafe** and/or glass
- Remove empty wine bottles and glasses
- Total and present wine bill to guests (or server) for payment

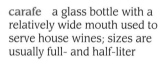

carafe   a glass bottle with a relatively wide mouth used to serve house wines; sizes are usually full- and half-liter

petits fours   small (individually portioned, bite-sized) cakes baked in an oven

Some upscale restaurants also utilize another food preparation position, the pastry chef or baker, that is infrequently found in commercial operations (although some hotels and specialty restaurants employ these persons). Pastry chefs must be highly skilled, and those at the top of their profession have accumulated many years of experience in progressively more responsible positions. The process of pastry and bread work is almost as much a science as it is a skill. For example, environmental elements such as elevation (number of feet above sea level), temperature, and humidity can affect the quality of their work. Cake decoration, delicate **petits fours,** and pulled sugar sculptures are examples of the creative work produced by a pastry chef who is a master craftsperson.

Chefs at work in kitchen of an upscale restaurant

Tableside food preparation at an upscale restaurant

WHEN IS A CHEF A CHEF?

The help wanted ad in newspapers often identifies restaurants seeking chefs for vacant positions. Persons preparing food for only very brief periods of time may refer to themselves as chefs. These restaurants and persons are confusing the terms *cook* and *chef*. A cook is a person who prepares food. A chef, by contrast, is a professional who has completed extensive formal study and experience requirements, including an apprenticeship for several or more years. A chef is likely to be a member of a professional association such as (in the United States) the American Culinary Federation (ACF) or the World Association of Cooks Society (international members). The best chefs in the United States are often members of the ACF and are typically certified as a Certified Executive Chef (CEC), Certified Chef de Cuisine (CCC), or Certified Master Chef (CMC).

A proud chef

UNIQUE CHALLENGES OF UPSCALE RESTAURANTS

OBJECTIVE 5
Describe unique
challenges that
confront upscale
restaurants.

In several common ways, upscale restaurants generally differ from other segments of the foodservice industry:

- *Independent ownership.* Many upscale properties are owned and managed by entrepreneurs, such as previously successful chefs who have had a long-time professional goal to operate their own business. Unlike restaurants in other segments, it is difficult to operate these properties as "family businesses."
- *Single- (or few) unit organization.* Most upscale restaurants are single-unit properties or, in relatively few cases, one of just several properties operated by the same individual. Many owners or operators in this segment recognize it is very difficult to consistently attain the necessary high-quality standards when multiple properties are managed. Some, especially chef owners and operators, believe that they must personally be involved in the day-to-day operation of their properties for desired standards to be consistently attained. This, of course, is not possible in a multiunit operation. Affiliation with partners and interacting with highly qualified chefs and managers may make it possible to operate several restaurants, but it is certainly not possible for one person to operate more than just a few properties in the upscale segment.
- *Need to consistently produce and serve meals at very high levels of quality.* Every foodservice operation must meet or exceed the product, service, and environmental quality standards expected by the guests. These expectations are, however, typically the highest for upscale restaurant guests. Significant operating efforts and a can-do attitude are necessary for restaurants to be the very best.
- *Limited volume.* Many restaurants in this segment have relatively few seats, and many are open for the evening meal only because of the **labor-intensive** nature of required food preparation and service tasks. There are, therefore, fewer opportunities to generate acceptable levels of revenue.
- *High check averages.* The number of dollars spent per average guest is, by definition, higher in this segment than in any other. Much of this revenue is utilized to compensate the restaurant for the costs incurred in purchasing high-cost food and beverage products and paying for the very high labor expenses. High check average, then, does not necessarily mean high profit, and many restaurants in this segment have financial challenges.
- *Emphasis on wines.* The importance of wine in the dining experience of guests at upscale restaurants has been noted several times in this chapter. Upscale properties frequently have hundreds of different wines valued at tens of thousands of dollars in inventory and can offer guests a wide range of alternatives based on their palates (tastes) and pocketbooks. The wine sold is most likely to be suggested, presented, and served according to formalized procedures that go far beyond efforts to only suggestively sell it. Obtaining desired inventory levels of the best wine is a challenge that faces many upscale properties.
- *Consumer education.* You have already learned that many guests in upscale restaurants visit not only to enjoy, but also to learn about, the food and beverage items that they experience. The objective for their visit is, then, more than "to eat because they are hungry" or to "have something to do." Rather, many guests have a passion about excellent menu item preparation and presentation and are serious about learning as much as they can about

labor intensive   the need for people rather than for equipment (machinery) to perform required work tasks

Bottles of wine in a restaurant wine cellar

table turns the number of times a guest dining table is used during one dining period

flatware guest table-service items, including knives, forks, and spoons

their interests. Proprietors of many upscale restaurants must compete for guests with these interests.

- *Required reservations.* Many upscale restaurants take and even require reservations. Those that are very successful are at capacity for almost every meal shift, and neither the restaurant nor its guests would benefit from a first-come, first-served system. Food purchase concerns, slow **table turns,** and guest commitment to the meal experience are additional reasons why reservation systems are frequently utilized.

- *More extensive guest service requirements.* French and Russian service styles, which require more elaborate skills and time-consuming service, have already been noted. Attention to numerous details (including the frequent refreshing of water, replacement of **flatware**, and refolding of napkins when guests leave the table—along with careful attention to all other guest needs—is a hallmark of service in upscale restaurants. These require service procedures and create service challenges that are not normally found in other foodservice segments.

Servers in tuxedos at an elaborate buffet table

SUMMARY OF CHAPTER LEARNING OBJECTIVES

1. **Define the term *upscale restaurant*.**
   An upscale restaurant is a foodservice operation that provides a very high quality of food and beverage products served at a very high standard of service with appropriate tabletop appointments in a tasteful environment. These restaurants are also referred to as *fine dining* or *white tablecloth* properties.

2. **Describe the types of guests who visit upscale restaurants.**
   A wide range of guests, from those who visit infrequently for special occasions, to those who visit to conduct business, to others who want to impress someone, and to others who visit because of its reputation, visit upscale restaurants. Other guests dine at upscale properties because they want to learn more about gastronomy.

3. **Describe how an upscale restaurant is organized for food preparation and foodservice activities.**
   Traditionally, upscale restaurants have been organized according to the traditional French

classical brigade developed by Auguste Escoffier. This organizational system has been modernized by collapsing, or combining, positions. Likewise, positions necessary for dining room service have evolved from the classical French organization to a more simplified version.

4. **Describe positions unique to upscale restaurants.**
   Two positions relatively unique to upscale restaurants include the sommelier (wine steward) and pastry chef (baker).

5. **Describe unique challenges that confront upscale restaurants.**
   Many upscale restaurants are unique in that they have independent ownership, are single- (or just a few) unit organizations, need to consistently produce and serve meals at very high levels of quality, and produce only a limited volume of meals. Other ways in which they are unique include high check averages, a significant emphasis on wine and consumer education, required reservation systems, and more extensive guest service requirements.

FEEDBACK FROM THE REAL WORLD

Our real-world advice comes from Kevin J. Brown, President and Chief Executive Officer of Lettuce Entertain You Enterprises, Inc. (LEYE). Kevin received a hospitality management degree and began working with LEYE in 1977. He worked in many of the company's restaurants and became a partner in 1981. Kevin consulted on a quick-service restaurant concept for Gap/Old Navy, Inc. As well, he created the highly successful Big Bowl, specializing in Asian noodles, stir fry, soups, and wraps, which was sold to Brinker International in February 2001. In 2005, Kevin and LEYE repurchased the concept, and now eight Big Bowl locations are managed and owned by LEYE.

What are examples of operating procedures (food production and food service) that your organization uses to assure that your high-quality standards are most consistently attained?

Managers of our restaurants utilize detailed checklists of tasks that begin at 6:00 A.M. and extend through the time the last manager leaves at the end of the day for every phase of the operation. This includes a "master prep walk-through" for all areas of the kitchen and various food preparation and food order requisitions. We also collect and utilize data relating to the quantity of food products in inventory, and we track product rotation (inventory turnover). We use daily

(continued)

revenue and sales and labor reports and adjust our forecasts as needed. We develop weekly, mid-monthly, and monthly statements that allow us to compare data for these periods against our forecasts and against the same periods in previous years. Throughout the day our managers constantly check the production line and dining area performance. We are very alert to the timing of our service. We also undertake food-temperature assessments on a very frequent basis. While the examples I've given are not inclusive, they do point to the need to consistently know what's going on in all areas of the restaurant at all times. It is this attention to details that allows us to more consistently meet the standards that our guests have grown to expect.

What, if any, changes in marketing tactics are used by upscale properties during times of economic downturns to attract guests with reduced discretionary dollars for dining away from home?

We utilize a very successful frequent-diners' program that rewards our guests for their regular visits with guest certificates and other incentives, including free air travel and hotel stays (at the highest reward level). This program helps to keep our guests loyal and returning to our properties even when the economy slows.

Another tactic: We closely examine our menus to assure that all items provide good value and that there are alternatives to those items that are highest priced.

Our Number One Club program is designed so that a manager talks to every guest. He or she especially targets first-time visitors and is empowered to provide a complimentary appetizer or dessert. Our philosophy: For the majority of our regular guests, marketing begins within our four walls and does not usually go beyond five miles! In properties with our highest check averages, we use guest chef visits, chef interaction benefits, and an extensive local public relations program.

What are the most important things a multiunit official can do to assure that the proper corporate culture permeates throughout the organization?

The best tactics involve a great deal of common sense. Top leaders must be visible, vocal, and consistent. They must also establish responsibilities, consistently reinforce the message, and make their managers accountable (who, in turn, must require accountability from their own subordinates!). Finally, I believe that effective leaders praise and reward their staff members. This, in turn, creates an incentive for still higher levels of achievement. Therefore, the process becomes cyclical; organizational standards can be attained and the quality bar can be raised higher.

MASTERING YOUR KNOWLEDGE

Discuss the following questions.

1. The chapter explained that experienced chefs often desire to become the proprietor (owner) of an upscale restaurant. What types of knowledge and skills would a person experienced as a chef bring to his or her new position as chef–owner of an upscale restaurant?
2. What types of knowledge and skill would an experienced chef not necessarily have learned in previous positions as a chef that would also be required to be the owner of a successful upscale restaurant?
3. What types of knowledge would be required of a food server in any type of foodservice operation?
4. What specialized knowledge and skills would be necessary for one to be a successful server in an upscale restaurant?

5. If you were the owner or manager of an upscale restaurant, what types of activities could you offer to allow your guests to become more knowledgeable about food and beverages?
6. What are the advantages and disadvantages for an upscale restaurant that offers a la carte and a table d'hôte menus? A menu that does or does not change daily?
7. What can a chef in an upscale restaurant do to assure that he or she can obtain the proper quality of ingredients for the planned menu?
8. How can a beverage manager or sommelier in an upscale restaurant learn about and keep up with information about wine? What types of special controls are required to manage wine inventories that may be less applicable to controlling food inventories?

LEARN FROM THE INTERNET

1. Check out the following websites for vintners and wine and food societies:
   - Bolla: www.bolla.com
   - Clos du Bois: www.closdubois.com
   - Chaine des Rotisseurs USA: www.chaine_us.org
   - American Wine Society: www.americanwinesociety.com

   What are examples of information that would be most useful for those in the hospitality industry? For consumers interested in general wine information?

2. Enter the name of your state (example: Nevada) and "fine dining restaurants" (example: Nevada fine dining restaurants) into your favorite search engine. Review the list of restaurants generated, and check out several websites to review the information presented about the properties you select.

3. Review the following websites of some of America's finest (fine-dining) restaurants:
   - Manresa (Las Gatos, CA): www. manresarestaurant.com
   - Charlie Trotter's (Chicago, IL): www.charlietrotters.com
   - The French Laundry (Yountville, CA.): www.frenchlaundry.com. Click on "French Laundry".
   - Per Se (New York, NY): www. frenchlaundry.com. Click on "Per Se").
   - Chez Panissee (Berkeley, CA): www.chezpanisse.com
   - MASA (New York, NY): www.masarestaurant.com

   What features of these properties are noted on the websites? What type of information is provided to address quality standards? What can you learn from the information on the sites?

KEY HOSPITALITY TERMS

The following terms were explained in this chapter. Review the definitions of any words with which you are unfamiliar. Begin to utilize them as you expand your vocabulary as a hospitality professional.

upscale restaurant
food and wine affinity
haute cuisine
a la carte (menu selection)
table d'hôte (menu selections)
gastronomy
classical brigade
apprenticeship
maitre d'hotel
captain (dining room)

finishing
expediter
serving
sommelier
from "scratch"
carafe
petits fours
labor intensive
table turns
flatware

13 Casual-Service (Midscale) Restaurants

Café Antipasti in Glasgow, Scotland

CHAPTER LEARNING OBJECTIVES

After studying this chapter you will be able to:

1. Review characteristics of a casual-service restaurant.
2. Discuss the role of the manager in a casual-service restaurant.
3. Describe the types of guests who visit casual-service restaurants.
4. Explain menu planning considerations applicable to casual-service restaurants.
5. Discuss special concerns about the service of alcoholic beverages in casual-service restaurants.
6. Consider career progression alternatives within the casual-service restaurant segment.
7. Provide examples of long- and short-term challenges confronting casual-service restaurants.

This chapter was authored by Jeff Elsworth, Assistant Professor, The School of Hospitality Business, Michigan State University, East Lansing, Michigan. He has been a manager, general manager, and franchise trainer of managers for several casual-service restaurant companies, including Damon's, Max & Erma's, and Houlihans.

FEEDBACK FROM THE REAL WORLD

The local college team won the conference championship. The first game in regional play-offs will be played in the community and is only one week away. Planning at LaSill's Seafood Bistro Restaurant has already begun. There will not be a busier Saturday night for the rest of the year than the one that is fast approaching.

The employee schedule is the first document affected; all staff members who normally work the evening shift are alerted that they will be needed that night; volunteers from the midday shift are also solicited.

The manager checks the inventory of china, glass, and flatware. The patterns are not special order, so additional quantities can be quickly obtained from a local supplier.

On Monday before the event several **distributor sales representatives (DSRs)** normally stop by; others call. All are alerted that a larger than usual order for food and beverage products will be placed midweek for Friday delivery.

The restaurant takes dinner reservations (normally this works out very well); however, the manager wished the system did not need to be in place this Saturday. (It does, of course; some people made reservations weeks ago, and **regulars** know about the reservation system and use it.) Receptionists and others who take telephone reservations are briefed about applicable procedures and reminded about the need to follow them very closely as the weekend approaches.

Dinner is served at LaSill's Seafood Bistro from 5:00 to 10:00 P.M. The big game is scheduled for early afternoon, so the restaurant will likely be hit early by customers, with a steady flow of guests with and without dinner reservations until at least 9:00 P.M. (perhaps later); many regulars, for whatever reason, always like to dine out early. Guests arriving without reservations will be put on a waiting list so that they can be worked into the dining room around those with reservations. Fortunately, the restaurant has a large bar and lounge area. It will be busy with guests waiting for tables, and it will be staffed and stocked accordingly.

Experience has shown that, on very busy nights, the dining room will do 3.5 **turns.** Since this is about the maximum, the manager has a good idea about the total number of guests to be served and, therefore, the total number of meals for which prepreparation will be needed.

With the total number of guests now estimated, detailed food production planning can begin. Guests will hope to be celebrating a victory. (However, even if the home team loses, many guests will still be happy about the conference championship!) This special occasion calls for some menu specials to help to raise the **check average.** (Also, properly planned specials will likely be those that can be prepared quickly to increase table turns.) The manager will work with the chef to estimate how the availability of these specials will affect the normal **sales mix** of menu items. Then the quantity of each regular menu item to be served can be estimated. This will become the basis for ordering ingredients and for the **prepreparation** tasks on the day of service.

With production plans in place, products are ordered midweek, are delivered on Friday, and preprep work for Saturday night begins. Friday nights are always busy anyway (although this week some regulars will likely postpone their visit until Saturday). This means that the restaurant's real rush will begin on Friday, with the increased preprep tasks added to the normal high volume of work on Friday.

By Saturday morning, everyone is hard at work because **mise en place** is important to get both the front and back (heart) of the house ready for that evening's production and service.

The restaurant's doors open for dinner promptly at 5:00 P.M. Some guests with and without reservations are waiting. The restaurant gets busy earlier than usual and stays busy later than usual. While some relatively small problems arise, the evening goes very well for both guests and restaurant employees. In fact, the manager overheard several groups of guests leaving making comments like "We had a good time this evening. Look how busy it was." "We

(continued)

should open a restaurant; after all, everyone has to eat!" "I bet it is easy to make money in the restaurant business; just open the front doors and the people will come."

What do you think the manager did right to get ready for a busy Saturday night? What else could the manager have done?

As you read this chapter, think about the answers to these questions and then get feedback from an experienced professional who works in the real world at the end of the chapter.

OBJECTIVE 1
Review characteristics of a casual-service restaurant.

distributor sales representatives (DSRs)   salespersons representing a product or equipment supplier who sell to the hospitality operation

regulars   repeat guests or frequent diners

turns   the total number of guests served during a meal period divided by the number of seats in a restaurant; a 150-seat restaurant serving 425 guests during a meal period has a turn of 2.83 (425 ÷ 150)

check average   the average amount spent by a restaurant guest: total food and beverage revenue ÷ total number of guests

sales mix   the percentage that one menu item sells of the total items served; one menu item has a known sales mix percent, the number of portions of that item can be calculated: total estimated guests to be served × sales mix percent = estimated units of the menu item to be sold

prepreparation   the task of getting food ingredients ready for production; for example, frozen shrimp might be thawed, pealed, and deveined to ready them for deep frying when needed; frequently shortened to *preprep*

mise en place   a French term meaning "everything in its place"; the cooks and bartenders must get ready for production; servers must get ready for service

CASUAL-SERVICE RESTAURANTS

What is a casual-service (midscale) restaurant? For the purposes of this book, let's call it a sit-down restaurant offering alcoholic beverages that markets to singles, couples, and businesspersons with a check average lower than that of an upscale restaurant and higher than that of a family-service restaurant in its geographic area. National brands that fit this definition may include Houston's, Bennigans, Chili's Grill & Bar, Olive Garden Italian Restaurant, Applebee's Neighborhood Grill & Bar, and Outback Steakhouse. Independents (entrepreneurs) in many communities also own and operate casual-service (midscale) restaurants.

The complexity of the foodservices industry makes it difficult to develop a precise definition for this (and all other) segments of the industry. It would be easier, for example, to state a range of check averages and to denote a restaurant type by reviewing where its check average falls relative to the range of check averages for each type. Unfortunately, as was true with the classifications of lodging properties earlier in this book, what the guest pays is not, by itself, helpful. Consider, for example, a restaurant meeting the above definition located in a rural area of a southern state and contrast it with a similar property in a large city in a New England state. A similar meal experience (food, service, and environment) may cost $10 in the former and $30 in the latter.

Casual service (midscale) restaurants along with their counterparts in the family-service segment are among the types of restaurants most likely to be operated by **entrepreneurs** who operate their properties without affiliation with a recognized brand. (Most high check average properties are also operated by individuals without chain affiliation.) The name recognition

Receptionist greets guests in a casual-service restaurant.

THEMES ARE IMPORTANT IN CASUAL-SERVICE RESTAURANTS

Many, but certainly not all, casual service restaurants incorporate a theme for their guests' experience. A theme, whether it be a pub, a casual restaurant in Italy, or a more rustic setting in Australia's outback, adds a unifying aspect to the dining environment. For example, the exterior building design, interior decor, and uniforms of service personnel, along with the menu, are integral to the theme being utilized. Many casual-service restaurants recognize that guests are looking for an experience, rather than just a meal when they dine out. A well-developed and implemented theme allows guests to escape from their daily lives into a different and pleasurable experience, and a well-executed theme can provide a great **competitive edge** for the restaurant.

associated with national brands makes it increasingly difficult for independents to operate in the quick-service marketplace. By contrast, sufficient knowledge, experience, and financial resources (along with, often, a little luck!) enable entrepreneurs to open restaurants that serve alcoholic beverages (these are the topic of this chapter) or without alcoholic beverages (as occurs in a family-service property) as discussed in Chapter 14.

Many persons enjoy casual-service restaurants in communities all across the country and visit those that are branded (examples were included earlier) and others within the community that are locally owned and operated. These range from a family serving ethnic foods, such as Italian or Greek items, to partners operating a restaurant and bar with a sports theme (and many television monitors), to a couple operating a restaurant featuring chicken, steak, barbecue, or another food item with full bar service.

Many hospitality students have an interest in owning their own place someday. For many, this dream will come true, and it is likely to be in a restaurant that is the topic of this chapter.

Unlike their counterparts in the lodging industry and the quick-service food segments, many casual-service restaurants are company owned and operated, rather than franchisee owned and operated. Like their counterparts in other segments, however, standardization of components such as building design, menu, and recipes and numerous operating procedures allow managers to work with proven systems and help to reduce surprises for guests. Many guests visiting these restaurants have typically visited this and/or another restaurant in the **chain**. They know what to expect and use their experiences to determine whether future visits are likely to be enjoyable.

entrepreneur a person who assumes the risk of owning and operating a business in exchange for the financial rewards that the business may produce

competitive edge the concept that a business does something very well, which encourages persons to purchase products and services from it, rather than from its competitors

chain a multiunit hospitality organization

OBJECTIVE 2
Discuss the role of the manager in a casual-service restaurant.

THE RESTAURANT MANAGER'S JOB

Managers of many casual-service chain restaurants operate businesses grossing several million dollars or more annually. They have lots of responsibility and typically have some experience in all positions and a relatively lengthy

White tablecloth dining at a curbside cafe

A bar in a casual restaurant should be integrated with the theme of the entire unit.

unit   one property in a multi-unit (chain) organization; sometimes called *store* or *outlet*

shift log   a record of critical information about a work shift completed by its manager for use by the manager of the next shift

experience in assistant management positions before becoming a general manager of a **unit.** In their positions, they must meet ambitious budget goals, directly supervise the work of other managers, be ultimately responsible for 75 or more employees, resolve innumerable day to day operating challenges, and represent their restaurant and brand within the community. Any way one looks at it, these general managers have a very challenging position. They must be able to summon creativity and a great deal of knowledge and experience to meet job demands.

Unit managers have many day to day operating responsibilities that are similar to those of their counterparts in other segments of the foodservice industry. They must, for example, forecast future business and assure that they have ample resources (especially food and beverage products, labor hours, and supplies) to effectively and efficiently serve anticipated guest counts. They must, as well, be knowledgeable about the most effective techniques to recruit, orient, train, and supervise staff members at all organizational levels within the unit. They must know how to facilitate teamwork among and between employees at all levels. To do this requires high energy, a passion for excellence, and the creativity to solve nonroutine operating problems. They must also serve as a role model for those whom they supervise.

In many ways, the unit manager's work is similar to that of an independent operator. The workday begins by checking the last **shift's log**, newly arrived mail, and telephone and e-mail messages, and then a "to-do" list must be constructed. At this point, the workday really begins as the manager addresses the issues necessary to open on time and consistently meet the property's standards.

The work of unit managers in casual-service properties also differs from that of their counterparts in at least some other segments. For example, they must be concerned about the responsible service of alcoholic beverages. This does not apply to managers in family-service and quick-service properties. (We will discuss special aspects of alcoholic beverage service in restaurants in a later section of this chapter.)

Outback Steakhouse

RISING STAR PROFILE

Todd Chwatun
General Manager
Big Buck Brewery and Steak House
Gaylord, MI

Have a Passion for Your Work!

Todd received an undergraduate degree in Finance, and during the next 12 years he worked in successively more responsible positions within the restaurant industry. His first nine years were with Old Country Buffet. His positions included hourly paid entry-level work in kitchen and foodservice positions, one year as a preopening trainer, and the next seven years as a manager with unit-level responsibilities. Next came two years with Damon's as a general manager, and his most recent experience has been with Big Buck Brewery and Steak House. After managing a Big Buck property in Grand Rapids, Michigan, he became part of a turn-around team that took the company through a bankruptcy to the present: a property with consistently excellent service and increasing sales growth in a community with an uncertain economy.

Todd is very proud of the most unforgettable moment in his career: "The day I was promoted to general manager with Old Country Buffet. At the time, I was the first person to be promoted through the ranks from an hourly employee to GM. At that time, I was also the youngest general manager in the country's history. It is a great honor to have your employer trust you enough to let you run the business."

Todd has special concerns about the challenges facing his segment of the industry: "The economy is our biggest challenge. People are spending less money because of job loss, smaller wage increases, and devaluation of the stock market. They are looking for increased value for the dollars they spend in dining-out experiences. At the same time, it is an increasing challenge for a restaurant to offer high-value items because of increasing costs.

"The other challenge is employee training, which is one of the most important aspects of running a successful business. First, the right person must be hired. Training should be individualized to the extent possible to reflect what a new staff member already knows and can do and to consider what must still be learned. New employees should be trained so that they can be successful on the job."

Todd was asked what, if anything, he would do differently in his career: "I wish I had gone to a culinary school for chef training. Even though I have worked in and managed kitchens, I still do not have all the knowledge about working with food that I wish I had. I will probably take some classes in the future."

Todd gives some good advice for young people considering a hospitality career: "Have a passion for your work; give it your best effort. Remember that experience is invaluable to your success. Most good managers have started in hourly positions and therefore understand how to interact with their employees.

"It is also important to get experience at both food preparation and food serving tasks. Both are important parts of the business and depend on each other. Last, while it is not necessary to earn a college degree, it is an asset to one's marketability and, of course, also adds to one's knowledge."

Another difference: Many properties in this segment do not have a chef; they may have a kitchen manager. Unlike their counterparts in a hotel, for example, which frequently employs a food and beverage manager and a chef, the general manager of a casual-service property must know details about food production and assume many food production duties, including those related to food safety. Then, if there are no kitchen-related problems, he or she can begin to think about the front of the house.

Unit managers working in multiunit organizations utilize menus, purchase specifications, basic operating procedures, and related tactics that have been developed by persons with organization-wide responsibilities to provide consistency between operating units. The procedures regarding these very important matters must be followed, but unit managers must also use their creativity in numerous other areas to meet the unique needs of their guests and their marketplace.

IT'S MORE THAN JUST A TITLE!

Unit managers in some casual-service organizations have more responsibilities than others. Sometimes, for example, a general manager is responsible for one unit. Other general managers may have operating responsibilities for one unit and, additionally, supervise one or more general managers of other units. (In at least one organization, this position is called *senior manager.*)

Advantages of this plan accrue to both the individual and organization. For example, as one's responsibility extends beyond the unit level, it is likely that additional compensation is received. Also, the organization can eliminate senior (area or regional) positions that do not have direct unit operating responsibilities or, at least, can expand the number of units that this senior official coordinates.

OBJECTIVE 3
Describe the types of guests who visit casual-service restaurants.

GUESTS OF CASUAL-SERVICE RESTAURANTS

Who are the typical guests visiting casual-service (midscale) restaurants? We began to answer this question early in this chapter when we indicated that this segment markets to singles, couples, and businesspersons. As is true with all segments of the foodservice industry, few, if any, guests generally visit restaurants in only one segment. For example, a businessperson may entertain clients at an upscale restaurant during the week, enjoy a casual-service property on the weekend, and take his or her children to a family- or quick-service restaurant on another occasion. Persons visiting casual-service properties generally go there for purposes other than just to eat. Some guests visit to break up a routine of home-cooked meals; others dine at these properties as part of shopping, a sporting event, or other trip. Others, especially young people, visit in groups, and still others stop at these units on trips away from home because they are familiar with the brand and don't want to risk a dining experience in an unfamiliar location. Casual-service properties provide "**eatertainment**" for all these types of guests.

Some casual-service restaurants are designed with one or more relatively small rooms that can be utilized for group functions. Other units do not have separate rooms, but have sufficient space to allow tables to be moved together to accommodate small groups of guests who wish to dine together.

eatertainment (foodservice) the concept that guests desire to enjoy the total dining experience (food and beverage products, service, and the environment, including cleanliness) and may desire pleasurable distractions (television and animatronics, for example) when they visit a foodservice operation

take-out service (foodservice) a dining option in which a guest calls, faxes, or e-mails an order to a restaurant and then goes to the property to pick it up

Turnover means new employees must be recruited selected, and trained.

Increasingly, another type of guest can be accommodated at casual-service restaurants: those who want to dine elsewhere! Many properties have historically offered **take-out service** to guests desiring it. Some properties encouraged their guests to call ahead so that the order would be ready when they arrived. Others had a more restrictive policy requiring those desiring take-out orders to arrive on-site, where they were promised expedited food production.

Today, however, take-out orders are seen to be a potentially very significant revenue generator.

DID YOU KNOW?

Many casual-service restaurants are especially busy during prime dining times, and this frequently requires guests to wait for tables. Many properties use restaurant pager systems that include small coaster-type units given to guests that flash, vibrate, or beep when their table is ready. Recent technology is making future generations of this equipment more interesting for guests. Examples include units with small screens that provide streaming sports scores, news, and trivia. Others have space for a small printed ad that can promote a restaurant's products or that can be sold to outside advertisers. Still other systems call a guest's cell phone when its time to dine, and another that keeps guests current on anticipated wait times.

One special concern: each unit can cost $50.00 or more, and there is a concern that more "bells and whistles" will entice some guests to steal them.

Source: Darren Robinson-Jacobs. Restaurant pagers that flash, vibrate, or beep may be getting some new bells and whistles. Retrieved October 3, 2005, from www.hotel-online.com

To this end, separate entrances leading to special take-out counters are being designed into many new construction units. Parking spaces near these entrances are being reserved for take-out customers. Another twist: some units feature staff members who carry take-out orders to customers as they wait in their autos. (Some readers may remember the curb service offered by some restaurants. Passengers drove up to intercoms located in the parking lot and ordered their meals. In some operations, service personnel even used roller skates to bring orders to the customers.) It is interesting that service procedures that once were innovative, but then became obsolete (in part, because of drive-through operations), are now becoming useful again.

MENU PLANNING CONSIDERATIONS

> **OBJECTIVE 4**
> Explain menu planning considerations applicable to casual-service restaurants.

You have learned that in the foodservice business "it all starts with the menu." This observation is just as correct in the casual-service segment as it is in any other part of the commercial and noncommercial foodservice industries.

Many restaurants in this segment feature menus planned outside the unit (they are utilized in all or most units within the organization). These menus typically offer a wide range of menu items in categories such as these:

Appetizers	Fajitas
Soups	Side dishes (accompaniments)
Salads	Healthy items
Lunch specials[1]	Desserts
Seafood entrées	Nonalcoholic beverages
Poultry entrées	Premium drinks (typically tied to a promotion
Steak entrées	with liquor distributors or distillers)
Hamburgers	Beers, wines, spirits

[1]In some casual-service restaurants, the same menu is used during the entire time that the property is open (late morning through late evening). Disclaimers may indicate that selected items are only available during a specified time.

selling interpersonal activities designed to promote the sale of products and services offered by the hospitality operation

advertising nonpersonal presentation of products and services offered by the hospitality operation

suggestive selling the process by which servers indicate menu items to guests that are preferred because of popularity and/or profitability factors

menu rationalization an approach used to maximize the number of menu items that can be prepared using relatively few ingredients

The menus of many casual-service restaurants offer 50 or more different items, and menus can contain numerous pages of menu suggestions. Menus must be carefully designed to be effective in-house **selling** and **advertising** tools. This is necessary to enable guests to quickly focus their attention on desired items so that service times are not slowed when guests must study the menu. Colors, creative descriptive copy, use of specific menu categories, and **suggestive selling** by servers are among the tactics used to make the best use of the menu.

Isn't it difficult to purchase ingredients for and to prepare a large number of menu items? It can be unless a **menu rationalization** approach is used. Then relatively few ingredients can be used to prepare a large number of menu items. For example, a chicken breast can be prepared by baking, barbecuing, or char-broiling. It can be sliced for a chicken Caesar salad and can be utilized in specialty casserole and/or numerous other dishes. Careful menu planning can minimize potential operating problems while still presenting a variety of dining alternatives to guests.

The menu determines the ingredients that must be purchased. Large, multiunit organizations may produce or manufacture some products utilized in their restaurants under their brand name. They may establish national contracts for other products that make it the responsibility of the manufacturers to find distributors to service all restaurants in all geographic areas. Alternatively, these organizations may utilize **full-line distributors** who sell a wide range of products to supply units within a specific geographic area. Unit managers may have some discretion in making purchase decisions about perishable items, including produce, baked goods, and dairy items, which are often purchased locally.

full-line distributor a supplier who offers a wide range of products; for example, some suppliers sell thousands (or more) of items, ranging from toothpicks to fresh produce to dishwashing machines; they offer a large variety but not a deep selection of items within a specific category

Business is conducted in casual-service restaurants, and these guests represent a large market for many properties.

Discuss special concerns about the service of alcoholic beverages in casual-service restaurants.

dram-shop laws a provision in the U.S. legal code that allows an injured party to seek damages from both the intoxicated person who caused the injury and from the persons who provided the alcoholic beverages to the intoxicated person

SPECIAL ALCOHOLIC BEVERAGE CONCERNS

Our definition of casual-service restaurants indicated that these properties typically offer alcoholic beverage service. Like any other business in the hospitality industry that makes alcoholic beverages available, special precautions are necessary to protect the guests and other members of the general public. In the United States, **dram-shop laws** allow persons injured by intoxicated persons to sue both the intoxicated person and those who served alcoholic beverages to that person. Social concerns also dictate responsible service of alcoholic beverages.

Casual-service properties frequently offer bar or lounge facilities in conjunction with their dining areas. These are utilized by guests who

- Are waiting for a table in the restaurant
- Are consuming their meal in the bar or lounge
- Have returned to the bar or lounge after consuming their meal in the restaurant
- Are visiting the property only for beverage service

Restaurant guests can include groups of young people, fans who have attended or are viewing sporting events, and others celebrating special occasions at the property. The responsible service of alcoholic beverages to persons who are of legal age and who are not obviously or visibly intoxicated can be a pleasant component of the dining experience in the restaurant and to those interacting with friends in the bar or lounge.

A chef working at the grill located across from the foodservice pickup line

The responsible service of alcoholic beverages is absolutely critical in any type of food or beverage operation. However, special concerns are relevant in casual-service restaurants because of the relatively young people who regularly visit these operations. Yes, hotels feature restaurants, bars, and lounges where alcoholic beverages are available. In addition, upscale restaurants may have waiting areas where alcoholic beverages are served, and they will likely have alcoholic beverage service available in the dining areas. However, young persons are much more likely to be in the customer base of casual-service restaurants.

Most states have changed the legal definition of intoxication to reduce the allowable **blood alcohol concentration (BAC)**. Casual-service (and all other) property managers must adjust (tighten) alcoholic beverage service procedures accordingly. One example: in some properties, it is a policy that the manager on duty must visit the table of and talk with any guests who order three or more alcoholic beverages.

blood alcohol concentration (BAC)   the amount of alcohol in the blood

As indicated above, the bar/lounge area of the typical casual-service restaurant is an integral part of the facility and the activities that occur within it. Restaurant managers must implement effective training programs to assure that all employees (not just the bartenders and servers!) are aware of appropriate procedures and that all aspects of the alcoholic beverage service program are consistently followed. This training may be required by the property's insurance carrier to reduce liability and, in turn, some insurance companies may reduce rates when all affected staff members have received the training.

CAREER PROGRESSION IN CASUAL-SERVICE RESTAURANTS

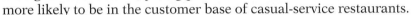

OBJECTIVE 6
Consider career progression alternatives within the casual-service restaurant segment.

Exhibit 13.1 shows an organization chart for a typical midscale restaurant. It shows the relationship among the three department heads: the kitchen manager, dining room manager, and head bartender; and the higher levels of unit management: the area manager, unit general manager, and assistant general manager(s). It is typical for top-level unit management (unit general manager and assistant general manager) to have experience in each position within the property. Depending on one's work experience and education, the time may be very brief in entry-level positions, with increasingly more time spent working in other management positions. A unit general manager will likely have spent a great deal of time as an assistant general manager, and the promotion to general manager may require relocation to another restaurant in the chain.

Casual-service restaurants offer significant opportunities for staff members who are interested in advancement within the unit and organization. Knowledge and skill are important to be successful in any position. However, standardized procedures utilized in multiunit chain organizations may speed the learning process and help property managers with necessary training. For

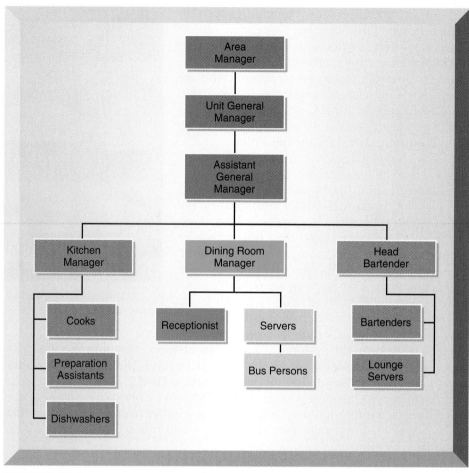

EXHIBIT 13.1
Midscale (Casual Dining) Restaurants: Route to the Top

example, this enables entry-level employees and college and university interns to become proficient more quickly in and among positions in a relatively short period of time. The growth of many of these organizations and the entire industry segment creates an ongoing need for new or additional management personnel within the units and the acceptance of external-unit responsibilities as well.

Two emerging trends may help to recruit and retain casual-service managers: partnership and profit-sharing programs that provide financial benefits (a percentage of bottom-line profits) for the successful operation of their restaurants. As partners, managers care more about their restaurants, the quality of team members hired, the guests' experiences, how the restaurant looks, and the speed of service.

The most common way for companies to grant ownership to managers is by relating compensation to factors such as staff development, revenue and profitability growth, and guest and team member satisfaction. The partners then receive a percentage of the bottom line.

Some companies ask managers selected for partnership to invest a specified amount of money that can be paid for with loans that are repaid by **payroll deductions**. Other companies offer an investment-free partnership plan with enhanced financial packages for top management. Regardless of how these programs are operated, they allow managers the opportunity to operate the restaurant as if it was their own, and fewer managers leave the company when they have a financial stake in it.

payroll deduction an amount withheld from an employee's compensation (paycheck) to pay for taxes, insurance, or other mandatory or voluntary financial obligations

CHALLENGES! CHALLENGES!

Casual-service restaurant managers are confronted with several challenges that significantly affect their success today and will increasingly influence their staying power in the future. Several of the most important include labor resources, a balance between quality and cost, using technology, and increased competition.

OBJECTIVE 7
Provide examples of long- and short-term challenges confronting casual-service restaurants.

Labor Resources

Casual-service managers, like their counterparts in other segments of the hospitality industry, require many staff members to provide a successful guest experience. Activities, including recruitment, selection, orientation, and training, are ongoing for all or most positions in many casual-service restaurants. Each aspect of the guest experience (great food and excellent beverages, appropriate levels of service, and a clean environment) is delivered by the restaurant's employees. Some properties have been able to attract staff members desiring a career in the industry, who then develop a passion for meeting (or, perhaps, exceeding) the property's standards relative to products, service, and environment. More common, however, is the employee who is "passing through" on the way to further education and/or a different career. The best casual-service managers are set apart from others by their ability to motivate their employees to work hard on behalf of the guests, because they know that, as in many segments of the hospitality industry, repeat business and word of mouth advertising are absolutely critical to success. Even though the casual-service segment has traditionally employed primarily younger workers, many companies now realize the importance of recruiting older workers. Staffing the restaurant with great people in the right positions and constantly training and motivating these persons to perform are challenges that will not go away and, in fact, are likely to become more important.

Finding the Correct Balance Between Quality and Cost

In some industries, managers are able to utilize technology to replace people. This is not, however, the case in the hospitality industry in general and the casual-service restaurants within it more specifically. Managers do utilize technology, but not with the objective of significantly reducing labor costs. While all types of expenses must be controlled, the two largest categories of expenses (food and beverage products and labor) demand special attention. Knowledgeable and trained staff must be available to meet the guests' needs. At the same time, however, these costs must be effectively managed. This is best done when managers recognize that their journey to

Guests receive their food orders in a casual-service restaurant.

quality involves an ongoing analysis of ways to reduce costs without sacrificing the attributes that make guests continue to return. Managers must also realize that another way to reduce the impact of expenses is to increase revenues. Marketing and sales tactics can be used to accomplish this.

Finding Ways That Allow Technology to Be Helpful

Revenue control and back-office accounting systems are examples of technology that have long been available to casual-service restaurant managers and their counterparts in other segments of the hospitality industry. However, applications involving revenue (guest) forecasting, product purchasing and inventory control, and guest reservation and seating systems are examples of applications that can help managers to become more effective. For example, in some properties that do not take reservations, arriving guests are met by a receptionist with a hand-held wireless transmitter. He or she estimates the wait time and enters data into the reservation wait system. Information about decreasing waiting time is displayed on large flat-screen monitors in the waiting lounge and/or other areas of the property.

Increased Competition

Potential guests of casual-service properties frequently discover new dining alternatives. Independents open new properties, multiunit organizations build properties in more locations, and existing competitors experiment with and incorporate new features designed to increase market share. Properties are also being squeezed by quick-service and fast casual-restaurant concepts on one side and fine casual and fine dining restaurants on the other side of the average check scale. Casual-service managers at both unit- and external-unit levels are under constant pressure to deliver greater value to their guests. They must do this consistently and better than the other organizations competing for customers within the same market. There is also a need to separate the organization from the clutter of the marketplace. How do they differentiate their operations from others? Ongoing marketing and advertising efforts are necessary to build a regular clientele of repeat visitors.

SUMMARY OF CHAPTER LEARNING OBJECTIVES

1. **Review characteristics of a casual-service restaurant.**
   A casual-service restaurant is a sit-down property offering alcoholic beverages that markets to singles, couples, and businesspersons with a check average lower than that of an upscale restaurant and higher than that of a family- or quick-service restaurant. National brands that fit this definition include Houston's, Bennigans, Chili's Grill & Bar, Olive Garden Italian Restaurant, Applebee's Neighborhood Grill & Bar, and Outback Steakhouse.

2. **Discuss the role of the manager in a casual-service restaurant.**
   Unit general managers are typically responsible for a multimillion dollar business. They directly supervise the work of other managers, are ultimately responsible for many additional employees, must resolve day to day operating challenges, and represent the restaurant or brand within the community.

3. **Describe the types of guests who visit casual-service restaurants.**
   Midscale restaurants appeal to businesspersons, couples, singles, and families who desire a dining experience with value-priced food, good service, cleanliness, and atmosphere, which, in total, represent the dining experience.

4. **Explain menu planning considerations applicable to casual-service restaurants.**
   The phrase "it all starts with the menu" applies to both midscale properties and their counterparts in other segments. Menus for multiunit organizations are typically planned outside the

unit, offer a relatively wide range of food items, and are carefully developed to serve as effective in-house selling and advertising tools.

5. **Discuss special concerns about the service of alcoholic beverages in casual-service restaurants.**

   As true of all foodservice operations, it is necessary to use great care to responsibly serve alcoholic beverages. Dram-shop laws permit injured parties to sue both those serving alcoholic beverages and the party who directly caused the injury. Restaurant managers must provide effective training to all staff to help assure that all laws are followed and that the restaurant meets its societal responsibilities.

6. **Consider career progression alternatives within the casual-service restaurant segment.**

Unit general managers must have the basic job knowledge and skills to perform work in all positions. Extended service as an assistant general manager is typically a prerequisite for promotion to general manager. This promotion may require relocation to another unit in the multiunit organization.

7. **Provide examples of long- and short-term challenges confronting casual-service restaurants.**

   Recruiting and retaining labor resources is a challenge that casual-service restaurants share with other industry segments. Other challenges relate to finding the correct balance between quality and cost, discovering ways to utilize technology, and responding to increased competition.

MASTERING YOUR KNOWLEDGE

Discuss the following questions.

1. What are the primary reasons that you and your peers visit a casual-service restaurant?
2. Why do you think that many casual-service restaurants are typically company owned and operated rather than franchisee owned and operated?
3. What do you think are the most challenging tasks of a unit general manager?
4. What are the rewards and challenges of serving as a unit general manager in a multiunit

organization and of being an independent entrepreneur?
5. What are some of the things that you have liked or disliked about jobs you have had? How would you, as an effective manager, have modified or changed these concerns so that staff members would have better liked the work and turnover might have been reduced?
6. What are reasons for restaurant employee turnover in addition to those suggested in the chapter?

FEEDBACK FROM THE REAL WORLD

Our real-world advice comes from Glen Bucello, who has served as the general manager of TGI Fridays, in Amherst, New York.

What do you think the manager did right in the case study at the beginning of the chapter to get ready for a busy Saturday night? What else could the manager have done?

This case study, like all others, provides the reader with some information—but probably not everything one would like—to carefully evaluate the situation. There may be numerous

other things that the manager did—or did not do—that would affect the success of the busy evening following the sporting event.

The manager was proactive by anticipating a significantly greater business volume and by planning for it. For example, he or she assured that all the necessary food, beverage, and supply products for the busy shift were ordered and would be available. As well, the manager alerted

(continued)

staff about the anticipated business and staffed for it by calculating the estimated guest counts and matching this with necessary production and service labor. The meeting with the chef to develop special menu items for the evening in efforts to increase check averages was also a useful tactic. Finally, work done on Friday to get ready for Saturday is a good example of the mise en place (everything in its place) that helps to reduce the work necessary during the countdown hours on Saturday leading to the evening shift.

The manager, then, did a good job in managing the products, labor hours, and activities leading up to the event. However, more could have been done. For example, he or she could have solicited feedback from the staff to assess their ideas about better ways to execute and build sales for the evening. (Perhaps some of the work done by the manager could even have been delegated to other managers!) There didn't appear to be any communication between managers, for example, as goals were established and as efforts to motivate personnel to perform to quality and quantity standards beyond a normal evening shift were implemented. This event represented a "go time," and coordinated efforts to involve and motivate all staff members could have been helpful.

The case study mirrors the way things are done in many hospitality operations. There is often more of a focus on products and procedures and less on efforts relating to human resources and teamwork, which are so critical to the success in both the short and long term.

Judging from the comments made by some departing guests, the evening was successful. I would like to have heard what the employees were saying as they ended their evening (probably a long time after the guests departed!). A successful restaurant must consistently please its guests, but also its employees and investors.

LEARN FROM THE INTERNET

1. Check out the websites for the following restaurant organizations:
   - P.F. Chang's China Bistro: www.pfchangs.com
   - Red Lobster: www.redlobster.com
   - T.G.I. Friday's: www.tgifridays.com
   - Chili's: www.chilis.com

   What features help to make each of these chain's units a casual-service restaurant according to this chapter's definition of the segment? What types of guests are likely to dine in the units? What do these restaurants seem to have in common? How are they different from other restaurant organizations that you have researched on the Internet?

2. Check out the following restaurant industry trade magazines:
   - *Nation's Restaurant News:* www.nrn.com
   - *Restaurant Business:* www.restaurantbiz.com
   - *Restaurants & Institutions:* www.rimag.com

   What are the topics of articles that appear directly relevant to casual-service restaurants?

3. Check out the home page for the National Restaurant Association (www.restaurant.org). What kind of information applicable to casual-service restaurants is noted? What products and services offered by the NRA would interest owners and managers of casual-service restaurants?

KEY HOSPITALITY TERMS

The following terms were explained in this chapter. Review the definitions of any words with which you are unfamiliar. Begin to utilize them as you expand your vocabulary as a hospitality professional.

distributor sales representatives (DSRs)	shift log
regulars	eatertainment (foodservice)
turns	take-out service (foodservice)
check average	selling
sales mix	advertising
prepreparation	suggestive selling
mise en place	menu rationalization
entrepreneur	full-line distributor
competitive edge	dram-shop laws
chain	blood alcohol concentration (BAC)
unit	payroll deduction

Family-Service Restaurants

14

International House of Pancakes

CHAPTER LEARNING OBJECTIVES

After studying this chapter you will be able to:

1. State factors that make family-service restaurants a unique segment of the restaurant industry.
2. Describe the types of guests who most frequently visit family-service restaurants.
3. Draw an organization chart for a family-service restaurant.
4. Review special procedures for buffet operations in family-service restaurants.
5. Identify current and long-term challenges that confront managers of family-service restaurants.

This chapter was authored by Lawrence E. Ross, PhD, Anne & Bill France Professor of Business and Coordinatior of Graduate Programs in Business, Department of Business and Economics, Florida Southern College, Lakeland, Florida.

FEEDBACK FROM THE REAL WORLD

Like all other restaurants, family-service operations are designed to attract specific types of guests:

- What can competitive family-service restaurants do to distinguish their property from others in this very crowded and competitive industry segment?
- How do guests determine whether they would like to dine at a restaurant in this segment rather than in another segment?

- What, if any, characteristics of effective managers are relatively unique to family-service restaurants?

  As you read this chapter, think about answers to these questions and then get feedback from the real world at the end of the chapter.

---

family-service restaurants commercial foodservice operations, such as buffets and table-service restaurants, with relatively low check averages that do not typically offer alcoholic beverages and that offer many menu items appealing to a wide variety of guests

buffet foodservices in which menu items are selected and generally portioned by guests as they pass along one or more serving counters; in some operations, items such as omelets are made to order and/or other items such as rounds of beef are carved to order

OBJECTIVE 1
State factors that make family-service restaurants a unique segment of the restaurant industry.

Many properties in every category of restaurants serve families. How, then, can one segment be referred to as **family service?** In this chapter we will discuss **buffet** and table-service operations that do not serve alcoholic beverages. Guests of all types are frequent diners at these restaurants, and employees must be fast-paced because of the large number of guests frequently served at peak business times. These properties offer many career opportunities and make up a very large and important segment of the commercial foodservice industry. These are among the reasons that this chapter will explore the world of family-service restaurants.

FAMILY SERVICE: UNIQUE COMMERCIAL DINING

Exhibit 14.1 shows alternative types of commercial foodservice operations and highlights the family-service segment on which our attention is now focused. This chart suggests that there is something special about family-service restaurants that sets them off from their counterparts in the commercial foodservices industry. It also reviews a significant component of our definition: family-service restaurants can offer buffet or table-service dining alternatives to their guests; some offer both (at least during very popular times such as weekend and midday or lunch periods).

Here are some factors that make family-service restaurants unique.

- A significant emphasis on comfort foods, rather than on themes (such as are used in many midscale restaurants)
- Child-friendly, with many high or booster chairs, several kids' menus or menu items, and (in table-service operations) premeal games and other distractions
- A special concern for food safety (particularly in self-service operations) because many of the guests are very young or elderly
- A growing need to address nutritional concerns such as for low-fat, lower-sodium, and sugar-free menu items
- Relatively fast table service compared to properties in other segments
- A relatively extensive menu with lower prices than their midscale restaurant counterparts
- **California-style menus:** these operations frequently feature breakfast, lunch, and dinner items during the entire time that the restaurant is open
- A de-emphasis on the sale of alcoholic beverages (many family-service properties do not have alcoholic beverage licenses)

California-style menu a menu in which items traditionally available for breakfast, lunch, and dinner are offered throughout the time that the property is open for business

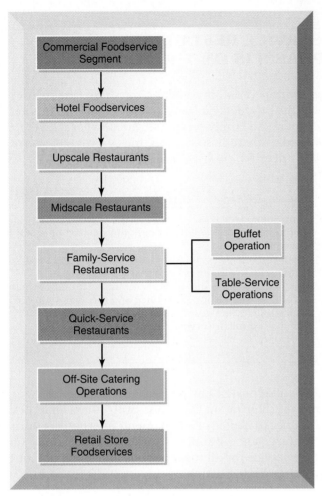

EXHIBIT 14.1
Alternative Types of Commercial Foodservice Operations

- Sit-down counter spaces: many properties provide stools at a counter, in addition to chairs at tables, to accommodate single diners
- Long hours of operation: many properties are open from early morning to late at night; some are open 24 hours daily

Buffet operations are available within most segments of the commercial foodservices industry. Properties may offer buffet service, for example, in the

Hostess in a family-service restaurant

FAMILY-SERVICE RESTAURANTS: THE EMPHASIS IS ON THE FOOD

Consumers in any type of foodservice operation are looking for value (the relationship between selling price and quality of the products and service they purchase) in their dining experience. This is especially true in the family-service segment, where the emphasis is on a relatively large variety of foods ("there is something for everyone!") served at a relatively fast pace and at a value price. By contrast, consider other segments in the commercial foodservices industry.

Segment	Products and Services Offered
Hotel foodservices	Convenience for hotel guests, special occasions for community residents, and banquets as part of group meetings
Upscale restaurants	Highest-quality gourmet food, serviceware, and service, frequently with an extensive wine list
Midscale restaurants	Unique food items in concert with the restaurant's theme, along with appropriate service and the availability of alcoholic beverages to yield a dining experience
Quick-service restaurants	Low-priced meals served in a hurry
Off-site catering operations	Food and beverages served at the client's choice of location

form of a help-yourself salad bar or, perhaps, during selected meal periods, such as Sunday brunch or on holidays. Still others may offer a Saturday night prime rib special buffet or other menu alternatives during some meal periods. By contrast, some buffet operations in the family-service segment use a buffet-style service for all meal periods and some do not even offer traditional table-service dining options!

OBJECTIVE 2
Describe the types of guests who most frequently visit family-service restaurants.

FAMILY-SERVICE RESTAURANT GUESTS

Many persons visit different types of foodservice operations at different times for different purposes. For example, travelers dine at a hotel restaurant where they are staying while on a trip and visit an upscale restaurant in their community for special occasions. They dine at a midscale property before or after a movie or shopping trip, take the family to a family-service restaurant after a sporting event or when no one wants to cook at home, and stop at a quick-service restaurant for a fast meal on the run.

Guests enjoying a salad that they portioned from a "help yourself" salad bar at a family-service restaurant

Family-service restaurants appeal to several types of guests:

Buffet serving line in a family-service restaurant

- Those who are traveling and desire menu items other than the items typically offered by quick-service restaurants. Many family-service properties are located at busy highway interchanges that allow travelers to drive only very short distances to or from major highways while on their trips.
- Families with children desiring menu items beyond those offered by quick-service restaurants and who want fast service.
- Guests who do not want alcoholic beverages and/or who prefer to dine in an alcohol-free environment.
- Persons desiring foodservices at times when few other options are available. For example, laws governing the sale of alcoholic beverages typically require that sales be curtailed at a specified time period. Most restaurants and hotel dining rooms offering alcoholic beverages close before or at these times. This provides family-service restaurants with opportunities to serve guests leaving drinking establishments.
- Elderly persons or families with elderly persons who are on a budget and/or who desire traditional (home-style) food.
- Community, civic service, and other groups who desire to have food served as part of their meeting agenda. (Many family-service operations offer a private room or a section of a public dining area that can be made semiprivate for this purpose.)

HOSPITALITY LEADER PROFILE

David Eisel, CC
Senior Development Chef
Bob Evans Farms, Inc.
(Restaurant Division)

David's team at Bob Evans Farms, Inc., consists of three chefs and a project manager. The team's responsibilities include developing new and exciting menu items, enhancing current menu items, and supporting their associates in the field.

His journey to his present position began as he worked in kitchens while attending college. "I have always loved cooking (and eating), but I just never considered pursuing a culinary profession

for my career. After graduation, I continued to work in restaurants in every capacity imaginable, and I finally decided it was time to turn my passion into a career. After considering many schools, I was pleasantly surprised to find a phenomenal culinary school in my own backyard: Columbus State Community College. I became a student in its chef apprenticeship major, which is an American Culinary Federation-affiliated program. I did my apprenticeship under Tom Corbett, CEC, at Wedgewood Golf and Country Club and, upon graduation, became a banquet chef at the club."

"In my next position, I worked for Cameron Mitchell Restaurants, first as a line cook and then

(continued)

as a sous chef. About the time my wife and I started our family, I learned about the position of corporate development chef from Carol Kizer, who was my former advisor from culinary school. I applied for the position and was accepted, and now my opportunities for advancement are unlimited. As well, I am able to see my wife and daughter much more than might have been possible if I remained in an operation's position. When I started my career, I never imagined being anything but a restaurant chef, and I even planned on having my own property someday. Now, however, my perspectives have changed."

What is your most unforgettable moment in the hospitality industry?

"There are a lot of unforgettable moments that stand out in my career. Passing my chef's certification practical on the first try, having a daily feature sell so well it made the menu, and meeting famous people are all unforgettable events. However, there is one moment that stands above them all: When you work for a single restaurant, creating a dish for a daily feature gives you almost instant gratification. When you work for a large corporate chain, you lose a lot of that connectedness with your guests. That feeling of accomplishment then gets further diluted because the timeline from a dish's inception to its final form can be a year or more. On the other hand, when your dish makes it onto the menu in 500 plus restaurants, there is a huge feeling of accomplishment. That being said, the most unforgettable moment in my career is when Knife and Fork Sandwiches made it onto the menu at Bob Evans. There is nothing quite like seeing a nationally televised commercial glorifying a product you developed!"

What are some challenges that confront your segment of the industry?

"There are quite a few challenges to working for a publicly traded, national restaurant corporation.

Food safety and food security take on a whole new dimension and are huge priorities. There is a lot that a large company can lose if there is an outbreak of food-borne illness. We also have to be very mindful of what is going on in the world around us. Outbreaks of a disease like avian flu or mad cow disease and natural disasters can seriously affect our supply chain. This makes it important for us to be able to prepare contingency plans for these possibilities. As for food safety, training is the key. We are constantly training our management and restaurant staff about proper food-handling techniques and following Hazard Analysis Critical Control Point (HAACP) and local guidelines.

What is your advice to persons considering a career in the hospitality industry?

"My advice to persons interested in a career in the culinary field is to get out and do it before you make the commitment to go to culinary school. There are plenty of entry-level jobs that will provide a sample of the joys and challenges of being in the restaurant environment. Some more advice, and this relates to my only regret, is to work for some amazing and successful people, even for free if necessary.

"I started my culinary career later in life and had familial responsibilities that prevented me from doing an internship in Europe or here in the United States. I think that I missed out on a lot of learning that you can't find in textbooks. So, make sure that cooking is what you want to do and then pursue it like an addiction for as long as you are able to do so. Then you'll find yourself with a wealth of knowledge and experience that will carry you through to the successes in your career."

OBJECTIVE 3
Draw an organization chart for a family-service restaurant.

ORGANIZATIONAL STRUCTURE OF A FAMILY-SERVICE RESTAURANT

There are some similarities and differences in the organizational charts for the buffet and table-service operations; however, most positions are similar to those utilized in other commercial foodservice operations. Exhibits 14.2 and 14.3 show, respectively, an organization chart for a buffet and a table-service operation in a typical family-service restaurant. When reviewing both figures, note that the head cook supervises prep (preparation) cooks and stewards (who are responsible for washing serviceware, pots, and pans and for cleaning kitchen and food storing areas) in both types of operations. In many

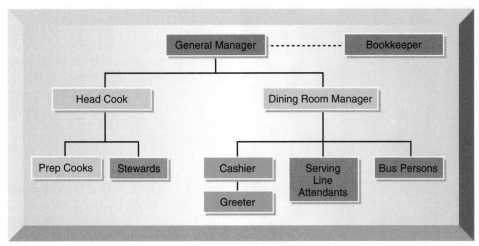

EXHIBIT 14.2
Organization Chart for a Family-Service Buffet Restaurant

family-service properties, these persons also clean floors, rest rooms, and other public areas in the property.

Staffing differences appear in front-of-house positions. In a buffet operation (Exhibit 14.2), there is typically a cashier who receives guest payments (usually at the entrance to the dining room or service area). In many buffets, guests seat themselves in an area of their preference. In others, they are taken to a table by a greeter, who may offer before-service beverages and may explain the food-serving process. (A greeter may also help guests who need assistance to move down the serving line and/or to take selected items to their dining table.) In either instance, it is the cashier who controls the speed and flow of guests to the dining room.

Serving line attendants keep busy transporting food from the food preparation area to the serving line. They are also responsible for keeping the serving counters and areas clean and tidy and for maintaining an attractive and fresh appearance for the available foods. In some buffet operations, their work is made easier by use of **pass-through** holding ovens or compartments that separate food preparation from serving areas. For example, hot food pass-throughs keep food in serving pans at the proper temperature from the time they are placed in the unit by the cook until they are picked up on the other side by the serving line attendant. Refrigerated and

pass-throughs (serving line compartments) hot, refrigerated, or room-temperature units in walls between production and service areas that allow service personnel to quickly obtain food needed to replenish serving lines

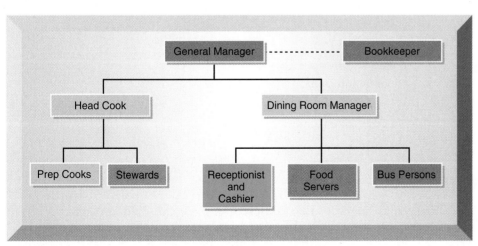

EXHIBIT 14.3
Organization Chart for a Family-Service Table-Service Operation

A bus person clears and cleans a dining room table in a family-service restaurant.

room-temperature pass-through units are also available. These pass-throughs can also be used to return empty serving counter pans to production areas. This helps to maximize the time that buffet counter personnel are in the public serving areas where they can provide ongoing guest service.

Exhibit 14.3 illustrates a typical organization chart for a family-service property with a table-service operation. Note that it is a simplified version of that used by an upscale or midscale restaurant. Since, these properties do not typically offer alcoholic beverages, work responsibilities are spread more simply between food preparation, food service, and cleanup. This streamlined organization is important to promote the speed of service, which is a reason that many guests select this type of foodservice alternative.

The organization charts just reviewed show no differences in food preparation but, rather, only in dining room positions. What happens when a family-service restaurant offers both

IF IT'S THE FOOD, IT MUST BE THE MENU!

Many table-service operations in the family-service segment offer a large variety of menu items. For example, numerous alternatives may be offered on menus in categories such as these:

Pancakes	Fresh fruit
French toast	Hamburgers
Waffles	Salads
Healthy-choice breakfasts	Other sandwiches
Eggs	Appetizers
Omelets	Specialty sandwiches
Local dishes	Soups and chilis
Side orders	Entrees
Children's items	Combination entrees
Homemade breads	Desserts
Beverages	

Lighter portions (lunches and dinners for health-conscious guests)

This list of menu item categories suggests that almost everyone can find preferred items. This is even more certain when one considers that family-service restaurants may offer a total of 200 or more different items within the above categories. Recall also that these items may be available in many properties 24 hours per day!

Server checks the temperature of a salad bar in a family-service restaurant

table-service and buffet alternatives for guests? Generally, the dining room organization will be similar to that pictured in Exhibit 14.3. A staff member with food preparation responsibilities typically resupplies and maintains the buffet serving line.

BUFFET SERVICES: SPECIAL OPERATING PROCEDURES[1]

> **OBJECTIVE 4**
> Review special procedures for buffet operations in family-service restaurants.

Managers of family-service restaurants offering buffet (self-service) alternatives have a unique challenge: how to control food costs when guests decide portion size. The reasons that many guests enjoy self-service features include the following:

- *Flexibility.* They can select the items and the amount of each item that they desire to eat.
- *Value.* Guests believe they receive a bargain when, regardless of how much they take, the price is the same.
- *Unlimited food.* All items displayed are available for guest selection and appear to be available in limitless amounts.
- *Speed and convenience.* There is no production waiting period as occurs when guests place orders with servers.

Managers, in turn, must successfully manage service labor and food costs when there is the potential for a larger numbers of guests. (The ability to serve many people quickly and efficiently can be an operating plus.) If quality can be retained, food can be prepared in larger volumes and an effective balance between dining and production systems can help to manage what otherwise might be more complicated and costly processes.

---

[1]This section is adapted from Simon Liu and Jack Ninemeier, "Managing Food Costs: Guidelines to Reduce Waste." *Michigan Restaurateur,* July/August, 1999.

A cook prepares pizza at a family pizzeria.

production schedule a management tool that indicates the quantity of each menu item needed, the amount, if any, available and the quantity to be produced

What about food waste? Managers in buffet operations must control potential waste, and the task begins before food is even produced. For example, technology can help to effectively forecast sales (number of guests), which, in turn, helps managers to purchase the proper quantity of products. This same sales forecast can also be used to plan the production of the appropriate quantities of each menu item. A **production schedule** predicts the sales mix and indicates the quantity of each item needed based on forecasted sales. It also notes the amount of each item, if any, available and then specifies the quantity to be produced. A production schedule may also include references to standardized recipes, personnel assignments, time standards, and other factors that can help to control food costs. Finally, it may also be useful in preplanning for the cross-utilization of any leftovers.

A proper management philosophy is also important. Managers must understand that food waste reduces profits and, thus, the more waste, the higher the food costs. Managers cannot just assume that this is a historical problem with no solution. They can also "learn from the garbage can." Managers in all segments of the industry, including family service, must fully understand guest preferences. Offering items that guests do not like just because it is buffet service makes no sense in efforts to reduce food costs.

Managers must also assure that menu analysis is continuous. They must

- Keep track of the variety and volume of items produced, transferred to the buffet, and left over at the end of the meal period.
- Assure that the menu is flexible. Some items, for example, should not be offered when market prices increase beyond a previously determined amount.
- Consider ways to utilize leftovers if quality (including sanitation) concerns can be addressed.

Managers can also implement food preparation and service tactics. For example, they can utilize standard recipes and be concerned about portion control. (Some items might be preportioned into casserole dishes or plates of a specified size. Chicken can be cut into quarters rather than halves.) Food tactics include replenishing buffet lines with less food more frequently. (Guests will perceive that the food being brought from the kitchen is fresher and, if this is not done, guests may subconsciously equate a large volume of food with "limitless" amounts.) Managers can also use the correct serving utensils at the right places (a ladle that is too large makes it easy for guests to take too much), and the correct size of serviceware is also required. (Plates, for example, that are larger than necessary may suggest to guests that they should take more food than they desire.)

CHALLENGES CONFRONTING FAMILY-SERVICE RESTAURANT MANAGERS

Restaurants in this segment are confronted by many of the same challenges as are other properties, including difficulties in attracting and retaining labor and competition from other properties attempting to attract the same market of diners. However, several other issues, discussed next, require constant attention from managers of family-service properties.

Providing Menu Items of Acceptable Quality at the Lowest Price

Diners in this market are very value conscious. They are attracted to family-service restaurants because of food quality and menu prices and, therefore, guest charges must be kept as low as possible and food quality and quantity must be as high as possible. The need to plan menus that can be offered in a very price competitive marketplace and the need to purchase the proper quality of food items to allow competitive pricing are ongoing concerns. In the case of buffets, this challenge is increased because of the "all you can eat" emphasis. (Some operations phrase this in a more conservative way: "All you care to eat.")

Operating with Few Staff over Long Hours of Operation

Table-service family-service properties are typically open 24 hours a day or, at least, from early morning until late at night. The need to keep staff members "on the clock" during slow service times makes it more difficult to address minimal cost concerns. Family-service restaurants address this **peaks and valleys** issue by paying careful attention to menu planning. A process of **menu rationalization** is used so that relatively few primary ingredients are required for a relatively large number of menu items. For example, ground beef can be used for numerous entrees in a family-service restaurant. Also, recipes utilizing only basic food preparation procedures permit food production with the minimum amount of food preparation labor. The use of convenience food items meeting the property´s quality requirements can also help to maximize the use of available labor. Service personnel benefit from **cross-training** so that the responsibilities of otherwise separate positions can be combined. In this manner, for example, one or only a few staff members can perform receptionist, food server, bus person, and cashier responsibilities.

peaks and valleys (business volume) fluctuating guest counts and revenue volumes; the peaks are business surges, and the valleys are slow business times

menu rationalization an approach used to maximize the number of menu items that can be prepared using relatively few primary ingredients

cross-training a technique of training persons for more than one position so that they can assist wherever they are needed

Families own some family-service restaurants.

Order counter in the kitchen at a family-service restaurant

Maintaining Appropriate Food Quality During Extended Hours of Operation

Food quality is an important component in the decision to visit a family-service restaurant. Quality concerns are addressed at the time that menus are planned. Many items can be made to order; others are prepared in small batches. Adequate equipment to hold items that must be prepared in larger quantities (soups and sauces, for example) must be available. Microwaves that can quickly heat, broilers that can quickly melt, and other equipment that can quickly finish menu items are typically available. Another technique, partial cooking and then holding at refrigerated temperatures until heating for service, is sometimes appropriate.

SUMMARY OF CHAPTER LEARNING OBJECTIVES

1. **State factors that make family-service restaurants a unique segment of the restaurant industry.**

   Factors include a significant emphasis on nutritional comfort foods, a child-friendly dining environment, food safety, relatively fast table service, and a relatively extensive menu with lower prices than in midscale restaurants. Some properties offer buffet service only.

2. **Describe the types of guests who most frequently visit family-service restaurants.**

   The types of guests most likely to visit these properties are travelers who desire menu items other than those offered by quick-service properties. Other markets include families with

children, guests who do not desire alcoholic beverages, persons desiring food services when few other options are available, elderly persons and families on a budget, and community, civic service, and other groups desiring food as part of their meeting agenda.

3. **Draw an organization chart for a family-service restaurant.**

   Organization charts for family-service properties offering table-service dining are basically similar to those in the midscale segment; however, no alcoholic beverage-related positions are needed. For example, a general manager may supervise a head cook (who is responsible for food preparation and kitchen-related

FEEDBACK FROM THE REAL WORLD

Our real-world advice comes from James Kolodynski, Owner, Big Boy Campus Corners, Rochester, Michigan.

What can competitive family-service restaurants do to distinguish their property from others in this very crowded and competitive industry segment?

Many of the basics of marketing and operations that apply to all restaurants (in fact, probably to all businesses) apply to units in the family-service segment. However, let me note three factors that are of special concern. First, one must keep the facility up to date and well maintained. Guests do not evaluate their experience and choose to become regular or repeat guests strictly on the basis of the food. The environment within which they consume their meal is also important. It must be clean and attractive; it must be bright and cheery. It must look like it welcomes the visitors.

Our guests are very concerned about value when they visit our property. They desire to receive, and should receive, a dining experience that is well worth what they must pay for it. Our guests will pay a little more to receive the quality they desire and, for them, this is a better alternative than to shop for the least expensive dining experience.

Our guests enjoy a menu that is fresh: a nice variety of comfort foods, new items, and comfort foods prepared and served in new ways. Our ingredients must be of the right quality; they will never be better than when they are received at our backdoor. We do offer specials, but we also recognize that the relatively wide variety of items available on our menus every day already provides something for everyone.

How do guests determine whether they would like to dine at a restaurant in this segment rather than in another segment?

I suggested some very important factors in the guest decision to visit our property in the response above: our guests judge us and our competitors on the basis of the total experience they receive from us. It is a very important and ongoing challenge to provide the food and service quality, along with cleanliness and atmosphere, that are integral to whether we get a chance to show guests what we can do. Then, when they are with us, we must deliver to the standards that our guests expect. This is important to win over a base of loyal and repeat guests who help to form the foundation for our success.

Another point: In a multiunit organization, every restaurant must do its fair share. Guests form a stereotype of our entire organization based on, for example, their visit to just one of our units. Our guests may think, "I remember the great meal we had at the Elias Brothers/Big Boy restaurant in one location; I bet it's great in another location as well." Unfortunately, the reverse is also true. If an experience in one unit is less than ideal, this can negatively influence the dining out decision on another occasion.

What, if any, characteristics of effective managers are relatively unique to family-service restaurants?

Many of the attributes of successful management are relevant to managers in other segments of the restaurant industry (and, in fact, to the hospitality industry as a whole and, no doubt, to other businesses as well). However, I think managers in our segment must meet and get to know their guests more personally than may be necessary or possible in other segments. It is not just a coincidence that some persons call our segment family-service restaurants. We do appeal to families and, once there, our guests must be treated like members of our family. The phrase "meet and greet" as a duty of hospitality personnel may be overstated and overutilized in subsegments of the industry. It does, however, exemplify what we must consistently do. When our managers are on the floor meeting our guests with a genuine welcome, they appreciate this. At the same time, our managers provide a role model for employees in our properties. They know that staff members are an integral part of the restaurant family.

cleanup duties), and a dining room manager is responsible for front-of-house positions. In a buffet operation, food production positions are the same; however, a dining room manager will supervise a cashier and greeter, serving line attendants, and bus persons.

4. **Review special procedures for buffet operations in family-service restaurants.**
   Managers must control service labor and food costs. They must have the attitude that costs can be controlled, must portion and make available foods in the correct quantities, and must provide the appropriate-sized serving utensils for guests. They must also accurately forecast guest counts, analyze food consumption patterns, and effectively analyze their

menus. Effective managers use technology to forecast and schedule purchasing and production to reduce food waste and to improve food quality.

5. **Identify current and long-term challenges that confront managers of family-service restaurants.**
   Challenges include those applicable to other segments (attracting and retaining labor and market competition) and several additional challenges: providing menu items of acceptable quality at the very lowest price, operating with few staff over long hours of operation, and maintaining appropriate food quality during extended hours of operation.

MASTERING YOUR KNOWLEDGE

Discuss the following questions.

1. How do you decide if you want to visit a family-service restaurant or, alternatively, dine in or take out from a quick-service property?
2. How important is the food, rather than the service and atmosphere, to the success of a family-service restaurant?
3. If you were the manager of a family-service restaurant featuring only buffet service, how would you differentiate your property from others in this segment that have table-service dining?
4. If you manage a family-service restaurant with a buffet, what are practical tactics you could utilize to reduce food costs?
5. What are examples of ways you could produce a wide variety of menu items with only limited production labor?

LEARN FROM THE INTERNET

1. Check out the websites for the following family-service restaurants:
   - Domino's Pizza: www.dominos.com
   - Denny's: www.dennys.com
   - International House of Pancakes: www.ihop. com

   What do their marketing messages have in common? How do they attempt to differentiate themselves from their competition?

2. Check out the following websites for organizations that feature buffet restaurants:
   - Old Country Buffet: www.buffet.com
   - Town and Country Buffet Restaurants: www.townandcountrybuffet.com
   - Furrs Family Dining: www.furrs.net

What kinds of guests do they seem to be trying to reach? How do they promote their menu? Is it a good idea to post daily menus on their websites? (Why or why not?) How do they differentiate their business from others that compete for the same guest base?

3. Check out the websites of several other family-service properties:
   - Big Boy Restaurants: www.bigboy.com
   - Perkins Restaurant and Bakery: www.perkinsrestaurants.com
   - Waffle House: www.wafflehouse.com

What kinds of information do they provide about the variety of menu items offered? How, if at all, do they compare their menu and menu items with those that a family might consume at home?

KEY HOSPITALITY TERMS

The following terms were explained in this chapter. Review the definitions of any words with which you are unfamiliar. Begin to utilize them as you expand your vocabulary as a hospitality professional.

family-service restaurants

buffet

California-style menu

pass-through (serving line compartments)

production schedule

peaks and valleys (business volume)

menu rationalization

cross-training

15 Quick-Service Restaurants

Exterior of a quick-service restaurant in Moscow

CHAPTER LEARNING OBJECTIVES

After studying this chapter you will be able to:

1. Describe the types of guests who visit quick-service restaurants (QSRs).
2. Review the organization of quick-service restaurants.
3. Provide information about career opportunities in quick-service restaurants.
4. Explain day-to-day operating issues of concern to quick-service restaurant managers.
5. Discuss basic challenges confronting the quick-service restaurant segment.

This chapter was co-authored by Theda Rudd, Visiting Instructor, The School of Hospitality Business, Michigan State University, East Lansing, Michigan, who has owned eight McDonald's Restaurants in the mid-Michigan area, and Robert Ross, Vice-President, Ross and Associates, who has owned a McDonald's Franchise in Grand Rapids, Michigan.

FEEDBACK FROM THE REAL WORLD

Many college students are experts on the topic of quick-service restaurants because they know a great deal about this segment of the hospitality industry from the perspective of the consumer. When parents ask, "Where do you want to eat?" many young children answer "McDonald's" or "Wendy's" or "Burger King," or they name a similar fast-food restaurant. This enthusiasm traditionally continues as persons grow older and, at any point in time, one is likely to find families, college students, senior citizens, and just about everyone in between in line at the service counter of the local quick-service property.

- Why do quick-service restaurants appeal to young children (who frequently encourage their parents to take them there)?

- What are common examples of operating details (frequently measured in pennies) that affect the profitability of a quick-service restaurant?
- What are some of the economics that frequently provide incentives for quick-service restaurant franchisees to operate a number of units?
- What are the most prevalent day to day operating concerns that confront unit managers of quick-service restaurants?

As you read this chapter, think about the answers to these questions and then get feedback from the real world at the end of the chapter.

WHO VISITS QSRs?

Quick-service restaurants (QSRs; frequently called fast-food restaurants) are a phenomenon of U.S. business and culture. These properties typically have relatively limited menus featuring food items that can be quickly prepared or processed. (The segment frequently refers to a single unit as a *site, location, operation, restaurant*, and, even more commonly, a *store*.)

As you have learned, it is difficult to describe a market of guests who visit any type of restaurant. Many consumers will, in the same week, visit an upscale restaurant for a celebration or business meeting, a midscale restaurant for a night out with friends, a family-service restaurant property for a weekend meal with relatives, and a quick-service property when they are in a hurry. QSRs market to persons that are in a hurry and to those who are cost conscious. They are, then, focusing on guests who are time- and/or money- (value-) driven. Many guests also enjoy the foods available and make these properties their dining-out priority.

Like their counterparts dining in properties in other segments of the restaurant industry, persons visiting QSRs are concerned about value. In the case of QSRs, guests have expectations about speed of service, cleanliness, quality, and costs that must be consistently addressed. The extent to which expectations are met influences their selection of a property when future quick-service meal decisions are made.

QSRs know who their actual and potential customers are, and they are very aggressive in creating and sending advertising messages to them. Young children, for example, want to be entertained while they are eating and enjoy playground-type equipment at the restaurant, along with toys or prizes they can take home. Senior citizens enjoy quiet and inexpensive dining options, which they often receive during **day-parts** that are less busy and when discounts are offered.

OBJECTIVE 1
Describe the types of guests who visit quick-service restaurants (QSRs).

quick-service restaurant (QSR) an operation that provides a limited menu and limited service (generally self-serve at counters or through vehicle drive-throughs) at low prices; also called *limited menu* or *fast-food restaurant*

day-part a segment of the day that represents a change in menu and customer response patterns (for example, time during which breakfast and other menus are offered)

EXHIBIT 15.1
Who Visits Quick-Service
Restaurants?

Who visits quick-service restaurants? The easy answer to this question is "lots of people for lots of reasons." However, let's answer this question in more detail:

Market	Reasons (Factors)
1. Senior citizens	To relax and pass the time To meet friends Because costs are reasonable Because products and beverages are tasty Because of senior discounts
2. Families with children	Children like the toys and/or other diversions and may be better behaved while eating Short wait for the food Reasonable costs Good food and beverage products Playgrounds are often available; children may play while adults rest or eat
3. People on the go	Drive-through service Fast in and out service Convenient Eat out without having to dress up
4. Single and young people	Cost and value Socialize with friends Casual wear
5. Tour groups	Cost Fast Room for everyone (no reservations) Brands are familiar to persons nationwide

CHECK IT OUT!

Many quick-service restaurants are revising menus and adding items that are targeted to health-conscious consumers. As well, new fresh-food chains now offer low-carb, vegetarian, all-natural, and organic food selections.

Want to learn more about this niche in the marketplace? If so, check out the following:

- Blendz (www.blendz.com). Smoothies and fresh-squeezed juices, soups, made-to-order salads, and panini sandwiches.
- Energy Kitchen (www.energykitchen.com). High-protein, low-fat dishes prepared by grilling, baking, or steaming.
- Just Fresh (www.justfresh.com). Bakery items, made-to-order salads, wraps, and sandwiches.
- O'Naturals (www.onaturals.com). All-natural, organic, and vegetarian items.
- The Original Soup Man (www.originalsoupman.com). Health-conscious soups.
- Salad Works (www.saladworks.com). Made-to-order salads and wraps, sandwiches, and soups.

OBJECTIVE 2
Review the organization of quick-service restaurants.

franchisees those who own (or lease) the property and building and buy the right to use the brand name for a fixed period of time and at an agreed-on price; they often pay royalties and contribute to regional and/or national advertising programs

Exhibit 15.1 reviews several markets that are attracted to quick-service restaurants and indicates reasons or factors for their popularity.

ORGANIZATION CHARTS FOR QSRs

Most QSRs are multiunit businesses owned by **franchisees.** Exhibit 15.2 illustrates the possible structure of three different organizations:

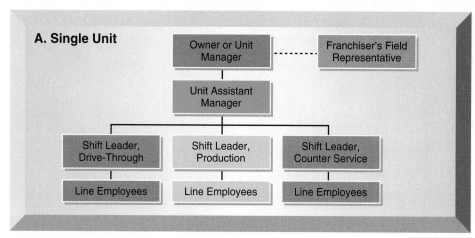

EXHIBIT 15.2A
Organization of Quick-Service Restaurants

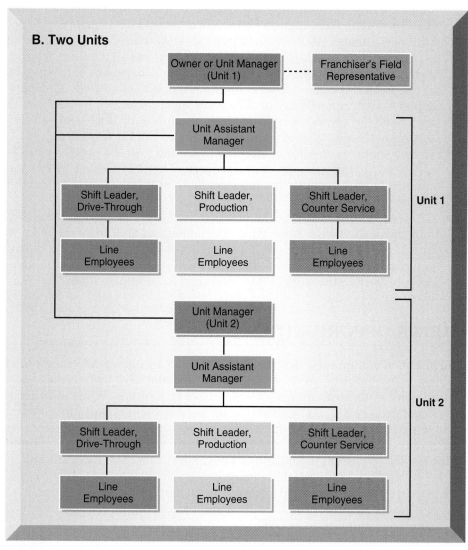

EXHIBIT 15.2B
continued

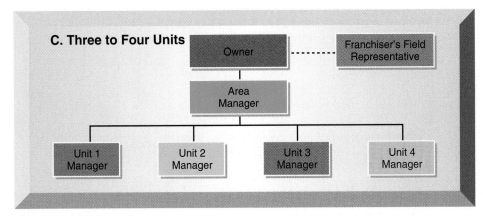

EXHIBIT 15.2C
continued

shift leader a person serving as a supervisor for specific departmentalized activities, such as drive-through, production, and counter service, during a specific work shift

franchiser those who manage the brand and sell the right to use the brand name

- A: Single unit. In the smallest type of QSR organization, an owner often serves as the unit manager and supervises the work of **shift leaders** responsible for drive-through, production, and counter service tasks (Exhibit 15.2A). A distinguishing feature of most QSRs is that they do not have one manager (such as a chef or head cook) who is responsible for all activities within a department (such as the kitchen) all the time. Instead, a shift leader is responsible for tasks within a department only when he or she is on duty. The overall coordination of all activities in all departments is the responsibility of the owner (unit manager). As depicted in the chart, the owner or unit manager receives staff (technical or advisory) assistance as needed from a representative of the **franchiser.**
- B: Two units. As the owner acquires a second unit, he or she typically serves as the unit manager of one property (Unit 1 in Exhibit 15.2B) and employs a unit manager for the remaining property (Unit 2 in Exhibit 15.2B).
- C: Three to four units. As the organization grows to three or, possibly, four units, the owner most typically employs an area manager who, in turn, supervises managers of individual units (Exhibit 15.2C). As the organization grows still larger, the owner will retain additional area managers to oversee the work of unit managers in additional units.

OBJECTIVE 3
Provide information about career opportunities in quick-service restaurants.

CAREER OPPORTUNITIES

Quick-service restaurants, like their counterparts in almost all segments of the hospitality industry, are labor intensive. Unfortunately, there is also a significant level of turnover in many quick-service restaurants. While this causes significant problems, it also provides faster advancement opportunities for individuals desiring a career in this segment. Exhibit 15.3 shows a possible career progression for a high-energy and relatively quick learner in a multiunit quick-service restaurant organization. Let's look at this chart more closely.

- An entry-level employee working in an applicable position for 3 to 6 months may be promoted to a shift leader upon demonstration of mastery in applicable job skills.
- A shift leader working in this position for 4 to 6 months may become very proficient in his or her responsibilities, especially as they apply to labor control and service delivery. This can yield a promotion to unit assistant manager.

HOW IMPORTANT IS DRIVE-THROUGH BUSINESS?

Drive-through business for a QSR is very important! In many units, the business generated from drive-through operations can approximate 50 to 70 percent of total business volume. Properties on highway or interstate locations may generate 80 percent of their business from a drive-through. QSR managers recognize that drive-throughs are, in effect, a "store within a store" and frequently plan labor and food production needs separately for this revenue source.

Unit locations are selected (or passed over) based on drive-through concerns. Buildings in older locations are remodeled (or closed) to accommodate drive-through traffic flows. Property design and layout ranging from exterior signage to location of drive-through windows to the actual kitchen and service window work-station layouts reflect this emphasis on drive-through business.

- Unit assistant managers must have experience in all positions. After shift leaders become proficient in their position, they must then gain the necessary experience to enable them to oversee multiple job functions. Promotion to unit assistant manager occurs when they can effectively train and supervise employees and when they can manage day to day operations.
- Unit managers must demonstrate their skills in managing employees in all positions and be able to achieve short- and long-term goals while planning and executing a profitable operation.
- High-performing unit managers may work in that position in one or more properties within the organization. Normally, a person who makes significant contributions to the organization may be eligible for promotion to area manager.

What's next? It is sometimes possible for a person to assume complete or partial ownership in a quick-service restaurant organization. (In some organizations, even entry-level employees may assume some ownership through a **stock purchase plan** or other equity plans.) If partial ownership within the organization is not a possibility, some directors of operations move into corporate-level positions with the franchiser, where their progression up the career ladder can continue.

stock purchase plan an employee benefit that provides low- or no-cost partial ownership (stock) in an organization as an incentive for successful and continuing performance

Subway in the food court at the University of California at San Diego (Subway has approximately 26,000 units in more than 80 countries around the world.)

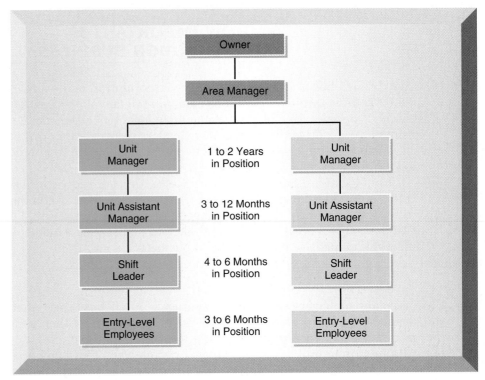

EXHIBIT 15.3
Possible Career Progression in Quick-Service Restaurants

MOVING UP THE ORGANIZATION

The layering of management responsibilities in even relatively small quick-service restaurant organizations provides opportunities for promotion to positions of progressively more responsibilities with applicable compensation increases. In the world of quick-service restaurants, there are numerous examples of high-level managers at the franchiser level who began as an entry-level (line) employee and, because of satisfactory performance, quickly advanced through the organization. In many organizations, students can advance to a shift leader (or even higher) position while still in high school.

Interior of a quick-service restaurant

DAY-TO-DAY OPERATING CONCERNS

Assume that you are the owner or manager of a quick-service restaurant. What types of day to day operating issues would be of concern as you manage your business? Seasoned QSR managers quickly identify and deal with several important issues.

A Pizza Hut restaurant in a Marriott Hotel lobby

Consistency of Product

Persons unfamiliar with the business may be surprised that product consistency is a major operating concern. Aren't all ingredients purchased according to the most exacting **purchase specifications** developed by the franchiser? Aren't standard recipes available to identify exactly how items should be produced? Aren't production staff trained in preparation procedures? The answers to each of these and related questions is typically "yes".

> **OBJECTIVE 4**
> Explain day-to-day operating issues of concern to quick-service restaurant managers.

purchase specification a statement (definition) of the quality requirements to be met by purchased products

Franchiser-mandated standards are high, as they should be. Remember, for example, this textbook's definition of quality: the consistent delivery of products and services according to expected standards. If tens of thousands of guests visit a quick-service restaurant within a single month, what is the likelihood that each guest will be satisfied on every visit he or she makes? Most, of course, will be. Some, however, will not be. Reasons range from an inability to meet a quality standard for one product on one day to the unreasonable expectations of some guests. The goal of consistently pleasing every guest all the time is admirable. Unfortunately, in real life, one can move toward it (reduce operating defects), but probably never attain it.

There is another relevant dimension to consistency: the need to produce products and services that are "seamless" between properties. The old advertising message of "the best surprise is often no surprise!" applies here. As persons visit the same brand of quick-service restaurant in different locations, they generally expect the same quality and quantity of products and services, which represent a consistent value at each property. If it is difficult to maintain consistency within an operation (and it is!), it is even more challenging to attain consistency among operations, especially when they are owned or managed by different organizations and/or are located in widely diverse geographic areas.

Drive-through window of a quick-service restaurant

HOSPITALITY LEADER PROFILE

Laurie Oxender
Corporate Operations
McDonald's
East Lansing, Michigan

She Survived the Beanie Baby Craze!

Laurie has completed formal college courses and numerous McDonald's training classes, including "Hamburger University." She has been employed with the McDonald's system for 23 years by a private owner–operator and, for the last 3 years, by McDonald's Corporation.

Laurie notes several most memorable moments in her career. Here are some highlights:

- "My promotion to restaurant manager. The first day I walked into *my restaurant* I felt many emotions at the same time (scared, nervous, excited, and anxious), but I tried not to let anybody else notice any of them!"
- "When I received an award for Outstanding Restaurant Manager for the first time with my owner–operator and then twice again with the company itself."
- "The Beanie Baby craze. Who would have thought that a little bean-bag toy (giraffe, monkey, and flamingo, for example) would cause such a stir? It was actually fun to go to work just because the customers were so funny. It was unbelievable; traffic jams at 6 A.M. in the drive-through just to get a toy! Answering machines attached to phone lines with recorded messages asking which Beanie Baby toy was currently available. (We actually couldn't use our phones!) TV and radio stations interviewing our customers. Patrons were clapping as we delivered flamingo beanie toys as we walked through the dining area (and hopefully we made it back to the storeroom to get more toys!)."

Challenges confronting the quick-service restaurant industry are numerous. Laurie notes the need to "stay competitive and focus on what the customer wants so that we can deliver it to them. Our customers have so many restaurants to choose from, and we want to be their restaurant of choice. We try to address the needs of everyone: we have happy meals for the children with great marketing tie-ins. The value meal selections are great meals at value prices with different sizes for different appetites. We have nutritional information available and on display for those who desire it, and our new products help to keep the menu fresh."

Laurie really enjoys training high-school employees and finds it extremely rewarding, for example, to have trained and developed a 16-year-old into a very successful restaurant manager. "I guess as I reflect back on my career I would have liked a position in McDonald's regional training development office. That's what I enjoy about the hospitality business: you have so many different avenues you can pursue, including human resources, operations, field service, and marketing, just to name a few."

Laurie's advice to persons thinking about a career in the hospitality industry: "Always stay open to new ideas because the restaurant business is always on the move. You have to be ready and on top of your game. You really need to be a committed leader if you want to be successful. Remember that the shadow you cast will be a model for others."

Food and Paper Costs

Management control of food and paper costs at the unit level is essential to profitability. The franchiser's operating system, including staffing guidelines, equipment requirements, and production systems, must be applied with shift to shift consistency to effectively manage food and paper costs. Delivering a quality product with minimal waste is the responsibility of every line employee, shift leader, and assistant manager. Profitability involves managing the pennies while producing a consistent, quality product at a level relative to the selling cost. At the same time, procedures for holding, packaging, and serving items must meet the franchiser's standards.

CO-BRANDING: AN INCREASINGLY POPULAR ALTERNATIVE

Co-branding is becoming more popular in the quick-service segment. This is an arrangement in which, for example, two or more franchisees of different organizations share common costs, such as building, dining areas, and a parking lot for a stand-alone building. Perhaps a pizza franchise operates alongside a chicken franchise, or a coffee franchise and a doughnut franchise operate in the same facility. Often the co-branded property offers a limited ("express") version of each franchise's menu. Frequently, there is a common order counter; guests can order any item from any menu at the same time. Sometimes, items from different menus must be ordered at different counters. In addition to helping the franchise owners to save capital and operating costs, this quick-service operation also benefits guests who need not go to two different operations in different locations to purchase "something for everyone."

There are variations of the co-branding strategy. For example, food courts in shopping malls and transportation centers (air terminals and highway rest areas) may feature several or more quick-service and other brands competing for guests. In this arrangement, rental charges, including a percentage of revenue, are paid to the facility's owner, rather than common costs being borne by the franchisee.

Controlling the waste of both raw food products (for example, ensuring that incoming and stored food is held under the proper conditions and is processed by the **use-by date**) and finished food products (for example, producing at a rate in line with sales to reduce waste) is required. Even seemingly insignificant activities such as the overuse of portion-control condiment packets, excessive rates of straw or napkin usage, dropped food products, and the improper use of packaging can affect unit profitability in an industry where the profit margin is often measured in cents per sale.

co-branding an arrangement in which two or more franchisees of different organizations share common costs, such as building, dining areas, and a parking lot for a stand-alone building

use-by date date (time) by which either a food product must be removed from inventory and be produced or sold or, alternatively, discarded

staffing grid a matrix that helps managers to plan allowable labor hours for specified positions based on estimated revenues to be generated during hours of operation

Labor Costs

Quick-service properties generate very low check averages compared to their counterparts in other segments of the commercial foodservice industry. At the same time, they are very labor intensive. For example, at least two persons (a production and a counter service person) are directly involved in the sale of almost every item. While managers have some ability to control or reduce food costs (for example, they can manage to reduce product waste and theft), their most significant contribution to profitability generally is derived from their ability to manage labor costs.

Attention to pennies (if not fractions of pennies!) is an integral part of the way quick-service restaurants are managed. To do this, many quick-service restaurant managers utilize a **staffing grid.** A sample staffing grid is shown in Exhibit 15.4. When reviewing this grid, note that staffing information is presented for three positions (drive-through attendant, front-counter attendant, and production worker). The grid

Guests at a quick-service restaurant

EXHIBIT 15.4
Sample Staffing Grid for a
Quick-Service Restaurant

Position	\$100	\$200	\$300	\$400	\$500	\$600	\$700	\$800	\$900
Estimated Hourly Revenue									
Maximum Allowable Labor Hours[a, b]									
Drive-through attendant[c]	1	2	2	3	3	3	3	4	4
Front-counter attendant[d]	2	2	3	4	4	5	5	6	6
Production worker	3	3	4	4	5	5	6	6	7

[a]Time spent by shift leaders is **included** in maximum allowable hours.
[b]Allowable hours are for illustrative purposes only and may not be indicative of revenue and staffing ratios in actual QSR operations. Other appropriate methods to plan and control labor costs include utilizing the factors of transaction counts per hour or sales per labor hour.
[c]When more than two drive-through attendants are working, other employees in this position are runners to bring food to the pickup window(s).
[d]In some operations, only one or two cash register operators are used; other employees bring food to the service counter.

does not reflect additional hours needed for training, custodial, or administrative duties; these are normally scheduled without regard for hourly sales levels. The range of estimated hourly revenue likely for the property (\$100 or less during a slow hour; \$900 or more during a rush hour) is listed along the top of the staffing grid. The maximum allowable hours for each position based on the estimated revenue for that hour are given. For example, if \$300 in revenues is forecasted for a specific hour, two drive-through attendants and three front-counter attendants along with four production workers can be scheduled. The grid shows the *maximum* allowable hours. Creative and effective unit managers and shift leaders may be able to meet quality and quantity standards with fewer labor hours, especially if they have a highly productive and motivated staff. To do this requires managers to coach their staff in quality and procedural standards and to establish expectations by the way they manage the operation.

economy of scale the concept that productivity per unit of input can increase as the volume of output increases

A review of Exhibit 15.4 illustrates an important concept: **economy of scale.** For example, when \$200 of revenues is estimated, three hours of production worker labor are needed. By contrast, when the amount of estimated hourly revenue increases to \$400 (twice the revenue volume), only four hours of production labor are needed. The input (number of labor hours) rises by one; it does not double when the output (revenue volume) doubles.

Unit managers typically use a staffing grid in the following manner:

Step 1: Revenues for each hour of operation are determined. Typically, revenue records are maintained on a by-hour basis for several previous weeks. A revenue history is generated and adjusted to yield estimated revenue for the time period covered by the staffing grid.

Step 2: The estimated hourly revenues from step 1 are compared to the grid.

Step 3: The grid indicates the maximum allowable number of labor hours that can be scheduled for each hour of operation based on revenue estimates.

Step 4: The unit manager determines allowable hours for the entire day and uses this information to develop employee schedules.

WHAT ABOUT TRAINEE HOURS?

Assume that the unit manager uses the staffing grid and notes that three production workers are required for a specific hour for which the schedule is being developed. Assume also that a new production worker must be trained. Does the manager schedule two experienced production workers and one trainee or three production workers and one trainee?

The staffing grid typically assumes that all employees on the grid are experienced and that the specified number of staff members (labor hours) is required to yield the necessary quality of output (products and services) based on the estimated volume of business during the hour.

What should the manager do? If two experienced employees and one trainee are scheduled, won't the two experienced employees need to do the work of three staff members and, at the same time, train a new person? If the staffing grid is effectively developed, quality standards will likely suffer. If, instead, the manager schedules three experienced staff members and the trainee, labor costs for that position will be excessive. However, the budgets of quick-service restaurants rarely include allocated training dollars for employees on the clock during training.

Sometimes a compromise can resolve the manager's dilemma. The trainee can be taught to correctly perform one or just a few tasks and can do this work during times of peak business volume. Then, as business slows, the trainee can learn additional tasks to eventually become proficient in his or her job.

DID YOU KNOW?

Numerous innovations are likely to transform quick-service restaurants. Some affect the way we order foods. For example, self-service kiosks will allow guests to order food and beverage products and pay with a credit or debit card. Others may bring fast-food products to us. For example, mobile restaurant units are now available to fast-food franchisees. Want nutritional information? At least one company is putting this information on its food boxes and wrappers. In some properties, drive-through order taking is outsourced to call centers hundreds of miles (or farther) away from the unit.

CHALLENGES! CHALLENGES!

OBJECTIVE 5
Discuss basic challenges confronting the quick-service restaurant segment.

Experts in quick-service restaurant management are quick to point out several challenges that confront this segment today and will likely be of concern tomorrow. Let's look at these next.

Labor

Managers have the never-ending task of recruiting and retaining entry-level employees. Some reasons are obvious, including these:

- A primary labor market is young persons (for example, high school, post-secondary students, and others who are just entering the labor force who are not seeking long-term employment). Another important labor market is **empty nesters** and senior citizens. At the other end of the age scale, older persons may seek employment for very short time periods to supplement their income.

empty nesters middle-aged persons whose children are grown and have left their parents' home

Deep fryer operation in a quick-service restaurant

- QSR managers must select staff members who are a fit for the job. The pace of the operations and the emphasis on quality service and product complicate the labor issue. Training, motivating, and rewarding employees are key factors in achieving consistent quality after the right people have been hired.

- In competitive labor markets, the idea that QSRs employ minimum-wage staff is a myth. Many managers have found that paying more to hire and to retain a more productive work force is worth the investment. Managers traditionally offer compensation that is competitive with other businesses that attract persons with minimal education or experience backgrounds. They also promote advancement opportunities and implement other tactics aimed at increasing retention. However, turnover rates remain high, and it will remain for the managers of tomorrow (who may be reading this book now!) to more effectively address the turnover issue.

Employees study before their work shift

Technology

Technology will continue to affect the industry segment. Unit managers utilize technology in much the same way as their counterparts in other segments. For example, computerized reports that help managers to plan for food production, labor scheduling, purchasing, sales reconciliation, and other purposes reduce the hours required for paperwork in the office. Efforts to utilize technology to reduce labor costs still further are underway.

For example, can computerized equipment reduce production labor? Simple examples, such as automated lifts on deep fryers to remove products when cooked and computerized labor scheduling, are already available. Automated cleaning systems for ventilation systems are also in use. As another example, point-of-sale (POS) systems speed ordering, help to track cash, detail product usage, and reduce training times, while providing the manager with information for staff scheduling and product ordering. In the future, technology may help in other ways. One example: a computer system is available that forecasts food production requirements by counting autos in the drive-through line and factoring in staple items and those featured in current promotions.

Legal Concerns

There are times when employees, consumers, and others have legitimate concerns about quick-service restaurants that should be addressed in a **judicial system.** Increasingly, persons stereotype the industry as being one of **deep pockets.** Recent examples include allegations about excessively hot coffee spilling on a purchaser attempting to consume the beverage in a moving automobile and cases of **obesity** blamed on excessive consumption of foods at quick-service restaurants. It is, of course, up to the courts to determine the merit of these and related allegations and to make appropriate judgments about their resolution. At the same time, managers of quick-service restaurants will likely have to spend much more time addressing concerns with legal implications.

judicial system the legal system by which persons can make claims and have binding decisions about them made in a court of law

deep pockets the slang expression referring to someone being affluent or an organization having excessive profits, which increases the size of potential lawsuits and judgments from these parties

obesity a physical condition evidenced by excessive body fat

Segment Image

The perceptions of unhealthy foods and concerns about unfair treatment of employees are among those that have historically cast a shadow over quick-service restaurants. The old saying "perception is reality" provides some guidance: while these allegations are generally untrue, many in the public believe them to be true. The public relations efforts required to change public perceptions are ongoing, and the success of the industry will, in large measure, be influenced by the effectiveness of these efforts.

PAY YOUR EMPLOYEES WELL, BUT DON'T PASS THE COSTS ON TO ME!

Managers of quick-service restaurants compete with each other for employees and guests. Higher pay rates and more extensive benefit plans are tactics that frequently help in recruitment efforts. Also, a public perception of low pay and few benefits creates advocates of higher minimum wages and other compensation to raise the standard of living for entry-level employees in the industry. (In fact, relatively few quick-service restaurants pay minimum wage; rates are appreciably higher in many areas of the country.)

At the same time, guests desire low-cost meals. Managers are then confronted with the largest challenge: How can I pay employees more without raising my prices? The answer, of course, is to operate more efficiently by reducing costs elsewhere. But

(continued)

managers of most quick-service restaurants have long ago found almost every penny of waste in their operation and are already working on the tightest budgets.

What can be done? Neither the manager nor the guests can have it both ways. The manager cannot pay more and charge less. The consumer cannot pay less and ask managers to pay employees more. Costs cannot increase while revenues remain constant. Quick-service restaurant organizations that effectively resolve this challenge will be increasingly successful in the future.

DID YOU KNOW?

Quick-service restaurant owners and managers are looking to technology to help speed their service and to improve their customers' experiences. Technology applications are implemented quickly. One example: when the first edition of this book was made available in 2004, relatively few QSRs accepted credit or debit card payments. As this current edition is being developed in 2007, most fast-food operators utilize this technology and offer **reloadable gift cards** as well in many markets.

Here's some other examples of what technology can do:

gift card (reloadable) a cashless payment system that allows guests to purchase (and repurchase) debit (payment) cards for use at a quick-service restaurant

- Zoom-through technology allows customers to call ahead for their order, arrive at a separate drive-through window, and use a payment card. Order-confirmation systems transmit these transactions to the property's point-of-sale system.
- Video cameras can take a picture of customers as they place orders at the drive-through. The image is seen by the cashier and the staff member at the pickup window. This technology allows operators to better identify and sequence customers and enable more accurately processed orders.
- New order systems in drive-through lines show pictures of products to help improve the accuracy of orders.
- Hands-free headsets and one-touch open microphone buttons can increase the productivity of staff members. Some work stations use touch-screen technology to transmit drive-through orders to production personnel.

Source: Nicole Richardson. The name of the game is speed: Technology drives quick service speed and accuracy. Retrieved May 31, 2006, from www.htmagazine.com

SUMMARY OF CHAPTER LEARNING OBJECTIVES

1. **Describe the types of guests who visit quick-service restaurants (QSRs).**
Many persons visiting quick-service restaurants are time- and/or money- (value-) driven. Others enjoy the available foods and visit these properties as a dining-out priority.

2. **Review the organization of quick-service restaurants.**
Quick-service restaurant organizations may feature one unit (the owner serves as man-

ager), two units (the owner serves as a manager of one unit and retains the services of a manager for the second unit), or a multiunit organization in which an owner employs an area manager who, in turn, directs the work of specific unit managers.

3. **Provide information about career opportunities in quick-service restaurants.**
Quick-service restaurants provide career opportunities for employees to begin at the

entry level of the organization and to be promoted relatively quickly to shift leader, assistant unit manager, unit manager, and even to area manager (in a multiunit organization). It is also possible for employees of a franchised organization to eventually work for the franchiser.

4. **Explain day to day operating issues of concern to quick-service restaurant managers.**
Issues relating to consistency of service delivery, products, and food and paper costs and effective management of labor costs are among the highest-priority day to day operating concerns of quick-service managers.

5. **Discuss basic challenges confronting the quick-service restaurant segment.**
Challenges confronting the quick-service restaurant segment include those relating to labor (staffing restaurant units), the search for ways that technology can make operations more effective, legal concerns about the public, who are increasingly likely to seek damages, and the perception that many foods served by quick-service properties are unhealthy.

FEEDBACK FROM THE REAL WORLD

Our real-world advice comes from Thomas Kovachic who served as the Director of Operations, for a McDonald's franchisee for approximately 30 years.

Why do quick-service restaurants appeal to young children, who frequently encourage their parents to take them there?

Advertising is the key here. For example, tie-ins with major motion picture studios frequently offer the next "big thing," and children want toys associated with these hit movies. Parents may not want to purchase toys released in conjunction with the movie (they are expensive), so purchasing a kid's meal is a nice compromise.

As we all know, young children are always looking for something new and exciting, and yet, at the same time, they want something familiar. A kid's meal or a Happy Meal works because the premium (toy) keeps changing, but the food does not.

A quick-service property offers much that is of interest to children, including fun (collectible) toys, finger food, taste, atmosphere, and fast service so that children don't have to sit at a table waiting for food to be served. There are, then, numerous reasons why children like our restaurants (and bring their parents along for a visit!).

What are common examples of operating details (frequently measured in pennies) that affect the profitability of a quick-service restaurant?

Pennies do count and can be saved or lost on the little things. Here are some examples:

- Condiment packets dropped on the floor or counter and then discarded
- Extra portion packets of salad dressing, hot cake syrup, catsup, and other items given to guests (costs for these extras are not built into the menu board pricing)
- Operating supplies such as floor cleaners and window-wash concentrates that are dispensed without metering devices
- Sandwich condiments used on products that are dispensed with equipment that has not been properly calibrated
- Fountainheads on the beverage system that have not been properly calibrated
- Finished drinks without the proper amount of ice (the employee then fills the remainder of the cup with additional soft drink, which is more expensive than ice)
- Overfilling shakes and sundaes or overportioning toppings for them

What are some of the economics that frequently provide incentives for quick-service restaurant franchisees to operate a number of units?

After working the bugs out of the first unit from the perspective of both the operations and back-office systems, there is an economy of scale: to manage a second unit does not require twice as much time as that needed to operate a single unit. For example, to track the food cost, one simply

(continued)

needs to add a second column to the spreadsheet that already exists. Also, cost savings carry over to the central office and support staff as the parent company grows. A single person can efficiently handle the details of payroll, accounting, marketing, and benefits for multiple units in about the same time required for one unit.

Supervision responsibilities can also be fulfilled in the same way. After the operating system is identified and put into place, an owner or operations manager can replicate the system in multiple units. Then time is needed to control and evaluate the operations, rather than to run them.

A final reason: One location may not generate sufficient cash flow. Also, profits from one property may not be sufficient to meet a franchisee's (owner's) personal expenses and longer-term investment goals. Additional units can be built and operated to generate cash flow and profits with reduced owner time and efforts because of the economy of scale advantages discussed above.

What are the most prevalent day to day operating concerns that confront unit managers of quick-service restaurants?

The most prevalent day to day operating concerns that confronted me were these:

- Recruiting and retaining quality staff
- Pressure to be profitable as the costs of doing business increased and as the need to keep prices low to retain guest count and sales volume also increased
- Employee dependability issues ("My car won't start, so I can't make it in." "My son's school nurse just called; he is sick, and I need to get him now."), which creates extra work for the employees who do come to work and a challenge to maintain the quality and quantity standards demanded by our guests
- Equipment breakdowns, especially critical pieces like the point-of-sale (POS) system, the main grill, the French fry vat, or the heating, ventilating, and air conditioning (HVAC) system
- Employee accidents, including burns and cuts
- Guest accidents, such as slips and falls and choking incidents
- Assembly of product supplies during a busy shift to get ready for the next shift

MASTERING YOUR KNOWLEDGE

Discuss the following questions.

1. What factors help you to decide whether and when to visit a quick-service restaurant?
2. Why do you think most quick-service restaurants are members of franchise organizations instead of being owned by independent ("mom and pop") entrepreneurs?
3. How do you think the responsibilities of a unit manager in a quick-service restaurant are similar to those of his or her counterparts in other foodservice segments? How might they differ?

4. What practical tactics might you, as a unit manager in a quick-service restaurant, utilize to help maximize product consistency? To reduce turnover and to assure that an adequate number of entry-level staff members are always available?
5. What are ways that you believe technology may further assist quick-service restaurant managers in the future?

LEARN FROM THE INTERNET

1. Check out the websites of the following quick-service restaurant organizations:
   - Arby's: www.arbys.com
   - Burger King: www.bk.com
   - Wendy's: www.wendys.com

   What types of employment opportunities do they advertise? What are features of positions in these organizations that interest you? Which do not interest you?

2. Check out the websites of the following hospitality industry publications:
   - *QSR Online:* www.qsrmagazine.com
   - *Hospitality Technology:* www.htmagazine.com
   - *Restaurant Business:* www.restaurantbiz.com

What types of information would be of use to managers of quick-service restaurants? Why? What types of information discussed in these websites would *not* be of interest to quick-service restaurant managers? Why?

3. Check out the websites of some additional quick-service restaurants:
   - McDonald's: www.mcdonalds.com
   - Sonic: www.sonicdrivein.com
   - Taco Bell: www.tacobell.com

What types of information do they provide about the nutritional content of the products they serve? What, if any, kind of additional consumer information about nutrition is provided?

KEY HOSPITALITY TERMS

The following terms were explained in this chapter. Review the definitions of any words with which you are unfamiliar. Begin to utilize them as you expand your vocabulary as a hospitality professional.

quick-service restaurant (QSR)
day-part
franchisees
shift leader
franchiser
stock purchase plan
purchase specification
co-branding

use-by date
staffing grid
economy of scale
empty nesters
judicial system
deep pockets
obesity
gift card (reloadable)

16 Off-Site Catering

Buffet at a catered event

CHAPTER LEARNING OBJECTIVES

After studying this chapter you will be able to:

1. Describe the range of businesses that offer commercial catering.
2. Review the primary markets for off-site catering.
3. Explain basic operating procedures used by caterers and mobile-unit caterers.
4. Provide a sequential overview of activities necessary for a successful catered event.
5. Review common positions in catering organizations.
6. Discuss specific concerns about the locations for off-site catered events.
7. Note challenges that confront off-site caterers.

The authors wish to thank Ken Hisey, general manager of the Embers Restaurant in Mount Pleasant, Michigan and Robert Lippert, chef emeritus at the property, for their input to the chapter's content. The authors also acknowledge the contributions made to this chapter by Patti Shock, CPCE, Professor and Department Chair, Tourism and Convention Department, William F. Harrah College of Hotel Administration, University of Nevada, Las Vegas.

Catering will enjoy significant success in the foreseeable future and is one of the fastest growing segments of the food service industry in the United States.

Details! Details! Details! A successful food-services operation of any type is always concerned about the details. You have learned that the concept mise en place (everything in its place) is an important tactic to get ready for food production and food service. Running out of clean dishes in the kitchen and having to fill salt shakers in the dining room at the peak of business volume can be very serious. Even so, dishes can be washed and salt shakers can be filled, and the setback in the quality food production and quality food service operations can be overcome.

However, what would you do if you were a foodservices manager 25 miles from your kitchen and you discovered that you had brought too few dishes and/or salt shakers? The management of details in the off-site catering segment is not something that *should* be done; rather, it is an absolute necessity and is but one of the challenges making professional careers in off-site catering most interesting.

Assume that you are the owner of a catering business that has dining facilities on-site and that you offer off-site catering as well. What are the advantages and disadvantages to your customers and to you of providing an event on-site or off-site?

As you read this chapter, think about your answer to this question and then get feedback from the real world at the end of the chapter.

This chapter will discuss hospitality businesses that produce and/or serve meals away from their business's primary location. As we do this, we must slightly stretch the definitions of **catering** and **banqueting** presented in Chapter 11. At that time we presented commonly accepted industry definitions for these terms:

catering (off-site catering) the physical transport of food to an off-site location

banqueting the process of preparing and delivering a food-related event in a group function room

- *Catering.* In the lodging industry, catering refers to selling a banquet event. In the off-site catering segment, catering involves the transport of food to an off-site location.
- *Banqueting.* Preparing for and delivering a food and/or beverage event held in a function room; this is a food production/service function. The term also applies to the catering segment even if there is no function room.

We have defined caterers to be for-profit businesses that produce food for groups at off-site locations. However, what does off-site mean? Large hotels and resorts may produce meals in kitchens for banquet events that are located at distant areas of their property. Hotels located immediately adjacent to convention centers may likewise produce food to be transported from the kitchen to another (nearby) property. Are these events and operations considered off-site catering? Technically, perhaps, they are (if, in the first example, "site" means away from the kitchen and, in the second example, "site" means away from the property). In these examples, if something required for an event is omitted from the original transport (shipment), it is still possible (though, perhaps, inconvenient) to retrieve them.

For the purposes of this chapter, *off-site catering* means the service of food at a location making it impractical (impossible) to return to the production kitchen for products, supplies, equipment, or other items needed for consumption or use at the remote service site.

banquet setup staff employees of the Food and Beverage Department who set up and tear down tables and set and remove chairs and other room furnishings at the conclusion of a banquet

banquet service staff employees of the Food and Beverage Department who set tables and serve meals for and remove serviceware at the end of a banquet

a la carte dining rooms food serving areas (rooms) where guests order from individually priced menu items

group function rooms food serving areas (rooms) where guests are served preordered (banquet) menus

caterers for-profit businesses that produce food for groups at off-site locations; some caterers have banquet space available for on-site use by groups desiring foodservices

Separating the tasks of selling food and beverage functions to groups from the delivery of the group function (food preparation and service and banquet setup and teardown) is convenient, because hotels frequently locate group function sales (catering) within the marketing and sales department. Function delivery is the responsibility of the food and beverage department (sometimes with help from housekeeping staff who clean the room). **Banquet setup staff** set up and remove dining room tables, chairs, and other room furnishings, and **banquet service staff** set the tables, serve the meal, and remove serviceware at the conclusion of the event.

In this chapter, we will explore businesses that may or may not have **a la carte** (a menu featuring individual choice items that are separately priced) **dining rooms** or **group function rooms** on-site. A common activity of off-site **caterers,** the topic of this chapter, is that they generate a significant amount of their revenues from the sale of food (meals) consumed off-site (at a significant distance from the production kitchen).

Catering operations typically have other things in common with each other besides generating significant levels of revenues from off-site foodservices. For example, they provide food (and often beverages) along with the equipment and staff needed to serve the guests. A banquet host selects the menu and determines the number of guests, the time and type of service, and the event's location. When a catering event is held in the operation's banquet hall, the price may include room rental. Most hotels now charge function room rental rates that can be negotiated for large groups. Sometimes rental charges are on a sliding scale based on the amount of food and beverage revenue that is generated. If the event is held off-site, there will almost certainly be an additional service charge for the facility, museum or park for example. Catering events are generally private (not open to the general public), involve a common menu, and are paid for by the host.

commissary a food preparation area (kitchen) utilized to produce food items at least some of which will be transported to and served off-site

WHO DOES COMMERCIAL CATERING?

Exhibit 16.1 identifies the types of organizations that may offer commercial catering:

- *Restaurants.* Some restaurants offer catering as a supplement to their on-site a la carte dining and, increasingly, take-out businesses. Examples include restaurants serving food for business group picnics, social groups at football tailgate parties, and others serving food from temporary booths at community festivals and ceremonies.
- *Vending* **commissaries.** Some vending operations have commissaries that produce foods such as sandwiches and desserts, which are sold through its vending machines.
- *Catering operations.* The primary subject of this chapter, some caterers offer on-site dining (banquet menus at a fixed price to groups and, perhaps, a la carte dining for individual guests), but they also offer off-site catering.
- *Mobile caterers.* Some hospitality operations sell coffee break and meal items to workers at construction sites or to pedestrians on busy street corners. Alternatively, they may provide vending machine or limited manual foodservices to locations, including office buildings and shopping centers. Some mobile caterers specialize in providing foodservices for entertainment productions, at-office parties, and in-home gatherings.
- *Hotels.* Many hotels generate significant food and beverage revenues from on-site banquet operations. Some, however, additionally offer off-site catering to community events, special fund-raising celebrations, and businesses or individuals who retain them for this service.

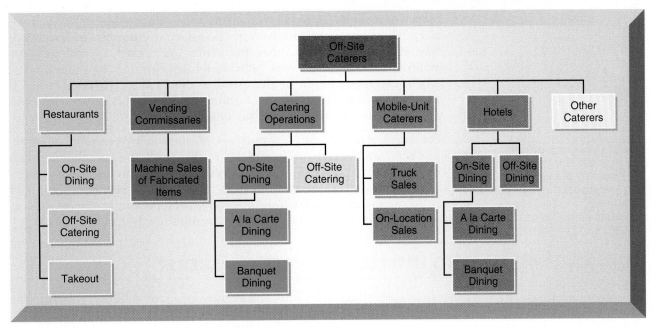

EXHIBIT 16.1
A Close Look at Commercial Off-Site Caterers

Note: Hotels must be set up for off-site catering services. For example, it is not typically feasible to move the hotel's table and chairs to the remote location. They may be needed at the hotel, and hotel-style furniture does not transport well. Therefore, furniture is typically rented with the charge passed on to the client. The hotel must also have (or rent) refrigerated trucks for transport, and staff must be prepared for proper sanitation and safety procedures on-site. Hotel banquet servers generally do not like to "cater out" because the work requirements are different. For example, banquet servers simply set up the tables and serve and remove serviceware at a hotel function. At an off-site event, they must help transport the food, do setup (and sometimes **plate** or finish plating), serve, and then clean up (sometimes in less than desirable weather instead of a climate-controlled banquet room).

plate (food service)
the act of portioning food onto the proper serviceware for service to guests

Delivery van for catering company

• *Other commercial caterers.* Numerous other businesses or individuals meet this chapter's definition of off-site catering. Examples include some delicatessens (delis) and other, frequently unlicensed, operations, such as fund-raising groups and individuals working out of their houses. (These caterers will not be discussed in this chapter. However, there is always a concern that a lack of training with unlicensed caterers can yield problems relating to food safety and sanitation.)

The world of off-site catering does not belong solely to commercial foodservices operators. As you will learn later in this book, noncommercial foodservices also provide off-site catering. Consider, for example, commissaries producing meals for transportation (airline and train) services, secondary schools producing meals for **satellite** feeding centers, and hospitals producing meals for centers in remote healthcare campus locations.

satellite foodservices a location to which food prepared in a commissary at another location is transported and served; for example, a satellite school serves meals produced in an off-site central commissary

OBJECTIVE 2
Review the primary markets for off-site catering.

WHO UTILIZES OFF-SITE CATERERS?

A simple answer is many persons and groups for many different reasons. The two primary markets are these:

• *Business groups.* Summer picnics have already been mentioned; holiday parties have not. The opening of a new business location; a retirement, appreciation, or other recognition event at the business location; and special anniversary and other occasions to celebrate an organization's success can all be held at the sponsoring organization's location. Many associations and corporate business organizations hold training meetings with breakfast, lunch, and/or dinner events, and these provide additional catering opportunities.
• *Individual social events.* Birthdays, weddings, anniversaries, reunions, housewarmings, and high school events are examples of special times that can be celebrated in special locations other than a restaurant's or a hotel's banquet room. In many areas, there is significant competition for these events, and a caterer's reputation does much to "sell" a prospective client.

Political and charitable groups sponsoring fund-raising events also commonly utilize off-site caterers for their special occasions.

Some, especially large, caterers employ one or more special events planners to provide a theme, activities, and environment that are in concert with the menu to be offered.

OBJECTIVE 3
Explain basic operating procedures used by caterers and mobile-unit caterers.

A CLOSE LOOK AT CATERING OPERATIONS

Caterers offering an on-site banquet room (hall) operate almost identically to the way that a hotel does. Food is produced in an on-site kitchen and is transported by mobile carts or carried on trays by food servers to the dining area, where it is served to guests. Also, as is true with hotel banquet operations, the food may be available on a buffet serving line or served to guests seated at tables.

Off-Site Caterers

Off-site catering can be done by a business that has no on-site dining facilities or by a hospitality organization as a part of its business. Those without dining

Outdoor catered event in a unique off-site location

facilities typically have everything a commercial foodservices operation has (a kitchen, staff, and necessary dining services items), but no dining areas for on-site food consumption.

Many off-site caterers offer prewritten banquet menus, but they must also have a great deal of flexibility because of the types of facilities that may or may not be available at the off-site location. (We will discuss menu planning concerns later in this chapter.)

Off-site caterers offer very customized services to their customers. First, they go to the customer's preferred location. Second, they typically utilize facilities that are much more limited than those available under more ideal locations, such as in a hotel, restaurant, or banquet room at their place of business.

Caterers have several options for preparing food: at their kitchen, off-site, or partially in their kitchen and at the off-site location.

Mobile-Unit Caterers

Mobile caterers bring simple foods directly to their customers, whether they be workers at a job site, visitors to festivals or conventions, other group gatherings, or individuals on city streets.

White tablecloth dining at catered event

There are two basic ways that mobile caterers operate. They may prepare (purchase) the food and:

- Hire route persons who deliver or sell products on scheduled routes or at predetermined locations. This arrangement is very similar to that of route persons employed by vending operators (see Chapter 21). Profits accrue to the mobile catering business.
- Lease vehicles to independent operators, who purchase all food items from the fleet operator. The truck leasee is, then, an independent businessperson who finds his or her own accounts and plans his or her own routes and schedules for delivery. Profits from the route then accrue to the independent businessperson (route person).

OBJECTIVE 4
Provide a sequential overview of activities necessary for a successful catered event.

PUTTING IT ALL TOGETHER: AN OFF-SITE CATERED EVENT

Exhibit 16.2 identifies the steps necessary in planning and carrying out an effective off-site catered event. Let's look at these steps.

Initial Meeting with Prospective Client

At this time, a catering owner or manager learns some of the basics that the prospective client has in mind: purpose and location of event, estimated number of attendees, ideas about menu (items and service style), alcoholic beverage concerns, and other related factors that are important to both the customer and caterer. If a reservation is made, it is very common for the caterer to require a deposit to hold the date(s).

Initial Site Visit

If the caterer is not familiar with the proposed location, a site visit will likely be needed. What preparation, holding, and small equipment is available?

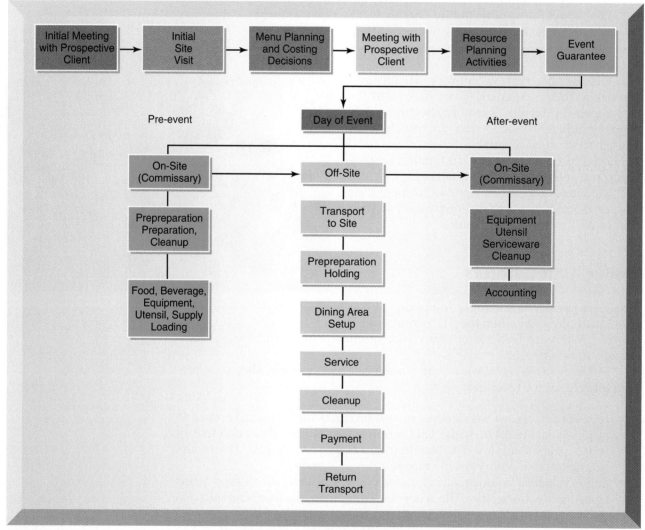

EXHIBIT 16.2
A Close Look at Commercial Off-Site Caterered Event

Where can the transport vehicles be unloaded and loaded and parked during the event? How exactly will food and other items be moved within the facility to the site of service? A drawn-to-scale sketch of the dining area may be needed to plan placement of serving lines, portable bars, and dining tables. During this trip to and from the site, the caterer can obtain an estimate of the transport time that will be required. Exhibit 16.3 shows an Off-Site Location Inspection Review Form.

DID YOU KNOW?

Many communities have ethnic social clubs, fraternal organizations, women's clubs, private city or country clubs, athletic clubs, hospitals, universities, libraries, independent banquet halls, civic auditoriums, stadiums, arenas, executive dining rooms in office buildings, churches, recreation rooms in large apartment or condominium complexes, parks, museums, and aquariums that have banquet rooms. Some of these facilities may be available for catered events with flexible and competitive price structures. Some are public facilities and are tax exempt. Some provide their own catering in-house; others are leased to and operated by contract food management companies under exclusive contracts; still others will rent their facilities to off-premise caterers. Hosts planning catered events and the caterers that serve them often have a wide variety of locations from which to select one that will be the most appropriate for the function.

Menu Planning and Costing Decisions

After the site visit, the caterer will be able to plan a menu that can be accommodated with the equipment available on-site and at the event's location. The menu planner for an off-site catered event has the same basic limitations as does his or her counterparts planning a room-service menu in a hotel: the quality of hotel food deteriorates as time lapses. This places a significant restraint on the items that can be served if they must be produced on-site for delivery to a remote location. This challenge might be lessened if the off-site facility has some food preparation and holding equipment. After a tentative menu is planned, product cost decisions can be made, which, in turn, will affect the price quotation that will be made to the prospective client. The time required for food preparation and transport to and from the facility can be estimated, as can service costs.

Signing the contract for a catered event is an early step in the catering planning process.

OFF-SITE LOCATION INSPECTION REVIEW FORM

Date of Visit: _____   Prospective Customer: _____   Event Date: _____   Event Time: _____

Location Contact   **Space to be Utilited for:**   **Access Times**
Name: _____   Reception: _____   _____
Address: _____   Meal Service: _____   _____
Telephone: _____   Other: _____   _____

Site Fees: _____   **Site Access Time on Day of Event:** _____

Access:
❑ Loading Dock   ❑ Main Entrance   Elevator: ❑ Yes ❑ No ❑ Not Needed   ❑ Other: _____

Available Foodservice Equipment:
❑ Range Ovens _____   ❑ Coffee Urns _____
❑ Burner Tops _____   ❑ Refrigeration _____
❑ Fryers _____   ❑ Heavy Duty Electric Lines _____
❑ Broilers _____   ❑ Dishwashers_ _____
❑ Water/Sinks _____   ❑ Racks _____
❑ Preparation _____   ❑ Microwave _____
❑ Pot Washing _____   ❑ Work Space _____
❑ Ice Machine _____   ❑ Portable Bars _____
❑ Work Tables _____   ❑ First Aid Kit _____
❑ Pots/Pans _____   ❑ Mops/Buckets/Brooms _____
❑ Fire Extinguisher _____   ❑ _____

Special Notes:
Is there adequate ventilation? ❑ Yes ❑ No   Is there adequate kitchen area? ❑ Yes ❑ No   Is there adequate
dining area? ❑ Yes ❑ No
What is the smoking policy? _____
Is the gas or electricity turned on? ❑ Yes ❑ No   Where are the switches? _____
What is done with the dirty grease from the fryer, if used? _____
Where are the circuit breakers? _____   Is the box locked? ❑ Yes ❑ No   Is there a key? ❑ Yes ❑ No

Comments:

Dining Room Needs: **Dishes:**   **Flatware:**

	Number	Size		Number		Number
Tables	_____	_____	Dinner Plates	_____	Knives	_____
Chairs	_____	_____	Salad Plates	_____	Forks	_____
Buffet Tables	_____	_____	Dessert Plates	_____	Spoons: Soup	_____
			Coffee Cups/Saucers	_____	Spoons: Tea	_____
			Water/Tea Glasses	_____	Spoons: Coffee	_____

Comments:

Alcoholic Beverage Service:
Does the establishment have a liquor license? ❑ Yes ❑ No   Who is responsible? _____
Can a one-day liquor license be obtained?   ❑ Yes ❑ No   Who is responsible for getting? _____

EXHIBIT 16.3
Off-Site Location Inspection Review Form

Who has responsibility for bar?
_____

Who has responsibility for the bartenders?
_____

Bar hours: _____ to _____
Who can change this time period?
_____

Special Service with the alcoholic beverage service?
Who is responsible for getting?   Who is responsible for serving? _____   _____

Restrictions on alcoholic beverage service: _____
Is bar set for keg beer? ❑ Yes ❑ No Notes: _____
Who has responsiblity for keg beer? _____ Who has responsibility for soft drinks? _____

Bar Needs:

	Number	Condition			Clean	
Type: _____	_____	❑ Good	❑ OK	❑ Poor	❑ Yes	❑ No
Type: _____	_____	❑ Good	❑ OK	❑ Poor	❑ Yes	❑ No
Wine: _____	_____	❑ Good	❑ OK	❑ Poor	❑ Yes	❑ No
Champagne: _____	_____	❑ Good	❑ OK	❑ Poor	❑ Yes	❑ No
Plastic: _____	_____	❑ Good	❑ OK	❑ Poor	❑ Yes	❑ No
Beer Pitchers: _____	_____	❑ Good	❑ OK	❑ Poor	❑ Yes	❑ No
Corkscrews: _____	_____	❑ Good	❑ OK	❑ Poor	❑ Yes	❑ No

Other:
Trash Removal _____
AV Needs _____
Speaker Needs _____
Dance Floor _____
Guest Parking _____
Restroom (Guests)   ❑ Yes ❑ No   Clean? ❑ Yes ❑ No   Who is responsible for upkeep? _____
Restroom/Lockers (Staff) ❑ Yes ❑ No   Clean? ❑ Yes ❑ No   Who is responsible for upkeep? _____
Handicap Access _____
Music/Band _____
Decorators _____
Facility Staff to be available during event _____
Other _____
_____
_____

Special Areas:
How is the head table to be set? _____
   Special requests: _____
_____
Speaker podium layout? _____

Dining Area Diagram

Other Comments

Meeting with Prospective Client

At this time, the cost of the event can be discussed (negotiated) with the customer. Changes, if any, in the plans of the caterer and/or the prospective client can be made. All contractual issues can be discussed, and the contract agreement can be signed by both parties. The client will then typically be required to make a deposit for food and beverage purchases, especially if special products are needed and must be purchased in advance.

Resource Planning Activities

Most professional caterers know that catered events are "simple but complicated"! They are simple because the same basic resource planning activities must be undertaken regardless of the event's size. They are complicated because of the significant number of details that must be attended to at every step in the event planning and delivery process. Catered events involving the service of thousands (or more) meals can take planning for up to one year (or much longer). Smaller events with which the off-site caterer has extensive experience can be planned in several weeks (or fewer). At both of these extremes (and for those of any size in between), the caterer must constantly be creative, concerned about details, and alert to continuous quality improvement activities to please the guests while effectively managing associated costs.

This empty room can be the site for an elegant catered event.

Event Guarantee

At the time specified by the event agreement, the customer must finalize the count of guests for whom food and beverage services will be provided. A guarantee deposit is normally paid at this time. The guarantee helps the off-site caterer in exactly the same way that it assists the hotel banquet planner: it provides the information that will drive food production, staffing, and revenue. With the guarantee in place, the caterer is assured to receive payment based on either the guarantee or the number of guests served (whichever is larger). Without a guarantee, the caterer does not know the quantity of food to prepare or the amount of labor that will be necessary. Guarantees are typically required 48 hours in advance of the event, although 72 hours may be preferred if the time lapses over a weekend or if the event will be held in a location where deliveries are more difficult or less frequent. Sometimes a caterer will accept a "minimum" guarantee 48 hours in advance, but the client can increase (but not decrease) the guest count up until 24 hours before the event.

Preparing food in a catering kitchen

Day of Event

Very large catered events may require on-site work several days or much longer in advance of the event. This may be necessary, for example, when landscaping must be provided or altered and when tents must be constructed. (Typically, the customer employs specialist subcontractors to perform this work; the caterer's job is limited to the food and beverage production- and service-related activities. However, as noted earlier, the caterer may offer special events planners to assume the responsibility of these and related tasks.) More typically, however, smaller events do not require on-site work by the caterer before the day of the event.

On the day of the event, some on-site commissary work must be done. This includes food prepreparation and preparation, along with cleanup of the on-site kitchen. As well, food, beverage, equipment, utensils, supplies, and the probably numerous other items needed for the event must be counted and loaded on the transport vehicle(s). This is where attention to details is a must. The Off-Site Location Inspection Review Form shown earlier in Exhibit 16.3 can help to remind the caterer about items that must be transported to the off-site facility. Also, packing sheets that identify everything to be shipped must be checked and rechecked (especially when several persons are involved

---

A WORD ABOUT TRANSPORTATION

Food, beverage, and all necessary equipment, utensils, serviceware, supplies, and other items must be transported to the off-site location. Most typically this is done by the owner or manager (in a small business when there is only one event happening at a specific time) or by a staff member who will be working at the off-site location. However, the caterer's employees who will be working at the location must also get there. Sometimes (but infrequently), they may meet at the caterer's location and be driven to the event site. More typically, however, they are given directions and a travel expense allowance and are personally responsible for arriving at the location at the specified time.

Note: The route should be traveled in advance to assess required transport time, and the trip should be made at the same time of day and with the same traffic conditions as for the actual event. Refrigerated trucks or those with a capacity to carry ample supplies of ice are a paramount concern.

in the packing process and when different persons pack equipment, food, and supplies). If washable dishes and flatware will be utilized, these also must be transported unless they are available at the off-site location.

During transport, sanitation concerns are important to minimize the time that **potentially hazardous foods** are kept within the **temperature danger zone** to minimize the possibility of a **food-borne illness.** Safety concerns are also important; for example, heavy equipment may shift during transport and cause injury to persons or damage to the delivery vehicle and/or its contents.

Another concern: everything must be carefully packed on the transport vehicle to reduce damage (jello molds, for example) and breakage (such as dishes). Location on the vehicle is also important. Light food items, for example, should be kept together and away from heavy nonfood items.

At the off-site location, food items may need to be preprepared and held at the proper temperature until serving. The dining area must be set up, food and beverage products served, and the facility cleaned up at the end of the event.

Unless other arrangements have been made, additional payments due from the client are typically expected at the end of the event, and all items that are the property of the caterer must be transported back to the on-site commissary. (Sometimes even the garbage from the event must be removed from the off-site location.) Clients should not be given surplus food because of sanitation concerns.

Back at the caterer's location, items used off-site must be counted, cleaned, and replaced into inventory, if applicable. Accounting activities, such as preparing the client's payment for bank deposit and maintaining payroll records, will be necessary.

As seen in the above "diary" of an off-site catered event, many of the necessary activities are very similar or identical to those required for a successful on-site foodservice event. However, some, such as food transport and prepreparation and preparation off-site, are very different. While careful attention to details is necessary in any type of foodservices, it is especially critical with off-site catering, since items forgotten can be many miles (rather than several feet) away from the serving site.

potentially hazardous foods foods of animal origin or other items high in protein that are most frequently involved in outbreaks of food-borne illness

temperature danger zone the temperature at which microorganisms causing food-borne illness most quickly multiply (approximately 41° to 135°F (5°C to 57°C)

food-borne illness an illness caused by consuming food that has been contaminated by microorganisms, chemicals, or other substances

CATERING OWNERS AND MANAGERS MUST HAVE SEVERAL SPECIAL AND MANY GENERAL MANAGEMENT SKILLS

To be successful in the catering business, an owner or manager must have numerous marketing-related skills to identify those potentially interested in his or her services, to identify and implement creative ways to reach potential markets, and to "make a sale and close the deal." Contrast this with the food and beverage manager in a hotel, where specialists in the marketing or catering department assume these responsibilities. As well, while every successful food and beverage manager is creative, an off-site caterer must be especially alert to ways to exceed the desires of event hosts and their guests in locations that change everyday.

Catering managers must be expert in all the broad functional areas that are necessary for hospitality managers in any other segment, but they do have special concerns. Let's see some examples:

Planning — Developing menus that can be produced within the limitations of those products that can be safely transported and served at off-site locations; developing work flow patterns at remote sites; considering contingencies for venues in which there may be few options.

Organizing	Considering every menu item, ingredient, supply, transportation, and service equipment and utensil, along with everything else needed to provide a successful function. While forgetting something in most operations involves, at best, a few steps or seconds for retrieval, a caterer's omission can cause significant problems when corrective action requires many miles or hours of travel time to address.
Staffing	Determining the number of staff members needed for an unfamiliar location, assuring that employees arrive at the remote site on time, and training them about work flow in the location are examples of staffing responsibilities that change with every venue.
Directing	Supervising employees in unfamiliar locations can be a challenge when there are unknowns about the facility that can occur even with the most careful site visits.
Controlling	It is difficult to establish expectations (standards) of performance for events in remote locations that serve as benchmarks to determine whether the event was successful. Creative caterers carefully analyze each event, learn from it, and incorporate their new experiences into the planning and implementation of subsequent functions.
Evaluating	While caterers perform evaluation tasks as they control, it is also important, but difficult, to obtain a big-picture assessment of numerous events that can help the owner or manager better plan for future events.

The business of food and beverage in any type of operation is interesting because there is, literally, "something new every day." However, in no segment of the hospitality industry is this a more accurate description than in the exciting and fast-paced off-site catering industry.

STAFFING THE CATERING BUSINESS

OBJECTIVE 5
Review common positions in catering organizations.

Exhibit 16.4 shows how a large off-site catered event might be organized. Unlike other organizational charts shown to this point, workers are separated according to activities that are done on- or off-site. Most activities are the same as those done in any other type of food or beverage service. A chef working with preparation assistants (cooks) prepares the food, and a utility person is responsible for washing pots and pans used in food preparation. (He or she will also need to clean washable serviceware, if used, when it is returned from the off-site event.) Cooks will portion food items into transport containers and, along with the utility person, will load transport equipment into the delivery vehicle.

At the off-site location, the owner or manager or site manager is in charge of the event. The owner or catering site manager is responsible to assure that all contractual terms are complied with. He or she is also responsible for the work done by all staff members and for assuring that the event is successful. The owner or manager supervises one or more cooks (if off-site food

A large family reunion can be catered.

preparation is needed) and the buffet and dining room setup personnel. (Typically, food servers and bartenders, if any, do setup and service work for small events.)

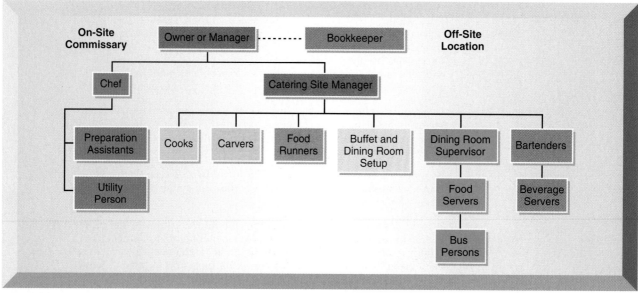

EXHIBIT 16.4
Organizational Chart for a Large Off-Site Catered Event

THE ANNUAL FUND-RAISER: A CASE STUDY IN OFF-SITE CATERING

Many restaurants do some off-site catering. Only relatively few, however, generate a significant percentage of their total annual revenues from the sale of meals served off-site. Those operations with much experience can make a large catered event seem almost easy. A real-world case study illustrates some of the many details to be addressed to make a big event successful. This example is an account of an actual event.

Six months before the planned event, the restaurant manager meets with the client (a committee representing a group sponsoring a once-a-year auction fund-raiser). The organization has offered the event for many years and has utilized the same restaurant caterer for 19 years. This is remarkable because, first, the restaurant is located 130 miles from the event's site and, second, because, although committee members know it is a good business practice to solicit competitive bids, they don't do so. They claim that no one can do it as well as this caterer!

During the meeting, tentative plans about a theme and potential menus are discussed. A tour of the kitchen in the facility owned by the event's sponsor is conducted to assess whether there have been major changes in equipment and layout since the previous fundraiser and to test-operate needed equipment. After all, the best surprise is no surprise!

After the visit, the manager plans a special buffet menu and all other aspects of the event, costing is done, and a proposal is sent to the client for modification and approval.

The menu to be offered is agreed on; major items will be these:

Entrees: Beef Tenderloin, Chicken, Seafood, and Pork

Hot starches: Rice, Noodles, and Potatoes (several varieties)

Hot vegetables medley: Fresh Asparagus, Baby Beans, and Vegetables

Cold vegetables: Green Salad with choice of six dressings (four are made on site), Pasta Salad, Potato Salad, Special Vegetable Selections, Pistachio Salad, Fruit and Vegetable Trays, Cottage Cheese, and numerous side dishes

Appetizers (self-serve): Ramaki, BBQ Ribs, Fruit Tray, and Vegetable Tray

Appetizers (passed): BBQ Shrimp and Fried Shrimp Specialties
Dessert: Cheese Cake with choice of several fruit sauces

One week before the event, the sponsor sends a guarantee. The caterer will prepare for 5 percent more guests than the guarantee of 700 persons. Careful planning is needed; the buffet should look as bountiful for the last person being served as it does for the first. The caterer will also provide food for the approximately 150 volunteer members of the organization who will help during the day and evening of the event. Also, the 40 (approximate) staff members of the caterer will consume at least one employee meal. The sponsor pays a deposit (approximately 20 percent of the estimated bill) and is invoiced for the remaining amount, which is to be paid at the end of the month.

All the food that will be needed is ordered and delivered to the caterer's restaurant kitchen. Food preparation begins several days in advance of the event. For example, some entree sauces can be prepared. Also, appetizers such as ramaki (water chestnuts wrapped with sliced bacon) can be assembled and placed in trays that are tightly wrapped before refrigeration. To suggest the volume of items to be transported to the serving site, assume that a typical guest consumes four of these Ramaki appetizers: about 2,800 must be prepared (700 guests × 4 appetizers each). If approximately 120 pieces can be placed in one 12 by 20 by 2-inch hotel (steam table) pan, 24 pans (2,800 ÷ 120) will need to be transported for just this one appetizer! Consider also that a standard convection oven holds 10 of these pans and that it takes 20 minutes to cook the items. This means that one oven will be in use for one hour (24 pans ÷ 10 pans = 2.4 oven loads; each load is 20 minutes and a partial load also takes 20 minutes).

Most preparation occurs during the last two days and must be interfaced with the restaurants' ongoing dining room business (which approximates, on average, 200 total meals per day over midday and evening meal periods).

The caterer brings almost everything that is needed for the event to the site, including the refrigerator: a refrigerated truck! Only the facility's preparation and serving line equipment will be used.

All serving line pans and utensils, dinnerware, and other guest-related service items, including alcoholic beverages, are shipped to the facility one day before the event. The food is loaded onto the refrigerated truck late on the evening before and is transported to the site early on the day of the event. The banquet chef personally packs or supervises the loading of all food and needed supplies and equipment following a very detailed (3 to 4 pages) checklist of necessary items. The chef must also assure that items are loaded correctly and fastened securely to avoid spillage and/or damage during the trip.

As soon as the truck arrives, food and equipment are checked in according to the same checklist, and food preparation begins. Dining room and serving line setup is done by staff members especially assigned to these duties. The self-service stations must be set up, and all serviceware for the butler service, involving appetizers to be passed, must be organized. Hot food preparation and finishing activities last all day. Personnel assigned for cold foods and salads arrive in early afternoon and begin work.

During the event, guests can help themselves to appetizers at a special station and, as well, other appetizers are **butlered** (served by food servers who circulate throughout the serving, dining, and auction areas). The hot and cold food serving lines are set up so that guests can pass down both sides. China (washable serviceware) is used. It takes approximately one hour to serve the guests.

Volunteers from the sponsoring organization wash the caterer's dishes and other serviceware before they are boxed for shipment back to the restaurant. The caterer brings its own smallwares (pots and pans and other cooking-related utensils), as well as a staff member to wash and account for them before they are shipped back to the restaurant.

Was the fund-raiser a success? You bet. While a contract will still be necessary for next year's fund-raiser, when the event concluded members of the host committee said, "Thank you very much, and we will certainly see you next year!" The restaurant manager knew there was an excellent chance for repeat business.

butlered (food serving style) a service style in which food is served to guests who are standing by a food server (butler) who moves among the guests

lineup meeting a brief informational training session held before the work shift begins

in-home catering off-site catering done in a host's home for a small number of guests

personal cheffing the use of a personal chef to prepare complete meals for each person for several (or more) days at the host's home

---

CHECK IT OUT!

To learn more about in-home dining, go to www.cooksforyou .net; www.niagaragourmet.sa/ catering. Click on "personal chef."

Learn more about personal chef careers by checking out the United States Personal Chef Association: www.uspca .com

---

OBJECTIVE 6
Discuss specific concerns about the locations for off-site catered events.

As with any foodservices event, a **lineup meeting** should be conducted after all staff are assembled at the off-site location and before they begin work. This session can be used to brief staff members about the event and its objectives and to review the menu, serving techniques, and work assignments. The catering manager in charge at the event's location must utilize all principles important in the art and science of supervision. This is necessary to assure that staff members work according to standard procedures and that they are empowered to make on-the-spot decisions to make the event as enjoyable as possible for the customer and guests.

DID YOU KNOW?

In-home catering is an alternative to dining in a restaurant or other foodservice location. Parties for as few as two persons can be arranged to provide the level of menu and service quality that one desires (and wants to pay for!). One advantage: guests can select every menu item, and determine exactly when they wish to dine.

"**Personal cheffing**" is even more unique. This involves hiring someone to go to one's home, prepare all the food at that location, and package it so that there are complete meals for each person for several (or more) days.

ALL ABOUT OFF-SITE CATERING LOCATIONS

The location at which the off-site event will be held presents, perhaps, the most significant challenge to the caterer. It is probable that, somewhere and sometime, almost any place where a catering event could be held has been utilized. Many sites provide opportunities for creative caterers to utilize their professional talents. At the same time, meal service can also be made more difficult because of restrictions imposed on the caterer and his or her customer. Some off-site locations will likely have adequate (or better) water, gas, and/or electric utilities, along with storage, preparation, and service facilities. (It is important to determine whether special arrangements are needed to turn on available utilities. Examples include those in schools, churches, and many businesses.) By contrast, other locations, such as in parks or on beaches, may have no facilities whatsoever. It is therefore critical that the caterer visit the proposed site if he or she has not had prior experience with it. (Exhibit 16.3 showed an Off-Site Location Inspection Review Form that can help the caterer to record observations during the visit.)

The caterer should determine (confirm) the responsibility for usage fees for the site. (Typically, spaces are rented by the customer, rather than by the caterer, but it is important to confirm which party is responsible for this.) If equipment or other items that are not owned by the caterer are to be delivered to the site, arrangements for the deliveries must be made. (When? Where? Where will they be stored? How will they be secured?)

A small family occasion can be catered.

ARAMARK chef displaying a meal to be served at Olympic Park in Sydney, Australia

If the off-site location has preparation equipment and space that can be utilized, raw food deliveries may be arranged directly to the site to reduce the amount of items that must be transported from the caterer's facility. Arrangements must be made for delivery of these products. If the caterer is responsible for guest parking, issues such as parking location, details for valet parking, if applicable, parking fees, guest entrances, availability of maps and directions, and even details about ice or snow removal, if applicable, must be addressed.

The Off-Site Location Inspection Review Form shown in Exhibit 16.3 lists inspection points applicable to facilities with preparation kitchens. Caterers must become very creative in facilities with inadequate or no food preparation facilities. Their most important concern is to plan a menu that recognizes that almost everything must be produced at the caterer's location. Experienced caterers with access to water, tabletops, and an electrical outlet for microwave ovens can do much to supplement food preparation previously done at their location.

Special concern must be given to the proposed dining space. If there is a scenic view or other attraction that will affect table placement, this should be noted. Will guests have to sit with the sun in their eyes? Tables and chairs, if available for use, should be checked to assure that they are safe and that they will meet the customers' needs.

Arrangements for and restrictions relating to the consumption of alcoholic beverages must be determined. For example, laws in some areas may prohibit locations with on-premise liquor licenses to allow liquor to be brought into the facility. In other instances, the customer may purchase the liquor, and the caterer provides bartenders, beverage servers, and serving supplies, including glassware. The caterer should determine whether a temporary liquor license is required and, if so, all restrictions applicable to it should be carefully adhered to.

On-site inspection visits should address numerous other issues including in-house personnel to be available during the event and the availability, adequacy, and cleanliness of rest rooms and coatrooms for the guests and locker areas for the caterer's staff members. Also, who is responsible for the upkeep of these facilities during the event and their cleanup after the function?

A careful inspection of the proposed off-site location is absolutely critical for a successful catered event, and shortcuts should not be taken as this inspection is made. If a specific location has been used (but not recently), an inspection is still important to assure that the caterer's previous experiences with it will be relevant for the event being planned.

<table>
<tr><td>

OBJECTIVE 7
Note challenges that confront off-site caterers.

</td><td>

CHALLENGES! CHALLENGES!

Several challenges confront catering company owners and managers that require their creative attention:

1. Attrition in guest counts occurs when clients begin planning a party for a large number of guests and receive price concessions for doing so. Then the event is downsized when the guarantee is given. This reduction in guest count can affect location and the number of staff members needed, the quantity of food to be purchased, and numerous other logistical concerns.

2. Many clients use third-party companies to plan their event, and these coordinators are focused on return-on-investment concerns. Increasingly, caterers do not even talk to the end client (host) but, instead, interact only with the function coordinator. As this occurs, obvious communication issues can arise.

3. There is a trend away from table-service events to buffets or receptions with more individual food offerings to accommodate the variety of lifestyles and styles of eating. Menus can be more flexible when guests self-select items, but the challenge of anticipating the popularity of specific items must then be addressed.

4. During a "normal" day, caterers might face many crisis situations. For example, bartenders or servers don't show up, late or incorrect food deliveries occur, inclement weather is forecast, guests arrive early or late, and critical items are unavailable at the catering location. These and numerous other issues can create high stress levels.

5. Safety and sanitation procedures required to meet applicable laws and regulations must be followed regardless of where the event is held. How to do so is often a challenge at many sites away from the caterer's location.

6. Keeping up with technology is an ongoing concern. Maintaining the website, investing in software programs, and training staff to use the technology are examples of concerns that must be prioritized with other financial and time obligations.

7. With peaks and valleys in business, it becomes difficult to retain staff. For example, there might be 10 events to staff during one week and no functions scheduled for the following week.

8. Successful operators must find a target market and successfully focus on the needs of its members to keep catering from being purchased like a commodity.

</td></tr>
</table>

SUMMARY OF CHAPTER LEARNING OBJECTIVES

1. **Describe the range of businesses that offer commercial catering.**
   At least five types of organizations may offer commercial catering: restaurants, vending commissaries, catering operations, mobile catering operations, and hotels.

2. **Review the primary markets for off-site catering.**
   The two primary markets for off-site catering are business groups and individual social events.

3. **Explain basic operating procedures used by caterers and mobile-unit caterers.**

   Some caterers offer on-site banquet rooms (halls) and produce and serve meals in the banquet areas in much the way that their counterparts in hotels do. These and other caterers also produce meals for service off-site at a customer's preferred location. Mobile-unit caterers bring simple foods directly to their customers. They may prepare (purchase) the food and hire route persons to deliver and sell items or, alternatively, they may lease vehicles to independent operators who purchase foods and sell them to their own customers.

4. **Provide a sequential overview of activities necessary for a successful catered event.**

   The caterer conducts an initial meeting with a prospective client. This is followed by an initial site visit so that menu planning and costing decisions can be made. A contract with the prospective client is then negotiated and numerous activities must then be planned in advance of the event. At the appropriate time, an event guarantee is made by the client. On the day of the event, numerous preparation activities occur at the caterer's commissary. As well, items are transported to the serving site and prepreparation, dining area setup, service, cleanup, and payment activities are required. Leftover food, equipment, supplies, and even garbage are then transported back to the commissary, where cleanup and accounting activities are undertaken.

5. **Review common positions in catering organizations.**

   In small catering operations, the owner or manager will be in charge of the event at both the on-site commissary and the off-site location. In larger operations or when there is more than one event at the same time, a catering manager may be responsible for activities at the off-site location. Necessary food items are prepared by the chef and preparation assistants at the commissary, and cooks, food servers, and bartenders are among the personnel required off-site.

6. **Discuss specific concerns about the locations for off-site catered events.**

   An Off-Site Location Inspection Review Form must be carefully completed to determine all details about the event location. These include information about access to a facility, available foodservices equipment, dining room needs, and other concerns, including trash removal, alcoholic beverage service license, parking (for guests and the catering delivery vehicle), and signage to direct guests to the event's location.

7. **Note challenges that confront off-site caterers.**

   Numerous challenges include those relating to attrition in guest counts, interactions with third-party event planners, trends toward buffets and receptions, and crisis situations that create stress. Other challenges involve the need to follow safety and sanitation procedures in off-site locations, keeping up with technology, difficulties in retaining staff, and the need to find and meet the needs of a specific target market.

MASTERING YOUR KNOWLEDGE

Discuss the following questions.

1. If you were a hotel food and beverage director or a restaurant manager, what would be the major concerns to be addressed as you considered the possibility of offering off-site catered events?

2. As an off-site catering manager, what tactics could you implement to best assure that all food, beverage, equipment, serviceware, and other items needed for an off-site catered event will, in fact, be available?

3. What are examples of off-site locations that would probably not be practical for an off-site catered event?

4. For what types of activities might the special events planner employed by a catering company be responsible?

5. What suggestions, if any, might you make for the manager responsible for the annual fund-raiser in the case study presented in this chapter?

FEEDBACK FROM THE REAL WORLD

Our real-world advice comes from Ken Hisey, General Manager, Embers Restaurant, Mount Pleasant, Michigan.

Ken's restaurant does a significant volume of off-site catering business throughout Michigan. He provides a matrix that indicates some of the pros and cons of an event held on- and off-site from the perspectives of both the customer and caterer.

Assume you are the owner of a catering business that has dining facilities on-site and that you offer off-site catering as well. What are the advantages and disadvantages to your customers and to you of providing an event on-site or off-site?

Pros and Cons of On-Site and Off-Site Catering
CUSTOMER'S PERSPECTIVE

On-Site (Caterer's Location)		Off-Site (Customer's Location)	
Pros	Cons	Pros	Cons
1. One-stop event; everything required for the special function will be provided just as it would at a hotel or restaurant	1. Limited by the caterer's location	1. May save money if customer provides some food and beverage products or services	1. May be significant additional costs for equipment and supplies not provided by caterer
2. May be less costly when total expenses for everything required are considered	2. Fewer opportunities for unique and special events (many guests will likely have had few, if any, off-site catering experiences)	2. Can enjoy the privacy of own home or the special features of a location that they select	2. May be logistics problems if caterer with insufficient experience is contracted
3. Know better what to expect because of more experience with on-site dining	3. Limited by the atmosphere of the caterer's facility	3. Can do something different; people typically eat in restaurants and hotels more frequently than they utilize off-site caterers	3. May be menu limitations and/or quantity limitations
		4. Alcoholic beverage laws may permit service at different times when a private party is being sponsored by the customer	

CATERER'S PERSPECTIVE

On-Site (Caterer's Location)		Off-Site (Customer's Location)	
Pros	Cons	Pros	Cons
1. Caterer is familiar with his or her location, layout, equipment, supplies, and tools; everything in the operation is standardized	1. Must compete with the many other businesses that offer on-site banquets	1. Working in different locations means more exciting work	1. Menu limitations may affect caterer's abilities to obtain business

CATERER'S PERSPECTIVE			
On-Site (Caterer's Location)		Off-Site (Customer's Location)	
Pros	Cons	Pros	Cons
2. Less chance of products, utensils, and/or supplies being unavailable	2. Limited to the number of diners that room occupancy permits allow	2. Less competition and the offering of an extra-special event may yield higher operating profits for the event	2. May be equipment limitations at off-site location
3. Lowered costs and less time since no transportation is needed; also, food production costs can be less because an employee can do multi-tasking			3. Operating problems can arise when staff are unfamiliar with off-site facility unless proper planning is done
4. Reduced planning time and no time required for site visits; the caterer's time is more efficiently spent			4. Important products, supplies, and/or equipment may be forgotten (details may be overlooked)
			5. May be inadequate transport equipment available (especially for very large events)

LEARN FROM THE INTERNET

1. Check out the home pages for several caterers:
   - Culinary Enterprises: www.culinaryenterprises.com
   - Prestige Caterers: www.prestigecaterers.com
   - EggWhites Special Event Catering: www.eggwhitescatering.com

   What kinds of information would be most important to you as a prospective client? What types of information do they provide that might be helpful to an individual desiring to be responsible for some necessary activities in a catered event?

2. Check out current articles in the following catering foodservice publications posted on the Internet:
   - *Special Events Magazine:* www.specialevents.com Click on "Caterers/catering."
   - *Catering Magazine:* www.cateringmagazine.com
   - *Catersource:* www.catersource.com

   What are topics of articles that would be relevant to off-site caterers?

3. Review the websites for the following associations:

   - International Caterers Association: www.icacater.org
   - National Association of Catering Executives: www.nace.net

   What services do they provide to members? What types of information are presented on the websites that are unique to catering organizations? That apply to all foodservice operations?

4. Check out the following websites for additional information about the off-site catering industry:
   - Meetings & Conventions: www.meetings-conventions.com
   - Meeting News/Successful Meetings/ MiMegasite: www.mimegasite.com
   - Meetings Community Listserv: www.meetingscommunity.com
   - Special Events: www.specialevents.com
   - BizBash: www.bizbash.com
   - Convene: www.pcma.org/resources/convene/ archives
   - Event Solutions: www.event-solutions.com

KEY HOSPITALITY TERMS

The following terms were explained in this chapter. Review the definitions of any words with which you are unfamiliar. Begin to utilize them as you expand your vocabulary as a hospitality professional.

catering (off-site catering)

banqueting

banquet setup staff

banquet service staff

a la carte dining rooms

group function rooms

caterers

commissary

plate (food services)

satellite foodservices

potentially hazardous foods

temperature danger zone

food-borne illness

butlered (food serving style)

lineup meeting

in-home catering

personal cheffing

Part 4

NONCOMMERCIAL FOODSERVICES OPERATIONS

Contract Management Company Foodservices

17

Children eating lunch in an elementary school cafeteria

CHAPTER LEARNING OBJECTIVES

After studying this chapter you will be able to:

1. Recognize that the preferred foodservice management alternative (self-operated or contract management company-operated) must be determined on a by-situation basis.

2. Explain that a win–win relationship between the sponsoring organization and the contract management company is needed.

3. Outline basic steps in the decision-making process to select and utilize a contract management company.

4. Describe the role of a foodservice liaison.

5. Note the importance of and types of communication between the sponsoring organization and the contract management company.

6. Discuss challenges confronting contract management companies.

The authors wish to thank Jeannette Colter, Senior Human Resource Generalist, Sodexho, for her assistance in coordinating the development of this chapter.

FEEDBACK FROM THE REAL WORLD

Pretend that a business manager of a large manufacturing company is concerned about minimizing operating expenses and providing foodservice alternatives that will be enjoyed by his or her employees. The foodservices have been managed and operated by the company's own employees (it has been self-operated), but significant losses have occurred recently. This is a large operation serving several hundred meals to employees six days weekly.

Your contract management company has just received a request for proposal (RFP) from the company that addresses your company's potential interest in managing the foodservices

operation, the services you could provide, and the costs associated with doing so.

What process would you use to develop a winning proposal response? What factors would enable your organization to manage the foodservices more effectively (successfully) than they are currently? How soon after the business is awarded to your company could you tool up to take over the program? What basic steps would be involved in the transition?

As you read this chapter, think about answers to these questions and then get feedback from the real world at the end of the chapter.

---

on-site foodservice a contemporary name for noncommercial foodservices operations

self-operated foodservices noncommercial programs in which the foodservices management and staff are employees of the organization offering the foodservice

contract management company a for-profit business that contracts with an organization to provide foodservices as specified; the management company can be a chain with many contracts or an independent management company with only one or a few contracts

managed foodservices foodservices operations that are managed by a contract management company

We have defined noncommercial foodservices to be those offered by organizations that exist for some reason other than to make a profit from the sale of food and beverage products. This segment of the hospitality industry is also called **on-site foodservice** in an effort to provide a descriptive name that is less related to its for-profit counterparts. Exhibit 17.1 reviews a portion of Exhibit 1.3. It shows many of the wide range of organizations that feed people (their employees and/or consumers of their services) for reasons other than to make a profit.

The chart also shows two basic ways that noncommercial foodservices operations can be managed. First, the organization can operate foodservices itself. In a **self-operated foodservices** program, the foodservice manager and his or her staff members are employees of the organization offering the foodservices. An alternative is for the organization to hire a for-profit **contract management company** to operate the foodservices. These foodservice operations are sometimes called **managed foodservices**. In this instance, foodservice managers are employed by the contract management company. Most contracts specify that nonmanagement staff members will also be employed by the contract management company. However, sometimes nonmanagement personnel are employees of the sponsoring organization.

WHICH FOODSERVICE MANAGEMENT ALTERNATIVE IS PREFERRED?

OBJECTIVE 1
Recognize that the preferred foodservice management alternative (self-operated or contract management company-operated) must be determined on a by-situation basis.

Auto mechanics have had friendly arguments for years about the topic "Which is best, a Ford or a Chevy?" Movie critics have annual debates about the "best movie of the year." Art shows, dog and cat shows, culinary competitions, and craft exhibits are all staged to allow judges and the public to answer the question "Which is the best?" The answer to this question generally relates to some factors that can be measured (the fastest car can be timed; dogs and cats can be compared to exacting breeding standards) and to other factors that are more subjective (car styling and art can be viewed differently by different people).

These points also apply to the question "Which is best: self-operated or contract management company-operated foodservices?" The answer is that it really depends on many factors, most of which are specific to the organization

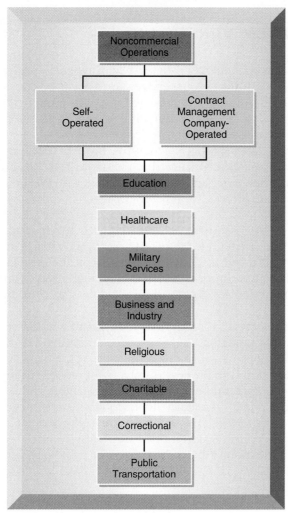

EXHIBIT 17.1
The World of Noncommercial Foodservices

considering the alternatives. Some concerns are objective (financial statements can indicate whether an operation meets monetary goals), but other factors are more subjective (which alternative offers the best-tasting food?). This distinction (the necessity for service to be offered at minimal cost or employee benefit) represents a fundamental difference in how foodservices are viewed by

This resident in a long-term care facility is eating a meal prepared by the facility's food-service department that could be self-operated or managed by a contract management company.

CHECK IT OUT!

Food Management Magazine publishes annual information about the largest contract management companies. To view the current report, go to www.foodmanagement.com. Scroll to "Articles," and click on "Article Archive Search." Type "Top 50 management companies" in the search box.

IS IT THEM VERSUS US?

The history of contract foodservice management probably began when a local restaurant owner or caterer began to provide limited foodservices for a local business. Over the years it has grown into a multibillion dollar business with several large companies offering foodservice management services internationally, others with nationwide **accounts,** and still others with a large regional or community-wide base of operations. Historically, managers of self-operated foodservice programs have disliked contract management companies, in part, because of a concern that their jobs were in jeopardy. The management company brings in its own top-level unit manager(s), because management expertise, of course, is what the organization is buying when it contracts with a foodservice management company.

There is also the matter of profit. An organization operated with public funds, such as a local school district, might question whether the profit paid to a contract management company might be better spent if it remained within the school district. (The contract management company would likely counter that it can yield increased efficiencies that will provide savings to the school district greater than what was paid in management fees to the company.)

So who does the better job of operating foodservices? The answer is that it probably depends just as much on the staff managing the foodservice operation as it does on whether the staff is employed by the sponsoring organization itself or the contract management company. There are no secrets in the process of effective foodservice management. Basic principles are well known and can be applied by all managers regardless of whether they are employees of an organization needing foodservices or a contract management company. Good (and less effective!) managers work for self-operated and for contract management-operated foodservices. A careful mix of creativity, effective operating procedures, and consistent application of basic management principles is a more important determinant of foodservice success than is the type of management operation (self-operated or contract company) used.

---

account the contract management company's term for the organization that has retained it to operate the foodservices program; also called *client*

representatives of sponsoring organizations. Some factors critical to the "Which is best?" question have both subjective and objective components. (A large management company does have expertise available, for example, to undertake kitchen design work or to do creative graphics for food promotions. However, how much do these services really cost when they are provided as part of a package price for operating the organization's foodservices program?)

OBJECTIVE 2
Explain that a win–win relationship between the sponsoring organization and the contract management company is needed.

A WIN–WIN RELATIONSHIP IS NEEDED
- -

Parties to the **management contract** must both benefit from it. An agreement in which one party wins and the other party loses will likely cause serious operating problems before the business relationship is dissolved. Exhibit 17.2 highlights potential risks incurred by both parties in a foodservices agreement.

The sponsoring organization may lose control over many aspects of providing its foodservices (and a desire to do so may be an incentive for an organization to retain a contract management company!). Accounts can determine the amount of control they desire. For example, depending on the agreement's terms, the organization may no longer hire or supervise staff or make decisions directly affecting costs. (These operating decisions will likely be made by the contract management company.) The sponsoring organization's staff must be convinced that management and other fees that it must pay will be offset by lowered operating costs. There is always a risk that operating expenses may be higher

RISING STAR PROFILE

Eric Loyall
District Manager
Corporate Services
Sodexho
Cincinnati/Louisville/Atlanta

A "Do Whatever It Takes!" Attitude

What is your educational background?

I graduated with an undergraduate hospitality management degree from the University of Massachusetts.

What is your work experience?

I am a district manager for Sodexho. My district is a bit unusual as I am currently responsible for the Food, Catering, and Vending services at five zoos, one museum, and 10 traditional corporate dining accounts.

What is the most unforgettable moment in your career?

While a student at UMASS, I held a summer job at a food stand inside a regional amusement park. One day management approached me and offered me an increase of 25 cents per hour to be in charge of the food stand. Though I was not sure I wanted to be responsible for others, I agreed. It turned out that, for $10 more each week, I had to do about 10 times the work! At the time, I didn't realize this small step to management would lead to a rewarding career full of unforgettable moments.

What are the most significant challenges facing your segment of the industry? How are they being addressed?

The biggest challenge is the same in all segments: Our customers are becoming more sophisticated (yes, even in the concessions and leisure world!). We address this challenge with more sophisticated menu offerings; themed locations; signature items; package pricing; the use of national, local, and in-house brands; the use of retail-style merchandising; and lots (lots!) of employee training programs.

What, if anything, would you do differently in your career?

I would learn Spanish because it would be very helpful in my efforts to manage a diverse work force.

What is your advice for young people considering a career in your industry?

There is no doubt that the foodservice industry is very exciting. Foodservice combines elements of the manufacturing and service industries, and this creates lots of action. In the course of this action, you will work with and for countless characters in many exciting situations. Hollywood has caught on to the industry's appeal. Just consider the food-related reality shows broadcast on major networks. However, to be successful, one must have what all our successful managers and chefs have: a passion for business, and a "do whatever it takes" attitude.

Elderly person enjoying a meal at a long-term care facility. Its Food and Nutrition Service Department could be self-operated or a managed services account of a contract management company.

management contract a formal, written agreement that specifies the responsibilities and obligations of both the organization sponsoring the foodservices and the management company that provides them; frequently, the company agrees to assume total responsibility for management of the foodservices operation in return for a management fee and, perhaps, other remuneration; the organization provides the building and equipment and may continue to incur legal and economic liability

EXHIBIT 17.2

Risks in an Arrangement to Operate Foodservices

deficit or subsidy the amount of expenses that cannot be paid for with revenues generated by a non-commercial foodservice program; called *loss* in a commercial foodservice operation

Organization Risks	Contract Management Company Risks
Loss of total control	Loss of profits
Potential operating cost **deficits** and **subsidies**	Sponsoring organization may become fiscally unsound
Reliance on the contract management company	Lack of input into long-range decisions that affect the foodservice operation
Concerns about lowered priority for its foodservice operation	Potential damage to its reputation
	Possibility that resources used to obtain and manage the account could be better spent elsewhere.

with the management company than without it, and the organization must frequently assume much or all of any operating deficit from the foodservices program. Even if the contract with the management company is terminated, what does the organization then do about its need to offer foodservices? Finally, there is a risk that a management company will reduce the attention it gives to the organization over the life of the contract. This can occur, for example, when it gives priority to efforts to attract and retain more lucrative accounts.

The management company is not without its own risks as an agreement is negotiated and administered. First, the management company risks reduced profit. (It may be possible to increase profits by channeling resources into other more profit generating ventures.) Second, it must assume that the sponsoring organization will remain fiscally sound. Also, the management company generally has little or no input into long-range decisions that affect it. If the management contract is terminated for whatever reason before its term, the management company has lost an account that has cost company resources to build. Also, the management company's reputation can be damaged, and the resources used to obtain and manage the account could have been more effectively used elsewhere.

OBJECTIVE 3
Outline basic steps in the decision-making process to select and utilize a contract management company.

THE CONTRACT MANAGEMENT DECISION

Exhibit 17.3 reviews general steps that an organization might find useful when making a decision to use a contract management company for its foodservices. Each step in the figure is important, and the steps should be

Elderly persons dining in an upscale retirement center

NONCOMMERCIAL FOODSERVICES OFFER EXCITING CAREERS

Noncommercial foodservices of both types (self-operated and contract management company-operated) offer exciting career alternatives because they often provide foodservices that are as diverse and challenging as are their commercial (restaurant and hotel foodservices) counterparts. (In fact, some might argue that the challenges are greater in noncommercial operations, because the same audience of potential guests is often at the heart of daily marketing and operating concerns.)

As a case study, consider a foodservices program operated at a world-famous healthcare institution whose main campus comprises many square blocks in a major city. The facility utilizes the services of a contract management company to manage an array of foodservices, including these:

Cash cafeteria operations in several facilities serving thousands of customers on an average day

Regular and special diets served to thousands of patients on an average day

Thousands of meals for employees, including physicians and other medical specialists, daily

Full-service foodservices, including banquets, coffee breaks, off-site catering, parties, and a wide range of other foodservices for employee special events

Special meals for government dignitaries, movie stars, and other personalities (patients) from around the world

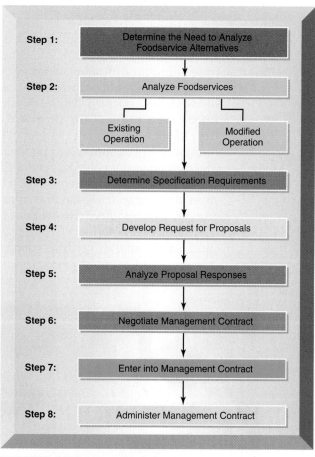

EXHIBIT 17.3
The Contract Management Decision

The unit manager for a managed services account talks to his area manager.

done sequentially. Let's examine this process.

Step 1: Determine the Need to Analyze Foodservice Alternatives. The organization must consider the factors that it will use to evaluate its own self-operated program and contract management company alternatives. Costs will be important, but so will quality and other standards. These must be defined and used (a) to determine when and if analysis of the current foodservices is needed, (b) to develop performance standards against which to review alternatives, and (c) to suggest priorities for the use of time and other limited resources. (The organization's administrators have many things to do; they need an objective way to determine the most significant problems. Should time be spent analyzing foodservices or, alternatively, is their time better spent on other activities?)

Step 2: Analyze Foodservices. The existing foodservices operation can be carefully reviewed by considering sales, costs, and other factors for which operational data are available. This analysis may generate ideas to modify the existing operation in a way that allows the existing self-operated program to be improved without the need for external (contract management company) assistance.

Step 3: Determine Specification Requirements. Analysis of the existing operation and estimates about operating results if systems are modified can yield information useful in describing an ideal foodservices program. These should be identified and incorporated into a **request for proposal (RFP)**. Exhibit 17.4 identifies factors to be considered when reviewing an existing foodservice program and to be included in requests for proposals from potential contract management companies.

Step 4: Develop Request for Proposals. Organization representatives must determine if a potential contract management company can provide required foodservices in an acceptable manner. They assess this by developing and sending out a request for proposals to eligible contract management companies.

request for proposal (RFP)
a formal document that incorporates the organization's needs for foodservices expressed in the form of detailed specification requirements; the objective of the RFP is to define the required foodservices so clearly that prospective bidders (management companies) can develop accurate costs and other estimates used in their proposal responses

A dietitian trains unit managers.

EXHIBIT 17.4
Essential Foodservice Specifications

Existing foodservices can be examined to assess the extent to which the following factors are satisfactorily met by a self-operated foodservice program. This will suggest information that should be supplied by prospective contract management companies to indicate how they would operate foodservices under a management contract. This basic information includes the following:

Nutritional requirements
Basic meal patterns
Basic portion sizes
Nutritional audits
Revenues, costs, **surplus,** and deficit relative to budget
Standard recipes
Diet modifications (if applicable)
Food purchase specifications
Serving times
Personnel requirements (for foodservice director and operating staff)
Training requirements
Food handlers' health certificates
Staff uniforms
Wage rates
Compliance with all applicable laws and regulations
Responsibilities of the organization and the contract management company
Accountability, records, payments, and fees, including allocation of costs, examination of records, payment of allowable costs and fees, and compliance fees

surplus the amount of revenues that remain after all costs allocated to the non-commercial foodservice program have been paid; called *profit* in commercial foodservices

Step 5: Analyze **proposal responses.** Contract management companies respond to the request for proposals with a formal proposal response. It indicates exactly how the management company intends to meet all the specifications noted in the request for proposal. Organization officials must study proposal responses and compare them with the facility's current operation and with proposal responses submitted by other management companies.

proposal response the information sent by a contract management company to an organization that addresses foodservice specification requirements detailed in the organization's request for proposal (RFP)

The workers in this large cheese production plant will require breaks and a meal period during their shift. These services may be provided by a contract management company.

Step 6: Negotiate Management Contract. The organization cannot enter into a formal agreement with a management company unless and until a contract that specifically outlines the responsibilities and obligations of both parties has been developed. A process to negotiate each point raised by the management company in its proposal response is necessary.

Step 7: Enter into Management Contract. This formal document specifies the expectations, obligations, and responsibilities of both the organization and its contract management company partner.

Step 8: Administer Management Contract. Procedures to require compliance with the contract are essential to assure the organization that the management company "does what it says it would do."

THE FOODSERVICE LIAISON

OBJECTIVE 4
Describe the role of a foodservice liaison.

foodservice liaison a foodservice management specialist employed by a sponsoring organization to represent its interests in the ongoing administration of the foodservices agreement with a contract management company

Top-level managers of organizations sponsoring noncommercial foodservices are experts in the work they do in education, healthservice, business and industry, and other disciplines. They are not, however, typically experts in managing a foodservices operation within their organization. By contrast, those within the food management company are experts in managing foodservices; after all, it is their business. How can sponsoring organizations level the playing field as they interact with contract management companies?

Some, especially large, organizations may employ a **foodservice liaison** who, with extensive past experience, is a foodservice management specialist. He or she may have worked for many years in a restaurant or hotel's food and beverage operation or even for a contract management company. Increasingly, however, most persons serving as liaisons come from purchasing, human resources, or facility management backgrounds.

Exhibit 17.5 reviews the possible relationship between the organization and the contract management company when a foodservice liaison is utilized. Note, first, that the foodservice liaison typically reports to a business or finance officer within the sponsoring organization. By contrast, the unit foodservice manager reports to the contract management company's district, regional, or area foodservice director. The foodservice liaison interacts with the unit's foodservice manager on day to day and short-term administration of the foodservice contract. Much of this work involves assuring that both

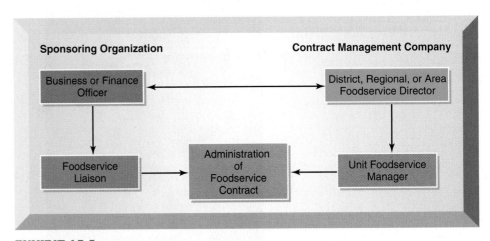

EXHIBIT 17.5
The Foodservice Liaison: The Link in the Relationship Between the Organization and the Contract Management Company

DID YOU KNOW?

Basketball legend and businessman Earvin "Magic" Johnson is offering his name and image (brand) to contract management foodservices in schools and colleges, sports and recreation feeding venues, and even healthcare facilities.

Themes being planned include "Magic Johnson Sports Bar" for colleges and, for schools and sports venues, "The Magic Johnson Marketplace," a basketball-themed eatery with a large, open grill.

His joint venture is with Sodexho and is being undertaken in efforts to change the "cafeteria-going" experience for consumers in a very large industry that is almost anonymous, even though it serves tens of millions of consumers nationwide.

As of June 13, 2006, no deals had been signed, but a campaign was begun to bring some "pizzazz" into a huge industry that is interested in making itself better known to the public that it serves.

Source: Bruce Horovitz. Johnson hopes to work his image magic with food service. *USA Today.* Retrieved June 12, 2006, from usatoday.printthis.clickability .com

parties comply with terms of the contract and, within these terms, discovering ways to more effectively deliver foodservices to those who utilize them. The organization's business or finance officer interacts with the contract management company's foodservice director as longer-term and special issues arise. For example, issues of agreement noncompliance that cannot be resolved between the foodservice liaison and the unit foodservice manager might be discussed by these officials. The foodservice liaison also provides technical assistance to the organization's business or finance officer as a new foodservice management contract is negotiated.

Chef using a grill at the Museum of Science in Boston

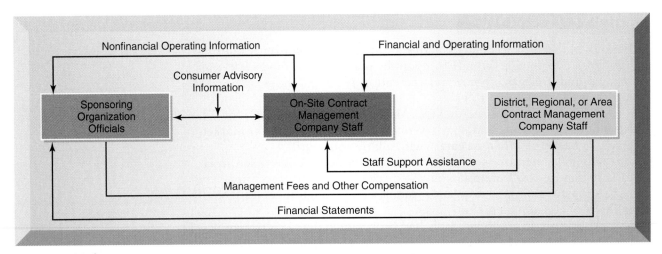

EXHIBIT 17.6
Relationship Between Organization and Contract Management Company Under a Foodservice Agreement

OBJECTIVE 5
Note the importance of and types of communication between the sponsoring organization and the contract management company.

MANAGING THE MANAGEMENT CONTRACT

Exhibit 17.6 reviews the relationship between the sponsoring organization and the contract management company after a foodservices contract has been agreed on. The relationship between the organization and on-site management is primarily of a nonfinancial nature. Also, there is often ongoing input to the sponsoring organization and on-site management from an advisory group of consumers. By contrast, much of the relationship between the organization and off-site contract management company personnel relates to financial matters. The organization pays fees and compensation to the company, which, in turn, provides financial statements to the organization.

Exhibit 17.6 also illustrates the relationship between the on-site management staff and the off-site (district, regional, or area) management company staff: financial and operating information flows between these personnel, and the off-site office provides staff support and assistance as needed.

There are numerous ways that sponsoring organization and contract management company personnel communicate. These are important to recognize, because effective ongoing communication is a critical factor in a successful agreement between the two parties. In an effective relationship, personnel from both the organization and the company will actively manage the agreement, identify operating and other problems, and work cooperatively to address them. Exhibit 17.7 reviews the types and frequency of communication between sponsoring organizations and the management companies who operate their foodservices.

The unit manager of a healthcare food and nutrition services department meets with her district manager.

EXHIBIT 17.7
Communication Between
Organization and Contract
Management Company

Type of Communication	Frequency of Communication
A. Telephone, e-mail, and facsimile (fax)	
1. Organization to on-site management staff	1. Anytime
2. Organization to district- or regional-level management company staff	2. Anytime
B. Meetings	
1. With organization's consumer advisory committee	1. At least monthly
2. Between organization and district- or regional-level management company staff	2. At least bimonthly
3. Between organization and on-site management staff	3. Anytime
C. Written **pro forma projections**	
1. Provided by the contract management company to the organization	1. At least quarterly
2. Annual budget (comparison of projected and actual to-date expenses)	2. Annually
D. Written financial statements	
1. Monthly operating statement (for month and year to date)	1. Monthly
2. Weekly revenue and cost report	2. Weekly
E. Written audit report	
1. Audit report of district or regional staff visit to organization	1. At least bimonthly
F. Informal oral conversation	
1. Between organization and on-site management staff	1. Anytime

pro forma projection
estimates of financial performance done in advance of a fiscal period

CHALLENGES! CHALLENGES!

OBJECTIVE 6
Discuss challenges confronting contract management companies.

The future of this industry segment and the challenges that will likely confront it can be considered from the perspectives of its customers, programs, clients, and work force.[1]

Customers

The typical customer continues to evolve. Globalization along with an increased presence of multinational companies and demographic changes in our own communities have made the customer base of contract management companies increasingly diverse. This base represents every culture and ethnic background and includes many persons whose dining preferences are not traditional U.S. cuisine. To attract and retain their business, we must identify and meet their needs. As well, our traditional customers are learning about new and different cuisines, and they are demanding a wider variety of dining options.

---

[1] This section was contributed by Stephen Di Prima, Division Vice-President, Sodexho's Corporate Services Division, Central Region, who also provided the "Feedback from the Real World" at the end of this chapter.

offshoring the relocation of some business functions such as production or manufacturing to a lower cost-location, typically overseas

Along with dining preferences, work habits are also changing. Some changes are being mandated from the boardroom, but just as many are being driven by the front-line workers themselves. **Offshoring**, virtual offices, flex hours, increased productivity, and technology improvements have all had an impact on noncommercial foodservice operations. In many cases, fewer workers are in buildings, and others maintain work schedules that don't align with traditional dining service operating hours. Contract management companies are aggressively addressing this issue and working even harder to build sales.

A third interesting dynamic is wellness and healthy dining in the workplace. There will always be fads (remember low-carbohydrate diets?), but an increasing number of customers are shifting their personal dining habits with health in mind. They want options that allow them to meet specific dietary goals, such as low salt, low fat, and high fiber, and they no longer want their healthy food decisions to be punitive, that is, to require the purchase of unappealing and bland foods. They expect wellness offerings to be integrated into all points of service and are not willing to sacrifice quality or taste as this occurs.

The impact of inflation, especially higher gasoline prices, also affects our customers, and operations. While income levels make a difference, more customers are demanding more value selections or choosing to bring meals from home. This is an ongoing issue that will continue to evolve with the economy and geopolitical environment.

Programs

Contract management companies are aggressively moving to address the changing profiles of their customers. No longer do companies look at each other as the competition for the customer. Increasingly, the competition is viewed as nearby casual- and quick-service restaurants and the brown bag. Contract management companies continue to partner with well-known national and regional brands, but they are also working hard to develop internal concepts with a retail "feel." For example, Sodexho continues to roll out innovative programs that are comparable to public venues with regard to what is offered and how it is packaged. Today's demanding workplace requires us to look at different ways to serve our customers. For example, credit cards are now the norm, and express lines, office delivery, **grab and go**, and take-home meals have become a standard part of our program.

grab and go the foodservice option in which a customer selects a prepackaged food item for consumption away from the site

sustainability the concept that the needs of today's population can be provided for without damaging the ability of future generations to meet their needs

Sustainability is another trend emerging in our market. Global environmental issues are becoming more important to our customers and clients. While recycling is important, these concerns go well beyond that. Locally grown products are capturing more interest, as is energy conservation. We have an operation in North Carolina that converts used frying oil to biodiesel fuel used to power vehicles on site. Locally grown products demonstrate a support for local industries and provide a higher level of perceived quality. This is a trend that will continue to evolve and grow.

Clients

client (of contract management company) the organization that negotiates and administers the foodservice contract with the management company

Our **clients** are proxies for the economic activity that is happening around the world. Many, if not most, of our client companies are affiliated with international companies or offshore jobs or have foreign subsidiaries. Clients continue to look for ways to reduce suppliers and often move to single-source solutions or a short list of preferred providers. This means that they are looking for companies with global footprints that can follow them wherever they go and that offer the expertise and experience required to work around the globe. Client expectations are for a single point of contact, master contracts, and program consistency. Contract management companies that do this well will grow, and those that don't will miss out on opportunities.

Management contracts are also changing. Traditionally, contracts were agreements that allowed companies to receive a fee for operating the foodservice program. Often these programs operated at a loss that was absorbed by the client. Today, fewer companies are willing to subsidize their programs. They structure contracts in which the management company takes the risk as it retains profits, but also assumes responsibility for losses.

Work Force

Internally, the greatest challenge foodservice management companies will face in the future is the same challenge that confronts them today: finding qualified people with a passion for the business and the desire to make this industry their career. This is true for every level, from the grill cook to boardroom executives. Foodservice professionals must also give back to their industry by supporting educational institutions, mentoring aspiring managers, and becoming personally involved in industry alliances and professional organizations.

SUMMARY OF CHAPTER LEARNING OBJECTIVES

1. **Recognize that the preferred foodservice management alternative (self-operated or contract management company-operated) must be determined on a by-situation basis.**
   There are pros and cons to both self-operated foodservice programs and those operated by contract management companies. The specifics of each situation must be carefully evaluated by decision makers to determine which alternative is best for the organization that sponsors the foodservice program.

2. **Explain that a win–win relationship between the sponsoring organization and the contract management company is needed.**
   Both parties to a management contract must benefit from it for a long-term relationship to evolve. Both the organization and the foodservice management company assume risks, and these must be assessed before and during the time of the contractual relationship.

3. **Outline basic steps in the decision-making process to select and utilize a contract management company.**
   Basic steps to select and utilize a management company include the following:
   • Determine the need to analyze foodservice alternatives
   • Analyze foodservices
   • Determine specification requirements
   • Develop requests for proposals
   • Analyze proposal responses
   • Negotiate management contract
   • Enter into formal agreement
   • Administer management contract

4. **Describe the role of a foodservice liaison.**
   A foodservice liaison is a representative of the organization sponsoring a noncommercial foodservice operation. He or she represents this organization in the administration of the agreement with the contract management company and may or may not have foodservices management experience.

5. **Note the importance of and types of communication between the sponsoring organization and the contract management company.**
   Organization officials generally interact with on-site contract management company staff relative to nonfinancial operating information. Financial aspects of the relationship involve interaction between organizational officials and off-site (district, regional, or area) contract management company staff members. Numerous types of telephone, e-mail, facsimile, meeting, written pro forma projections, written financial statements, written audit reports, and

informal oral conversation help to assure that communication is timely and effective.

6. **Discuss challenges confronting contract management companies.**

Customers are becoming increasingly diverse, and a wider variety of needs must be successfully met to retain the business. As well, changing work habits (for example, virtual offices and flex hours), an increased interest in healthy foods, and the ever-present demand for value in food purchases are becoming more important. There is increased competition from off-site foodservices that is being addressed by companies as they partner with national and regional brands and as they roll out innovative internal concepts. Environmental concerns are now very important and must be addressed. Large clients often want to interact with preferred suppliers who, increasingly, have global footprints, as do their large clients. Today, fewer companies want to subsidize foodservices, so profit and loss contracts are popular. The largest internal challenge of management companies continues to be the search for qualified personnel with a passion for the business.

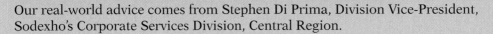

FEEDBACK FROM THE REAL WORLD

Our real-world advice comes from Stephen Di Prima, Division Vice-President, Sodexho's Corporate Services Division, Central Region.

In his current position, Steve's responsibilities include overseeing operations in 20 states and over $400 million in annual revenues. Steve has an undergraduate degree and more than 20 years of foodservice industry experience in both sales and operations. Steve maintains a key focus on client relations, team enhancement and management training, and development activities.

What process would you use to develop a winning proposal response?

Many factors combine to create a winning proposal: one that is customer focused and aligned with the client's needs and objectives.

Long before we develop our response, we employ a strategic process to confirm client objectives, identify creative solutions to meet their needs, outline measurable outcomes, and incorporate proof statements. Throughout this phase, we challenge ourselves to truly differentiate our ideas and proposal. We assign a strategy team for each project made up of individuals with the best skill set to address each new business opportunity.

In some cases, our response must follow a required format (request for proposal), and in other cases, the format is left to our discretion. In either case, the response itself usually includes an executive summary, recommendations, financial projections, and references. The document must be clear, concise, and error free, and must offer a compelling reason to choose our company.

Executive summaries communicate our message and may be the only part of the proposal the decision makers will read. They must be able to see why our company should be selected in a few, well-written pages.

Our clients often tell us that they appreciate our proposals for the following reasons:

- Well-organized and easy to find key information
- Attractive and professionally presented
- Thoroughly demonstrates how well we understand them and their needs
- Customized presentation, rather than a boilerplate document

- Innovative solutions
- Competitive offer

The single most important factor in developing a winning proposal is to clearly understand the client's objectives and to use these to guide your strategy and response.

What factors would enable your organization to manage the foodservices more effectively (successfully) than it is currently?

Numerous factors enable a contract management company to more effectively manage a foodservice operation. Management depth, organizational support, technical expertise, and economy of scale are all advantages that management companies enjoy.

A self-operated organization typically offers limited promotional opportunities for foodservice managers within their field of expertise. In addition, management turnover can have a significant impact, since the transition can require an organization to bring in a candidate from the outside. Support during the transition can be limited. Also, the person being replaced may be the only experienced foodservice management person in the organization.

Conversely, a management company is better able to attract and retain quality candidates because of the clear career path offered by the organization. This career track also provides a ready pool of qualified candidates to replace promoted or reassigned managers.

A management company also has the ability to allocate resources. If, for example, an account has a major event or is opening a new facility, the management company can direct additional managers or specific expertise to support the operation. These resources can include marketing, culinary support, and training, as well as many other areas.

An operation often requires additional technical expertise not available on-site. Sourcing this expertise can be challenging for a self-operated program, and it can be difficult to find and expensive. Management companies that operate a large number of sites typically have faced similar issues in other locations and can share that experience in subsequent situations. Even more importantly, they have the technical resources to support the actions necessary to address these issues.

Finally, a management company can leverage its scale to the advantage of individual accounts. Purchasing power, manufacturer support, distributor marketing, and training are all areas in which a management company can have a positive impact on an individual account.

How soon after the business is awarded to your company could you tool up to take over the program?

There is no standard timetable for transitioning an account. Based on expectations and circumstances, a contract management company can open a new program in two days or two months. Ideally, the organization wants to open with all its new programs and concepts in place. Ultimately, the client determines the speed of the transition.

Factors to consider for the client include current contract terms, company calendar, expectations for service, and upcoming events. Items that the management company must consider include status of current employees, the management selection process, number of locations, renovations, and contract negotiations.

The most successful transitions occur when both sides work together to forge a win–win relationship. Early and candid communication is crucial to a successful transition. This includes a clear understanding of expectations and joint development of performance requirements.

What basic steps would be involved in the transition?

The basic steps in the transition are these.

- Have regular and ongoing communication with client and team
- Review and establish mutual understandings about performance expectations
- Develop and execute bound contract
- Name the opening team and front-line workers
- Develop program specifics
- Requisition equipment
- Identify corporate resources required for the opening
- Renovate and merchandise as necessary
- Conduct preopening surveys and focus-group sessions (if client permits)
- Orient employees
- Train employees

MASTERING YOUR KNOWLEDGE

Discuss the following questions.

1. If you were the manager of a self-operated food-services company, what reasons would you cite to emphasize that self-operated foodservices are the preferred alternative for your organization?

2. If you were a district foodservices director for a contract management company making a sales call on a prospective organizational client, what points would you address that speak in favor of using your company to operate the organization's foodservice program?

3. What are the advantages and disadvantages of using a foodservice liaison from the perspective of the organization and the contract management company?

4. What kinds of day to day operating problems do you think are most likely to arise when an organization enters into a foodservice agreement with a contract management company?

5. How, if at all, does an emphasis on pleasing the consumer and attaining quantity and quality standards change when a self-operated foodservice program ends and a program offered by a contract management company begins?

LEARN FROM THE INTERNET

1. Check out the websites for the following contract management companies:

   - Delaware North Companies: www.delawarenorth.com

   - Centerplate: www.centerplate.com

   - Gluckenheimer Enterprises: www.gluckenheimer.com

   What selling points do they utilize to emphasize how they can benefit organizations who employ them?

2. Review the websites for the following contract management companies that were the top revenue producers in 2005.

   - ARAMARK: www.aramark.com

   - Compass Group, The America's Division: www.cgnad.com

   - Sodexho: www.sodexho.com

What do you think are some of the personal and professional advantages to working for one of these Big Three companies relative to other organizations that generate smaller revenue levels? What are possible disadvantages?

3. Check out the website addresses for the following hotel contract management companies:

   - White Lodging Services Corporation: www.whitelodging.com

   - Hostmark Hospitality Group: www.hostmark.com

   - Tharaldsen Lodging Companies: www.tharaldsen.com

What are the similarities or differences in (a) the way they approach prospective clients and (b) the benefits they suggest will accrue to owners compared to their counterparts who are foodservice management companies?

KEY HOSPITALITY TERMS

The following terms were explained in this chapter. Review the definitions of any words with which you are unfamiliar. Begin to utilize them as you expand your vocabulary as a hospitality professional.

on-site foodservice	surplus
self-operated foodservices	proposal response
contract management company	foodservice liaison
managed foodservices	pro forma projection
account	offshoring
management contract	grab and go
deficit or subsidy	sustainability
request for proposal (RFP)	client

Foodservices in Educational Organizations

18

College students: the market for postsecondary foodservices

CHAPTER LEARNING OBJECTIVES

After studying this chapter you will be able to:

1. Review the variety of foodservices offered in postsecondary schools.
2. Outline a typical organization chart for small and large postsecondary foodservice operations.
3. Describe factors that affect the management and operation of postsecondary school foodservices.
4. Discuss positions unique to postsecondary school foodservices.
5. Explain current challenges confronting administrators of postsecondary school foodservices.
6. Review a typical organization chart of an elementary and secondary school foodservice program.
7. Discuss factors that affect the management of elementary and secondary school foodservices.
8. Describe management positions unique to elementary and secondary school foodservices.
9. Explain current challenges confronting administrators of elementary and secondary school foodservices.

Millions of students live in residence halls at postsecondary schools and, while there, consume many meals over numerous weeks with only relatively few breaks from their campus dining routines. Sometimes payment for foodservices is part of the residence hall fees. This incentive (the meal is already paid for) encourages many to be regular diners.

Many more millions of students in elementary and secondary schools also participate in school foodservice programs. Many have access to lunches served each school day; breakfasts are also served in some schools. Again, an incentive (lowered per meal charges for a predetermined number of meals) may encourage them to participate frequently in these foodservices.

What can foodservice managers of programs in educational organizations do to maximize student participation levels? How will increased student participation rates affect the prices charged per meal? What factors in the near or longer term will most influence levels of student participation in postsecondary school foodservice programs?

As you read this chapter, think about answers to these questions and then get feedback from the real world at the end of the chapter.

---

board plan a payment schedule for meals that is included as part of the charge paid for a residence hall room; schools may offer numerous board plans such as 5, 10, 15, or 20 meals per week at a preestablished charge

Educational organizations meet our definition of noncommercial foodservices because they exist for a reason (education) other than to generate profits from the sale of food and beverage items. To attain their educational objectives, however, they must meet the foodservice needs of students, faculty, and staff. These may range from **board plans** offering numerous meals each week to an a la carte system of cash payments for a snack during a study break.

The variety of foodservices needed must be identified and planned by creative managers to address their constituencies' needs in a cost-effective manner. Programs may be offered by a contract management company or, alternatively, they may be self-operated. (Many colleges and universities utilize a contract management company in an effort to reduce the high costs of operating foodservices and to create new ideas to stimulate participation and revenues.) In both cases, the objectives of providing cost-effective foodservice options that are enjoyed by those consuming them are the same. This chapter will explore the basics of managing foodservices in postsecondary and elementary and secondary educational organizations.

OBJECTIVE 1
Review the variety of foodservices offered in postsecondary schools.

FOODSERVICES IN POSTSECONDARY SCHOOLS

Foodservices in educational organizations, like their counterparts in other noncommercial entities, evolve to meet the needs of those requiring them. A very small commuter college, for example, may utilize only several hundred square feet of space to provide a limited breakfast and/or lunch menu during specified hours and limited beverage or snack offerings at other times throughout the school day. Vending machines located in high-traffic areas throughout the building(s) may supplement this limited foodservice program. At the other extreme,

---

Postsecondary school foodservice information was supplied by Roz Jaffer, formerly Operations Supervisor, Auxiliary Services Division of the Department of Housing and Foodservices, Michigan State University. Kathy Kane, Director of Food and Nutrition Services, Fowlerville, Michigan, assisted with the discussion of foodservices in elementary and secondary schools. The authors also acknowledge the assistance of Alan Fink, Regional Vice-President of Operations, HDS Services, in the development of this chapter.

foodservice options in very large universities serve tens of thousands of students daily and operate on budgets of many millions of dollars annually.

Exhibit 18.1 reviews foodservices available in one large university. The variety of locations and extent of the foodservice operations noted far exceed the common perception (a cafeteria in a commons area and vending machines in a residence hall) of some who quickly dismiss this segment as a meaningful career option. In fact, foodservices of the types described in Exhibit 18.1 and those that are even much smaller require professional, creative, and high-energy managers to operate them effectively.

ORGANIZATION OF POSTSECONDARY FOODSERVICES

Not surprisingly, the complexity of a foodservice organization relates to its size (volume of business). Exhibit 18.2 shows a possible organization chart

OBJECTIVE 2
Outline a typical organization chart for small and large postsecondary foodservice operations.

EXHIBIT 18.1
Foodservice Alternatives in a Large University

Location	Type
Residence halls	• Cafeteria service open 7 A.M. to 7 P.M. daily for full foodservices; 7 P.M. to 10 P.M. daily for short-order and other foodservices
	• Convenience stores
	• A la carte restaurants
	• Snack bars
	• Branded kiosks
	• Carry out and room service (pizza)
	• Vending services
	• Coffee shops
	• Juice bars
	• Bake shops
Libraries	• Snack bars
Memorial union	• Quick-service outlets, cafeteria, and banquets
Conference center	• Full-meal service
	• Coffee break service
Performing arts center	• Catered events
Faculty club	• Fine dining
	• Banquets
	• Swimming pool snack bar
Concession operations (for sporting and special events)	• Catering (in stadium box seat sections)
	• Concession stands (for baseball, football, basketball, agricultural, and other recreational events)
	• Ice cream carts
	• Contracted foodservice venues: branded submarine and other sandwiches, candy, BBQ ribs, ice cream, East Indian cuisine, and Native American food stands
Golf course	• Snack bar
	• Catered events
Tennis facility	• Snack bar
	• Catered events
Hotel or conference center	• Full-service restaurant
	• Room service
	• Banquet operations
	• Pool-side service
	• Snack bars
	• Coffee shops

College students in a cafeteria line

subcontract a contract under a contract: a person may contract with someone else who, in turn, contracts with a third party to perform part of the contract's obligation

allocation the process of distributing revenues earned and/or expenses incurred between departments on a basis that approximates each department's share of the revenues and/or expenses

for a small college with relatively limited foodservices. In this organization, a foodservice manager (who probably does much hands-on work) supervises one or more cooks, cafeteria attendants, dishwashers, and student employees. In turn, she or he reports to the school's business manager. Other important tasks, such as facility cleaning and maintenance and equipment preventive maintenance, are performed by staff members in other departments of the school or may even be performed under a **subcontract;** applicable costs may or may not be **allocated** to the foodservice operation.

Exhibit 18.3 reviews the organization of the foodservice division in a large university. When reviewing this chart, note that a residence hall foodservice manager is directly supervised by a residence hall manager who has responsibility for the entire residence hall. The foodservice manager does, however, have access to the technical help from the university's foodservice department. For example, the residence hall foodservice manager has the support of the foodservice coordinator's office for menu and recipe development, production forecasting, and food costing.

The foodservice manager, in turn, manages the work of a production manager, a service manager, and a student personnel supervisor (who directs student supervisors and student employees). Additionally, the residence hall foodservice manager manages a payroll clerk and the stock handler. In a very large university, there may be 20 or more residence halls organized like the unit illustrated in Exhibit 18.3.

The amount of knowledge, skill, and experience needed to effectively manage foodservices in a postsecondary school is equal to that required for similar positions in other organizations in other segments of the hospitality industry. These positions do, then, represent attractive career goals for those studying for or already within the hospitality industry.

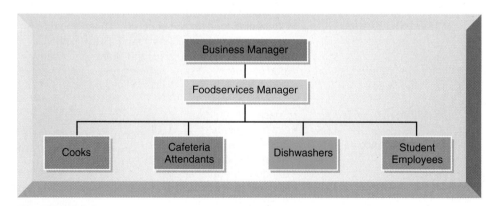

EXHIBIT 18.2
Organization Chart of a Small Postsecondary School Foodservice Operation

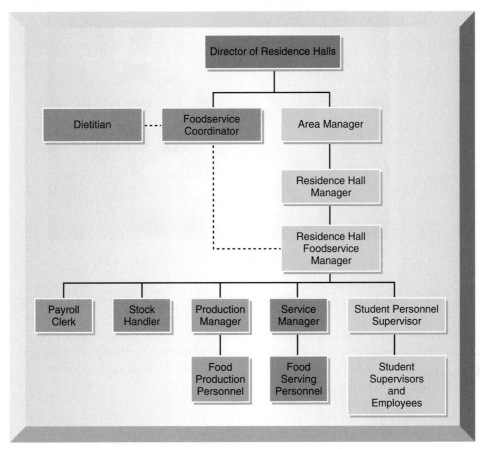

EXHIBIT 18.3
Organization Chart of a Large Postsecondary School Foodservices Operation

A CLOSE LOOK AT POSITIONS IN POSTSECONDARY SCHOOL FOODSERVICES

Many positions in the hospitality industry offer attractive career choices for those desiring them. Foodservice positions in postsecondary schools are no exception! In addition to competitive compensation including benefits, persons in these positions frequently enjoy the following:

Working hours that are in concert with the needs of those being served (late-night and holiday work is less than in some other segments)

Opportunities to work with academic colleagues in matters of campus-wide interest

Ability to assist in planning and presenting educational programs for students in hospitality, general management, and other study areas

Quality of life features (time at work is often limited to 40 hours weekly), and weekend work is often shared among supervisors, which limits weekend work obligations

Advancement opportunities: great promotional opportunities are often available

Academic advancement opportunities: benefits often include the opportunity to take classes for advanced degrees

Discounts on products and services often available for personal purchase at reduced rates through university stores

Technical support for home computers is often available free of charge

College students enjoy a break from classes in a dining room

SPECIAL MANAGEMENT AND OPERATING CONCERNS

The restraints that influence the management and operation of postsec-ondary school foodservices are similar to those that influence foodservices in other noncommercial segments. For example, foodservice administrators must comply with applicable laws relating to employees, safety, sanitation, and security. Typically, the budget is one part of a larger budget applicable to the institution's ancillary (supportive) services. The primary sources of revenue are payments from the users of the foodservices and, perhaps, some financial assistance in the form of **overhead costs** borne by the educational institution and not allocated to foodservices. Foodservices may also receive miscellaneous other revenue, such as that from vending machine rebates, convenience stores, and in-house catering bookings. Additionally, foodser-vice operations often have revenue-generating business in the summer months from participants in sports schools and summer conferences.

Within these restraints, then, the most important factors affecting food-service managers relate to providing foodservices that meet consumer and financial goals. Increasingly, educational foodservices must be **self-supporting;** the sponsoring organization is unwilling to pay for program deficits. Foodservice managers in this segment operate on a day-to-day basis in a manner very similar to their counterparts in commercial foodservices. They must provide value for their consumers while operating within financial goals. Therefore, the most challenging aspect of operating foodservices in a residential hall relates to the balance between providing the appropriate vari-ety of food items on a daily basis while maintaining costs within the budgeted constraints.

UNIQUE POSITIONS IN POSTSECONDARY FOODSERVICES

Not surprisingly, many of the positions required to manage postsecondary school foodservices are the same as those required for other segments of the foodservice industry. Personnel are required for general and on-site management and procurement, for example, and perform functions critical in any operation. Other positions, however, are less frequently found in many hospitality organizations. These include (in very large post-secondary educational foodservices) managers, and their primary responsibilities, as follows:

College foodservice personnel prepare pizza for delivery to residence hall rooms.

- *Residence hall manager.* Manages the financial, personnel, and operational activities of a residence hall to provide quality living accommodations, foodservices, and support services. (This position is, in some ways, similar to that of a hotel's general manager. However, the need to provide counseling to resolve personal problems for students and to, in effect, serve as sort of "adopted parents" for them are responsibilities unique to this position.)

- *Residence hall foodservice manager.* In charge of the overall foodservices operation within a residence hall, including staff management, production, and food and equipment purchases. Other responsibilities may include budget development and management, financial and production forecasts, staff hiring and development, special event catering management, repairs and maintenance, labor relations, and daily meal service operations.

- *Food stores manager.* Directs the daily operation of the food stores. He or she purchases all food and beverage products used at all campus locations. Other responsibilities may include the negotiation of equipment contract purchases, overseeing food store warehousing, and coordination of food, equipment, and supplies distribution to residence hall facilities.

- *Foodservices coordinator.* Responsible for all centralized functions involving computerized recipes, precosting, and menu management. The department also coordinates and implements all campus-wide special events. Additionally, data applicable to past meals and events are provided to other foodservice personnel through the utilization of a centrally managed database.

- *Concessions manager.* Administers and coordinates food, beverage, and merchandise sales at sporting and other public events and may serve as the university liaison to the supplier with the vending contract.

- *Central bakery manager.* Manages the daily operation of the central bakery, which provides baked goods to all the foodservice outlets on campus. The central bakery generates auxiliary revenues through sales of bakery products to parents and students for occasions such as birthdays and graduations.

- *Laundry manager.* Manages the daily operation of the laundry facility, which provides for the linen and laundry needs of the foodservices, building, and on-campus hotel operations. Linen is cleaned and delivered to on-campus locations on a rental charge basis.

- *Convenience store (C-store) manager.* Responsible for the C-stores, fast food, specialty, and coffee shops located throughout the campus.

Explain current
challenges confronting
administrators of
postsecondary school
foodservices.

CHALLENGES FOR POSTSECONDARY SCHOOL FOODSERVICES

Some basic challenges confronting administrators of postsecondary educational foodservices are familiar to their counterparts in other segments. Still others are relatively unique. Let's look at these challenges.

Financial Management

You have already learned about one important challenge that confronts all college and university foodservice managers: the need to provide the wide variety of items that students, faculty, and staff desire within budgeted cost allowances. Like their peers in other segments, financial resources (money) are in increasingly limited supply. Similar also to their counterparts, administrators in this segment must reexamine "how things are done" to find potential new sources for revenue, while implementing processes to reduce costs without sacrificing quality goals. Publicly funded postsecondary schools are finding that revenues from governmental sources are being reduced. This, in turn, requires all administrators in every department to establish priorities and even to reduce some expenditures that might have been considered necessary in the past. Increasingly, foodservices are being required to pay their own way, while students (and/or their families) are paying ever-increasing tuition and related costs. This, in turn, limits the opportunity for foodservice administrators to raise charges without increased (and vocal) concerns from student consumers.

Financial concerns may encourage business and finance managers in facilities offering self-operated programs to evaluate the use of contract management companies. An incentive to reduce costs still further may prompt facilities already utilizing a contract management company to consider the use of a competitive organization.

Availability of Foodservice Employees

Like their counterparts in other segments, postsecondary foodservice administrators often have difficulty in recruiting and retaining full-time employees. Unlike some other segments, students desiring part-time employment are often available. However, turnover is often accelerated, because large numbers of student employees are more likely looking for a part-time, temporary job than searching for a career. A large percentage of student employees must typically be recruited at the beginning of each school semester or term and will resign at its end. On average, a large campus foodservice operation may employ hundreds of student employees each semester. Holidays, school breaks, school trips, and the need to study for examinations create numerous scheduling challenges for foodservice administrators utilizing student employees.

Food Costs

Financial challenges have already been noted. However, food costs are of particular concern. Facilities offering a board plan typically operate with a daily **ration** goal. That is, the operating budget allows an average amount per student that can be spent on food each day.

Consumer Excitement

Students, faculty, and staff consuming frequent meals at an educational facility (and elsewhere) need variety to retain their interest. Foodservice managers face a constant challenge to make a visit to a foodservice outlet

ration   the average amount of money that a noncommercial foodservice operation can spend to purchase food for one person for one day; rations are typical budget goals in schools offering board plans, in the military, and in correctional institutions

something to look forward to, rather than something to be dreaded. Cycle and/or theme menus and help-yourself stations featuring baked potatoes, soups, pizza, submarine and other sandwiches, and numerous other items are among the many examples of tactics that are increasingly used. As well, creative ways to generate student input and the use of off-campus commercial foodservice partners are being used by creative college and university foodservice managers. Other tactics include the following:

Snack bar in a college residence hall

- Special events and dinners
- Cook-to-order pasta, sushi, and breakfast bars
- "Café to Go" concepts (carryout services for popular menu items)
- Theme dinners combined with in-residence hall programming that emphasize ethnic events including, for example, Mexican, Asian, African American, and Greek themes
- Daily menu specials, such as ice cream flambé, potato bar, and cook-to-order vegetarian entrees
- Development of incentive plans to increase student participation
- Marketing of convenience stores for student retail purchases

DID YOU KNOW?

Are "24/7" Foodservices available on your campus?

The term 24/7 refers to 24 hours a day, seven days a week. In other words, "all the time," and that is when foodservice venues are available at some colleges and universities. Some schools do make limited foodservice available around the clock. Others operate 24/7 only on weekends or during finals week. At still other locations, "all night" really means until 3:00 A.M. or 4:00 A.M. However, these operating hours may signify a trend that recognizes some consumers will visit campus foodservices at, literally, any time.

Typically, these programs operate out of a memorial union, enlarged convenience store, or other centralized site. Many offer pizza, burgers, and premade salads and sandwiches, but some offer a 24-hour breakfast menu, and even fresh-made sandwiches.

Labor-cost concerns are important (can revenues generated offset all costs?), but, increasingly, foodservices administrators are able to justify longer hours for more satisfied customers.

Alan E. Fink
Regional Vice-President of Operations
HDS Services
Farmington Hills, Michigan

Alan received his undergraduate degree in 1975 and, after managing several fine dining seafood restaurants, he served as general manager of a private club for five years. For the past 24 years he has worked in the contract management field with HDS Services. His responsibilities have involved supporting foodservice programs in corporate dining, private club, retirement community, and kindergarten to high school and college operations.

Alan offers some insights for those considering a hospitality management career.

What is the most unforgettable moment in your career?

It's difficult to pinpoint one unforgettable moment because every day brings new challenges. One example: coordinating the opening of several different accounts within a 30-day period. Orchestrating the management teams, establishing initial relationships with new clients, training new hourly teams, and introducing our company programs and practices at several locations in different industry segments simultaneously was challenging and exhausting. It was a great accomplishment for our teams to successfully open these operations while meeting the customers' needs.

What are the most significant challenges facing the noncommercial foodservice industry? How are they being addressed?

The entire industry is facing several challenges today. Most notable is attempting to "do more with less." In other words, the typical foodservice operation must reduce its internal operating budgets while continually being challenged to upgrade the quality and quantity of services provided to customers. This is difficult, and it takes a concerted effort by managers and hourly associates to achieve these goals.

One tactic is to seek additional revenue streams. Many managers react to budget cuts by trying to minimize food, labor, and direct expenses. However, a better approach is to increase the revenue base as an alternative or in addition to cost-cutting initiatives. Catering opportunities, snack bars and sundry shops, and even ancillary services such as child care and dry cleaning might be ways to augment revenue opportunities.

Another challenge is that our customers are now much more demanding, knowledgeable, and diverse, and we must provide several nutritious and appetizing meal options. Many customers in the schools and corporate cafeterias we support are requesting ethnic choices such as Asian, Hispanic, and Mid-Eastern selections, along with vegetarian alternatives. We meet these requests while maintaining food and labor cost controls. To do so requires that we study menu costs, production sheets, and productivity levels and utilize leftovers efficiently.

What, if anything, would you do differently in your career?

I would have supplemented my education with a culinary degree from a highly respected culinary school such as Johnson & Wales. In most foodservice operations food expense represents the highest cost, yet so few managers really understand the complexities and dynamics of the kitchen. I learned from years of working closely with chefs and kitchen associates. (In other words, through "osmosis.") However, a more formal culinary education would have been very beneficial.

What is your advice for young people considering a career in your industry?

1. As you gain experience, don't concern yourself with only monetary rewards. Learning from experts and reputable organizations far surpasses instant financial success. The salaries will be there for those who focus on surrounding themselves with good mentors.
2. Never sacrifice quality in the work you do. Today's customers are too sophisticated and knowledgeable about outstanding food and service to accept anything less. This doesn't mean buying only prime-graded meats, fresh products, and $50 per pound dessert chocolate. Even the best and most costly foods can be destroyed if they are not handled properly. Buying the right product at the right price, preparing foods using tested recipes, consistently training your staff about customer service, and treating each associate with respect are paramount to a successful food operation.
3. Get to know the people in your foodservice classrooms and in the industry. The person studying with you today could be an important internal or external customer in the future. Foodservice management is really a small community, and networking is always important.

FOODSERVICES IN ELEMENTARY AND SECONDARY SCHOOLS

OBJECTIVE 6
Review a typical organization chart of an elementary and secondary school foodservice program.

Elementary, middle (junior), and high schools often make a midday meal available for their students, faculty, and staff. Many programs are self-operated, some are operated by contract management companies, and all are confronted by the same economic and other challenges (along with some additional ones!) that confront their peers in postsecondary schools.

ORGANIZATION OF ELEMENTARY AND SECONDARY SCHOOL FOODSERVICES

The organization of the foodservice program relates in large measure to its size. Exhibit 18.4 shows a typical organization for a small **decentralized foodservice program** in an elementary or secondary school. Note that the principal is the direct supervisor of the foodservice manager within the school. The manager may, in turn, direct the work of cooks, who frequently produce and serve the food and perform applicable cleanup duties. Other personnel may be required for dish, pot, and other washing duties. Teachers, teacher assistants, and/or parents (community) volunteers may be responsible for dining room supervision and related tasks. As seen in the chart, while the school foodservice manager in each school is still directly supervised by the school's principal, there is no external, centralized assistance from a district-level foodservice director.

decentralized (school foodservices) program a foodservice organization in which a manager has independent responsibility for menu planning, purchasing, recipe development, and all other aspects of operating the program within a single school

Exhibit 18.5 illustrates reporting relationships in a **centralized school foodservice program.** General responsibilities for menu planning, procurement, recipe development, training, and a wide range of other tasks are assumed by a district foodservice director. He or she is responsible to the school district's business manager and, in turn, coordinates the work of school foodservice managers in each school. In this model, school principals serve in a staff advisory relationship to the school foodservice manager. The principal and his or her staff, for example, establish meal serving times, may help to identify (process) students eligible for free or reduced-price meals (this is discussed

centralized (school foodservices) program a foodservice organization in which general foodservice management duties are coordinated within the school district, and a foodservice manager directs the operation of a foodservice program within a single school

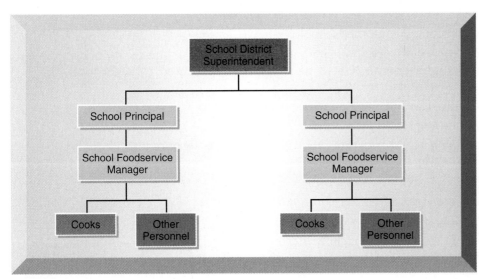

EXHIBIT 18.4
Organization Chart of a Decentralized Elementary and Secondary School Foodservices Program

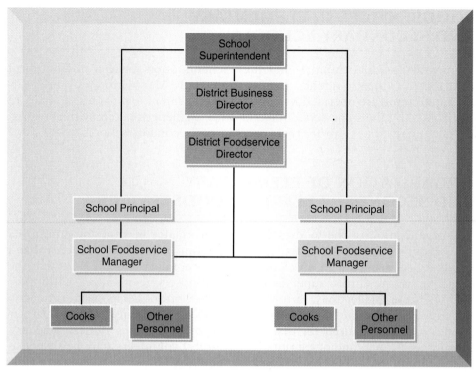

EXHIBIT 18.5
Organization Chart of a Centralized Elementary and Secondary School Foodservices Program

THERE IS MORE THAN LUNCH IN ELEMENTARY AND SECONDARY FOODSERVICES

Many persons typically think of the school lunch when they think about foodservices in elementary and secondary schools. The midday meal is, by far, the largest part of the operation of foodservices in elementary and secondary schools. However, other types of foodservice alternatives may also be offered including these:

School breakfasts

Meals served to participants in other school-related programs

Contract feeding for meals served on-site and/or transported off-site for service to persons participating in programs such as Head Start sponsored by other local, state, and federal government agencies

Summer feeding programs offering breakfast and/or lunch to enrolled students

Special milk programs

Afterschool a la carte (cafe) programs that allow students to purchase items for consumption on the way to or at home

Vending

Catering for school district and general public-related events

Elementary and secondary school foodservice administrators are constantly addressing the concern to be self-funding, while offering meals and food items with nutritional integrity.

later), and can help to promote the foodservice program throughout the school year. (The use of a foodservice director to coordinate a foodservice operation in individual units is similar to the responsibilities of a manager in a district, area, or region in a multiunit commercial foodservice operation. As districts become larger, a centralized organization realizes greater benefits.)

Large school districts with numerous school buildings tend to centralize both food production and foodservice management. Careful analyses often show that operating costs may be reduced significantly if, for example, food is produced in a central **commissary** for distribution and service at individual schools. When this plan is utilized, schools with the largest student enrollment (typically, middle, junior, and senior high schools) house the commissary. In addition to producing meals for the school's consumption, additional meals are prepared for consumption at **satellite** units.

After a morning of class these grade school students are ready for lunch.

commissary a food preparation area (kitchen) utilized to produce food items at least some of which will be transported or served off-site

Meals prepared at the central commissary are transported to satellite schools in one or more of several common ways:

- Foods can be prepared during the morning of service and can be kept hot during transport to the satellite. Foods can be transported in **bulk** in hot-food carts or, alternatively, can be preportioned into containers made of Styrofoam or other heat-retaining material.
- Meals can be prepared on the afternoon (or earlier) before the day of service and can be preportioned and refrigerated until shipped to the satellite school. (There, meals are **reconstituted** to serving temperature immediately before service.)
- Meals can be produced and preportioned sometime before service and can be frozen for later delivery to the satellite center. They can then be reconstituted for service as needed.

satellite (school foodservices) a location to which food prepared in a commissary at another location is transported and served; for example, a satellite school serves meals produced in an off-site central commissary

bulk (food portions) a large volume of food that has not been preportioned for individual service

reconstituted the application of heat to a chilled or frozen food item to raise it to the proper serving temperature

In compliance with certain restrictions discussed later, schools may also purchase all or part of the meals to be served from external suppliers. However, concerns about food quality and the cost of alternative food production and delivery systems are always issues with which school foodservice managers must deal.

FACTORS AFFECTING ELEMENTARY AND SECONDARY SCHOOL FOODSERVICES

OBJECTIVE 7
Discuss factors that affect the management of elementary and secondary school foodservices.

Managers of foodservices in this segment have most, if not all, of the same types of restraints encountered by their postsecondary school foodservice counterparts. In addition, however, two other factors are of great significance:

Federal Government Regulations

commodities (federally donated) foods purchased by the U.S. Department of Agriculture for distribution to schools and other eligible recipients

Many elementary and secondary school foodservice programs participate in the U.S. Department of Agriculture (USDA) Child Nutrition Programs. In return for receiving monies and federally donated **commodities** to help to subsidize school foodservice programs, participating schools must comply with numerous regulations. Examples of these regulations include the following:

- The need to provide free or reduced-priced meals to low-income students as defined by the federal government. (Schools must use methods to make meals available in a way that protects the anonymity of recipients.)
- Requirements about the nutritional value of meals eligible for governmental reimbursements
- Requirements to make food available in schools without school foodservices
- Significant record-keeping requirements to justify reimbursements that have been requested and received

Usually, personnel from the applicable State Department of Education work with local schools to improve the foodservices and to assure compliance with applicable regulations. In some states, inspections of private schools are conducted by representatives of the USDA.

Children in a school cafeteria line

Governance by the School Board

Foodservices operated by elementary and secondary schools are an integral part of the school's organization, which is, ultimately, regulated by an elected or appointed school board. As such, the most important decisions affecting the schools and the foodservices within them are made by persons without full-time management responsibilities for the school. (This organizational structure is, of course, a cornerstone of the American way of life. Local communities should be responsible for schools and should make the most important decisions that affect them. Our point relates to the possibility that decisions affecting school foodservices may be made on numerous bases that do not, and probably should not, consider school foodservices as the highest priority.) Examples include decisions regarding the continuance of decentralized foodservices in schools where they cannot be cost justified, decisions about the use (or nonuse) of contract management companies, supplier selection decisions, and compensation for foodservices personnel.

UNIQUE MANAGEMENT POSITIONS

OBJECTIVE 8
Describe management positions unique to elementary and secondary school foodservices.

Several management positions unique to school foodservices in elementary and secondary schools are described next.

District Foodservice Director

Some of the duties of these administrators were discussed earlier in the chapter. They have centralized administrative duties (for example, developing budgets, managing compliance with federal, state, and/or local regulations and developing food purchase specifications). They also provide technical training to unit managers. Foodservice directors in very large districts may be responsible for foodservices in, perhaps, hundreds of schools and manage multimillion dollar foodservice budgets.

School Foodservice Consultant

This professional is employed by the State Department of Education or the USDA. He or she visits participating school districts to assure compliance with applicable USDA regulations and may perform numerous other tasks, such as these:

- Developing and presenting training programs on topics applicable to school foodservices
- Providing technical assistance, for example, in the design of foodservice facilities and the conduct of special projects for local foodservice programs

Grade-school children eat lunch in a multipurpose room that is used for other purposes after the mobile tables are removed.

- Providing input to the analysis of requests for proposals and/or proposal responses by schools soliciting assistance from contract management companies

Like all effective consultants, persons in this position must identify problems and then provide recommendations for their resolution.

Nutrition Educator

Many elementary and secondary school foodservice programs assist classroom teachers with nutrition education activities. Many educators believe that dietary habits are learned and can be influenced by what is taught in the classroom and can be complemented by foodservices available in the school's dining room. District foodservice directors, in general, and nutrition educators, more specifically, may make presentations in classrooms (especially in elementary schools), provide nutrition-related resources to classroom teachers, and otherwise promote the role that school foodservices can play in health and nutrition. Many nutrition educators are **registered dietitians (RDs)** with significant knowledge about nutrition-related concerns.

Note: As students advance to higher grade levels, nutrition education efforts typically shift away from the classroom and toward efforts to promote the selection of nutritious food alternatives at the time of meal service. Some secondary schools, for example, offer only nutritious meal alternatives, with several choices for the entree and/or other items. Other schools, however, offer a wide range of a la carte items that often have advantages (increasing student participation and revenues) and a disadvantage (reducing the emphasis on nutritional meal selection).

registered dietitian (RD) a member of the American Dietetic Association (ADA) who meets requirements relating to minimum academic and internship experiences; the RD has successfully passed a registration examination and accrued specified registration maintenance credits by participating in ongoing professional education activities

OBJECTIVE 9
Explain current challenges confronting administrators of elementary and secondary school foodservices.

CHALLENGES CONFRONTING ELEMENTARY AND SECONDARY SCHOOL FOODSERVICES

Like their counterparts in postsecondary schools, foodservice directors and managers in elementary and secondary schools confront many challenges. Some of these are described next.

The Need to Be Self-Supporting

A decreasing number of schools provide a **board-budgeted deficit** to support the school's foodservice program. This, in turn, requires school foodservice programs to generate revenues sufficient to meet operating costs. The challenge increases if and when additional costs are allocated to school foodservices and when revenues and/or donated food commodities do not keep pace with rising costs.

board-budgeted deficit (school foodservices) a grant made by the governing unit to the school foodservices program to compensate for losses incurred when revenues do not meet expenses

Revenue Shortfalls in Secondary Schools

The issue about nutritional concerns versus a la carte meals generating higher revenue levels has already been noted. Schools that allow students to leave the campus and that have shortened lunch periods provide additional obstacles to maximizing revenues from students. Other alternatives, including the availability of vending and fund-raising activities involving food sales by student groups, may reduce student participation in school foodservice programs still further.

Changing Student Food Preferences

Foodservice managers have the constant challenge of keeping up with **food fads** and **food trends.** As with their counterparts in higher education, student food preferences seemingly change quickly and often radically. Special efforts are required to continually identify and offer items desired by students that fall within cost, nutritional, and, sometimes, regulatory guidelines.

food fad a relatively short-lived interest in or preference for specific food items

food trend a longer-lived change in the preference for or interest in specific food items

Educator and Student Apathy

The important role that properly managed school foodservices can play is sometimes overlooked. School foodservices are sometimes viewed as little more than a filling station for students needing something to eat at midday. This is unfortunate, because foodservice managers quickly point out that students who are hungry and/or malnourished cannot perform at their very best in the classroom. Ongoing promotion and publicity efforts, such as the National School Lunch Week sponsored by the American School Foodservice Association, are employed as necessary to counter this improper stereotype.

Regulation Changes

Schools participating in programs receiving federal funds and/or commodities must comply with a wide range of regulations as a condition to receiving this assistance. Sometimes, rules change almost overnight and can require significant effort for timely compliance.

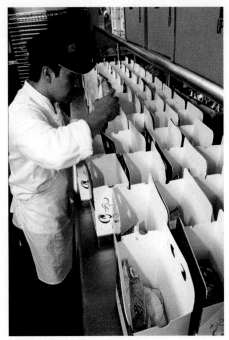

School foodservice employee preparing box lunches for a field trip

Increased Use of Technology

As is true with other segments of the hospitality industry, elementary and secondary school foodservice administrators receive significant assistance from technology. Two examples: computerized point-of-sale (POS) systems make it easier to track free or reduced-price meals that need to be served in a way that protects the anonymity (identity) of recipients. This increases the number of students who apply and receive meals, which, in turn, increases revenues (reimbursements) to the school districts. Also, technology allows Internet access to parents; they can learn the amount of money in their child's lunch account and what food items have been purchased. Parents, especially at middle-school levels, often use this information to encourage children to purchase and consume foods of appropriate nutritional value, rather than **junk foods,** which are frequently purchased when there is no or little parental supervision.

junk foods (school foodservices)   foods with little or no nutritional value

CHECK IT OUT!

To learn more about this system, go to www.mealpay.com.

Source: Michelle Lefort. MealPay tracks kids eating. *USA Today*, October 4, 2005.

SUMMARY OF CHAPTER LEARNING OBJECTIVES

1. **Review the variety of foodservices offered in postsecondary schools.**

   The variety of foodservices offered in postsecondary schools ranges from the small commuter school offering, perhaps, basic breakfast, lunch, and snack fare, to a major university offering numerous foodservice outlets in residence halls, libraries, memorial unions, conference and performing arts centers, faculty clubs, and concessions at sporting events.

2. **Outline a typical organization chart for small and large postsecondary foodservice operations.**

   In a small postsecondary school, the foodservice manager typically reports to the institution's business manager and supervises cooks, cafeteria attendants, dishwashers, and student employees. In a larger operation, the foodservice manager may report to a residence hall manager and, in turn, may direct the work of production and service managers (who supervise others with these responsibilities) and a student personnel supervisor (who directs the work of student supervisors and employees).

3. **Describe factors that affect the management and operation of postsecondary school foodservices.**

   Restraints include the need to apply applicable laws and to develop and stay within budgetary restraints, which may include the need to be self-supporting. The overall concern is to provide value to consumers while operating within financial goals.

4. **Discuss positions unique to postsecondary school foodservices.**

   Positions unique to postsecondary school foodservices include residence hall manager, food storage manager, residence hall foodservice manager, food stores manager, foodservice coordinator, concessions manager, central bakery manager, laundry manager, and convenience store manager.

5. **Explain current challenges confronting administrators of postsecondary school foodservices.**

   Current challenges include the need for school foodservices to pay their own way, to attract full-time and part-time (often student) employees, to manage food costs, and to consistently generate consumer excitement for the foodservices offered.

6. **Review a typical organization chart of an elementary and secondary school foodservice program.**

   In a centralized school foodservice program, a district foodservice director provides technical assistance to the foodservices manager in each school. By contrast, in a decentralized school district, the school foodservice manager is the expert on the foodservice operation within the school. Large school districts typically operate a commissary (for off-site production), with the food then transported to satellite (individual school) serving units.

7. **Discuss factors that affect the management of elementary and secondary school foodservices.**

   Some factors that affect the management of elementary and secondary school foodservices are federal government regulations and governance by the local district's school board.

8. **Describe management positions unique to elementary and secondary school foodserices.**

   Management positions unique to elementary and secondary school foodservices include school foodservice director, school foodservice consultant, and nutrition educator or registered dietitian (RD).

9. **Explain current challenges confronting administrators of elementary and secondary school foodservices.**

   Challenges confronting elementary and secondary school foodservice administrators include the need to be self-supporting, revenue shortfalls in secondary schools, changing student food preferences, educator and student empathy, regulation changes, and increased use of technology.

FEEDBACK FROM THE REAL WORLD

Our real-world advice comes from Roz Jaffer, formerly Operations Supervisor, in the Department of Housing and Foodservices, Michigan State University.

Roz has a bachelor's degree in hospitality business and a master's degree in labor and industrial relations and has more than 19 years of experience in housing and food services administration.

What can foodservice managers of programs in educational organizations do to maximize student participation levels?

Foodservice managers must become much more creative in the way they plan and deliver products and services to their students. Examples include these:

- Offer more carryout or "to go" services
- Utilize vending machines with more extensive offerings of high-quality food items
- Offer room service (for example, pizza delivery to residence hall rooms during evenings and weekends)
- Utilize customer-service days or weeks to "experiment" with new items; these can be complimentary or offered at discounts to encourage student purchases and feedback
- Offer gourmet continental breakfast setups conveniently located by the front doors of the residence halls and classroom buildings
- Offer gourmet buffet breakfast setups in special dining rooms of a residence hall on the weekends and during slow periods
- Meet the individual needs of the students by offering specialized dietary menus
- Offer late-night snacks and services

How will increased student participation rates affect the prices charged per meal?

Believe it or not, as student participation in board rate plans increase, it may be necessary

to increase prices. Why? Because the food prices established in board plans are based on a student no-show rate. For example, student charges built into a 20 meal per week board plan assume that the student will consume 20 meals per week for every week in the semester, even though that it is not likely to occur. This no-show rate can range from 5 to 55 percent depending on the day of the week and the specific meal period. No-shows, then, generate revenue even though there are no offsetting food costs for the meals that are not consumed. As student participation increases (that is, as students consume more meals), the no-show rate decreases. Costs for food consumed therefore increase, and this creates the possibility of having to offset higher food costs with higher student charges.

What factors in the near or longer term will most affect the levels of student participation in postsecondary school foodservice programs?

The students' participation rates are obviously affected by their interest in consuming the available meals or food items. Therefore, it is necessary for foodservice administrators to keep up with student interests, food fads, and trends. These can change quickly, and we must learn about them so that we can consistently offer items that our students will desire.

(continued)

There are some student-related trends that foodservice administrators must also address, such as the following:

- A trend toward lower participation rates in campus foodservices over the weekend. Students may have, in many areas, numerous alternatives that are of competitive interest to them.
- Many students prepare some or all of their meals in residence hall rooms, even though most cooking appliances are not permitted. It is to our advantage to offer value-based meals that make this alternative less attractive.
- Increasingly, students desire a la carte (not board) plans. We can address this by using a la carte (cash or debit) operations and by offering convenience stores, kiosks, coffee shops, food courts, creative meal plans, restaurants, outdoor hot dog and ice cream stands, and food pubs and by making vending and contractual arrangements with off-campus food or beverage operations, including those that are branded. An interesting idea: we are now planning to offer commission-based (contractual fee) arrangements with off-campus foodservice operators. With this plan, students would make a deposit into a campus account; they could then use these funds to purchase products at participating operations, which would pay a commission to the university.
- It is imperative for foodservice managers to keep up with the food trends of local and national restaurants. For example, the current trends toward ethnic foods, healthy foods, and small portion sizes are all considerations that should be of interest as foodservice managers plan future menus. Additionally, changes must be made quickly to keep up with trends. This is critical to avoid loss of business and decreases in student participation rates.

Postsecondary school foodservice administrators must consistently generate student interest by first discovering what students prefer and then finding creative ways to deliver it at a cost acceptable to both the educational facility and the student market.

MASTERING YOUR KNOWLEDGE

Discuss the following questions.

1. If you were the foodservice administrator in a postsecondary school, what tactics would you utilize to increase student acceptance of and participation in the program?
2. What are some potential advantages of assuming an administrative position in a postsecondary school foodservice program? Potential disadvantages?
3. What might you do to recruit and retain student employees for the school foodservice program that you manage?
4. Compare and contrast a centralized elementary and secondary school foodservice program? A decentralized program?
5. How would you evaluate the type of delivery system utilized to transport meals from a central commissary to a satellite serving unit?
6. The text notes several ways in which the work of a district's foodservice director is similar to that of an area manager in a multiunit foodservice organization? What are additional ways? How are job responsibilities different?
7. What are some ways that the work of a school foodservice consultant is similar to that of a consultant specializing, for example, in kitchen layout and design?

LEARN FROM THE INTERNET

1. Check out the websites of the following contract management companies:
   - ARAMARK: www.aramark.com
   - Chartwells(Compass Group): www.chartwells-usa.com
   - Sodexho USA:www.sodexhousa.com

   What information do they provide about services offered for postsecondary schools? For elementary and secondary schools?

2. Check out the website for your own school. What, if any, information about your school's foodservice program is noted?

3. Check out the website for the National Association of College and University Foodservices (NACUFS): www.nacufs.org. What current topics are being discussed by the predominantly postsecondary school foodservice administrators who visit this website?

4. Check out the website for the School Nutrition Association: www.schoolnutrition.org. What current topics are being discussed by the predominantly elementary and secondary school foodservice administrators who visit this website?

KEY HOSPITALITY TERMS

The following terms were explained in this chapter. Review the definitions of any words with which you are unfamiliar. Begin to utilize them as you expand your vocabulary as a hospitality professional.

board plan
subcontract
allocation
overhead costs
self-supporting (foodservices)
ration
decentralized (school foodservices) program
centralized (school foodservices) program
commissary

satellite (school foodservices)
bulk (food portions)
reconstituted
commodities (federally donated)
registered dietitian (RD)
board-budgeted deficit (school foodservices)
food fad
food trend
junk foods (school foodservices)

19 Food and Nutrition Services in Healthcare Facilities

Exterior of large private hospital

CHAPTER LEARNING OBJECTIVES

After studying this chapter you will be able to:

1. State common goals of food and nutrition service programs in healthcare facilities.

2. Describe the organization of food and nutrition service programs in hospitals and senior life-style and care facilities.

3. Review job duties of selected positions unique to healthcare food and nutrition service programs.

4. Discuss tools and tactics used to help assure that patients and residents receive meals that meet prescribed nutritional requirements.

5. Explain basic steps in common systems used to transport food within healthcare facilities.

6. Discuss challenges confronting administrators of food and nutrition service programs in healthcare facilities.

This chapter is authored by Julie Tkach. Julie is a doctorial student at Michigan State University and has served as Director of Nutrition Services in a hospital for eight years. She acknowledges the assistance of Nancy Bacyinski, Regional Director of Operations for HDS Services in the Cincinnati market.

FEEDBACK FROM THE REAL WORLD

The responsibilities of healthcare food and nutrition service administrators are fascinating, complex, fast-changing, and challenging. Their decisions can literally affect the health and even the lives of those being served. Their professional contributions are vital to achieving goals relating to patients (in hospitals) and residents (in senior life-style and care facilities) and to the financial well-being of their facilities.

The name of the department discussed in this chapter differs throughout the healthcare industry. Common examples include nutrition services, dining services, dietary services, and food and nutrition services. (The latter name will be used throughout this chapter.) However, the many basic goals, organizational patterns, job duties in selected positions, operating protocols, and challenges are similar among these departments, regardless of their names. These are the topics of this chapter.

What are some ways in which the work of a food and nutrition services administrator is similar to that of a manager in a food and beverage operation in a hotel or a restaurant? What are some ways in which the work is different? What are examples of how regulations applicable to the operation of healthcare facilities have affected the operation of the food and nutrition services department? What are some ways that the management of the department will likely change over the next 10 or 15 years? What are some things that those who lead healthcare food and nutrition service departments will be required to know and/or to do in the future that are of less importance today?

As you read this chapter, think about answers to these questions and then obtain feedback from the real world at the end of the chapter.

A hospital's mission is generally to provide short-term (acute) healthcare to heal those who are sick or injured and to promote wellness, develop personnel, and advance research and education. By contrast, the mission of a senior life-style and care facility is to provide the proper level of residential care for those who desire or require it. Today, as noted in Exhibit 19.1, a wide range of life-style and care alternatives are available for older persons. The names and features of these options vary, and individual facilities may offer services at one or more of these service options. While one normally thinks of these residential alternatives as being appropriate for the elderly, others, such as accident victims and young persons with degenerative diseases, may also require long-term care services. Each type of life-style and care option offers foodservices to residents desiring or needing it. Throughout this chapter, we will use the term **long-term care facility** to apply to residential facilities offering any or all of these services to older persons and others.

Food and nutrition services offered by healthcare facilities are classified as noncommercial operations according to the industry organization and description used throughout this text. The reason: healthcare facilities do not exist primarily to provide foodservices to their patients or residents, but they must do so as an integral part of their mission. Healthcare food and nutrition service departments exist primarily to plan and provide well-balanced meals meeting exacting **nutrition** requirements to help patients and residents regain and/or maintain their health. They also serve those who are employed by and visit the facility. It is clear, then, that food and nutrition services administered and staffed by professionals are integral to the attainment of a healthcare facility's goals.

long-term care facility a facility offering one or more of a variety of life-style and care alternatives to seniors and other residents who desire or need these services

nutrition the science concerned with the study of food and nourishment, especially in humans

Senior Life-Style and Care Option	Overview	Persons Who Benefit
Active life-style	A life-style option that attracts retired and near-retirement persons who want to own a place where they will retire.	Those above a specific age established by the community.
Independent living	Homes, condos, apartments, and the like, where residents maintain an active life-style. Facilities may have special senior accommodations such as bathroom railings, wider doorways, and emergency alert systems.	Seniors who can continue to live at home, but who may desire or need a little help to do so.
Congregate care	Combines private living quarters with centralized dining services, shared public spaces, and access to social and recreational activities.	Seniors in good health who desire both independence and companionship.
Assisted living	Combines lodging and services such as meals, housekeeping, and laundry.	Seniors who may need help with daily activities, such as bathing, medication, and dressing, but not nursing care.
Skilled nursing care	Provides care for persons with physical or mental disabilities who need assistance with daily activities and in case of emergencies.	Those who require assistance with daily activities.

Note: Continuing care communities exist that provide two or more of these services to eliminate the need for residents to relocate.

EXHIBIT 19.1
Range of Senior Life-Style and Care Alternatives

OBJECTIVE 1
State common goals of food and nutrition service programs in healthcare facilities.

GOALS OF HEALTHCARE FOOD AND NUTRITION SERVICES

Several goals are shared by the administrators of food and nutrition services in healthcare facilities of all types.

Nutrition

active lifestyle (senior life-style) a life-style option that attracts retired and near-retirement persons who want to own a place where they will retire

independent living (senior life-style) a life-style option for active seniors who are able to live without assistance in a hotel, retirement center, condominium, apartment, or other facility; accommodations may be modified to include bathroom railings, wider doorways, and emergency alert systems

Many patients in hospitals depend on exacting nutritional intake as an integral part of their recuperation. Many residents in long-term care facilities depend on dining services for their total nutritional intake. A special concern about the nutritional well-being of persons served is, then, at the forefront of food and nutrition service goals in healthcare facilities. This concern begins when menus are planned; care must be taken to assure that the proper nutrients in the required amounts are available in the menu items produced and served to patients and residents. This emphasis continues as food purchase specifications are developed and as items of proper quality that yield maximum nutritional benefit are brought into the facility. Nutritional issues are also critical as items are stored, produced, and made ready for service. Follow-up nutritional auditing by facility professionals is frequently undertaken to assure that nutritional goals are consistently attained.

Healthcare facilities must meet a wide range of regulations, including many relating to the nutritional aspects of foodservices. Consider, for example, the need to provide three nutritious and appetizing meals and additional snacks each day (with significant details to explain these requirements) and the minimum times that must lapse between breakfast, mid-day, and evening

Dietitian consults with a patient.

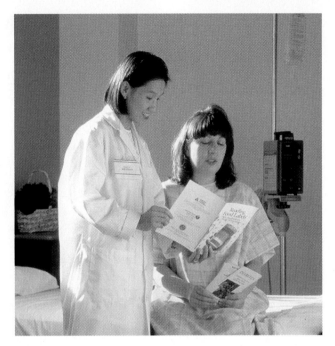

meals and the maximum time between the evening and breakfast meals. These are examples of numerous foodservice-related requirements that healthcare facilities must meet to receive licenses to operate by the applicable state governing agency.

Economic

Concerns about **cost containment** are ever-present in all departments of all healthcare facilities, including food and nutrition services. As well, governmental, consumer, and societal concerns about increasing healthcare costs create significant challenges for facility administrators. Today's food and nutrition service managers recognize that economic concerns must be given a high priority so that the facility can grow and survive in the fast-changing external environment in which it must compete. To this end, they must develop, use, and monitor against carefully developed operating budgets that specify revenues to be generated by and costs allocated to their department.

Social and Personal

For many consumers of healthcare food and nutrition services, meals are a high point of the day. Consider the hospital patient, for example, with many physical and psychological concerns that can be offset, at least temporarily, by the enjoyment of a meal. Active residents in long-term facilities frequently center much of their socializing around meals in the dining room.

Educational

Administrators of many healthcare facilities are concerned that applicable nutritional principles be understood and practiced by those whom they serve. These concerns are evident as **clinical dietitians** visit with patients to explain special diet requirements. **Outpatient** nutritional counseling is also frequently available.

congregate care (senior living and care option) a long-term care option that provides private living quarters with centralized dining services, shared public areas, and access to social and recreational activities

assisted living (senior living and care option) a long-term care option that provides private living accommodations and other services, including dining, housekeeping, laundry, and the management of medications

skilled nursing care (senior living and care option) a long-term care option that provides specialized care for persons with mental or physical disabilities, including those who are bedridden and who are in need of significant assistance with daily activities

cost containment efforts to reduce costs wherever possible while assuring that the quality of products and services being produced are appropriate for their intended use; sometimes called *cost minimization*

clinical dietitian a food and nutrition expert whose work may involve foodservices management, nutrition therapy (planning special diets, for example), and nutrition education; dietitians working in healthcare foodservices are typically credentialed as a registered dietitian (RD) by the American Dietetic Association (ADA)

outpatient a person receiving hospital services without being admitted to the facility

Computers track nutritional data for people concerned about their diets. Example: check out the website for the United States Department of Agriculture (USDA) MyPyramid program: www.mypyramid.gov

Community Services

It is common for many healthcare facilities to assist their communities in activities ranging from providing space and meals as part of local disaster plans, to promoting nutrition education and health awareness, to sponsoring a wide range of educational and other activities.

Other Goals

Administrators of healthcare food and nutrition services share some goals with their counterparts in other segments of the hospitality industry. These include recognizing the needs of their employees and becoming involved in applicable professional associations. They also have interests in addressing societal goals, including equal employment opportunities; in making efficient use of the limited resources available to them; and in working as part of the management team to move toward attainment of their facility's mission.

OBJECTIVE 2
Describe the organization of food and nutrition service programs in hospitals and senior life-style and care facilities.

ORGANIZATION OF HEALTHCARE FOOD AND NUTRITION SERVICES

While position titles vary, some aspects of organizational charts for food and nutrition services in healthcare facilities are relatively similar to those in other foodservice segments. This is understandable for several reasons. For example, regardless of the facility's size, the same basic tasks are involved in purchasing products, preparing them for service, and delivering them to the consumer. While these tasks might be undertaken by more or fewer people in more or fewer positions, the basic similarities remain. Also, while the mission and objectives of healthcare facilities are different from their counterparts in other industry segments, goals involving nutrition, economics, and a general concern for those being served, the employees, and others are also basically the same.

Exhibit 19.2 shows a sample organization chart for food and nutrition services in a large medical facility. No facility may have this exact organization,

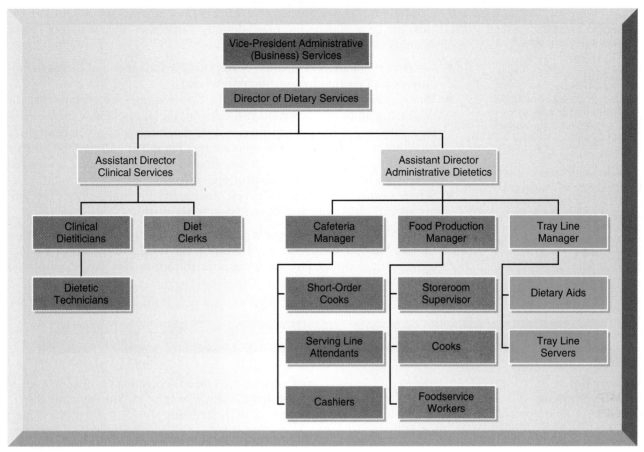

EXHIBIT 19.2
Sample Organization Chart: Hospital Food and Nutrition Services Department

and **downsizing** (also called *rightsizing*) efforts have collapsed the chain of command in many facilities. However, Exhibit 19.2 does help to identify and separate the responsibilities and functions that are integral to all hospital food and nutrition service operations. Note that the director of food and nutrition services reports to a vice-president for administrative (business) services and directly supervises the work of assistant directors for clinical services and administrative dietetics.

Many directors of hospital food and nutrition services are members of the American Society of Healthcare Food Service Administrators (ASHFSA), the Dietary Managers Association (DMA), and/or the Society for Healthcare Foodservice Management (HFM). Others are registered dietitians (RDs) who are credentialed by the Commission on Dietetic Registration and are members of a professional organization, the American Dietetic Association (ADA). Their responsibilities include activities involved with directing menu planning, food purchasing, food production, and service tasks. As well, they are responsible for financial management, employee recruitment, training and supervision, and food safety and sanitation. In some (especially smaller) facilities, they may also be responsible for nutritional assessment and clinical care, with technical assistance provided by a consulting dietitian.

The assistant director for clinical services in the food and nutrition services department of a large hospital directs the work of clinical dietitians and **dietetic technicians.** This administrator may also supervise the work of diet clerks whose responsibilities include assuring that each physician's requirements for special diets (low salt or diabetic, for example) are addressed when foods are prepared and portioned for delivery to specific patients.

downsizing the act of reducing the number of employees, positions, and/or labor hours for cost containment purposes; also called *rightsizing*

dietetic technician a practitioner in food and nutrition who may assist dietitians with medical nutrition therapy, manage all or part of a foodservices operation and be involved in nutrition education activities; many are credentialed as a dietetic technician, registered (DTR) by the American Dietetic Association (ADA)

dietetics the science of food and nutrition as it applies to health and well-being

public cafeteria foodservices in a healthcare food and nutrition services that are available for visitors to the facility

patient units sections of the hospital that house patients with specific needs; examples include oncology (for cancer patients), and medical or surgical for persons recovering from surgery

Exhibit 19.2 also indicates that an assistant director of administrative **dietetics** in large hospitals may directly supervise the work of three professionals:

- *Cafeteria manager.* This person is responsible for service of meals to employees and visitors in a **public cafeteria**.
- *Food production manager.* Persons in this position are responsible for producing all food (except short-order cooking, if applicable, in the public cafeteria) for the facility. Increasingly, hospitals and other healthcare facilities are employing chefs who are quickly moving the public's image of healthcare food and nutrition services away from an undeserved stereotype of unappealing, institutional meals.
- *Service manager.* This person is responsible for portioning foods (including special diets) that will be served in **patient units.**

Exhibit 19.3 shows a sample organizational chart for food and nutrition services in a long-term care facility. Note that the food and nutrition services director reports to the facility administrator. Except in very large facilities, a

RISING STAR PROFILE

Amy Reich
HDS Services

Overcoming Obstacles Lead to Career Success!

Amy received her undergraduate degree in hospitality management after working in restaurants since she was 15 years old. While in college she was a food server, and then she became the administrative assistant at the same property. After graduation, Amy worked for Ruby Tuesday Restaurants for about 18 months. Amy has worked for HDS Services, a contract food management company. She began as the assistant manager at a business and industry account and was quickly promoted to the unit director. After two years, she became a general manager with responsibility for one account and the overview of four others (one with four foodservices outlets), including a school, a long-term care facility, and business and industry accounts.

What is the most unforgettable moment in your career?

We bid against a competitor who operated the foodservice program at the company's headquarters, while our company managed the foodservices at another location. We were the underdogs and thought that the home favorite would win. However, the client decided that our food quality

and service level were too much to beat. We all celebrated!! It was a long road, but we were able to manage both facilities.

What are the most significant challenges facing your segment of the industry?

Recruiting, retaining good staff, and keeping our employees motivated! This challenge can be addressed by use of the Total Quality Management Process. Also, training programs for hourly paid staff members, an ongoing "promotion from within" policy, and programs to help managers to retain staff are very helpful.

What, if anything would you do differently in your career?

Nothing! All the obstacles I have overcome have led me to where I am now!

What is your advice for young people considering a career in your segment?

Work hard! Know how to multitask, or you will work extremely long hours. When you first begin, observe everything and be patient; don't think that you will know or can learn everything right away. Sometimes learning something the hard way is actually better for you "down the road." Expect that there will be training, but how good a manager you eventually become is really up to you. Things are sometimes not what you expect them to be when you first start out. Give your new position time, and you may soon understand why things are the way they are.

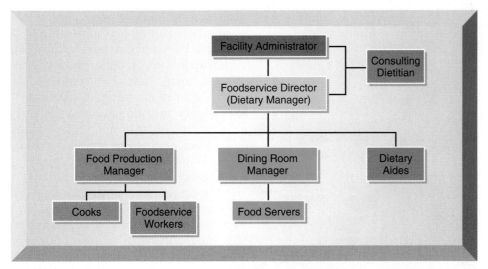

EXHIBIT 19.3
Sample Organization Chart: Long-Term Care Food and Nutrition Services Department

consulting dietitian (a professional who works with, probably, several long-term care facilities and/or small hospitals and, perhaps, other organizations) may plan (or review) menus and assist as necessary with special diet requirements and nutrition education activities.

The director of food and nutrition services for a long-term care facility has general responsibility for the overall operation of the food and nutrition service program. An integral part of this role involves efforts to ensure that employees adhere to safe food-handling practices and that they comply with the standards of the **Joint Commission on Accreditation of Healthcare Organizations (JCAHO)** and other regulatory and advisory organizations. The director of food and nutrition services directs the work of a food production manager (who, in turn, supervises cooks and foodservice employees), a dining room manager (who supervises food servers), and dietary assistants (who may, among other duties, transport food to and assist residents who are unable to eat in the dining room).

Some upscale independent living facilities offer table-service dining with alternative menu choices; food servers take orders and deliver preplated meals much as do their counterparts in restaurants and hotel food and beverage operations. Depending on local alcoholic beverage ordinances and other concerns, wines and/or other alcoholic beverages may even be available. In other facilities, meals are portioned in a serving counter area and transported to the residents' tables by food servers.

consulting dietitian a registered dietitian who provides technical assistance as a consultant (rather than as an employee) to an organization desiring or requiring this assistance

Joint Commission on Accreditation of Healthcare Organizations (JCAHO) a quality oversight board for healthcare organizations in the United States

A CLOSE LOOK AT UNIQUE POSITIONS

The organization charts in the previous section identified some positions relative to food production and service that are common to all types of foodservices operations. We also noted, however, some positions and/or responsibilities within positions that are unique to healthcare foodservices. Let's look at several of these positions.

OBJECTIVE 3
Review job duties of selected positions unique to healthcare food and nutrition service programs.

Clinical Dietitian

A clinical dietitian is responsible for nutritional care and follow-up of patients or residents and for communicating appropriate information to other healthcare

diet order   the diet (allowable foods and beverages) prescribed by a physician, including detailed nutrient information, extent of consistency modification, and the dates of the diet's initiation and duration

Preplated food is transported to a patient unit for service to patients.

professionals. A person in this position commonly holds an RD: a credential that requires education, experience, national testing, and, in many states, a license. He or she must assess a patient's or resident's nutritional status and develop nutritional care plans after analysis of charted and observed data. RDs may also instruct patients or residents about appropriate diets, evaluate the appropriateness of **diet orders,** and assure the nutritional adequacy and adherence of menus to prescribed diets. They must also calculate patients' nutrient needs and record actual food intakes. Clinical personnel in long-term care facilities closely monitor residents' weight and inform physicians or nurses about changes so corrective medical actions, if necessary, can be taken.

Dietary Managers

dietary manager   a professional certified by the Dietary Managers Association who has the education, training, and experience to fulfill applicable responsibilities and who has successfully completed a nationally recognized credentialing exam

A dietary manager in a long-term care facility may undertake a credentialing process that involves education, experience, and testing to become a Certified Dietary Manager or Certified Food Protection Professional (CDM, CFPP). These staff members have management responsibilities similar to those in other foodservice segments who are responsible for back-of-house food production and management. However, they have special duties as well. For example, they may help to gather nutritional data from patients or residents and identify dietary needs. They must also assure that the dietitians' nutritional plans or physicians' diet orders are implemented. They may, as well, have a role to play in nutrition education.

Dietetic Technicians and Assistants

Dietetic technicians, registered (DTRs) have successfully completed a credentialing process that requires education, experience, and national testing. They typically work as part of the facility's healthcare team to help prevent and treat disease and to administer medical nutrition therapy. They may process and update paper work relating to patient or resident transfers, diet changes, discharges, and nourishments. As well, they may check menus for nutritional adequacy and adherence to diet prescriptions and often have food management responsibilities.

Dietary assistants may portion food for service to patients or residents, load and transport food carts from the kitchen to patient units, assist patients or residents with meal consumption, and return transport carts to the kitchen area.

OBJECTIVE 4
Discuss tools and tactics used to help assure that patients and residents receive meals that meet prescribed nutritional requirements.

EMPHASIS ON NUTRITION

The nutritional needs of patients or residents must be consistently met, and this does not happen by chance alone. Much information is needed, and a formalized process of gathering necessary data must be in place. Several steps are frequently involved:

Step 1: Diet Order Completed A physician typically prescribes a diet for each patient or resident, which is included in the patient's or resident's medical chart. (In some states, registered dietitians are also permitted to do this.) Diet orders may be hard-copy forms but, increasingly, electronic entries are entered into a computer for electronic transmittal from the patient unit to the food and nutrition services department. A facility may use a predeveloped diet order form that helps the physician order a diet, or the physician may write out a specific diet order based on diets available in the facility's diet manual. With either alternative, information about the required diet is entered into the patient's or resident's medical record.

Step 2: Patient Data Available for Meal Service Hard-copy or electronically generated menus containing information about the patient's or resident's name and room number, type of diet, assistance, if any, needed, and other information are made available when food is readied for service. Traditionally, food for a specific patient has been portioned onto a tray and brought to all patients in a specific patient unit at the same time for service at about the same time. Increasingly, however, facilities are providing meal service in alternative ways, such as family style, self-service, and room service (where, in a style similar to hotel room service, patients can order desired menu items over a relatively broad range of time).

Step 3: Diet History Developed A patient's or resident's diet history is helpful to plan and implement a required nutritional program if one is required. This is typically done by an interview with the patient or resident and/or a friend or relative. JCAHO guidelines require that patients be screened within 24 hours of admission to determine the need, if any, for further nutritional assessment. The initial screening includes a review of a patient's height, weight, weight changes, dentition (chewing ability), gastrointestinal problems (those that relate to the stomach and intestines), and food allergies and intolerances. Not all patients will require food intake monitoring, nutrition intervention, or

house diet a diet that has been adopted (accepted) by the medical director and the foodservice administrator for use at the facility; deviations from these diets are used for special diet needs

regimen (diet) a nutrition care plan used to preserve and restore the health of a specific patient or resident.

MORE ABOUT SPECIAL DIETS

While some healthcare facilities offer 50 or more different special diets, normally relatively few are commonly used, depending on their **house diets** that can be modified for special needs. For example, a "low-fat diet" might be a "regular diet" with special exemptions and/or substitutions.

One frequent challenge of healthcare food and nutrition services personnel is the need to identify the specific patient or resident so that they will know what this individual can (and cannot) consume. This may be easy to do in a hospital when patients are assigned to rooms and even to beds. It becomes more difficult in a long-term care facility offering congregate meal services. Another challenge in some instances involves tracking food consumption when dietary intake is a critical component in a healthcare **regimen.**

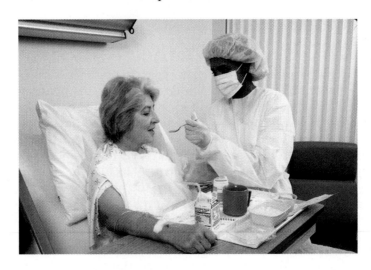

Patient with contagious illness is fed by a dietetic assistant.

nutrition education. However, nutritional data can be gathered in cases where it is necessary to do so in several ways:

- 24-hour food recall record (to record information about food intake during the previous 24-hour period)
- Weekly food frequency report (used to recap weekly food consumption for the patient or resident)
- Usual food intake record (used to describe a typical day's food intake)
- Three-day food intake record (developed by foodservices personnel and used to plan actual food consumption)
- Nutritional screening form (determines factors that affect nutrient needs)

Step 4: Diet History Data Analyzed and Summarized The diet history developed in step 3 must be analyzed and summarized.

TECHNOLOGY AND NUTRITIONAL INFORMATION

Increasingly, much of the work involved in collecting, analyzing, and making decisions about nutrition information is becoming automated. Consider, for example, the use of personal digital assistants (PDAs, also called *hand helds*). Available software can be integrated with the food and nutrition service department's primary database for many purposes, including client or patient nutritional assessment and tracking and 24-hour recalls and food records. After data are entered into the PDA, they can be transferred to the main computer. *Stand-alone* PDAs can be used to calculate patients' or residents' calorie or nutrient needs and ideal body weights. *Read-only* PDAs can provide information about the nutritional content of foods when, for example, diets are planned.

When diet changes are entered into patient records, electronic menus or tickets can be generated. Technology allows the tracking of many variables, including dietary restrictions, food preferences, allergies, and intolerances.

Technology can also help with numerous other tasks. For example, in a long-term care facility, the residents' weight can be determined and data can then be generated to yield charts and trends that can be compared with norms. This is useful input for dietary decisions. As well, a list of those at nutritional risk can be generated so they can be monitored and corrective actions can be taken.

Food intake may be found to be adequate and appropriate or, alternatively, potential nutrition-related concerns may become evident. If the latter occurs, a further **nutritional assessment process** is necessary to determine detailed nutritional information and the appropriate nutritional care plan.

nutritional assessment process   using information gained from diet history data to make professional conclusions, state goals, and outline recommended approaches to assure that a cost-effective patient or client care plan can be developed

FOOD TRANSPORT SYSTEMS

In many types of food and nutrition services operations, including independent living and assisted-care facilities, the residents typically come to the site (dining room) where the food will be served. By contrast, patients and residents in healthcare facilities who are confined to their rooms must have food delivered to them. How is this done in a way that maintains food quality and is cost effective?

Exhibit 19.4 identifies the basic steps in the process by which patients or residents in some healthcare facilities order food for subsequent delivery to their room. Let's look at the steps more closely.

Step 1: Select Menu Item Increasingly, food and nutrition service departments provide menu choices for their patients or residents within the dietary restrictions, if any, established by the physician. In some facilities, a hard-copy menu is provided that enables the patient or resident to make a selection (for example, between two or more entrees and two or more desserts). To assist with production scheduling, menu selections for meals to be served the next day may need to be submitted by a specified time during the previous day.

> **OBJECTIVE 5**
> Explain basic steps in common systems used to transport food within healthcare facilities.

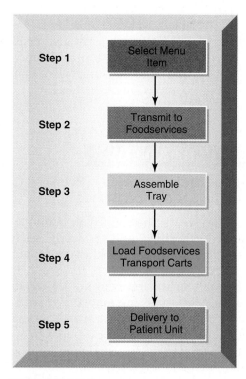

EXHIBIT 19.4
Patient or Resident Menu Order and Delivery

electronic tray ticket (healthcare food and nutrition services) a list of menu items desired by a patient or resident that is generated electronically by a patient, resident, or dietary assistant for electronic transmittal to the kitchen.

Step 2: Transmit to Foodservices If a manual ordering system is used, hard-copy menu requests indicating each patient's or resident's selections may be collected and physically carried to the kitchen. Increasingly, however, wireless technology is used by the patients or residents and/or dietary assistants (who take the order from the patient or resident) to electronically transmit menu selections to the kitchen where **electronic tray tickets** are produced. Menu orders are totaled, and the number of portions of each menu item required for production is determined.

Step 3: Assemble Tray Some healthcare facilities use a tray assembly line to ease the task of portioning foods into individual compartmentalized trays or dishes for patient service. In some manual operations, patient requests from hard-copy menus are written onto cards that are placed onto the tray assembly line. In most hospitals using manual systems, the menu that the patient selected is sent down the tray line. In automated systems, electronic tray cards are automatically printed and then placed on the assembly line.

Step 4: Load Foodservices Transport Cart Food transport systems used in healthcare facilities must keep foods to be served at their proper serving temperature from the time of preportioning to the time of service. With one system, hot food items are portioned at a very hot temperature into insulated trays or plates and covered with a tightly fitting, insulated cover. Another system utilizes heated pallets onto which the individual trays are placed as they are loaded into the transport carts (which are typically insulated but unheated). Cold foods may be transported on ice. Carts with refrigerated and heated sections are also in use in some healthcare facilities.

Step 5: Deliver to Patient Unit After foodservice transport carts are filled, they are quickly moved to the appropriate patient unit where the preportioned meals are served to the patients or residents in their rooms. Empty carts are typically left in the patient unit so serviceware can be returned to the kitchen at the completion of the meal.

DID YOU KNOW?

Patient Satisfaction Is a Primary Consideration in Healthcare Food and Nutrition Services

For many years, the routine in many hospitals has been to serve breakfast at a specified and, typically, early time in the morning. Some hospitals now use breakfast or snack carts to offer mid-morning continental-style breakfasts for those patients who do not want to be awakened earlier and who do not require special diets. In some hospitals, these offerings are augmented with quick-service items such as hot sandwiches maintained at proper temperature in a food transport cart. Sometimes these carts are brought to a patient unit at a predetermined time. In other facilities, patients can order these items if and when they desire them. In addition, many hospitals now use a hotel room service style in which the patient calls the kitchen with his or her meal choices for any or all meals, and these are prepared and delivered to the room.

Some long-term care facilities offer modern "café food court" or "country store" venues in which employees, residents, family members, and other visitors can purchase a limited variety of menu items. These are frequently cash operations (purchases are paid for at the time of item selection), but some facilities allow residents to purchase items on account, with charges added to their monthly (or other cycle) bill. Some facilities also offer "mini-convenience store" operations with packaged food and nonfood items available.

COOK–CHILL SYSTEMS CAN HELP WITH FOOD PRODUCTION AND SERVICE

Some healthcare facilities use a **cook–chill system** to assist with food production and/or transport needs. When this system is used, food is produced in bulk and then brought quickly to a refrigerated temperature to address sanitation and quality concerns. This system can be used to ease the task of food production when higher product volumes are anticipated. It can also be used when food must be transported.

Consider, for example, a healthcare facility in a campuslike setting with several buildings located over a relatively wide area. With today's emphasis on cost containment, it is unlikely that separate production kitchens would be built to serve the food and nutrition service needs for each building. Rather, a commissary-type system would probably be developed where food was produced in a central location for transport to other building sites for later **reconstitution** (reheating) and service as required.

DID YOU KNOW?

Technology Makes Better Menu Item Selection Easier

Today, some restaurant food servers use hand-held technology to take guests' orders and transmit them to the kitchen for preparation. This same technology is used in some hospitals that offer menu choices. For example, dietary assistants can visit patients or residents in their rooms, request menu preferences from among those that are permitted, and submit menu requests to the kitchen. This can be done instantly in a wireless environment or after orders for all patients in a unit are taken. This system also tallies the number of portions required to assist with food production planning.

Hand-held systems can also be used by food servers who take orders for residents consuming meals in the dining rooms of long-term care facilities. After identification of the resident is confirmed, requests can be entered and are automatically checked against the approved diet plan. If the item is permitted, the order is placed. If the preferred item is not permitted, the resident is informed and an alternative selection is made.

Systems using television monitors to order room service in hotels are also being used by patients and residents in some healthcare facilities to place food orders.

cook–chill system   a food production and delivery system in which food is produced in bulk, quickly refrigerated, and then transported to a serving site for later reconstitution and service

reconstitution   the application of heat to a chilled or frozen food item to raise it to the proper serving temperature; also called *reheating*

OBJECTIVE 6
Discuss challenges confronting administrators of food and nutrition service programs in health-care facilities.

inflation the economic condition that exists when selling prices increase throughout a country's economy

Medicare a federal medical insurance program that primarily serves those over 65 years of age (regardless of income) and younger disabled persons and dialysis patients; medical bills are paid from trust funds that covered persons have paid into

Medicaid a federal and state assistance program that pays covered medical expenses for low-income persons; it is run by state and local governments within federal guidelines

CHALLENGES! CHALLENGES!

Healthcare food and nutrition service administrators face several significant challenges that affect today's operations and will likely affect those in the future as well. Let's look at several.

Providing High-Quality Food and Service in a Cost-Effective Manner

For many years, the cost of healthcare rose much faster than the cost of **inflation**. The result was governmental, third-party (insurance company), and public (consumer) outcry to control costs. A wide body of regulations relating to federally funded insurance programs (**Medicare** and **Medicaid**), along with the requirements of private insurance companies, has placed caps on reimbursements paid for medical procedures for covered persons. As a result, healthcare facilities now receive less reimbursement for services provided to insured parties. Therefore, food and nutrition service administrators must continually monitor all the financial processes of their department and promote the department's retail services. Administrators, including those responsible for foodservices, are also confronted with the need to decrease expenses.

Cost-containment efforts have focused on almost every area within healthcare facilities, and those that are supportive to patient and resident care, such as food and nutrition services, have been very carefully examined. Administrators must cost-justify all expenses, and the pressure to do more with less is clearly evident in today's healthcare environment.

Discovering New Revenue Sources

In addition to containing (reducing) operating costs, today's healthcare food and nutrition service directors are also concerned about increasing revenues from nontraditional sources. Examples include implementing home meal replacement programs that yield products for sale to employees, patients, and/or visitors. For example, employees who have completed a work shift and relatives of hospital patients may purchase a prepared meal they can consume at home. These efforts can be particularly successful when necessary equipment is available in the facility's kitchen, when staff members are knowledgeable about and skilled in applicable food production tasks, and when the peaks and valleys of production allow for additional production activities without substantially increased labor costs.

Healthcare facilities have traditionally provided no-cost nutrition and diet counseling for patients and residents. Today, most facilities charge for these services and, additionally, make these services available for members of the public who otherwise would not have access to them.

Another revenue-generating tactic involves participation in federally and/or state funded meal programs for low-income and other persons. One example is meals-on-wheels programs that provide meals to eligible participants at their homes.

Healthcare food and nutrition service operations may cater functions for facility employees wanting to celebrate special occasions with their peers. Food and beverage functions may be provided for specific departments and for facility-wide events. Off-site catering is also done by an increasing number of healthcare institutions.

Hospitals are very labor intensive, and the cafeteria operations available to the employees and visitors are increasingly reviewed for overlooked revenue sources. Traditionally, many healthcare facilities subsidized employee meals by paying for all or part of the meal cost as a staff member benefit. When these programs (benefits) are phased out, associated costs to the facility are eliminated. As well, food and nutrition service directors have become very creative in developing retail venues that attract employees and visitors and generate increased revenues. These include self-branded sandwich, salad, and other stations increasingly found in business and industry operations (see Chapter 20) and in other commercial and noncommercial segments. Another example: space may be leased to commercial operators, or contracts that provide a specified percentage of revenue or other financial remuneration are negotiated with them.

Residents dining in an upscale retirement center

Changing Culture of Healthcare Food and Nutrition Services

Closely aligned with cost containment, food and nutrition services in many facilities have been realigned through facility and/or departmental reorganization. Downsizing to reduce staff and planning and implementing new food production and delivery systems have sometimes been helpful. Some facilities that have operated their own food and nutrition service programs have begun to use the services of contract management companies, and facilities that already use these services may renegotiate contracts when it is in their best interest to do so.

Managing the Business

Directors of healthcare food and nutrition services have experienced many of the same operating pressures as their counterparts in other segments of the hospitality industry. Consumers increasingly want greater value (price relative to quality of products and services). The concept of **nonselect menus** is being replaced with **alternative choice menus** in response to this trend. It is difficult to recruit and retain qualified and trained food and nutrition services staff, and new adaptations of technology must constantly be analyzed to assess their potential impact on the department. Some potential operating problems are resolved daily and routinely. Creative food production personnel are able to plan and provide meals meeting the nutritional requirements for a wide variety of patients with different nourishment needs with only minimal impact on production and service efficiencies.

 Other business concepts used by savvy food and nutrition service directors include the ongoing search for ways to increase productivity to maximize outputs relative to financial inputs without sacrificing quality and efforts that yield work process improvements. Benchmarking that allows productivity and financial comparisons with similar facilities is also increasingly prevalent.

 Satisfaction rating systems are now in use that question patients upon or after discharge about their experiences with the healthcare facility, including

menu (nonselect) a menu that offers no choice of item selections for the consumer

menu (alternative choice) menus that allow consumers to make a selection between food item alternatives

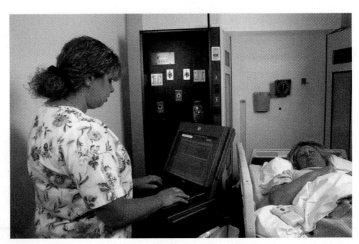

Patient nutrition data may be collected at bedside for electronic distribution to the Food and Nutrition Services Department.

perceptions of food and nutrition services. Respondent input is quantified on a quarterly or other basis and can be compared to similar facilities. Food and nutrition service directors can be evaluated, in part, based on their department's performance on these ratings. As well, analysis of rating information is used to identify possible improvement alternatives.

Integrating Food and Nutrition Services into the Total Healthcare Experience

Early in this chapter we noted that food and nutrition services were (or, at least, could be) a high point in a patient's or resident's day. Positive or negative experiences can affect one's perception of the entire healthcare facility in much the same way that good or bad experiences with a hotel's food and beverage operation can influence one's perceptions about the entire lodging property.

While decisions about preferred hospital stays for patients are not likely to be made on the basis of food and nutrition services, decisions about facilities serving the elderly will very likely consider this factor. In recognition of this, many facilities provide complementary meals to family members who tour the facility as residential-care decisions are made. They may also provide free or nominally priced meals to family members when they visit their loved ones. Efforts to make these meals and experiences enjoyable within the restraints of cost containment are very important to all food and nutrition service administrators.

hazard analysis critical control points (HACCP) a food safety assurance process that identifies potential sanitation-related problems in food production and service.

SUMMARY OF CHAPTER LEARNING OBJECTIVES

1. **State common goals of food and nutrition service programs in healthcare facilities.**
   Goals of food and nutrition service programs in healthcare facilities typically relate to nutrition, economics, social and personal concerns, education, community service, and other goals, such as recognizing employee needs, giving something back to the industry, and addressing numerous societal issues.

2. **Describe the organization of food and nutrition service programs in hospitals and senior life-style and care facilities.**
   The director of food and nutrition services in a large hospital may report to a vice-president

for administration (business) and may, in turn, directly manage the work of an assistant director responsible for clinical services and a second assistant director responsible for administrative dietetics (which includes the cafeteria, food production, and tray assembly and delivery). The director of dining services in a long-term care facility may report directly to the facility's administrator and may, in turn, directly supervise the work of food production and dining room managers and dietary assistants. Most long-term care facilities utilize a consulting administrative or clinical dietitian to provide applicable technical expertise.

3. **Review job duties of selected positions unique to healthcare food and nutrition service programs.**
   Clinical dietitians are responsible for nutritional care and follow-up of patients or residents and for communicating appropriate information to other healthcare professionals. Dietary managers typically have management responsibilities involving purchasing, receiving, storing, and production that are similar to others responsible for back-of-house food management. Dietetic technicians may check menus for adequacy and process and update paperwork relating to patient or resident transfers, diet changes, discharges, and nourishments. Dietetic assistants may be involved in tray assembly and/or transport duties, among others.

4. **Discuss tools and tactics used to help assure that patients and residents receive meals that meet prescribed nutritional requirements.**
   Basic nutritional information is gathered as part of an initial patient and resident screening process. When necessary, dietary intake tools are used to plan, analyze, and monitor nutritional intake.

5. **Explain basic steps in common systems used to transport food within healthcare facilities.**
   Basic steps in the process by which patients or residents order food for subsequent room delivery include selecting menu items, transmitting menu selections to foodservices, assembling trays, loading foodservices transport carts, and delivering meals to the rooms in the patient unit. Increasingly, nontraditional meal service methods, including family-style and hotel service-style methods, are in use.

6. **Discuss challenges confronting administrators of food and nutrition service programs in healthcare facilities.**
   Challenges confronting healthcare food and nutrition service administrators include those relating to declining reimbursements, the search for ways to generate revenues from nontraditional sources, the changing culture of foodservices, ongoing efforts to manage the business, and integrating food and nutrition services into the total healthcare experience.

FEEDBACK FROM THE REAL WORLD

Our real-world advice comes from John Rendall.

John is an experienced healthcare facility manager who has led and managed 285 full-time equivalent employees (FTEs) in the environmental services, food and nutrition services, and laundry and linen services departments in a hospital.

(continued)

What are some ways in which the work of a director of food and nutrition services is similar to that of a manager in a hotel food and beverage operation or a restaurant?

Both coordinate the activities of their departments to facilitate the service of high-quality food. This entails managing finances, food production, retail services, and purchasing, as well as ensuring compliance with Food and Drug Administration (FDA), **hazard analysis critical control point (HACCP,** see p. 354**),** and other regulatory requirements.

What are some ways in which the work is different?

The most obvious difference is participation. Aside from the employees working in the healthcare organization, a large percentage of the customers (patients) are there involuntarily: a serious health condition requiring treatment. Each patient's expectations and nutritional requirements are unique, and a food and nutrition services director is challenged to make the dining experience pleasurable and satisfying. While guests in a hotel or restaurant visit at their preference and choose from a variety of menu items, a patient's menu options may be more limited and controlled. Also, it is difficult to make food appealing to them when they don't feel well.

What are examples of how regulations applicable to the operation of healthcare facilities have affected food and nutrition services?

From a clinical nutrition standpoint, the emergence of managed care resulted in shorter lengths of stay for patients. This makes the completion of the patient's nutritional assessment, planning the patient's diet, and monitoring the patient's response to her or his nutrition care quite demanding. With patients spending so little time in the hospital, many food production operations have shortened their menu cycle. There has also been an increased emphasis on outpatient nutritional education, because there is less time for a planned diet to affect therapy while a patient is in the hospital.

From an operational perspective, limits on managed care costs, a shift to more outpatient procedures, and cutbacks in Medicare and Medicaid reimbursements have put increased pressures on healthcare food and nutrition services to control costs while maintaining or increasing customer satisfaction.

What are some ways that the management of healthcare food and beverage services will likely change over the next 10 to 15 years?

Directors of hospital food and nutrition services recognize that the efforts of their department are required to support the recuperation and healing of a patient; however, this is not the healthcare organization's core business. As a result, they must constantly seek ways to decrease operating expenses and increase revenues. A highly subsidized food and nutrition service is undesirable, so more emphasis on the retail aspect of the cafeteria operations will be required. Creative ways are needed to encourage employees to remain in the facility and eat in the cafeteria. How? One way is to offer menu items for a diverse market of customers that allow them to purchase food from a department retail venue (for example, convenient grab-and-go items).

What are some things that tomorrow's managers of healthcare food and nutrition services will be required to know and/or to do that are of lessened importance today?

Tomorrow's customers will be more informed about nutrition and demand healthier food options. Comfort foods may still outsell salads, but managers will need to be responsive to changing eating habits.

It will be increasingly important to manage all activities of the food and nutrition services department and to be familiar with other departmental operations. Tomorrow's directors will increasingly be required to manage multiple departments or manage the food and nutrition services at multiple facilities. Managing assets, including the efficient use of space and equipment, will be more critical with less capital improvement dollars available for remodeling, replacement, and renovation. Presentation and marketing skills will be extremely valuable to attract customers and to increase participation in retail offerings.

MASTERING YOUR KNOWLEDGE

Discuss the following questions.

1. What approach should a healthcare food and nutrition service manager take when his or her boss continually emphasizes the need to reduce costs? What are ways that this can be done without sacrificing his or her department's goals?
2. How might the dietary needs of hospital patients and residents in long-term care facilities be the same? How are they likely to be different?
3. How, if at all, do you think technology can be helpful in the process used to gather basic nutritional information for a patient or resident?
4. Assume that you are a director of food and nutrition service and have had recent complaints about the temperature of meals delivered to patients or residents in their rooms. Using what you have learned in this chapter, what kinds of things might you look for and address in each step?

LEARN FROM THE INTERNET

1. Check out the websites of the following contract management companies:
   - ARAMARK: www.aramark.com
   - Compass Group (Americas Division): www.cgnad.com. Click on "companies & brands," and then click on "Morrison Management Specialists."
   - Sodexho: www.sodexhousa.com

   What types of specialized services, if any, do they note for the management of healthcare food and nutrition services?
2. To learn general information about food and nutrition services in hospitals, including nutrition resources, menus, mission statements, and other consumer-related issues, type "hospital dietary services" into your favorite search engine. Click on several of the websites for the hospital food and nutrition service departments that you locate.
3. Check out the home page of the American Dietetic Association: www.eatright.org. When you arrive at the website, click on "careers & students." What types of specialized skills and tasks are part of the work that registered dietitians and dietetic technicians, registered, must do? What types of formal education and experience are required or recommended for them to be qualified?
4. Review the website of the Dietary Managers Association: www.dmaonline.org. What are typical responsibilities of dietary managers? Certified dietary managers? What types of ongoing professional development and educational opportunities does this association make available for its members?

KEY HOSPITALITY TERMS

The following terms were explained in this chapter. Review the definitions of any words with which you are unfamiliar. Begin to utilize them as you expand your vocabulary as a hospitality professional.

long-term care facility
nutrition
active life-style (senior life-style)
independent living (senior life-style)
congregate care (senior living and care option)
assisted living (senior living or care option)
skilled nursing care (senior living or care option)
cost containment
clinical dietitian
outpatient
downsizing
dietetic technician
dietetics
public cafeteria
patient units
consulting dietitian

Joint Commission on Accreditation of Healthcare Organizations (JCAHO)
diet order
dietary manager
house diet
regimen (diet)
nutritional assessment process
electronic tray ticket (healthcare food and nutrition services)
cook–chill system
reconstitution
inflation
Medicare
Medicaid
menu (nonselect)
menu (alternative choice)
hazard analysis critical control points (HACCP)

20 Business and Industry Foodservices

Some large corporations have jets with in-flight meals provided by their foodservice operations.

CHAPTER LEARNING OBJECTIVES

After studying this chapter you will be able to:

1. Provide an overview of the business and industry foodservices segment with an emphasis on what it is and why it is important.

2. Review alternative financial goals of business and industry foodservice operations.

3. Explore the range of foodservice alternatives offered in business and industry foodservices.

4. Review the organization of management positions in business and industry foodservice operations.

5. Review challenges applicable to foodservice managers in business and industry organizations.

6. Explain unique challenges faced by contract management companies operating business and industry foodservices.

This chapter was authored by Curtis Lease, District Manager, ARAMARK Business Services, Houston, Texas.

FEEDBACK FROM THE REAL WORLD

You are responsible for the foodservice operations in a relatively large company. It is the headquarters for a product manufacturer and has several thousand office workers and about the same number of plant (assembly line) personnel in a complex of buildings on the same site.

Office employees have access to a large serving area and dining room open throughout the working day. A series of separate service stations offer a range of items, from components of a continental breakfast through a fairly substantial variety of hot meal items. The lunch features made-to-order sandwiches, pizza, hot food stations, salads and desserts, and other items. An office coffee service and vending machines are also available throughout the office building. The personnel in the manufacturing plant have access to two straight-line cafeteria counters and a large bank of vending units in a central serving site, many featuring foods that can be reconstituted.

Food for both the office and assembly-line staff is produced from a central kitchen in the office complex. A short-order station is available in the assembly plant for items such as hot sandwiches, which are prepared in small batches.

There has been a downturn in the national economy, and this company, like many others, has suffered. The first round of layoffs has occurred and, although it was small, the rumor mill about "what's next" is in full gear. There have been no wage increases for the company's staff for the last one and a half years; none are expected.

The foodservice operations have always had very focused financial goals and these have not changed: it must break even; there can be no subsidies from the company. In fact, over the past several years, more overhead costs that were not charged to the foodservice operations are being allocated to it.

At the same time, the number of employees being served has decreased. This is due, in part, to the initial layoffs and, as well, to employee concern that, in the tough economy, they can do better by bringing food from home and/or by sending someone in a work group to one of the nearby quick-service restaurants. (In fact, several of these operations take fax and telephone orders, and a fairly large group of regulars pick up orders that have been separately bagged as soon as they arrive at the restaurants.)

The problem is clear: costs are going up and revenues are going down. At the same time, foodservices must break even without a **subsidy,** and the contract management company must make a fair profit or it will not be able to continue providing foodservices. What, if anything, can you do to better manage the operation (to reduce costs without sacrificing quality standards) and to do more effective marketing (to increase guest counts, check averages, and revenues)?

As you read this chapter, think about your answers to these questions and then get feedback from the real world at the end of the chapter.

Does it sound familiar? Students participating in a foodservice program at a postsecondary, high school, or grade school want a wide variety of menu selections and "surprises" so that they don't get bored. They will "vote with their feet" (eat fewer meals), even though they may have relatively few options if they are not satisfied. At the same time, if the foodservice experience is enjoyable, there will be steady participation because they have many other things to worry about besides where to eat.

Foodservice managers in **business and industry** operations have the same types of challenges. First, there is the potential to attract many guests who, while perhaps not a **captive market,** are at least in a central location when meal periods are scheduled and/or when people normally like to eat. More similarities: concerns about lack of variety, eating in the "same old place," and a sense of boredom that can arise as one settles into a dining routine. Also, like all segments of the hospitality industry, guests dining in

subsidy funds provided by an organization in support of its foodservice program

business and industry foodservices the segment of the noncommercial foodservice industry that provides meals or partial meal components to employees while they are at work; frequently referred to as *B&I*

captive market the relatively rare situation in which consumers have absolutely no choice of product or service alternatives; examples in foodservices include inmates in a correctional institution and naval personnel on long-term sea duty

Office workers in this high-rise office building probably have access to midday foodservices.

OBJECTIVE 1
Provide an overview of the business and industry foodservices segment with an emphasis on what it is and why it is important.

business or industry operations are looking for value. They desire good products, appropriate levels of service, and a pleasing and comfortable dining environment at the lowest possible cost.

You can see, then, that managers working in both the educational and business and industry foodservice operations have several challenges in common. The good news: many of the tactics useful to address opportunities in one segment are equally applicable in the other.

ALL ABOUT BUSINESS AND INDUSTRY FOODSERVICES

Business and industry foodservices (frequently abbreviated B&I) are those available, as the name implies, to employees while they are at work. Organizations offering foodservices to their employees and visitors include manufacturing plants, office and multi-tenant buildings, and public institutions such as government buildings.

A PROBLEM WITH NAMES

Throughout this book, we have divided the vast world of foodservices into two types: commercial and noncommercial. As you have learned, the former (commercial) relates to operations that exist to generate profit on the sale of food and beverage products. The latter (noncommercial operations) exist for other reasons, but must provide food and beverage services as part of their efforts.

The term *noncommercial* has bothered administrators in this segment for years. While some believe it is better than the more antiquated *institutional foodservices*, many industry observers still seek a term that better exemplifies and describes this very large industry.

The solution: a relatively new term, *on-site foodservices*, has been proposed. An advantage: the term is contemporary and does describe these operations. A disadvantage: a literal interpretation (food produced and served at the same location) also applies to almost all segments of the commercial foodservice industry. Another term, *managed services*, is also becoming popular. It is also contemporary and describes the appropriate operations. It also shares a potential disadvantage with the previous term: the world of work has many other services besides foodservices that must be managed.

Some persons may view terminology concerns as a semantic exercise with little practical value. In fact, in today's world of hospitality business, marketing is everything (or almost everything!). The ability to attract persons to work within the industry and others to consume the food produced by it may well be influenced by what the industry segment is called.

Any ideas? Hospitality professionals have debated this issue for many years. Perhaps you have the answer!

Commerce park buildings and those on a corporate campus may have a central site for foodservices.

Foodservices in business and industry settings easily meet the definition of noncommercial foodservices utilized throughout this book: they are offered by organizations that, unlike their commercial foodservice counterparts, do not exist primarily to produce, serve, and generate profits from the sale of food and beverage products. They also fit our definition because they are not typically available to the public.

SELF-OPERATED AND CONTRACT MANAGEMENT COMPANY-OPERATED OPTIONS: IS IT "ALL OR NOTHING"?

Today a significant majority of all business and industry operations are managed by contract management companies, and this percentage is increasing. Much of this growth occurred when management companies assumed the operation of existing self-operated foodservices that were unable to meet their financial goals. Other growth has occurred as businesses with successful contract management company relationships expanded to additional locations and retained existing or other management companies for the new sites.

As business organizations become larger, the management of their foodservice alternatives becomes more complex. It is not uncommon, for example, for a large global company to have some outlets managed by its own employees (self-operated sites) and, at the same time, to utilize one or even several contract management companies to operate foodservices in other locations. To add to the complexity, vending and office coffee service operations may be handled by still other organizations.

Foodservice liaisons may be employed by organizations to represent them in the day to day management of foodservices when contract management companies are utilized. While their job is never easy, it becomes a significantly greater challenge when their responsibilities are expanded from one unit to the management of foodservices in a diverse network such as that described above.

As discussed throughout this text, there are no secrets to the successful management of a foodservice or other type of hospitality operation. Successful programs can be operated by the organization itself or with the use of a contract management company. The principles of doing so are the same, and it is the knowledge, skills, and abilities of the management team, not the management alternative (self-operated or contract management company), that are most instrumental in determining the success or failure of the foodservice program.

Bank employees appreciate a well-run foodservice operation.

three-martini lunch a phrase referring to the (sometimes excessive) consumption of alcoholic beverages by business persons during the work day

Many business and industry foodservices are available because of employer convenience and/or benefit. In companies with relatively short, scheduled lunch breaks, there is relatively little time for employees to leave for off-site foodservices, and the option of packing a lunch is not attractive to many people. Organizations with locations remote from commercial foodservice alternatives encounter another problem: no place to go. Another issue related to employees leaving the work site are the concerns that they will return late (or not at all) and that they might return in an impaired condition (if, for example, they have had a **three-martini lunch**). As well, off-job accidents that occur when employees must drive to a restaurant for lunch can be reduced.

The issue of employer convenience is increasingly superseded by another concern: cost. Economic issues are typically at the heart of a decision to utilize self-operated or contract management company-operated foodservices. (These alternatives for operating noncommercial foodservices were the topic of Chapter 17.)

Exhibit 20.1 summarizes an employer's concerns about foodservices. The answer to the question of whether to offer foodservices to employees is typically no when the employer does not envision the responsibility or advantages of doing so. If it is seen to be a convenience or a necessity by the employer, the question of how to do it becomes a priority. Basic concerns about the need to minimize complaints from employees and to minimize costs are at the forefront of the decision. The two basic options (self-operated or contract management company-operated) are then assessed, and the best alternative is selected.

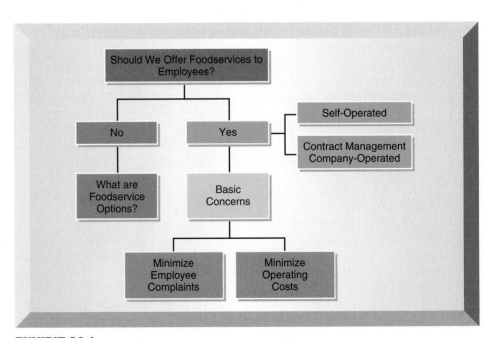

EXHIBIT 20.1
The Business and Industry Puzzle

FINANCIAL GOALS OF BUSINESS AND INDUSTRY FOODSERVICE OPERATIONS

OBJECTIVE 2
Review alternative financial goals of business and industry foodservice operations.

We have already noted that business and industry foodservices share the financial concerns of their counterparts in other segments. Exhibit 20.2 illustrates a historical perspective on the economic goals of foodservices in this segment. Although the term *business and industry* is oversimplified (the segment is diverse: foodservices programs operate all along the continuum shown), it does illustrate an evolution in financial goals.

- In the past, employers often treated foodservices as an employee fringe benefit; some organizations offered free meals and others operated foodservices at a loss. (Since employee payments did not cover operating costs, this subsidy was seen as an employee benefit.)
- Recently, organizations have reduced costs everywhere, including foodservices. Programs were expected to break even, surpluses were decreasingly provided, and programs were less frequently offered as an employee benefit.
- Today, foodservices are increasingly expected to generate at least some profit. Sometimes this expectation is met because some costs, not historically allocated to the foodservices, are now allocated to the program. In other instances, some money in the form of **rebates** or **commissions** from the contract management company may be expected.
- Future foodservice operations will increasingly have profit-making goals. Higher levels of rebates from contract management companies will be negotiated, even though they will likely be at the expense of foodservice consumers.

rebate monies paid to a sponsoring organization by the contract management company; typically based on the profitability of the foodservice operation to the contract management company

We have been discussing economic goals from the perspective of the sponsoring organization, and this overview applies directly to self-operated programs. What about financial goals when a contract management company is involved? Exhibit 20.3 addresses this question, where we see that a range of financial arrangements is possible between the sponsoring organization and the contract management company.

commission a payment made by a contract management company to a client that is typically based on a percentage of revenues generated from sales at the client's location

- Assume, for example, that the sponsoring organization is willing to subsidize foodservices as a benefit to employees. The management company might negotiate a contract for a set fee (also called **cost plus**). Under this arrangement the sponsor provides monies in addition to those generated from employee revenues to pay the fee. Alternatively, the company could specify lower than required meal charges for employees and pay (subsidize) the contract management company for the difference.
- Assume that the sponsoring organization wants to break even; it does not want to subsidize the program nor does it wish to generate a profit. The

cost plus a financial agreement in which a contract management company establishes a charge to the sponsoring organization based on actual incurred costs plus a fee for its services

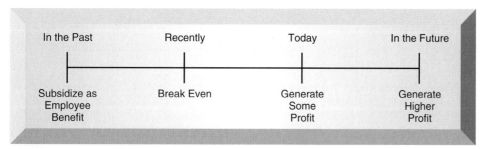

EXHIBIT 20.2
A History of an Organization's Goals for Business and Industry Foodservices

Clarie Schulze
Food Service Director
ARAMARK Business Services
San Antonio, Texas

The Hospitality Industry Is Customer Service

What is your educational background?

I graduated with an undergraduate degree in food science and technology, with a minor in business administration.

What is your work experience?

I completed internships with the quality assurance departments of several manufacturing companies that service the restaurant and foodservice industry. The work involved hazard analysis critical control point (HACCP) systems enforcement, implementation, and development. I also worked on projects relating to control testing on product attributes to maintain product consistency and employee training relating to food safety.

What are the most significant challenges facing your segment of the industry?

My view of challenges is, perhaps, different from that of some of my colleagues. This is good, and it is understandable since managers have diverse backgrounds and views about the future and what we should do now to help to shape it. The challenges I would like to address focus on food quality and food safety, since food (along with customer service) is what our company and our industry is all about. A significant challenge relates to ensuring that all the food we produce and serve is safe for consumption. This requires the consistent application of HACCP principles and procedures. Operators must also be able to segregate allergens (food ingredients that create allergies in some persons) and/or other ingredients to which some persons are chemically sensitive. The complete segregation of allergens and the reduction or elimination of chemically sensitive ingredients such as monosodium glutamate (MSG) need to be long-term goals for the hospitality industry.

Here at ARAMARK we are implementing HACCP temperature logs, and unit leadership is being proactive to incorporate the HACCP system into the way we do things. However, this is a challenge because it requires formal training in each unit.

What are your career plans?

I intend to increase my focus on management and the human resources principles that affect employee–management relationships and our contacts with our clients (account managers) and customers (consumers of our products).

What is your advice to young people considering a career in your industry segment?

It is important, first, to know about your business. An integral aspect is knowing how to interact with the guests and your staff members. Remember, the hospitality industry *is* guest service.

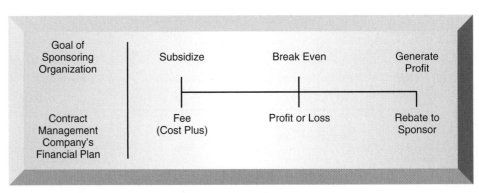

EXHIBIT 20.3
Range of Financial Agreements in Contracted Foodservices

contract management company may negotiate a profit and loss agreement in which it generates a profit (or loss) based on its financial success.

- Assume that the sponsoring organization desires to profit from its foodservices. The contract management company will then pay a commission from the revenues it generates from paying guests (and, of course, charges to consumers may need to be higher than otherwise to generate this excess revenue unless commissions are paid on the basis of higher business volume).

You can see, then, that there is a range of agreements between sponsoring organizations and contract management companies to address the organization's financial expectations for the foodservices program.

DID YOU KNOW?

Business and industry foodservice operations provide services to increasingly more sophisticated customers who are, in effect, looking for a "retail" environment: a "real restaurant with real food choices." Business and industry diners like brand-name choices such as McDonald's and Starbucks and a surprising staple to some observers: pizza.

Here's some interesting information about the cafeterias at four of Atlanta's best known corporations:

- Chick-Fil-A. Not surprisingly, Chick-Fil-A sandwiches and other chicken products are a big favorite. Pizzas are baked in a stone-tiled oven in plain view. The kitchen makes irresistible desserts and, sometimes, unusual creations, such as spicy cornbread salad. Twice a year, homemade jambalaya is offered with zydeco music playing in the background.

- UPS. The cafe at UPS headquarters prepares 2,000 meals daily, all served on china and washable flatware (no to-go boxes). Many customers like the "action station" that prepares stir fry. One fact: macaroni and cheese must be made only with real milk, butter, and cheese.

- Coca-Cola. The Boulevard operation offers numerous stations, most of which offer made-to-order items. Hot food choices on a typical day include pan-carved roast bison, curried pumpkin soup, and chicken Oscar. No surprise: soft drinks are free and are positioned everywhere in the dining area, and there is no Pepsi!

- Georgia-Pacific. The cafeteria for these employees is also open to the public. It features a large salad bar and daily specials ranging from pork loin to salmon. No surprise: all the plates are made of cardboard.

Source: John Kessler. Company cafeterias go upscale with more choices, specialties. *Atlanta Journal-Constitution*, February 13, 2006. Retrieved February 14, 2006 from www.ajc.printthis.clickability.com.

straight-line serving line a traditional cafeteria line in which guests move down a serving line, selecting all components of their meal

scramble cafeteria system a plan in which specific menu components are available in separate locations of the cafeteria serving area; also called a *modular system*

food court an area in which employee- and/or consumer-dispensed foodservices are available

BUSINESS AND INDUSTRY FOODSERVICE ALTERNATIVES

OBJECTIVE 3
Explore the range of foodservice alternatives offered in business and industry foodservices.

Just as educational facilities offer numerous foodservice options, so do those in business and industry. Sometimes a **straight-line serving line** is used. Increasingly, however, food products are offered using a **scramble cafeteria system.** For example, separate stations in a **food court** may be established for the following:

Workers on offshore oil rigs must be fed three or more meals a day.

Salads
Hot entrees
Sandwiches (often made to order)
Pizza and Mediterranean
Grab and go
Exhibition and display cooking (Asian and pasta, for example)
Soups and breads
Ethnic (including Mexican, Asian, and Indian)
Sushi
Carvery (carved meats)
Grill and American
Specialty bars (such as top-your-own baked potato)
Barbecue
Desserts
Beverages

concierge (contract management companies) an individual responsible for providing specialized personal and professional assistance to organizations and selected staff members within it

Guests can quickly move from station to station to select desired items. There may be Italian and/or vegetarian or other stations that offer popular selections (often with a daily special).

THERE IS MORE THAN FOODSERVICES TO CONTRACT MANAGEMENT COMPANIES

There are many small contract management companies whose relationship with a business or industry organization is limited to its contract for foodservices. These companies specialize in managing foodservices, and they do it well. Other, especially very large national (and even global), contract management companies offer organizations a wide range of services in addition to the provision of meals. Examples include facility management (including custodial services), uniform rental, laundry services, and business services (including managing organization-owned conference centers). Some management companies even offer **concierge** services to provide a wide range of assistance to key officials within the organization.

Organizations experiencing a successful relationship with the operation of its foodservices may seek another division of the same contract management company for assistance with other services. While profits rendered to the contract management company for operation of foodservices may be less than desired, the management company may be compensated as it provides other services. (*Important Note:* Large contract management companies offer excellent career opportunities in divisions other than those that are traditionally considered to be part of the hospitality industry.)

Auto workers consume food and beverages during meals and other breaks.

Dining areas range from modest to first class. Those in many business and industry settings are designed and furnished in a manner similar to or even more attractively and comfortably than their counterparts in commercial operations.

Are food courts with attached dining areas the only foodservice options in business and industry? The answer is no. Other ways in which foodservices are provided to employees include the following:

- *Executive dining.* Table-service restaurants with gourmet menus and furniture, fixtures, and table appointments of the very highest quality may be available in a few business and industry locations. Smaller board and conference rooms may be available where executive dining is also provided.
- *Traditional banquets.* Foodservices for large groups may be offered with food quality, variety, and service equal to that offered by hotels and commercial caterers.
- *Other catering.* Creative managers in business and industry settings may provide foodservices for office parties and picnics (both on- and off-site) and even deliver pizza, sandwiches, and/or other items to employees at their work stations.
- *Vending.* A variety of food products (such as sandwiches and desserts produced on-site) may be made available to employees by mechanical means.

Executive dining rooms available in some business and industry operations offer meals and service equal to their upscale restaurant counterparts in the community.

home meal replacement food purchased away from home for at-home consumption

branded food food and/or beverage items manufactured by organizations with, typically, nationally recognized names; examples include Starbucks (coffee) and Pizza Hut (pizza)

self-brands food and/or beverage products manufactured by an organization sponsoring or operating foodservices at the site

- *Office coffee services.* Employees in office settings may have refreshment breaks provided by the organization's foodservice personnel.
- ***Home meal replacement.*** Some, but relatively few foodservice operations may produce whole meals and/or meal components that employees may purchase for takeout and consumption at home, the quality of which is equivalent to or better than that of carryout services offered by commercial restaurants.
- *In-flight foodservices.* Organizations owning private aircraft may serve onboard meals and beverages prepared by the organization's foodservice program.
- *Branded food courts.* Operations may offer **branded** or **self-brands** of products such as specialty coffees and pizza. Food courts in B&I are similar to those found in shopping malls; competitors offering alternative food products are located next to each other, with guests consuming their selections in a common dining area.
- *Cafes and bistros.* These operations range from upscale to limited service to grab and go.
- *Convenience stores (C-stores).* Consumers may utilize retail stores offering foodservices, including snacks and beverages and, perhaps, other items, such as company logo merchandise, gifts, gift baskets, gourmet retail items, sundries, and personal care items.

OBJECTIVE 4
Review the organization of management positions in business and industry foodservice operations.

ORGANIZATION OF BUSINESS AND INDUSTRY FOODSERVICES

The organization of a business and industry foodservice operation is similar to that of other noncommercial operations. A primary difference relates to the names given to these positions. Exhibit 20.4 shows several organizational possibilities. Part A illustrates the most basic organizational system: a self-operated program in a single unit. The foodservice director is supervised by a business manager. (In some organizations, the foodservice director may be supervised by a human resources, facilities, or procurement administrator.) In turn, the foodservice director supervises the work of a head cook (with food production responsibilities) and a cafeteria supervisor (with serving responsibilities).

Part B of Exhibit 20.4 illustrates a self-operated program with outlets in several locations. Note that the foodservice director supervises the work of foodservice managers in each unit who, in turn, supervise persons with food production (head cook) and food serving (cafeteria supervisor) responsibilities.

Part C shows how a contract management company-operated program might be organized in an operation without a foodservice liaison. The foodservice director (who is an employee of the management company) reports to the organization's business manager (or human resources, facilities, or procurement administrator) and also to an external district manager who is an employee of the contract management company. The foodservice director, in turn, supervises the work of the head cook and cafeteria supervisor.

Finally, in Part D you see the organization modified because a foodservices liaison is used.

Business and industry foodservices provide catered meals for company picnics.

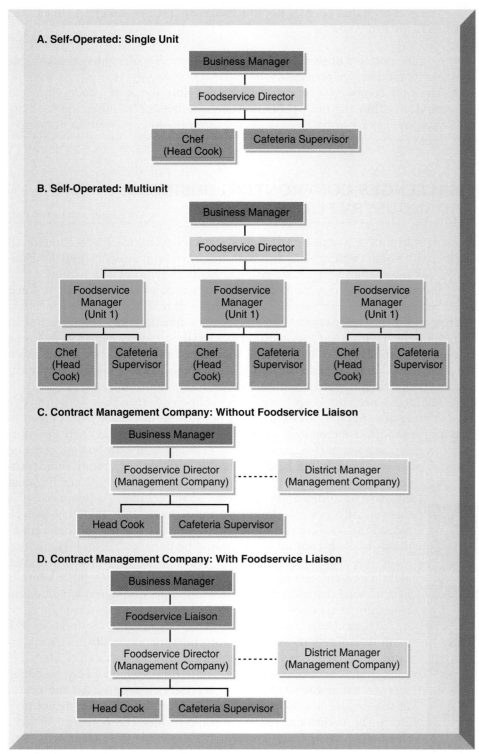

EXHIBIT 20.4
Organization of Management Positions in Business and Industry Foodservices

The foodservice liaison (an employee of the organization) is supervised by the business manager (or other administrator within the sponsoring organization). The liaison, in turn, is responsible for the foodservice operation as it is managed by the foodservice director (a management company employee). The relationships between the foodservice director, district manager, and on-site managers (head cook and cafeteria supervisor) are the same as in Part C.

You will note that each of the four basic organizational charts discussed has two factors in common:

- A representative of the sponsoring organization is ultimately responsible for its foodservice program.
- The unit foodservice manager is responsible for food production and service within the unit. (This is true regardless of whether the foodservices are operated by the sponsoring organization or a contract management company.)

OBJECTIVE 5
Review challenges applicable to foodservice managers in business and industry organizations.

CHALLENGES CONFRONTING BUSINESS AND INDUSTRY FOODSERVICES

Managers in business and industry foodservice operations share some challenges with their counterparts in other industry segments, as well as challenges unique to the segment. We will discuss both types in this section.

Consumers can become bored, and it is a constant challenge to keep them returning. They are very cost conscious and tend to compare what they receive (products and service) not only with what they pay (the concept of value), but also with what they would pay elsewhere. Many guests in business and industry foodservices believe that their employers should be giving them a benefit and therefore perceive that the value they receive should be significantly greater than it would be elsewhere.

Managers need to keep pace with technology. Business and industry foodservices are changing in many ways because of technology. Managers in this segment utilize technology in much the same way as do their counterparts in other segments (for example, for assistance in purchasing, revenue control, employee scheduling, and production forecasting, among many others). However, some technology is available but is either not cost effective to utilize and/or not easy to implement. For example, it is theoretically possible to utilize input from cash registers (which record the number of unit sales) to forecast when additional quantities of **batch-cooked** foods should be prepared. Also, it is theoretically possible for consumers to order food by computer for later pickup at a cafeteria or other location. Numerous technical details have slowed the widespread use of these technologies, which could benefit both foodservice operations and those being served.

batch cooking   the process of preparing smaller quantities of food several times during a serving period, rather than the total number of portions required at the same time

There is a need to educate those responsible for foodservices in an organization, as well as the consumers (employees). Organization officials, for example, might utilize the services of an external caterer for a special event. These funds would likely be better spent if the organization's own foodservices supported the event. In the case of a self-operated program or subsidized contract program, the additional revenues could reduce the potential of loss. Depending on the agreement with a contract management company, use of the internal supplier could increase the amount of commission paid to the organization.

Employees are typically unaware of the financial expectations of the foodservice program. They are likewise unaware of the often significant expenses required to operate the foodservice program. (In fact, many believe that "since there are no or few costs, we are entitled to very low charges for the foods we purchase." The challenge of educating administrators and consumers of the foodservices is very important.

Marketing challenges are significant. Issues relating to organizational downsizing that result in fewer guest counts and increased

Access to a pleasant foodservice experience is important to persons doing tedious assembly work.

consumer resistance to price increases were noted in the Feedback from the Real World section at the beginning of this chapter and will be discussed at its conclusion. Organization representatives typically believe the solution to be additional marketing and/or promotion tactics. Sometimes, ironically, ideas that are suggested (advertising on the organization's closed-circuit television network, including information with paychecks, and desk drops of advertising materials when work stations are cleaned, for example) are not permitted.

MANAGEMENT COMPANIES FACE UNIQUE CHALLENGES

Contract management companies operating business and industry foodservices are confronted by the challenges discussed above. Additionally, they must address at least two other issues:

1. Their companies lack name recognition by potential employees; this complicates tactics to recruit new staff members. Many persons recognize the names of some of the world's largest manufacturers, financial institutions, and insurance companies, for example, that may employ them to work in self-operated foodservices. (In the case of famous and not so famous commercial foodservices, name recognition may also be influential in making employment decisions.) Significantly fewer, if any, potential applicants are familiar with the names of contract management companies in organizations employing them to manage foodservices.

2. Clients are different. Traditionally, contract management companies interacted with foodservice liaisons, human resources officials, and business and finance administrators who had some knowledge about the management of foodservices. This made it relatively easy to negotiate and administer contracts for foodservices. Today, however, an increasing number of sponsoring organizations are delegating foodservice coordinating tasks to administrators with extensive knowledge about facility management and procurement. Their past experiences have less, if any, relationship with foodservices, and an educational effort is necessary to help them to recognize factors important in managing foodservices.

OBJECTIVE 6
Explain unique challenges faced by contract management companies operating business and industry foodservices.

Foodservices for correctional facilities can be self-operated or managed by a contract management company.

SUMMARY OF CHAPTER LEARNING OBJECTIVES

1. **Provide an overview of the business and industry foodservice segment with an emphasis on what it is and why it is important.**

   Business and industry foodservices (B&I) are those made available to employees while they are at work. These services may be offered by organizations because of convenience to employees and/or because they also benefit the companies. (Short lunch breaks may allow little time for off-site consumption, and there is a concern that employees may return late, not at all, or in an impaired condition.)

2. **Review alternative financial goals of business and industry foodservice operations.**

   Financial goals have moved along a continuum from the past, when foodservices were subsidized as an employee benefit; to recently, when goals related to breaking even; to today, when some profits are expected; to the future, when higher levels of profits will likely be expected. Contracts with management companies can be developed that recognize the financial goals of the sponsoring organization.

3. **Explore the range of foodservice alternatives offered in business and industry foodservices.**

   B&I foodservices can be delivered in food courts utilizing a straight-line serving system or a scramble cafeteria system. Dining areas can range from modest to more attractive (comfortable) than those in commercial operations. In addition to traditional cafeteria operations, foodservice alternatives include executive dining, traditional banquet and other catering activities, vending, office coffee services, home meal replacement, and even in-flight foodservices.

4. **Review the organization of management positions in business and industry foodservice operations.**

   B&I foodservices are organized in a manner similar to other noncommercial foodservice operations. Typically, a unit foodservice director is supervised by a business manager or other administrator of the sponsoring organization. He or she, in turn, directs the work of a foodservice manager, who supervises others with food production and food serving responsibilities. Organizations utilizing the services of a contract management company may provide a foodservice liaison to represent the organization in its dealings with the management company.

5. **Review challenges applicable to foodservice managers in business and industry organizations.**

   Challenges include the need to be creative to encourage repeat business, the need to find ways to utilize available technology, the need to educate organization officials and employees about the role of foodservices, and marketing issues relating to organizational downsizing.

6. **Explain unique challenges faced by contract management companies operating business and industry foodservices.**

   Contract management companies in the B&I segment are confronted by two additional challenges: the lack of name recognition, which hinders employee recruitment efforts, and the need to educate the new generation of organizational representatives responsible for foodservices.

FEEDBACK FROM THE REAL WORLD

Our real-world advice comes from Curtis Lease, District Manager, ARAMARK Business Services, Houston, Texas.

Curtis has experience in the resort, hotel, commercial restaurant, and B&I industries. He has worked for both self-operated B&I foodservices (Motorola, Inc.) and contract foodservices (ARAMARK) in a variety of client organizations, including rural, metro, central-city, professional office, manufacturing, and light industrial environments. In his current position as district manager with ARAMARK, he is responsible for over $18 million in sales at over 15 client locations in the Houston area.

A very challenging situation was introduced at the beginning of this chapter. A variety of foodservice alternatives was available to office and factory workers. Participation was decreasing because of previous layoffs, fears of additional labor force reductions, and a general downturn in the economy. Employees were looking for ways to find increased value in their dining purchases. At the same time, foodservice costs were increasing and no internal-organizational funds were available for its support.

What, if anything, can you do to better manage the operation (to reduce costs without sacrificing quality standards) and to develop more effective marketing (to increase guest counts, check averages, and revenues)?

First, the situation described is a real-world challenge that confronts operators regularly. Change is very prevalent in the business world, and foodservice operations must continually flex to meet the changing needs of the client (sponsoring organization) and the customer (employees). Typically, foodservice contracts are written and based on very specific population and/or revenue levels. When these change, this often triggers specific clauses in the contract that may affect financial agreements or even require contract renegotiations.

In any event, foodservice operators must continually track, monitor, and evaluate sales trends, buying habits, and feedback of their customer base. Demographic changes, the economy, the financial health of the client, and local competition (for example, commercial restaurants and trends in the marketplace) affect customers' spending habits in the daily foodservice operation.

The goal of all foodservice managers in a situation like this should be to provide fact-based data along with options to the client that will allow the two (foodservice operator and client) to make smart and financially sound decisions. The foodservice operator must provide fact-based data, including financial information, and must suggest options for the client. If this is not done, the foodservice operator is not operating in the spirit of a true partnership and is not helping the client to learn about all possible options that might offer solutions to the challenge.

Two special notes: First, as the challenge implies, clients and customers do not want to be affected negatively from quality and service goals. However, when populations and/or revenue levels change, often the end result for the operation is some type of change or impact on, at least, service levels (for example, reduced food offerings). Quality should not be affected, but customer perceptions might suggest otherwise. Bottom line: the foodservice manager has a tremendous challenge to manage perceptions and to drive value (special events and menus, vendor promotions, theme weeks, combo and value meals, for example) during challenging economic times. Second, when it comes to marketing, one of the first things most clients point to when revenue drops is a concern about marketing and what the management team is doing to increase participation and/or check average. It is critical that, before going to clients to look for financial relief or renegotiations, marketing activities must have already been implemented.

Here are a few options to present to the client in our situation:

- Consolidate operations. If possible, combine restaurant operations so that one or more of the satellite operations can be closed.
- Reduce food station offerings within the restaurant(s) to lower food waste and labor costs.
- Engineer menus. Introduce new food stations and menu offerings. Drive new and higher participation and check averages by introducing new items (with greater sales than current items and with larger profit margins).
- Promote the restaurant operation to nonusers. Target nonusers and look for ways to capture sales from them. (What can we sell to a brown-bagger? Every new dollar generated is helpful!)
- Market the operation outside the four walls. Can the operation be opened to the public?
- Promote external and off-site catering. A few additional catering events (especially large events like company picnics) can help to significantly reduce operating costs.
- Look for additional services and products that can be offered to the clients and customers. (Could the foodservice operation add a specialty coffee cart? Concierge services? Retail store? Office coffee service?)

(continued)

- Change the concept of the food outlet. Can a satellite restaurant be changed into a cold-food grab-and-go bistro? What about enhanced vending?
- Dare to compare. Embrace the local competition and demonstrate (with a dare-to-compare campaign) the value of the on-site restaurant. Are customers eating off-site comparing similar quality and portions? (Usually, the perception of "getting greater value" at a local quick-service restaurant is incorrect. The problem: the

customer is not comparing like items and quality. What is the pricing comparison to the market?)

These suggestions are only a few of the many options available. The key is to present many ideas. Remember that these options will vary by site and by client. Over time, experienced managers are more skilled at presenting effective options that can be great solutions to the challenge.

MASTERING YOUR KNOWLEDGE

Discuss the following questions.

1. Assume that you are the business manager of a large company. How would you determine whether foodservices should be offered? If a B&I program was judged necessary, how would you determine whether it should be self-operated or managed by a contract management company?

2. If you were a unit manager of a B&I foodservice operation, what would you do to retain consumer interest in the program? How would you assess what, if any, changes in the menu would be helpful?
3. What is the likely impact of organizational downsizing on a foodservice program? What can be done to minimize resulting problems?

LEARN FROM THE INTERNET

1. Check out the home pages of the following contract management companies:
   - Compass Group (Americas Division): www.cgnad.com
   - ARAMARK: www.aramark.com
   - Sodexho: www.sodexhoUSA.com

   When you arrive at the site, click on "Markets Served" and then "corporate dining" site.

   What, if any, information do they provide to business managers potentially interested in contracting foodservices to an external supplier? What cross references, if any, do they provide to other types of contracted services offered by the organization?

2. Check out the websites for several foodservice-related trade magazines:
   - *Restaurant Business:* ww.restaurantbiz.com. Enter "customer" into the website's search box.
   - *Restaurants & Institutions:* www.rimag.com. Enter "customer" into the website's search box.
   - *Food Management Magazine:* www.food-management.com. Click on "articles," then click on "archive search," and then enter "customer" into the search box.

   Review information applicable to B&I foodservice managers interested in reducing guest complaints and increasing the number of employees utilizing the foodservice operation.

KEY HOSPITALITY TERMS

The following terms were explained in this chapter. Review the definitions of any words with which you are unfamiliar. Begin to utilize them as you expand your vocabulary as a hospitality professional.

subsidy

business and industry foodservices

captive market

three-martini lunch

rebate

commission

cost plus

straight-line serving line

scramble cafeteria system

food court

concierge (contract management companies)

home meal replacement

branded food

self-brands

batch cooking

21

Vending and Office Coffee Services

Customer uses a cell phone to order (pay for) vended items.

CHAPTER LEARNING OBJECTIVES

After studying this chapter you will be able to:

1. Explain why organizations utilize vended services.
2. Discuss the advantages and disadvantages of using vending services.
3. Outline the organizational chart for a large vending company.
4. Explain basic behind the scenes activities that occur at a vending organization.
5. Review the roles and responsibilities of route managers and route drivers in delivering vended services.
6. List the types of vending machines available to dispense food and beverage products.
7. Suggest how technology can assist vending managers to make their operations more cost effective.
8. Review challenges that confront vending and office coffee service businesses.

The authors acknowledge the assistance of Craig Hesch, CFO, A.H. Management Group, Chicago, Illinois, for his assistance with this chapter.

FEEDBACK FROM THE REAL WORLD

You are the business manager for a relatively small but exclusive private college. It has a current enrollment of about 3,500 students, and there are several hundred faculty, staff, and administrative employees.

The college operates manual foodservices under a contract with a management company, and it has a separate contract with a local vending services provider. There have been no problems with the former (manual foodservices), but the arrangement with the vending company has never been successful. Now there is an increasing number of customer complaints about low-quality and outdated products, malfunctioning and unattractive machines, and, of course, high prices. The contract with the company expires in several months. What advice would you give to the college's business manager as he or she determines the future of vended services on the campus?

As you read this chapter, think about the answers to these questions, and then get feedback from the real world at the end of the chapter.

Vending services can be used to replace and/or to supplement their **manual foodservice** counterparts. Vending machines may be owned by the hotel, restaurant, or a noncommercial operation that makes them available. In this case, the organization would likely produce (provide) the products that are dispensed by the machine. (This alternative may involve a contract with an external supplier to provide mechanical support for the machines.)

More commonly, however, vending machines and the food and beverage products dispensed are provided by a contracted vending service. In this instance, a private company owns or leases the vending equipment, utilizes a warehouse to receive and store manufactured products, purchases or leases delivery vehicles, and employs **route drivers** to transport products and refill machines. The company may use a **commissary** to prepare items such as sandwiches that are sold through the machines. **Office coffee services (OCS)** are considered part of the office refreshment industry, and vending service companies often provide these services. Coffee and related service items and a limited number of other products, such as tea and soft drinks, commonly utilized in coffee break settings in business and industry organizations may be provided for a set fee per kit of coffee and related supplies.

WHY VENDED SERVICES?

Vended services help organizations utilizing them in at least two ways. They serve as a supplement to manual foodservices. There may be employees and others who do not want to participate in a dining room or cafeteria program. They may, for example, just want to purchase a beverage, sandwich, or snack. Vending also makes food and beverage products available to the organization's employees and visitors as a convenience when manual foodservices are not available (in other words, at times when a more extensive offering of food and beverage products is not **cost-justifiable,** for example, during a late-night shift when few employees work and the costs

vending services services in which food, beverage, and/or products are dispensed to consumers by vending machines

manual foodservices services in which food and/or beverages are served to consumers by foodservice employees

route drivers staff members employed by a vending organization to transport products, resupply products, and retrieve money from vending machines at an account utilizing the vending company's services

commissary a food preparation area (kitchen) utilized to produce food items at least some of which will be transported and served off-site

office coffee services (OCS) a service provided by an external supplier who provides coffee break-related beverages to business and industry and other accounts that desire these items

OBJECTIVE 1
Explain why organizations utilize vended services.

cost justifiable relating to the need to assure that the costs incurred are necessary

Warehousing is an important part of vending operations.

incurred for manual foodservices may not be offset by the revenue generated. The cost of manual foodservices during this time will likely be considered unjustifiable).

Vended services can replace manual foodservices. This may occur when, for example, the number of persons to be served is too small to permit a manual foodservice operation at any time of the day.

Vending services may be available from one or two machines in the corner of an employee lounge or even in a wide space in a hallway. At the other extreme, an extensive bank of vending units that occupies a significant amount of space and offers many hot and cold food and beverage items may be available. (There may even be one or more attendants available to resupply machines, dispense some items, and/or perform other tasks.)

ADVANTAGES AND DISADVANTAGES OF VENDED SERVICES

OBJECTIVE 2
Discuss the advantages and disadvantages of using vending services.

There are numerous advantages and several potential disadvantages for organizations utilizing vending services. The advantages include the following:

commission rebates a fee typically based on a percentage of revenues generated by a vending machine that is paid by the vending company to the organization in which the machine is located

- Convenient access for employees and guests to food and beverage products at any time
- The ability to offer food and beverage services to employees and guests at little or no cost. In fact, **commission rebates** or rental fees are even possible.
- Little, if any, capital costs to the organization (assuming that space to locate units is available)
- Fast service and a wide product selection (which reduces consumer complaints)
- Reduced need to offer manual services except at optimally desired times

---

WHO UTILIZES VENDED SERVICES?

Consumers of vended products typically utilize these services for convenience. Machines are located in areas close to cafeteria and break areas and in other locations that minimize the time consumers need to access the units. While numerous items can be dispensed by vending units, the most frequently vended items are hot and cold beverages, candy, snacks, and related items that supplement, but do not replace, a typical meal.

Vending units are lined up for the public's use.

HISTORY OF THE VENDING
SERVICES INDUSTRY*

The first vending machine may have been a device used to dispense sacrificial water in ancient Egyptian temples. Machines to vend snuff and tobacco boxes after coins were inserted appeared in English taverns and inns during the early 1600s.

During the 1800s, British inventors developed vending machines to sell books, postage stamps, and candy. Later in that century, gum ball (chewing gum) dispensers became popular, and the Adam's Gum Company may have been the first business to generate significant revenues from vending machine sales.

Over the years, many products, including cigars, perfumes, wine, and even divorce papers, have been dispensed by vending machines. In the old days, slugs in the shape of coins and even coins to which strings were attached could be used to cheat vending machines. The need to develop mechanisms to prevent product or money theft was a concern to the vending industry that continues to this day.

By the early 1900s, automats (automated restaurants) were available in which customers purchased portions of food from individual coin-operated compartments mounted on the wall. They could then eat while seated at tables or while standing up. (To do the latter was to consume a "perpendicular meal.")

Early soft drink machines were very crude by today's standards. For example, cracked ice was placed on top of bottles in the vending machines each morning, and glasses were available that consumers could rinse (if they desired) before using them.

By the mid-1920s, vending machines were used to sell cigarettes, soft drinks in paper cups, candy, and other snacks. Also at that time, a vending unit was placed inside a refrigerator in the first efforts to vend products such as butter, eggs, and other items needing refrigeration. Vending tops for existing reach-in soft drink coolers became popular in the 1930s. Machines to vend hot coffee made from liquid, concentrate, and dry ingredients were introduced in the 1940s, and in the early 1950s machines were introduced that made fresh coffee from coffee grounds.

In the 1960s, paper-money change makers provided increased opportunities for vending companies to serve consumers and, with improved refrigeration and heating capacities, the modern era of vending began.

*Adapted from G.R. Schreiber. *A Concise History of Vending in the U.S.A.* Lake Bluff, IL: Sunrise Books, 1999.

Potential disadvantages of the use of vending services include these:

● Service is impersonal; there is no contact with foodservice personnel.
● It is not generally possible to provide the wide variety of prepared food items available in manual foodservices.
● Employees with previous access to manual foodservices may not readily accept the change to vended services.

OBJECTIVE 3
Outline the organizational chart for a large vending company.

ORGANIZATIONAL STRUCTURE OF VENDING OPERATIONS

Vending organizations range in size from very small mom and pop operations grossing $1 million (or less) annually to very large national and even international organizations grossing hundreds of millions of dollars every year. Exhibit 21.1 shows part of a possible organizational chart for a large vending company. Large companies typically offer both manual and vended services and also office coffee services (OCS) and catering. This figure emphasizes the vended and office coffee service chain of command in the organization.

When reviewing Exhibit 21.1, note that the company's chief operating officer (COO) directs the work of a president who, in turn, manages activities

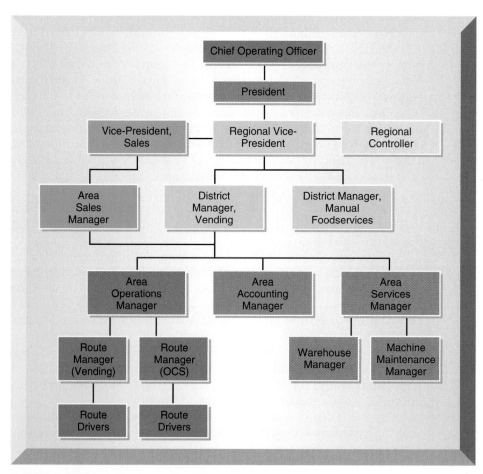

EXHIBIT 21.1
Possible Organization of a Large Vending Company

of several (or more) regional vice-presidents. (The chart identifies only one of these officials.) The regional vice-president, in turn, directly supervises a regional vice-president for sales and for accounting (regional controller).

The regional vice-president also directly supervises a district manager (DM) for vending and a district manager (DM) for manual food-services. (A regional vice-president may be responsible for $60 million or more in revenue annually.)

Each DM for vending, in turn, may work with an area sales manager and supervise an accounting manager. He or she also supervises the area operations managers (who direct the work of route managers for vending and for OCS) and an area services manager (who is responsible for warehousing and machine maintenance). Depending on the number and size of accounts that are his or her responsibility, the district manager may be re-

Vending units in a local neighborhood are popular "refreshment centers."

sponsible for $6 million in business (from 2,000 vending machines) to $15 million (from 4,000 vending machines). Finally, note that Exhibit 21.1 shows that the route drivers report to route managers. It is amazing to recognize that the relatively few coins that a consumer places into a vending machine can be aggregated into a business that generates half a billion dollars or more in a single year.

Smaller organizations will likely have an organization chart with fewer layers of management, but vending businesses of any size must combine work tasks into positions focusing on the following:

- Sales
- Accounting
- Operations
- Services
- Warehousing
- Machine maintenance
- Route service tasks

OBJECTIVE 4
Explain basic behind the scenes activities that occur at a vending organization.

BEHIND THE SCENES OF VENDING OPERATIONS

Exhibit 21.2 illustrates the activities required before vended products are transported to the vending **account location.** While some of the functions noted, such as administrative support and marketing and sales, are applicable to all types of hospitality operations, some are more unusual, such as machine maintenance and the money room. Let's look more carefully at each of these activities that occur at the headquarters of the vending organization.

account location   a site where a vending company's machines are located; a large account may have banks of vending machines in several (or more) places throughout its location

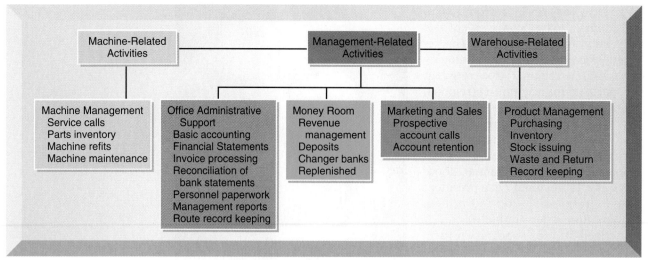

EXHIBIT 21.2
Behind the Scenes in Vending Operations: Getting Ready for Sales

Machine Management

These activities relate to the management of vending machines, which are becoming much more complex and expensive. (Today's machines range in cost from $3,000 to $10,000 or more and require very knowledgeable mechanics with sophisticated equipment to properly maintain and repair them.) Technicians are required for service calls to sites where equipment is malfunctioning and for unit maintenance. Machines may be brought back to the organization's repair shop for retrofitting (modernizing) and for more extensive repairs. Also, the management of the spare parts inventory is important because of the number and cost of replacement items, which must be available for use by repair and service technicians.

Office (Administrative Support) Activities

accounts receivable (AR) money owed to an organization because of sales made on credit

accounts payable (AP) the total of all invoices owed by an organization to its suppliers for credit purchases it has made

Vending units accept bills and lessen the need to inconvenience customers. Increasingly, machines also accept credit and debit cards.

Some of the activities performed by office staff at vending headquarters are common throughout the hospitality industry. Examples include basic accounting, such as managing **accounts receivable** and **accounts payable,** and the generation of financial statements. Other examples include the routine processing of invoices for payment, reconciling bank statements, and managing personnel paper work, including payroll records.

One task, route record keeping, is unique to the vending segment. Route record keeping involves a tedious, complex process of matching, on a by-route driver basis, the quantity of product loaded onto delivery trucks daily with the amount of product loaded into machines and returned to the warehouse with the applicable amount of product revenue that should be generated by the quantity of products sold. As diagrammed in Exhibit 21.3, the quantity of fresh products that are likely required to refill the vending machines on each route are loaded onto a delivery truck. The sales value of these products is known (can be estimated). At each stop, some products are used to refill the machines (replace products that were sold). Other fresh products must be used to replace products still remaining in the machines that have reached their **expiration date.** The sum of the products used to replace products that have been sold and to replace expired products represents the quantity of product that has been used to fill the machine. This process, repeated for each product dispensed through each vending machine on the route, can be utilized to determine the quantity of fresh product that should be returned when the route is completed:

expiration date the calendar date at which a product should no longer be available for sale because of a concern that quality deterioration has occurred

$$\begin{pmatrix} \text{Quantity} \\ \text{loaded} \\ \text{onto truck} \end{pmatrix} - \begin{pmatrix} \text{Quantity} & & \text{Quantity} \\ \text{used to} & & \text{used to} \\ \text{replace} & + & \text{replace} \\ \text{sold items} & & \text{expired} \\ & & \text{products} \end{pmatrix} = \begin{pmatrix} \text{Quantity of} \\ \text{fresh} \\ \text{product} \\ \text{returned} \end{pmatrix}$$

The quantity of fresh product returned becomes available for route delivery at a future date unless product expiration dates have been exceeded.

The quantity of products used to replace sold units becomes the basis to determine the amount of revenues to be collected from machine sales:

$$\begin{pmatrix} \text{Quantity of} \\ \text{product sold} \end{pmatrix} \times \begin{pmatrix} \text{Product} \\ \text{selling price} \end{pmatrix} = \begin{pmatrix} \text{Machine} \\ \text{revenues} \end{pmatrix}$$

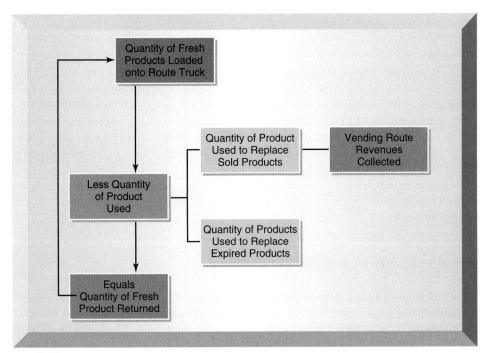

EXHIBIT 21.3
Vending Products Sold Should Match Vending Revenues Received

accountability (in vending) the process of matching products loaded onto route trucks with the amount of products returned and vending revenues turned into the money room

This **accountability** process must be completed for all machines at the account site and for all account sites to yield the daily route revenues. This effort to account for all product sales and returns and for revenue that should be collected requires that vending products be counted several times before they are sold or returned to the warehouse as expired products.

Technology is increasingly used to simplify and speed up the process of reconciling products and revenue on vending routes. The need to count, reconcile, and recount adds time and labor costs to the process, which vending organizations are constantly trying to reduce.

Money Room Activities

As the name implies, the money room is where the cash is brought after route drivers remove it from the vending machines and return it to the vending organization's headquarters. Monies must be counted and compared with the product and revenue reconciliations described above. Bank deposits must be made, and machine change banks used at account sites must be replenished.

drop chute in vending, a chute or slot in the door or wall of a money room through which funds collected on routes can be passed without entering the money room

The large amounts of cash processed in the money room typically require elaborate security precautions to minimize the possibilities of external or internal theft. In addition to limited access, many vendors utilize a **drop chute** to reduce the need for staff members not working in the area to enter the money room. Currency counters are used to reduce the time and to increase the accuracy required for the money-counting task. (The vending industry has long supported the availability and increased use of a dollar coin since coin-counting equipment is faster and more accurate than is paper-currency counting equipment. The dollar coin is also preferred by customers because paper bills are more often rejected by vending machines.) Like other businesses in the hospitality industry that generate large amounts of cash, armored security services are typically employed to transport cash from vending offices to banking organizations where deposits are made.

Marketing and Sales Activities

This function includes generating new and maintaining existing business. In the vending industry, like other segments of the very competitive hospitality industry, service of existing customer accounts is critical. Also like other businesses in hospitality, every employee is a salesperson. Top-level vending managers and/or their sales representatives are constantly seeking new accounts and working to maintain existing ones. Route drivers also play a significant role, because they represent their organization to the consumers. They have the most day to day interactions with the client so it is important that route drivers have a good personality and the ability to communicate well. They are, in effect, the vending organization's first line of goodwill and communication.

Product Management Activities

In many ways, the vendor's warehouse is managed like a storeroom in a hotel, restaurant, or other foodservice operation. Products must be ordered, and incoming stock must be received and placed into inventory. There it must be effectively managed to control against quality deterioration and internal theft and to minimize the amount of money tied up in inventory. Procedures must also be in place to assure that the quantity and value of all products issued

VENDING CLIENTS AND VENDING CUSTOMERS

Vending organizations interact with **clients** and **customers.** Clients are the account decision makers who negotiate and contract with the vending organization for its services, and customers are the users of the vending machines who purchase products from them. Sometimes making clients happy makes the customers happy. Consider, for example, the arrangement in which clients request that products be sold at the lowest possible price to provide the best value for those purchasing vended products. This will result in happy customers with few, if any, complaints made to the clients to be passed on to the vending company.

Sometimes, however, when clients are happy, customers are made unhappy. Consider the situation in which clients desire high commission rebates, which must be passed on to vending customers through higher prices for the products they purchase. Customer complaints about prices then go to the client, who passes them on to the vending company. The result is a challenge for the vendor to satisfy the financial concerns related to selling prices (the customers), commissions (the client), and profitability (the vending company).

(placed on the delivery truck) are known. Unlike their foodservice counterparts, however, when products are issued they generally do not go to the kitchen but, rather, to delivery trucks for transport to accounts. (As noted earlier, some vending organizations do have kitchens or commissaries that produce the foods, such as sandwiches and baked goods, that will be sold through vending machines.)

Managing waste and returns (which occur because product expiration dates have been reached) is of vital concern and requires very careful controls to minimize costs. Knowing what sells (and what doesn't), moving products as needed between machines, and effective communication between route drivers and management personnel are tactics to manage waste and returns.

We have mentioned the task of recordkeeping several times because it is a critical activity in an industry segment in which literally every penny (actually, every fraction of a penny!) counts. Machines must be inventoried each time they are serviced; delivery trucks must be inventoried at least weekly, and vending warehouse personnel must take a complete inventory at least monthly. Fortunately, technology is increasingly available to assist with the inventory task; we will discuss its role later in the chapter.

clients (vending) the account decision maker(s) who negotiates and contracts with a vending company

customers (vending) individuals who purchase products from vending machines

Vending units on a college campus

WHO BUYS WHAT FROM VENDING MACHINES?

Location (Vending Site),	%	Products Purchased, %	
Manufacturing	41	Bottled and canned beverages	49.5
White collar	26	Snacks	21.0
Educational	12	Food	7.8
Healthcare	7	Hot beverages	10.0
Other	14	Cold cup beverages	3.7
	100	Ice cream	2.0
		Milk	1.0
		Other products	5.0
			100.0

Source: National Automated Merchandising Association (NAMA), *Vending 101.* Chicago. To view current data, go to the NAMA website (www.vending.org.) and click on "Publications"and then "About Vending."

OBJECTIVE 5
Review the roles and responsibilities of route managers and route drivers in delivering vended services.

route manager   the manager within the vending organization who plans delivery routes, supervises route drivers, takes corrective action as necessary based on route revenues and product costs, and provides service to help retain existing accounts

ROUTE MANAGERS AND ROUTE DRIVERS SERVICE VENDING ACCOUNTS

Route managers and route drivers are two positions that are unique to vending service organizations. Exhibit 21.4 shows some of the most important tasks performed by individuals in these positions. It also illustrates that the main focus of their efforts is to effectively deliver service to their accounts and customers.

A large part of the work of route managers involves answering the question "What is the most time- and cost-efficient way to deliver products to our accounts?" Problems of long distances (in suburban or rural locations) and of driving in congested areas (in cities) are only part of the challenge. Other issues address concerns about times when products should be delivered, the possible need for multiple deliveries during the work day (and work night!), and, in general, the reduction of costs associated with maintaining a fleet of delivery trucks and minimizing the work times of route drivers (who are frequently paid on an hourly basis).

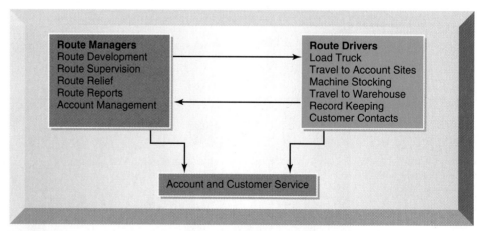

EXHIBIT 21.4
A Close Look at Vending Route Managers and Route Drivers

Route managers directly supervise route drivers. Tasks performed in their role as supervisor are basically the same as for any other supervisor. They are responsible for training, performance appraisal, motivation, and building teamwork, among numerous other personnel-related challenges. Also, just as chefs must sometimes do the work of their cooks and front-desk managers must sometimes check in guests, so must route managers sometimes work routes to relieve drivers who are not available when needed.

Route managers provide input to route reports that detail the productivity and profitability of accounts on specific routes and the drivers who service them. Also, they interact with representatives of each of their accounts. This is absolutely important to implement the vending agreement on a day to day basis and as they determine how to better meet the account's needs in efforts to add value to the vending relationship. In some organizations, responsibility of **account retention** can account for 40 to 50 percent of a route manager's time.

Route drivers have often served in route relief (fill-in) positions or have other experience before they are given their own routes. Many of their tasks involve physical work. They must, for example, load (or help to load) the truck at the warehouse and drive to vending locations. They must transport products to and open the machines, remove and replace expiration-dated products, and restock products that have been sold. Cash must be collected, record keeping relative to product stocks and cash collected is required, and machines must be cleaned and closed. These tasks are repeated at each account they service. Then, at the end of the day, drivers must return to the warehouse where additional record-keeping tasks must be performed. For example, they must record the "adds and totals" on records to reconcile sales for each specific machine. Also, they must develop a product requisition sheet helpful in stocking their delivery truck for the next day's deliveries.

In addition to the above work tasks, route drivers are also the on-site customer service representative for the vending organization. They are likely to come into contact with more customers at the vending site than are route managers, central office sales personnel, or other managers. In this respect, then, they are very much like food servers: because of their many contacts with consumers, they play a significant role in the relationship between the organization and those it serves.

account retention activities undertaken to ensure that representatives of organizations utilizing the services of a hospitality organization will continue to do business with the organization; contract management companies and vending or office coffee service organizations are examples of hospitality business with account retention concerns

alternative beverages water and a wide variety of mostly noncarbonated beverages, including juices, teas, and a wide range of newly popular flavored drinks

postmix the process of mixing carbonated water with syrup for soda (soft drinks) at the time the beverage is served (dispensed)

OBJECTIVE 6
List the types of vending machines available to dispense food and beverage products.

MODERN VENDING EQUIPMENT

Today, machines are available to vend almost every product for which operators have found it financially advantageous to do so, including these:

- Snacks (glass front)
- Canned and bottled soft drinks and **alternative beverages**
- Cupped soft drinks (**postmix**)
- Hot drinks (coffee, hot chocolate, tea, and related beverages)
- Refrigerated foods
- Frozen foods
- Units that vend combinations of the above

Vending units are popular around the world.

VENDING PROFITS ARE IN PENNIES PER DOLLAR

	Vending Company Annual Revenue				
	≤$1M	$1–$3M	$3–$5M	$5–$10M	≥$10M
Revenues	100.0%	100.0%	100.0%	100.0%	100.0%
Product costs	(50.0)	(49.9)	(47.4)	(47.5)	(44.5)
Gross margin	50.0	50.1	52.6	52.5	55.5
Labor costs	22.6	22.6	21.8	23.8	21.7
Commissions	5.2	6.4	8.0	7.6	10.1
Other costs	24.7	19.9	19.2	18.1	18.4
Operating profit	(2.5)	1.2	3.6	3.0	5.3

What the numbers say: Levels of operating profits increase as the volume of revenues increases. This is primarily because of reduced product costs (due to volume purchases) and lowered "other costs" (which also relate to increased operating efficiencies resulting from higher sales volumes).

Note: "Operating profit" is before applicable income taxes; the amount of profit for the owners or investors of vending organizations is less than the bottom line shown above.

Source: National Automated Merchandising Association (NAMA). *Vending 101.* Data are current as of 11/1/05. To view current information, go to www.vending.org and click on "Publications"and then click on "About Vending."

high-traffic areas locations adjacent to areas with large numbers of potential customers

CHECK IT OUT!

To gain a great overview of the vending and office coffee service industry, check out *Vending 101* on the website of the National Automatic Merchandising Association (NAMA): www.vending.org. When you arrive at the site, click on "Publications" and then "About Vending."

Vending machines can be located by themselves in **high-traffic areas** or, alternatively, they can be arranged into banks of compatible equipment that offer a wide array of products to customers.

Officials in vending companies have the same types of concerns about the selection and purchase of equipment as do their counterparts in other segments of the hospitality industry. Vendors are looking for good price value. However, they also recognize that a good equipment supplier is one who also provides information (such as assistance in resolving applicable operating problems) and service (such as demonstrating equipment and supplying parts, conversion kits, and other supplies on a timely basis).

Most machine manufacturers and many of their distributors offer equipment purchase financing plans. Other vendors utilize banks, commercial finance companies, equipment leasing companies, and/or, sometimes, their own internal financial resources to acquire the extensive amount and types of vending equipment that are needed.

OBJECTIVE 7
Suggest how technology can assist vending managers to make their operations more cost effective.

VENDING TECHNOLOGY

Previously, common business practices in the vending industry required an incredible amount of manual record keeping to track and account for many food and beverage products costing relatively little and selling for just a small margin above costs. Technology is increasingly coming to the assistance of vending operators in their efforts to account for revenues and control costs.

Bar Codes

Bar code technology enables persons receiving products in warehouses to quickly update information about quantities available in inventory as products are received. They can also quickly record decreases in inventory levels as products are issued to delivery trucks. This technology also enables warehouse staff to determine the quantity or sales value or cost of products in a **perpetual inventory** system.

Curbside Polling and Kiting

Can you imagine how the productivity of route drivers could be increased if the following scenario occurred: the route driver arrives at the account site and utilizes wireless technology to determine the quantity of each product remaining in each vending machine. He or she can then take the required quantities of each product necessary to replenish the machine on the first trip to the vending machine location. (Currently, route drivers must guess based on experience the quantity of products needed to refill machines. Additional trips from the vending machine to the delivery truck and back again may be necessary if the initial guesswork is inaccurate.) **Curbside polling** technology is available today and will be utilized increasingly in the future as vending operators determine cost-effective ways to remain competitive while providing increased levels of service to their accounts.

A related trend is even more futuristic. **Kiting** eliminates the need for curbside polling. This remote technology enables vending machines to "communicate" refill needs directly to the warehouse. For example, a standard may be that a machine will be serviced when it is 60 percent empty or has one column empty. (Standards regarding product expiration dates are also considered.) This allows the company to go to machines only when it is cost-efficient

bar code   lines of information that can be scanned into a computer system; bar code technology is used to update inventory databases and for many other purposes

perpetual inventory   a system that keeps track of all incoming and outgoing products so that one knows, on an ongoing basis, the amount of product that should be available in inventory

curbside polling   the process that allows route drivers using a hand-held terminal (HHT) to determine the current level of products in vending machines while still in their trucks

kiting   remote technology that enables vending warehouse staff to learn the product refill needs of specific machines; kits containing needed products are assembled, taken to the applicable machine, and loaded into it

---

SOME COMMON VENDING TERMS

4Cs A traditional industry abbreviation for basic vending products: coffee, cup soda, candy, and cigarettes

Full-line vendors Operators who offer items such as hot canned food, canned soda, and refrigerated and frozen food, in addition to the basic 4Cs

Specialty vendors Operators who concentrate efforts in specific equipment or products, such as French fries, pizza, popcorn, and other specialty items

OCS (office coffee service) vendors Operators who provide brewing cups and coffee items to businesses for coffee break amenities. It is common for full-line vending operators to move into OCS, and for OCS operators to offer vending services to meet demands of their customers.

Bulk vendors Operators who vend candy, gum, novelties, and related items. Crossover between full-line and bulk operators in both directions is not uncommon (but less frequent than in OCS and vending)

Music and game vendors Operators who offer music machines, video games, coin-operated amusement, and related devices

Street vendors Operators who service public locations, such as restaurants and taverns. The service can encompass cigarettes, snacks, jukeboxes, video games, pool tables, or any combination of these and related offerings.

Source: National Automated Merchandising Association (NAMA), *Vending 101*. Chicago, n.d.

to do so. Warehouse employees assemble *kits* of products needed to refill the machines. The kits are loaded onto the truck, and the driver can go directly to the machine and load the refill kit prepared for it.

Home Office Information

How many dollars of revenue are lost and how many customers become upset when vending machines malfunction? While a precise answer is not known, technology is available to reduce lost sales and customer complaints. Wireless technologies can automatically notify repair personnel at the vending company's headquarters that a malfunction is occurring on a specific machine and that repair or maintenance is needed. Machines are also often equipped with technology that helps to ensure that selected products are dispensed and do not get hung up in the machine. (If this occurs, money is automatically refunded to the customer.)

Machine Revenue and Product Cost Tallies

Wireless technology enables machines to upload information about product sales and product usage on a by-machine basis to the vending organization. This allows a double-check on the revenue collection and product usage reported by route drivers.

Technology to Increase Vending Revenue

cashless vending technology that allows customers to purchase products from vending machines without using cash (coins or currency)

micropayment (vending machines) small (several dollars or less) purchases from a vending machine made by credit or debit card

How many dollars of potential vending revenue are lost because the customer has the incorrect change or paper currency in a larger denomination than that accepted by the machine? **Cashless vending** technology is now available that allows a customer to dial a number on a cell phone (the number to call is noted on the vending machine) to make vending purchases. Approval of the charge allows the customer to make a vending purchase with the amount charged to a credit or debit card or even to his or her telephone bill. Another innovation: **micropayments** made by credit or debit cards directly inserted into vending machines. Advantages to the vending organization include elimination of human counting errors, significantly reduced time to count and reconcile monies, and less opportunities for cash theft. There are, however, increased costs because card readers are more expensive to purchase and there is a transaction processing fee.

OBJECTIVE 8
Review challenges that confront vending and office coffee service businesses.

CHALLENGES! CHALLENGES!

As with all segments of the industry, vending and office coffee service operations are confronted by several challenges:

- **Health initiatives around the nation.** While it is very important to eat healthy foods, these items do not sell as well as other items, they take up limited machine space, and their gross margins are not better than other products.
- **Consolidation in suppliers, manufacturers, and operators.** When there are more equipment and product manufacturers, there is greater competition, and this helps to keep vending costs down for operators and consumers. Consolidation, then, creates the opposite effect: higher costs and increased consumers' prices.

- **Smaller account size is now the norm.** There are fewer large accounts in the manufacturing sector, which are the bread and butter of vending. Competition for these large accounts has become extreme.
- **Technology.** This will be the key component for success in the future. With clientel size shrinking and competition increasing, it is of utmost importance that maximum efficiencies be obtained in both labor and purchasing. Unfortunately, this will squeeze the smaller companies, because significant capital is typically required for this kind of conversion

Of course, within these challenges, a lot of opportunity exists. The vending companies that can work through these challenges will succeed well into the future.

SUMMARY OF CHAPTER LEARNING OBJECTIVES

1. **Explain why organizations utilize vended services.**
   Vended services are used as a supplement to manual foodservices in some organizations. In others, vended services replace manual foodservices.

2. **Discuss the advantages and disadvantages of using vending services.**
   Advantages include convenient food and beverage product access for employees and guests, the ability to offer foodservices at little or no cost, little, if any, capital costs to the sponsoring organization, and fast service and a wide variety of product selection and less need to offer manual services. Disadvantages may include impersonal service, the inability to provide the variety of products possible in manual foodservices, and the potential for consumer complaints if vending services replace manual foodservices.

3. **Outline the organizational chart for a large vending company.**
   A regional vice-president supervises a district manager who, in turn, supervises area managers for sales, operations, accounting, and services (machines). The area operations manager directs the work of route managers, who are responsible for route drivers.

4. **Explain basic behind the scenes activities that occur at a vending organization.**
   Three basic types of activities happen behind the scenes:
   - Machine-related activities: service calls, parts inventory, machine refits, machine maintenance

   - Management-related activities: office and administrative support, the money room, and marketing and sales
   - Warehouse-related activities: purchasing, inventory, issuing, and record keeping

5. **Review the roles and responsibilities of route managers and route drivers in delivering vended services.**
   Route managers are responsible for developing the route, supervising and providing relief for route drivers, completing route reports, and managing their accounts. Route drivers perform numerous physical tasks, including loading and driving delivery trucks, machine stocking, record keeping, and serving as a point person for customer service.

6. **List the types of vending machines available to dispense food and beverage products.**
   Common vending machines include those for snacks (glass front), canned soft drinks, cupped soft drinks (postmix), hot drinks, refrigerated and frozen foods, and units that vend combinations of these items.

7. **Suggest how technology can assist vending managers to make their operations more cost effective.**
   Technology can assist in several ways, including the following:
   Bar code technology. To quickly maintain product perpetual inventories and determine the quantity, sales value, or cost of products in inventory

Uplinking technology. To help route drivers to determine the quantity of products needed as vending machines are resupplied *Home office information.* Includes the ability to inform vending home office personnel about the need for on-site service of malfunctioning vending machines

Machine revenue and product cost tallies. To quickly determine the quantity of products sold and the resulting revenues expected from these sales on a by-machine basis

Cashless vending technology to increase vending revenue. For example, customers can utilize their cell telephones to make vending purchases

8. **Review challenges that confront vending and office coffee businesses.**

   Four challenges that confront the vending and office coffee service industry are dealing with national health initiatives; consolidation of suppliers, manufacturers, and operators; smaller account sizes; and the increased need for expensive technology.

FEEDBACK FROM THE REAL WORLD

Our real-world advice about the selection of a vended services provider for the college described at the beginning of this chapter is provided by Dan Mathews, NCE. Dan is Senior Vice-President & COO for the National Automatic Merchandising Association in Chicago, Illinois.

What factors should the business manager consider as a vending services provider is selected for the campus of the exclusive private college?

The business manager could consider asking the on-site foodservice contractor to also provide the vending services, and this might be done without bidding the contract. The two parties could simply reach a mutually acceptable agreement and proceed. While this tactic is simple, it may not yield the best results, and the school official may, instead, attempt to solicit competitive bids. Since the present manual foodservice company is doing a good job, this supplier could be among those requested to provide detailed information about their vended services.

The business manager will be wise to develop and distribute a request for proposal (RFP) to prospective companies to facilitate the bidding and subsequent proposal evaluation process. The process of doing so will help to answer the question "What exactly do we want?" As well, it will identify a list of basic concerns

that should be addressed by each prospective vending organization that provides a proposal response. The vending services decision should then become easier to make when information about similar topics (those of concern to college administrators) is provided.

This relatively small organization may not develop and circulate an RFP that is as detailed as one issued by a very large organization. However, many factors are important and should be considered as RFPs are developed and as proposal responses are evaluated. As you review the list of concerns that follow, you can begin to see that a "simple" challenge ("obtain the services of a vending provider that will best meet our needs") really involves a significant amount of planning effort to accomplish.

Here is a list of important concerns for the college administration:

- Types of products to be vended, including size of portion and the need for nationally known brands
- Quality specifications for ingredients used in perishable products such as fresh sandwiches, if applicable (there may be no need for these types of vended food items since the existing manual foodservices may provide adequate options for students, faculty, and staff)
- A requirement for healthy options in addition to other items

- The number, type, and planned location of each machine
- Procedures to be used to assure product freshness, and to confirm that all health, sanitation, and food safety requirements are complied with
- Advertising restrictions, if any, on machines or products
- Method to guarantee efficient and timely customer refunds
- Requirements to be met by the vending services route personnel and other representatives
- Information about marketing and promotional programs the vendors would implement on campus in conjunction with some of their suppliers

The business manager should also provide information about the college's current vending operations, including number of machines, types, locations, and sales data for each machine.

Responsibilities of the vending contractor should also be specified. These typically include the following:

- Installing, maintaining, and servicing new vending machines with the latest technological innovations, including cashless operations
- Securing permits, licenses, insurance, and other prerequisites for conduct of the business and for the payment of all taxes incurred by the business
- Furnishing food and beverage products and the management and labor necessary for proper machine operation
- Supplying products of the proper quality according to specifications and keeping the machines filled and working at all times.
- Operating and maintaining vending units according to all laws, regulations, and other rules of applicable authorities and complying with the rules and regulations of the college
- Maintaining vending machines in first-class condition at all times
- Providing adequate vending services in times and in locations that are agreed on
- Complying with requirements about the use of space, utilities, and storage of vending property, if any, on the campus

- Identifying, defending, and holding the college harmless against loss, damage, expense, or claims applicable to the vending operation

Special attention must be paid to expectations about payment plans. For example, if a rebate commission plan is used, the vending contractor will pay a commission to the college. Commissions should be listed by product group, with corresponding guaranteed commissions, if any, specified in dollars (not percentage of machine sales). Sometimes the vendor company sets a guaranteed minimum. (This is called a *guaranteed commission*.) Alternatively (but not commonly), a profit or loss arrangement could be used. With this arrangement, the operator does not pay a commission or require a subsidy and keeps all proceeds from the machine sales.

In addition to learning about the above details, the business manager should be very concerned about each prospective company's experience and reputation. If possible, he or she should visit two or three of the local clients that have been referred by the bidders. The financial status of each proposed vending company is also important. To this end, a copy of the company's financial review or statement will indicate its financial strength. The business manager should also visit the company's branch office(s) to assess cleanliness and the overall operation.

College administrators should recognize that the vending company is selling service in addition to products. Service experiences should be discussed with each company's current clients: How long does it take to fix machines? Are machines ever empty before being refilled? Are customers providing feedback that identifies positive or negative service? How helpful are company personnel in working to correct the client's concerns?

Finally, the business manager should recognize that negotiating and signing an agreement for vending services is just the beginning of the relationship that follows. Representatives of the college and the vending contractor must interact in a way that both parties and, of course, the customers being served benefit from the relationship.

MASTERING YOUR KNOWLEDGE

Discuss the following questions.

1. Think about your own reactions to vended services and assume that other students have the same perspectives. What are the pros and cons of using vended services that you can cite? How do you think vending organizations should address the disadvantages, if any, that you identified?

2. As a vending operator, what kinds of information and service would you want from vending machine equipment suppliers to help your personnel to service, maintain, and modernize your vending machines?

3. Using the example of one candy bar, describe each time that a candy bar is accounted for from the point when it is received in the warehouse until revenues from its sales are accounted for at vending headquarters.

4. What type of cash-control procedures should be implemented to reduce internal theft by employees working in the money room?

5. Pretend that you are a sales representative for a vending organization. What points about your company's service would you make to a prospective account to encourage that company to do business with your organization?

6. How exactly can a route driver influence the quality of service provided by a vending organization at a specific account?

7. How would you defend the need for and explain procedures to utilize wireless technology to route drivers with many years of experience and little experience with technology equipment and systems?

LEARN FROM THE INTERNET

1. Check out the website for the National Automatic Merchandising Association (the trade association representing the vending industry): www.vending.org. What are the current challenges confronting the vending industry? How do these challenges differ from their counterparts in manual foodservices? What kinds of information does NAMA provide that does or does not apply to managers in manual foodservices?

2. Check out the websites for the following vending companies:
   - Modern Food Management Systems, Inc.: www.modernvending.com
   - Canteen Vending Services: www.canteen.com
   - Sodexho: www.sodexhousa.com

   Which of these offer vended services in addition to manual foodservices? Office coffee service in addition to manual foodservices? What types of information about vended services do these companies provide? Why do they suggest that a prospective account would benefit from utilizing their services for vending and/or office coffee services?

3. Check out the websites for the following vending machine manufacturers:
   - Royal Vendors: www.royalvendors.com
   - Crane Merchandising System: www.cranems.com
   - Seaga Manufacturing, Inc.: www.seagamtg.com

   What kinds of equipment do they have available? What equipment do they believe will be most useful for tomorrow's vending industry?

KEY HOSPITALITY TERMS

The following terms were explained in this chapter. Review the definitions of any words with which you are unfamiliar. Begin to utilize them as you expand your vocabulary as a hospitality professional.

vending services
manual foodservices
route drivers
commissary
office coffee services (OCS)
cost justifiable
commission rebates
account location
accounts receivable (AR)
accounts payable (AP)
expiration date
accountability (in vending)
drop chute

clients (vending)
customers (vending)
route manager
account retention
alternative beverages
postmix
high-traffic areas
bar code
perpetual inventory
curbside polling
kiting
cashless vending
micropayment (vending machines)

Part 5

RECREATION AND LEISURE ORGANIZATIONS

Private Club Management

22

Private golf club in Point Elizabeth, South Africa

CHAPTER LEARNING OBJECTIVES

After studying this chapter you will be able to:

1. Explain why many persons join private clubs.
2. Review two basic ownership structures for private clubs.
3. Describe common types of private clubs.
4. Describe how equity clubs are organized.
5. Review an organizational chart for a typical private club.
6. List the competencies required to be an effective club general manager.
7. Review unique aspects of private club food and beverage operations.
8. Review challenges confronting the private club industry.

FEEDBACK FROM THE REAL WORLD

There are many great employment opportunities throughout the vast world of hospitality management. A common denominator typically involves interaction with a large number of persons: employees and guests of the operation. Private club management is no exception.

What are the rewards and challenges of interacting with club members who, unlike many of their counterparts at hotels and restaurants, are likely to be very frequent visitors to their clubs? How, if at all, does a club manager interact differently with a relatively new member and one who has been a member of the club for many decades? What tactics can a club manager use to interact with a building superintendent whose knowledge and skills in very technical areas are vastly different from those of the club manager?

As you read this chapter, think about answers to these questions and then get feedback from the real world at the end of the chapter.

---

private club a membership organization not open to the public; persons join a club after being accepted by its membership and must typically pay an initiation fee and monthly membership dues; they must also pay for products and services purchased at the club that are not included as part of membership dues

The world of **private club** management offers opportunities for those with knowledge and skills in hospitality management, and this segment is unique in numerous respects. Its modern history can be traced back to the mid-1700s when social clubs developed in England and when the origin of golf in Scotland brought people together to pursue their interest in this new sport.

In the past, only relatively wealthy persons joined private clubs. By contrast, today clubs are of interest to and within the financial ability of a large percentage of the population,

What is the world of club management all about? Why is membership in private clubs becoming increasingly popular? What do club managers do? These are among the issues addressed in this chapter.

OBJECTIVE 1
Explain why many persons join private clubs.

WHY JOIN A PRIVATE CLUB?

People join private clubs for numerous reasons, including the following:

* *Access to recreational facilities.* Persons who join country (golf), tennis, and yachting clubs, for example, may find private club facilities to be

Private clubs frequently provide tennis facilities for members and guests.

much better than those available to the general public elsewhere in the community.

- *Convenience.* Ready access to a dining room table or a golf tee at busy times is typically easier in a private club than in a public facility.
- *Business reasons.* Conducting small business meetings and entertaining business clients in a private club are very useful tactics for many businesspersons. Club environments also provide the opportunities for businesspersons to interact socially with others who might be influential in their businesses.
- *Employment benefit.* Some organizations provide private club membership as a benefit to selected executives and others.
- *Family tradition.* Some families may have been members of a specific club for many generations; club membership is a tradition.
- *Friendly atmosphere.* Many people enjoy the recognition and service provided by club managers and staff, which are enhanced by personal relationships formed during their numerous visits to the club.
- *Statement of social status.* Some clubs are very exclusive, with high initiation and membership fees (and very long waiting lists to join!), which make them available to only the very affluent.

WHO OWNS THE CLUB?

OBJECTIVE 2
Review two basic ownership structures for private clubs.

Private clubs can be member owned or nonmember owned. Clubs of either type of ownership can be operated by a contract management company whose personnel interact with the club owners (members in equity clubs and the owners in nonequity clubs) in much the same way that management companies operate lodging properties for their owner(s). Let's look at both types.

Equity Clubs

Equity clubs are owned by their members and are governed by a board of directors elected by the members. Each member is a shareholder and owns equal equity in the club. Voting members elect board members from among their peers, who then make major club decisions. A club manager, then, works directly for the members since they own the club. Most private clubs are equity clubs. As such, they are nonprofit corporations exempt from federal income taxes and some state and local taxes.

equity clubs (private clubs) private clubs owned by their members and governed by an elected board of directors

Nonequity Clubs

Nonequity clubs are owned by an individual or corporation, rather than by club members. Members have much less decision-making authority than do their counterparts in equity clubs. Most nonequity clubs are not tax exempt because they are typically for-profit organizations. These clubs are typically owned by developers (for example, of a real estate project) or by corporations. Club managers in nonequity clubs do not work for club members; they work for the club's owner.

nonequity clubs (private clubs) clubs owned by an individual or corporation that are generally not tax exempt; most are corporate- or developer-owned clubs

COMMON TYPES OF PRIVATE CLUBS

OBJECTIVE 3
Describe common types of private clubs.

Exhibit 22.1 shows several common types of private clubs. Let's take a close look at each of these.

RISING STAR PROFILE

Michael W. Graney
General Manager and Chief Operating Officer
The Country Club at Muirfield Village
Dublin, Ohio

Michael received an undergraduate degree in political science from Miami University (Ohio) and then returned to school to receive an associate's degree in culinary arts from Columbus State Community College in 1996. He offers some interesting insights for persons studying hospitality management today.

What is your most unforgettable moment in the hospitality industry?

In 2003, I was the executive chef at The Country Club. I applied for the position of general manager for the club and was awarded the job. I will never forget the day the announcement was made, and I became the supervisor of the persons who had been my peers: other department heads. While I may have lacked a little confidence about my leadership abilities at that time, I discovered that my staff members were ready to work with me, and we became a great club management team. I am blessed with great employees, but it seems I always have been. Luck and timing are important factors in career success, but I believe that teams follow captains for a reason.

What are the most significant changes that have occurred in private clubs?

Competition for our members' luxury time is a very significant challenge that we all face in the club industry today. Time is becoming the most valued asset for many of our members. Most of them have the financial and time-related abilities to do most anything they wish, but it has to be convenient for them to do so. If our products, services, and facilities are convenient and time efficient, then we will succeed and outperform our competition, and their luxury time will be spent with us.

What, if anything, would you do differently in your career?

I should have traveled more at the beginning of my working career to experience the different regional cultures in the United States. I am always amazed about the similar behavior and reactions of people from the same part of the country.

What is your suggestion for those interested in a career in the hospitality industry?

I recommend that one begin a career in the industry in a position such as a restaurant server. If you do not enjoy the immediate gratification of exceeding a member's or a guest's expectations, then hospitality management is probably not going to provide an enjoyable career. If you cannot hear a complaint straight from the customer's mouth and immediately decide how you will remedy the situation, you cannot think on your feet well enough to succeed in the industry. If you begin your working career as a server or in another high-guest-contact position, these two issues will be addressed very quickly.

Country Clubs

country club   a private club with a clubhouse, golf course, and typically other recreation facilities, along with food and beverage outlets, pro shop, locker facilities, and other amenities; also commonly called a *golf club*

Country clubs have a **club house** and a golf course; many have other sports facilities, such as tennis courts and a swimming pool. Country clubs typically offer one or more food and beverage outlets, pro shop (for selling golf and other sporting equipment, logo merchandise, and other items), and locker rooms. There are more country clubs than any other type of private club in the United States.

City Clubs

club house   the club facility used for primary food and beverage production and service, social functions, swimming pool and lockers, and the club's administrative offices, among other purposes

City clubs are typically located within a city's business area or a suburban office complex. Services range from clubs with food and beverage outlets to others

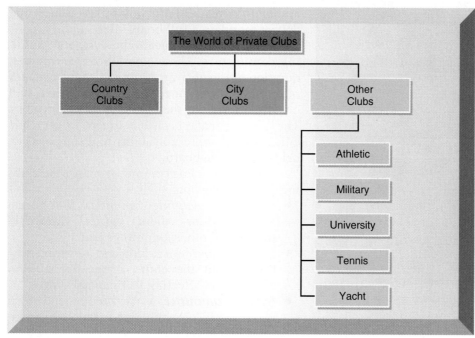

EXHIBIT 22.1
Types of Private Clubs

with conference rooms, indoor sport facilities, and sleeping rooms for members and guests. These clubs typically exist to meet the business, entertainment, and social needs of club members in a city or suburban environment.

Other Types of Clubs

There are various other types of clubs as well.

- *Athletic clubs.* Fitness or sports facilities are provided for members.
- *Military clubs.* Each branch of the U.S. military offers clubs for officers and enlisted personnel. Most are similar to city clubs; some offer additional services.
- *University clubs.* These clubs serve university communities, including graduates, faculty, and staff. Facilities typically include food and beverage outlets, meeting and banquet areas, and sometimes fitness facilities and other accommodations.
- *Tennis clubs.* These clubs offer tennis courts and related amenities. Many offer food and beverage services, including banquet rooms.
- *Yacht clubs.* These clubs address the needs of boaters and offer marina services (storing, refueling, and dock services). Some have a clubhouse, food and beverage services, and swimming pools.

ORGANIZATION OF EQUITY CLUBS

You have learned that most private clubs are equity clubs. Exhibit 22.2 illustrates a common way that equity clubs are organized. An elected board of directors develops club policies and provides overall governance and direction for the club. Officers typically include a president, vice-president, secretary, and treasurer. Many clubs have an **executive committee** comprised of these officers. Its function is to, if necessary, address emergencies

---

CHECK IT OUT!

Want to review information about more than 140 of the world's very best golf clubs? If so, check out the website for Golf Club Atlas.Com: www .golfclubatlas.com. You can see great photos of the golf courses and learn much about the amenities offered by these courses.

---

city club   a private club within a city's business area or suburban office complex that offers food and beverage services and, often, conference and indoor sports facilities; some offer sleeping rooms

OBJECTIVE 4
Describe how equity clubs are organized.

executive committee (private clubs)   a group composed of a club's president, vice-president, secretary, and treasurer who, if necessary, address emergencies and/or consider relatively minor issues that do not mandate a full board meeting

Poolside a la carte dining at a private club

standing committee (private club) a permanent committee that provides advice to the board of directors about matters within the area of their assigned responsibilities

capital improvements remodeling and/or building or facility additions, changes in land use and other projects requiring substantial sums of money

and/or to consider relatively minor issues that do not mandate a full board meeting.

Private clubs typically have several **standing committees.** These committees vary in size, duration of member appointment, and frequency of meetings. Committee members serve in a staff or advisory role to the club's board of directors. They do not make decisions except in very specific areas where responsibility to do so has been delegated by the board.

Typical standing committees in private clubs include the following:

- *Long-range planning committee.* Makes recommendations about **capital improvements** and other long-range plans.
- *Finance committee.* Makes recommendations about the club's financial condition and matters affecting its financial status.
- ***Bylaws committee.*** Makes recommendations about the bylaws and club-mandated regulations that govern the club.
- *Nominating committee.* Makes recommendations about the candidates to be considered for election to the board of directors.
- *Membership committee.* Makes recommendations about candidates for club membership and about the membership status of club members.
- *House (club house) committee.* Makes recommendations about the maintenance of the club house, the grounds that surround it, and the food and beverage operations.
- *Social committee.* Makes recommendations about the entertainment activities of the club.

PRIVATE CLUBS OFFER NUMEROUS MEMBERSHIP CATEGORIES

Members of a private club do not all have the same rights and privileges. Among the most common membership categories are the following:

Regular membership. The member has full use of all club facilities and amenities and has voting rights and the right to hold an elected office within the club.

Social membership. These members have use of the clubhouse and its food and beverage facilities, but may have limited use of facilities such as the swimming pool, tennis courts, and fitness centers. There may be no or very limited use of golf facilities.

Nonresident members. Those living beyond a specified distance may be allowed to pay lower dues than regular members.

Junior membership. These members, generally children of regular members, are granted membership on the basis of their parents' affiliation but have not yet attained the age required for regular membership.

Senior membership. This category is reserved for members who have been affiliated with the club for a specified number of years and who have reached a specified age.

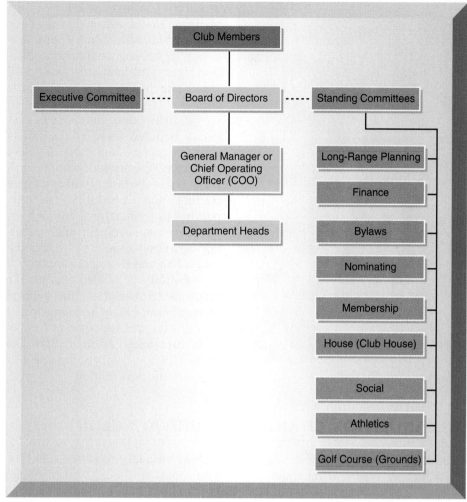

EXHIBIT 22.2
How Equity Clubs Are Organized

bylaws committee (private club)   a committee in a private club that makes recommendations about regulations that govern the club

- *Athletic committee.* Makes recommendations about athletic concerns. Many large clubs typically have separate athletic committees addressing golf, tennis, swim, and fitness activities.
- *Golf course (grounds) committee.* Makes recommendations about golf course maintenance, course irrigation, and policies to regulate play.

Exhibit 22.2 also indicates the relationship between the general manager and the board of directors in an equity club: the general manager reports to this governing body.

The **Club Managers Association of America (CMAA)** is the association that serves the needs of private club managers. It emphasizes the need for a business model to guide the relationship between the club's board of directors and the general manager. In effect, the club's board develops the broad policies that should govern the management and operation of the club. The general manager should serve as the club's chief operating officer (COO) to implement programs and procedures in concert with the policies developed by the board.

Club Managers Association of America (CMAA)   the association that serves the needs of private club managers

The need to constantly recognize and follow the model of the club's general manager as COO is important. The board of directors represents the members who own the club and should make decisions about the most important matters affecting the club. These include the development of the

Golfers at a private club

mission statement and long-range planning tools driven by it. They also include decisions about revenues to be collected from initiation fees and member dues and about the bylaws that govern the club.

A distinction, however, is necessary between these broad policy-related concerns and more detailed, day to day operating decisions. Concerns about the latter (which include staffing and scheduling, product purchase specifications, and numerous other management and operating concerns) should be within the general manager's responsibility.

Exhibit 22.2 also shows the relationship between the general manager and his or her department heads, who are responsible for specific functional areas within the club. This topic will be explored in depth in the next section.

<table>
<tr><td>

OBJECTIVE 5
Review an organizational chart for a typical private club.

</td></tr>
</table>

ORGANIZATION CHART FOR A PRIVATE CLUB

Exhibit 22.3 shows a possible organization chart for a large country club. The chart focuses on the department heads who report to the general manager. It also identifies positions in the next rung of the organization, the intermediate-level managers who report directly to department heads.

Notice that the general manager directs the work of 10 department heads. Five of these (food and beverage director, director of human resources, controller, membership director [Marketing], and director of purchasing) involve responsibilities that are similar to those of counterpart positions in large lodging organizations. Notice, however, that a new position, assistant general manager (Club House Manager), manages the work of

Golfer at a private club's pro shop

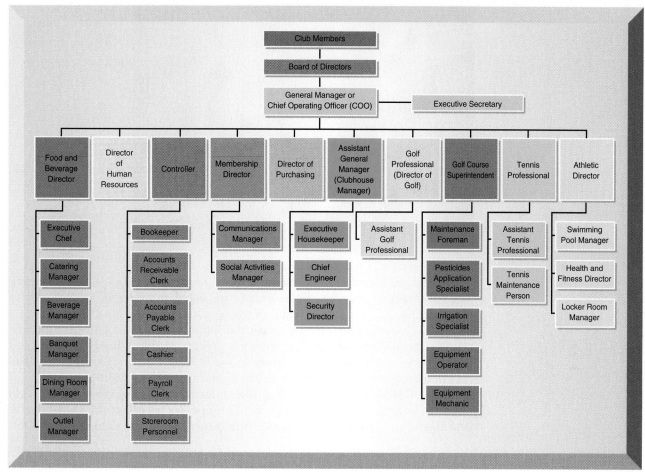

EXHIBIT 22.3
Organization Chart for a Large Country Club

three department heads (executive housekeeper, chief engineer, and security director) typically found in a hotel.

Four other positions (golf professional, golf course superintendent, tennis professional, and athletic director) are generally found only in private club management, although resorts may have some or all of these positions as well.

COMPETENCIES FOR CLUB MANAGER SUCCESS

The Club Managers Association of America has conducted extensive research to identify **competencies** required for successful club managers. These fall into the following nine broad categories, listed in order of importance:

- Management
- Accounting and finance
- Human and professional resources
- Food and beverage management
- Club governance
- Building and facility management
- Marketing
- Sports and recreation management
- External and governmental influences

OBJECTIVE 6
List the competencies required to be an effective club general manager.

competency a requirement that specifies what an individual must know and/or be able to do to be successful in a position

Small-function room in a private club

What are the most important and most frequently used club manager competencies? These specific competencies are listed in order of importance in Exhibit 22.4. As you review each of these competencies, note that none are unique to club management. The general principles of managing hospitality (and other) organizations are similar among segments of the industry. This is good news for persons aspiring to a career in the industry: principles useful for successful management in one segment can be transferred and utilized in another.

The CMAA has developed a Management to Leadership model that provides insight into how management competencies affect the club's operation (see Exhibit 22.5). The model illustrates that general managers/COOs

EXHIBIT 22.4
Most Important and Most Frequently Used Club Manager Competencies

Competency	Competency Domain
Budgeting	Accounting and Finance
Financial Statements	Accounting and Finance
Communication Principles	Human and Professional Resources
In-House Communications	Marketing
Cash Flow Forecasting	Accounting and Finance
Employee Relations	Human and Professional Resources
Balancing Job and Family	Human and Professional Resources
Time Management	Human and Professional Resources
Supervision Tactics	Human and Professional Resources

EXHIBIT 22.5
Management to Leadership
Source: Club Managers Association of America

HOW IMPORTANT IS GOLF IN COUNTRY CLUBS?

You have learned that country clubs comprise the majority of private clubs in the United States. Most members join these facilities for access to golf. The responsibilities of the golf professional and golf course superintendent are, therefore, absolutely critical to the success of the club. Some country clubs that do not use the COO concept have an organizational structure in which three persons report directly to the board of directors: the general manager (responsible for food and beverage operations and business aspects of the club), the golf professional, and the golf course superintendent. While the responsibilities of these three professionals are obviously different, numerous operating problems arise when more than one person with general operating responsibilities directly reports to the board. These problems are best resolved when an organization similar to that illustrated in this chapter is used.

are responsible for three major areas: operations, assets and investments, and club culture. The building and perfecting of skills and competencies is ongoing.

The foundation of the model is the successful management of club *operations* that are defined in the core competencies identified in Exhibit 22.4. The second tier of the model involves mastering the skills of *assets management*. The general manager/COO must be able to manage the club's physical property and the financial well-being and human resources of the club. The third part of the model involves preserving and fostering the *culture* of the club: its traditions, history, and vision.

CLUB FOOD AND BEVERAGE OPERATIONS

> **OBJECTIVE 7**
> Review unique aspects of private club food and beverage operations.

Several aspects of a foodservice operation in a private club often set it apart from some of its counterparts in other segments of the hospitality industry. Let's look at several of these.

Number of Food and Beverage Outlets and Range of Products Offered

Large private clubs typically have several (or more) a la carte dining outlets serving everything from ice cream cones (at the pool snack bar) to gourmet dinners in an upscale dining room. All or most of the food products for this diverse range of outlets would likely be prepared in the same kitchen, and a single manager might have general oversight for all food and beverage operations. Other staff might be cross-trained to work in all or several of these outlets, and the club's standards must be consistently attained within each outlet.

Meeting Club Members' Needs and Requirements

Many members join their club because of the recognition they receive. Referring to guests by name, seating them at a preferred table, remembering special occasions, and allowing members

Banquet setup in a private club

DID YOU KNOW?

The unique appeal of private clubs is founded on service. People can get elsewhere the many things that clubs offer—fine dining, catering, golf, tennis, fitness facilities, and so on. What they can't find in a public facility is the level of service they can expect from a private club. Most private clubs are willing to absorb the labor costs and hire the staff members it takes to provide extraordinary service.

A moment of truth happens with every encounter a member has with the club. It can be an encounter with a staff person, a product, or some aspect of the club's physical facilities. Did the server greet me courteously? Are the golf cars charged, clean, and ready to go? Are the rest rooms clean? Did the employee in the pro shop answer the phone right away? Service is about details, so club managers must train the club's staff to take care of the details. An attendant at the club's pool, for example, must be trained to go get a towel for a member who forgets to bring one, rather than just tell the member where the towels are located.

The service goal is to make the members say "wow." A club should try to exceed member expectations. This is harder to do in a club than in a hotel or restaurant. Hotels and restaurants have different people in every day. A club member might be at the club several times a week, year after year. This makes it harder to provide "wow" service. The club has to constantly work to keep the service level high.

One of a club manager's primary tasks is to make sure staff members have what they need to do the job properly. If you are not directly serving members, you should be serving the people who are. Club managers should talk to staff members frequently to find out about obstacles that are hindering them from providing great service. An obstacle can be a flawed process or something physical—it can be as simple as a piece of furniture that's in the way. Club managers should make the work environment as efficient as possible so that employees are not frustrated, because employee frustration can get taken out on club members.

A club's management team is small relative to the number of employees. Because of that, it's important that club managers give each employee the proper training. Training is an ongoing management function; it's a cycle. Club managers set the standards, communicate the standards to the staff, provide the tools and training, and then gather feedback from members to make sure the standards are right and the training is working. Of course, the most important measure of staff performance is member satisfaction. Taking a membership-satisfaction survey on an annual basis provides wonderful feedback. A manager should work to constantly raise the level of satisfaction.

A feature of private clubs, one that makes providing great service both easier and at times more challenging, is that there is a finite number of members. Over time, club managers are able to get to know members and their families and can provide very personalized service. Not only can club managers smile, say hello, and call members by name, they can also ask them about the grandchildren, the new house, or the bank merger. Members like to talk about themselves, but not on a superficial level. They don't want a generic "How are you?" from a club manager.

One of the biggest service challenges clubs face is the basic fact that clubs deal with people. Communication is not always perfect. You've got to meet or exceed what members expect again and again. It is very difficult to maintain standards so high that members are impressed every time they walk in. That's the service challenge that club managers face every day.

Cathy Gustafson, PhD, CCM
Professor, University of South Carolina
Former General Manager of The Faculty House of Carolina,
Columbia, South Carolina

Source: *Contemporary Club Management.* Joe Perdue, ed. Alexandria, VA, Club Managers Association of America, and Lansing, MI, Educational Institute of the American Hotel & Lodging Association, 1997 (pp. 97–98).

to order special items (even if they are not on the menu!) are among the ways that club food and beverage personnel address their members' special concerns.

Other Food and Beverage Services

Club members may request a special menu for small or large groups. Outdoor picnics, food and beverage cart service on the golf course, and parties at poolside are examples of opportunities that club food and beverage managers have for implementing their creativity.

Food and Beverage Service Issues

Turnover in private clubs is frequently lower than in other segments of the hospitality industry. Advantages are obvious, including the employees' familiarity with the club's policies, members, and procedures. It is thus easier to attain efficiency and quality service goals.

Boardroom in a private club

Long-term employment can also create some difficulty in retraining, resistance to changed procedures, and the possibility that poor work habits evolve over time. Also, when compensation is, in part, based on seniority, there can be a wide range of differences in wages or salaries paid to beginning and more senior staff members. Clubs that do not offer retirement packages may have another difficulty: some employees may work beyond when they should. If they become inefficient, morale problems can result as they interact with new staff members who receive less compensation. Long-term employees may also be tempted to become too familiar with members and not respect the professional distance that should be kept between the club's members and employees.

THE ROLE OF FOOD AND BEVERAGE IN A CLUB

The food and beverage department in a private club is critical to its success. First, it helps to attract new members. For example, a nonmember's first experience in a club may be as a guest in its dining room or at a banquet function. Consistent food quality and service are factors that are important to prospective club members, and the reputation of a club's food and beverage service is an important marketing tool.

(continued)

Careful attention to members' needs is very important in all clubs, and member satisfaction with food and beverage services is an important aspect in member retention. Food and beverage products and services must be of consistently high quality. This is achieved by recruiting, selecting, and retaining the very best personnel and by establishing and working toward the attainment of food quality standards that consistently meet or exceed the members' expectations.

Financial concerns are also important. In some clubs, the food and beverage department generates the primary source of revenue. At others, the revenue generated is much less. Depending on the specific club, the financial goals of the food and beverage department may be to make money, break even, or even to lose money. (Some outlets, such as the snack bars and "halfway house" facilities in country clubs, exist solely to serve the membership. They must be subsidized with revenue from other sources.) A mix of pricing factors and the volume of food and beverage services provided in a la carte and banquet dining functions help to determine the profitability of a club's foodservices.

OBJECTIVE 8
Review challenges confronting the private club industry.

CHALLENGES! CHALLENGES!

Several important challenges, discussed next, confront private club managers today and will likely do so in the future.

Need to Continually Provide Value to Members

Private club members, like their counterparts utilizing the services of other hospitality operations, desire value for the money they spend on meals, services, and recreation away from home. Club managers must find ways to reduce costs and maintain reasonable selling prices to attract new and to keep existing members.

Competition with Other Hospitality Operations

Private clubs do not just compete with other private clubs. Rather, organizations such as restaurants, public sports facilities, and other entertainment venues all provide alternatives for club members. Club managers and their staffs must continually find ways to delight their members. This becomes especially challenging with those who have been members of a club for many years.

Las Vegas National Golf Club, Las Vegas, Nevada

Competition for the Best Possible Staff Members

Private clubs, like other operations in the hospitality industry, must recruit and retain the very best employees. To do this increasingly involves a close look at compensation programs and all methods used to supervise employees.

Royal Vancouver Yacht Club, Vancouver, British Columbia, Canada

Implementation of quality efforts, including empowerment, appeal to the new generation of better-educated people with more job employment opportunities than were available to yesterday's employees.

Ways to Reduce Costs with Increased Utilization of Technology

Club members continue to want service delivered by hospitable staff members. Reductions in staff levels in these service-related positions may be difficult. However, just as managers of hotel, restaurant, and other hospitality organizations are looking at technology to increase revenues and reduce costs without sacrificing quality, so too are private club managers. One example: many clubs are developing creative websites to inform members of club activities and to allow them to book reservations for desired events online.

SUMMARY OF CHAPTER LEARNING OBJECTIVES

1. **Explain why many persons join private clubs.**
   Reasons why people join private clubs include access to recreational facilities, convenience, business reasons, as an employment benefit, as part of a family tradition, for the friendly atmosphere, and as a statement of social status.

2. **Review two basic ownership structures for private clubs.**
   Equity clubs are owned by their members and are governed by a board of directors elected by the members. Each member is a shareholder owning equal equity in the club. By contrast, nonequity clubs are owned by an individual or corporation, and members have much less decision-making authority.

3. **Describe common types of private clubs.**
   Country clubs (also called golf clubs) are the most common type of private club in the United States. Other examples of clubs include city, athletic, military, university, tennis, and yacht.

4. **Describe how equity clubs are organized.**
   In one common type of organization, equity club members elect a board of directors who, in turn, retain the services of a general manager (chief operating officer) who supervises the work of department heads. The board of directors utilizes an executive committee and numerous standing committees to provide input about specific club-related concerns. The Club Managers Association of America recommends

that the board of directors develop broad policies to govern the management and operation of the club. The general manager, in turn, serves as the club's chief operating officer.

5. **Review an organizational chart for a typical private club.**
   The club's general manager typically supervises the work of department heads with responsibilities for food and beverage, human resources, finance, membership, purchasing, golf, golf course maintenance, tennis, and athletics. Also, a club house manager is supervised by the general manager and is responsible for housekeeping, engineering, and security.

6. **List the competencies required to be an effective club general manager.**
   The nine most important and frequently used club manager competencies relate to budgeting, financial statements, communication principles, in-house communications, cash flow forecasting, employee relations, balancing job

and family, time management, and supervision tactics.

7. **Review unique aspects of private club food and beverage operations.**
   Aspects of a club's foodservice operation that set it apart from other segments of the hospitality industry may include the number of food and beverage outlets and the range of products offered, the need to meet club members' needs and requirements, different food and beverage services, and special food and beverage service issues.

8. **Review challenges confronting the private club industry.**
   Several important challenges include the need to continually provide value and satisfaction to members, competition with other hospitality operations, competition for the best possible staff members, and the discovery of ways to reduce costs with increased utilization of technology.

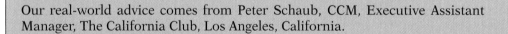

FEEDBACK FROM THE REAL WORLD

Our real-world advice comes from Peter Schaub, CCM, Executive Assistant Manager, The California Club, Los Angeles, California.

Peter received his undergraduate degree in hotel and restaurant management. He joined the management team at Houston Country Club in Houston, Texas, as an assistant manager. Since 1998, Peter has served as the executive assistant manager at The California Club in Los Angeles, California.

Both prior to and during his university studies, Peter held internship positions at Oak Ridge Country Club in Hopkins, Minnesota, Woodhill Country Club in Wayzata, Minnesota, and Twin Orchard Country Club in Long Grove, Illinois.

It is worth noting that Peter is a second-generation club manager. His father, Hans J. Schaub, CCM, is the general manager at The Minneapolis Club in Minneapolis, Minnesota.

What are the rewards and challenges of interacting with club members who, unlike many of their counterparts at hotels and restaurants, are likely to be very frequent visitors to their clubs?

The most rewarding aspect of having frequent "visitors" (our club members) is the ability we have to anticipate our members' needs. If proper attention is given to every detail, our staff can learn the likes and dislikes of every member. This al-

lows us service opportunities that are not typically available in hotels and restaurants, such as serving a member his favorite drink as soon as he is seated or handing a member her favorite newspaper as she walks through the front door each morning on the way up to the health club.

It is important to remember that personal attention is a major reason why people join private clubs. An obvious challenge is that our members' expectations may change often and we, as club managers, must always strive to meet and exceed these ever-changing expectations each day. Consider, for example, a member who originally joins the club to have a place to conduct business. He soon marries, and the club must now also fulfill the needs of his spouse. Later, the couple may have a child, and their needs once again shift to include a family-friendly environment. If the club is unable to fulfill these changing needs, the chances of losing an important member increase.

How, if at all, does a club manager interact differently with a relatively new member and one who has been a member of the club for many decades (or longer)?

From a professional standpoint, nothing should be different. Both the long-standing club members who joined 50 years ago and the member who joined last month deserve the utmost respect.

It is, however, extremely important that a club manager pay close attention to a new member. Each member joins for a different reason, and each has different expectations of her or his club experience. Each member has different likes and very different dislikes. The sooner we, as managers, can pinpoint their needs and preferences, the sooner we can exceed their expectations. The sooner we are able to exceed

their expectations, the more they will use the club, grow with the club, and bring new members to the club.

What tactics can a club manager use to interact with a building superintendent whose knowledge and skills in very technical areas are vastly different from those of the club manager?

The technical knowledge it takes to work as an engineer in a building built in 1929 is obviously great. The details one must learn to work on pipes, electrical issues, boilers, and refrigeration, for example, are enough to fill many books in the engineering school's library, and this is obviously time that a club manager does not have.

To interact properly with an engineering staff, a club manager must understand enough to know what is being discussed and how to explain it to the applicable committee(s) and have the ability to make an educated decision when necessary. The best people to learn from are those who know best: the engineering staff. A club manager must ask plenty of questions, learn the lay of the land from his or her staff, and not be afraid to get dirty if it means learning more about the physical plant and how things work.

MASTERING YOUR KNOWLEDGE

Discuss the following questions.

1. What factors or features would be of greatest interest to you if you were evaluating alternative clubs for membership? What features would be important in your decision to maintain or give up your membership?
2. What role, if any, would you as the general manager want to have in interacting with a private club's standing committees? Why?
3. How important to a club's success is the Club Managers Association of America's

model of the club manager as the chief operating officer (COO)?
4. How would you as a club manager direct the work of the club's golf professional and golf course superintendent, given that the knowledge and skills required for these positions would be significantly different from your own?
5. What are examples of activities in which club managers employ the most important and most frequently used competencies described in this chapter?

LEARN FROM THE INTERNET

1. Review the websites of several types of clubs (or look up private clubs in your area) by typing the following in your favorite search engine:
   - Private university clubs
   - Private golf clubs
   - Private city clubs
   - Private yacht clubs

   What kinds of products and services do they note to be available? Why should someone belong to the club?

2. Check out the website of the Club Managers Association of America: www.cmaa.org. What kinds of issues of interest to club managers are being addressed? How, if at all, do these issues differ from those that would interest managers in other segments of the hospitality industry? How does the CMAA help the private club industry?

3. Check out the websites of the following hospitality industry-related trade magazines:
   - *Club Management:* www.club-mgmt.com
   - *Club Director:* www.natlclub.org
   - *Restaurant Business:* www.restaurantbiz.com

   What are examples of issues noted that would be of concern to all private club managers? To those in specialized types of clubs?

KEY HOSPITALITY TERMS

The following terms were explained in this chapter. Review the definitions of any words with which you are unfamiliar. Begin to utilize them as you expand your vocabulary as a hospitality professional.

private club
equity clubs (private clubs)
nonequity clubs (private clubs)
country club
club house
city club

executive committee
standing committee (private club)
capital improvements
bylaws committee (private club)
Club Managers Association of America (CMAA)
competency

Cruise Lines
A Close Look at Resorts on Water

23

The ship's captain on the bridge

CHAPTER LEARNING OBJECTIVES

After studying this chapter you will be able to:

1. Present a brief history of cruising.
2. Explore typical reasons why people cruise.
3. Review basic features of modern cruise ships.
4. Describe common ship- and land-based management positions in the cruise industry.
5. Explain procedures used to sell cruise vacations.
6. Note basic sources of revenues on cruise ships.
7. Consider challenges confronting the cruise line industry.

This chapter was authored by Bernard N. Fried, EdD, CHAE, Associate Professor, Tourism and Convention Department, William F. Harrah College of Hotel Administration, University of Nevada, Las Vegas.

FEEDBACK FROM THE REAL WORLD

Cruise lines require many persons working on ships and on the shore. Many persons have a stereotype of jobs with glamour and adventure when they think about employment in the cruise industry. There are great positions in the industry but, as in all other segments of the hospitality industry, hard work and extensive knowledge and skills are required to be successful.

Why are travel agencies the biggest generator of cruise sales? How do travel agents interact with the cruise lines as they sell cruises? Do discounts and agency rebates help to generate cruise business? What types of positions are available in travel agencies specializing in cruise sales? From the perspective of a travel agent, what do you see to be the future of the cruise industry?

As you read this chapter, think about the answers to these questions, and then get feedback from the real world at the end of the chapter.

What do you think of when you see advertisements for cruises and/or learn that one of your friends will be taking a cruise? Do you think about travel to unique locations, great onboard luxury accommodations, and spectacular (and seemingly never ending) food and beverage services including midnight buffets? Do you think about meeting new people, romance and/or participation in numerous onboard activities, including gaming, lounging around the swimming pool(s), and/or dancing until the very late hours (or later)? Today's cruises offer all of these and much more.

cruise ship a passenger vessel designed to provide leisure experiences for persons on vacations

Many people in many different positions are required both on the **cruise ship** and on shore. Many of these are in guest (passenger) contact positions. However, just as is true in other segments of the hospitality industry, many positions unnoticed by the traveling public are, at the same time, absolutely critical to the success of the organization.

In this chapter, you will learn basic background information about the cruise line industry. It is a very large and fast-growing segment and provides employment opportunities for many people from around the world. Perhaps, after studying this chapter, you will have an interest in becoming one of them!

OBJECTIVE 1
Present a brief history of cruising.

HISTORY OF CRUISING

Humans have historically used coastal waterways, rivers, and lakes for commerce, warfare, and exploration and to travel for business purposes. It has been relatively recently, however, that the oceans and other large bodies of water have been used as a medium for persons to enjoy their leisure time.

The first scheduled passenger sailing across the Atlantic took nearly 28 days in 1818. The world's first propeller-driven passenger vessel was launched in the early 1840s. By the early 1900s, transatlantic ocean travel was relatively common, but not always safe (remember the *Titanic*!). Early cruises were very expensive voyages that provided those who could afford it a holiday as they traveled from one destination to another.[1]

---

[1]Roger Cartwright and Caroline Baird, *The Development and Growth of the Cruise Industry*. Oxford, England: Butterworth Heinemann, 1999. Information about the history of ship travel is from Marc Mancini, *A Guide to the Cruise Line Industry*. Albany, NY: Thompson Learning, 2000.

Ocean liners of the early 1900s were basically built to transport immigrants. The wealthy who could afford it traveled first class, but the vast majority of persons on board traveled in steerage class. After World War I (1914–1918), during which most available ocean-crossing ships were used for troop transport, ocean liners became bigger and started to provide more of the amenities that are part of today's cruising experience.

In 1958, commercial jet service began across the Atlantic, and travel between the United States and Europe took hours rather than days. Ships whose primary objective was to provide transportation were much less popular. During the 1970s and 1980s, the concept of leisure cruising evolved rapidly. Air conditioning, swimming pools, dance floors, and superb food and beverage services, among many other amenities, made "floating vacations" more popular. By the 1990s, **megaships** carrying 2,000 or more passengers were being built.

In fact, increasingly large cruise ships continue to be built. *Freedom of the Seas,* a Royal Caribbean Cruises Ltd. liner, was christened in May 2006, in New York Harbor. It is 237 feet tall and 1,112 feet long, with 15 passenger decks. It can cruise with more than 4,000 passengers.*

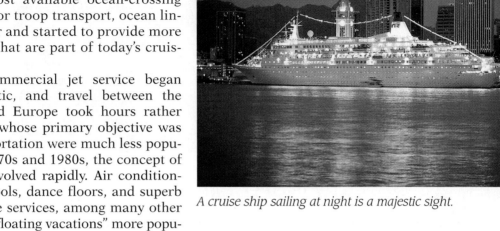

A cruise ship sailing at night is a majestic sight.

megaship a cruise ship that carries 2,000 or more passengers

---

*Largest passenger ship christened in New York Harbor. cnn.com. Retrieved May 13, 2006, from www.cnn.com/2006/travel/05/12.

ALL ABOUT THE CRUISING EXPERIENCE

Cruise lines offer cruises that last from a very few days to several months (or longer). Typical schedules involve at-sea and at-port times, with activities that permit passengers to be just as active or inactive as they wish for almost every moment during the journey. Some itineraries are round trip; the cruise ship leaves from a port, cruises and visits other ports of call, and returns to the port from which it left. Some cruise lines offer one-way itineraries; a cruise ship leaves from one port and ends its cruise at another. (Passengers leave the ship, or disembark, and use another means of travel to their next destination.) Some cruises offer pre- and/or postcruise packages that allow passengers to select options to have hotel and perhaps land excursion activities before or after the cruise.

Where can one cruise? Almost anywhere that there is deep water! Popular cruises include those to Alaska, within the Caribbean, the western and eastern Mediterranean and throughout Europe, Africa, and in the Pacific, among numerous destinations.

Cruise ships are normally redeployed (repositioned) to make them available for popular cruising seasons in different places at different times throughout the year. For example, cruise ships visiting Alaska during the summer months may then cruise across the Pacific to Hawaii and then on to the South Pacific until warm weather cruises again become popular in Alaska.

Casino on a cruise ship

WHY PEOPLE CRUISE

There are several common reasons why cruises are popular vacation choices for many people:

- *Relaxation.* Passengers can unpack and enjoy their cruise with few, if any, responsibilities until its conclusion. There are no worries about where to go, how to get there, or what to eat. The wide range of activities means that there is something for everyone whenever they want to enjoy it. Passengers are pampered with service to the extent they wish to be.
- *Travel and education.* Cruises typically cover long distances and allow passengers to see and experience places they have only dreamed about visiting. Many tourists think about ports of call they have visited during cruises when they consider potential sites for future vacations. Opportunities to learn about the sites visited are extensive both on the ship before it arrives and during the port-of-call stop.
- *Social.* One can make new friends or enjoy a romantic experience. Many newlyweds celebrate their marriages by taking cruises.
- *Status.* The cost of cruising has declined dramatically over the past decade; almost anyone who can afford to take a vacation can find a cruise package within his or her budget. However, relatively few people have been on cruises, and the "bragging rights" that accrue are an incentive for some persons to take cruises.
- *Safety.* Traditionally, cruises have been seen as a safe vacation choice. The controlled environment, shipboard safety and construction features, and ready access to medical personnel have been a plus for many travelers.
- *Family tradition.* Some persons take all (or almost all) of their holidays on cruises. Some veteran cruisers have taken 30 or even more cruises and plan their next one while on the current one.

stateroom a guest room on a cruise ship; also called *cabin*

A CLOSE LOOK AT MODERN CRUISE SHIPS

Modern cruise ships are vastly different from ocean liners built just a relatively short time ago. Space, not speed, is a prime concern to accommodate many large **staterooms** (guest rooms) and the large number of public spaces for activities available to the passengers. Modern cruise ships are carefully planned

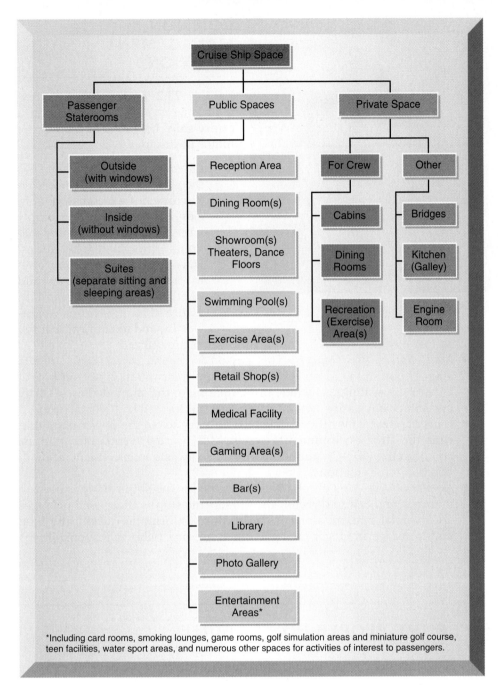

EXHIBIT 23.1
Classification of Spaces Available on Cruise Ships

to facilitate passenger **embarkation** and **debarkation** and for movement once persons are aboard the ship.

How is the space on a cruise ship classified? Exhibit 23.1 helps to answer this question. Space is allocated for passenger staterooms (these are typically suites, which are outside cabins with windows and, sometimes, private external sitting areas, and other sleeping rooms without windows in terms of decreasing costs). Public spaces include all areas of the cruise ship to which passengers have normal access. Private spaces exist for the crew and for other purposes, including the bridge (from which the captain commands the ship), the ship's kitchen (galley), and the engine room.

embarkation   the process of boarding a cruise ship

debarkation   the process of exiting a cruise ship

Cruise ship docked at an ocean terminal

COMMON MANAGEMENT POSITIONS

Exhibit 23.2 notes common ship-board management positions on a cruise ship. Let's look at each of the major positions.

- *Captain.* This individual has the final authority on the ship to carry out all company policies and rules and to comply with all international and national laws and regulations. His or her primary responsibility is to see to the care and safety of everyone on board, to assure that the vessel is seaworthy, and to confirm that the proper navigation and operating procedures are utilized.

OBJECTIVE 4
Describe common ship- and land-based management positions in the cruise industry.

- *Staff captain (first officer).* This person is second in command of the ship. He or she is responsible for it when the captain is not on board. Other responsibilities include those relating to the ship's doctor, security and safety, navigation, and maintenance (performed by the boatswain).
- *Chief engineer.* This officer's responsibility relates to the power plant that runs the ship; environmental systems for heating, ventilating, and air conditioning (HVAC); plumbing; fire safety; waste management; and on-board communications.
- *Hotel manager.* This official is responsible for the ship's shore excursion manager and cruise director, the purser (the ship's officer who manages all financial matters along with the ship's information desk), the food and beverage manager, and the chief steward (who is responsible for

---

WHY SOME PEOPLE DON'T CRUISE

Perceptions are reality, and some people are not interested in cruises because of their perceptions about the following:

- Expense
- Exclusivity (cruising is thought to be an upper-class pastime)
- Single and adult market (the belief that cruises are not suitable for families with children)
- Confined space and lack of quiet spaces
- The prevalence of sea sickness and other discomforts
- Schedules that must be tightly adhered to; concerns about dining at specified times and spending a required amount of time at a port-of-call are examples of routines that disinterest some persons

The cruise line industry is working to educate the public about what the cruise is and what it is not. As it becomes more successful, more persons will likely try and enjoy cruise experiences.

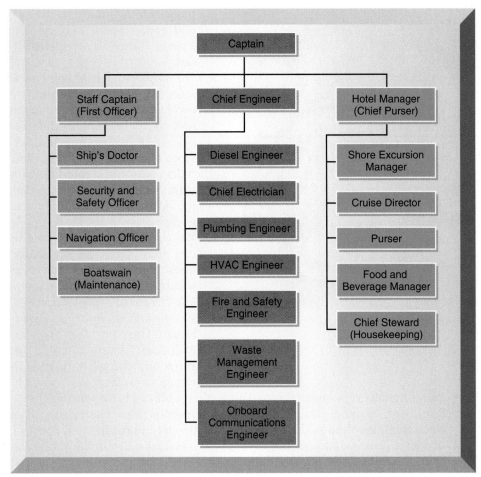

EXHIBIT 23.2
Common Management Positions on Cruise Ships

housekeeping). (Hospitality management graduates are most likely to obtain onboard positions within the hotel manager's department.)

Management positions needed for the land-based support of cruise line organizations are basically divided into the same functional areas as in other large hospitality operations. Exhibit 23.3 identifies some of these. Let's look at each of these positions.

- *Vice-president, hotel operations.* This position relates to planning and coordinating onboard guest services and land programs made available to

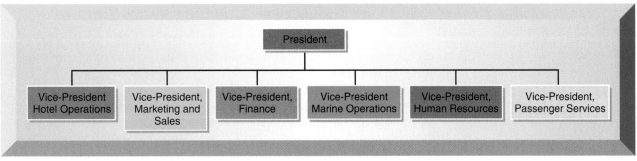

EXHIBIT 23.3
Common Land-Based Management Positions in the Cruise Line Industry

Swimming pool on a cruise ship

passengers. Quality assurance and procurement may also be among his or her responsibilities.

- *Vice-president, marketing and sales.* Marketing personnel are involved with market research and the development and promotion of the products and services offered by the cruise line. Sales personnel interact with travel agencies and with others to facilitate individual and group sales.
- *Vice-president, finance.* This official may serve as the cruise line's chief financial officer to administer all financial matters relating to the organization.
- *Vice-president, marine operations.* This position involves technical issues relating to ships and the ports (docks) at which ships stop.
- *Vice-president, human resources.* This top-level official is responsible for recruitment, training, compensation, and numerous other matters (many of them legal) involved in the employer–employee relationship.
- *Vice-president, passenger services.* These services may involve reservations, movement of luggage, and coordinating air and land and arrival schedules, among other responsibilities.

OBJECTIVE 5
Explain procedures used to sell cruise vacations.

SELLING THE CRUISE EXPERIENCE

Some seasoned cruisers enjoy one or more holidays at sea every year. Planning and arranging their cruise experience require less time and difficulty than the efforts required for noncruisers, who typically do much preplanning for a land-based vacation by automobile with their family. By contrast, other,

DID YOU KNOW?

Cruise ships have been and are being used for nontraditional purposes. For example, cruise ships were used as temporary shelters for persons affected by Hurricane Katrina in the New Orleans area after it made landfall in the fall of 2005. Visitors and others in Lebanon during the events of July 2006 were transported by cruise ships to nearby Cyprus to catch planes to their homes.

Visitors to Jacksonville, Florida, for large sporting events, sometimes have the option of staying on a cruise ship because of a hotel room shortage in the area.

A new concept: *condo cruise ships*. Condo cruise lines are selling condo suites on cruise ships. Owners pay a standard condo fee (between $7,000 and $10,000 annually) to help generate the $15,000,000 annual cost to operate a mid-sized luxury cruise ship. For more information about this lodging alternative, go to www.condocruiselines.com.

CRUISE SHIPS: WHO IS IN CHARGE OF WHAT?

Some cruise lines retain **concessionaires** to provide some of the ship's services. Examples of such services include photography, beauty salons, and retail gift shops. Some cruise lines subcontract almost every service, including casino management, food and beverage operations, and entertainment. (When extensive use is made of concessionaires, the ship's hotel manager may be responsible only for housekeeping and social activities.)

especially first-time, cruisers consider cruise holidays to be very significant events for which extensive planning is important.

Cruise lines typically develop very colorful and informative brochures to advertise cruises far in advance of the actual event. In fact, many passengers book their cruise vacations more than one year in advance of the cruise. While some cruisers book directly with the cruise line company (and the number may increase because of the Internet), the vast majority of passengers utilize a travel agency or other intermediary to help in making selection decisions and arrangements for their cruise.

Why do many passengers book their cruises through travel agencies? The answer is that, unfortunately, booking a cruise is more complicated than making a reservation for an airplane flight or a hotel room (which travelers increasingly do themselves). A significant amount of information is needed, which, historically, many travel agents have been able to provide. As well, some, especially first-time prospective cruisers, desire advice about the cruise that is best for them. Numerous cruise lines offer cruises to many destinations, and onboard cruising environments make the decision-making task even more daunting; many persons do not know where to find information to answer their questions other than a travel agent.

Consider just one variable: cost. There can be 30 or more different charges for one specific cruise depending on cabin size and location and pre- and post-cruise packages. Cruise lines utilize **yield management** practices, which also have a significant impact on costs for a cruise. The extent of discounting, if any, from brochure-stated prices also affects ticket price. Cruise lines have historically offered numerous and very creative discounting plans that create wide differences between brochure and actual cruise prices and even between what two passengers in neighboring cabins pay for the same cruise.

concessionaire a for-profit business that has been granted the right to provide agreed-on products and services to the organization's (cruise ship's) passengers (customers)

yield management a demand forecasting system designed to maximize revenue by maintaining high rates (charges) during times of high demand and by decreasing rates (charges) when there is lower demand

Buffet on a cruise ship

NAUTICAL GLOSSARY

Aft   Toward or near the stern (back) of the ship.

Air/sea package   A single price charged a tourist for airfare to and from the point of departure, the airport-to-dock and return), the cruise and, perhaps, lodging before or after the cruise.

Basis two (also called *double occupancy*)   Pricing per person based on two passengers sharing a stateroom designed to accommodate two or more passengers.

Beam   The width of the ship at its widest point.

Berth   A bed on a ship; also can refer to the docking space of a ship at port.

Boat deck   The deck where the lifeboats are located.

Bow   The front of the ship.

Bridge   Place on the ship from where it is controlled.

Bulkhead   An upright partition or wall dividing the ship into cabins and compartments.

Cabin itinerary (also called *round-trip itinerary*)   The route with ports of call (stops) for a ship leaving from and returning to the same port.

Cabin steward   The person who maintains staterooms.

Course   The direction in which the ship is headed; usually expressed in compass degrees.

Cruise Lines International Association (CLIA)   A trade organization that consists of representative cruise lines and travel agency affiliates.

Cruise-only trip   Cruise with no associated arrangement for air transportation.

Deck   The equivalent of a story (floor) in a building.

Deck plan   The ship's floor plan showing cabins and public spaces.

Disembarkation (also called *debarkation*)   Exiting the ship.

Dock   A berth, pier, or quay.

Embarkation   Boarding the ship.

Fathom   A measurement of distance (usually depth) in the water; equal to 6 feet.

First seating (or *sitting*)   The earliest of two meal times in the ship's dining room.

Forward   Toward or near the bow (front) of the ship.

Free port   A port or place free of custom's duty and regulations.

Funnel   A smokestack (chimney) of the ship.

Galley   The ship's kitchen.

Gangway   The opening through the ship's side and the corresponding ramp by which passengers embark or disembark.

Gross registered ton (GRT)   A measurement of 100 cubic feet of enclosed revenue space within a ship.

Hold   Interior space below the main deck for storage or cargo where passengers are not allowed.

Hull   The part of the ship that rests in the water; the frame or body of the ship, exclusive of the superstructure.

Inside cabin   Passenger accommodations without a window or porthole; located in the interior of a ship.

Knot   A unit of speed equal to one nautical mile (6,076 feet) per hour, as compared to a land mile of 5,280 feet.

Lido deck   Pool deck area that offers informal, buffetlike dining, both indoors and outdoors.

Manifest   A list or invoice of a ship's passengers, crew, and cargo.

One-way itinerary   Itinerary with the ship starting at one port and finishing at another.

Open seating (or *sitting*)   A dining plan in which passengers may sit anywhere in the dining room; tables are not assigned.

Past passenger rate (also called *alumni rate*)   A discounted rate given to persons who have previously sailed a cruise line.

Pax   The industry abbreviation for "passengers."

Port   When facing forward, this is the left side of the ship.

Port charge   What ports charge to dock a ship.

Port day   A day when the ship stops at a port of call.

Postcruise package   A package that includes lodging at the ship's arrival port after the cruise.

Precruise package   A package that includes lodging at the ship's departure port before the cruise.

Pitch   The front-to-back (bow-to-stern) motion of a ship.

Porthole   Round window or opening on the side of the ship.

Quay (pronounced *key*)   A berth, dock, or pier.

Registry   The country whose laws the ship and its owners are obliged to obey, in addition to complying with the laws of the countries where the ship calls and/or embarks passengers.

Repositioning cruise   A cruise during which the ship moves from one general cruise area to another.

Roll   The side-to-side motion of the ship.

Seating times   Scheduled times when certain meals are served in the formal dining room of a ship. Usually there are two seatings: main (early) and second (late).

Shore excursion   A port-based tour or activity.

Space ratio   A measure of how much space is occupied by one passenger if a full complement of passengers is sailing; equals GRT divided by standard passenger capacity.

Stabilizers   Finlike, gyroscopically operated devices that extend from both sides of the ship below the waterline to provide a more stable motion.

Stack   A funnel from which the ship's combustion gases are exhausted to the atmosphere.

Starboard   When facing forward, the right side of the ship.

Stateroom (also called *cabin*) A guest room on a ship.

Stern   The back end of the ship.

Suite   The most expensive type of passenger accommodation; generally consists of a sitting area, one or two bedrooms, a bathroom, a kitchenette, and a verandah.

Superstructure   The part of the ship above the hull.

Table assignments   Assigned tables in the dining room for scheduled meals that accommodate two to ten people.

Tender   A small boat that ferries passengers between port and ship.

Weather deck   Any deck open to the outside.

Windward   Toward the wind.

A 24-hour pizzeria on a cruise ship

LAND OR CRUISE VACATIONS: WHICH ARE MORE EXPENSIVE?

Many persons have a perception that cruises are much more expensive than land vacations. Is this correct?

When a tourist thinks about a land vacation, he or she typically thinks about the (relatively) low hotel room rental price, but may disregard the (relatively) high additional costs for meals, land transportation, entertainment, and other charges. By contrast, most charges for a cruise are **bundled** (all-inclusive), which suggests a relatively high initial purchase price, but relatively fewer additional costs. This creates, for many, "sticker shock" at the first step of price comparison.

Most persons consider more than costs when making vacation plans. However, when cost differentials are significant, this factor is important. Cruise lines, their industry association (Cruise Lines International Association), and knowledgeable **travel agents** are working to educate consumers about the real costs of this holiday alternative.

The cruise industry is increasingly being challenged by land vacations that are all-inclusive. Some land resorts, such as Club Med and Sandals, offer packages including room, food and beverages (including alcoholic beverages), beach, entertainment, and other activities and even have no-tipping policies. The number of vacationers purchasing all-inclusive land vacations is increasing each year.

---

bundled (charges)   costs for several (or more) products or services in an all-inclusive charge

travel agent   a person or company (travel agency) that sells travel products and services to the public and is compensated for this service by fees charged to the buyer and/or by commissions paid by the travel supplier

OBJECTIVE 6
Note basic sources of revenues on cruise ships.

Some travel agencies are full service. As the name implies, they sell any travel product or service available to the public. By contrast, others specialize in one product or service. For example, some agencies primarily sell cruises and have a great deal of knowledge about this special travel product. The best (usually higher-volume) agencies may have relationships with one or more cruise lines that enable them to pass on discounts and value-added benefits (such as stateroom upgrades) to their clients.

Guests dining on an observation deck of a cruise ship

GENERATING REVENUE ON THE CRUISE

As you have learned, many charges that one would incur on a land-based vacation are bundled into their cruise costs; however, cruise lines still generate significant amounts of revenues from most passengers. Let's see how.

- *Alcoholic beverage sales.* Sale of alcoholic beverages is the single biggest source of onboard revenue on many cruise ships. Modern liners are designed to have numerous beverage outlets conveniently available, highly visible, and opened at the times when passengers are most likely to utilize them.
- *Photographs and videos.* Photographers are available on many cruise ships from the time one embarks to when one debarks and at many

times in between. Photo opportunities occur during the captain's reception, at the dinner table, and frequently at other times when candid photo opportunities arise.

- *Ship's casino.* While most passengers do not take a cruise primarily to gamble (some do!), some passengers do gamble and many others like to watch. Some cruise lines market to high-rollers, and other companies schedule special cruises catering to passengers who enjoy gambling.
- *Merchandise with the ship's logo, souvenirs, and necessities.* These suggest the range of items sold in retail shops on cruise lines. Revenues may also be generated from onshore shops that are promoted by cruise line personnel as ships enter a port of call.
- *Beauty salons and spas.* Passengers can have massages, facials, hair styling, and even mud baths onboard cruise ships.
- *Shore excursions.* Some cruise lines own buses and boats, for example, that passengers utilize for extra-cost activities.

RISING STAR PROFILE

Mike Laundry
Hotel Director
Pride of Aloha (Hawaii)
Norwegian Cruise Lines–America

Mike received an undergraduate degree in marketing and management with a minor in accounting from North Adams State College in Massachusetts in 1992.

Although he spent six months working in a hotel in Miami, he basically came right out of college and went right onto the ships. "I wasn't sure exactly how I was going to like working and living on a cruise ship, but once I got on board I realized that a life at sea could be very rewarding and fulfilling, both personally and professionally. I started out as a junior purser and, after working my way up through the ranks, became a hotel director earlier this year. I am responsible for all of the ship's hotel systems, including cabins, food and beverage, entertainment, and spa. Depending on the size of the ship, I am responsible for the management of upward of 800 employees.

"I joined Carnival Cruise Lines in 1994 and participated in the launch of three new ships, including the 2,052-passenger *Imagination* in 1995, the 2,642-passenger *Carnival Destiny* in 1996 (at the time the world's largest cruise ship), and the 2,124-passenger *Carnival Pride* in 2002. For these ship introductions, I traveled to shipyards in Italy and Finland and then sailed across the Atlantic to the United States. The launch of a new ship is a massive undertaking with a great deal of responsibility and provides an excellent opportunity to

showcase my job skills. Above all, these ship introductions provided me with unforgettable memories for years to come."

In his present position, Mike is onboard the Pride of Aloha, a cruise ship that makes inter-island cruises around the Hawaiian Islands.

Mike commented on the most significant challenges facing the cruise industry: Only a relatively small percentage of the population has ever taken a cruise. This means that there is tremendous room for growth. Today's massive cruise ships are dramatically different than even just a few years ago. They offer more and varied dining, entertainment, and activity options than ever before. The industry must continue to push the envelope in terms of onboard amenities in efforts to find ways to attract new cruisers."

Mike was asked about changes he would make in his career: "I wouldn't change a thing. I have put in a lot of hard work over the years, and it has definitely paid off. I have worked with very talented people from all over the world, including an excellent management team that has provided encouragement and allowed me to learn and grow in my professional career."

He also provided advice for young people considering a career in the cruise industry: "A life at sea can be very rewarding. Modern cruise lines provide a comfortable working environment. Granted, there is lots of hard work; cruise ships operate on a 24/7 basis. However, working aboard ship provides a unique opportunity to help guests' vacation dreams come true, to see the world, and to interact with people from all walks of life. Not many jobs can make that claim!"

OBJECTIVE 7
Consider challenges
confronting the cruise
line industry.

CHALLENGES! CHALLENGES!

Several challenges that confront the cruise line industry must be effectively managed to help to assure the short- and long-term success of the industry.

Cruise ship at port

Increased Competition

Larger and larger capacity cruise ships are on order and being delivered. Cruise line companies will need to more aggressively compete for cruise line passengers. A key element in this competition will be the tactics used to encourage first-time cruisers to consider this holiday alternative and to convert their potential interests to cruise ticket sales.

Competition will also come from land-based vacation alternatives offering all-inclusive prices. Since most or all of these resorts are at oceanfront locations, they can offer many of the same type of water-related activities as do their cruise ship counterparts.

Increasing Incremental Revenues

How can cruise lines encourage cruisers to spend more while on the ship? Upgrading (to higher-priced staterooms) and tactics to encourage cruisers to purchase noninclusive amenities available on the ships will be very important in helping to assure the long-term success of specific cruise line organizations.

Dining room on a cruise ship

At-Sea Security Concerns

The possibility of terrorist acts now confronts all segments of society, including the hospitality industry in general and cruise liners more specifically. The very large numbers of passengers and crew on many cruise ships makes these ships attractive to those who would commit terrorists acts. Increased passenger and baggage screening and ship protection while at port are among the tactics that will be increasingly used to protect ships and their passengers and crew.

DID YOU KNOW?

Believe it or not, sea piracy can be a security concern for cruise ships. While there were almost 450 attacks on commercial shipping in 2003, until recently cruise ships have been relatively safe from this concern. However, pirates in two small boats carrying machine guns and a rocket-propelled grenade attempted to board the Seabourn Cruise Lines *Seabourn Spirit* in November 2005 off the coast of Somalia. Its captain was able to use a combination of speed, change of course to the open sea, and a long-range acoustic device (LRAD) that generates an ear-splitting noise in a directed beam toward the pirates. Additionally, crew members used high-pressure fire hoses to prevent pirates from boarding the ship.

Source: Ship used high-tech device to ward off pirates' attack. *USA Today,* November 9, 2005, page 12A.

At-Sea Illness Concerns

Hundreds or thousands of passengers confined to cruise ships can create opportunities for the transmission of illnesses. For example, numerous cruises have been shortened or terminated because of the Norwalk virus, which has flulike symptoms that last several days or longer. Careful attention to proper sanitation practices at port and during cruises is very important, as is the effective cleaning and sanitizing of the ships on which passengers have contracted diseases.

SUMMARY OF CHAPTER LEARNING OBJECTIVES

1. **Present a brief history of cruising.**
   Ships have long been used for commerce, warfare, exploration, and business travel. Only recently, however, have they been used by persons enjoying their leisure time. While the first scheduled trans-Atlantic passenger sailing was in 1818, it was not until the early 1900s that ocean travel became relatively common. In the late 1950s, commercial jet service provided a much faster alternative across the Atlantic, and it was not until the 1970s that leisure cruising became more popular. Today, megaships carrying 2,000 or more passengers are being built in anticipation of a still greater increase in the cruise industry.

2. **Explore typical reasons why people cruise.**
   Passengers take cruises to relax, for travel and education, for social and status reasons,

to be safe during their travels, and as a family tradition.

3. **Review basic features of modern cruise ships.**

   Modern cruise ships are built for space, not speed, and have significant spaces allocated for passenger staterooms and for the crew's privacy. Additionally, and to remain competitive, public spaces are available for a wide range of purposes and activities to meet or exceed the passengers' interests during the cruise.

4. **Describe common ship- and land-based management positions in the cruise industry.**

   Common shipboard management positions include those of captain, staff captain, chief engineer, and hotel manager. Common land-based management positions include those of vice-presidents of hotel operations, marketing and sales, finance, marine operations, human resources, and passenger services.

5. **Explain procedures used to sell cruise vacations.**

   Most cruise vacations are booked by travel agents. The purchase of a cruise, especially for first-time cruisers, can be complicated, and numerous pricing alternatives make the decision more difficult.

6. **Note basic sources of revenue on cruise ships.**

   Even though many services of cruise ships are all-inclusive, significant amounts of revenue can be generated from passengers through alcoholic beverage sales, photographs and videos, the ship's casino, merchandise with logos, beauty salons and spas, and shore excursions.

7. **Consider challenges confronting the cruise line industry.**

   Challenges include increased competition (especially as larger-capacity cruise ships come on line), finding ways to increase incremental revenues, and at-sea security and illness concerns.

FEEDBACK FROM THE REAL WORLD

Our real-world advice comes from Mary Ann Ramsey, CTC, DS, President, Betty Maclean Travel, Inc., Naples, Florida.

Among many other industry honors, Mary Ann serves as a member of the board of trustees of the Institute of Certified Travel Agents and is a member of Travel + Leisure's travel agent advisory board. She has also served on the advisory boards of Seabourn Cruise Lines, Royal Viking Line, and Norwegian Cruise Lines. In 1999, Ramsey launched the Adventure Travel Company, which offers experiences for travelers from safaris to climbing Mt. Kilimanjaro.

Why are travel agencies the biggest generator of cruise sales?

Making the decision to take a cruise is a very big decision for many persons. Also, while they generally know what they want (a great time and pleasant memories at a reasonable price), many persons really don't know what is best for them because they do not know what is available. Also, many, especially first-time, cruisers have family and friends who have taken a cruise with the assistance of travel agencies; therefore, "if they used a travel agent, so should I!"

Purchasing a cruise is more complicated than, for example, buying an airline ticket. The numerous cruise lines offer different prices for different cabin types at different times of the year on cruises to different ports.

My agency deals primarily with upscale cruises to Europe, Tahiti, Africa, and similar non-Caribbean destinations. Travelers cannot receive all information required to make their decision simply by contacting the cruise line directly. Take, for example, documentation: our travel consultants work carefully with our clients to assure that their passports and visas are in order. Countries have different requirements regarding multientry (points and times), number of days in the country, the length of time that passports are valid after entry into the country, and related technical concerns that we can address as we provide individualized attention to our clients.

How do travel agents interact with the cruise lines as they sell cruises?

Believe it or not, very little of our contact with a cruise line is by computer. Instead, we use telephone lines to contact cruise companies, who, in turn, use fax services to send confirmation. My agency, like many others, belongs to a marketing organization (a consortia). The service we belong to is called "Virtuoso." We are members based on the agency's volume and type of travel; we have access to an excellent cruise line database. One service provided by this organization is a newspage that is updated throughout the day. It provides much information about all matters of interest to cruisers and potential cruisers. This is a great help to us, as we can then pass this information on to our clients.

Do discounts and agency rebates help to generate cruise business?

Basically, our marketing consortia (Virtuoso) negotiates rates with cruise lines that are utilized by its subscribers. We are able to pass on significant savings for group fares, special rates for other cruisers, exclusive shore excursions, and onboard credits (for example, a private onboard cocktail reception and use of the ship's spa). Our clients also have access to a Voyager's Club, which utilizes a travel agency representative (host) to help all cruisers onboard who are clients of travel agencies participating in the Virtuoso Consortia.

Rebates may be used by some travel agencies; we do not. In effect, a rebate is part of a travel agency's commission that is given back to a cruiser to lower the price. In my experience, we don't do well when we compete with other agencies by price. Some cruisers may give price the highest priority in their cruise decision; they will, then, shop travel agencies. By contrast, we emphasize service, and we want to establish a long-term relationship based on the service, including the information that we provide.

What types of positions are available in travel agencies specializing in cruise sales?

Agencies like mine have great opportunities. For example, a young person might begin after college as a sales assistant who does research and cruise package processing after a deal is made with a client. Those who do well will be promoted to travel consultant, have direct client contact, and do some package processing. Persons with 10 years of successful experience can become senior consultants, who primarily have contact with clients desiring our most complicated trips.

From the perspective of a travel agent, what do you see to be the future of the cruise industry?

I see a lot more competition between cruise lines seeking passengers and travel agencies seeking clients. The future is bright, however, because only a relatively small percentage of people have taken a cruise. This will change, and the base of first-time cruisers and their repeat-cruise counterparts will yield a steady business for those cruise lines and travel agencies who can find creative ways to increase their markets.

MASTERING YOUR KNOWLEDGE

Discuss the following questions.

1. How important is price to the typical cruise passenger? How do prospective passengers evaluate the alternative charges that, in total, make up the purchase price for the cruise?
2. What types of value-added services might you as an owner or manager of a travel agency provide to increase the amount of cruise business you do?
3. Pretend that you are considering taking a cruise or flying to a coastal city for a vacation. What types of costs would need to be considered with both alternatives to determine the lowest-cost alternative? What factors in addition to cost would influence your purchase decision?

4. What types of menu planning factors might differ for the foodservice operation on a cruise ship versus that offered by a high check average restaurant?

LEARN FROM THE INTERNET

1. Check out the websites for several cruise line companies:
   - Carnival Cruise Lines: www.carnival.com
   - Norwegian Cruise Lines: www.ncl.com
   - Royal Caribbean International: www.royalcaribbean.com

   What types of pricing structures do they offer and how do they sell alternative packages to prospective passengers? What types of onboard amenities do they publicize? How, if at all, do they suggest that a cruise experience on their ship is better than on their competitors' ships?

2. Check out the websites for still other cruise lines:
   - Galapagos Cruises Inc.: www.galapagos-inc.com
   - World Explorer Cruises: www.wecruise.com
   - Society Expeditions: www.pacificislandstravel.com

   What information do they provide about the geography of the cruises, the ports of call and pre- and/or postcruise packages relating to the educational and cultural aspects of these destinations?

KEY HOSPITALITY TERMS

The following terms were explained in this chapter. Review the definitions of any words with which you are unfamiliar. Begin to utilize them as you expand your vocabulary as a hospitality professional.

cruise ship
megaship
stateroom
embarkation
debarkation

concessionaire
yield management
bundled (charges)
travel agent

Casino Entertainment Management

24

Slot machines on gaming floor of New York Hotel and Casino, Las Vegas, Nevada

CHAPTER LEARNING OBJECTIVES

After studying this chapter you will be able to:

1. Present an overview of the gaming industry.
2. Discuss reasons why people visit casinos.
3. Explain the organization of a casino.
4. Review the revenue and support centers in a typical casino.
5. Briefly review social problems sometimes associated with gaming.
6. Discuss challenges confronting the casino entertainment industry.

This chapter was authored by Vincent H. Eade, MA, Professor/Founding Director of the UNLV International Gaming Institute, William F. Harrah College of Hotel Administration, University of Nevada, Las Vegas. Mr. Eade is a co-author with his brother Raymond of *Introduction to the Casino Entertainment Industry,* Prentice Hall, Inc., Upper Saddle River, NJ, 1997.

FEEDBACK FROM THE REAL WORLD

In this chapter, you will learn that the casino entertainment industry is very large and profitable and that it is experiencing unprecedented growth. However, does the fascination and appeal that attracts visitors in ever-increasing numbers also apply to those who work within it? More specifically:

- What types of positions within the industry are most attractive to graduates of postsecondary hospitality programs?
- How, if at all, do management positions in this industry differ from their counterparts in applicable positions in restaurants and hotels? How are they the same?

- How important are lodging and food and beverage services to the success of large casinos?
- What is a typical promotion or career advancement pattern for a talented person desiring a career in the casino entertainment industry?

As you read this chapter, think about the answers to these questions and then get feedback from the real world at the end of the chapter.

---

casino   a business operation that offers table and card games along with (usually) slot operations and other games of skill or chance and amenities that are marketed to customers seeking gaming activities and entertainment; many casinos also offer food and beverage services and lodging accomodations for the convenience of their visitors

racino   a race track that has added slot machines to increase revenues

gaming   any activity that involves wagering (betting) something of value on a game or event with an unknown outcome

wager   to pledge (promise) something as the result of an event for which the outcome is unknown; also called *bet*

OBJECTIVE 1
Present an overview of the gaming industry.

table games   games of chance involving wagering between the casino and its customers

black jack   a table game in which the winner is the person closest to 21 without exceeding that number; also called *twenty-one*

The **casino** entertainment industry has captured the imagination of the business world and the consumer. Until the late 1980s, gaming was restricted in the United States to Las Vegas and Atlantic City. However, since that time it has expanded rapidly across the country, surfacing on Native American tribal reservations, riverboats, dockside locations, and **racinos,** as well as in numerous cities in other countries. To put the size of the gaming industry in perspective, casinos retain more revenue annually than the total of all money spent at movie box offices and on books, attractions, and recorded music.

Our study of this chapter will introduce positions that are unique to casino organizations. The potential for visitor and employee theft of significant amounts of cash in very short periods of time requires the need for layers of control, and the positions to implement and manage these controls are not necessary in other hospitality organizations.

The casino entertainment industry is the "new kid on the block" relative to most other segments of the hospitality industry. It is growing quickly in size and, at the same time, evolving in sophistication. This chapter will provide an overview of the casino entertainment industry and help you to decide if a career within it might be right for you.

OVERVIEW OF THE GAMING INDUSTRY

The **gaming** industry is very broad and diverse, as outlined in the following:

Casinos

A large casino typically offers the following types of **wagering** activities:

- **Table games.** Table games involve wagering between the casino and its customers. Common examples of table games include **black jack** or twenty-one, **dice** or crap games, **roulette**, the **big six** (also called Wheel of Fortune or Money Wheel), **baccarat, mini-baccarat, pai-gow, pai-gow poker,** and other games in which wagers are placed on a table or table layout as an integral part of the game.

- **Card games.** Card games differ from table games. With card games, the casino does not wager against the players but, instead, offers games in which players wager against each other while a casino employee (dealer) deals the cards. The casino relies on a fixed percentage taken from each hand played as its revenue source for card games.
- *Slot machines and video games.* Slot machines use simulated or actual spinning reels activated by a handle pull or a button push with **payoffs** based on a computerized random-number generator program or the alignment of graphics or symbols on a reel (for example, "three cherries across"). Video games include video poker, keno, bingo, and lottery terminals.

The casino in the Las Vegas Hilton

- **Bingo.** Bingo is a game in which players match numbers on cards they have "purchased" with numbers drawn at random.
- **Keno.** Keno is a variation of bingo in which an electronic board or screen is used to display numbers 1 to 80. Twenty numbers are randomly selected, and players mark a keno ticket indicating which numbers they believe will be drawn. Keno is, then, similar to a lottery drawing. Casinos have a keno lounge with keno runners who circulate throughout the casino accepting wagers on each game. Most casinos now have keno slot machines.
- **Race** or **sports books.** Race books feature wagering on horse racing; sports books take action on professional or collegiate sporting events. Casinos establish a line on games or other wagering propositions and take a percentage on wagers and losing bets.

dice table games in which a player wins or loses based on dice rolls; also called *crap games*

roulette a table game in which a large wheel is spun by a dealer who simultaneously spins a small white ball around the inside top rim of the wheel; wagers are placed on a number or color upon which it is hoped the ball will fall

big six a carnival-style game in which a large, upright wheel is spun by a dealer and players wager on which number the wheel will stop; the higher the payout, the greater the odds against hitting the number

baccarat a high-stakes table game using playing cards in which the highest (best) hand is nine, and the winner is the player closest to nine. In casinos, this game is played in a formal, separate room; dealers wear tuxedos

mini-baccarat a lower-stakes table game similar to baccarat, except the player does not have a turn as the bank and there is one dealer; in casinos, this game is less formal: it is played on the main floor and dealers wear the usual casino uniform

pai-gow a game in which four cards or tiles are dealt to players, who must have two hands higher than the dealer's or bank's hand; casinos get a commission on winning hands

Horse and Dog Track Racing and Racinos

Pari-mutuel wagering is the most common system. Many states have legalized off-track betting. Casinos typically feature video monitors televising races at multiple tracks, and they provide food and beverages for their patrons as they study data, place wagers, and watch races.

Lotteries

Government-sponsored lotteries involve matching numbers predrawn by purchasers with those later selected in a public drawing; they provide lucrative forms of tax revenues after making very large (sometimes multimillion dollar) payoffs to lottery winners.

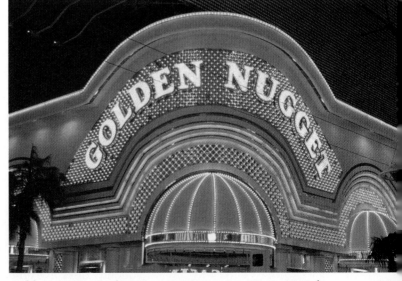
Golden Nugget Casino, Fremont Street, Las Vegas, Nevada

RIVERBOAT, DOCKSIDE, AND NATIVE AMERICAN CASINOS

Historically, gaming in the United States was legalized only in Las Vegas, Nevada, and Atlantic City, New Jersey. This changed in 1989, when Iowa approved riverboat gaming. This form of casino gaming quickly won legislative approval in numerous other states. Riverboat casinos typically cruise on rivers or in harbors and offer table and card games, as well as slot operations. Dockside operations are better classified as barges that are moored to a dock and do not cruise on a waterway. The variety and number of permissible games vary according to the dockside vessel's size and state gaming regulations. Some gaming vessels charge an admission fee, and riverboats cruise for a predetermined number of hours.

Native American (Indian) tribal casino gaming began in the late 1980s out of economic need and unique legal circumstances. Historically, tribes were regarded (or regarded themselves) as sovereign nations living on reservations arranged through treaties with the U.S. government. Court decisions set the legal foundation for gaming by asserting that, if a state currently regulates a form of gambling, then tribes living within that state can engage in gambling. Tribes and states negotiate compacts that establish the terms and conditions of operating a casino (for example, the gaming taxes to be paid to the state). More than one-third of the nation's federally recognized tribes now sponsor some type of gambling. Legislation (the Indian Gaming Regulatory Act of 1988) helps to assure that tribes are the beneficiaries of gaming revenues.

---

pai-gow poker a combination of Chinese pai-gow and poker using 52 cards and a joker

card games games of chance in which customers (players) wager against each other while a casino employee (dealer) deals the cards

payoff (gaming) any wager or winnings paid to a player

bingo a game in which players match numbers on cards with randomly drawn numbers

keno numbers 1 to 80 are displayed on an electronic board or screen; players mark a keno ticket indicating which 20 numbers they think will be drawn; keno is similar to lottery drawings

race book or **sports book** a casino department that accepts wagers on horse races or professional and collegiate sporting events

OBJECTIVE 2
Discuss reasons why people visit casinos.

Charitable Games

Churches and religious and nonprofit organizations offer bingo games, raffles, and Vegas Night promotions to raise money.

Other Gaming Venues

These include slot and video operations, bingo parlors, bowling sweepstakes, and social games such as dominoes, backgammon, checkers, chess, darts, and numerous others.

WHY VISIT CASINOS?

There are a number of socioeconomic and psychological reasons why people visit casinos. Some are presented in Exhibit 24.1. Let's look at each of these factors in more detail:

- *Gaming.* Many people like to gamble, wager, or participate in games of chance or skill. For some, it means a chance to "strike it rich" or, at least, to win some extra spending money. Others see gaming as a chance to break the bank or test their skills when their ability is pitted against the casino.

- *Recreation and entertainment.* Persons with discretionary income often seek new and different ways to enjoy their money; casinos offer an attractive alternative. The environment offers an exciting form of entertainment and, for many, a mental escape from pressures of their work and/or personal lives. In addition to gaming alternatives, casinos frequently offer live entertainment in show rooms or lounges and numerous

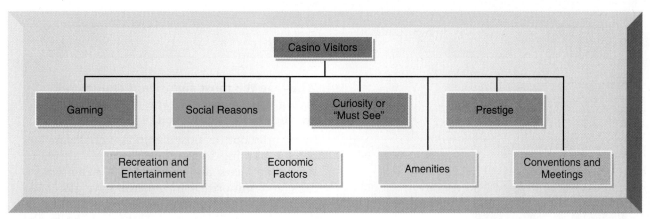

EXHIBIT 24.1
What Attracts Casino Visitors

restaurants (often including those affiliated with national chains). Other entertainment activities may include bowling, movie theaters, karaoke "sing-alongs," and shopping in retail outlets. Properties in applicable locations may incorporate water- or snow-related activities into their entertainment offerings. When traditional recreation, sporting, and entertainment amenities such as musical concerts, boxing matches, and golf are added to the potential experience, it is easy to understand the appeal of casinos to many visitors.

- *Social reasons.* Senior citizens and retirees more than any other group are drawn to casinos for the social interaction that occurs between customers and between customers and the property's employees. Civic organizations, clubs, and associations utilize casino meeting rooms for social gatherings.
- *Economic factors.* Since gaming is a vital source of revenues for hotels and casinos, these properties often offer excellent (low-priced) guest-room rates and value-priced buffets to attract visitors.
- *Curiosity or "must-see."* Today's mega-casinos have become "must-see" attractions for many persons. As casino gaming has progressed from being just legal to legitimate, more people want to see them.
- *Amenities.* Many people are drawn to the health spas, hair salons, beauty parlors, amusement centers, and theme attractions offered by casinos. Since these properties typically operate 24 hours a day, they serve as

pari-mutuel wagering
betting on horses in which odds based on the amount bet on each horse are established; winners share the total wagers placed in the pool among themselves based on the established odds

Slot machine players in action

RISING STAR PROFILE

Marcus W. Threats

My Advice: Be a Generalist!

Marcus has two associate of applied science degrees (in hotel administration and in casino management). He also earned a bachelors of science degree in hotel administration and a master in business administration. After graduation in 1987, he served for seven years as a naval officer and aviator in the U.S. Navy.

Marcus has worked in every major department in the gaming industry. He began as a bus boy at the age of 16 and worked his way up to the position of waiter. He has kitchen work experience as a dishwasher, kitchen runner, cook's helper, and fry cook and has also worked as a front-desk clerk to obtain hotel experience.

On the gaming side, Marcus has experience as a dealer, box supervisor, table-games supervisor, pit manager, and assistant casino shift manager. He gained his finance and accounting experience by working as a senior financial analyst and as a casino accounting manager.

What is the most unforgettable moment in your career?

The most unforgettable moment in my career was the last day I dealt dice at the Las Vegas Hilton. Dice dealers in those days split tips with the four dealers that made the team of the dice crew with whom you worked. That night, for the last two times I worked the stick position, the players never lost a bet. This allowed my crew to make more money than any of us had ever made in one night.

What are the most significant challenges facing your segment of the industry? How are they being addressed?

In my opinion the most significant challenge facing the gaming industry is employee diversity. For many years and still today African Americans and minorities in general have not been given the same management opportunities as those in the majority race. This is evident by the relatively few number of minorities working at the director level and above.

All the major gaming companies are working to address the issue of diversity. However, this is just the first step in a long journey. If the gaming industry is to mature as an industry and be recognized for its economic contributions to society, this industry must be willing to diversify its work force. This is important not only in entry-level positions, but also up to and including the executive level. I believe that it is just a matter of time before this maturity will occur.

What, if anything, would you do differently in your career?

I would change nothing in my career. I have been fortunate to have had some excellent mentors and instructors with whom I have maintained contact throughout my career. I continue to seek out these individuals and ask for their advice about my career.

What is your advice for young people considering a career in your industry segment?

My advice for a young person considering a career in the gaming industry is to get a college education along with work experience. The success of any person in the gaming industry lies in education, because the need to make educated business decisions will be crucial. Also, I recommend that young persons take the time to work in and learn about all the major areas of the industry, including hotel, food and beverage, and, finally, gaming. I believe that, in the future, it will be important to be a generalist. One will need to have a thorough knowledge about all the departments in the industry, rather than being a specialist with knowledge about only one area or department.

banking facilities to cash payroll and personal checks. Suites and public spaces may also serve as locations for weddings and parties.

- *Prestige.* Casinos attract gamblers by providing complimentary rooms, entertainment, food, beverages, gifts, and even airfare. This VIP (very important person) treatment provides status, and many recipients talk about the "comp" (complimentary) suites or "free" gourmet meals they receive.
- *Conventions, meetings, trade shows, and special events.* Casinos with public spaces book conventions, meetings, trade shows, or special events that draw attendees to the facility. While at these events, many people will visit the casino.

Not all casino visitors are attracted by all the factors noted in Exhibit 24.1. Many, however, are attracted by more than one factor. Each visitor, then, consciously and/or unconsciously is interested in attaining personal goals when he or she visits a casino. The extent to which these goals are met affects the quality of the casino experience.

ORGANIZATION OF CASINOS

Exhibit 24.2 shows a possible organization of a large casino property. While it is simplified (many additional positions are required), it does indicate how major responsibilities might be divided. Note, for example, that the general manager of the casino supervises directors of departments who are responsible for hotel operations, human resources, marketing, casino operations, finance, security, surveillance, food and beverage operations, and engineering and maintenance. With the exception of the director of casino operations, finance (who supervises the cage manager), and the director of surveillance (who has responsibility for control of significant amounts of currency assets), the responsibilities of the other casino directors are similar to those of their counterparts in other hospitality operations. (Some responsibilities of the director of security also differ. Detailed information about positions involving **casino cage** management, security, and surveillance will be presented in the next section of this chapter.)

Exhibit 24.2 also illustrates the management personnel who report to the director of casino operations. These individuals (the managers of customer development and VIP services, bingo, race and sports, slot operations, baccarat, table games, keno, and poker) occupy positions unique to their industry segment.

Let's look at one position, manager of table games, to see how career progression within this division might evolve. Exhibit 24.3 illustrates the chain of command for positions supervised by the manager of table games. Casinos typically develop detailed job descriptions that identify the tasks for each of these positions. Basic responsibilities for each include the following:

- *Manager, table games.* Responsible for the overall operation of the casino's table games and the personnel that staff them

casino cage the casino's banking center maintained by a cage manager; transactions with casino customers are conducted by casino cashiers at cage windows; the cage is responsible for the property's currency, coins, tokens, and gaming chips; casino pit clerks are an extension of the cage and work in the gaming pits on the casino floor; cage personnel prepare cash banks (for example, for restaurant cashiers) and bank deposits, cash checks for patrons, and place valuable items in safety deposit boxes; currency is also counted in a secure area of the cage

OBJECTIVE 3
Explain the organization of a casino.

Outdoor formal courtyard at Bellagio Resort Hotel in Las Vegas, Nevada

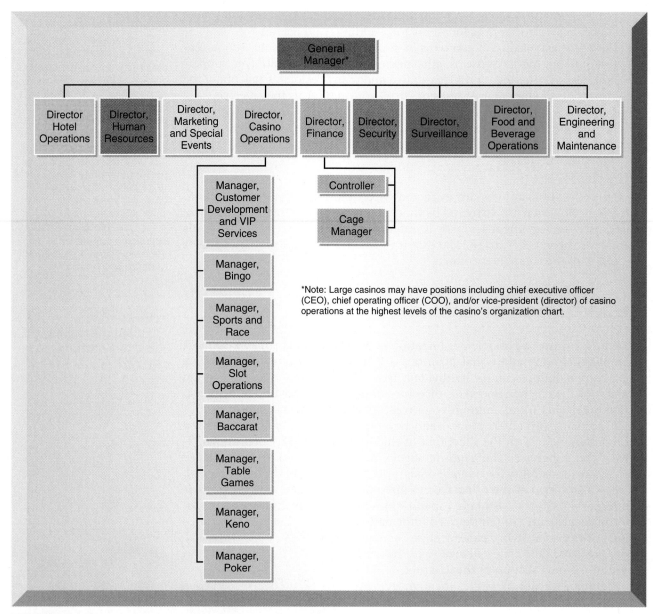

EXHIBIT 24.2
Organization Chart for Casino Operations

- *Shift manager.* Responsible for the operation of table games and required personnel during a specific shift
- *Pit manager.* Responsible for the operation of table games and required personnel in a designated **pit** (specific tables in a designated location in the casino)
- *Floorperson.* Responsible for supervising an assigned group of tables within a pit
- *Dealer.* Responsible for the operation of a specific table game at one table within a pit
- **Boxperson.** Responsible for placing cash waged in a dice game into a drop slot in the dice table, placing waged chips in the rack, and protecting the integrity of the game

pit (casino table games) specific tables in a designated location in the casino

boxperson responsible for placing cash waged in a dice game into a drop slot in the dice table, placing waged chips in the rack, and protecting the integrity of the game

A similar chain of command exists for the other divisions within the casino operations department. Unseen in Exhibit 24.3 are other persons, including those in the surveillance and finance (casino cage) departments, whose very important work also affects positions in the games department. We will look at these positions more carefully in the next section.

REVENUE AND SUPPORT CENTERS

Revenue centers are, as the name implies, departments within the property that generate revenues. In a casino, there are gaming revenue centers (for example, table games and slots) and nongaming revenue centers (for example, lodging and restaurant sales). By contrast, **support centers** are nonrevenue-generating departments that are necessary to assist or support revenue centers. Exhibit 24.2 identified typical departments in a casino. Let's add a few more and sort them into revenue and support classifications.

Common revenue centers in a casino include the casino operations department, which, as you have learned, is responsible for the following:

Bingo	Table games
Race and sports books	Keno
Slots	Card games, including poker
Baccarat	

Other revenue centers include the hotel operations and the food and beverage operations departments. With the exception of these two departments, a casino's revenue centers are unique to this segment of the industry.

Support centers in a casino include the following:

- Human resources
- Marketing and sales
- Finance (accounting and auditing)
- Security
- Surveillance
- Engineering and maintenance

Some but not all of the functions performed by human resources, marketing and sales, and

OBJECTIVE 4
Review the revenue and support centers in a typical casino.

revenue centers a department within an organization that generates revenue; two examples in a casino are the casino operations and hotel operations departments

support centers nonrevenue-generating departments that are necessary to assist (support) revenue centers; two examples in a casino are the human resources and security departments

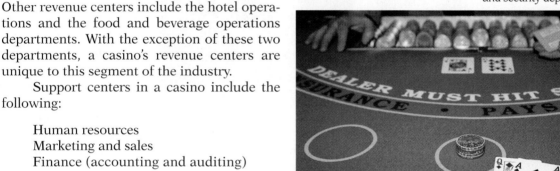

Winning hand on a black jack table

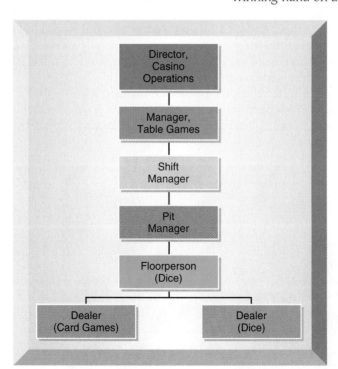

EXHIBIT 24.3

Organization Chart: Focus on Manager of Table Games

engineering and maintenance personnel in hotels and other lodging properties are similar to those performed by their counterparts in casinos. However, much of the work undertaken by security and finance personnel and all the activities involving surveillance personnel are unique to casino operations. Let's look at these responsibilities.

Surveillance scenes at a casino

A Close Look at the Security Department

Many of the responsibilities of a casino's security department are applicable to other hospitality operations. For example, security staff may escort employees to parking areas at night; assist local police authorities as they investigate criminal activities; maintain crowd control; ensure that all city, county, state, and federal codes and laws are complied with; and handle intoxicated or unruly guests. Other activities, however, are unique to casinos. These include the following:

- Escorting cash transfers from the casino floor to the casino cage
- Escorting guests who have won significant amounts of money to their car, airport, or other local destination
- Moving drop boxes from table pit games and transporting them to the casino cage
- Overseeing the slot drop done by a team of employees who remove coins from slot machines
- Guarding the casino cage and working to prevent robberies of and/or assaults on cage personnel
- Providing public relations assistance for the casino with its guests
- Assisting slot department personnel by witnessing the replenishment of slot booth bank rolls, hand-paying large jackpots won by slot players,

A slot machine pays a lucky player.

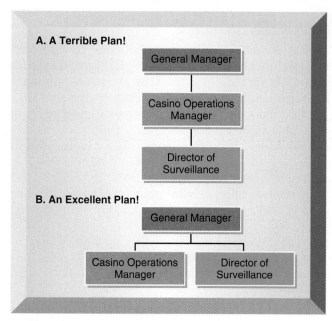

EXHIBIT 24.4
Effective Surveillance Is Critical

performing slot machine hopper fills (replacing coins in machines), and assisting with slot drops

- Assisting with credits and fills for table games (**credits** involve transporting gaming chips from a gaming table back to the casino cage; **fills** involve bringing gaming chips from the casino cage to fill the gaming tables' chip racks)

A Close Look at the Surveillance Department

A casino's surveillance department acts as a check and balance on the casino. As shown in Exhibit 24.4, it is critical that the director of surveillance report directly to the general manager. This reduces the potential for **collusion;** a separation of authority and power represents the foundation for sound and effective internal control procedures in a casino and in any other type of hospitality operation.

credits (casino gaming tables)   the security task of transporting gaming chips from tables to the casino cage

fills (casino gaming tables) the security task of transporting gaming chips from the casino cage to the tables

collusion   secret cooperation between two or more employees for the purpose of committing fraud

---

WHAT DOES THE SURVEILLANCE DEPARTMENT DO?

The primary function of a casino's surveillance department is detection of theft of company assets from gaming tables, slot machines, the casino cage, and all other revenue areas of the property.

Surveillance operations are done either with dedicated cameras permanently fixed on key revenue areas of the casino or by scanning cameras that randomly rotate and videotape less critical areas of the property. If a scam is detected, surveillance personnel contact the casino manager's office and call government regulators, who will then be available to arrest the cheater(s). (If casino floor supervisors believe that a problem is occurring in the gaming area, they will contact surveillance to request assistance in viewing the possible problem.)

Although it is impossible to catch every thief, especially with the high-tech devices now being used by scam artists, personnel casino surveillance departments historically uncover the major portion of scams. Certainly, the presence of cameras in the casino acts as a reminder to all visitors that surveillance personnel are on the watch!

DID YOU KNOW?

Chips that gamblers use to wage bets can be high-tech with radio frequency identification (RFID) inserts. Radio signals from the chips allow casinos to keep real-time track of them on gaming tables, to assess player points, and to help keep chips secure from theft or counterfeit. Use of this technology allows casinos to know their position on every gaming table in just a few seconds throughout the entire gaming floor. As well, pit bosses at casinos using this technology will no longer have to estimate drops at the end of each shift, and will have more time to focus on customer service and employee training.

To review one website that discusses this technology, go to www.progressivegaming.net and click on "technology."

Source: Tom Wilemon. High-tech chips let casinos keep track: radio signals thwart thieves. Retrieved February 7, 2006, from www.hotel-online.com

---

The first surveillance rooms in Las Vegas casinos featured an extensive network of catwalks over the casino. This enabled "eye-in-the-sky" personnel to visually view gaming areas through one-way smoked glass in the ceiling of the casino. Today's surveillance rooms use high-technology video cameras with zoom and wide-angle lenses, colored television monitors, computers capable of instantly reproducing photographs of suspected cheaters, and computer linkups to the slot tracking system so that surveillance employees can note cases of tampering. Videotape and digital recorders line the walls of the modern surveillance room, and this department maintains a video library of their observations, which can be used by casino department personnel for review purposes.

A Close Look at the Finance Department (Casino Cage)

The casino cage can rightfully be called the nerve center of the property. It has the responsibility for many vital functions.

- *Bank roll custodianship and accountability.* Bank roll requirements of a casino consist primarily of currency, coinage, and gaming chips (which must be accurately inventoried and closely monitored). One can imagine the extent of documentation and controls required of cage personnel as they account for millions of dollars on a daily basis.
- *Servicing the casino pits.* This involves providing table chip fills requested by a supervisor, receiving table chip credits authorized by a gaming supervisor, processing customer credit instruments (IOUs), and providing other help and information to casino supervisors.
- *Interaction with almost every revenue and nonrevenue department.* Casino cage personnel prepare cash banks and bank deposits, make customer payouts, and change customer's winning chips for currency and customer coins (for example, from slot winnings) to cash.

Exhibit 24.5 shows how a casino cage might be organized. The cage manager reports to the director of finance (or CFO or controller). He or she, in turn, supervises the work of the credit manager, who approves credit for casino customers, and the collections manager, who is responsible for collecting outstanding customer debts. (A basic principle of internal control is that

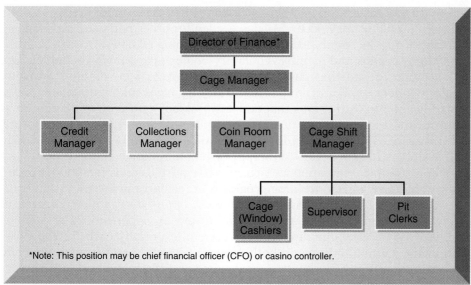

```
                    ┌──────────────────────┐
                    │  Director of Finance* │
                    └───────────┬──────────┘
                                │
                    ┌───────────┴──────────┐
                    │     Cage Manager     │
                    └───────────┬──────────┘
         ┌────────────┬─────────┼───────────────┐
  ┌──────┴─────┐ ┌────┴─────┐ ┌─┴────────┐ ┌────┴──────┐
  │   Credit   │ │Collections│ │Coin Room │ │Cage Shift │
  │  Manager   │ │ Manager  │ │ Manager  │ │ Manager   │
  └────────────┘ └──────────┘ └──────────┘ └────┬──────┘
                              ┌──────────────────┼──────────────┐
                        ┌─────┴─────┐     ┌───────┴────┐   ┌─────┴─────┐
                        │   Cage    │     │ Supervisor │   │   Pit     │
                        │ (Window)  │     │            │   │  Clerks   │
                        │ Cashiers  │     └────────────┘   └───────────┘
                        └───────────┘
```

*Note: This position may be chief financial officer (CFO) or casino controller.

EXHIBIT 24.5
Organization of a Casino Cage

the individual who authorizes customer credit privileges should not be the same person who collects the debt. For this reason, then, these two positions are separated.)

Exhibit 24.5 also shows the coin room manager, who supervises the **slot drop** and count and is responsible for control of uncounted coinage during the drop. A team of employees circulates throughout the casino, removing coins from slot machines that have been won by the machine and have dropped or fallen into a bucket at the bottom of the machine. The team is known as the hard-count team (coins are hard and currency is soft; therefore, casinos have hard-count teams and soft-count teams). The hard-count team transports the coins to a hard-count room where the coins are counted by machines (actually they are weighed!) and wrapped for deposit purposes or for circulation back into the casino. The cage shift manager per-forms the duties and responsibilities of the cage manager in his or her absence. This includes the responsibility for the physical (custodial) control of all assets held in the cashier's cage during the assigned shift. The cage shift manager also supervises front-line cage personnel, including cashiers, supervisors, and **pit clerks** (who provide information helpful in generating **marker** transactions for a specified number of tables within the casino).

slot drop the collection of slot machine coins taken by casino personnel who transport the coins to the casino cage

pit clerks a person reporting to the casino cage shift manager who provides information helpful in generating fill, credit, and marker transactions for a specified number of tables within the casino

marker similar to an IOU; casinos do a credit check on customers and extend credit by use of a marker based on their financial background and ability to pay; customers can sign these markers and use the money to gamble

GAMING AND SOCIETY

Some persons become addicted to gaming. When the need to gamble becomes a priority in one's life,

Coin bucket from Mirage Casino

OBJECTIVE 5
Briefly review social problems sometimes associated with gaming.

personal relationships and employment can suffer. Stress and anxiety leading to health problems may occur. Monies needed for other purposes may be lost, and crimes may be committed to support the gaming addiction.

Many casinos and gaming regulatory bodies take a positive and aggressive attitude in assisting customers and employees who develop problem gaming tendencies. For example, regulatory agencies may require that casinos contribute to institutions that address problem gambling or develop programs to assist individuals with addiction problems. Many casinos incorporate referral services through **employee assistance programs** to help their own staff members to gain access to therapy or rehabilitation centers when necessary. For example, regulating agencies may require casinos to conduct problem gambling awareness training programs for casino employees.

Concerns about crime are noted by those opposed to gaming. Organized crime, for example, has always been motivated by opportunities to quickly and easily generate large amounts of revenue, especially cash. In the early days of the gaming industry in both Atlantic City and Las Vegas, there were concerns about ties between organized crime and those involved in the management of gaming businesses.

Today, however, several things have changed. First, government regulations place significant controls on casinos. Also, the largest casino organizations are legitimate businesses in every sense, as are their counterparts in other segments of the hospitality industry. Most of the larger casino organizations are publicly traded and have stockholders. The integrity of owners and top-level managers provides another obstacle to infiltration by professional criminals.

There are also concerns about other types of crimes, sometimes called street crimes. Prostitution, crimes committed by persons to support their gambling habits, and crimes upon visitors to casinos are examples.

Elected officials and the voting public in general constantly evaluate the advantages of gaming, including a community's economic development and lowered unemployment rates, with the potential for criminal activity and social issues. These analyses include many of the same types of cost–benefit and decision-making processes that are applicable to numerous other issues within our society.

employee assistance program a counseling and/or referral plan sponsored by an organization for its employees with personal problems

OBJECTIVE 6
Discuss challenges confronting the casino entertainment industry.

CHALLENGES! CHALLENGES!

Some challenges confronting casinos are similar to those of other segments of the hospitality industry; others are different. Let's look at both types.

Need to Attract and Retain a Qualified Work Force

Training needs to occur at three levels: skilled front-line employees, supervisory to mid-management personnel, and executives. Training venues include in-house programs, those offered by for-profit businesses such as dealer schools, and those provided by slot manufacturing companies (for technicians) and postsecondary educational facilities. It is likely that future casino managers and executives will have both postsecondary and graduate degrees. Also, a national certification program and exam for casino executives are likely.

Increased Government Regulation

Government is concerned that the industry be properly regulated. As an example, casinos must comply with federal laws designed to prevent money laundering. Recently, in the United States, a federally appointed committee conducted a lengthy study. It visited a number of gaming jurisdictions, assessed the impact

Spa Bellagio at Bellagio Resort Hotel in Las Vegas, Nevada

of gaming, and published its results and observations as part of the *Congressional Record*. There have also been legislative discussions about a wagering ban on collegiate athletic events.

Increased Efforts to Address Problem Gambling

Although problem gamblers represent a very small percentage of those involved in casino-style gambling, this is still a high-profile societal issue. Resistance to legalized gambling will likely continue, and those who research in this area will need to focus on solutions, as well as on the nature, causes, and extent of the problems.

Use of Technology

One of the greatest challenges confronting the future of gaming relates to technology. Gaming is already offered over the Internet. If legal issues involved in regulating computerized gaming are resolved, a whole new venue for gaming may emerge. Technological changes in slot machines have already been dramatic and, eventually, virtual reality will enhance the sight and sound experience to create the ultimate in technological slot play. Casino play-at-home may be the next frontier, with television sets used to display slot machines online from casinos. (While making gaming more accessible, this concept removes the excitement and live casino environment and would likely face legal challenges relating to underage gambling controls. However, it does point to the possibility of many different gambling opportunities both within and outside the traditional casino environment.)

Technology has also dramatically changed the slot industry. One of the most significant changes has been the conversion from slot machines that drop coins when a player cashes out to a coinless and reusable voucher or ticket system. This has resulted in the elimination of hopper fills (coins being placed in the machine hopper) and the need for a hard-count team and has yielded improved customer service. Technology will continue to drive the slot manufacturing industry based on customer need and demand.

The gaming leaders of tomorrow will need to pay close attention to customer expectations and how the use of technology can help exceed these expectations.

Increased Competition

An additional challenge relates to increased competition, which will cause many casinos to reinvent their operations and look for new ways to attract and retain new markets of customers.

More Nongaming Revenue

In recent years, the Las Vegas gaming industry has witnessed an interesting phenomenon: more money is being generated from nongaming revenue sources. Casinos have realized that guests are willing to spend money on items that, historically, were viewed as secondary sources of income. Today, Las Vegas casinos rely on the sale of food, wines, concerts, beverages at ultralounges (bars or nightclubs), shows and entertainment venues, bowling alleys, movie theaters, and special events to drive their bottomline. Much like Las Vegas, other gaming operators face the challenge of continuing to make their operations increasingly productive in a competitive environment and will need to examine ways to add new revenue streams to their businesses.

International Growth

Gaming has not only seen explosive growth in the United States in the past decade, but we have also witnessed the expansion of gaming globally. International gaming corporations have expanded or started casino operations in countries throughout the world. Gaming companies based in the United States have made business ventures into Macau and the Pacific rim. The members of the gaming industry are becoming fewer and more connected, and casino operators will face the challenge of global competition for customers.

SUMMARY OF CHAPTER LEARNING OBJECTIVES

1. **Present an overview of the gaming industry.**
   Casinos are a significant part of the gaming industry. A large casino typically offers numerous types of wagering: table games, card games, slot machines and video games, bingo, keno, and race and sports books. Other venues for gaming include horse and dog track betting, lotteries, charitable games, and numerous other gaming venues, including slot and video operations, bingo parlors, bowling sweepstakes, and social games such as dominoes, backgammon, checkers, chess, and darts.

2. **Discuss reasons why people visit casinos.**
   A number of socioeconomic and psychological reasons explain why people visit casinos. These include a desire to gamble, recreation and entertainment, social reasons, economic factors, curiosity (must-see), amenities, and prestige.

3. **Explain the organization of a casino.**
   A casino is generally headed by a general manager. He or she directly supervises the work of department heads, including those for hotel operations, human resources, marketing, casino operations, finance, security, surveillance, food and beverage operations, and engineering and maintenance.

4. **Review the revenue and support centers in a typical casino.**
   Revenue centers are departments within the property that generate revenues. These include gaming revenue centers in the casino operations department and nongaming revenue centers such as in hotel operations and food and beverage operations. Support centers are nonrevenue-generating departments that are necessary to assist or support revenue centers.

Common examples in casinos include human resources, marketing, finance (accounting and auditing), security, surveillance, and engineering and maintenance.

5. **Briefly review social problems sometimes associated with gaming.**

   Examples of social problems sometimes associated with gaming include addiction and concerns about organized crime and street crimes.

6. **Discuss challenges confronting the casino entertainment industry.**

   Challenges confronting the casino entertainment industry include the need to attract and retain a qualified work force, the likelihood of increased governmental regulation, and the need to more proactively address problem gaming concerns. Other challenges relate to the use of technology, which may make gaming more accessible offsite and can be used to further improve casino equipment and machines, and increased competition, which may cause casinos to reinvent their operations. Generation of significant revenue streams from nongaming sources and fast-paced international growth in gaming are additional issues confronting today's decision makers in this segment.

FEEDBACK FROM THE REAL WORLD

Our real-world advice comes from the chapter's author, Vincent H. Eade, MA, Professor/Founding Director of the UNLV International Gaming Institute, William F. Harrah College of Hotel Administration, University of Nevada, Las Vegas.

Vince joined the UNLV faculty in 1986. He came to Las Vegas in 1975 to work for the Aladdin Hotel, where he was the assistant general manager and the rooms division manager until 1980. Thereafter, he worked as the corporate director of labor relations for the North Las Vegas Casino Corporation (the Silverbird, the Silver Nugget, and Silver City Casinos). He also served as the Aladdin's director of personnel and labor relations.

What types of positions within the industry are most attractive to graduates of postsecondary hospitality programs?

Graduates seeking a career in the casino entertainment industry often begin in entry-level management positions, in pit operations, and in the slot department, such as a slot floor person. Other graduates pursue careers as casino analysts or in casino marketing. Graduates are also frequently employed in nongaming departments in a hotel–casino in human resources, food and beverage, and the rooms division. Still other graduates work in the gaming industry, but not directly in a casino (for example, in sales positions for slot manufacturing companies or as game trainers for companies that develop new games or gaming devices). Other graduates work in the government regulatory sector.

How, if at all, do management positions in this industry differ from their counterparts in applicable positions in restaurants and hotels? How are they the same?

Let's first address how positions are the same. The casino segment, like the hotel and restaurant segments, is part of the hospitality industry. All segments are in the people or customer service business. Managers in the hospitality industry must understand customer service strategies,

(continued)

whether they work in a casino, hotel, restaurant, club, or other segment. Furthermore, as is the case with any other hospitality segment, the business cannot operate successfully without excellent employees. Managers must have strong human resources management skills, understand employee motivational strategies, including team building, and demonstrate strong coaching, mentoring, and leadership abilities.

The casino industry does have some unique features, challenges, and situations that confront its managers. For example, most casinos operate 24 hours a day, 7 days a week, and are fast-paced businesses. Managing in this environment requires the ability to work nontraditional shifts and to handle heavy volumes of customers (many of whom wager large sums of money). The products (table games and slots, for example) offered in a casino are unique, and managers must understand how the games operate, including the mathematics and game performance expectations. Rooms division managers in a hotel–casino may have to alter their thinking when it comes to selling some rooms. For instance, the top suites in a hotel–casino may not be for sale to the general public but, rather, are put on reserve to be "comped" for top casino customers.

How important are lodging and food and beverage services to the success of large casinos?

Lodging and food and beverage services are vitally important to the success of a casino for several reasons. At one time, casinos virtually gave away rooms, food, and beverages, believing this loss of revenue could be made up by the casino. Today, casino managers want to generate a profit in as many areas as possible or hope, at least, to reduce losses in other areas. Lodging, food, and beverage have become important nongaming revenue centers for casinos. Additionally, these operations serve as a marketing tool for casinos. Guests staying in a casino with lodging accommodations and food and beverage operations can plan extended stays and can enjoy the convenience of meals on-property if they choose to do so. Finally, these amenities add to the entertainment experience people can enjoy at a casino.

What is a typical promotion or career advancement pattern for a talented person desiring a career in the casino entertainment industry?

A person starting a career in pit or table game operations should have an extensive understanding of table game operations and customer relations. Some would argue that they must also have dealer experience. Thereafter, a typical promotion path would be to a floor person, pit manager, director of table games, assistant shift manager (or shift manager), and, finally, casino manager. Those pursuing a career in slots would likely start as a floor person, then progress to shift manager, and eventually to director of slot operations.

Once a student is 21 years old, it would be advantageous to do an internship and/or to secure a part-time job at a casino. This experience will help students understand the various components of the business and provide insights into potential career paths.

MASTERING YOUR KNOWLEDGE

Discuss the following questions.

1. What challenges might confront an experienced hotel manager who assumed that position in a hotel operations department of a casino? Conversely, what challenges will likely confront the experienced hotel operations manager in a casino organization who accepted a top management position in another segment of the lodging industry?

2. What challenges might confront an experienced food and beverage director who moved into the food and beverage department of a casino? Conversely, what challenges will likely confront the experienced food and beverage director in a casino organization who accepted a top management position in another segment of the foodservice industry?

3. What are examples of ways that casinos use two or more persons to control (manage) cash revenues in efforts to reduce theft?

LEARN FROM THE INTERNET

1. Check out the websites of several casinos that are not operated by Native Americans:
   - Resorts Atlantic City: www.resortsac.com
   - Bellagio Hotel & Casino: www.bellagio.com
   - MGM Grand–Las Vegas: www.mgmgrand.com
   - The Venetian Resort: www.venetian.com

   What attractions in addition to gaming do they make available for visitors?

2. Check out the websites of the following casinos and review the information provided about responsible gaming awareness:
   - Greektown Casino: www.greektowncasino.com
   - Mirage Hotel and Casino: www.themirage.com

   - Treasure Island Hotel & Casino: www.treasureisland.com
   - Trump Plaza: www.trumpplaza.com

3. Check out the websites for several Native American casinos:
   - Foxwoods Resort and Casino: www.foxwoods.com
   - Pechanga Resorts & Casino: www.pechanga.com
   - Soaring Eagle Casino & Resort: www.soaringeaglecasino.com

   How is the information provided in these websites similar to that offered by very large casino organizations? How is it different?

KEY HOSPITALITY TERMS

The following terms were explained in this chapter. Review the definitions of any words with which you are unfamiliar. Begin to utilize them as you expand your vocabulary as a hospitality professional.

casino	keno
racino	race book or sports book
gaming	pari-mutuel wagering
wager	casino cage
table games	pit (casino table games)
black jack or twenty-one	boxperson
dice	revenue centers
roulette	support centers
big six	credits (casino gaming tables)
baccarat	fills (casino gaming tables)
mini-baccarat	collusion
pai-gow	slot drop
pai-gow poker	pit clerks
card games	marker
payoff (gaming)	employee assistance program
bingo	

25 Sports and Recreational Foodservices
Part of the Leisure Service Market

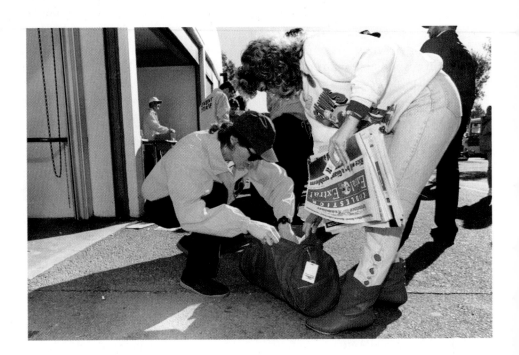

Security concerns limit refreshments that can be brought into a sporting event.

CHAPTER LEARNING OBJECTIVES

After studying this chapter you will be able to:

1. Discuss the scope of the sports and recreational foodservices segment.
2. Explain the organization of a typical sports and recreation operation.
3. Review concession menus and revenue considerations.
4. Note factors that affect concession sales at a sporting event.
5. Outline concession management practices on event day.
6. Discuss catering operations in sports and recreational feeding.
7. Identify challenges confronting sports and recreational foodservices operations.

This chapter was authored by Guy D. Procopio, Concessions Manager, MSU Concessions, Division of Housing and Foodservices, Michigan State University, East Lansing, Michigan.

FEEDBACK FROM THE REAL WORLD

The biggest collegiate football game in the state every year: Michigan State University against the University of Michigan. This year the game will be played on Michigan State's campus in East Lansing. The game will be a sellout (75,000 fans), regardless of the win or loss record of either team. After all, it is a tradition, "bragging rights" for the next 12 months are at stake, and the fans will have a great time even if the weather does not cooperate!

You are the concessions manager in the University's Division of Housing and Foodservices. Among your responsibilities are the food and beverage concessions for all sporting events held on campus.

Assume that you are a very experienced professional and that you effectively manage all resources that are within your control. What are three situations that can occur before or during the game, in spite of your best management procedures, that can negatively affect revenue generation and/or fan pleasure? What, if anything, can you do before and/or after these situations arise?

As you read this chapter, think about answers to these questions and then get feedback from the real world at the end of the chapter.

Is it really "work" when you are managing the food and beverage operations at a stadium where professional or collegiate football, baseball, basketball, hockey, and/or another sport is played? Would a person who likes horse racing and/or auto racing enjoy working in a facility where racing is the main attraction? Almost everyone likes some type of music; what about a job where the "who's who" of professional musicians and star performers from all segments of the entertainment world attract fans for their concerts and other productions?

These types of professional positions exist in the sports and recreational foodservice segment of the hospitality industry. However, just as there is much more to hotel management than a beautiful lobby atrium and the world of restaurants is more than dining rooms with white table cloths, so are sports and recreational foodservices more than "just what fans see" when they attend an attraction or event.

Behind the scenes of the stadiums, coliseums, theaters, and other venues are food and beverage managers working in sports and recreational foodservice (also called concessions) operations. Management positions in these businesses are challenging, tough, and rewarding. They offer opportunities that those aspiring to professional careers in the hospitality industry should know about. This is the purpose of this chapter.

> **OBJECTIVE 1**
> Discuss the scope of the sports and recreational foodservices segment.

ALL ABOUT SPORTS AND RECREATION FOODSERVICES

Opportunities to provide foodservices are present almost anywhere that large numbers of people convene for sports or other recreational purposes. They exist because people increasingly have more **leisure time** and are seeking enjoyable ways to spend this time. **Recreation** is one popular alternative, and the need for foodservices increases as more persons have more leisure time.

There are numerous ways to categorize the **recreational foodservices industry.** A common method focuses on the locations where the food and beverage services are offered:

> **leisure time**   personal time away from work or other responsibilities to do as one wishes
>
> **recreation**   activities that revitalize one's mind and body away from work
>
> **recreational foodservices industry**   foodservices offered for persons enjoying recreational pursuits; also called *rec foods*

Fans purchase snacks from hawkers without leaving their stadium seats.

- *Stadiums and coliseums (arenas).* **Stadiums** are outdoor recreational facilities typically constructed for sporting events that, on occasion, feature other large entertainment events. **Coliseums** (also called arenas) feature indoor seating and are very appropriate not only for some types of sports, but for numerous other types of recreation and entertainment activities.
- *Fairs and festivals.* Large events such as state fairs and smaller events such as agriculture-related exhibitions are examples of activities that attract large numbers of people for sometimes several weeks at a time.

stadiums outdoor recreational facilities

coliseums indoor recreational facilities; also called *arenas*

- *Theater operations.* Motion picture theaters and complexes offer lobby concession operations that generate a very significant percentage of the total revenues that accrue to these operations.
- *Other recreational outlets.* Automobile and horse racing tracks, summer music festivals, indoor and outdoor seasonal events sponsored by communities around the country, and national and state parks, zoos, museums, and aquariums are other examples of events or locations where food and beverage operations can be profitably offered.

While there are numerous exceptions, typically larger-volume and year-round venues tend to be operated by contract management companies. Lower-volume and short-term operations may be managed by contract management companies, but are often managed by the facility's operators. (The length or term of contracts that sports and recreational foodservice clients negotiate with management companies is frequently longer in this segment than in others. Contracts of 10 or more years, with extensions beyond that point, are possible, especially when the management company invests in up-front capital improvement projects.)

OBJECTIVE 2
Explain the organization of a typical sports and recreation operation.

ORGANIZATIONAL STRUCTURE

Exhibit 25.1 shows the organization of a sports and recreation organization in a large stadium. The food and beverage director for the stadium reports to the stadium's general manager. He or she may be an employee of the stadium (if it is self-operated) or, alternatively, an employee of a contract management company. In turn, the food and beverage manager supervises the work of a business manager, a catering manager, a human resources manager, and a concessions manager.

The business manager's duties are, in many ways, similar to those of his or her counterparts in other segments of the hospitality industry. These include responsibility for accounts receivable and payable, development and analysis of financial statements, and payroll management.

Some stadiums offer sit-down foodservices in restaurants and/or bars. These and/or other locations may also offer foodservices in stadium box seat locations. The catering manager supervises a team of food production (catering chef) and outlet managers (for food and beverage service).

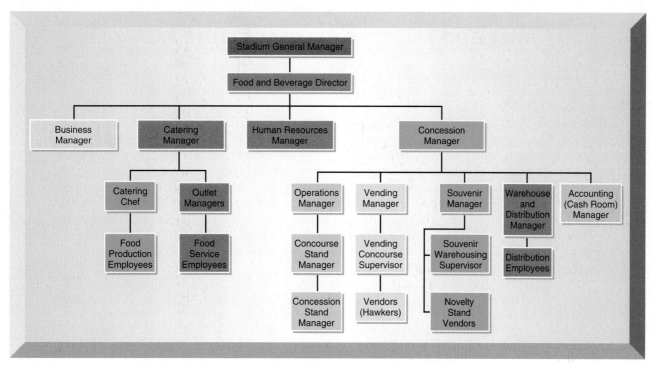

EXHIBIT 25.1
Organization of Sports and Recreation Foodservices in a Large Stadium

Now let's look more closely at the supervisory responsibilities of the concessions manager. Positions supervised include the following:

- *Operations manager.* This individual is responsible for food and beverage sales in permanent and/or temporary food and beverage stands located around the stadium, which is typically divided into areas called concourses. A concourse stand manager directs the work of concession stand managers within his or her concourse.
- *Vending manager.* Persons in this position are responsible for selling (vending) food and beverage products to event attendees who are seated in the stadium during the event. Vending concourse supervisors manage the work of vendors **(hawkers)** who move through assigned areas in the stadium selling (hawking) their products.

hawkers (sports and recreational foodservices) employees in the concessions department of a sports and recreational foodservices venue that move through an assigned area of a stadium selling (hawking) their products

Food and beverages are served in comfortable sky boxes.

WHERE DO ALL THE EMPLOYEES COME FROM?

Sports and recreational foodservice operations typically need many entry-level employees on an infrequent basis. Irregular work schedules and work shifts of perhaps only several hours for several days a month do not appeal to most persons in the work force. So where do these employees come from?

Many sports and recreational foodservice operators in all types of publicly and privately operated venues utilize community organizations whose members volunteer for work at these events as a fund-raising activity for their organization. For example, a community service or church-related group may be assigned a specific concession stand. (In many areas, there is a long waiting list for organizations desiring to work these concession stands.) One member of this volunteer group serves as the concession stand manager and schedules his or her peers to work when the stand is in operation. Typically, volunteer groups receive a specified percentage of the **adjusted revenues** generated by the concession stand.

Can volunteer groups really by relied on to staff concession booths on a regular basis? The answer is yes, and the financial rewards, along with the waiting list to replace nonperforming groups, serve as incentives for reliable and responsible service.

adjusted revenues (sports and recreational foodservices) gross revenues less sales taxes

- *Souvenir manager.* Stadiums typically feature souvenirs at novelty stands located around the stadium that sell retail logo merchandise to attendees. These stands may be self-operated by the stadium. Frequently, however, souvenir sales are contracted to others. (This is the reason why, in Exhibit 25.1, there is a souvenir warehousing supervisor; food and beverage items in storage owned by the stadium or contract management company would not be comingled with inventory items owned by the souvenir vendor.) The souvenir manager manages a souvenir warehousing supervisor and novelty stand vendors.
- *Warehouse and distribution manager.* Persons in this position are responsible to move food and beverage products from centralized areas where they are received and stored to concession stands and other locations where they are sold.
- *Accounting (cash room) manager.* Events attracting tens of thousands of spectators generate very large sums of money that must be carefully accounted for from the time of collection to deposit to follow-up audits. This task is among the responsibilities of the accounting (cash room)

Watching the game while eating and drinking

manager. The division of duties suggested in Exhibit 25.1 is important for control: the operations manager handles issued products, but not money. The cash room manager handles money, but not products. The warehouse manager handles products before they are issued. The business manager reconciles product sales (operations manager) and money (cash room manager).

A CLOSE LOOK AT MENUS AND PRICING

OBJECTIVE 3
Review concession menus and revenue considerations.

When one thinks of menus at sports and recreational foodservice outlets, items such as hot dogs, popcorn, soft drinks, and beer are often at the top of the list. These are popular items and, not surprisingly, generate very high **contribution margins.**

Most items sold in concession operations can be classified into four types:

contribution margin (sports and recreational foodservices) total revenue less all chargeable costs; also called *net revenue*

- Main entrée (for example, hot dogs and pizza)
- Salty snacks (for example, popcorn and peanuts)
- Beverages (hot, cold, and alcoholic)
- Sweets (for example, candy bars)

Nonalcoholic beverages may generate as much as 50 to 60 percent of gross revenues.

The food and beverage items sold at events have several things in common. First, there are few, if any, significant production requirements. Some items (for example, hot dogs and cheese for nachos) need only be heated; popcorn can be quickly prepared in appropriate machines. (In large stadium operations, huge machines in a centralized location may prepare this product. It is then distributed in bulk to concession stands for individual portioning into bags or boxes.) Other items (cold and hot drinks) need only to be dispensed; little or no production skill is required for these items and, therefore, minimal training in food and beverage production is required. Another advantage: little equipment, along with space to place the equipment, is necessary. Also, little time for food and beverage production is needed. This is important because of the significant quantities of food and beverage products that are typically sold during very short time periods at an event.

Concession and stand services (vending) items are almost always sold for cash. The need to make change during a sales transaction significantly slows service. Therefore, prices are typically in dollars (for example, one hot dog for $3.00) and in quarter- or half-dollar (for example, one soft drink is $2.50) increments.

Managers responsible for sports and recreational feeding operations typically develop revenue goals on the basis of estimated attendance at events. (As will be discussed later,

Refreshments keep the fans happy.

per capita   per person, such as the amount of revenue (or expense) per person

point-of-sale (POS) terminal a computer system that contains its own input and output components and, perhaps, some memory capacity, but without a central processing unit

attendance is influenced by weather, time of event, and the economy.) If, for example, 60,000 people typically attend a campus football game and if, historically, concessions revenue has approximated $250,000, the **per capita** revenue of $4.17 ($250,000 ÷ 60,000 persons) can be estimated. This benchmark can be adjusted by, for example, calculations to reflect suggestive selling techniques, facility modifications, and menu price increases to arrive at estimated revenues for future events. Once revenue is known, associated product costs and other costs can be calculated and compared to budget goals. (Per capita concessions revenues in pro sport events such as the World Series or Super Bowl can be $7.00 to $10.00 per game, compared to approximately $5.00 in collegiate football and basketball events.)

OBJECTIVE 4
Note factors that affect concession sales at a sporting event.

FACTORS AFFECTING CONCESSION SALES

Numerous factors influence the volume of revenues and type of sales at a sporting event.

AN INTERESTING FACT!

As a rule of thumb, concession operations managers plan concession stand work stations so that 75 percent of the items sold will be within reaching distance of the employee collecting customer payment (for example, cold beverages, hot dogs, and popcorn). Time is important; it cannot be wasted, as it would be if employees had to walk even a short distance to retrieve an item ordered by a customer.

REVENUE CONTROL IN CONCESSION OPERATIONS

How much money should a concession manager expect to collect from a concession stand at the end of an event? Many concession stands (especially those in high-volume, frequent-event stadiums, which can afford hardware and wiring costs), have **point-of-sale (POS) terminals** (cash register systems.) This equipment makes transactions more accurate, speeds service, and assists with after-event reconciliation. However, even when these machines are available, the service of large numbers of people in very short time periods can easily lead to mistakes and theft of cash.

A common method of revenue control in concessions operations involves the counting of product containers. For example, assume 500 32-ounce soft drink cups are available in the concession stand at the beginning of the event. Then, if 100 are available at the end of the event, 400 cups have been used (500 − 100 = 400). This example is oversimplified because adjustments (such as additional packaging brought to the stand during the event) and waste must also be factored into the calculations. If 32-ounce soft drinks are sold for $3.00, these 400 "missing" soft drink cups represent $1,200 in revenues (400 cups at $3.00 each = $1,200.00). The same process is utilized to determine the quantity of all other food and beverage products (and there may be as many as 40 different items) that have been sold during the event. Then the total quantity of revenues generated (and that must be accounted for at the end of the event) can be assessed.

Weather

Weather has an obvious impact on stadium (outdoor) games, but it also affects the number of fans attending coliseum or arena (indoor) games. For example, concessions managers in colleges and universities in the northeastern and midwestern United States typically think about three "seasons" in a football season of just several months: warm, in-between, and cold. Not surprisingly, sales correlate with these temperatures: warm season = cold beverages; in-between season = more food; cold season = hot beverage sales. When the weather turns unexpectedly bad, food and beverage directors become unhappy just as the fans do; however, it is for a different reason: there are more unanticipated sales of logo clothing and merchandise (which have a lower net revenue) and lower sales of beverages (which have a higher net revenue).

Skiers need food and beverage services.

Time of Game

Typically, the earlier the better. Unfortunately, from the view of concession managers, television and athletic conference contracts dictate game times.

Teams' Success

The history and tradition of the two competing teams, the home team's won or loss record for the current year, and the reputation of the opponent are important factors in attendance.

STAND SERVICE VENDORS ARE IN BUSINESS FOR THEMSELVES!

In many sports and recreational foodservice operations, persons selling food and beverage products to fans seated throughout the stadium are in business for themselves! Throughout the event, these vendors (also called hawkers) go to an assigned central location to obtain additional quantities of the products they are selling. There are two basic methods for paying the hawkers. They might, for example, purchase 50 bags of popcorn paying $1.50 for each bag. They then sell the bags of popcorn to the spectators for $2.00, keeping the profit of $0.50 per bag for themselves. When this process is used, vending managers can control cash revenues at the centralized pickup location in the same way that they do in concession locations: by accounting for product containers.

In a second popular method, the amount of product supplied to hawkers is tracked; at the end of the event they receive a percentage of the revenue generated by the amount of product sold.

Basketball fans anticipate the beginning of the event.

Economy

Individuals purchase personal tickets to sporting events with their discretionary income; business purchases are treated as an entertainment or marketing expense. Money spent for both of these purposes is reduced when there are slowdowns in the economy.

Other Factors

Season schedule (for example, the number of consecutive home games) can sometimes encourage or hinder attendance. Fans may not go to games several weeks consecutively; tickets may be given to others whose per capita spending is different from that of season regulars.

Season ticket holders have a significant influence on concessions revenues. For example, persons purchasing these tickets for collegiate events are typically individuals paying with personal funds. By contrast, corporations purchase large numbers of season tickets for professional sports. These fans are not, then, spending out-of-pocket funds and typically spend more.

CONCESSIONS MANAGERS MUST BE PROACTIVE IN A REACTIVE ENVIRONMENT!

Imagine that you are a concessions manager for a major university. Seventy percent of your annual concession revenue is generated from football games. There are only six home games in the season; there are only three hours of peak retail time when stands are open for business during each game. In other words, 70 percent of your annual revenue will be generated in only 18 retail hours!

Another interesting statistic: 90 percent of concession revenues from a football game are generated from pregame through the end of half-time. Imagine that you are the concessions manager and that the home team is losing by many points prior to half-time. Many spectators will leave before and/or at half-time. Product costs will be excessive, revenues will be down, and the "clock is ticking" for the remainder of football minutes in the calendar year.

MANAGING CONCESSIONS ON EVENT DAY

The day or night of the big event has finally arrived! Let's see what happens behind the scenes before and after the fans buy the concession products.

The best concession stands are those that are independent production centers. They do not rely on external food and beverage production, have adequate equipment and storage, and are self-contained to meet their highest peak sales requirements. (Popcorn may be popped on the day of the event and transported in bulk for individual bagging or boxing at the concession

Nighttime footbal! On a cold evening, more coffee and fewer soft drinks are consumed.

stands.) With few exceptions, then, products need only be heated (hot dogs and pretzels, for example), dispensed (cold and hot drinks, for example), or sold in prepackaged containers (candy bars, potato chips, and peanuts, for example).

Modern sports and recreational facilities are designed with significant attention paid to the needs of concession operators. Space for warehousing, vending pickup, concession stand space, nonpublic elevators for distribution, and private access ways are frequently designed into new facilities when they are constructed. Full-service kitchens to support food production needs for luxury-level suites and club-level seating are built in convenient areas, and **pantries** to serve other locations are also constructed.

Concession stands are stocked before events (sometimes for several events if space permits), but during-event distribution is sometimes necessary as well. Distribution includes the food and beverage products and the disposable supplies (soda cups and popcorn boxes, for example) that will be needed (if space within the stands is ample for this volume of items).

> **OBJECTIVE 5**
> Outline concession management practices on event day.

> pantry (sports and recreational foodservices) a space used to portion prepared food for later service to customers, for example, preportioned hamburger patties may be heated on a grill in a pantry area

---

WHO GETS PAID WHAT?

Food and beverage managers typically make arrangements of several types for selling food and beverage items during events:

Concessions *receive* a percentage of revenues. A branded retailer of ice creams or sandwiches, for example, may pay a percentage of revenues that it generates to the concessions operation in return for the space and opportunity to sell its own products during the game.

Concessions may *give* a percentage of revenues. Many concessions operations utilize volunteer groups to staff concession stands. In return, the group receives a percentage (typically 10 to 15 percent) of the adjusted revenue generated.

Concessions may sell food and beverage products to independent operators. Vendors (hawkers) pay for products at a vending stand and then sell the product at a higher price to spectators in the stands (the excess revenue belongs to the vendors) or they may receive a commission on sales.

Condiments cannot be forgotten.

Concessions managers are concerned about theft of revenue; a stand in a popular location can generate several thousands of dollars (or more) in sales in a very short period of time. Therefore, revenues may be picked up and transported to the money counting room at least three times: when the event begins, during the event, and at the end of the event.

OBJECTIVE 6
Discuss catering operations in sports and recreational feeding.

catering (sports and recreational foodservices) the production of food and beverages for sale to groups of people

JUST LIKE A RESTAURANT!

Catering (the production of food and beverages for sale to groups of people) is increasingly popular in concession operations. Examples range from sit-down restaurants in a stadium to the provision of meals to fans in stadium and coliseum boxes and suites. Guests in sit-down operations may order from menus with a relatively wide range of menu items. Menus available in boxes and suites may be of more limited variety, but still offer "something for everyone." Service in these remote locations ranges from preordered foods that are preportioned for delivery to the areas to buffet lines with "all you care to eat" selections available before (and often during) the event. Some items (for example, soft drinks) may be stocked in the stadium box or suite, and the charge is based on the volume of depleted inventory. Buffets may be supplemented with short-order food production, pasta bars, and a range of desserts (sometimes presented or served from rolling dessert carts!). When preordered menus are used, creative plans, such as a four-game rotating menu (with discount for preordering for the games), are becoming more popular.

OBJECTIVE 7
Identify challenges confronting sports and recreational foodservices operations.

CHALLENGES! CHALLENGES!

Concessions operators have at least one challenge in common with their counterparts in most other segments of the hospitality industry:

- *Frequent difficulty in securing the necessary labor resources.* Like other segments, labor shortages are frequently a problem. This chapter has discussed one creative solution (utilize nonprofit organizations desiring fund-raising opportunities). However, in times of low unemployment rates (fewer people are looking for jobs), positions in this and all other segments of the hospitality industry may go unfilled.

Other challenges confronting sports and recreational foodservices include the following:

- *Critical need for interaction with others.* For example, in college and university sports, interaction between the athletic department and the foodservice division becomes necessary. In professional sports and for concert and other entertainment events, concerns of the concessions department have become more important because of the possibility of significant revenue generation.

- *Need to manage variables that are often beyond the control of the concessions manager.* These challenges have always been part of the concessions business and will likely continue to be so in the future. Numerous variables have been discussed in this chapter.

- *Increasing use of technology.* Concessions managers increasingly use technology to expedite forecasting, ordering, and reconciliation and to manage inventories and determine revenues. Still to come, however, are creative ways to reduce the guesswork associated with making longer-term decisions about revenue estimates.

- *Countering public perceptions about the price and value of concession purchases.* Spectator concerns about the selling prices of concession products are not unusual. They increase when safety and security concerns place limits on the items (frequently none!) that spectators can bring into an event. Concession profits (net revenue) can be high (30 to 55 percent of an item's selling price may remain when all allocated expenses are addressed). However, these monies are typically split between the concessions operations and athletic department (in a self-operated college or university program) or between concessions and the stadium in other types of events that depend on concession revenues to support the operations. When a contract management company operates concessions, fees for its services must be paid according to contract (immediately after the game, monthly, or quarterly, for example).

  Creative concessions managers are addressing the price and value challenge by offering **combo units** (several menu items packaged together at a selling price less than the sum of their individual prices). This tactic is in common use by the quick-service segment as well. Another approach: sell larger product packages (at a lower cost per ounce or fluid ounce than when smaller-sized packages are purchased).

combo units a combination meal in which several menu items are packaged together at a selling price less than the sum of their individual prices

---

WHO OPERATES CATERING SERVICES?

Like other segments in the hospitality industry, the organization of catering services in concession operations can be complicated. For example, a sports and recreational venue may provide all of its own concessions and catering services (self-operated). Alternatively, it may provide the concessions and subcontract catering to another organization. Alternatively, it may operate concessions and interact with a contract management company to provide catering services (or vice versa).

SUMMARY OF CHAPTER LEARNING OBJECTIVES

1. **Discuss the scope of the sports and recreational foodservices.**

   Opportunities to provide foodservices exist almost anywhere that large numbers of people convene for sports or recreational purposes. These include stadiums and coliseums (arenas), fairs and festivals, theater operations, and other recreational outlets, including automobile and horse racing tracks, summer music festivals, indoor and outdoor seasonal events, national and state parks, zoos, museums, and aquariums.

2. **Explain the organization of a typical sports and recreation operation.**

   The food and beverage manager is supervised by a stadium general manager and, in turn, supervises the work of a business manager, a catering manager (responsible for bulk food production), a human resources manager, a concessions manager (who is responsible for concessions sales, vending (in-stand) sales, souvenir sales, warehouse distribution, and cash room reconciliations).

3. **Review concession menus and revenue considerations.**

   Most menu items sold in concessions operations can be classified as main entrees, salty snacks, beverages, and sweets. Some operations have licenses to sell alcoholic beverages. Selling prices are established at a rate that makes it easy to make change (for example, rounded dollars or $0.25 increments).

4. **Note factors that affect concession sales at a sporting event.**

   Numerous factors affect concession sales, including weather, time of game, teams' success, economy, and season schedule.

5. **Outline concession management practices on event day.**

   The best concession stands are independent production centers. Revenue is tracked on the basis of the number of package units (for example, soft drink cups) sold based on pre- and postevent counts (after adjustments) of package units. Revenues may be picked up and transported to the money counting room before, during, and at the end of the event.

6. **Discuss catering operations in sports and recreational feeding.**

   Catering ranges from sit-down restaurants in a stadium to the provision of meals in stadium boxes and suites. Menus range from the offering of a relatively wide range of items to more limited preordered food items. Buffets and even an extensive variety of desserts can be offered.

7. **Identify challenges confronting sports and recreational foodservice operations.**

   Challenges include the frequent difficulty in securing necessary labor resources, the critical need for interaction with others, the need to manage variables beyond the concessions manager's control, increasing use of technology, and the management of public perceptions about the price and value of concession purchases.

MASTERING YOUR KNOWLEDGE

Discuss the following questions.

1. What are some ways that managing food and beverage products and labor in sports and recreational foodservice operations are the same as in hotel and restaurant foodservices? What are some ways in which they are different?

2. What potential problems can arise as concessions managers account for stand revenues utilizing the package unit approach discussed in the chapter?

3. If you were asked to design the food production and service aspects of a large sports and recreational facility, what are some of the major concerns you would address and how would you address them?

FEEDBACK FROM THE REAL WORLD

Our real-world advice comes from Guy Procopio, Concessions Manager, MSU Concessions, Division of Housing and Foodservices, Michigan State University.

In his current position, Guy Procopio oversees food and novelty sales at all concessions-related events at Michigan State University. He has served as the president of the National Association of Collegiate Concessionaires and as a board member of the National Association of Concessionaires. His undergraduate degree is in material and logistics management.

Our feedback issue relates to situations that can occur before or during a game. An experienced pro is not likely to experience difficulty with, for example, nonfunctioning equipment (it is under a preventive maintenance program), nor will concession stands run out of products (they will have been stocked with adequate supplies based on sales history information). But here are three situations that can occur that are beyond one's control.

Situation 1: *Weather Changes before or during the Game*

Consider, for example, a rainy and/or cold day that turns sunny and warm during the event, or the reverse. Cold beverages sell better in warmer weather; warm beverages sell better in cold weather. Since markups are higher for cold beverages (soft drinks) than for warm beverages (coffee and hot chocolate), concessionaires hope for warm weather. The worst-case weather is torrential rain (fans either buy less food and drinks or, at least, don't take them into the stands but, instead, consume the products under cover of the stadium) or an extremely cold blizzard (which might keep some fans at home). (Michigan State concession managers always expect at least 60,000 fans for every game regardless of the weather and the win–loss record of both teams.)

Management Tactics

Concessionaires monitor the weather closely for several days before the game. They adjust concession stand inventories as game day draws closer. Inventories include both products and other items. For example, cold weather means more coffee and cocoa souvenir mugs will have to be stocked in the stands. Hot weather requires more large soft drink cups, in-cluding souvenir mugs. Effectively designed stands are basically self-operated and require limited assistance from concessions staff during an event. Stands have equipment to make required hot beverages and have ample storage for cold beverages, including the water and ice needed for beverages and to cool the bottles of water. Experienced stand managers know how to proactively respond to weather change during a game. For example, if it begins to rain or turn cool during the game's first half, they will begin to prepare additional quantities of hot beverages to be ready for increased sales during half-time. They know that, if they are not ready, sales will be missed.

At Michigan State, merchandise such as rain gear (ponchos and hats) is sold by subcontractors. They must also anticipate and prepare for the impact of changing weather in their sales. Use of these tactics allows salespersons to be ready with the right product regardless of the weather.

Situation 2: *Inadequately Staffed Concession Stands*

As you have learned, many concession stands are staffed by volunteers from nonprofit organizations that receive significant funds from the

(continued)

efforts of their volunteer members. Unfortunately, groups can, on rare occasions, not show up or provide an inadequate number of stand employees.

Management Tactics

The immediate response is to ask volunteers from other stands to help out (frequently there are more than the necessary workers in some stands). Each group who provided extra assistance would receive a prorated share of the stand's revenue percentage that would otherwise be given to the organization originally assigned to the stand. It is also possible to bring in a backup service group of individual members to work where needed. For example, a volunteer group of 12 to 16 persons might be hired for a flat fee of $250.00 to work anywhere and everywhere during the game. Over the longer term, concession managers use groups with a great track record of past assistance. Problem organizations are eliminated, and managers assure that organizations are well aware of the funding assistance they receive. They also explain that other groups would like to work with the university (there is a waiting list) and are available if necessary.

Situation 3: *A Game with a One-Sided Score at Half-Time*

If one team is winning by a large margin, many fans will likely leave early, and concessions personnel will have been busy during the first half of the game getting ready for significant half-time sales that will not occur. Significant hawker sales can also be lost during the second half of the game if fans leave early.

Management Tactics

There is little that can be done to reduce the cost of the perishable foods that have been produced during the first half of the game and that will now not be sold. Stands will stay open as late as possible to maximize sales for the fans who do stay. Hawkers will still be sent into the stadium at half-time and during the second half to provide products to fans who may make impulse purchases while at their seats. Bagged ice that is still in good condition can be placed back in the freezer. Some prepared foods might be available for donation to local charities. However, since items will have to be counted to determine sales that were made to determine concession stand commissions, this could be difficult to do because of sanitation problems caused by time lapses and handling and rehandling during postgame inventory procedures. (Concession managers typically do not discount selling prices to encourage additional sales, since fans will likely expect discounting in the future. Also, labor cannot be reduced, since it is almost like a fixed cost, because of the need to clean up the stand before the next event.)

LEARN FROM THE INTERNET

1. Check out the websites for the following companies:
   - Ovations Food Services: www.ovationsfoodservices.com
   - ARAMARK: www.aramark.com
   - Centerplate: www.centerplate.com

   What type of information, if any, is provided about the sports and recreational foodservice units that they operate? What kinds of position vacancies do they advertise?

2. Compass Group North America (www.cgnad.com) purchased Levy Restaurants in 2006. Levy Restaurants is a leader in sports and entertainment foodservice, with more than 30 percent of professional sports teams in its portfolio. To view its website, go to www.levyrestaurants.com. What factors are suggested that make this organization successful? What are the current events publicized in the site's newsroom?

3. Check out the website for the National Association of Concessionaires: www.naconline.com. What are the major topics and challenges that this association is addressing for its members? Also, review the website for the National Association of Collegiate Concessionaires: www.nacc-online.com. What are its special concerns and interests?

KEY HOSPITALITY TERMS

The following terms were explained in this chapter. Review the definitions of any words with which you are unfamiliar. Begin to utilize them as you expand your vocabulary as a hospitality professional.

leisure time
recreation
recreational foodservices industry
stadiums
coliseums
hawkers (sports and recreational foodservices)
adjusted revenues (sports and recreational
    foodservices)

contribution margin (sports and recreational
    foodservices)
per capita
point-of-sale (POS) terminal
pantry (sports and recreational foodservices)
catering (sports and recreational foodservices)
combo units

26 Management of Amusement and Theme Parks

A statue of Walt Disney welcomes visitors to Walt Disney World Resort near Orlando, Florida

CHAPTER LEARNING OBJECTIVES

After studying this chapter you will be able to:

1. Define the terms *amusement park* and *theme park.*
2. Provide a brief history of amusement and theme parks.
3. Explain basic planning issues of concern to theme park managers.
4. Discuss safety and security aspects of amusement and theme park management.
5. Review employment opportunities in the amusement and theme park segment of the hospitality industry.
6. Review long- and short-term challenges confronting the amusement and theme park industry.

This chapter was authored by Duncan R. Dickson, Assistant Professor, Rosen College of Hospitality Management, University of Central Florida, Orlando, Florida.

FEEDBACK FROM THE REAL WORLD

As disposable income in the United States grows and as individuals have more leisure time, theme and amusement parks become an increasingly important part of the hospitality industry. With its extensive theme park operations, Orlando, Florida, has become the number one tourism destination in the world. Theme parks can be an important economic catalyst for a region and offer a variety of exciting career opportunities for those involved.

Many segments of the hospitality industry allow guests (visitors) to escape their daily routines by offering enjoyable experiences that are not part of their daily lives. However, amusement and theme park operators can do this in a way that no other organization can. In the old days, parents took their children to sites where they could enjoy relatively simple (by today's standards!) rides and foods (don't forget the cotton candy!). Today, children of all ages (especially the parents!) enjoy the out-of-this-world attractions and amenities offered by amusement and theme parks worldwide. And, in fact, a one-day visit is typically insufficient to see and do everything.

What are the major sources of revenue generated by amusement and theme parks? How, if at all, does the management of food and beverage operations differ between more traditional operations like hotels and restaurants and amusement and theme parks? How do managers meet the labor fluctuations during seasonal changes in business volumes? What is the general process used to determine whether and when rides and shows should be added to a park?

As you read this chapter, think about answers to these questions and then get feedback from the real world at the end of the chapter.

Today, people in the United States and in many other countries have more **leisure time** than they have ever had before. (France, for example, recently instituted a mandated 35-hour work week.) The **leisure industry** has grown in concert with increased opportunities to spend time away from work because, as the amount of this time expands, people are looking for more things to do. The pursuit of **recreation** includes visits to attractions and theme parks, which are the topic of this chapter.

WHAT'S THE DIFFERENCE?

Is there a difference between an **amusement park** and a **theme park**? Yes, technically there is. An amusement park is a collection of rides and activities located in a central area or park with no unifying theme. Typically, each attraction or ride requires its own admission or ticket, and tickets may be sold separately or in blocks. Traditionally, amusement parks have not been gated.

By contrast, theme parks charge an admission price at the gate that allows visitors access to all attractions within the park. Most theme parks focus on a dominant theme (such as, in the case of Disney, fantasy, adventure, and movies, among others). The theme, then, is reflected in the architecture, landscaping, costumes of park employees, rides, shows, foodservices, retail merchandising, and other visitor-related experiences.

HISTORY OF AMUSEMENT AND THEME PARKS

Amusement parks began with the festivals in Europe during the Middle Ages (about A.D. 500 to 1500). People gathered together to sell and barter or trade goods and to celebrate harvests. It was natural for entertainment to become part

leisure time personal time away from work or other responsibilities to do as one wishes

leisure industry businesses that appeal to the leisure market; these include organizations offering entertainment, recreation, cruises, and gaming

recreation activities that revitalize one's mind and body away from work

OBJECTIVE 1
Define the terms *amusement park* and *theme park*.

amusement park a collection of rides and activities located in a central area with no unifying theme and separate admission or ticket requirements for each attraction

theme park a destination that creates an atmosphere and environment of another place and time, enclosed in a central area with an admission price paid at the gate that allows visitors access to all attractions

Restaurant food-service operations at theme parks such as Disneyland in California are enjoyed by visitors and are important revenue centers for the parks

OBJECTIVE 2
Provide a brief history of amusement and theme parks.

of these celebrations and, from these events, came the early amusement parks. (The oldest [Bakken] still in business dates from the mid-1600s in Denmark.)

Most amusement parks offered simple rides, gardens, and entertainment and typically operated on a limited schedule. (For example, in St. Petersburg, Russia, the ice slides were popular in winter.) Most of these amusement parks ceased operation, in large part, because of civil unrest that arose during the 1800s in Europe.

In the United States, amusement parks became popular because of two influences: the concentration of people in industrialized cities and a need for ridership of the new electric railways on weekends. New Age amusement parks were built at the ends of these electric railways. The most famous was New York's Coney Island, built in 1884.

By 1920, there were about 1,400 amusement parks in the United States. A combination of several events (among them the introduction of radio and talking motion pictures, a worldwide depression beginning in 1929, and events that would lead to a world war) reduced the number of amusement parks to less than 400 by 1938.

The Modern Theme Park

Walt Disney invented the modern theme park in 1955 when he opened Disneyland in California. Disney had been involved in the film industry and had specialized in animation. He brought these two disciplines (theatrics and story telling) together and created an environment that was clean, orderly, safe, and family oriented. Before Disneyland, vast numbers of people could only see fantasies in movies, but at Disneyland they could "step into them" as they cruised down a jungle river or rode in a spaceship into the future. His theme park allowed the total involvement of one's senses into an entertainment experience.

Disney's theme park concept has now spread worldwide, and many refinements to the concept have been made since 1955 by the Disney organization and other theme park operators.

Portable popcorn wagon at a Disney theme park

THEME PARKS ARE REALLY A BIG BUSINESS

Since 1955, the playing field for theme parks has changed significantly. Disneyland quickly became a destination and proved to potential investors and marketing experts that a theme park had a broad customer base. Competition became integral to the theme park industry in 1961 when Six Flags over Texas opened in Dallas.

Major corporations dominate today's theme park industry. The Walt Disney Company does not have the greatest number of parks; however, it dominates in attendance, with nine of their properties ranking in the top 15 most attended parks. (The top eight parks ranked by attendance are Disney Parks.)

Six Flags Corporation has the most theme parks (40); however, many do not operate year round. The other large, multipark operators are these:

Top Amusement and Theme Park Chains, 2005

Walt Disney Company (12 parks)	100.0+ million visitors
Universal Studios Theme Parks (6 parks)	29.45 million visitors
Busch Gardens Adventure (9 parks)	16.00 million visitors
Six Flags Theme Parks (40 parks)	13.83 million visitors
Cedar Fair, L.D. (18 parks)	6.78 million visitors
Paramount Parks (6 parks)	5.90 million visitors

Note: Water parks are included.
Source: *Amusement Business,* December 12, 2005.

Disney learned an early lesson. He bought back all the leases he had sold to raise money for land purchases and for construction and preopening expenses as quickly as he could. Why? Because Walt learned that, to have a successful theme park, one must have total control over its environment and its revenue potential.

A theme park communicates its stories primarily through visual and vocal statements. However, in reality, efforts are made to incorporate all five of our senses. Theme park planners know that authenticity is not the key to good theming; believability is the key, and it all starts with a good story.

HOW THEME PARKS OPERATE

OBJECTIVE 3
Explain basic planning issues of concern to theme park managers.

The primary reason that visitors come to theme parks is to enjoy the rides and the attractions. However, they spend money (lots of money!) on parking, admission fees, food and beverage products, merchandise and souvenirs (retail sales), and other purchases. Some, especially large theme parks, also have hotels or other lodging accommodations in the park or nearby.

To be successful, theme parks must provide a safe, clean, and happy environment and experience for their visitors. To do this requires the consistent delivery of outstanding service. This is an incredibly difficult goal to attain, and careful planning to prevent potential obstacles to service is required.

Most theme parks are very large. This typically distinguishes them from amusement parks, although one of the latter (Blackpool in the United Kingdom) hosted 6 million guests in 2005. A significant amount of capital investment is required to purchase land, build buildings and access ways, construct rides (modern high-thrill rides often cost millions of dollars!), and develop other elements in the park's **infrastructure.** In effect, construction never

infrastructure utility systems, roads and sidewalks, land improvements, and other site construction required before building construction begins

multiplier effect the spin off financial benefits derived from the operation of a business or industry within a community or other area

Goliath Roller Coaster, Six Flags Magic Mountain, Valencia, California

ends, because there is an ongoing need to reinvest in the park to maintain a competitive position.

Community leaders like theme parks because they yield jobs due to the **multiplier effect**. Economic forecasters estimate that several (or more) jobs are also created within the local community for every job that is created in a theme park. As in other segments of the hospitality industry, positions are service related and require people, not machines, to deliver required services. Theme parks also boost tourism to an area and sometimes become the destination by themselves. (Walt Disney World Resort near Orlando, Florida, and Dollywood in Pigeon Forge, Tennessee, are examples.) Theme parks also generate significant tax revenues, which help to support their host community's public services. Close and cooperative interaction between community leaders and park owners and managers is, then, important.

Every detail of a theme park from the perspective of its potential visitors must be carefully thought out. Admission fees at many parks are pricey (sometimes in excess of US $60 a day), and marketing tactics to sell the park as a value are absolutely critical to bring visitors to the park. Once there, procedures to quickly help visitors move through admission gate queue lines, pay the fees, and enter the park become necessary. Pedestrian and service, security, and emergency vehicle traffic flow concerns throughout the park are important, as is ease of movement if the need for park evacuation or other emergency arises. This process is called **way finding**.

way finding a term used in the amusement and theme park industry that refers to pedestrian and service, security, and emergency vehicle traffic flow throughout the park

DID YOU KNOW?

Amusement and theme park managers and their guest are concerned about ticket prices. During the 2006 summer season, Six Flags Great Adventure in New Jersey charged $59.99 per day for adult admissions. To counter price resistance, it added more entertainment and Looney Tunes characters and was making efforts to reduce waits for rides and food. Universal World, Walt Disney World, and Sea World Orlando charged $60.00 per day for a one-park visit, but their prices dropped for multiday ticket purchases.

By contrast, Cedar Point Amusement Park (Ohio) reduced its adult admission prices by $5.00 and sold cotton candy for 25¢. Holiday World (Indiana) began offering free soft drinks throughout the park.

While admission fees have climbed steadily over the past years, many parks offer discounts for persons buying tickets online, discount coupons when purchases are made at local stores, or reduced ticket prices when visitors bring specified products, such as cans of soft drinks or pizza boxes.

Source: Theme parks try new pricing at gates. Retrieved May 9, 2006, from www.cnn.worldnews.printthis.clickability.com

WHO LIKES THEME PARKS?

When you think of visitors to theme parks, do you think of children and/or a family including children? In fact, more adults visit theme parks than do children! People of all ages from the very young to the very old enjoy theme parks because they create an unforgettable experience.

Food and beverage outlets from **kiosks** offering just one or very few items at relatively low cost to sit-down table-service operations offering menus with a wide product and selling price range are typical. These must be developed and constructed.

Large theme parks have several thousand employees. Where will they be trained, change into their uniforms, eat, and have access to other human resources needs?

The number of visitors drives the planning of theme park operations. For example, an estimate of the number of park visitors is determined, and this drives revenue benchmarks for all revenue-producing outlets in the park. With revenues known, expenses likely to be incurred to generate the expected revenue levels can be developed.

The time that visitors wait for access to park rides and other

kiosks very small refreshment (concession) stands offering just one or a very few food or beverage products

Kumba Roller Coaster at Busch Gardens, Tampa, Florida

VIRTUAL QUEUING HELPS THE PARK AND THE VISITOR

FASTPASS™ is a virtual queuing system developed by Disney, and Universal uses a similar system called Universal Express. It allows a visitor to swipe his or her entrance ticket at an attraction with a long line (wait). The computer then assigns a time for the visitor to return, and he or she can then go to the front of the line.

The computer tracks visitors and assures that no visitor has more than one FASTPASS at a time. The visitor, in effect, waits in a virtual line and is therefore free to move throughout the park (and perhaps purchase food and beverage products and merchandise), rather than waiting in a real line, where one cannot move around and spend money.

Who benefits? The visitor and the park. Technology helps again to resolve problems, so everybody wins.

Note: Want to learn more about virtual queuing? See Dickson, D., et al., "Managing Real and Virtual Waits in Hospitality Service Organizations". *Cornell Hotel and Restaurant Quarterly*, 46(1);52–68, 2005.

Retail shops generate substantial revenue

attractions must be known, and procedures must be in place to optimize this time without sacrificing safety and other concerns. Studies by a park's industrial engineers are undertaken to assess the best wait times, which should not be too long or too short. (A wait that is too short allows visitors to rapidly move through the attractions and then leave the park. A wait that is too long keeps visitors away from retail shops and food and beverage outlets. Disney parks have implemented a virtual queuing system called the FASTPASS®. This allows visitors to enjoy a virtual wait that allows them to peruse the park's shops and food emporiums.

Detailed training for each task in each position is necessary. Employees are typically cross-trained so that they can assume duties in several positions when needed. This is especially helpful in parks with significant seasonal or other business operations, including hotels, night clubs, and restaurants. Cross-trained staff allows the minimum number of employees to be on duty while helping to assure that the park's quality of service standards are consistently attained.

Operating concerns continue as requirements of the **Americans with Disabilities Act (ADA)** must be met. Wheelchair access is important to assure that all visitors have equal access to all the park's attractions.

Signage (including signs in different languages) is also important. Retail sales (merchandise and souvenirs) create significant revenues at most theme parks. Point-of-sale merchandising and suggestive selling tactics by retail clerks can be helpful to increase sales. The park's design or layout can also affect revenues. For example, do the main traffic patterns move visitors between food and beverage and retail outlets as part of the park's traffic flow? Are visitors routed through applicable souvenir areas after visiting rides, shows, and other attractions?

Americans with Disabilities Act (ADA) a federal law providing civil rights protection to persons (visitors, guests, and employees); among other provisions, it guarantees equal opportunities for disabled individuals in public accommodations and employment

SAFETY AND SECURITY IN THEME PARK MANAGEMENT

OBJECTIVE 4
Discuss safety and security aspects of amusement and theme park management.

Ongoing security is necessary to consistently maintain a safe environment, which is a prerequisite to attracting visitors to amusement and theme parks. In most (but not all) parks, visitors travel on foot. Crowd and traffic flow concerns become important. First-aid stations must be conveniently located, and uniformed and plain-clothed security personnel are needed to circulate throughout the park.

Large parks typically have one or more full-time safety inspectors. Staff members hired for security positions, as well as all other park employees, typically participate in security awareness programs. Topics may include protecting personal and company assets, monitoring for counterfeiting schemes, fire and rape prevention, substance abuse (for employees and visitors), and procedures to reduce shoplifting.

Most theme parks utilize electronic surveillance equipment in addition to security personnel to constantly monitor all areas, from the external parking lots and park perimeters to the inside of retail merchandise areas. Furthermore, park security personnel has historically had to know the detailed precautions necessary when weather alerts arise. Today, increased terrorism threats pose new dangers that must be addressed by proactive security personnel.

Security staff are at the heart of a theme park's **risk management** program. In this capacity, they play a significant role in reducing liability costs arising from accidents. Theft by visitors and employees is also a potential ongoing concern, and park security personnel are involved in activities to deter internal and external thefts.

While safety and security concerns are important everywhere in the park, procedures applicable to park rides and attractions are a priority. Preventive maintenance, effective instructions to visitors, and careful observation to assure that all procedures are followed all the time are very important. When inspection and safety standards are not addressed, injury, deaths, and lawsuits are likely.

Some parks utilize sophisticated technology to assist in security management; others do not. Security personnel on horseback and dogs (for example, for drug and bomb detection) are used in some parks as part of ongoing safety and security efforts.

Entrance to Fantasyland at Disneyland Park in Anaheim, California

risk management the process of conserving an organization's assets by reducing the threat of losses that arise from uncontrollable events

RISING STAR PROFILE

Melissa Pennell
Catering Guest Service Manager
Disney's Contemporary Regional Catering
Lake Buena Vista, Florida

The Straight and Narrow Path Usually Isn't the Shortest Path!

Melissa received an associate of arts degree with a history major in May 2000 and a bachelor of science in hospitality management from the University of Central Florida in August 2002. She is currently working on a master's of science in hospitality management from the University of Massachusetts, Amherst.

She has worked for the Walt Disney World Resort for more than six years in positions including attractions hostess, special events coordinator, supergreeter, restaurant manager, and catering manager. She also has experience with Old Navy Clothing Company and the Gettysburg National Military Park. While studying on her master's degree, she worked for the catering department at the University of Massachusetts, Amherst.

Melissa's hospitality industry experiences are very interesting: "I started working for Walt Disney World in April 1997 as an attractions hostess for the Great Movie Ride. I worked in other positions while at the Disney–MGM Studios and also worked the Doug Live! Show, the

(continued)

Indiana Jones Epic Stunt Spectacular, The Voyage of the Little Mermaid, and The Making of Armageddon attractions. I then became a coordinator for special events and worked on other events, including Super Soap Weekends, Star Wars Weekends, New Year's Eve Events, Regis and Kathie Lee Tapings, Disney Channel Concerts, Annual Passholder Events, and other out of the ordinary occurrences within the studios.

In 1999, I worked as a guest liaison for Radio Disney. I was the contact between day guests and B. B. Goode (the midday DJ for the nationally syndicated show). When I left the studios in 2000, I headed to the waterparks as a supergreeter. I spent a few days a week at each of the three waterparks coordinating games and special events for the guests. I also worked as a guest services hostess at Typhoon Lagoon after the summer season. In March 2001, I accepted an intern position at Disney's Caribbean Beach Resort's food and beverage department, where I oversaw six quick-service locations, a full-service restaurant, a pool bar, and room service. At the end of the internship, I was moved to the Stands East Department of Magic Kingdom Restaurant Operations, where I spent just under a year running 11 snack locations. From there I came to my current location as a catering guest service manager for Disney's Contemporary Resort and Magic Kingdom Park. After two years in this role, I decided to return to school full time and accepted a position as a teaching/research assistant at the University of Massachusetts, Amherst. I spent 18 months in Massachusetts, working on my degree and completing various research projects for the university. At the end of my program, I returned home to Florida and Walt Disney World and assumed my previous position.

What is the most unforgettable moment in your career?

I will never forget the feeling I had at the end of the first major event that I supervised. All the hours of work were well worth it when I heard the gasps coming from the attendees as they entered the event. Although they will never know the work it took to put it together, just the excitement of having the event run from start to finish without major issues is satisfying.

What are the most significant challenges facing your segment of the industry? How are they being addressed?

The downturn in the economy has significantly reduced the number of bookings, especially in the long range. We have turned to focusing on short-term bookings and local social events. There is also an initiative to find creative means of providing service; we are cutting back in certain areas but covering for these in other areas. Most significantly, my company has turned to putting new technology to work in our locations. Adjusting to these new processes has brought new challenges to a functionally nontechnical industry. Individuals with little experience with computers are having to learn how to adapt to the technology.

What, if anything, would you do differently in your career?

I would not change a thing about my career. Everything I have done to date has been a learning experience, and I would not be where I am today without this experience. I took chances. Some were positive; some were negative. However, all the experiences added up to make me the leader that I am today. Choosing to leave the industry for a period of time was important to my development, and I would do it again in a moment. I learned so much about myself while I was in graduate school. Although I knew throughout my undergraduate experience that I wanted to complete a master's degree, it was important to me to have a solid understanding of the industry prior to returning to the classroom. The years I spent in the industry gave me this basis for extending my education with real-world experience. I cannot exactly put my finger on it, but I knew when it was the right time to go back to school. Not that it wasn't a scary move—leaving the comfort of a regular job—but I experienced so many things that I would not have been able to do staying in Orlando and in the "real-world." I am happy where I am, and all of my choices to this point have led me here, so it must have been the right thing to do!

What is your advice for young people considering a career in your industry segment?

Don't be afraid to take chances. The straight and narrow path isn't the only path (and usually isn't the shortest path). Experience is a great teacher.

EMPLOYMENT OPPORTUNITIES

As with many hospitality companies, careers with theme park organizations can be categorized into operating and support positions. Exhibit 26.1 shows major departments in an organization chart for a large theme park. You will note that most departments have familiar titles (they are used in other hospitality organizations); one (rides and attractions) offers positions not applicable to other segments of the hospitality industry. Let's look at some elements within each of these types of positions.

Visitor Contact Departments

The majority of revenue generated by most theme parks is derived from three distinct areas: admissions, food and beverage, and retail operations. The first area (admissions) is managed by the accounting and finance department. The other two areas are part of the operations department. Staff members in several other departments (entertainment and special events, security, parking, and custodial) also have significant visitor contact.

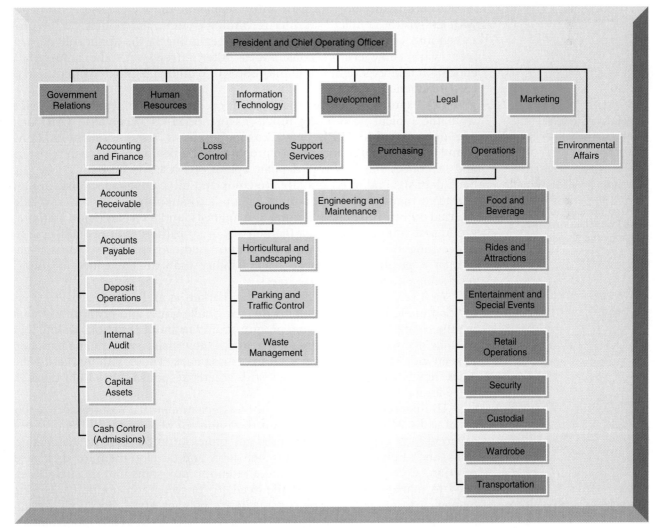

EXHIBIT 26.1
Organization Chart (Major Departments) in Large Theme Park

These operating departments typically have a management hierarchy that allows for entry-level positions or significant promotion from within. There are numerous opportunities for the right person. For example, if you are looking for a career track providing good upward mobility, but you don't want the constant relocation that some segments require, you could do well in a theme park environment. By contrast, persons desiring promotion within a multiunit hotel or restaurant organization may need to relocate to receive the promotion.

The human resources management issues and challenges in a theme park career are similar to those in other segments of the hospitality industry. One difference relates to the schedule changes that theme parks must endure. Operating schedules typically change by season, so there is often a high reliance on part-time and casual labor. Another difference is the high concentration of employees in one location. Walt Disney World Resort, near Orlando, has more than 55,000 "cast members," making it one of the world's largest single-site employers.

Support Departments

As with hospitality operations in other segments, there are also departments with less visitor contact that offer rewarding careers. Individuals can be promoted into some of these positions after beginning in the applicable department with entry-level responsibilities. Alternatively, with the appropriate education and experience, one may enter into some positions without entry-level experience.

accounts receivable (AR) money owed to the organization because of sales made on credit

accounts payable (AP) the total of all invoices owed by the organization to its vendors for credit purchases made by the property

For example, consider the accounting and finance department. Aside from the typical accounting functions of **accounts receivable (AR)** and **accounts payable (AP),** heavy cash operations require tellers utilizing sound cash-control procedures to prepare the banks for all the cash registers and to collect the funds. A deposit operations team is needed to prepare bank deposits and to recirculate the coins and bills. Other specialists are required to manage the expenditure of funds to support the operations. Add internal audits, financial planning and analysis, and a research and statistics group and you can see that a theme park organization requires a diverse finance function. Persons with an accounting education may begin their career in a position with more responsibility than an entry-level accounts receivable or accounts payable clerk.

As a second example, consider the marketing and sales team. Positions in this functional area are equally diverse, challenging, and rewarding. Imagine the promotions, advertising programs, and/or public relations events that must be planned and implemented to attract new visitors to a theme park and to keep the regulars or repeat visitors coming back. Those with marketing degrees may begin work in positions with greater responsibilities than those in entry-level positions.

Human resources is an example of a department that requires a complex set of skills. How would you recruit thousands of persons to fill hundreds of different jobs; orient the newly hired personnel; train them in the knowledge, skills, and abilities required to do their jobs; and develop them for their next position? Consider also the employee retention programs that must be developed to manage turnover and the need for ongoing consultation with line managers to assure that the organization's policies and procedures are applied appropriately and consistently. There are, indeed, great opportunities, especially for line managers with an interest in human resources.

Some line managers make a career shift from attractions management to ride design and installation. (Engineering and design experts may lack

Visitors line up at a ticket booth at Coney Island in New York City

the solid operational knowledge necessary to design and install a successful attraction.)

Not all theme parks have all the departments (functional areas) noted in Exhibit 26.1. The organization chart does, however, suggest the functions that are often necessary to make a major theme park successful. It provides an overview of the great diversity of talent necessary to run a park. Career opportunities abound for all types of individuals with all types of backgrounds. A suggestion: don't worry about where you start; you will find that there are numerous promotion from within opportunities in whatever department and at whatever level you begin.

CHALLENGES! CHALLENGES!

Not surprisingly, two challenges are of interest or concern to employees of the amusement and theme park industry, just as they are to managers in almost all other segments of the hospitality industry: recruiting and retaining a sufficient number of employees at all organizational levels and exploiting technology to use it most cost effectively.

However, these issues are of special concern of this segment because of the significant growth forecasted. As more people around the world gain additional leisure time, they will be looking for opportunities to spend it. This, in turn, will likely lead to an increase in the number of theme parks in locations throughout the world where they do not currently exist or where expansion of existing parks will be viewed as the best alternative to meet rising demand. China and India, with their burgeoning economies, are great examples of areas that are prime for expansion of theme parks. Also, a country like Dubai, which wants to shift its economy from a total dependence on oil and perhaps become the resort area of choice in the Middle East, is developing a theme park. Industry planners must consider whether new parks duplicate existing ones or, alternatively, whether new concepts will be most profitable. (If so, what are they?) As expansion occurs and especially if there is an economic downturn (remember that we have a global economy), competition between parks may affect revenues.

In addition to a continued human resources need and expansion of the industry, other future challenges include the following:

- The development of new, inventive, and exciting rides and other attractions to interest mid-teen visitors

> **OBJECTIVE 6**
> Review long- and short-term challenges confronting the amusement and theme park industry.

- New marketing strategies to attract the baby boomers as they retire. This segment of the population has the greatest amount of disposable income and a longer projected life-span than any generation in history. Also seniors can be targeted as potential second-career employees to address the industry's labor shortage.
- The need to create cost efficiencies without harming visitor services in an industry that is very labor intensive. For example, the heavy employee base creates significant fringe benefit costs; how can these be managed in a fair way for employees while minimizing price increases to visitors?

Main Street, U.S.A., at Disney's Magic Kingdom Park near Orlando, Florida.

SUMMARY OF CHAPTER LEARNING OBJECTIVES

1. **Define the terms *amusement park* and *theme park*.**
   An amusement park is a collection of rides and activities located in a central area with no unifying theme and separate admission or ticket requirements for each attraction. A theme park creates an atmosphere and environment of another place and time. It is generally enclosed in a central area, with an admission price paid at the gate allowing visitors access to all attractions.

2. **Provide a brief history of amusement and theme parks.**
   Amusement parks began in the Middle Ages (about A.D. 500 to 1500) when people gathered to sell and barter or trade goods and to celebrate harvests. The modern theme park was invented by Walt Disney in 1955 when he opened Disneyland in California. He created environments in which visitors could become completely immersed in an entertainment experience.

There has been a rapid expansion in theme parks and in their ability to more fully immerse visitors in an unforgettable experience.

3. **Explain basic planning issues of concern to theme park managers.**
   Successful theme parks provide a safe, clean, and happy environment and experience for visitors. Outstanding service is required, as is a significant amount of capital investment. All details from parking to admission fees to movement of visitors throughout the park, as well as tactics to increase the money they spend, must be carefully considered while maintaining an appropriate price–value relationship. Issues relating to the management of several thousand or more employees, visitor access to park rides and attractions, and the use of signage are of great concern. Employees must be properly cross-trained so that they can effectively work in several positions.

4. **Discuss safety and security aspects of amusement and theme park management.**

   Ongoing security is necessary to maintain the safe environment necessary to attract visitors to parks. Crowd control and vehicular traffic flow concerns are important. Security awareness programs for security personnel and all other park employees are required. Knowledge of procedures to use for weather alerts and all other dangers must be known and practiced, and an ongoing risk management program is required. Safety and security procedures applicable to park rides and attractions are a priority. Some parks utilize sophisticated technology to assist in security management, while others utilize more basic tactics.

5. **Review employment opportunities in the amusement and theme park segment of the hospitality industry.**

   A wide range of positions in the many departments required to manage a theme park is available. Departments include human resources, support services, accounting and finance, information technology, operations (revenue-generating functions), security, and marketing, along with many others. One may begin in an entry-level position and work up within the department. By contrast, others with higher levels of education or experience may begin in positions with more responsibilities. A wide range of positions and responsibilities allows one to pursue an aggressively challenging career without the need to relocate.

6. **Review long- and short-term challenges confronting the amusement and theme park industry.**

   Challenges include recruiting and retaining a sufficient number of employees at all organizational levels and exploiting technology to use it most cost effectively. These are issues that this industry segment shares with others. The future of the industry looks bright, because leisure time is likely to increase and more visitors will be looking for recreational alternatives. Decisions about expansion (duplication of existing and/or development of new concepts) must be made. Park expansion may lead to competitive pressures on revenue in times of economic downturns. Other challenges include making the theme parks more attractive to mid-teens and the ever-growing senior population while, at the same time, engaging this latter group as potential second-career employees. Competition from other segments of the leisure industry and the need to create cost efficiencies without harming visitor services are additional challenges to this industry segment.

FEEDBACK FROM THE REAL WORLD

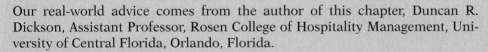

Our real-world advice comes from the author of this chapter, Duncan R. Dickson, Assistant Professor, Rosen College of Hospitality Management, University of Central Florida, Orlando, Florida.

Duncan has more than 30 years of hospitality industry experience, beginning as a busboy at age 14 at a Howard Johnson's Restaurant in Annapolis, Maryland. After obtaining degrees from the University of Maryland, College Park, and the School of Hotel Administration at Cornell University, he continued his career as a restaurant manager for Walt Disney World Company. After stints in the Lake Buena Vista Club, Pinocchio Village Haus (Magic Kingdom Park), and the Village Restaurant, Duncan moved to human resources with responsibilities for food and beverage recruiting. During 18 years in the Disney staffing arena (for the last 6 years he was in charge of the entire staffing effort), he created numerous leading-edge recruiting programs including the U.S. and International College Programs. Duncan also assisted with the staffing for Disneyland Paris. Duncan has also served as the vice-president of staffing for Kelly Services and the director of international staffing for Vistana, Inc. (now Starwood Vacation Ownership). He has been teaching at UCF since 1997 as an adjunct faculty member and joined the school as a full-time faculty member in 2001.

(continued)

What are the major sources of revenues generated by amusement and theme parks?

Admissions, food and beverage, retail, parking, special events, and tours are the major sources of revenues generated by amusement and theme parks.

How, if at all, does the management of food and beverage operations differ between more traditional (hotel and restaurant) and amusement and theme park operations?

In a theme park operation, one works on the basis of per capita (per person) spending. Attendance drives daily revenue. A food outlet manager receives a historical per capita revenue figure generated per visitor. Based on that projection (estimated number of visitors times per capita revenue), the restaurant manager can accurately schedule labor for work shifts. Chefs can also project food preparation requirements and labor schedules.

How do managers meet the labor fluctuations during seasonal changes in business volumes?

This is probably the most difficult task for managers in amusement and theme parks. Typically, one uses a combination of full-time, part-time, and seasonal workers. Trying to keep the full-time staff at a minimal level (to provide them the maximum number of hours possible), a good manager then uses employees in the other two categories and adjusts with overtime and short shifts as needed. Basically, one staffs to the lowest attendance and then adjusts as necessary.

What is the general process used to determine whether and when amusement park attractions should be added to a park?

Theme parks cannot exist with one-time visitors. Multiple visitation is essential to profitability (approximately 60 percent of all visitors are return guests). To renew interest for these guests, theme parks add new attractions approximately every 5 years. Also, to capture new markets, park planners must develop leading-edge technology that extends the draw of the original park. Therefore, the process to add an attraction is ongoing. It may be a new parade based on a hit movie (*Aladdin* at Disney-MGM Studios), the redo of an old attraction (*Jimmy Neutron* replacing *Hanna & Barbera* at Universal Studios Florida), or a totally new attraction to attract a new market (*Krakken* at SeaWorld Orlando looking to capture the mid-teens). Parks must stay current to keep the turnstiles revolving, so the process is a continuum: the what, where, when, and how is a process of maintaining a pulse on the visiting public and giving them what they want before they know they want it.

MASTERING YOUR KNOWLEDGE

Discuss the following questions.

1. How do you think theme park officials assess the types of attractions, entertainment, and special events that comprise the experiences to be offered to park visitors?
2. What do you think are the primary factors that influence whether a park visitor's experience is memorable?
3. How might you defend the need to increase admission (gate) prices to visitors who complain about the alleged high charges for young family members?
4. What, if any, are the most interesting aspects of a career in amusement and theme parks that are most attractive to you?

LEARN FROM THE INTERNET

1. Check out the home pages of the following well-known theme parks:

   - Busch Gardens: www.buschgardens.com
   - Disneyland: www.disneyland.com. When you arrive at the site, click on "Parks."
   - Hershey Park: www.hersheypark.com
   - Knott´s Berry Farm: www.knotts.com
   - Six Flags: www.sixflags.com
   - Universal Studios: www.universalstudios.com.When you arrive at the site, click on "Parks and Resorts."
   - Walt DisneyWorld: www.disneyworld.com.When you arrive at the site, Click on "Parks."

   What messages are they providing to viewers in efforts to attract them to the park? What types of career opportunities do they offer? What, if any, descriptions of available training for these positions are provided? What kinds of information are provided about specific attractions, entertainment, and special event activities that are available in the park?

2. Check out these sites of popular but smaller theme and amusement parks:

   - Belmont Park: www.belmont.park.com
   - Castle Park: www.castlepark.com
   - Dorney Park & Wildwater Kingdom: www.dorneypark.com
   - Lake Compounce Theme Park: www.lakecompounce.com
   - Lakemont Park: www.lakemontparkfun.com
   - Lakeside Amusement Park: www.lakesideamusementpark.com
   - Valley Fair: www.valleyfair.com

   How, if at all, do the attractions differ from those of the larger parks? How do the advertising messages differ (if they do)? What are differences in ticket prices, in employment opportunities, and in the perceived value and enjoyment of the park experience?

KEY HOSPITALITY TERMS

The following terms were explained in this chapter. Review the definitions of any words with which you are unfamiliar. Begin to utilize them as you expand your vocabulary as a hospitality professional.

leisure time	way finding
leisure industry	kiosks
recreation	Americans with Disabilities Act (ADA)
amusement park	risk management
theme park	accounts receivable (AR)
infrastructure	accounts payable (AP)

27

Overview of the Entertainment Industry

Concerts of all types attract many fans and are an integral part of the entertainment industry.

CHAPTER LEARNING OBJECTIVES

After studying this chapter, you will be able to:

1. Define *entertainment* and discuss a brief history of the entertainment industry.
2. Provide an overview of the entertainment business.
3. Discuss trends in the entertainment industry.
4. Review major responsibilities that are part of the positions within the entertainment industry.
5. Describe challenges that confront the entertainment industry.

This chapter was authored by Kathleen Nelson, PhD, CSEP, CMP, Assistant Professor, and Pat Merl, Adjunct Professor. Both serve with the Tourism & Convention Department, William F. Harrah College of Hotel Administration, University of Nevada, Las Vegas (UNLV).

Kathleen is a co-author of the *International Dictionary of Event Management* and has authored other publications addressing the entertainment and special events industry. As co-owner of Dan Nelson Productions, she has more than 25 years of business experience in the industry. She is a recipient of the *Sam and Mary Boyd Award* from UNLV and has received several other professional

FEEDBACK FROM THE REAL WORLD

What does the executive director of entertainment and special events for a major casino hotel do during an "average" day? While there is no average day in this fast-paced, demanding, and high-energy position, a diary of one day at work will provide an overview of one of the most responsible and challenging positions in entertainment management.

Read through this chapter and, with it as background, obtain feedback from the real world about the ongoing challenges of someone who is at the top of his on her profession.

WHAT IS ENTERTAINMENT?

The International Dictionary of Event Management[1] defines **entertainment** as "an activity performed for the enjoyment of others." This broad definition probably suits the public's ever-changing opinion about the events and activities within the always expanding and all encompassing scope of entertainment.

Some people think of entertainment as an activity such as a sporting event or production show at which one sits and watches. However, by today's standards, entertainment is frequently something in which one participates. Examples include visits to amusement and theme parks and involvement in gaming activities. Entertainment is, then, anything in which one can become immersed, participate, observe, and/or experience. Most importantly, it is regarded as something pleasurable that provides a diversion or enhances an activity.

The entertainment and media industry along with the advertising for it generates almost three quarters of a trillion dollars in the United States annually. American entertainment products are sweeping across the country and around the globe. Hundreds of millions of people listen to the same music and watch the same films and videos. Recorded music has become one of the world's most widely distributed products, and music travels so well because its language is universal. The music market is dominated by U.S. artists, promoters, and songwriters. Another winner in the entertainment segment: the motion picture industry, which is a growth industry in the United States.

Entertainment products dominate the licensed merchandise market. Recent **licensed products** have included SpongeBob SquarePants (have you purchased an aquarium, inflatable pool toy, license plate frame, or flip-flops?), Spider-Man, and Ozzy Osbourne. Concert acts like Madonna and U2 generate $15 or more per attendee in the sales of their licensed merchandise.

OBJECTIVE 1
Define *entertainment* and discuss a brief history of the entertainment industry.

entertainment an activity performed for the enjoyment of others

licensed product an item produced under an agreement (license) between the owner of intellectual property (trademark) and another party that permits, for payment of a fee, the latter to use the owner's property. For example, manufacturers of a Spider-Man tee shirt must pay a fee to the owners of the Spider-Man trademark to do so

---

awards. Kathy currently serves on the certification commission of the International Special Events Society.

Pat has served as company captain for the Lido de Paris at the Stardust (Las Vegas) and has held production, operations, and company management positions for an organization that produced shows on cruise lines and in U.S. and Canadian showrooms. She has operated her own entertainment booking company, has served as an assistant director of show operations for a major Atlantic City casino and resort, and has served as vice-president of marketing and operations for a Las Vegas production company.

[1]J. Goldblatt and K. Nelson. *The International Dictionary of Event Management.* New York: John Wiley & Sons, 2001.

Many food and beverage operations feature live entertainment as a way to attract guests.

Entertainment offerings provide something for everyone. Lounge, **headliner**, production and Broadway shows, comedy clubs, theaters, concerts, malls, museums, animal and wildlife habitats and exhibits, botanical gardens, family entertainment centers, movie theaters, bowling alleys, and nightclubs are all part of the entertainment industry. Entertainment has been an important part of hospitality for centuries. The Roman coliseums attest to its long history.

At the beginning of the 1800s, local performers in the United States entertained in small theaters, saloons, and other places where people socialized to attend plays, concerts, and traveling shows. In the late 1800s P.T. Barnum, considered the world's greatest showman, imported the first European burlesque show from England to America. Initially, this entertainment form was derived from plays that made fun of classical drama. However, it later became a creative mix of theatrical entertainment with sensual overtones, striptease, double-entendre comedy, and mocking imitations geared toward a male audience. **American burlesque**, as it became known, marked the beginning of a long history for Barnum and for production shows as we know them today.

Burlesque adapted elements of minstrel and variety shows that included dancers, singers, musicians, comedians, and novelty or specialty sight acts, and this variation gave burlesque its American brand. The shows were performed in beer halls and concert saloons.

Barnum's true claim to fame—the circus—was also imported from Europe. Barnum's circus traveled from town to town (city to city) entertaining the locals with its talented cast of clowns, acrobats, high-wire walkers, jugglers, animals, and a myriad of other exciting, amusing, and enjoyable entertainment. Today, millions of people still travel for miles to witness the spectacle of the Ringling Brothers and Barnum & Bailey Circus whenever it plays in numerous cities throughout the United States. Although the types of acts, costumes, music, and names have changed, the influence of the early circus is still evident in our country's entertainment culture.

The late 1800s also saw the rise in popularity of another entertainment form. **Vaudeville** was a combination of variety and minstrel shows geared toward a more general audience. The majority of vaudeville performers were immigrants who brought their own style of slapstick and ethnic comedy to America. Vaudeville would become the launching pad for a multitude of famous Broadway and film and television comedians such as Phil Silvers, Milton Berle, Sid Caesar, George Allen and Gracie Burns, Fanny Brice, and Ray Bolger, who became stars in the 1930s.

headliner (entertainment) a star (performer) who receives prominent billing for a performance

American burlesque a creative mix of theatrical entertainment with sensual overtones, striptease, double-entendre comedy (jokes or skits with two meanings), and mocking imitations geared to a male audience that was a popular form of entertainment in the United States from about the late 1800s to the 1920s

vaudeville a theater show with a variety of short acts including songs, dances, minstrel, actors, stand-up comedy, juggling, and other light entertainment geared to a general audience

LAS VEGAS: THE ENTERTAINMENT CAPITAL OF THE WORLD

By the 1950s, Las Vegas was established as a gambling center, and it was then when famous European production shows such as the Lido de Paris, Casino de Paris, and Follies Bergere opened on the Las Vegas Strip. Lounge shows featured major stars such as Frank Sinatra, Dean Martin, Sammy Davis, Jr., Don Rickles, and Louie Prima, who performed at major strip hotels. Live music, dance, and comedy could be seen any hour of the day during any day of the week. Top-quality entertainment was (and is) always available in Las Vegas.

Since the 1990s, many casino hotels in Las Vegas have been transformed into destination resorts. Their goal: to anticipate and fulfill every need and/or desire that could possibly arise during their guests' visits so they will have no need or desire to leave the premises. These properties are now self-contained, with their own gourmet restaurants, shopping, spas, production shows, nightclubs, movie theaters, bowling centers, arenas, and family entertainment centers, among other attractions.

Forerunners to today's production shows became popular in the early 1900s with the Ziegfeld Follies, George White's Scandals, and Earl Carol's Vanities, entertainment that created and legitimized the glamorous showgirl image. Vaudeville's variety, specialty, and novelty acts merged to create the format that has evolved to today's almost (and many times) unbelievable production shows.

The ongoing legalization of gaming throughout the United States has contributed to the magnitude of live entertainment available to the middle-class public. However, even some areas without legalized gaming are creating their own tourist attractions based on an entertainment profile. A prime example is what used to be the small and peaceful farm town of Branson in southwest Missouri. Branson has become a tourist attraction with theaters that attracts tens of millions of visitors annually from all over the country. Tourists enjoy a broad selection of shows and acts performed by headliners such as Jim Stafford, Bobby Vinton, Mickey Gilley, Yakkov Smirnoff, Andy Williams, and Mel Tillis, each of whom provides family entertainment and now call Branson their home. Several Branson venues offer morning shows to packed houses during its April to December season.

SCOPE OF THE ENTERTAINMENT BUSINESS

OBJECTIVE 2
Provide an overview of the entertainment business.

Operating tactics of the entertainment industry are now being merged with the corporate culture of many organizations to train employees in team building and presentation skills and in stress reduction and work ethics. Some hospitality organizations employ "cast members" rather than "staff members." New terms combine "tainment" (the last two syllables in "entertainment") with an entertainment theme, environment, or experience or with a product, service, or activity. The result: continuous changes to our language and to the definition and scope of the entertainment industry. Example terms include **eatertainment** (discussed in Chapter 13), *shoppertainment*, *infotainment*, *sportainment*, *bevertainment*, and *dealertainment*. Leisure sports, recreational activities, and gaming are now considered entertainment. Let's look at a few of the mergers between traditional activities and entertainment.

eatertainment (foodservice) the concept that guests desire to enjoy the total dining experience (food and beverage products, service, and the environment, including cleanliness) and may desire pleasurable distractions (television and animatronics, for example) when they visit a foodservice operation

Radio studios employ technicians and others, including sales and management staff.

Eatertainment

In the 1990s, entertainment and dining began to merge and produced numerous themed restaurants. Examples include the following:

- Hard Rock Cafe. Enjoy a touch of Americana while eating American classic foods and listening to rock music.
- Planet Hollywood. In these restaurants, diners are surrounded by Hollywood memorabilia.
- Motown Cafe. Guests can enjoy soul music while having lunch or dinner.
- Harley Davidson Cafe. Just look for the front half of a Harley motorcycle mounted above the restaurant's entrance.
- Rain Forest Cafe. These properties are a great place to shop and eat, replete with aquariums, waterfalls, lush greenery, and animated jungle animals and birds.
- Nascar Cafe. Dedicated to sports and race car fans.
- House of Blues. Offers its Gospel Brunch and southern food.
- ESPN Zone. Large restaurant and family entertainment chain that features food, sports, interactive games, and attractions.

What makes these restaurants different from their more traditional counterparts? The environment of each is themed to create a memory and experience that offers guests far more than the usual sandwich, entrée, dessert, or beverage.

CHECK IT OUT!

To learn about entertainment venues at these casino hotels, go to:

Excalibur Hotel & Casino:
www.excalibur.com

Imperial Palace:
www.imperialpalace.com

Rio Casino Resort:
www.harrahs.com

Click on "find a casino;" click on "select a brand;" enter "Rio."

EATERTAINMENT, DEALERTAINMENT, AND BEVERTAINMENT IN LAS VEGAS

Las Vegas visitors and residents have access to popular eatertainment franchises such as those listed in the following box. Also, they can enjoy the Excalibur's Tournament of Kings Dinner Show, which is one of the last dinner shows on the Las Vegas Strip. After dinner, they can visit the Imperial Palace (soon to be "imploded" to make way for a new and bigger Harrah's) to be dealertained as they play blackjack with Marilyn Monroe, Elvis Presley, and other entertainment icons, and they can go to the Rio for a beverage served by one of its many bevertainers.

DID YOU KNOW?

There are Pros and Cons to Eatertainment

You have learned that some restaurants provide great food and entertainment in a genre called eatertainment. It is easy to see the pros of eatertainment: enjoyable food and beverages served in an entertaining atmosphere. But could there be any disadvantages?

One answer to this question involves ice cream shops such as Stone Cold Creamery and Marble Slab Creamery that offer made to order ice cream creations filled with pretzels, Oreo bits, M&M's, and other ingredients assembled by "scoopers" (employees) who will do almost anything except put ice cream on the ceiling or stand on the counter to entertain their customers. (One tactic: singing off-the-wall songs.) The problem: long lines of persons waiting as other customers order ice cream and select other ingredients, and as ice cream is scooped onto a cold ledge, and the ingredients are mashed in the ice cream while the "scoopers" entertain.

At Cold Stone Creamery, the leader in this segment of the frozen dessert industry, it takes about 10 minutes to prepare one customer's order. (This is about 8 minutes longer than the industry average.) To compensate, some stores offer preportioned items for carry-out customers who are in a hurry. Today, increasingly, consumers have a choice of good ice cream or a good ice cream experience, and there are pros and cons for both alternatives.

Source: Bruce Hororitz. Ice cream shops thaw sales with scoops of fun. *USA Today* June 9, 2006.

To learn more about the companies mentioned above, check out:

Stone Cold Creamery: www.stonecoldcreamery.com
Marble Slab Creamery: www.marbleslab.com

Location-Based Entertainment (LBE)

Technologically sophisticated, away from home attractions are increasing in popularity. The largest examples are U.S. amusement and theme parks that have now been exported around the globe. The Mall of America in Bloomington, Minnesota, offers shoppertainment with its seven-acre amusement park. Each year it attracts more visitors than all of the persons who, in total, visit Disney World, Elvis Presley's Graceland, and the Grand Canyon (and these sites are, as well, considered location-based entertainment alternatives.

High-tech entertainment centers and urban entertainment centers are additional examples of location-based entertainment venues. A great example of the former is GameWorks (www.gameworks .com). Examples of the latter include Universal Studio's City Walks in Hollywood and Orlando (www.citywalk.com)

All first-time visitors to Hawaii should go to a luau.

family entertainment centers (FEC) community-based recreation or entertainment centers with attractions such as miniature golf, go-cart rides, video games, skating centers, bowling allies, movie theaters, and health clubs; also known as *fun centers*.

and Downtown Disney in Orlando (enter "downtown disney" in your favorite search engine). These and related destination locations feature an array of restaurants, games, private party rooms, shopping, nightlife, and related attractions for adults, families, and youth of just about all ages. Other venues in this entertainment genre include **family entertainment centers (FECs)** or fun centers: community-based recreation or entertainment centers with attractions such as miniature golf, go-cart rides, video games, skating centers, bowling alleys, movie theaters, and health clubs. Other family-oriented businesses include small amusement parks, family restaurants, resorts or hotels, shopping centers, and fairs. In 1990, approximately 250 businesses identified themselves as FECs. Today, the International Association for the Leisure and Entertainment Industry (IALEI) counts more than 10,000 organizations as FECs.

Children's entertainment centers or children's play centers include Chuck E. Cheese's (www.chuckecheese.com), Peter Piper (www.peterpiperpizza.com), and Kid's Quest (www.kidsquest.com); click on "cyber quest"). These facilities are geared toward child development and education and provide a perfect example of edutainment: the merger of education and entertainment. Other examples include very creative educational television shows for children and adults and games and toys that teach the children who play with them.

Numerous other examples of entertainment-based organizations and businesses can be cited. Consider, for example, the arts, including symphony, opera, ballet, concert series, theater, and museums. These and their counterparts require generalized management positions and individuals with specialized skills in music production, stage lighting and design, talent management, and broadcasting. Also, don't forget about Halls of Fame for sports and rock and roll and country music. IMAX theaters that project three dimensional (3-D) images up to eight stories high and featuring surround sound are a unique form of motion picture entertainment.

Cruise Ship Entertainment

You learned in Chapter 23 that cruise ships are exemplary destination resorts. Not only is the ship itself a destination for the passengers, but this destination resort takes the passengers to exotic ports or other destinations! Carnival Cruise Lines, Royal Caribbean Cruise Lines, and Norwegian Cruise Lines are the big 3 of more than 20 cruise lines in operation today.

LOCATION-BASED ENTERTAINMENT AND SHOPPERTAINMENT IN LAS VEGAS

Las Vegas offers shopping attractions such as the Roman-themed Forum Shops at Caesars. Once there, shoppers can have their photo taken with a Roman centurion standing at attention at the central fountain. They may also want to take a break from shopping by floating down a canal with a gondolier at the Venetian's Grand Canal Shops. Each venue offers its own brand of shoppertainment (and hospitality, since each mall has at least a few thousand hotel rooms and several restaurants under the same roof!). Guests visiting these and similar locations are sure to find all types of entertainment, eatertainment, and/or edutainment while enjoying the shoppertainment!

HOSPITALITY LEADER PROFILE

Harold Skripsky

Harold Skripsky turned his entrepreneurial spirit into many successful family entertainment businesses. He is a founding father of the International Association for the Leisure and Entertainment Industry (IALEI). Today, one of his earliest ventures, the Enchanted Castle, is recognized among the premier family entertainment centers in the United States.

Skripsky started his career with McDonald's Corporation in 1973, and he rapidly became a field service manager supervising 110 franchise stores in the Chicago area. Focused on a lifelong entrepreneurial dream, he left McDonald's in 1981 and opened Oodles Restaurant in Naperville, Illinois. As it flourished, Skripsky's partner joined the business full time, and they began planning their next venture.

In 1983, they opened the 10,000 square foot Enchanted Castle, a family entertainment center in Lombard, Illinois. By 1993, after a number of expansions, it was, at 46,500 square feet, the largest indoor family entertainment complex in the state. The complex features a 600-seat restaurant with a private birthday party area, 280 video and redemption games, carnival games, simulators and novelty games, bumper karts, an 18-hole mini-golf course, batting cages, and a prize redemption center.

In 1992, Skripsky developed a new prize redemption center and the ImaGYMnation Station, an advanced indoor children's playground. The following year, Enchanted Castle was expanded again for Q-Zar—the ultimate live action laser game, the second in the nation.

In 1993, the Enchanted Castle owners were honored in the White House Rose Garden with the Small Business Administration's (SBA) Entrepreneurial Success Award. The award was presented to them at the state, regional, and national levels. At the national level, Skripsky and his partner became the third inductees in the SBA National Hall of Fame. Their award was based on a successful business history, efficient management of operations, and a commitment to their business community.

That same year, Skripsky became a founding member of the board of directors and charter member of the International Family Entertainment Center Association (IAFEC). He became its president in 1996/1997, has chaired numerous committees, and stays active in the association.

In 1994, Skripsky and his partner sold the Enchanted Castle to Discovery Zone. He was appointed vice-president for operations to create and develop a Family Entertainment Center Division. In 1996, Skripsky repurchased the Enchanted Castle and focused his attentions on its growth. In early November 1997, he sold the business to Ogden Corporation, and Skripsky then worked with Ogden for three years in its Entertainment Division.

In 2000, he served as the driving force and negotiator when the association (now named the International Association for the Leisure and Entertainment Industry, IALEI) purchased FUN EXPO with two other industry associations. He became chairman of the board of the Leisure and Entertainment Trade Shows (LETS), a group that governs the operation of FUN EXPO for the three associations.

Also in 2000, Skripsky joined with several of his former employees from the Enchanted Castle to begin a redemption game design studio, Alan-Grant, Inc. AGI creates new ideas for redemption games, builds prototypes (working models), and licenses these prototypes to industry manufacturers, who then produce, market, and sell the games to operators.

Harold also remains very active in a business, Entertainment Management Services, Inc., that he formed in 1996, that provides consulting services to the family entertainment industry.

Skripsky has written numerous articles, primarily addressing the operation of FECs. He currently participates in seminar programs at FUN EXPO, is a member of the International Association of Amusement Parks and Attractions (IAAPA), and works closely with trade associations like American Amusement Machine Association (AAMA) and Amusement and Music Operators Association (AMOA).

CHECK IT OUT!

To view the website for the Enchanted Castle, go to www.enchanted.com.

In their early days, cruise lines catered predominantly to retirees and passengers over 65 years of age. Cruising was a passive type of entertainment with an abundance of food and tours conducted at the various ports of call. Basic entertainment was typically limited to musicians, acts, and singers.

Contemporary cruise ships cater to a much younger audience, and they provide the same type of entertainment one would expect to see on land. These include Broadway shows, Las Vegas-style production shows (some enhanced by live orchestras), headliners, comics, acrobats, jugglers, movies, and other entertainment alternatives.

Although there are "cruises to nowhere," most cruises sail to ports of call and, while doing so, entertain their passengers with great dining experiences (the Captain's Dinner and the Midnight Buffet), activities (scavenger hunts, limbo contests, and pig roasts), in addition to the entertainment just noted, to ensure that their passengers are having the time of their lives.

Today's liners have theaters with state of the art technology. This enables a producer to build a show equal to those seen in theaters and showrooms throughout the world. Many of America's top show producers and talent compete for an opportunity to produce for or work on a five-star cruise line.

TWO CASE STUDIES: ENTERTAINMENT ON CARNIVAL CRUISE LINES

The *Carnival Victory* was launched in 2000 and has some of the best nightlife at sea, with entertainment focused on the casino, Vegas-style shows, and theme bars.

Its Irish Sea Bar is a pub-style sing-along piano bar with rotating piano, and passengers in the mood for a high-octane dance club will find the entrance to Club Artic nearby. They can't miss the 500 video monitors and neon lights.

Carnival's award-winning tradition of producing the most spectacular revues afloat continues on this ship. It features a three-deck-high Caribbean Lounge with spectacular productions on par with those in the most modern Las Vegas showrooms. These shows are possible because of the sheer size of the Caribbean Lounge with its 34-foot-wide, 48-foot-deep, and 16-foot-high stage.

The spaciousness of this magnificent theater has resulted in the creation of a sea home four decks high with a fly tower for scenery and costumes. Controlled by an Acrobat 3D rigging computer, 34-fly lines with variable-speed motors are programmed to shift scenery and coordinate as many as 170 costume changes that may be required for each show.

Operated by one of the backstage managers, the computer also handles the turntable. Twenty-six feet in diameter, this rotating stage can be preprogrammed to stop at every point within a 360-degree radius depending on the requirements of each scene. Encompassed within the revolving turntable is a special five-step lift that rises out of the deck even when the turntable is rotating. The orchestra pit is capable of descending one deck below the main floor of the Caribbean Lounge, and it is also computer controlled.

The Caribbean Lounge boasts an extensive array of specialized lighting equipment, from cyber lights to lasers with full digital graphic capabilities. Four custom computers, controlled by a main unit dubbed "show control," coordinate all lighting effects.

A state of the art sound system with 12-channel surround sound and a 16 by 8 matrix allows the creation of sound that seems to be coming from 16 separate locations. Over 12 tons of speakers and more than 100,000 watts of amplifiers round out the fully digital sound system. An automated mixing desk and a computer system control all the sound equipment.

Popular shows have included a cast of 16 dancers and two featured singers accompanied by a 10-piece orchestra. Fast-paced, high-spirited Vegas-style revues offer toe-tapping tunes, a variety of scenery, dazzling costuming, energetic dance numbers, and elaborate, exhilarating pyrotechnic, video, and lighting effects. A lighting technician, audio engineer, two backstage managers, two follow-spot operators, and six stagehands complete the cast.

The *Carnival Liberty* began service in 2005. It's entertainment venues include the following:

Venue	Capacity
Venetian Palace (main show lounge)	1,400
Emile's (Lido/poolside restaurant)	1,396
Silver Restaurant (aft dining room)	1,122
Golden Restaurant (forward dining room)	744
Czar's Palace (casino)	484
Victoria Lounge (aft show lounge)	425
Hot & Cool (dance club)	211
The Stage (live music/karaoke bar)	88
Harry's (supper club)	108
Persian Room (port restaurant annex)	28
Satin Room (starboard restaurant annex)	36
Promenade Bar (promenade bar)	23
Jardin Cafe (promenade patisserie)	50
Flower Bar (lobby bar)	10
Piano Man (piano bar)	100
Gloves Bar (sports bar)	55
Antiquarian Library	17
Paparazzi (wine bar)	30
Empress Bar (club lounge)	40
The Cabinet (grand bar)	147
Tapestry Room (Multifunction room)	100

Entertainment is very important to Carnival Cruise Lines, and it even has a website for this purpose:www.carnivalentertainment.com. Check it out to learn about employment opportunities (cruise director, entertainer, teen activity director, and other supportive positions) and to learn the stories about some of the persons who also work shore side.

To learn about position vacancies in all the major cruise lines, go to www.cruiseshipjob.com. While at this site, click on "entertainment department" to view salaries for common entertainment positions.

DID YOU KNOW?

Implotainment®

The term *implode* refers to the demolishing of a building by planting explosive charges that make it explode inward. A new term, *implotainment,* was coined by Pat Merl, one of the authors of this chapter, and can be added to our list of entertainment alternatives. Hotel implosions have been used as backdrops for movies such as *Mars Attacks* (Landmark Hotel). Also, the remains of the Sands Hotel implosion is seen in the movie *Conair,* and Steve Wynn's self-produced, made-for-television

(continued)

movie, *Treasure Island: The Adventure Begins*, includes footage of the Dunes Hotel implosion.

The Dunes Hotel implosion was produced as a major event for Las Vegas. Thousands of people gathered and partied as the hotel tumbled to the ground into a pile of rubble and smoke. Las Vegas and its landmark hotels are continually selected as backdrops and sites for television shows and series and for films. The city is, therefore, popular for both passive and active forms of entertainment.

OTHER ENTERTAINMENT VENUES

The world of entertainment is vast and extends far beyond the glamour and extravagance of Las Vegas, Atlantic City, and Broadway (in New York City), production shows featuring famous entertainers and, of course, movies (motion pictures).

Entrepreneurs operate numerous businesses that entertain a wide variety of people in selected segments of the market, including these:

- Laser tag centers
- Go-kart tracks
- Batting cages
- Skateboard parks
- Water parks
- Roller skating centers
- Arcades

- Ice skating fields
- Paint ball fields
- Miniature golf courses
- Campgrounds
- Children's entertainment centers

To learn more about some of these and related venues in the entertainment industry, check out the following websites:

International Association for the Leisure and Entertainment Industry: www.ialei.org

American Amusement Machine Association (AAMA): www.coin-op.org

Amusement & Music Operations Association (AMOA): www.amoa.com

Domed Ontario Place IMAX movie theater in Toronto

OBJECTIVE 3
Discuss trends in the entertainment industry.

TRENDS IN THE ENTERTAINMENT INDUSTRY

After they are introduced, popular entertainment concepts and ideas begin to saturate markets and become less interesting. Concepts are copied, worked, and reworked until people become bored with them, and they then begin to look elsewhere for entertainment. It is vital for hospitality venues and their entertainment managers to stay on top of the industry, to change when necessary (and it frequently is!), and to maintain a competitive edge. Information regarding trends can be found in industry publications such as *Amusement Business, Backstage, Backstage West, Entertainment Management Magazine, Ezone, Hollywood Reporter, Pollstar, Theater Magazine,* and *Variety.*

Let's use Las Vegas as a case study to explore one current trend in the entertainment industry: increasingly extravagant productions. In the early 1980s, a Canadian-based circus emerged that would eventually change the face of the circus industry and propel the image of circus to new heights through a reinvention of the circus concept. Ultimately, this new concept, with the incorporation of state of the art technology, moved from the circus tent into the showroom. This concept changed the face of circus and became one of the major contributions to the showroom entertainment production industry.

In the early 1990s, Cirque du Soleil came to Las Vegas to perform its traveling show, Nouvelle Experience, under a tent attached to the back of the Treasure Island Hotel. The circus was not a novel form of entertainment for Las Vegas; numerous well-known shows had traveled there to perform. However, this circus was different. Cirque incorporated original scripting, theme, costuming, makeup, and music in the customary circus format and combined it with a lavish production to create a truly visionary concept.

Cirque has not only raised the bar for the traditional U.S. circus, but has also set new standards and trends for entertainment production in general. It continues to break ground with each new edition of the show. One of Cirque's Las Vegas-based shows (O at the Bellagio) pushed creativity and technology to the limit by combining world-class talent with the latest in staging technology and water. The result: a show that merges traditional acrobatic skills with aquatic prowess to create a memory that can not easily be put into words.

Cirque du Soleil's Zumanity, at the New York New York Hotel & Casino, is in keeping with the trend toward more adult-oriented entertainment in Las Vegas. Cirque's KA at the MGM and LOVE at Treasure Island bring the count to a total of five Cirque shows on the Las Vegas Strip. This trend reflects the Las Vegas production shows of yesterday, but today's technology and megabudgets bring it to a new level.

A majority of the novelty and specialty acts and production shows in Las Vegas originated in Europe, especially in England, Germany, France and, most recently, Russia and Canada. For example, Le Femme is a Parisian import from the Crazy Horse in Paris. Other Las Vegas international productions include the Tropicana's Follies Bergere, which debuted more than 45 years ago, and Mama Mia!, a very successful musical that made its way to Las Vegas via Broadway and London's West End.

Mama Mia is part of a relatively current Broadway trend called **back catalog shows** or compilation shows. Historically, the show's **book** was written first, and the music, which reinforced the story, was composed later. A back catalog show's storyline is based on a selected catalog of music that has already been written and released (in this case music from the well-known 70's group, ABBA). Two other examples: *We Will Rock You* is a show based on 25 hit songs recorded by the rock

back catalog show a Broadway show in which the story is based on music that has already been written and released; also called *compilation show*

book a Broadway show term referring to spoken lines in a play or musical

Many visitors to Las Vegas don't spend all their time in the casinos.

HISTORY OF ENTERTAINMENT IN ATLANTIC CITY

With the passage of the 1976 casino referendum, the race to open the East Coast's first casino was on. Resorts International became New Jersey's first casino hotel and, when it opened in 1978, a new era of entertainment began.

Casino gaming was now within a six-hour drive for 25 percent of the population of the United States. Buses and cars from East Coast cities formed caravans of gamblers ready for casino play.

Much excitement surrounded the opening of Resorts International. As its doors opened, the axiom of "build it and they will come" could not have been more true. Steve Lawrence took to the craps table to ceremoniously mark the official opening. Sharply dressed gentlemen and ladies filled the more than 33,000 square feet of casino space and stood more than three deep in areas for the chance to play at one of the 84 table games or 893 slot machines. Some people waited for up to six hours to enter the casino.

The Resorts entertainment experience continued off the casino floor with live music in the Rendezvous Lounge. Sam Butera and The Treniers became synonymous with the best in live lounge entertainment at Resorts. In the theater, the headliner calendar looked like pages from the "Who's Who" in Hollywood. Steve Lawrence and Eydie Gorme opened the Superstar Theater, and they were followed by Tina Turner, Bill Cosby, Jerry Lewis, Vic Damone, Jackie Gleason, Gene Kelly, Flip Wilson, and dozens more. In 1980, within a six-month period, more than 20 stars played Resorts' Superstar Theater, including Dom DeLuise, Lola Falana, Zubin Mehta, Johnny Carson, Dean Martin, Tom Jones, Steve Martin, Lou Rawls, Ben Vereen, Buddy Hackett, Don Rickles, Cher, Engelbert Humperdink, Diana Ross, Tony Bennett, and Barry Manilow—many of whom were making return appearances.

In 1980, Lou Rawls was the first entertainer to create his handprints in cement for Resorts in a display at its Boardwalk entrance. Since the dedication of the Entrance of the Stars, nearly 60 handprints have been cast, including a dozen in the new millennium, such as Tom Jones and Whoppi Goldberg. Always a forerunner in bringing top-notch entertainment to Atlantic City, the 25th Anniversary of Resorts and of gaming in Atlantic City was celebrated in 2003 with comedian Jerry Seinfeld, who performed in the Superstar Theater. Unquestionably the hottest ticket in town, the line of people waiting to purchase tickets was reminiscent of the lines of people waiting to gamble 25 years earlier.

CHECK IT OUT!

To view the website of Resorts Atlantic City, go to www.resortsac.com

group Queen that debuted in London's West End in 2002 and later opened at the Paris Hotel in Las Vegas, in August 2004. The Broadway show, *Movin Out*, is a rock ballet based on Billy Joel's music of the late 1970s to early 1990s that opened in New York in October 2002, and also played briefly on London's West End in early 2006.

OBJECTIVE 4
Review major responsibilities that are part of the positions within the entertainment industry.

POSITIONS IN THE ENTERTAINMENT INDUSTRY

The live entertainment industry is also referred to as *show business*. These two words help one to distinguish between the two basic types of positions available in the industry: those that relate to show and those that relate to business. Customarily, performers possess innate talents that are further developed through serious study in schools and/or universities that specialize in teaching these types of performing arts. Their talents are further developed through intense study, discipline, and dedication to the art form they have chosen. Persons in show positions are most likely to benefit from postsecondary education with, for example, a degree in fine arts. Examples of the types of jobs that fall into this category are dancers, singers, actors, musicians, comics, novelty and specialty acts, circus acts, and others.

By contrast, entertainment business positions involve knowledge of principles that are important to producing, managing, marketing, promoting, advertising, and selling the show part of the business. These positions are equally important because without one there cannot be the other. A wide variety of these positions is available in both show and film. (Just look at the credits in the Playbill

Production shows in major cities and on cruise ships and in other locations attract many theatergoers.

from the next Broadway show or film that you see!). Knowledge gained in colleges of education, business, hospitality management, fine arts, and in film or law schools can be of invaluable assistance throughout one's career in any aspect of the entertainment industry.

As is true in other segments of the hospitality industry, entry-level positions allow persons to gain experience, become familiar with the jargon and culture, and determine whether an acceptable career choice has been made. Don't hesitate to volunteer or apply for internships for any job, even though it may not seem challenging at the time. If you are interested in the industry, it is important to learn what it is about from an employee's perspective.

The following is a short list of many popular business-related positions and some responsibilities in each:

- **Production manager.** Interacts with entertainers, theatrical agencies, and their support personnel to coordinate contractual and **rider** requirements. Studies contracts to ensure that requirements for rooms, food and beverage, and transportation, and the likes are met, and expedites production operations. Manages daily operation of preproduction, including budgeting, payroll, purchasing, contracts, schedules, file maintenance, and correspondence. Interprets **collective bargaining agreements** and assists with public relations activities.
- **Stage manager.** Coordinates all aspects of a show from rehearsal through opening and into day to day operations. Requires a basic knowledge of stage technology, the art form (dance, music, and acting. for example), human resources, budgets, contracts and union rules, scheduling, payroll, and safety, among numerous other disciplines.
- **Production office coordinator.** Prepares and distributes production reports, **call sheets**, shooting schedules, and script revisions. Requires knowledge applicable to budgets, union contracts, regulations, and disability reports.
- **Public relations or publicity agent.** Writes press releases, assembles press kits, and distributes them to media representatives and organizations. Arranges interviews with newspapers and magazines, sets up photo opportunities and TV and radio appearances for performers and

rider (contract) an amendment attached to a contract to modify it to avoid rewriting or redrafting the entire document. Riders to entertainment contracts typically address a performer's equipment, meals and drinks, and general comfort requirements

collective bargaining agreement a contract between an employer and employees who are members of a labor union that establishes the rights and responsibilities of both groups in their employment relationship

call sheets rehearsal or work call schedules, typically created by the production stage manager or coordinator, to notify cast and/or stage crew members about show, music, or technical rehearsals

Children's parties are big business and are services offered by many hospitality operations.

commission (booking agent) a fee, based on an agreed-on percentage of an artist's payment for an engagement, that a booking agent receives for securing the engagement

advancing tours the process by which a production company's technical representative travels ahead of the tour (show) to learn about the performance space and available equipment, meets with theater or facility contacts, and identifies and resolves potential problems in advance of the show's arrival

others involved with the production, and develops strategies for additional press coverage.

- **Production assistant.** Assists the production manager by using administrative and computer skills to assist with communication and script editing activities, in addition to supporting the production manager in all areas of his or her responsibility.
- **Booking agent.** Secures bookings (engagements) and may develop tours for the entertainers under contract. Represents artists and acts as a broker (middleman) who is customarily paid on a **commission** basis.
- **Entertainment attorney.** Advises about numerous legal matters. Entertainment contracts and contract riders can be extremely detail oriented, and they require careful analysis. Other issues of concern may include intellectual property and copyright, merchandising, labor, shipping, and taxes.

- **Personal assistant.** After an artist reaches a certain status or level of fame in the entertainment industry, he or she usually needs a personal assistant. These professionals bridge the gap between the artist's personal and business needs. Duties run the gamut from taking a pet to the vet to **advancing tours.**
- **Director of entertainment.** Manages all aspects of entertainment for a hospitality organization, including selecting and booking entertainers and coordinating their logistical needs while at the property. Develops and monitors the property's entertainment budget, addresses entertainment employee scheduling and payroll issues, approves entertainment-related purchases, and addresses the concerns of entertainers, employees, and event organizers. Negotiates all performance-related contracts and bargaining agreements.
- **Promoter.** Markets, publicizes, advertises, and creates promotions to generate awareness of the show, create excitement, and sell tickets. A promoter goes ahead of the show and does everything necessary to create an interest that generates ticket sales. Persons with basic business knowledge and an understanding of marketing, advertising, public relations and promotion are great candidates, and the experience gained can take one far in the entertainment industry.

Other positions offering opportunities for those considering a career in the entertainment industry include craft services, who cater food on film shoots, and transportation captains, who coordinate cast and crew travel between sets and locations, transportation vehicles, and housing of actors and location-based offices.

WANT TO LEARN MORE?

To learn about numerous positions in the entertainment industry, check out these websites:

Clear Channel: www.clearchannel.com. Click on "careers."

Concerts West: www.concertswest.com. Click on "employment."

Ticketmaster: www.ticketmaster.com. Click on "careers."

Indeed: www.indeed.com/jobs. Click on "entertainment."

Arts Opportunities: www.artsopportunities.org

Entertainment Careers.Net: www.entertainmentcareers.net

My Music Job.Com: www.mymusicjob.com

CHALLENGES! CHALLENGES!

OBJECTIVE 5
Describe challenges that confront the entertainment industry.

It is difficult to categorize challenges that confront the entertainment management industry because it is so broad. Ever-changing economy, consumer preferences, competition, technology, concerns about attaining financial goals, and an ongoing search for the best people for position vacancies present challenges to managers in the entertainment segment, just as they do to peers in other organizations within the tourism and hospitality industry.

Let's look at some specifics:

- Many entertainment organizations are confronted with significant competition, and new methods of electronic delivery make it difficult to control content. For example, how can recording companies control free but illegal downloads of their recordings? These companies lose significant revenues when consumers download music preferences from the Internet and then use them multiple times on compact disks, i-pods, and cell phones. Will television revenues be reduced as advertisers become less certain their messages will be seen because of prescreening when personal video recorders are used, or will advertising companies find ways to circumvent these new technological devices?
- Revenues from subscription-based entertainment businesses such as satellite radio, paid cable, and pay per view systems are increasing as they win customers away from traditional radio and television broadcasts. As well, the public willingly pays broadband fees for Internet access and obtains news and other entertainment from this source.
- Cell phones are now being used for entertainment purposes, and communication and game machines now have Internet connectivity, which allows consumers to find new entertainment alternatives with these technologies.
- Traditional sources of entertainment, such as books, newspapers, recorded music, and visits to movie theaters, are challenged because of electronic alternatives.

backline gear the onstage musical and amplification equipment rented for the performing band (speakers and amps, keyboards, drum kits, and the like)

- Entertainment production budgets are challenged as both live and recorded entertainment content are driven more and more by technology. The cost of technology is leading to higher ticket prices and limiting audience demographics to only those who can afford them.
- Lack of content, or the entertainment product itself, is also a threat to the industry. It is becoming more and more difficult to come up with fresh ideas, whether in the film, theater, or music industry.

SUMMARY OF CHAPTER LEARNING OBJECTIVES

1. **Define entertainment and discuss a brief history of the entertainment industry.**
   Entertainment can be described as an activity performed for the enjoyment of others. By today's standards, it is both passive and active, and it is something pleasurable that provides a diversion or enhances an activity. The modern entertainment industry in the United States evolved from the late 1800s, first with burlesque, and then with vaudeville. Production shows of ever-increasing extravagance evolved and, beginning in the 1950s in Las Vegas, modern entertainment across the widest possible spectrum of alternatives has evolved.

2. **Provide an overview of the entertainment business.**
   Entertainment is integrated into much of what we do everyday. In fact, the base phrase, -*tainment,* is often merged with terms involving eating, shopping, sports, and other activities to connote an increasing entertainment dimension for many things that people do. Many entertainment organizations are geared toward families. Casinos, cruise lines, shopping centers, restaurants, nightclubs, and numerous large industry segments exist to provide entertainment for targeted markets.

3. **Discuss trends in the entertainment industry.**
   One of the most significant trends is a reinvention of the circus concept, first brought to the United States in the 1880s. Cirque du Soleil began with a Nouvelle Experience production that incorporated scripting, theme, costume, makeup, and music into a lavish production,

and Cirque has opened new and increasingly extravagant production shows since that time. The nightclub industry has redefined nightlife for young adults. It is not unusual for a reserved table to start at a minimum of $600 (if one is available).

4. **Review major responsibilities that are part of the positions within the entertainment industry.**
   Entertainment positions require education and training in numerous disciplines. Popular positions include production manager, stage manager, production office coordinator, and public relations or publicity agent. Other positions include production assistant, booking agent, entertainment attorney, personal assistant, director of entertainment, and promoter.

5. **State challenges that confront the entertainment industry.**
   Entertainment organizations are confronted with significant competition, including new forms of electronic delivery. Revenues from traditional radio and television broadcasts are decreasing, while those of subscription-based businesses are increasing. New entertainment venues, including cell phones and communication and game machines with Internet connectivity, are becoming more popular, while traditional entertainment sources, such as recorded music and movie theaters, are challenged. Entertainment production budgets are being stretched as the cost of technology is driving ticket prices beyond what many consumers can afford.

FEEDBACK FROM THE REAL WORLD

This diary of a day in the life of an executive director of entertainment and special events was contributed by Rick Gallagher.

Rick was a performing musician, entertainer, and songwriter for 20 years, and he began his career in Atlantic City as an entertainment technician at the Tropicana in 1988. In 1990, he helped open the Taj Mahal's entertainment department, where he was promoted to lead entertainment technician and then to entertainment technical supervisor. In 1995, Rick became entertainment operations manager at Caesars Atlantic City, where he was promoted to entertainment director. In 2001, he was hired as executive director of entertainment and special events at Resorts Atlantic City.

It's 9:00 P.M. as Rick Gallagher accompanies the evening's headliner to the stage. He hears the voice of the stage manager through the theater stage intercom system: "Fade house music. House lights to half." There is applause from the audience as they sense it is show time. "House lights out. Take the main curtain out. Go audio. Open microphone 1. Spot 2 pick-up stage left entrance." As the headliner steps into the light and belts out her first note, Gallagher cannot think about the launch of another show because his buzzing beeper sends him to the nearest house phone.

Rick's work day began at 9:00 A.M. when he learned that the headliner and her entourage were at the airport in New York, but they and the limousine driver who he had arranged to pick them up could not locate each other. The limousine company was contacted and the driver was called. The exact location of the entourage was pinpointed, and a potential disaster was averted. Gallagher instructs the entertainment coordinator to double-check that the headliner's suite is clean and ready, that the correct flowers and food for her suite have been delivered, that the **backline gear** (see p. 502) rental (the on-stage musical and amplification equipment rented for the performing band) required by the headliner's contract has arrived and is in good order, that the piano is tuned, and that the orchestra leader has confirmed the rehearsal time and instrumentation.

At 10:00 A.M. Rick meets with senior management and finance personnel to discuss the proposed entertainment budget for the following year. Armed with recent income (profit and loss) statements, payroll reports, and theater and departmental revenue and expense reports, he justifies the funds needed for the following year's entertainment plan. For 90 minutes, line items such as headliners' salaries, orchestra costs, equipment repair and maintenance expenses, entertainers' rooms, food and beverage costs, lounge band costs, music licensing costs, and employee overtime are discussed. He makes some gains and takes some losses.

At 11:30 A.M. he meets with the property's director of labor relations, the business agent for the Entertainment Technicians Union, the union shop steward, and a lead technician from the hotel about scheduling and payroll issues.

At noon, Rick, his entertainment coordinator, a security supervisor, and a security guard greet the headliner and her entourage. They escort them to their suite while a bellman and personal assistant take charge of their luggage. Once in the suite, pleasantries are exchanged, and the limousine snafu is downplayed while the entertainers nibble on their suite order of favorite fruits, snacks, and bottled water (room temperature), and they express appreciation for the flowers. The coordinator and security detail vacate the suite after escort times are set for rehearsal, dinner, and the show. Rick remains as additional details are negotiated with the headliner and her manager: an expensive bottle of wine and an additional room for the president of her new record label. He thinks that he can accommodate these requests and asks if she would meet and take photographs with some of the VIP customers after the show and attend a customer cocktail party the following night.

At 12:45 P.M., Rick receives the following week's employee schedule. He confirms that all shifts and events are covered. Labor hours are explained and justified, revisions are made, and the schedule is faxed to the union call steward. The payroll budget is intact.

(continued)

A 20-minute lunch with colleagues is followed by 40 minutes of returning phone calls and e-mails. Then Rick goes to the theater to observe rehearsal and to check on details: dressing rooms (clean), the backstage food order (delivered), the orchestra (tuned and ready), and the stage lighting (focused and programmed). The stage techs have set up the rented backline gear per the applicable contract's technical rider and have "rung out" the on-stage monitors. The headliner enters, there are no complaints, and Rick can move on.

At 3:00 P.M. he attends a meeting with the company president and marketing executives. Customers have requested specific headliners, and the president wants to explore other headliners to attract new customers. Some are too expensive and others don't fit with the market. They reach agreement. Rick returns to his office and begins making calls to the appropriate agents. Availability, cost per show, expected ticket sales, number of rooms, technical requirements, among other details, are discussed. At 5:00 P.M., his secretary needs his signature. She wants to move paper work forward before leaving for the day. Rick signs purchase requisitions for supplies, contracts for bands and disk jockeys, check requests for vendors, and vacation requests for employees.

At 6:30 P.M., Rick has a dinner meeting with the headliner's agent. Discussions include booking other headliners represented by the agent, the future of the hotel's entertainment, industry trends, and minor complaints by the headliner's entourage. The rapport is positive, and the conversation is punctuated by beeps and cell phone calls.

The two make their way to the theater. The line is getting long. Inside, the theater crew has just finished mopping and prepping the stage. The security detail is in place; the maitre d's and the seating captains are ready. Doors open at 7:30 P.M. sharp.

It's 9:05 P.M. and he has reached the house phone to answer the beep after the headliner began her show. The band hired for that evening's special casino event has not yet arrived, and the event's organizers are concerned. Additionally, they are feuding with a technician who is refusing to make last-minute lighting changes for the themed decor. Rick arrives at the ballroom and, fortunately, the band has arrived as well. However, the three parties are embroiled in a dispute, and Rick finds the right combination of people skills, internal customer service tactics, and firmness required for a solution. He coerces the band to set up itself, a lift is brought in to help the technician change the lighting, and personnel from another department move tables and chairs so the technician can maneuver safely. The event begins a few minutes late, but the customers are not inconvenienced.

Returning to the theater, Rick knows he missed the show. However, the customers are raving as they head to the casino. Backstage, the headliner is freshening up. Rehearsal times and crew calls are set for the next day. Customers are brought back stage as previously arranged to meet and greet and take photographs with the headliner. The record label president is in good spirits from his bottle of wine and is heading for his room.

Its 11:00 P.M. The headliner is safely escorted back to her suite. Rick heads for home. His beeper is on but silent, and it's been a good day.

MASTERING YOUR KNOWLEDGE

1. Why is Las Vegas considered the entertainment capital of the world?
2. Why do casinos and cruise ships dedicate significant resources to the development and offering of some of the world's most extravagant production shows?
3. Why has entertainment become so entwined with everyday activities such as shopping? How have the fields of education and information distribution benefited from the incorporation of entertainment aspects?
4. What types of family-based entertainment organizations are available in your community? Which additional types of businesses would be successful?
5. If you were responsible for booking entertainment for hospitality operations, such as at a hotel, restaurant, private club, or casino, what factors would be of most concern to you? Why?

LEARN FROM THE INTERNET

1. Review the websites of the following entertainment industry professional associations:

   - International Association for the Leisure and Entertainment Industry (IALEI): www.ialei.com
   - Amusement and Music Operators Association (AMOA): www.amoa.com
   - American Amusement Marketing Association (AAMA): www.coin-op.org
   - Entertainment Services & Technology Association: www.esta.org

   What is the purpose of these associations? What types of organizations would benefit from their products and services? How do they contribute to the broad entertainment industry?

2. Check out the websites for the following entertainment industry e-publications:

   - *The Hollywood Reporter:* www.hollywoodreporter.com
   - *Backstage:* www.backstage.com
   - *Variety Magazine:* www.variety.com

   What are the professions of persons that would be interested in these online publications? How do business readers use the information learned from these resources?

3. Enter "entertainment management" into your favorite search engine. Scroll through a few of the websites you find. What businesses are represented by these sites? What are examples of careers that you have never thought about until you viewed this information?

KEY HOSPITALITY TERMS

The following terms were explained in this chapter. Review the definitions of any words with which you are unfamiliar. Begin to utilize them as you expand your vocabulary as a hospitality professional.

entertainment
licensed product
headliner (entertainment)
American burlesque
vaudeville
eatertainment (food service)
family entertainment centers (FEC)
back catalog show

book
rider (contract)
collective bargaining agreement
call sheets
commission (booking agent)
advancing tours
backline gear

Part 6

THE MEETINGS BUSINESS

Professional Meeting Management

28

Meetings are an aspect of business that cannot be avoided.

CHAPTER LEARNING OBJECTIVES

After studying this chapter you will be able to:

1. Identify three types of meeting planners.
2. Describe basic responsibilities of meeting planners as a meeting is planned.
3. Explain basic procedures for meeting attendee registration.
4. Review basic information about housing meeting attendees.
5. Describe basic responsibilities of meeting planners as the meeting evolves.
6. Describe basic responsibilities of meeting planners as a meeting is concluded.
7. Discuss special aspects of a conference center education coordinator.

This chapter was authored by Curtis Love, PhD, Associate Professor, Department of Tourism and Convention Administration, William F. Harrah College of Hotel Administration, University of Nevada, Las Vegas.

FEEDBACK FROM THE REAL WORLD

A professional meeting planner has a very big job: to plan all the details of a meeting in such a way that it is successful within the financial boundaries established for it. One of the most important factors that will determine a meeting's financial success relates to the meeting site. The meeting planner is a professional, but so is the marketing and sales representative with whom the meeting planner must negotiate on behalf of the meeting's sponsor.

How would you answer the following questions:

- What are some of the most important tactics that a meeting planner can utilize during the negotiation process with representatives of the prospective meeting site to minimize costs without compromising the meeting's objectives?

- On what items is a hotel or other meeting site representative most likely to negotiate? Least likely?
- What are common mistakes that meeting planners make while planning a meeting?
- What are the most frequent problems that occur as attendees preregister for a meeting; what tactics can a professional meeting planner use to address these potential problems?
- What are the most important tasks that a meeting planner should do immediately after a meeting is concluded?

As you read this chapter, think about answers to these questions and then get feedback from the real world at the end of the chapter.

Meeting management is an integral part of the hospitality industry because meetings represent a very big business. They require sleeping rooms for those who travel long distances and food and beverage services for those attending them. In addition, the significant time and expenses incurred by attendees require that the meetings be professionally planned and managed to maximize their effectiveness. In this chapter, we will explore what meeting planners do in corporations and associations with sufficient meeting activities to require this position and in companies owned by entrepreneurs who plan and manage meetings for their clients.

OBJECTIVE 1
Identify three types of meeting planners.

meeting planner a specialist who plans, manages, and follows up on all details of meetings and/or conventions

TYPES OF MEETING PLANNERS

There are three basic types of **meeting planners;** those who work for

- Corporations
- Associations
- Individual clients (independent planners)

Let's look at each of these types of meeting planners.

Corporate Meeting Planners

Corporate meeting planners are employed by a single company and may be involved in planning numerous meetings for personnel in different locations in different company divisions at the same time. Large organizations may employ many meeting planners, whose work is directed by a corporate meetings director (or similar title).

MEETINGS: ROI IS A MUST!

Business meetings are held for a purpose, and they must be worth more than they cost! It is relatively easy to determine a meeting's cost: attendee travel-related expenses and compensation while attending the meeting, site costs, speakers' fees, and numerous other charges can be calculated. Meeting budgets must be carefully planned to assure that these costs are managed. However, what is the worth of information presented at meetings? How can the value of the meeting to attendees be quantified? How can planners assure that there is an acceptable **return on investment (ROI)** so that meeting costs justify the expenses? These are questions that persons funding, planning, and attending meetings must increasingly answer.

Attendees at corporate meetings are generally required to attend; their travel, lodging, and related expenses are typically paid by the organization. Therefore, one challenge confronted by other types of meeting planners, promoting and estimating attendance, is less of a challenge. However, since corporate meetings typically involve persons who have attended previous meetings, planners are challenged to assure that sessions are creatively planned to maintain their interest.

return on investment (ROI) the measure of managerial efficiency that correlates profitability with the investment made to generate the profit

Association Meeting Planners

Thousands of business or trade and professional **associations** exist to provide education, lobbying, group purchase, and/or other services for members who share common professional, hobby, or other interests. Many of these associations have regional or national meetings and/or **conventions** or **trade shows.** In small associations, the planning may be the responsibility of the executive director (typically a compensated administrator). This official may retain the meeting planning task within the organization or may utilize an independent meeting planner to assist. Typically, volunteer members of executive boards, committees, and other influential members of associations provide input to meeting goals and determine the topics to be discussed. In larger associations, specialized meeting planners who are employees of the organization are utilized.

association an organization with volunteer leadership (and usually a paid staff) that serves persons with a common interest or activity

convention a meeting of association members or those working within a profession

trade show an industry-specific event that allows suppliers to an industry to interact with, educate, and sell to individuals and businesses that are part of the industry; also called *exhibition*

Association members decide if they wish to attend these meetings and, if so, they must pay their own expenses (or solicit funds from their employers, if applicable). The association meeting planner's task is to encourage attendance; this is a challenge in times when prospective attendees want to assure that return on investment concerns will be met.

Independent Meeting Planners

Independent meeting planners are in business to help customers such as small corporations, associations, and others who cannot afford or who do not need a full-time meeting planner. Independent planners may be entrepreneurs operating a one- or several-person business to larger organizations specializing in offering meeting planning services to numerous smaller businesses and associations.

The tasks of independent meeting planners are twofold. They must, first, generate clients and, second, assist clients with their meeting planning needs.

Many meetings are informal.

People like to attend meetings because of their direct benefits and also because many persons enjoy travel to and from the sessions and the opportunity to discover the community or area in which the meeting is held. While teleconferencing has a niche in the meetings industry, hotels, conference centers, and other locations will continue to be preferred sites for the conduct of meetings.

WHY DO PEOPLE ATTEND MEETINGS?

Meetings need to have well-thought-out objectives, and these objectives must drive the planning and conduct of the meeting. Meetings are held for numerous reasons, including the following:

Sales meetings.   To introduce new products and services, to motivate salespersons, and to reward effective performers.

Stockholder meetings.   To inform investors about the financial status of the business and to discuss problems, plans, and other matters of interest.

Management meetings.   Managers and administrators at different organizational levels and/or in separate locations meet to develop plans, address problems, and discuss business concerns and opportunities.

Board of directors meetings.   Top-level officials of associations and businesses meet to discuss the present and to plan for the future of their organizations.

Association conventions and trade shows.   Professional associations may have an annual meeting that can attract thousands or more attendees to hear speakers and to participate in discussion sessions; booths manned by suppliers to the industry may be available to enable attendees to learn more about the products and services offered by the vendors.

Professional development meetings.   Postsecondary educational institutions, for-profit training organizations, and others offer meetings that address ad hoc topics; these programs are marketed to a general and, often, very large group of potentially interested attendees.

Motivational meetings.   Numerous professional motivational speakers offer programs ranging from several hours to several days, which are marketed to organizations and/or to individual attendees.

TECHNOLOGY AND MEETING MANAGEMENT

Modern technology enables the use of satellite and Internet-based conferences to minimize travel to common meeting sites. With this plan, meeting attendees can participate in **teleconferencing.** Sophisticated systems allow real-time, interactive conversations and discussions between participants. However, technology has not reduced the need for or benefits to employees in the same or different organizations in widespread locations to convene in traditional meetings for discussions about common issues.

RESPONSIBILITIES OF MEETING PLANNERS

OBJECTIVE 2
Describe basic responsibilities of meeting planners as a meeting is planned.

Persons who plan meetings must be creative, well organized, and able to manage, seemingly, a million and one details at the same time. The ability to effectively communicate is a necessary trait, as is the ability to negotiate for the best use of the resources available to the organization for which the meeting is intended. As Exhibit 28.1 illustrates, the work of a meeting planner can be divided into three components:

teleconferencing the conduct of meetings by using audio and visual communication technology to link persons in different locations

- Planning the meeting before it begins
- Managing the meeting as it evolves
- Following up after the meeting

Planning the Meeting

The process of planning begins by defining the meeting's objectives. Effective meeting objectives focus on the attendees. What exactly is the purpose of the meeting? What will we accomplish if the meeting is ideal? Who should attend the meeting, and what is in it for them? How can we make our meeting more desirable than a competitor's event?

Videoconferencing provides another meeting alternative.

A common method of writing effective meeting objectives is to use the **SMART** approach. Each letter of the SMART approach reminds the planner of critical components of a well-written objective:

SMART the tactic of writing objectives that are **s**pecific, **m**easurable, **a**chievable, **r**elevant, and **t**ime focused

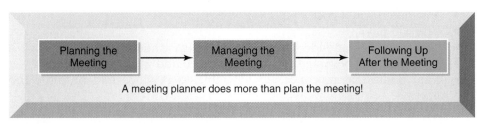

Planning the Meeting → Managing the Meeting → Following Up After the Meeting

A meeting planner does more than plan the meeting!

EXHIBIT 28.1
A Meeting Planner's Activities

Specific. Only one major concept is covered in each objective.
Measurable. Must be able to quantify or measure whether the objective has been attained.
Achievable. Is it possible to accomplish the objective?
Relevant. Is the objective important to the organization's overall goals?
Time. By when should the objective be completed?

Meeting objectives should typically include cost factors (if applicable) and indicate who is responsible for achieving the objective.

The site-selection process can begin after meeting objectives are developed because they guide the planner in decisions about physical location, type of facility, transportation options, and many other meeting components. Site selection may occur days, weeks, months, or even years before the event. For major conventions, a city is usually selected three to five years in advance. Small corporate meetings are usually planned less than six months in advance. Factors such as location of attendees, costs, accessibility (transportation), type of meeting facility, and meeting space requirements are critical to the site-selection process.

After meeting objectives and the basic location are determined, a **request for proposal (RFP)** is written to describe all major needs of the meeting. It will typically contain information such as the following:

- Meeting name
- Meeting start and end dates
- Key contact information
- Expected attendance
- Number and type of sleeping rooms required
- Number and size of meeting and exhibition space (if any) required
- Food and beverage requirements
- Acceptable rates for rooms, meeting space, and food and beverage
- Expectations of comps (free services)
- Cutoff date for the submission of RFPs

The RFP is circulated to hotel properties and convention facilities that may be interested in submitting a bid. If a meeting facility decides to submit a proposal, representatives of its sales department review meeting specifications and create a response.

The ultimate goal for the property submitting the bid is to balance what the planner wants and can afford with the revenues needed by the property. Many factors must be considered. If low room rates are important to the planner, then perhaps a guarantee of providing all food and beverage during the meeting will balance out reduced room rates. Conversely, if the group does not want the facility to provide food and beverage, then additional charges for guest-room or meeting space rental will likely be assessed.

After the planner has reviewed the RFPs returned, negotiations between the planner and the prospective meeting site sales representative can begin.

The meeting planner's budget will be at the heart of the negotiation process. It will address questions such as these:

- How much will it cost?
- Who will pay?
- How much will attendees be charged for registration?
- What food and beverage events are planned and what will be served?
- What additional revenues are available to produce and promote the meeting?

The three basic steps for planning the meeting's budget are previewed in Exhibit 28.2. Let's look at each of these three steps more closely.

request for proposal (RFP) a formal document that incorporates the organization's needs expressed in the form of detailed specification requirements; the objective of the RFP is to define the required services so clearly that prospective bidders can develop costs and other estimates used in their proposal responses

RISING STAR PROFILE

Julie Price

Managing Meeting Details Has Its Rewards!

Julie's first hospitality position was as a food server at a restaurant in her home town while she was in high school. During college, she worked at the snack shop at the student activity center, as a front-desk attendant at a residence hall, and as a food server at a Bennigan's restaurant. During the summer after her sophomore year, she completed an internship with the Michigan Municipal League (the state's association of cities and villages), which, in hindsight, was very significant to her career. Julie received an undergraduate degree with a major in integrative public relations and a minor in broadcast cinematic arts.

She remained in contact with supervisors from her internship at the Michigan Municipal League after her internship. She desired a position in event planning and, as fate would have it, that organization was searching for someone with these responsibilities.

As the education coordinator, Julie coordinated about 80 training programs annually for city officials throughout the state. Site visits at hotels and conference facilities are needed and after the space is secured, the education coordinator is responsible for all logistics, including food and beverage, audiovisual, and special arrangements. It is also important to promote the training programs to increase attendance and to plan large events that may have as many as 1,200 attendees. For one of these (the Michigan Municipal League's state convention), she served as the media relations representative and wrote news releases, distributed press tips, and interacted with the news media.

Julie has an unforgettable moment: "Seeing everything come together with nearly 700 attendees at our annual convention; everything ran smoothly!"

Julie is well aware of the most significant challenges confronting the meetings industry: budget cuts and resulting drops in attendance. "Local governments run on very strict budgets and so does our association. We have to be practical. We cannot plan elaborate meetings and events, and I must constantly address prices."

Julie has some great advice for young persons considering a career in the meetings industry: "Attention to detail is a must, as is effective communication and negotiation skills. Always make sure to read the fine lines of contracts, and carefully negotiate with a facility before you sign any documents.

"Know that you are not going to make a lot of money right after graduation. However, positions like mine are a lot of fun and very rewarding. You don't have to sit behind your desk all day. You are always meeting people and planning things. This industry is amazing. There are so many 'perks,' and you make so many connections."

Step 1: *Establish Financial Goals* Financial goals should incorporate the SMART process. They may be established by the meeting planner, association management or corporate mandate, or the account (client) of the independent meeting planner. Financial goals are very important to develop and continually consider because they establish the financial expectations of the meeting. Some events may be not for profit (for example, an awards ceremony to honor top achievers in a company). Most association meetings, by contrast, rely heavily on conventions to produce operating revenues. A third economic goal can be to break even: revenue collected from all activities should cover the expenses.

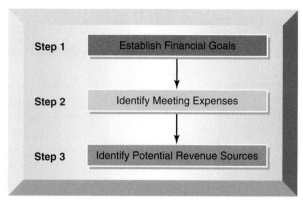

Step 1	Establish Financial Goals
Step 2	Identify Meeting Expenses
Step 3	Identify Potential Revenue Sources

EXHIBIT 28.2
How Is the Budget for the Meeting Planned?

Step 2: *Identify Meeting Expenses* Expenses vary according to the meeting's objectives and will be affected by location, season, type of facility, services selected, and other factors. Examples of costs include the following:

Registration materials
Speakers' travel expenses and fees
Signs, posters, and banners
Gratuities and gifts
Printing and photocopying
Room rental
Decorations and flowers
Shipping and freight charges
Complimentary registrations
Temporary staff
Food and beverage functions
Promotion
Multimedia equipment
Staff travel and expenses
Insurance
Supplies
Labor charges

Step 3: *Identify Potential Revenue Sources* How are meetings funded? Corporations include meeting costs in their operating budgets. Corporate planners must work within the constraints of the budget. Associations must be more creative in finding money to plan and implement an event. If the registration fee is too high, people won't attend. If it is too low, the association itself may not achieve revenue expectations. Association planners often look to funding sources, in addition to registration fees, such as these:

- Corporate or allied association funding
- Private funding
- Exhibitor fees (if trade show)
- Sponsorships (for example, of a speaker and/or a luncheon)
- Selling logo merchandise

Meetings can occur in a hotel conference room.

CLOSE LOOK AT THE MEETING PLANNING TEAM

Some members of the meeting planning team make decisions; others may be needed to implement the decisions. Decision makers are typically executives within the organization who approve the meeting and its budget, supervise the meeting planning team, and have responsibility for all legal, financial, and policy matters.

Meeting planners negotiate and recommend contracts, solicit bids, and hire and supervise suppliers. They also prepare drafts to monitor budget revenues and expenses, establish a planning schedule, recommend and implement policies and procedures, manage the on-site meeting as it evolves, and prepare follow-up documents and reports.

A wide variety of technical staff may be necessary depending on the size and type of meeting. These include specialists to:

Develop program topics and select speakers

Design copies for marketing and promotional pieces

Develop accounting and record-keeping systems for the meeting

Coordinate press relations

Assist with meeting technology needs

Review contracts and agreements

Prepare training materials and conduct sessions

Assess insurance coverage and risk management issues

- Advertising fees (banners or ads in the convention program, for example)
- Local, state, and national government assistance
- Renting membership address lists for marketing purposes
- Establishing official partnerships with other companies to promote products
- Contributions in cash or in kind (services or products)

Special Concerns: The Meeting Program

The program for the meeting involves all its scheduled activities, including presentations, food and beverage-related functions, trade show hours, non-meeting recreational alternatives, and **unscheduled time.** As with all other aspects of meeting planning, the objectives of the meeting drive its program of events. Meeting planners often help to select topics, presentation formats, and speakers that will most appeal to the meeting attendees.

Times for meeting schedules are important. How many days should the meeting last? How many hours per day should be allocated? How much time is needed for each program component and speaker? Since meetings may be planned years in advance, you can see that the meeting planner's scheduling concerns range from years to minutes.

unscheduled time time during a meeting when no events or activities are planned; this represents the attendees' personal time

OBJECTIVE 3
Explain basic procedures for meeting attendee registration.

MEETING REGISTRATION PROCEDURES

Registration is the process of gathering all necessary information and fees required for an individual to attend a meeting. It may begin several weeks or months before the event and continue to the last day of the meeting. Discounts are often provided to attendees who register in advance. (This can help planners to determine if attendance will reach anticipated levels. If not,

registration the process of gathering all necessary information and fees required for an individual attending a meeting

This political convention attracts thousands of delegates and is structured around hundreds of small and large meetings.

marketing efforts can be increased and efforts to negotiate within the hotel or meeting facility to reduce costs may be undertaken.)

Data collected on the registration form may include name, title, occupation, address, e-mail, phone, fax, membership category, desired workshop sessions, social functions, and more. Some organizations inquire about company size, attendee's supervisory or financial responsibilities, and the extent of their purchase decision making. Registration data are valuable and can be used before, during, and after the meeting.

Prior to the meeting, the data can be given or sold to exhibitors or advertisers so that they can promote their company, products, and services before the meeting date. During the meeting, registration data can be used as a promotional tool to gain media attention for the organization, sponsors, and exhibitors. It can also help the local **Convention and Visitors Bureau (**CVB) to justify the costs of marketing and soliciting groups to visit the area. After the meeting, registration data can be used to update association membership records and solicit new members or it can be sold to interested parties. Most importantly, it can be used to help the planner with the logistics and promotion of the next meeting.

Convention and Visitors Bureau (CVB) organizations, generally funded by taxes levied on overnight hotel guests and/or from membership fees paid by members; their purpose is to increase the number of visitors to the areas they represent

FOCUS ON MEETING ATTENDEES

Meeting planners must know and remember many things. When considering specific sessions, they must consider these factors:

Attention span. Most meeting attendees cannot concentrate on a topic for an extended amount of time. Short, fast-paced sessions generally work best.

Attendee retention. People typically remember more when they have participated in a presentation, rather than when they have just listened to it. How can this concern be addressed during meetings?

Use of visuals. Technology can be used to help presentations come to life.

Meeting environment. Table arrangements, comfort of chairs, lighting, room temperature and ventilation, and a wide range of other details applicable to the meeting space can have a dramatic impact on a meeting's success.

These details must be anticipated, planned for, and addressed during the meeting to help to assure that it is successful.

Preregistration is the process of registering attendees in advance of a meeting and provides information about who will be attending the meeting. For example, it can help the meeting planner to determine room capacities for educational sessions and can inform speakers about the estimated number of people that may attend a session. Whether paper based or electronic, and regardless of whether it is completed in advance or at the meeting site, the prospective attendee must typically complete a registration process.

The registration area is the first experience an attendee has with a meeting or convention. A slow or complicated registration process can set the tone for the entire meeting. Therefore, the registration area should be heavily staffed the first day and should remain open throughout the event. The check-in process for large groups is often expedited by sending necessary material to preregistered attendees prior to the event. These attendees will then only need to show identification and registration confirmation to receive meeting materials.

Press conferences are a type of meeting.

Registration is often **outsourced** by the meeting planner for large events. Some hotels or convention centers work with temporary agencies that provide staff to perform the registration activities. Some registration management companies also handle housing.

BASIC HOUSING PROCEDURES

When attendee housing is needed, four basic methods are typically utilized:

- Attendees arrange for their own room. The meeting sponsor makes no prior arrangements about price or availability.
- A group rate is negotiated by the planner, and attendees respond directly to the reservations department of their preferred hotel.
- The meeting sponsor handles all housing. Attendees book rooms through the meeting sponsor, who provides the hotel with a rooming list of confirmed guests.
- A third-party housing bureau (outsourced company) handles all arrangements either for a fee or paid by the CVB.

The first method is easiest for the planner. However, if rooms are not **blocked,** there will assuredly be a premium for renting meeting space and other services, because the hotel will have no assurance about the largest amount of potential revenue (guest-room rental) it may receive.

The last three options require that the meeting planner establish a rate for the attendees that reflects prior negotiations with the sales department about the total value of the meeting to the property. As with food and beverage events, the planner must estimate how many people will rent a guest room. If the planner blocks 100 rooms and only 75 attendees rent a room, the planner may be responsible for part or all of the cost of the unrented rooms. This is referred to as the **attrition rate.**

Having attendees call or reserve rooms online directly with the hotels is a good option. They will benefit by the negotiated room rate, and the hotel can handle the reservation processing directly. The meeting planner will be only minimally involved. When larger meetings require multiple properties,

preregistration the process of registering attendees in advance of a meeting

outsource to employ a person or organization to perform activities that would otherwise need to be done in-house (within an organization)

OBJECTIVE 4
Review basic information about housing meeting attendees.

block guest rooms reserved for members of a specific group

attrition rate the number of guest rooms in a block of rooms that are not rented

planners often provide a range of hotel prices to accommodate the budgets of all attendees.

Outsourcing the housing process to a third-party vendor or CVB is most common with medium- and large-sized meetings. Housing for a city-wide meeting is best left to professionals who have the most current technology and are well equipped to handle thousands of housing requests. Reservations through a housing service can be made by mail, phone, fax, and Internet.

OBJECTIVE 5
Describe basic responsibilities of meeting planners as the meeting evolves.

MANAGING THE MEETING

A meeting will not be successful if it is not properly planned. However, a properly planned meeting cannot be successful unless it is also properly managed as it evolves.

The meeting planner typically arrives at the meeting site one or more days early to confirm that all arrangements have been made and to plan last-minute details. Materials must be shipped to the meeting site, unpacked, and organized, and the meeting's headquarters, media, and perhaps other offices must be set up.

All particulars of the meeting should have been planned and be on paper in the **meeting specification guide.** Information should include the following:

meeting specification guide
a book (binder) containing all information and details applicable to a meeting, including agenda and schedule, contracts, purchase orders for products and services, and applicable communications

- *Meeting overview.* General information including:
  Group profile
  Names and responsibilities of meeting planners
  Number of guest rooms in a block with rates
  Details about the **master account** (including persons authorized to charge and types of allowable charges)
  Information about complimentary products and services
  Dates and times of all events and sessions

master account the folio established by the lodging property that allows certain preapproved charges made by or on behalf of a meeting sponsor to be charged to the meeting sponsor, rather than being the responsibility of the individual incurring the charge

- *Detailed instructions.* Specific information about interacting with personnel in each area of the hotel including:
  Procedures for auditing and signing hotel bills
  Receiving equipment sent to the meeting site
  Lodging contacts and scheuled hours on-site
- *Meeting services contacts.* Information is needed for all vendors and suppliers who will be providing products and services for the meeting including:

  Audiovisual services
  Floral arrangements
  Convention Bureau staff
  Entertainment
  Photographers
  Office equipment rentals
  Exposition (exhibit) services
- *Event requirements.* Details of all events that are part of the meeting including:
  Banquet event orders (BEOs), which detail all requirements for a food and beverage function
  Audiovisual, room setup, and other details about each meeting room for each meeting session
  Details such as delivery times, quantity, price, and locations

banquet event order (BEO)
a form used by the sales, catering, and food production areas to detail all requirements for a banquet; information provided by the banquet client is summarized on the form, and it becomes the basis for the formal contract between the client and the hotel

Technology helps with meeting presentations.

for receipt for all items purchased from all contracted service organizations

During the meeting, the meeting planner will likely be busy from very early in the morning until very late at night coordinating activities, managing details, and expediting promised services that might be behind schedule or overlooked by providers.

Other details that may require the meeting planner's attention during the meeting include these:

Much of a meeting manager's work involves negotiating on the telephone.

- Assessing on-site attendance is necessary to gather information for future meetings. If, for example, only a specified percentage of attendees participate in general, breakout, or trade show sessions, this is must-know information for future meetings.
- Managing **guarantees.** Information about food and beverage functions is necessary when the event's sponsor may be charged for meals in excess of the guarantee. For example, the meeting planner will want to know if an event with a guarantee of 1,000 diners was actually attended by 1,025 diners because of the additional charges involved.
- Supervising on-site staging (for example, of general meeting breakout sessions and trade show setup)
- Interacting with key organizational representatives to assess perceptions about the meeting and whether any immediate corrective action(s) may be necessary
- Helping to assure that messages and information between on-site meeting planners are coordinated and efficient
- Assuring that signage is placed when and where planned
- Providing special treatment for very important persons (VIPs), including speakers
- Providing for last-minute script changes, if necessary, for speakers

guarantee a contractual agreement about the number of meals to be provided at a banquet event; typically, a final guarantee must be made several days in advance of the event, at which time the entity contracting with the hotel agrees to pay for the larger of the actual number of guests served or the number of guests guaranteed

precon (preconference) session a session attended by meeting planners and applicable hotel personnel to review details and make final decisions about an upcoming meeting

---

DON'T FORGET THE PRECON MEETING

A **precon (preconference) session** should be held at least one day before the meeting to enable planners and organization representatives and property staff to assure that all the groups' expectations, needs, and special requirements can be met. Members of the hotel's management team (general manager, sales manager, convention services managers, and department heads or their representatives) should attend. Details about the meeting planner's expectations for each event and the hotel's representatives' responsibilities are discussed. Often a separate meeting is held with food and beverage department personnel regarding specifics of food and beverage functions. In addition to precon sessions, additional daily meetings are often held when a large meeting is being managed and/or when on-site problems occur.

- Adjusting the environment; heating, ventilating, air conditioning (HVAC), smoking, housekeeping, noise, and lighting issues (among others) may need to be addressed
- Coordinating the movement of large numbers of people between general sessions and breakout or other meeting spaces
- Managing on-site data collection from attendees; attendees' evaluations of sessions and attendance registration forms at sessions for certification and/or other purposes may need to be collected
- Troubleshooting; problems (or potential problems) always occur as meetings evolve, which meeting planners must address in a way that makes these issues unnoticeable to attendees

FOLLOWING UP AFTER THE MEETING

OBJECTIVE 6
Describe basic responsibilities of meeting planners as a meeting is concluded.

The meeting isn't over until it's over! As attendees return to their homes, the meeting planner still has work to do:

- Auditing and approving master accounts
- Tipping: While some tips are paid by attendees (such as for a la carte dining service and bellpersons) and while there are likely automatic food and beverage **service charges,** tips may also be paid to others providing services for the meetings. Tips (or gifts that can be shared) are often given to housekeepers, security and shipping personnel, audiovisual technicians, and front-desk staff members, along with sales managers and convention service managers.
- Auditing all other invoices presented for payment
- Summarizing and evaluating attendees' meeting evaluations
- Conducting a **postcon (postconference) meeting** with hotel staff

service charge a mandatory amount added to a guest's bill for services performed by a staff member of the hospitality organization

The meeting planner should create a written document to record all key events to help to plan the next meeting. The postcon serves as a report card to tell what went right and wrong during the meeting. Attendees typically include the planning staff, a sales department representative, the food and beverage director, the audiovisual manager, and accounting staff. Discrepancies in billing, service failures, and problems and praises are addressed.

postcon (postconference) meeting a session attended by meeting planners and applicable meeting site personnel to evaluate a meeting that has concluded

FOCUS ON CONFERENCE CENTER EDUCATION COORDINATORS

OBJECTIVE 7
Discuss special aspects of a conference center education coordinator.

We have just previewed important tasks that are part of a meeting planner's job. Recall that one important responsibility is to negotiate with and select a property location for the meeting. By contrast, **conference center education coordinators** have a role that is the opposite: to attract meetings to his or her employer (a conference center). They do this through marketing and sales activities to attract meetings and by assisting meeting sponsors and planners with housing, food and beverage services, meeting activities, management, and all other activities that are the responsibility of a sales and marketing staff member in the hotel. This role is similar to someone in a property's marketing and sales department with one big difference: the conference center education coordinator typically works with the meeting planner to define educational needs, select topics, and identify prospective speakers. In the case of nonorganizational-specific conferences, they also

conference center education coordinator the person performing the work of a meeting planner who represents a potential meeting site (conference center) and works with meeting sponsors and planners to plan on-site activities, including educational programs

> ## ALL ABOUT CONVENTION AND VISITORS BUREAUS (CVBs)
>
> Convention and Visitors Bureaus are located in many areas and can have a dramatic influence on attracting meetings to their areas. Hotels, restaurants, and area recreational sites typically fund CVBs. In some areas, tax revenues may be used for financial support. CVBs undertake advertising and promotional campaigns to attract groups to business meetings and conventions and individual travelers to the area. CVB personnel may help meeting planners with activities such as these:
>
> Manning registration and information booths
>
> Providing brochures and inexpensive souvenirs (novelties) to be used with other promotional information
>
> Coordinating housing between several hotels when large meetings require guest rooms in other than the primary meeting hotel
>
> Providing ongoing services for meeting planners as programs are planned and convened

use a much broader marketing approach to reach a widely diverse group of potential attendees.

What Does a Conference Planner Do?

Many universities have continuing education or professional development conference centers that generate significant revenues. They employ professional education coordinators who serve as account executives working to meet the specific educational needs of several assigned clients. An important

> ## HURRICANE KATRINA AND THE MEETINGS BUSINESS
>
> Hurricane Katrina struck New Orleans and the Gulf Coast in Fall 2005 and showcased just how fragile tourism and the meetings industry can be. Following the disaster, hundreds of meetings and conventions had to be canceled or postponed. This, in turn, led to hundreds of millions of dollars of lost revenues to New Orleans and the region. It affected meeting facilities, industry suppliers, gaming venues, hospitality industry employees, local restaurants, retails stores, and every other component of the hospitality industry. It also created innumerable challenges for many planners who had to cancel or postpone their events or reschedule them to another location. The New Orleans Metropolitan Convention and Visitor's Bureau did a fantastic job of informing the meeting planning community about the clean-up efforts and the rebuilding of the convention infrastructure. It posted informative streaming videos on its website on a regular basis (www.neworleanscvb.com) and created a marketing campaign, Make Way for the Rebirth, to promote New Orleans. The first major group to meet in New Orleans was the American Library Association, which brought 18,000 members to the city in June 2006. The event was an overwhelming success, and it proved that New Orleans was coming back strong.

responsibility is to learn the educational needs, goals, and objectives of their clients so that they can customize a specific topic to better meet the unique needs of the client.

Education coordinators generally work on three types of programs:

open-enrollment program an educational program developed by a continuing education and professional development conference center on a generic topic that is marketed to attendees from different organizations

- **Open-enrollment programs.** Designed to present a generic topic to attendees from different organizations; these programs may be widely marketed to attract attendees from broad national and international locations.
- Generic topics for a single organization
- Customized programs for a specific organization

Planners in executive education centers typically have access to academic and industry experts with the knowledge and presentation skills to yield very high quality programs.

Airport hotels frequently have meeting rooms to accommodate persons flying to a central site for a several-hour meeting.

They also utilize extensive networks to assist in locating special presenters for special topics.

BOOKING OUTSIDE THE BLOCK AND ROOM BLOCK PIRATES

An unfortunate consequence of online travel sites is that attendees can often book a room at a lower cost in the same hotel in which the meeting planner has established a room block. This is called "booking outside the block." When negotiating a contract, a smart planner will include protection that prohibits the hotel from selling rooms during the conference dates to the general public for less than the agreed on conference rate. If this is not possible, then the planner should include a clause that credits (includes) rooms used by meeting attendees who are not part of the block to the overall room pickup for the event.

Room block pirates are another problem. These are companies that target meeting attendees with reduced rates for rooms either at the headquarters hotel or, perhaps, another nearby property. They often rent association membership lists from the parent organization and then promote their services under the pretense of being connected to the group. Although this is highly unethical, it is not illegal. The best way for a meeting planner to protect the room block (and the attendees) is to alert members prior to the housing process about fraudulent companies trying to attract them with lower rates or alternative locations. Remind attendees that, if the negotiated room block is not met, the group will still pay for any unused rooms. This, in turn, will have a negative impact on the event's financial success and could lead to higher registration rates in the future. Again, protecting the meeting with specific contractual clauses is essential.

SUMMARY OF CHAPTER LEARNING OBJECTIVES

1. **Identify three types of meeting planners.**
   There are three basic types of meeting planners: those who work for corporations, associations, and individual clients (independent planners).

2. **Describe basic responsibilities of meeting planners as a meeting is planned.**
   The meeting planner begins by defining the meeting objectives using the SMART (specific, measurable, achievable, relevant, and time-focused) approach. Site selection must consider, first, the geographic location and then the hotel, conference center, or other site within that location for the meeting. A request for proposal describing the major needs of the meeting is circulated to potential meeting sites, and proposal responses are analyzed upon return. Then the negotiation process begins and, upon successful completion, a meeting budget can be finalized. Another important concern relates to the schedule for the meeting program.

3. **Explain basic procedures for meeting attendee registration.**
   Registration involves gathering the information and fees required for an individual to attend a meeting. A wide range of information can be collected that is helpful before, during, and after the session. Many meetings allow attendees to preregister and, for big conferences, the registration and preregistration tasks are outsourced.

4. **Review basic information about housing meeting attendees.**
   Four basic methods can be used for housing: attendees can arrange for their own room, attendees can respond directly to their preferred hotel, the meeting sponsor can handle housing needs, or a third-party housing bureau can be utilized.

5. **Describe basic responsibilities of meeting planners as the meeting evolves.**
   During the meeting, the meeting planner will be busy with many tasks. The meeting specification guide lists numerous details to help avoid surprises during the session. A preconference session is held before the meeting begins so that meeting representatives and those from the host site can undertake detailed planning. A wide range of other activities is necessary and should be done in a way that is not noticeable to attendees.

6. **Describe basic responsibilities of meeting planners as a meeting is concluded.**
   After the meeting is completed, the meeting planner must audit master accounts and other invoices, tip necessary personnel, summarize and evaluate attendees' meeting evaluations, and conduct a postconference meeting with hotel staff.

7. **Discuss special aspects of a conference center education coordinator.**
   The meeting activities of conference center education coordinators are similar to those of a meeting planner. However, there are at least two differences: they have an additional role to attract meetings to their conference center and, in the case of university-sponsored centers, conference planners are involved in helping meeting planners to plan educational sessions and select potential speakers.

MASTERING YOUR KNOWLEDGE

Discuss the following questions.

1. What are examples of communication and negotiating skills that effective meeting planners must be able to utilize?

2. What are ways in which the work of meeting planners for corporations, associations, and individual clients is the same? Different?

3. What types of questions must be answered by small associations or companies as they consider the use of an independent planner for an upcoming meeting?

4. If you were a meeting planner, what types of concerns would be important to you when evaluating alternative meeting sites within a specific city?

5. What are examples of topics you as a meeting planner would address in a precon meeting? A postcon meeting?

6. What are examples of surprises that may occur as a meeting evolves that must be effectively managed by a meeting planner?

7. You are an association meeting planner. Preregistration for an upcoming conference is lower than expected. What are some tactics you can use to address this challenge?

FEEDBACK FROM THE REAL WORLD

Our real-world advice comes from the author of this chapter, Curtis Love.

Curtis Love is an associate professor in the Department of Tourism and Convention Administration at the William F. Harrah College of Hotel Administration, University of Nevada, Las Vegas. Love's teaching and research concentrations are in the areas of meeting planning and exposition management. Prior to joining the faculty at UNLV, he was the vice-president of education for the Professional Convention Management Association. He has presented numerous workshops for industry associations, including the International Association of Exposition Management, Professional Convention Management Association, Association for Convention Operations Management, International Special Events Society, Meeting Professionals International, and Canadian Society of Association Executives. He specializes in assisting organizations in the development and implementation of evaluation instruments to measure customer service and satisfaction with educational programming and in collecting and analyzing association membership data.

What are some of the most important tactics that a meeting planner can utilize during the negotiation process with representatives of the prospective meeting site to minimize costs without compromising the meeting's objectives?

A key negotiation tool is for the meeting planner to fully comprehend the overall economic value of the meeting from the facility's perspective. Hotels and other meeting facility personnel look at the combined economic impact of a group before they submit a bid for the business. How many and what type of sleeping rooms will be used? How many food and beverage functions will take place? What menu selections and decor will be needed? Will recreational facilities such as spa and golf courses be utilized? In a gaming facility, is the group likely to gamble or use other entertainment venues? Providing a detailed history of past meetings to the facility greatly enhances one's bargaining power.

Being flexible with meeting dates can also be economically beneficial for meeting planners. Most hotels have peak seasons and off-seasons. Holding a meeting during a hotel's off-season can yield comparable levels of facilities and service at reduced prices. Likewise, facilities in major resort cities like Orlando and Las Vegas will negotiate lower rates for meetings held Monday through Thursday, because this leaves peak days (Friday, Saturday, and Sunday) open for the leisure market, which will pay higher room rates.

On what items is a hotel or other meeting site representative most likely to negotiate? Least likely?

Room and meeting space rates are typically the most flexible due to supply and demand. Rates at a four-star property during the off-season can be extremely affordable. If enough sleeping rooms are reserved, meeting space may be provided free. Amenities such as admissions to spa and recreational facilities may also be highly negotiable. Fixed costs such as food and beverage are less flexible. Food costs can vary dramatically due to the availability and seasonality of menu selections. Typically, hotels will only guarantee pricing a few months prior to the actual event.

What are common mistakes that meeting planners make while planning a meeting?

Failing to keep the host facility informed about changes in housing, session locations, meeting room sets, audiovisual needs, security, and other facility concerns can be problematic. The facility needs adequate time to communicate changes to the service personnel responsible for implementing the meeting. Planners also must

CHAPTER 28   Professional Meeting Management   **527**

keep detailed written records of all communication with facility staff. Without proper documentation, it is easy to forget "who has been told what." It also serves as a record should there be problems down the road.

Not anticipating emergency situations can also be a big problem. Transportation strikes, adverse weather conditions, security threats, political protests, and other unexpected situations can have a devastating impact on a meeting. Detailed written emergency plans should be made well in advance of the meeting and should be communicated to all staff.

Keeping the big picture of a meeting in mind can also be troublesome. A meeting planner working to produce a major convention with a large trade show and many ancillary events can easily lose sight of the overall goal of the meeting. If the planner focuses only on his or her own part of the convention, such as arranging educational sessions, and does not comprehend the trade show component, scheduling and communication problems can (and likely will!) arise.

What are the most frequent problems that occur as attendees preregister for a meeting? What tactics can a professional meeting planner use to address these potential problems?

Preregistration is very important, especially for the association planner. Many decisions are based on preregistration numbers. This information helps the planner to adjust room blocks, catering guarantees, educational sessions, room sets, and many other key components.

A planner always looks to the past when examining preregistration numbers. All things equal, how do the preregistration numbers compare with last year at the same point? (If numbers are down, then perhaps more promotion is needed to encourage prospective attendees to sign up.) Multiple methods of registration must be made available. For example, if only Internet-based registration is available, those without computer access may be excluded. Registration should be made available by every means possible: mail, fax, phone, and Internet. Using a professional registration service generally alleviates most potential problems.

What are the most important tasks a meeting planner should do immediately after a meeting is concluded?

An after-conference (postcon) meeting with the facility's staff is advisable for any meeting of substantive size and complexity. It may be the planner's last time to sit face to face with the convention service manager and other key facility staff to review what went right or wrong. It's much easier to address concerns while they are fresh on the planner's mind. On return to the office, any bills due should be reviewed promptly for payment. (One doesn't want to get the reputation of being a slow-paying customer.) Other duties include writing thank you notes or letters of recognition to those who made your meeting a success. Making notes to help to plan the next meeting is also important.

LEARN FROM THE INTERNET

1. Check out the websites for the following associations:
   - International Association of Healthcare Central Service Materiel Management: www.iahcsmm.org
   - International Carwash Association: www.carcarecentral.com
   - American Marketing Association: www.marketingpower.com

   Literally tens of thousands of associations are part of the meetings market. If you want, select several about which you are familiar or want to learn more and obtain information about their educational and/or trade show sessions.

   What kind of information do they provide to help market upcoming conferences, conventions, or trade shows?

2. Check out the following websites for several hotel and conference centers:
   - New York Marriott Marquis: www.nymarriottmarquis.com
   - Opryland Hotel: www.gaylordhotels.com
   - Sheraton Waikiki Beach Resort: www.sheraton-waikiki.com

Also, check out websites for hotels in your area.

What type of information is provided to sell meeting planners on the use of their facilities?

3. Check out the websites for the Convention and Visitors Bureaus in your community and other communities close to you. How do these organizations attempt to encourage meeting planners to offer meetings within their areas?

4. Check out the websites for independent meeting planners including:

   • Conference & Logistic Consultants, Inc.: www.gomeeting.com

   • Meeting Expectations, Inc.: www.meetingexpectations.com

   • Meeting Solutions, Inc.: www.meetingsolutions.net

   • Premier Meetings: www.premiermeetings.com

   • Professional Meeting Planners: www.pmpmeeting.com

What advantages do they cite for using their organization?

KEY HOSPITALITY TERMS

The following terms were explained in this chapter. Review the definitions of any words with which you are unfamiliar. Begin to utilize them as you expand your vocabulary as a hospitality professional.

meeting planner
return on investment (ROI)
association
convention
trade show
teleconferencing
SMART
request for proposal (RFP)
unscheduled time
registration
Convention and Visitors Bureau (CVB)
preregistration

outsource
block
attrition rate
meeting specification guide
master account
banquet event order (BEO)
guarantee
precon (preconference) session
service charge
postcon (postconference) meeting
conference center education coordinator
open-enrollment program

Exhibition (Trade Show) Management

29

Close-up of trade show booth

CHAPTER LEARNING OBJECTIVES

After studying this chapter you will be able to:

1. Provide a brief overview of exhibitions (trade shows) and the role they play in the marketplace.

2. Discuss how exhibitors and exhibition sponsors work together to assure successful exhibitions.

3. Describe popular location sites for exhibitions.

4. Learn basics about the role of exhibition service contractors in exhibition management.

5. Explain specifics to consider when exhibition floor plans and layouts are drawn.

6. Review the responsibilities of a position that is unique to exhibition management.

7. Discuss basic challenges confronting the exhibition management industry.

This chapter was authored by Curtis Love, PhD, Associate Professor, Tourism and Convention Department, William F. Harrah College of Hotel Administration, University of Nevada, Las Vegas.

FEEDBACK FROM THE REAL WORLD

Associations of all types generate significant revenues from the conduct of their annual (or more frequent) conferences. Many sponsor exhibitions (trade shows) as an integral part of these conferences. This allows them to generate booth rental from suppliers, manufacturers, and others wishing to exhibit at the trade show. These shows *must* be successful or the association will feel the budget consequences for the upcoming year or longer. Relationships with exhibitors will also be affected when attendance is down and the fees spent by exhibitors are not utilized in a cost-effective manner.

Pretend you are a full-time planner for an association organizing an exhibition. How do you determine what activities related to planning and implementation of an exhibition should be retained and done in-house? What activities can be considered for outsourcing? How would you select a service contractor for the responsibilities to be outsourced?

As you read this chapter, think about answers to these questions and then get feedback from the real world at the end of the chapter.

Ever since humans have grown food and produced items for sale, it has been necessary to have a place of contact between the seller and the buyer, regardless of whether the items were sold or traded. At first these interchanges probably occurred on roads, street corners, and town meeting places. Gradually, these fairs became regular events at which people exchanged goods and services on a larger scale. Historically, people relied on artisans to create consumer goods on a one-at-a-time basis. If you needed shoes, you went to a cobbler; if you needed a bowl, you went to a potter.

In the late 1800s, with the advent of the Industrial Revolution and mass-production techniques, everything changed. As goods were mass produced, their costs decreased dramatically. This, in turn, made more goods affordable for more people. As goods entered the marketplace, consumer demand grew and the need for more, better, and cheaper products arose.

Also during this time, large indoor exhibitions that lasted several months were held in permanent structures built for the express purpose of showcasing manufactured goods. These exhibitions were highly organized and were attended by invitation only; the general public was not admitted. Their purpose was to encourage national and international trading opportunities between wholesalers and retailers.

OBJECTIVE 1
Provide a brief overview of exhibitions (trade shows) and the role they play in the marketplace.

exhibition an industry-specific event that allows suppliers to an industry to interact with, educate, and sell to individuals and businesses that are part of the industry; also called *trade show*

trade show an industry-specific event that enables suppliers to an industry to interact with, educate, and sell to individuals and businesses that are part of the industry; also called *exhibition*

exhibitors an individual or organization sponsoring a booth at an exhibition

consumer show an exhibition open to the public (usually for an admission fee)

ASSOCIATIONS SPONSOR EXHIBITIONS

Exhibitions, sometimes referred to as **trade shows,** are events that are often part of annual association-sponsored conferences and meetings. In addition to the trade show, a significant educational component is featured. Planning and executing a major trade show can take a year or more. **Exhibitors** are suppliers and others desiring access to those attending the event. They sponsor and staff a booth to showcase their products and services during the exhibition.

Consumer shows are another popular type of exhibition. Examples include home, garden, and bridal events. These events are generally open to the public and an admission fee is typically charged. Exhibitors are retailers and/or manufacturers desiring direct access to consumers.

Exhibit 29.1 identifies key players in exhibitions. Show organizers can be either associations or for-profit companies. They bring together attendees

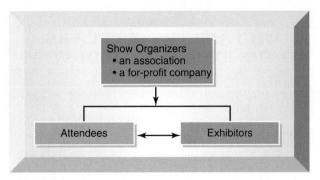

EXHIBIT 29.1
Key Players in Exhibitions

desiring to learn what's new to help them in their business and exhibitors whose goals are often to:

- Display their goods and services to attendees
- Educate attendees about their goods and services
- Generate sales
- Benchmark against other competitors at the exhibition
- Introduce and test new products and services
- Visit with regular clients
- Network within the industry

EXHIBITORS AND SPONSORS ARE PARTNERS

OBJECTIVE 2
Discuss how exhibitors and exhibition sponsors work together to assure successful exhibitions.

Developing a product or service is the first step in getting it to the buyer. The second, and often most challenging step, is to sell it. Exhibitions bring exhibitors together with a targeted group of buyers who (if the product or service has been carefully thought out) may be interested in what the exhibitors want to sell. **Qualified buyers** are individuals who either have purchasing power or some type of influence in the purchase decision-making process. It is not the number of attendees that spells success for an exhibition's sponsor but, rather, the number of qualified buyers. Exhibitors don't want to waste time trying to sell products to people who have no intention of buying them.

qualified buyers individuals with purchasing power or who influence purchasing decisions

Large exhibitions, such as those sponsored by the National Restaurant Association (NRA) and the Club Managers Association of America (CMAA), are scheduled at approximately the same time each year. This provides meaningful target dates for manufacturers and suppliers to roll out or launch new products and services.

Exhibitors typically ship large quantities of promotional materials

Persons in line to enter trade show at Long Beach Convention Center

---

WHO ARE THE SUPPLIERS TO THE EXHIBITION INDUSTRY?

What types of companies are necessary to make exhibitions successful? In other words, where are the jobs in the exhibition industry?

Exhibition management companies

Exhibit halls

General service contractors

Exhibit designers and manufacturers

Specialty contractors (including carpenters, plumbers, and florists)

Transportation

Industry-specific publications

Associations

Hotels and restaurants

Union laborers

---

and samples of products, if applicable, to exhibitions. The former are distributed to attendees as they move down aisles past exhibitors' booths. These materials can generate sales long after the exhibition ends. Some samples may be consumed immediately, in the case of food or beverage products. Promotional items may later remind a potential buyer about the exhibitors' products.

Costs to exhibit at exhibitions can be significant. Booth rental charges are one example. (Show sponsors may generate significant revenues from selling booths at the exhibition; the costs are typically based on exhibit floor location and/or the square feet of booth space.) Additional costs include those incurred to transport, house, feed, entertain, and pay the salaries of the exhibitor's personnel, sample and promotional materials costs, and often freight costs for transporting the booth and its contents. Costs of booth setup, electrical wiring, carpeting, furniture, and security also add up quickly. Exhibitors occupying hundreds of square feet of booth space with staff available to accommodate the number of attendees who would likely visit this location can spend hundreds of thousands of dollars or more. There is always a special concern that this expenditure be cost-effective and be the wisest use of funds.

Associations sponsoring trade shows often have one or more exhibitor representatives serving on their board and/or the events planning team. Their input is utilized whenever possible in efforts to encourage attendees to visit the trade show during the hours it is open. Tactics include these:

- Scheduling key exhibit times when no other conference-related activities occur
- Scheduling coffee breaks, entertainment, and special speaker events in the exhibit area
- Conducting drawings on the trade show floor (winners must be present!) for significant prizes

exhibitor's prospectus
marketing information provided to prospective exhibitors with the purpose of encouraging their participation in an exhibition

An **exhibitor's prospectus** is the primary marketing tool used by show organizers to promote their show to potential exhibitors. Key information such as time, date, and location of the show is provided. Facts and figures about last year's show attendance and exciting activities to entice attendees to the next show are also included. The exhibitor's prospectus contains all the forms necessary for exhibitors to place a deposit on the booth size requested. Show rules and regulations and general information about services available to the exhibitor are also included.

After an exhibitor has agreed to participate in the exhibition, a contract will be signed and an **exhibitor's service kit** containing a wide range of information applicable to the upcoming exhibition and the responsibilities of exhibitors will be sent to the exhibitor. Other information about payment schedules and insurance coverage is provided. The exhibitor's service kit has historically been a large, bound notebook. Increasingly, however, it is available online at the sponsor's website. All forms can be filled out electronically or printed and mailed or faxed to the show's organizer.

At the trade show

LOCATION! LOCATION! LOCATION!

Locations for the conduct of exhibitions are a significant factor in their success. Large cities with their cultural, recreational, shopping, dining, and other attractions are of interest to many potential attendees who wish to arrive earlier and/or remain later than exhibition dates. Some locations are very attractive to the attendees' families who, increasingly, accompany them. Still other locations are attractive because of weather, resort activities, scenery, and/or historic significance. Many associations rotate meeting locations in patterns that recognize the impact of distance (the travel costs) on attendance. A large association, for example, may move from eastern to midwestern to western locations in the United States or, alternatively, may cycle in a midwest, east coast, midwest, west coast, midwest cycle.

After the geographic location for an exhibition is determined, its site within the preferred city must be determined. Common locations for exhibitions include the following:

- Convention centers
- Hotels
- Private halls
- Universities and colleges

exhibitor's service kit a packet of information containing rules of the exhibition sponsor and contracts and promotional pieces offering products and services of the exhibition service contractor(s)

OBJECTIVE 3
Describe popular location sites for exhibitions.

IT ALL BOILS DOWN TO MONEY!

You have learned that vendors incur significant costs to exhibit at exhibitions. They typically have numerous alternatives for getting the word out about their products or services, including advertising in trade publications and on Internet home pages and providing samples to potential buyers. Manufacturers can also conduct mini-trade shows in conjunction with selected distributors.

During times of economic slowdowns, exhibitor participation at exhibitions often decreases. This, in turn, creates significant economic challenges to associations and other sponsors whose budgets anticipate revenue from booth rentals. Sponsors must, then, be creative in efforts to quantify the worth of exhibiting at their shows. To do this, they typically conduct research to determine the buying power of attendees and to consider inducements to encourage exhibitors to attend.

SUCCESSFUL EXHIBITIONS ARE GOOD FOR THE LOCAL ECONOMY

Exhibition attendees spend money on housing, meals, shopping, transportation, entertainment, and attractions and for numerous other purposes, which, in turn, boosts the local economy. Local businesses providing products and services in support of exhibitions and/or their attendees benefit, as do their employees, both of whom, in turn, help the local economy by paying taxes and spending money.

Large cities in metropolitan areas typically have **Convention and Visitors Bureaus (CVBs)** whose purpose is to secure exhibition business and to increase attendance at exhibitions in the area. These agencies, often funded by governmental assessments (sometimes called **occupancy taxes**) and/or from membership fees paid by CVB members, are typically very creative and aggressive in their marketing efforts.

Convention and Visitors Bureau (CVB) organizations generally funded by taxes levied on overnight hotel guests and/or from membership fees paid by members; their purpose is to increase the number of visitors to the areas they represent

occupancy taxes assessments levied against lodging properties whose purpose is to support the local tourism industry; sometimes called *bed tax*

- Arenas
- Private auditoriums
- Agricultural pavilions
- Fairgrounds
- Parks
- Cruise ships

Properly designed convention centers have significant expanses of open space and flexible access to utilities. They often have meeting, auditorium, arena, and banquet spaces, along with necessary conference (audio and video), food production and service, exhibit, loading dock, and other areas and support services to meet the needs of planners of exhibitions of different types and sizes. Many, especially large, facilities hold multiple events simultaneously and/or can refigure events and spaces for different groups overnight (or even more quickly!). Large hotels can provide space for small- to medium-sized exhibitions. However, unless they have been constructed specifically or remodeled for these purposes, they are frequently limited relative to loading docks, ceiling heights, weight restrictions, and electrical and utility services.

Exhibit 29.2 is a checklist used by exhibition planners to evaluate alternative exhibition sites.

WHAT DO EXHIBITION SERVICE CONTRACTORS DO?

Planners typically utilize **service contractors** to help them with on-site exhibition products and services. They provide a wide range of assistance to exhibition sponsors and exhibitors. Exhibit 29.3 reviews examples of this assistance.

In contrast to service contractors providing full-line (general) service, some specialty service contractors provide assistance in only one or several of

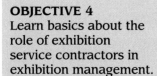

OBJECTIVE 4
Learn basics about the role of exhibition service contractors in exhibition management.

service contractor (exhibition) a business or individual who provides goods and/or services to exhibition managers and exhibitors that create the environment for an exhibition, including the exhibit floor and its related elements

The Venetian Resort-Casino in Las Vegas offers 1.9 million square feet of meeting space just minutes from its guests' hotel suites.

EXHIBIT 29.2
Checklist for Evaluation of
Exhibition Site Alternatives

	Acceptable	Potential Problem	Comments
Part I: General Considerations			
❑ Can attain event objective	❑	❑	
❑ Location (relative to target markets)	❑	❑	
❑ Accessible and attractive	❑	❑	
❑ Political, legal, union restrictions	❑	❑	
❑ Available when needed	❑	❑	
❑ Pricing concerns	❑	❑	
❑ Attendee expectations	❑	❑	
❑ Exhibitor preferences	❑	❑	
❑ Labor pool	❑	❑	
❑ Economy (international, national, local)	❑	❑	
❑ Other: _____	❑	❑	
Part II: Facility Requirements			
❑ Gross square footage acceptable	❑	❑	
❑ Ceiling height	❑	❑	
❑ Floor load capacity and carpeting	❑	❑	
❑ Obstructions	❑	❑	
❑ Doors (pedestrian and freight)	❑	❑	
❑ Loading docks	❑	❑	
❑ Storage	❑	❑	
❑ Utilities	❑	❑	
❑ Security	❑	❑	
❑ Communication capabilities	❑	❑	
❑ Show services and exclusive contracts	❑	❑	
❑ Facility rules and regulations	❑	❑	
❑ Americans with Disabilities Act (ADA)	❑	❑	
Part III: Public Service and Administrative Areas			
❑ Location and number of restrooms	❑	❑	
❑ Telephones and Internet access	❑	❑	
❑ Registration area	❑	❑	
❑ Foodservice outlets	❑	❑	
❑ Business services	❑	❑	
❑ Signage restrictions	❑	❑	
❑ Insurance	❑	❑	
❑ Licensing	❑	❑	
❑ Taxes	❑	❑	
Part IV: Meeting Manager's Considerations			
❑ Distance from show floor	❑	❑	
❑ Ceilings	❑	❑	
❑ Walls and sound proofing	❑	❑	
❑ Floors and doors	❑	❑	
❑ Obstructions	❑	❑	
❑ Windows and lighting	❑	❑	
❑ Electrical and communications	❑	❑	
❑ Audiovisual equipment	❑	❑	
❑ Competing groups	❑	❑	
❑ Business services	❑	❑	

Some trade shows are for consumers rather than professionals.

subcontract   a contract under a contract: a person may contract with someone else who, in turn, contracts with a third party to perform part of the contract's obligation

Attendees can taste new products at hospitality-related trade shows.

the listed areas. These specialty contractors might be retained directly by the sponsor and/or exhibitor or might be **subcontracted** by the general service contractor.

Exhibition planners typically create a request for proposal (RFP) outlining their requirements and expectations. Proposal responses received from prospective service contractors are evaluated. This input, along with previous experience, availability, referral and reputation, familiarity with site, available resources, professional accreditation, and, of course, costs, is utilized to determine the service contractor(s) to be used for the exhibition.

EXHIBIT 29.3
Examples of Assistance Provided by Exhibition Service Contractors

To Exhibition Sponsors	To Exhibitors
General decoration	Freight handling
Framing and drapes setup and teardown (for booths)	Warehousing
	Signage (booth)
Floor coverings	Furniture rental
Lighting	Booth setup and teardown
Signage (general)	Booth options (electrical and plumbing, for example)
Audio and video	
Sound system	
Staging	
Cleaning	
Security	
Office and registration setup	
On-site coordination	
Labor, union contracting, management	
Manage shipping	

It can take a large staff to man an exhibitor's trade show booth.

MECHANICS OF FLOOR PLANS

Allocations for exhibitions of any size are critical in assigning space and accommodating booth traffic during exhibitions. Exhibition halls and other facilities offering meeting spaces typically have **floor plans** drawn to scale to familiarize planners with and alert them to potential layout concerns. A site inspection with a representative of the facility and the service contractor, if applicable, is generally very helpful.

If the show organizer uses the same facility for each exhibition, a **static floor plan** involving the use of the same layout for each exhibition can be helpful once the best arrangement of space and traffic flow has been determined.

Exhibit 29.4 shows common booth designs. Recall that larger (square feet) booths typically rent for more than smaller booths; booths in preferred locations rent for more than their less desirable counterparts.

OBJECTIVE 5
Explain specifics to consider when exhibition floor plans and layouts are drawn.

floor plan   a schematic drawing of the exhibition space that indicates all obstructions, entrances, utility ports, and available usage areas

static floor plan   a schematic of exhibit space used by a show sponsor each time space in the same facility is utilized

Autos on display at Los Angeles, California, auto show

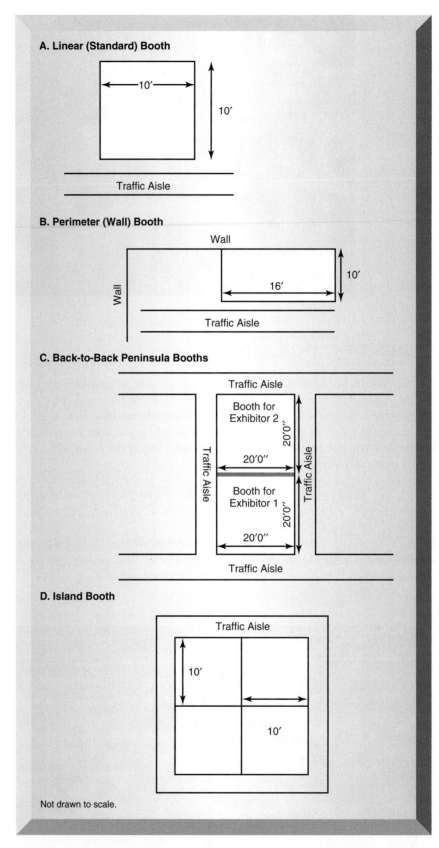

A. Linear (Standard) Booth

B. Perimeter (Wall) Booth

C. Back-to-Back Peninsula Booths

D. Island Booth

Not drawn to scale.

EXHIBIT 29.4
Common Exhibitor Booth Designs

HOW ARE EXHIBITOR BOOTHS ASSIGNED?

Many show organizers make booth assignments for the following year during the current year's show. The process is relatively easy because most potential exhibitors are there. Many exhibitors have preferred locations based on traffic flow, proximity to other exhibitors, or similar considerations. Most exhibitors would like to be the first booth people see when entering the trade show floor or, alternatively, they want to be located next to a high-profile exhibitor. To be fair to all exhibitors, several methods of booth assignment are commonly used. **First come, first served** uses postmarks or date and time stamps on a fixed-space contract to show which exhibitors will be first to select their booth location. Another method is by **lottery;** exhibitors draw a number, and those with the lowest numbers are first to select. All other booths are then selected based on the number drawn by the exhibitor. **Priority points** is a third option: exhibitors receive points for each year they exhibit and for the size of their booth. Exhibitors with the most points have the first choice of booth locations.

A CLOSE LOOK AT THE EXHIBITION MANAGER'S JOB

A number of different types of managers cooperate as a team to promote, create, and implement an exhibition. The exhibition manager is an employee of the sponsoring organization and coordinates all aspects of trade shows, which include selling booth space, assigning booth locations, ensuring that all exhibitors follow rules and regulations, and monitoring security and registration activities. The exhibition manager tries to create lasting relationships between exhibitors and the trade show sponsor and general service contractor. An exhibition manager must be outgoing, with good oral and written communication skills, and be able to negotiate effectively. His or her primary function is to create trust and to provide excellent customer service.

first come, first served (exhibition booth assignment method) booths are assigned on the basis of the date booth contracts are signed

lottery (exhibition booth assignment method) booths are assigned on the basis of the lowest numbers drawn by exhibitors

priority points (exhibition booth assignment method) exhibitors receive points for past exhibits and booth size; those with the most points have the first choice of booth selection

CHALLENGES CONFRONTING THE INDUSTRY

Several significant challenges confront the exhibition management industry.

Economic Slowdown

The success of exhibitions is closely tied to the overall health of the national economy. When times are tough, things get rough in the exhibition industry. Exhibitors tend to buy smaller booths and fewer services when their budgets get tight. At worst, some exhibitors scale back on the number of trade shows in which they participate each year. Effective trade show managers address this challenge by demonstrating how participation in the trade show will increase their business. They use research to assess what exhibitors need to succeed at a show (and then provide it), and they foster long-term relationships to develop trust. Then, when the economy improves, exhibitors will remember how well they were treated!

Need to Reduce Costs

Technology can be used to improve efficiency and provide better customer service. For example, marketing materials can now be updated quickly and distributed inexpensively online. Web-based registration, exhibitor contracts,

OBJECTIVE 6
Review the responsibilities of a position that is unique to exhibition management.

OBJECTIVE 7
Discuss basic challenges confronting the exhibition management industry.

Forklifts may be needed to move huge crates holding exhibitors' booth contents.

and booth assignment tasks can dramatically save processing and printing costs. And a virtual trade show on the sponsor's website can keep the show alive 365 days a year. Links to exhibitors and streaming video can be used to make Web surfing a more active experience for prospective attendees and exhibitors.

Education

Exhibitors and attendees want to maximize the return on investment as they attend an exhibition. An increased emphasis on education can include providing continuing education to attendees. Topics can be developed that are industry focused and/or provide for personal growth. Association administrators can also design educational programs for new exhibitors to teach them how to sell to a specific market. This is especially important for international attendees whose direct selling culture may be different from that in the United States.

Networking with professional colleagues is an important aspect of trade shows.

RISING STAR PROFILE

**Sue Ralston
Associate Director
Trade Show Sales
and Service
National Automatic
Merchandising
Association
Chicago, Illinois**

Studying and Learning Doesn't End When You Finish School

Sue graduated with a university degree in communications. While in school, she was unaware that she would pursue a career in trade show management after graduation. However, it turned out to be an excellent major, because she learned much about negotiation and persuasion and how to be effective in real-life situations, such as interacting with groups and public speaking.

Even when she graduated, Sue wasn't exactly sure about the profession she wanted to pursue. She spent much time thinking about it and talking with family members. In hindsight, she recalls, "I should have sought the advice of a career counselor while I was still in college."

At the suggestion of her aunt, who had worked in association management for many years, Sue applied to organizations in the Chicago area. Her aunt had explained that associations employed persons whose work involved membership databases, educational programs, foundations, and committee management. Others organized trade shows and annual meetings. This task-oriented work appealed to Sue, and she was retained as an administrative assistant at Bostrom Corporation, an organization that did administrative work for small associations.

Her first account was the North American Society for Trenchless Technology. (This association is concerned with underground utility construction.) She worked with a small staff, which enabled her to learn much about membership management, newsletter writing, organizing volunteers, communicating with the board of directors, and (her favorite part!) planning the society's annual conference and trade shows.

After two years, she was promoted to administrative director and eventually to assistant account executive. After five years, the society decided to retain its own compensated management staff, and her organization was no longer needed. Sue continued to work with Bostrom and assisted other account executives with specialized tasks; however, she then decided that a career move was in order.

Sue began to work with the National Automatic Merchandising Association (NAMA), her current employer. NAMA is the national trade association of the food, refreshment, and merchandise vending; office coffee service; and contract food service management industries. (See Chapter 21 for a discussion of this industry segment.) Its membership is comprised of service operating companies, equipment manufacturers, and suppliers of products and services to these companies. Its mission since 1936 has been to advance and promote the automatic merchandising and office coffee service industries.

Sue's present responsibilities include her work as NAMA's primary contact with more than 300 exhibitors at their two annual expositions. She must develop trade show floor plans, marketing materials, and manuals. She also must sell booth space, organize the trade show floor, work with convention facility personnel and outside contractors, and provide outstanding customer service at all times.

Sue has an interesting story when asked about the most unforgettable moment in her career: "I remember when I was studying for my Certification in Exhibition Management. The process was long and difficult. It consisted of a series of three exams (one hour each) spread over three months. Each test was based on four large manuals addressing trade show and meeting planning topics. The final exam was a two-hour case study followed by a two-hour floor plan exam. When I was studying, there were fewer than 150 CEMs in the industry, so it was a highly respected designation. I had to wait two months to receive the test results.

(continued)

"One day NAMA's chairman of the board was updating us in our conference room. At the end of his presentation, he said he had some other important news. He began by saying, 'Sue Ralston' (the moment seemed to happen in slow motion; after all, what could the association's chairman have to say about me? In all of one-half of a second I was confused and nervous and excited). He continued, 'has passed the CEM exam.' My boss's boss had learned about my test results even before I had asked the chairman to make the announcement to our staff! It was incredibly special to me that he did this. All my hard work, late night study sessions, and stress about passing the exam were over. My colleagues cheered and I breathed a great sigh of relief (and ordered new business cards right away to boast about my new credentials)."

Sue was asked about the most significant challenges facing the industry: "Since I am concerned about managing trade shows and selling booth space, a significant challenge has been the mergers and acquisitions of manufacturers, suppliers, and other companies who can exhibit. There are fewer booths to be sold, and this means shrinking shows. The slow economy has not helped, because companies are looking for ways to reduce expenses. Unfortunately, market-ing dollars are often the first to be cut. We must do all we can to reinvent our show to keep it new and fresh and to provide incentives for exhibitors to be part of it. We have to continually develop new programs to entice new exhibitors and to keep the current exhibitors coming back."

Sue has already provided some advice about what she would do differently in her career: spend some time with a career counselor while in college. She also notes that an internship or a part-time job in the industry before she graduated would have helped to jump-start her career.

Sue has some excellent advice for young persons considering a career in the meeting management industry: "Get some work experience before you graduate even if it is unpaid. Try a variety of different positions, if possible, so that you can really familiarize yourself with numerous opportunities. The experience will give you something to put on your résumé and may help you to focus on what it is you really want to do.

Unfortunately, many people do not love what they do for a living. At the least, you must make sure that you like your position and career a lot! If you are reading this book, you obviously care about your career and are one step ahead of the game. Congratulations."

SUMMARY OF CHAPTER LEARNING OBJECTIVES

1. **Provide a brief overview of exhibitions (trade shows) and the role they play in the marketplace.**

   It has always been necessary for sellers and buyers to interact. Modern exhibitions (trade shows) are organized by associations and for-profit companies to bring exhibitors and attendees together at a common meeting site.

2. **Discuss how exhibitors and exhibition sponsors work together to assure successful exhibitions.**

   Exhibition sponsors generate significant revenues from exhibitor booth rentals. Exhibitors seek venues to introduce and sell their products and services to prospective customers. Sponsors solicit and utilize input from exhibitors as exhibitions are planned. They work together to assure that the exhibition is successful, that is, cost effective for the exhibitor, and to assure repeat exhibitor revenues for the sponsor in successive years.

3. **Describe popular location sites for exhibitions.**

   Exhibition sponsors seek geographic locations that will be most attractive for the largest number of potential attendees. After a location is selected, a specific meeting site within that location is determined. A wide range of factors, many relating to the physical requirements established for the exhibit space, is assessed as a site is selected.

4. **Learn basics about the role of exhibition service contractors in exhibition management.**

   Exhibition planners frequently contract activities related to the planning, conduct, and completion of an exhibition to service contractors. They, in turn, can provide a wide range of services to the sponsors and their exhibitors. General service contractors may perform all the required activities by themselves or, alternatively, may subcontract services to a third party.

5. **Explain specifics to consider when exhibition floor plans and layouts are drawn.**
   Detailed drawings of floor plans for exhibitions are required to allocate space. Common booth designs allow exhibitors to select the size and configuration of a booth that will best meet their needs.

6. **Review the responsibilities of a position that is unique to exhibition management.**
   An exhibition manager is an integral part of the team needed to promote, create, and implement an exhibition. He or she coordinates all aspects for trade shows, which include selling booth space, assigning booth locations, ensuring that all exhibitors follow exhibition rules and regulations, and monitoring security and registration activities.

7. **Discuss basic challenges confronting the exhibition management industry.**
   Basic challenges include finding ways to be successful in an economic slowdown, using technology to reduce costs, and utilizing education as a tactic to help exhibitors and attendees to maximize their return on the investment incurred in attending an exhibition.

FEEDBACK FROM THE REAL WORLD

Our real-world advice comes from the author of this chapter, Curtis Love.

Curtis Love is an associate professor in the Department of Tourism and Convention Administration at the William F. Harrah College of Hotel Administration, University of Nevada, Las Vegas.

How do you determine what activities related to planning and implementation of an exhibition should be retained and done in-house?

If your car broke down, would you rather go to a mechanic who repaired cars once a year or one that repairs cars every day? Of course, you'd choose the mechanic who worked on cars every day. The same is true for activities involved in producing an exhibition. Any function that you can outsource to a professional company who does that job on a regular basis should be considered. What is critical is that the show manager (the employee of the sponsoring organization) retain control over outsourced functions. Companies that are retained represent the exhibition's sponsor. Attendees and exhibitors don't recognize (nor should they) that these are contracted services. They will view them as part of the association or organization producing the exhibition. For example, if the outsourced security guards are not doing their job, this will reflect negatively on the sponsor. Monitoring all outsourced functions on a continuous basis is necessary.

What activities can be considered for outsourcing?

Numerous components of an exhibition can be outsourced. A housing bureau, for instance, can

(continued)

manage attendee housing. A registration service can handle registration. For most show managers, hiring a major general service contractor such as GES or the Freeman Companies can alleviate almost any outsourcing needs. These companies have subdivisions within their corporate structure that specialize in transportation, audio-visual, graphic and booth design, carpentry, and everything else needed to produce a show. They can provide one-stop shopping, which is convenient and economical. Most associations retain the educational component of their convention in-house, because their focus and core competencies involve understanding and servicing the educational needs of their members.

How would you select a service contractor for the responsibilities to be outsourced?

Firsthand experience is always the best. Developing a lasting relationship with a company promotes smooth transitions from year to year. Once service contractors understand how you operate, they can be proactive (not reactive) to your needs. Some show managers contract with service contractors on a multiyear basis.

Networking with your peers can also help to locate good service contractors. Testimonials from a trusted friend can be much more reliable than ads in industry magazines. The Convention and Visitors Bureau (CVB) in the host city is a good place to start when considering alternative companies to hire. They can provide lists of companies and contact information. If possible, attend a show where the service contractor is currently working to observe service levels and competencies. Ask for references and check them out thoroughly. Many contractors must have industry credentials to do a particular job. Check for up-to-date employee certification designations.

MASTERING YOUR KNOWLEDGE

Discuss the following questions.

1. Assume that you are a vice-president for sales in a large organization and that you have been approached to exhibit at an annual association-sponsored exhibition. Your organization has never exhibited at this event. What factors would you consider as you make the decision?
2. The chapter lists several tactics that may be helpful in encouraging attendees to visit a trade show. What additional tactics might be helpful?
3. How would you determine the size and configuration of an exhibit booth for your organization at an exhibition?
4. What are some specifics of booth design that may help to attract visitors to your booth?
5. What factors would you, as an association meeting planner, utilize to select an exhibition service contractor?
6. You are an association meeting planner. Assume there is an industry or economic downturn and it appears that fewer exhibitors will participate in an upcoming exhibition. What can you do to encourage increased participation?
7. If you were an association meeting planner, what factors would influence the amount you would charge potential exhibitors desiring booth space at your exhibition?

LEARN FROM THE INTERNET

1. Check out the following websites of independent meeting planners:
   - Conferon, Inc.: www.conferon.com
   - Meetings & Events, USA: www.yournextmeeting.com
   - VNU Expositions, Inc.: www.vnuexpon.com

   What, if any, technical assistance and services do they offer to help association planners with exhibition (trade show) management?
2. Check out the websites of the following hospitality associations:

   - National Restaurant Association: www.restaurant.org
   - Club Managers Association of America: www.cmaa.org
   - National Association of College & University Food Services: www.nacufs.org

   What kind of information do they provide about trade exhibitions that will be part of their next annual meeting?
3. Check out the websites of several hotel organizations:

- The Peninsula Chicago: www.chicago.peninsula.com
- Loews Hotels: www.loewshotels.com
- Hilton Hawaiian Village: www.hiltonhawaiianvillage.com

What type of information about meeting spaces do they provide for the use of potential meeting planners? About other information of help to meeting planners?

KEY HOSPITALITY TERMS

The following terms were explained in this chapter. Review the definitions of any words with which you are unfamiliar. Begin to utilize them as you expand your vocabulary as a hospitality professional.

exhibition
trade show
exhibitors
consumer show
qualified buyers
exhibitor's prospectus
exhibitor's service kit
Convention and Visitors Bureau (CVB)
occupancy taxes

service contractor (exhibition)
subcontract
floor plan
static floor plan
first come, first served (exhibition booth assignment method)
lottery (exhibition booth assignment method)
priority points (exhibition booth assignment method)

30 Special Events Management

Spectators line up for admittance to an Olympic event.

CHAPTER LEARNING OBJECTIVES

After studying this chapter you will be able to:

1. Define the term *special events management.*
2. Provide a brief history of special events.
3. Describe the type of markets in which special events are conducted.
4. Explain recent trends in the special events industry.
5. Review a flow chart of the activities required to plan a special event.
6. Review some major responsibilities that are part of positions within the special events industry.
7. Discuss significant challenges confronting the special events industry.

This chapter was authored by Kathy Nelson, PhD, CSEP, CMP, Assistant Professor, Tourism and Convention Department, William F. Harrah College of Hotel Administration, University of Nevada, Las Vegas.

FEEDBACK FROM THE REAL WORLD

Large events such as the International Olympics attract tens of thousands of athletes, coaches, trainers, and members of the news media and hundreds of thousands of spectators. How do officials plan for the food and lodging needs of these people? More specifically:

- How far in advance of a large, world-class event such as the International Olympics does planning for its foodservices begin?
- What are some logistics about the volume of foodservices that are offered?

- What are the most critical aspects of planning the event?
- How important is teamwork in the planning process, and what function does each team member assume?

As you read this chapter, think about answers to these questions and then get feedback from the real world at the end of the chapter.

Special events management is an exciting and growing industry. It attracts persons who possess creative talents and organizational skills. Special events professionals enjoy a work environment in which no two days are the same. They create and customize events that provide their clients with entertaining, unique, and memorable experiences. Events also have the ability to reflect and mold our society. **Hallmark events** (those that are sustainable and revivable), such as the International Olympics, the World Cup, and, most recently, the 9/11 remembrance ceremonies, are important milestones in shaping the culture of the United States and the world.

> **hallmark events** special events that are repeated because they are significant, sustainable, and revivable

> **OBJECTIVE 1**
> Define the term *special events management.*

WHAT IS SPECIAL EVENTS MANAGEMENT?

Special events management is the profession that involves public assembly for reasons of celebration, entertainment, and education (among other purposes). Special events management includes several activities: event research, design, planning, coordination, and evaluation.

Special events management is a multidisciplinary profession. The elements of most events are basically the same: entertainment, decorations, lighting, sound, special effects, catering, and often transportation. Employment in special events management transcends many hospitality positions in hotels, food and beverage, tourism, and the meetings and conventions industries.

> **special events management** the profession that plans and manages public assemblies for reasons of celebration, entertainment, and education (among other purposes)

> **OBJECTIVE 2**
> Provide a brief history of special events.

SPECIAL EVENTS: A HISTORICAL REVIEW

As long as there have been groups of people, special events have celebrated human triumphs and milestones. Events celebrate past, present, and future lives and all the accomplishments (wonderful, terrible, and bittersweet) that accent life's journey. The special events management profession originated within the discipline of **public relations** when specialists became necessary to manage the activities (**special events**) that creative organizations use to obtain publicity and to build corporate images.

The term *special event* represents an extraordinary moment in our lives. Robert Jani (one of Walt Disney's imagineers) is credited with first using the term in 1955. He proposed the creation of a nightly parade in Disneyland (the

> **public relations** activities designed to build good relations with a company's numerous constituencies by use of tactics such as press releases, product publicity, corporate communications, and public service

> **special event** an activity, program, or occasion that represents a memorable experience that requires an unusual degree of planning and creativity

Main Street Electric Parade) to solve the problem about how to keep visitors in the park after 5:00 P.M. When a reporter asked, "What do you call that program?" he replied, "A special event." By that, he meant something that someone experiences that is different from a normal day of living.

EVENT MARKETS

OBJECTIVE 3
Describe the type of markets in which special events are conducted.

cause-related events those undertaken for reasons of charity (private or public relief for persons in need)

life-cycle events activities that celebrate or recognize significant milestones in one's life

Many event planners classify events by markets. The most commonly considered are noted in Exhibit 30.1. Event markets include those sponsored by associations, corporations, and casino hotels. Other events are **cause related.** Retail and sporting events, fairs, festivals, parades, and social and tourism events are also part of the event market, and we will look at each in this section. Corporations typically spend the most money on events, but the social market is the largest because it encompasses **life-cycle events** such as birthdays, bar or bat mitzvahs, weddings, anniversaries, and funerals.

Association Events

Associations sponsor innumerable events of all types, including award presentations, political rallies, community service, installation of officers and leaders, training programs, conventions, exhibitions, and seminars.

Corporate Events

Corporate events are sponsored to achieve specific goals, including celebratory events such as product introductions, customer appreciation, grand openings, and incentive programs.

Casino and Hotel Events

Special events are a significant part of a casino's marketing activities today. In addition to corporate events that occur at casinos, such as grand openings and numerous types of celebrations, special events attract and reward casino players. For example, boxing matches and rock concerts attract the highest level of VIP players, and high-roller parties are often utilized as a customer-appreciation tool.

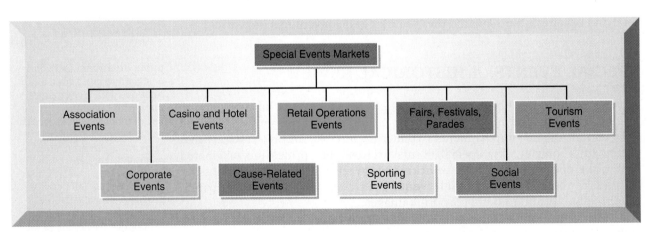

EXHIBIT 30.1
The Special Event Markets

SPECIAL EVENTS OCCUR EVERY DAY IN CASINOS

Slot clubs and tournaments increase casino revenue during slow periods, build customer loyalty, and develop a customer database. Slot tournaments are a perfect example of how the casino uses special events as a marketing tool. Players are encouraged to join slot clubs and are given a membership card. When they do so, this card tracks each member's play (number of hours and dollars spent playing the slots). It also has a built-in reward system so that customers can earn points toward meals, shows, and hotel rooms and receive the appropriate level of VIP treatment.

Casino club members are often invited to participate in monthly slot tournaments that are highly themed and feature a high-ticket prize at the tournament's end. These events have become highly competitive between casino properties and rely on the next creative theme to attract new and retain existing players in the tournaments. An awards banquet, including themed entertainment, food, and beverages, frequently concludes these special events.

Cause-Related Events

Many **not-for-profit organizations** raise a huge portion of their annual budgets from fund-raising events. As inducements to participate, part of the fees paid by those attending may be tax deductible as a charitable contribution.

> **not-for-profit organizations** a group of persons working for reasons other than to make profit from their efforts; many nonprofit organizations have charitable objectives

Retail Operations Events

The main purpose of retail event promotions is to introduce and sell merchandise. During the 1960s and 1970s, retailers could attract thousands of consumers to their stores with one-day events that included the appearance of soap opera stars and athletes. Today, retailers design long-range promotional events using an integrated approach to attract consumers on a steady basis. Consider the Sony Metreon Complex in San Francisco. Shoppers can enjoy the maximum of entertainment and events with 15 movie screens, an IMAX theater, eight restaurants, and numerous stores and attractions that would rival many amusement parks.

Sporting Events

Sporting events bring lots of visitors and therefore lots of money into a community. A few of the top sporting events each year are the National Collegiate Athletics Association's (NCAA) Men's Final Four Basketball Tournament, Junior Olympic Games, and the ESPN Summer X Games. Sporting events are a perfect platform for corporate sponsorship. No other single event in America is more attractive to corporate America than the annual Super Bowl football game. In 1999, Las Vegas attracted 250,000 visitors to the Super Bowl who spent millions of dollars while visiting the area.

Crowds gather at the Edinburgh festival in Scotland.

SUE SHIFRIN-CASSIDY: KIDSCHARITIES.ORG

KidsCharities.org grew from an idea in early 1999 during the Kosovo crisis. Songwriter Sue Shifrin-Cassidy and her husband (world-renowned entertainer David Cassidy) wrote the song "Message to the World" to benefit WarChild USA's efforts for Kosovo refugees. The song, produced by a multiaward winner (Narda Michael Walden), became bigger than life with featured artists including Rosie O'Donnel, Wyclef Jean, Sam Moore, David Cassidy, and many more.

From that effort and the joy of helping others, Sue founded KidsCharities.org, the first worldwide website benefiting the world's children. KidsCharities.org donates 100 percent of its online donations to children's charities, including Juvenile Diabetes Foundation, Special Olympics Nevada, City of Hope, Planet Hope, Reggie Jackson's Mr. October Foundation for Kids, and others.

Fairs, Festivals, and Parades

These events provide many opportunities to bring communities together to celebrate various cultures and interests through performances, arts, crafts, and socializing, while, at the same time, boosting tourism dollars. For example, the Kentucky Derby Festival (horse race) attracts 1.5 million visitors to Louisville, and the Rose Bowl parade (prior to the annual football game) attracts 1 million visitors for that one-day event in Pasadena (Los Angeles). Whether people attend a Pumpkin Festival in Circleville, Ohio, or the Cannes Film Festival in France, chances are they will come away exhausted, entertained, and gastronomically satisfied.

Social Events

The social (life-cycle) market continues to grow as health conditions improve and people live longer. Once, celebrating a fiftieth wedding anniversary was rare; today it is almost commonplace. Celebratory events that recognize the passage of time are usually ritualistic in nature.

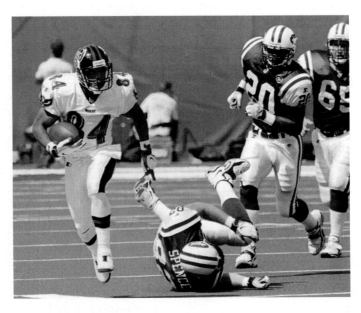

Many special activities are scheduled around important sporting events.

IT'S ONLY MONEY!

Life-cycle events are important to clients. Today, some weddings are upscale and themed events that last for days. In 2001, an award-winning wedding was produced at a Las Vegas casino resort property. It utilized 32 florists and a 4,000 work-hour setup crew to carefully attend to the bridal couple's every wish at a cost that exceeded $1 million!

Tourism Events

Communities that do not have the facilities to offer large events can still utilize tourism events to attract visitors. Redevelopment projects are reviving the downtown areas of many U.S. cities. With this redevelopment comes the opportunity for creating tourism events. As an example, consider Cleveland, Ohio, which has been named one of North America's 10 most improved cities. Cleveland's entertainment district, called the Flats, lines the Cuyahoga River and has transformed old industrial sites into party meccas. In 1994, the city unveiled its $450 million Gateway Sports Complex, which includes both Jacobs Field (home of the Cleveland Indians baseball team) and Gund Arena (home of the Cleveland Cavaliers basketball team). The Cleveland Browns' new football stadium and the Rock and Roll Hall of Fame and Museum have helped Cleveland earn a spot on *Travel & Leisure's* top 10 vacation destinations.

Here are two additional examples. Fort Worth, Texas, transformed its downtown stores into Sundance Square with entertainment attractions, modern shopping areas, restaurants, and museums. Chattanooga, Tennessee, centered its downtown redevelopment around the $45 million Tennessee Aquarium. New hotels, museums, modern shopping, theaters, and other attractions provide the setting for numerous tourism events.

> **OBJECTIVE 4**
> Explain recent trends in the special events industry.

> **sponsorship** money, goods, and/or services rendered by an organization in exchange for a return, including public relations, advertising, and/or charitable tax benefits

TRENDS IN THE SPECIAL EVENTS INDUSTRY

One of the biggest trends in the event industry today is the merging of corporate and public events. This is accomplished through many forms of **sponsorship.** Money, goods, and/or services are provided by an organization in exchange for public relations, advertising, and/or charitable tax benefits. In times when there is dwindling public funding for the arts, for example, corporate sponsorship of museums is rising rapidly. In addition to the arts, corporate sponsorship plays an increasingly important role in numerous public events, including festivals and holiday celebrations.

The arrangement between Saber of America and Philadelphia's Franklin Institute Science Museum illustrates the new forms of sponsorship. When the museum's traveling science show rolls into schools, it travels in a fleet of four Saber Legacy station wagons donated by the auto maker. A second example: The Houston

Parades are highlights of many events.

Wedding ceremonies are an important market for event planners.

Livestock Show and Rodeo has 41 sponsors. Each pays between $60,000 and $1 million to sponsor an event, ranging from a milking parlor to the playing of the national anthem.[1]

Another trend in the special events industry is a renewed interest in professionalism. The nation's current economic uncertainty, rapid technological advances, and increased competition, among other factors, have prompted event professionals to differentiate themselves by professional credentials and practices. Certification designations are more important today than they have even been in the special events industry. In many cases, they distinguish a certified event professional as being the "best of the best!"

Since the events of September 11, 2001, it is increasingly common to produce events perceived to be more meaningful, as opposed to events that are just celebratory or that can be seen as financially wasteful. This trend toward cause-related events, rather than those with incentive and reward purposes, will likely remain popular.

As is true in other segments of the hospitality industry, risk management concerns are a hot topic at industry-related education and professional development conferences. In the wake of the horrific fire that killed 99 club goers and injured nearly 200 more in West Warwick, Rhode Island, in 2003

Safeco Field is named after its corporate sponsor, Safeco Corporation, a property and casualty insurance company.

[1]K.D. Washington and R.K. Miller, *The 2003 Entertainment Media and Advertising Market Research Handbook,* Richard K. Miller and Associates, Inc., 2003.

MEET YIFAT OREN, CERTIFIED SPECIAL EVENT PROFESSIONAL (CSEP)

Yifat Oren

Yifat Oren began her career in the special events industry in the early 1990s as the publisher of *Wedding Celebrations,* a complete guide for special events. As a result of that successful venture, Yifat noticed the need for a knowledgeable, stylish, and visionary individual to ease the stress associated with the planning and production of a successful event. She launched Yifat Oren & Associates Special Events, a complete event planning company that specializes in exquisite social gatherings. With the technical knowledge attained through extensive experience, Yifat combines flair for art and style to provide the most discerning clientele with incomparable experiences.

Yifat believes, "Each wedding day is a complex blend of family, emotion, social occasion, religious ceremony, passion, and coincidental elements. The challenge is to see the event through the bridal couple's eyes, to reflect their personal style, to get to know them and to deliver what their wedding dreams are made of."

With a growing and hip celebrity clientele, Yifat Oren & Associates has been touted as one of the most up and coming event planners in Los Angeles. The strategy: take events to the next level by personalizing them to each specific client with details from the moment the first guest arrives. The goal is to consistently create imaginative styles and trends. Her organization will tailor every aspect of an event to the whims and wishes of the most discriminating clients.

(which occurred just four days after 21 people were killed in a stampede at a Chicago nightclub), event professionals are now very serious about risk management; they recognize that it is everyone's responsibility, but that these concerns begin at the time of event planning.

A CLOSE LOOK AT EVENT PLANNING

The work of an event planner is in many ways similar to that of a meeting planner. Exhibit 30.2 is a flow chart that identifies major steps in planning a special event. When reviewing this figure, note that the event's purpose and

High-society receptions require significant special event planning.

CHECK IT OUT!

Special Events Magazine offers the opportunity to view an extensive number of activities and information about many topics of importance to special event planners. Want to learn about hotel events, catering, or risk management concerns in special events planning? Just enter these or other topics of interest in the website's "Search This Site" box at www.specialevents.com.

OBJECTIVE 5
Review a flow chart of the activities required to plan a special event.

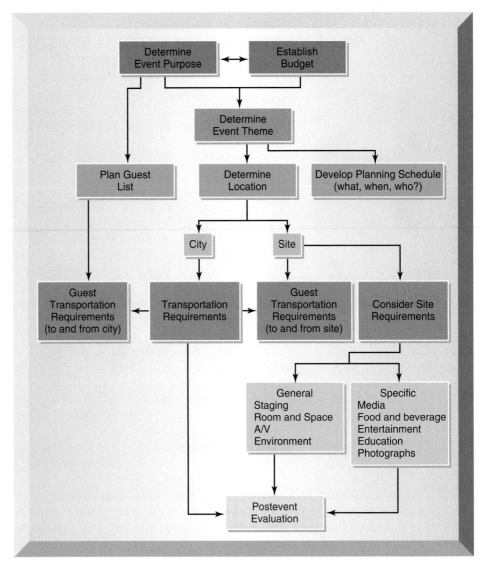

EXHIBIT 30.2
Steps in Planning a Special Event

budget are typically considered before its theme and the guest list. The theme, then, may drive the event's location and its planning schedule. Details, including transportation requirements (to move guests to and from and within the event's location) and numerous general and specific details relating to the conduct of the event at a specific site, are required. Postevent evaluation is a must, especially if events are repeated. Then all parties will learn about planning procedures that should be continued (because they work!) or that may need modification (because they were ineffective!).

The phrase "attention to details" is an appropriate way to describe the work of special event planners. This is especially important as one considers that planners frequently are working on several special events at the same time.

OBJECTIVE 6
Review some major responsibilities that are part of positions within the special events industry.

SPECIAL EVENTS MANAGEMENT POSITIONS

The International Special Events Society (ISES) categorizes members into event disciplines. This classification (see Exhibit 30.3) suggests some of the specialized positions within the industry.

EXHIBIT 30.3
Common Positions Within
the Special Events Industry

Position	Examples of Position Titles and Responsibilities
Events planners (coordinators)	Persons in this position serve as event planner, coordinator, meeting planner, wedding consultant, fund raiser, exposition service manager, and other entities.
Special events managers	This individual should have a minimum of three years experience in the special events industry as an event coordinator, designer, production manager, or technical director.
Special events producers	Individual special events producers have a minimum of five years experience in the industry. They have produced or had a major role in producing at least 10 events.
Design, decor, or graphic arts specialists	Floral designers and floral and plant suppliers; set, prop, and display designers; lighting designers; balloon artists; graphic and advertising artists; flags and banners producers; suppliers of decorative materials, invitations, and calligraphy; and persons with similar responsibilities.
Technical service and products specialists	Audiovisual services; sound and staging; lighting; photography and video; computers and software; event staffing and security; special effects; fireworks and pyrotechnics; generator rental; other positions.
Hardware rental and construction personnel	Equipment rental; party hire; tenting; staging; set and props construction; stadium and seating; temporary structures; catering equipment; apparel (formal and costumes); linen rental; restroom; trailers and other positions.
Entertainers	Theme or amusement parks; booking agencies; musicians; vocalists, disk jockeys, magicians, sporting event and concert promoters or managers; specialty acts; performing artists; casino and carnival entertainment and equipment; amusement and interactive games; virtual reality; ticketing services; professional speakers; novelties and caricature artists and other entities that provide or produce entertainment.
Food service and product personnel	Catering (on- and/or off-site); ice sculptures; bakery and wedding cakes; food staffing and other positions.
Venue (location) managers	Hotel and specialty venues; bleachers, skyboxes, and other venues.
Travel and transportation personnel	Destination management services; incentive travel companies; valet parking services; ground operators; ground transportation (bus, van, and limousine) services; tours, charters, and other positions.
Event public relations and marketing specialists	Advertising agencies; media companies; public relations firms; marketing companies; awards and promotional products companies; accounting and financial services; speakers' bureau; publications and media; insurance; professional support services and other positions.

CHALLENGES! CHALLENGES!

As is true with all segments of the hospitality industry, the special events segment is confronted by several challenges.

Bar mitzvah celebrations are a large part of the special events market.

Risk Management Concerns

Risk management remains a challenge even though the awareness of its importance has already been raised throughout the industry. Surprisingly, this topic has not received serious attention until recently, in part because event managers tend to be very creative by nature. Educational conferences, professional literature, and other venues for advancing the profession have focused more on the new and different creative aspects of event planning, rather than on the nuts and bolts of basic planning principles. After September 11, 2001, however, this all changed.

There also is the human tendency to want to shift blame to someone else. Consider, for example, the tragic fire in Rhode Island referenced previously. Accusations were made about the band whose pyrotechnics ignited the blaze, the owners of the establishment, the company that supplied the foam used as soundproofing material, the fire marshall who gave the club a seal of

Fireworks are part of Fourth of July celebrations in many cities in the United States, including New York City.

approval, the town of West Warwick, and the state of Rhode Island. In the future, event planners will more consistently and adequately address risk management concerns to assure that they are doing their part to provide a safe environment for event guests.

Raising the Level of Professionalism

Historically, the special events industry has comprised small entrepreneurial businesses who learned the business from experience, rather than through formal education and professional development. Experience is absolutely critical to the success of an event planner; however, so is more formalized training. The primary professional association for the International Special Events Society (ISES) has developed an effective certification program that is driven by excellent professional development programs in increasingly successful efforts to raise the standard of excellence in the industry.

Marketing Issues

The goals and objectives for many events have shifted to cause-related events. This poses marketing challenges for event companies who need to reinvent themselves. Also, the events industry rises and falls in concert with the economy. Consider, for example, the September 11, 2001, tragedy. Special events companies lost all or most of the business on their books after that event, and it was more than a year before planning for new events began.

PROFILE OF A SPECIAL EVENTS COMPANY

Most businesses providing special events services are independently owned and provide opportunities for creative persons to identify and serve the special events needs of selected markets. Here's an example.

VP Events, Inc., is a full-service event, design, and production company. The firm was founded in 1994 as Vintage Productions, specializing in vintage weddings and so-

Mary Litzsinger

cial events. Since that time, the company has evolved into an award-winning design and production firm specializing in a broad range of entertainment, corporate, and social events. Clients look to VP Events, Inc., for something different and unique that allows them to emphasize their individual expressions. While the firm has enjoyed notoriety for its specialty, unique wedding design and other off-premise events, the true focus is on elegance, style, and individuality.

President and owner Mary N. Litzsinger, CSEP, has a bachelor's degree in marketing. She received the designation CSEP (Certified Special Events Professional) in 2001 from the International Special Events Society. She has served on the faculty of the UCLA Extension Program, where she encouraged students to join the special events planning industry. For the

(continued)

past 15 years, she has developed and produced events, fund-raising opportunities, public relations, and corporate branding programs for local, regional, and national organizations.

Karey Williams graduated from the University of Southern California and serves as event and marketing manager. She has been a full-time event and marketing manager for over four years. Her first major wedding received high reviews and earned a featured spot in a national publication. She brings a background in the cosmetics and fashion industry to the firm. Karey uses her knowledge and experience to help clients with their specific needs related to dress design and hair and makeup consultations. In addition to working with social clients of VP Events, Inc., Karey develops opportunities for the firm in corporate, sports, and fund-raising events.

Karey Williams

SUMMARY OF CHAPTER LEARNING OBJECTIVES

1. **Define the term *special events management*.**
   Special events management is the profession that plans and controls public assemblies gathered for the reasons of celebration, entertainment, and education (among other purposes). Activities integral to the process include those related to event research, design, planning, coordination, and evaluation.

2. **Provide a brief history of special events.**
   Celebration of special events has been part of human history. The special events management profession originated within the discipline of public relations when specialists became necessary to manage activities that creative organizations used to obtain publicity and to build corporate images. The term *special events* was coined by Robert Jani (a Walt Disney imagineer) in 1955 when he used it to described the Main Street Electric Parade in Disneyland.

3. **Describe the type of markets in which special events are conducted.**
   Special events markets are those sponsored by associations; corporations; casinos and hotels; cause-related and retail organizations; sporting events; fairs, festivals, and parades; and social and tourism-related activities.

4. **Explain recent trends in the special events industry.**
   Recent trends include sponsorship (the merging of corporate and public events) and an increased interest in professionalism within the special events industry.

5. **Review a flow chart of the activities required to plan a special event.**
   The purpose of the event and its budget are initially established. Then the guest list and transportation requirements can be considered. At the same time, the event's theme may determine its location (which will also affect transportation). When the event site is known, general and specific event planning activities can begin. A postevent evaluation should be undertaken at its conclusion.

6. **Review some major responsibilities that are part of positions within the special events industry.**
   Numerous positions within the special events industry involve their coordination, management, and production. Design, decor, graphic arts, and technical service and products specialists may also be needed. Related positions include hardware rental, construction personnel, entertainment, foodservices, location management, travel and transportation, and event public relations and marketing specialists.

7. **Discuss significant challenges confronting the special events industry.**
   Challenges confronting the special events industry include concerns about risk management, raising the level of professionalism within the industry, and marketing concerns relating to the need for event companies to reinvent in a new age or in a weak economy.

MASTERING YOUR KNOWLEDGE

Discuss the following questions.

1. How does the work of a special events planner (coordinator) or manager differ from that of a meeting planner? How is it similar?
2. How might nonprofit corporations and government organizations seek corporate sponsorships for, respectively, member or public events?
3. What types of features would attract you to a special event in another community? If you were responsible for marketing the event in that community, what tactics might you utilize?
4. Pretend that you are a special events planner who has been retained by a regional shopping center to plan an event celebrating a major addition. How could you utilize the steps noted in Figure 30.2 to plan the event? Develop an example.

FEEDBACK FROM THE REAL WORLD

Our real-world advice comes from Marc Bruno, Regional Vice-President, ARAMARK Business Services, Philadelphia, Pennsylvania

How far in advance of a large, world-class event such as the International Olympics does planning for its foodservices begin?

The International Olympic Committee (IOC) is responsible for overseeing the Olympic process and selecting the host cities for each Summer and Winter Olympics, which are held every four years. Approximately 10 to 12 years prior to each Olympic Games, cities from around the world begin to compete for the votes of the various IOC delegate members to become the host city. Only one city per country can be selected (for example, the United States Olympic Committee selected New York City as the city to compete for the U.S. location for the 2012 Summer Olympics). Seven years prior to the Games, the voting to determine the host city occurs and election results are announced. The successful hosts of the Summer and Winter Games now known are Summer, 2008, Beijing; and Winter 2010, Vancouver.

Once the city is announced, a local Organizing Committee is formed and begins planning for hosting the Olympics. It focuses on five major areas:

Athletic competition   Transportation
Security   Foodservices
Housing

Typically, the local organizing committee (for example, the Athens Olympic Committee was called ATHOC) will outsource the foodservices to one or more companies. The three primary areas are these:

- The Olympic Village, where the athletes, coaches, officials, and staff reside for approximately 30 days
- The venues (competition sites)
- Corporate hospitality

ARAMARK has been involved in previous Olympic Games in some or all of these three areas and is usually the largest provider of foodservices. For example, ARAMARK has served as the foodservices manager for 13 games in which it managed the foodservice needs for the Olympic Village.

Planning for each Olympic Games takes approximately 2 years, usually with a core group of 5 to 10 people. As the Games approach, the group expands to hundreds of managers and thousands of employees.

(continued)

Here are the major Olympic activities and international sporting events that ARAMARK has managed:

Summer Olympic Games

1968	Mexico City
1976	Montreal
1984	Los Angeles
1988	Seoul
1992	Barcelona
1996	Atlanta
2000	Sydney
2004	Athens

Winter Olympic Games

1980	Lake Placid
1984	Sarajevo
1988	Calgary
1994	Lillehammer
1998	Nagano

Major International Sporting Events

1970	Caribbean Games—Panama City, Panama
1971	Pan American Games—Cali, Colombia
1974	Caribbean Games–Santa Domingo, Dominican Republic
1979	Pan American Games–San Juan, Puerto Rico
1981	Bolivarian Games–Barquisimeto, Venezuela
1983	Pan American Games–Caracas, Venezuela
1984	Olympic Torch Run–9,000 Miles USA
1987	Pan American Games–Indianapolis, Indiana
1990	Goodwill Games–Seattle, Washington
1994	12th Asian Games–Hiroshima, Japan
1998	Commonwealth Games–Kuala Lumpur, Malaysia
1998	13th Asian Games–Bangkok, Thailand
1999	Pan American Games–Winnipeg, Canada
2002	FIFA World Cup–Korea and Japan

When we are involved with Olympics in countries outside North America, we partner with a local company that brings extensive knowledge of the local customs, service levels, purchasing and distribution systems, and human resource contacts.

What were some logistics about the volume of foodservices offered?

As a case study, let's consider the 2004 Summer Olympic Games in Athens, Greece. The 2004 Olympic Village in Athens was the largest Olympic Village in history. It hosted 23,800 athletes, coaches, officials, and Games personnel. The Parolympic Village hosted 12,250 additional persons. The ARAMARK/Daskalantonakis Group serviced the dining and catering needs for both villages 24 hours a day for approximately 60 days during the summer of 2004. Over 2 million meals were served to Olympic athletes, coaches, and officials during this time. In addition, we managed the construction of temporary dining and kitchen facilities to service these dining outlets. The athletes' main village was the world's largest temporary dining facility ever, housing over 6,000 seats and capable of serving over 80,000 meals a day. In addition, we operated a staff dining and retail casual dining facility capable of feeding an additional 20,000 meals per day. We utilized approximately 2,500 employees and purchased well over $10 million in food for the month-long event.

What were the most critical aspects in planning the event?

The most critical aspects in planning were as follows:

- *Human resources.* Recruiting, hiring, accrediting, training, and servicing temporary employees and chefs for the approximate 30-day period.
- *Culinary.* Planning a menu for over 15,000 athletes from around the world, each with their own preferences and food needs during training and competition. The menu is huge, and we brought in chefs from around the world to assist in the production of such mammoth quantities and varieties of food items.

- *Technology.* Assuring that all the proper systems were working and in place and that there was a backup plan in case it failed for some reason is critical. Technology can make the planning process much easier if it works well.
- *Finance.* Making sure that budgets and expenditures were correct and that tracking of all costs was complete.
- *Construction.* Designing and operating in temporary facilities that need to be precisely planned and constructed without delays.
- *Operations.* There were many moving parts when operations got underway, and systems, processes, and people needed to be in harmony or major chaos could have occured.
- *Food safety.* Serving so many meals and utilizing products from around the globe was a challenge. We ensured that the food was handled and prepared safely from the farm to the plate and along every step of the way.
- *Communication.* Proper communications among all departments and shifts and to the customers was critical. This is especially true when one considers that we dealt with athletes from 197 different nations, with their different languages.

How important was teamwork in the planning process and what function did each team member assume?

Teamwork was of the utmost importance. It was critical that all departments and functions be in harmony with each other before and during planning and execution. Everyone's individual responsibilities were very important, but they became much greater when combined with the interdependence of the other necessary functions during the actual operations. The core team focused on many issues initially, and then we separated the issues and let each team focus solely on its area. The project was so incredibly huge (it was like having a Super Bowl going on 24 hours a day for 30 days straight!) that it helped to have individuals oversee the following departments:

Operations	Purchasing
Culinary	Information technology
Human resources	Design and construction
Recruiting	Warehousing and logistics
Training	Finance
Accommodations	Food safety and sanitation
Transportation	

LEARN FROM THE INTERNET

1. Check out the websites for the following special event planners:
   - Action Events: (www.actionevents.com)
   - Bravo Productions: (www.bravoevents-online.com)
   - Summit Events: (www.seonthenet.com)
   - Corinthian Events: (www.corinthianevents.com)

   What are some features that make them very competitive with others? What features make them less attractive? What types of information about their past experiences are provided? How might this information be of interest to you if you were responsible for a similar event? What are examples of information provided that might help you as an event sponsor to evaluate whether these organizations would be helpful to you?

KEY HOSPITALITY TERMS

The following terms were explained in this chapter. Review the definitions of any words with which you are unfamiliar. Begin to utilize them as you expand your vocabulary as a hospitality professional.

hallmark events

special events management

public relations

special event

cause-related events

life-cycle events

not-for-profit organization

sponsorship

Part 7

FOCUS ON YOU AND YOUR PROFESSIONAL CAREER

Planning Your Hospitality Career

31

Graduation day represents the start of many persons' careers.

CHAPTER LEARNING OBJECTIVES

After studying this chapter you will be able to:

1. Recognize the importance of planning as a first step in career decision making.
2. Provide an overview of the career planning process.
3. Utilize tactics helpful in exploring personal interests.
4. Indicate tactics helpful in analyzing beginning-of-career professional alternatives.
5. Use an alternative evaluation grid to quantify the decision-making process.

The authors wish to thank Authella Collins Hawks, Director, Student Industry Resource Center (SIRC), The School of Hospitality Business, Michigan State University, for her assistance with this chapter.

FEEDBACK FROM THE REAL WORLD

Trina and Jeffers are both about to graduate from a two-year community college program located in the suburbs of a large city. They are interested in the foodservices industry, and both think they might like to work in the noncommercial segment of the industry. Here are some of their thoughts about factors that may affect their employment decisions after graduation:

Factor	Trina	Jeffers
Preferred location	Local area	Anywhere; no preference
Additional hospitality education	No (not now)	Maybe
Good technical training	Yes	Yes
Career that will always have day to day operating responsibilities	Yes	No
Technical help when working through decisions	No (wants to be in charge)	Yes (concerned about the impact of a bad decision)
Flexibility	Probably would like to stay with the same organization and enjoy the "perks" of seniority	Yes; would consider a different position with the same or a different organization
Compensation (salary and benefits)	Better-than-average because of the belief that she is better than average	Better-than-average because of the belief that he is better than average

Based on their own personal interests, how should Trina and Jeffers assess the type of organization (self-operated or contract management company) in which to begin their careers?

Think about your responses to this question. Then review one process of analysis in the Feedback from the Real World section at the end of this chapter.

You have been studying about and perhaps working in the hospitality industry. Initial learning and/or working experiences prompt many persons to think that a career within the hospitality industry is just right for them. Conversely, the initial experiences of others may have the opposite effect: they learn what they do not want to do! Some basic principles and procedures for career planning are applicable in both of these cases. Many people who are happy with their early career choices change their mind later and become interested in another track within the hospitality industry or even decide to leave the industry. Few, if any, persons plan out details of a career that may last 40 years or more and then follow that plan without deviation. This chapter will provide information to help you to consider what is important as you consider professional employment alternatives.

OBJECTIVE 1
Recognize the importance of planning as a first step in career decision making.

CAREER DECISIONS BEGIN WITH PLANNING

Many people use a schedule to keep them organized and on track during the day. Schedules help individuals to prioritize the things that are most important. They also help them to better manage projects with dead-lines. Activities can be added, deleted, or changed to keep the schedule current. Then, when they start their day, they know what they must do during the day. Many things can affect the daily sched-ule. For example, meetings may be scheduled or postponed at the last moment, or these sessions may last longer or be shorter than originally expected. Nothing in the future is cast in stone, but the schedule planner makes every effort to be in control of or, at least, to have influ-ence over it.

This grocery store clerk may decide to change careers and enter the hospitality industry.

Career planning is similar to planning a daily schedule in many ways. First, the purpose is the same (to keep organized and on track). Second, changes are made to keep the schedule (career plan) current and on track as priorities change. Many things can affect it, but consistent efforts are made to retain control over (or at least to influence) the schedule (plan). Recognition that careers should be planned and not left to chance is a critical first step in your efforts to do everything possible to remain in control of your professional future.

OVERVIEW OF CAREER PLANNING PROCESS

An overview of the career planning process is presented in Exhibit 31.1. Recognition of the need for career planning is the first step in the process. Its importance was noted previously. This should be followed by an exploration of personal interests, skills, and values and even an evaluation of your person-ality type (which should then drive the remainder of the decision-making process). Knowledge of all (or as many as possible) alternatives is helpful input to the ultimate selection of the preferred industry, segment, organiza-tion, and position for one's first professional position assignment. After an initial position is accepted, it is important to work effectively to attain the goals that prompted you to accept the position. Career progress should be continually evaluated, and the career planning process becomes cyclical as the steps are repeated.

Many people enrolled in a hospitality management education program have already taken an important first, but not irrevocable, step in career plan-ning. Courses, internships, and job experiences should reinforce the initial decision to consider work within the hospitality industry. Then the career planning priority shifts to issues such as the most desired segment, organiza-tion, and position, which will become the focus of the career planning efforts. By contrast, peers may be less certain about the industry in which they will seek employment. Fortunately, the process to answer questions such as "What do I want to do within the hospitality industry?" and "In what industry do I wish to work?" have many of the same decision-making elements.

OBJECTIVE 2
Provide an overview of the career planning process.

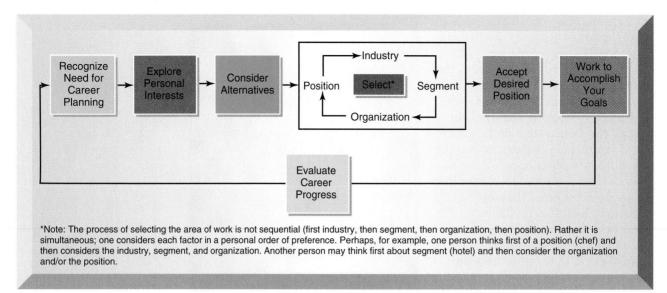

*Note: The process of selecting the area of work is not sequential (first industry, then segment, then organization, then position). Rather it is simultaneous; one considers each factor in a personal order of preference. Perhaps, for example, one person thinks first of a position (chef) and then considers the industry, segment, and organization. Another person may think first about segment (hotel) and then consider the organization and/or the position.

EXHIBIT 31.1
Steps in Career Planning

RISING STAR PROFILE

Lanelle Henderson
Chief Executive Officer
Welcome 2 the Neighborhood, LLC
Henry County, Georgia

Career Changes Are Part of Life

Lanelle graduated from Georgia State University with a degree in hospitality administration. She had previously worked in computer graphics for approximately nine years before starting to study for her hospitality career.

While studying for her undergraduate degree, she worked in her university's executive MBA program as a meeting management intern and then as its marketing director. She also worked with the hospitality school as an office manager responsible for marketing and recruiting activities. After graduation, Lanelle began work as a sales manager with Residence Inn by Marriott, Atlanta (Downtown), and then as the director of sales at the Hampton Inn and Suites, Atlanta (Downtown).

She left the hotel industry to spend more time with her teenage son who was entering high school. "I love the hotel industry but, as director of sales, the position required too many hours. Since my son wants to go to college out of state, I felt quality time with him now was very important." Lanelle moved to Henry County, Georgia, which is one of the fastest growing counties in America. More than 175 new businesses apply for business licenses each month.

"I wanted to be an active participant in my community. I founded my business in 2003. We welcome new families into the area and provide them with a welcome basket full of community information, maps, product samples, and discount coupons from local businesses. As well, we have now restructured the business to do target marketing, event marketing, and promotional marketing activities. One example: we organize a "Newcomers Social" and invite newcomers to a local restaurant. We greet them, introduce them to the property, and present them with welcome gifts from the local businesses. We market for the local businesses to build loyal relationships, extend a warm community welcome, and keep the tax dollars local."

Lanelle has excellent advice for those considering a career in hospitality: "Smile, learn, and be happy! Hard work, determination, and the willingness to make a difference will go a long way. If helping people gives you joy and if making people smile is what you like, then a career in the diverse hospitality industry will reward you on the spot.

Over the past two and a half years, we realized that our two signature events, Annual Picnic in the Park and Women on the Move, bring people together and allow our clients to engage with potential customers. Event marketing is very effective, enjoyable, and memorable and that is what W2TN brings to Henry County.

To view Lanelle's website, go to www.W2TN .com.

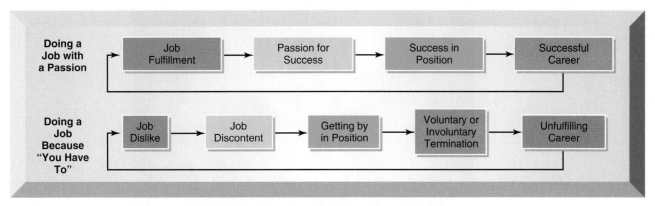

Doing a Job with a Passion	Job Fulfillment	→	Passion for Success	→	Success in Position	→	Successful Career

| Doing a Job Because "You Have To" | Job Dislike | → | Job Discontent | → | Getting by in Position | → | Voluntary or Involuntary Termination | → | Unfulfilling Career |

EXHIBIT 31.2
Find Fulfillment on the Job

CONSIDER YOUR PERSONAL INTERESTS

OBJECTIVE 3
Utilize tactics helpful in exploring personal interests.

Many of the young hospitality leaders profiled throughout this book have emphasized that work should be enjoyable. How does one find enjoyable work? The best way is to carefully consider what you like to do and then to find a career that has these major elements.

Can you imagine a professional athlete practicing many hours every day to become better at a sporting skill that was not of interest? How about a scientist in a laboratory on the cutting edge of a new discovery? Or what about an architect planning new building designs, a chef developing new recipes, or a hotel general manager making important decisions about many challenges and opportunities every day? There may be some athletes, architects, chefs, and general managers who do not like what they do. However, their counterparts who continually find pride and joy in their work will be much happier in that part of their life where they will be spending a significant amount of time.

Exhibit 31.2 summarizes the importance of finding fulfillment on the job. Look at the figure and ask yourself, "Which do I prefer?" When you have a great passion for the job you do, there is likely to be contentment. This creates an interest in succeeding, which typically leads to success in the position, which, in turn, builds a successful career and increased job satisfaction.

Contrast this with a person doing a job because he or she has to. If you have no interest in or, even worse, dislike a job, you will likely be disinterested and not do well in it. You may attempt to just get by, meeting minimal expectations, which, in turn, leads to an unfulfilling career. This becomes a

Enjoyable classes may suggest rewarding careers in the culinary arts or other aspects of the hospitality industry.

Faculty advisors can give helpful advice about career alternatives.

cyclical process, leading to further dislike and disinterest and, eventually, to a job and/or a career change.

Persons normally spend a significant amount of time in their work over many years. It is critical, then, to find a career in which you are interested, and this begins by determining exactly what your interests are. Exhibit 31.3 provides

Part 1

List those things you do well (your strengths):

1. _____

2. _____

3. _____

Part 2

Personal Attributes (Characteristics)	How Does This Attribute Help You to Do Well?
What are your greatest <u>skills</u>?	
What are your greatest <u>strengths</u>?	
About what do you have the greatest <u>knowledge</u>?	
For what do you have the greatest <u>aptitudes</u> (natural abilities)?	
What things in life do you most highly <u>value</u>?	
What are your interests? (What do you most like to <u>do</u>?)	

EXHIBIT 31.3
Explore Your Personal Interests

CREATE A PERSONAL MISSION STATEMENT

A mission statement is an abstract (hard to quantify) explanation about what an organization (or a person) wants to accomplish and how the organization (or person) wishes to accomplish it. For example, a hotel may want to be "the first choice of planners desiring business meetings by offering specialized services, meeting spaces, technologies, accommodations, and foodservices for meeting attendees." Likewise, the mission statement for a restaurant might focus on "providing the best value for business travelers by consistently offering enjoyable food and beverages served by friendly staff in a clean and relaxing environment."

You can develop and utilize a mission statement in much the same way as do hotels and restaurants. For example, the mission statement developed by a hospitality student may focus on "helping guests to have an enjoyable hospitality experience and employees to find joy and respect in the workplace by learning and utilizing basic quality management principles that recognize the worth of guests and employees."

Mission statements, like career plans, can (and often do) change. However, they provide a benchmark against which to compare career planning alternatives, and they provide a partial answer to the question "Am I on the right track in my career planning efforts?"

a worksheet to help you to begin formalizing and organizing thoughts about your personal interests. First, it asks you to list those things you do well. The worksheet then allows you to consider how your skills, strengths, knowledge, aptitudes, values, and interests may have helped you to do well. People feel better when they do things they do well (things that allow them to capitalize on their strengths). Emphasizing strengths and identifying personal attributes that complement them is a great tactic to use when planning a career.

OBJECTIVE 4
Indicate tactics helpful in analyzing beginning-of-career professional alternatives.

WHAT ARE YOUR ALTERNATIVES?

After you explore your personal interests, it is helpful to focus on career possibilities. Here are some good questions to ask: If everything was ideal, what would I be doing? What jobs would I be preparing to do? Where would I be working? and What kind of people do I like working for and with? Other questions include these: What type of boss would I have? and What type of employees would I supervise?

After these and related questions have been answered, you will have a benchmark against which to compare career and position alternatives. Exhibit 31.4 suggests some tactics that may be helpful in identifying alternatives. When reviewing the figure, note that five general tactics are suggested:

- Utilize personal communication skills.

Many hospitality courses use project-based instruction with small teams of students.

EXHIBIT 31.4
Tactics to Identify Career
Alternatives

Tactic 1: Utilize Personal Communication

☑ Talk to human resources persons about positions and career path alternatives.
☑ Gain practice (experience) by talking, reading, and writing about positions, companies, and careers.
☑ Build your personal and professional network of contacts.

Tactic 2: Consider the future of alternative industries, careers, and positions.

☑ Review U.S. Department of Labor publications, including the *Occupational Outlook Handbook* and its quarterly updates.
☑ Talk with educators, industry, and organization officials.
☑ Read trade magazines and review reliable information on the Internet.
☑ Discuss career alternatives with school career counselors and advisors.

Tactic 3: Learn about alternative organizations.

☑ Study mission statements.
☑ Review company materials.
☑ Talk with and shadow industry employees.
☑ Network with your contacts at school and work and within the community.
☑ Read industry publications.
☑ Interview informally someone who has a job that you might like to have.

Tactic 4: Take advantage of unique educational opportunities.

☑ Talk with visiting industry speakers and adjunct faculty; attend career fairs.
☑ Participate in internships, work experiences, and project-based instruction sessions.

Tactic 5: Emphasize what is important to you.

☑ Remember your personal interests.
☑ Think about typical work-related responsibilities.
☑ Do not forget your personal mission statement!

Many adults find that additional formal education is helpful in their careers.

- Consider the future of alternative industries, careers, and positions.
- Learn about alternative organizations.
- Take advantage of unique educational opportunities.
- Emphasize what is important to you.

Some of the most important factors that you should address as you evaluate your career and segment and position alternatives are these:

- Harmony with your interests
- Career progression outlook
- Perceived rewards
- Professional development opportunities
- Geography (location)
- Salary versus living expenses

Let's take a closer look at each factor.

Harmony with Your Interests

You explored your personal interests when reviewing Exhibit 31.3. Remember to consider how your interests can be met by the alternative types of work you could be doing.

Career Progression Outlook

Think about the **career ladders.** To do this, speak to a career counselor (if available). Also, talk with graduates from your school who are working for organizations in which you are interested and obtain information from alternative companies.

Training in "How to Interview" sessions can be helpful when the real time arrives.

Many have printed materials available (check their websites; also contact recruiters or other human resources personnel).

Perceived Rewards

When many persons think about rewards, they think about money and, especially, starting compensation. However, a wide range of other monetary and

career ladder a plan that projects successively more responsible professional positions within an organization or industry; career ladders also allow one to plan and schedule developmental activities judged necessary to assume more responsible positions

---

DID YOU KNOW?

Women comprise less than half of hotel general managers, but industry experts indicate it is now easier for women to fill top jobs. In 2002, the American Hotel & Lodging Association (AH&LA) reported that 43.5 percent of its member hotels were run by women. However, the percentage of women holding chief executive officer (CEO) and other top-level corporate positions was believed to be smaller.

Changing demographics are one reason for cracks in the **glass ceiling:**

- More women than men graduate from postsecondary hotel and restaurant management programs.
- The tourism and hospitality industry is a "people business," and many women are drawn to the industry because of their interest in working with people.
- Major hotel chains have developed diversity and mentoring programs that, respectively, can help to recruit and retain women managers.

glass ceiling an expression that describes unofficial or unacknowledged roadblocks for women attempting to advance within an organization

---

Source: David Armstrong. Cracks in glass ceiling: hotels are opening doors for women in management. Retrieved on May 11, 2006, from www.sfgate.com/cgi-bin/article.cgi?file

PROFESSIONAL PERCEPTIONS MAY NOT BE REALITY!

When asked, some hospitality students indicate that they are "people persons" and that is what excites them about the industry. They want to work in organizations and positions in which people (guests) must be served, and people (staff members) must be available to serve them. However, many parts of a hospitality manager's job do not relate to people. Consider, for example, activities dealing with financial planning, laws and regulations, insurance and risk management, and technology, to name just a few. If "working with people" is the highest-priority factor in your career selection decision, you should probably do more career exploration to be sure that you won't be surprised (or disappointed) with a career in hospitality management.

Another stereotype involves thinking about the hospitality industry relative to starched white tablecloths and beautiful table appointments (in restaurants) and beautiful atriums and other architectural wonders (in the lobbies of hotels). These amenities are designed into the environment so that guests can enjoy them. However, much of your work will likely be behind the scenes in offices that look like any other and/or in kitchens, laundry rooms, and other work areas where the environment is sometimes much less beautiful. You are also likely to spend time in corridors, parking lots, meeting rooms, and numerous other spaces as you "manage by walking around."

The hospitality industry can be and is a great business for people who enjoy it. Learn as much as you can about the industry while your career decisions are still being considered. Then you will be in it and want to stay within it for all the right reasons!

nonmonetary benefits should be considered as part of the total reward package. For example, consider these:

- Vacation pay
- Insurance benefits (health, dental, optical, prescription drugs, and others)
- Retirement plans [401(k) and/or other]
- Tuition assistance
- Meals
- Personal and sick days
- Bonuses, profit sharing, and stock options
- Relocation expenses
- Other benefits (free or reduced-priced lodging and/or meals, company car, uniform and laundry services, professional association memberships)
- Off-site training and professional development
- Travel reimbursements

All these and other payroll-related employment alternatives should be considered when this factor is analyzed.

Professional Development Opportunities

professional development programs a planned series of educational and training activities made availble to staff members for the purpose of improving current job skills and knowledge and/or to preparing them for other positions

Some hospitality organizations have a better reputation than others for helping staff members to succeed by providing planned and progressive **professional development programs.**

Geography (Location)

Hospitality managers are concerned about "location, location, location" when they consider expansion alternatives. In the same way, geography is frequently

LEARNING DOESN'T END
WHEN YOU FINISH SCHOOL!

Learning doesn't end when you finish school. In fact, it will just be starting! There are many things that one can learn only through on-job experience. Sometimes one learns *what* to do; sometimes one learns *what not* to do. Either way, ongoing experience can modify your common sense and supplement the knowledge and skills learned previously.

In addition to on the job experience, one can learn through a wide range of professional development opportunities offered by professional associations and by the hospitality organization with whom you are employed. Check out these opportunities and recognize that they can help you to learn and grow and contribute more on the job (which, in turn, leads to advancement). Professional hospitality managers recognize that learning is continuous, and the best way to discover better, cheaper, and faster ways to do things on the job is to keep up with the fast-paced changes in the industry.

a concern when making career decisions. Many persons seek initial employment after graduation with a multiunit organization (which, by definition, has multiple sites). Promotions to increasingly responsible positions frequently involve relocation. To some persons, this is positive (they like to experience new places and, perhaps, cultures); they place a high priority on these experiences. Many persons like the industry because of this travel factor. By contrast, others perceive relocation to be less advantageous since they must move away from family members and uproot others. Some persons like to stay close to home after graduation; others like to live somewhere that has always been of interest to them. Each person must determine how important these (and all other) factors are when making career decisions.

Salary versus Living Expenses

Will your new career provide adequate compensation to meet your basic living needs so that you can be an independent and self-sustaining individual? If not, are you willing to work in more than one job to meet your financial obligations? These factors must be considered to plan your future.

USE AN ALTERNATIVE EVALUATION GRID

It is unlikely that each factor just noted will be equally important when you make career planning decisions. How, then, can you consider the relative importance of each factor as you analyze alternatives? Exhibit 31.5 shows a sample alternative evaluation grid that can be

Many students work their way through school by serving in hospitality positions.

OBJECTIVE 5
Use an alternative evaluation grid to quantify the decision-making process.

RISING STAR PROFILE

Jason Koenigsfeld
Doctoral Candidate
Auburn University
Auburn, Alabama

Teaching, Research, and Community Service Will Be My Responsibilities!

Jason graduated from the William F. Harrah College of Hotel Administration at the University of Nevada, Las Vegas. He completed a management internship after graduation at the John's Island Club in Vero Beach, Florida, before continuing his formal education at Auburn University. There he received his master of science in hotel and restaurant management, and he is now completing work on his doctoral degree in hotel and restaurant management at Auburn.

Jason was asked about his interest in completing a doctoral degree, and beginning his career as a faculty member in a postsecondary hospitality management program.

"Teaching is an important responsibility of college professors, and most college and university students are aware of this. However, many faculty members are also responsible for conducting research and for participating in community service activities. These three responsibilities summarize my interest in the career I will begin after receiving my degree."

Teaching. "I served as a teaching assistant for Professor Joe Perdue at the University of Nevada, Las Vegas, and still return there each semester as a guest speaker. I've taught classes as a graduate student at Auburn that I will likely teach after receiving my degree. Soon I will also start teaching as an adjunct faculty member in the School of Hospitality Administration at Georgia State University. The phrase "Been there and done that" suggests the empathy I have for the students and my interest in assuring that their learning experiences are the very best they can be."

Research: "As an undergraduate and graduate student, I've read research-based articles that were interesting but, to me at least, not directly applicable to the numerous challenges confronting the hospitality industry today. I realize that research requires funding assistance and that researchers frequently go "where the money is." However, I am going to do my best to discover new information that will directly benefit the hospitality industry, the consumers of its products and services, and the students who study it."

Community service. I believe that faculty members should give back to their employer (college or university), their industry, and their community, among other constituencies. I will enjoy doing this as a volunteer and will work hard on school-related committees and work groups within selected hospitality associations. I recognize that the more I do so, the more I can bring what I learn into the classroom, and improve my educational messages to the students.

I've always thought that one never ceases to learn. In fact, the more formal education I've received, the more I recognize this. I intend to keep on learning by completing faculty internships in the hospitality industry and by gaining and maintaining industry contacts. As well, other great learning experiences will arise as I accompany classes on field trips and visit other areas to learn more about "what is happening" in the fast-paced hospitality industry. As well, I will learn much from my faculty peers and as I interact with others in professional associations and on related projects. These experiences will provide additional opportunities for me to learn and to pass this information along to my students.

It's only natural that, as one considers and begins a new career, there is much excitement and some apprehension. (Did I make the correct choice?) I recognize that the hospitality industry is diverse and that it provides opportunities for almost anyone regardless of personal and professional interests. I hope that my enthusiasm yields benefits to those with whom I interact. As this occurs, I will be making a contribution to my profession and the industry.

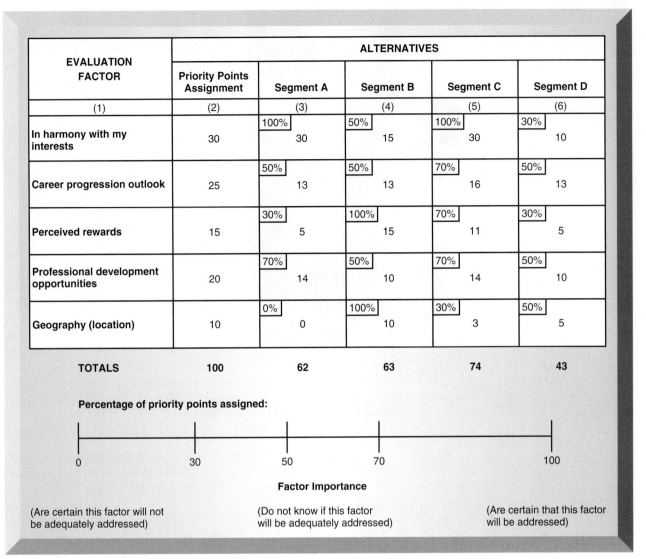

EVALUATION FACTOR	Priority Points Assignment	ALTERNATIVES			
		Segment A	Segment B	Segment C	Segment D
(1)	(2)	(3)	(4)	(5)	(6)
In harmony with my interests	30	100% 30	50% 15	100% 30	30% 10
Career progression outlook	25	50% 13	50% 13	70% 16	50% 13
Perceived rewards	15	30% 5	100% 15	70% 11	30% 5
Professional development opportunities	20	70% 14	50% 10	70% 14	50% 10
Geography (location)	10	0% 0	100% 10	30% 3	50% 5
TOTALS	**100**	**62**	**63**	**74**	**43**

Percentage of priority points assigned:

| 0 | 30 | 50 | 70 | 100 |

Factor Importance

(Are certain this factor will not be adequately addressed)   (Do not know if this factor will be adequately addressed)   (Are certain that this factor will be addressed)

EXHIBIT 31.5
Alternative Evaluation Grid

used to summarize the impact of each factor on career alternatives. Let's look at it more closely. Note that it lists the five evaluation factors just discussed. It also provides (in column 2) a place for you to indicate how important each factor is in your evaluation. For example, on a 100-point scale, assume that you rate professional development opportunities at 20 points and the extent to which an alternative is in harmony with your interests at 30 points. (The numbers listed in column 2 illustrate how the grid can be used. You should spread the 100 points between the five factors according to your perceptions about each factor's relative value.) Finally, the alternative evaluation grid provides a means to evaluate your interests in four alternative career segments (for example, hotels, restaurants, cruise lines, and meeting management). Note in the exhibit that industry segments are evaluated. You may, of course, substitute organizations or positions for industry segments.

Let's assume that you want to consider industry segments for their employment potential. You can assign the percentage of priority points (see the

Parents will have lots of suggestions about their children's career.

scale at the bottom of Exhibit 31.5) to each factor for each segment being considered. Think about the extent to which you believe your interests will be adequately addressed by each segment. If, for example, you are 100 percent certain that segment A will meet your interests, you would assign 100 percent (30) priority points to this segment. As a second example, if you are certain that a factor will not be adequately addressed, it should receive no priority points. Note that for segment A this score (0) was assigned to geography. As a third example, assume that you are uncertain (you do not know) about the extent to which a factor will be addressed; a 50 percent rating can be given, and this score was used to assign career progression points for segment A. Let's further assume that you are fairly certain that perceived rewards will not be adequately addressed and that professional development opportunities will be addressed. These two factors received, respectively, 30 percent and 70 percent of the total possible points for segment A.

What does the grid tell you when it is completed? It suggests the following:

- Segment C is preferred; the segment is in harmony with your interests, and you are "pretty sure" (70 percent) that career progression, perceived rewards, and professional development opportunities will be addressed.
- Segment A (with 62 points) and segment B (with 63 points) are too close to call. Your personal interests in professional development will be better met in segment C. However, perceived rewards are less and the geography is not really acceptable.
- Segment D is clearly the last choice. You are almost certain (30 percent) that your personal interests and perceived rewards factors will not be met, and you are uncertain about career progression, professional development opportunities, and geography factors.

What does the grid tell us? Working in segment C appears to be the preferred segment unless you desire to learn a lot more about segment D. Also, you can do more research on several factors applicable to segments A and B.

IN CONCLUSION

This chapter has discussed a process that will help you to begin to make career plans. How do you determine the exact company and position that is your employer of choice within a segment? We will address this concern in the next chapter.

SUMMARY OF CHAPTER LEARNING OBJECTIVES

1. **Recognize the importance of planning as a first step in career decision making.**
   While one cannot plan the future with absolute certainty, use of basic career planning principles allows one to have, at least, some influence over it.

2. **Provide an overview of the career planning process.**
   There are seven basic steps in the career planning process: recognize the need for career planning, explore personal interests and strengths, consider alternatives, and make a decision. (This involves the simultaneous consideration of the industry, segment, organization, and position, which will be a first step in one's professional career.) The last steps in the career planning process involve the need to accept the desired position, work to accomplish goals, and continually evaluate career progress.

3. **Utilize tactics helpful in exploring personal interests.**
   When you do a job you like, it is likely to be more fulfilling and to lead to a successful career than if you do a job because you have to.

   You can explore your personal interests by considering your skills, strengths, knowledge, aptitudes, values, and interests relative to the accomplishments of which you are most proud.

4. **Indicate tactics helpful in analyzing beginning-of-career professional alternatives.**
   Basic tactics involve utilizing personal communication; considering the future of alternative industries, careers, and positions; learning about alternative organizations; taking advantage of unique educational opportunities; and emphasizing what is important to you. Factors that should be addressed include the extent to which alternatives are in harmony with your interests, career progression outlook, perceived rewards, professional development opportunities, and geography (location).

5. **Use an alternative evaluation grid to quantify the decision-making process.**
   Use of an alternative evaluation grid allows you to match important evaluation factors with alternatives (industry segments, organization, and/or position, for example) according to the personal priorities you assign to each factor.

FEEDBACK FROM THE REAL WORLD

In this section, we do not ask for real-world advice from an industry expert. Each person planning his or her career should obtain advice, but must make a decision alone. Let's see how Trina and Jeffers approach this challenge.

At the beginning of this chapter, you learned that both Trina and Jeffers were undecided about the noncommercial foodservices segment within which they wanted to be employed initially. Let's assume that they both arrived at this decision by considering their accomplishments and personal interests with the help of the alternative evaluation grid (see Exhibit 31.5). They now know the segment of the foodservice industry (noncommercial) in which they are interested. Let's also assume that they have identified additional factors that may influence their decision about the type of

noncommercial organization (self-operated or contract management company-operated) in which they want to be employed. Now consider the seven factors noted at the beginning of the chapter. Let's see what Trina and Jeffers think about each factor and use their viewpoints to focus in on a specific type of employer.

- *Location.* Trina will likely discover numerous organizations within her area that operate their own foodservice program. Trina is also likely to find foodservice programs within the area operated by national, regional, or even local contract management companies. The availability of positions within the area is important because she does not want to relocate. Jeffers has no preference about where he goes when he

(continued)

graduates. He likes his community but has also traveled enough to know that there are many places around the country where he might like to live and work.

- *Additional hospitality education.* Both Trina and Jeffers realize that they will need to become proficient in their first job before they can explore the possibilities of additional hospitality education. Trina does not desire further hospitality education now; she may like to take some classes later. Jeffers is potentially interested in additional education at some point in his career. He is aware of traditional (*distance learning*) courses and electronic learning alternatives to continue his education. However, he would like to live and work in a community where a *residential education* program is available.
- *Technical training.* Both Trina and Jeffers recognize the need for good technical training in their new position to supplement the very useful and practical knowledge from their formal education.
- *Operating responsibilities.* Trina thinks she would like a job with day to day management responsibilities for menu planning, purchasing, staff scheduling, and other operating concerns, while Jeffers knows that he must spend many

years in a career of progressively more responsible operating duties. At some point he wants to be more removed from the day to day operations.

- *Technical assistance.* Trina is a real take-charge person who will know when she needs technical help (for example, when establishing a new accounting or bookkeeping system or designing a kitchen or dining room). However, she wants a position where she can be fully responsible and accountable. Jeffers likes to make decisions as well. However, he would like to get all available information from all possible sources before high-priority decisions are made.
- *Job flexibility.* Trina would like to find the right organization, grow and be promoted within it, and enjoy the more structured routine that it would provide. Jeffers likes to keep his options open. A different position in a new organization located in a different city would be a challenge that he would accept.
- *Fair compensation.* Both Trina and Jeffers want fair compensation based on the value they bring to the job.

Let's consider what we have just learned to help Trina and Jeffers to decide whether a self-operated or contract management company-operated foodservice position might be best. The following chart identifies some of the pros and cons of positions in self- and contract manage-

Pros and Cons of Positions in Self-Operated and Contract Management Company-Operated Foodservices

Factor	Self-Operated Foodservices	Contract Management Company Foodservices
Preferred location	Many organizations are typically located in only one area.	The contract management company has locations (accounts) in numerous locations.
Additional hospitality education	Must determine if tuition is a fringe benefit; if traditional education is desired, the organization must be located near a school or college campus.	Large management companies provide educational benefits; if traditional hospitality education is desired, it may be possible to transfer employment to a desired location.
Wants good initial training	Training quality depends on programs established by the organization and, perhaps, on whether unforeseen problems arise that reduce training time.	Large management companies have structured training programs and resources and may be able to train new employees in units that are not experiencing unforeseen problems.
Career with day-to-day operating responsibilities	Unless the organization is multiunit, the top-level management positions would probably have some daily operating responsibilities.	Higher-level management positions often involve multiunit responsibilities; these managers supervise other managers who are responsible for foodservices within specific units.
Technical assistance	The manager in a self-operated unit is the expert. It is only when specialized expertise is needed that external (consulting) help is solicited.	Large contract management companies have headquarters-level executive chefs, layout and design specialists, nutritionists, information technology, marketing and other experts who can help managers in individual units.

Job flexibility (position responsibility)	A career with a self-operated organization likely means working in the industry segment and, perhaps, in the same location and building.	A career in numerous industries and locations is possible.
Compensation (salary and benefits)	Compensation (starting pay) is typically slightly less than that paid by a contract management company.	Compensation (starting pay) from a contract management company is slightly higher than in self-operated organizations.

ment company-operated foodservices relative to the seven factors that each thinks is important.

Let's see how Trina and Jeffers might personally evaluate each of these seven factors.

- *Preferred location.* Many facilities are located in only one location. Employment with a self-operated facility may dictate, then, the location of employment. (Large, international organizations are, by definition, worldwide. With some exceptions, however, very large organizations tend to contract foodservices, rather than operate them autonomously.) Persons desiring geographic moves without changing locations may prefer a contract management company.
- *Additional hospitality education.* Tuition assistance is a benefit offered by many self-operated and contract management companies. However, if a traditional education on a campus is desired, the self-operated facility must obviously be located close to the campus. By contrast, a contract management company has numerous locations and may, perhaps, even serve the educational institution where further education can be pursued.
- *Initial training.* The quality of initial orientation and training in a self-operated facility depends on the facility itself. By contrast, most contract management companies provide structured training and education opportunities for newly employed management staff.
- *Operating responsibilities.* Managers in most self-operated facilities still have day to day operating responsibilities. Top-level managers are either directly responsible for or supervise managers who do daily scheduling, make purchase commitments, and plan special banquet events (among numerous other duties). By contrast, higher-level managers with contract management companies are in positions that supervise unit managers who, in turn, are responsible for daily operating activities.

While there is much challenge and some stress in all positions within the hospitality industry, many believe that those who are "one step away from the firing line" (field rather than unit managers) are in preferred positions.

- *Technical assistance.* The unit manager in the self-operated program is, by definition, the unit's expert on menu planning, food production, layout and equipment, marketing, management information systems, and other highly specialized and technical fields applicable to quantity food production. By contrast, unit managers in contract management companies often have technical expertise available within the company that can provide this assistance to them in the unit.
- *Job flexibility (position responsibility).* Managers with contract management companies often have more flexibility in position, industry segment, and location compared to their counterparts in self-operated programs.
- *Compensation (salary and benefits).* Self-operated and contract management company-operated employers are concerned about compensation and recognize that it is an important motivator for student recruitment. Pay at beginning management positions must, then, be competitive. However, with exceptions, managers in upper-level positions tend to receive higher levels of compensation in contract management companies, because the responsibilities measured in terms of dollars of business volume are greater for persons responsible for foodservices in many operating units.

Although there are many factors to consider (and we have noted only some of the most important in our discussion), it appears that Trina will be pursuing a position in a self-operated foodservice program; Jeffers will probably seek an initial career position with a contract management company.

MASTERING YOUR KNOWLEDGE

Discuss your answers to the following questions.

1. What role do you think formal career planning, as opposed to "seeing what happens," plays in the career of successful hospitality executives?
2. How is career planning *different* from maintaining a daily schedule plan?
3. What are several of your greatest accomplishments? What impact, if any, did your personal attributes play in these accomplishments?
4. Do you believe that your career is likely to be more successful if you enjoy the positions you hold during your career?
5. Review the tactics to identify career alternatives in Exhibit 31.4. What are additional activities you can undertake relative to each tactic?
6. Do you agree that learning doesn't end and that you will need to be involved in ongoing professional development programs throughout your career?
7. What, if any, additional evaluation factors would be important to you in the alternative evaluation grid (Exhibit 31.5) if you are considering a specific organization within an industry segment? A specific position within an organization?

LEARN FROM THE INTERNET

1. Check out the websites of several organizations in industry segments that are listed throughout this text in Learn From the Internet sections. Look for the employment opportunities section of the webpage. What information is presented that is of interest to you now as you seek an initial professional position with this employer? What type of information is available to more experienced persons seeking a career change to the organization?
2. Review the websites for the following hospitality education programs and/or others if you have special interests:
   - Cornell University School of Hotel Administration: www.hotelschool.cornell.edu
   - Florida International University School of Hospitality Management: www.hospitality.fiu.edu
   - Conrad N. Hilton College, University of Houston: www.hrm.uh.edu
   - Johnson & Wales University, the Hospitality College: www.jwu.edu/hosp/

   What employment opportunities do they cite? What, if any, discussion about career progression is noted? What type of placement assistance do they provide? Why should students want to major in hospitality management?
3. Check out the websites for several professional associations serving the hospitality industry noted in this text. What, if any, advice do they provide about career planning that can help you to evaluate opportunities within the segment they represent?

KEY HOSPITALITY TERMS

The following terms were explained in this chapter. Review the definitions of any words with which you are unfamiliar. Begin to utilize them as you expand your vocabulary as a hospitality professional.

career ladder   **professional development programs**
glass ceiling

The Job Search
Your First
Professional Position

32

You can learn about potential employers at career fairs.

CHAPTER LEARNING OBJECTIVES

After studying this chapter you will be able to:

1. Review the process for making decisions about industry segment, company, and position as one plans a career in the hospitality industry.
2. Learn basic ways to secure information about potential employers.
3. Cite advantages and disadvantages of working for large and small companies.
4. Learn about factors that are important to employers recruiting job applicants.
5. Learn how to develop an effective résumé.
6. Obtain information useful in developing a cover letter.
7. Utilize basic principles when participating in employment interviews.
8. Learn tactics helpful in postinterview job search activities.

The authors wish to thank Authella Collins Hawks, Director, Student Industry Resource Center (SIRC), The School of Hospitality Business, Michigan State University, for her assistance with this chapter.

FEEDBACK FROM THE REAL WORLD

You have a general idea of the segment of the hospitality industry in which you are going to begin your career. Perhaps it will be with hotels, restaurants, or noncommercial foodservices. Perhaps, instead, you are interested in a position with a cruise line, amusement park, or casino. The basic steps to find the job that is right for you and your prospective employer are the same.

How would you answer the following questions?

- What are some of the most important tactics hospitality students should use in their job search?

- What are suggestions about developing a résumé?
- What are helpful tactics for employment interviews?
- What are some of the most important tactics that hospitality students should *avoid* in their job search?
- What advice can you give to students who have more than one job offer?

As you read this chapter, think about answers to these questions and then get feedback from the real world at the end of the chapter.

In Chapter 31 you learned basic information to help you begin planning your career. What's next? In the case of the diverse hospitality industry, you must think about the appropriate industry segment and the company and position within that segment that might initially be best for you. For example, you may be interested in a midscale restaurant (industry segment) and numerous companies are potential employers. How do you select one and for which position should you apply? These are the types of issues addressed in this chapter.

OBJECTIVE 1
Review the process for making decisions about industry segment, company, and position as one plans a career in the hospitality industry.

MORE CAREER-RELATED DECISIONS TO MAKE!

Exhibit 32.1 reviews factors in the career decision-making process introduced in Chapter 31. Some students use a sequential approach such as that noted in

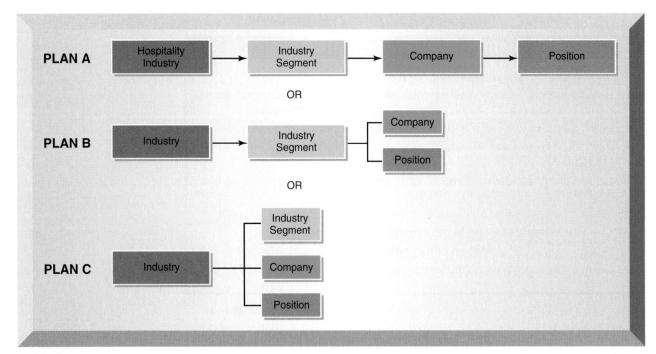

EXHIBIT 32.1
Decisions! Decisions! Decisions!

| **WHAT'S THIS ABOUT A STARTING POSITION?** |

Many students begin their hospitality career as a management trainee after completing their college degree. In this capacity, they rotate through a planned sequence of positions. As this occurs, they begin to master the set of skills that their employer believes is necessary for them to become a manager. At the same time, they learn basics about responsibilities and tasks in various positions in each department. They also begin to learn about the organizational culture and the relationship of the departments to each other and the management challenges and operating procedures of each department.

Many students negotiate an agreement before employment that, upon successful completion of the management training program, they will begin work in a mutually agreeable position. This will be the beginning of a career track that will take them, at least initially, up the ladder within the organization.

Some students, especially those who have completed internships and/or have work experience with their permanent placement employer, may not be required to participate in this rotating management training or, at least, it might be shortened. Instead, they may move directly into the management position negotiated with their employer.

---

plan A. First, they determine the industry (hospitality), then the segment within it, then the company operating within that segment, and, finally, a position. Other students, by contrast, focus on the hospitality industry first and, the industry segment second and then combine (merge) decisions about company and position so that they are considered simultaneously (plan B). Still other students like a less structured approach (plan C) in which there are two basic decisions: hospitality industry and a second decision about segment, company, and position.

WHAT INFORMATION IS AVAILABLE?

OBJECTIVE 2
Learn basic ways to secure information about potential employers.

Let's assume that you have decided to begin your career within the hospitality industry; where should you start your job search? The many sources of information about companies in all industry segments can provide background information about potential employers:

Networking

There are numerous contacts who can provide information about and/or help you to identify alternative hospitality employers:

networking the process of building professional relationships

- *Classmates.* Many of your peers have probably worked for companies to complete internships or similar requirements and/or to earn money while they were in school.
- *Faculty members.* Those teaching hospitality-related courses probably have numerous contacts (their own networks) that can yield information for your job search.
- *Campus recruiters.* Representatives of many companies visit the campuses of many postsecondary schools. They may also visit **career fairs** sponsored by educational institutions.
- *School alumni.* Graduates of your school may hold positions in companies in which you are potentially interested.
- *Your family and friends.* For many students, this is the best source of information for potential employers.

career fairs trade show-type events that allow prospective job applicants, moving from booth to booth, to meet recruiters representing numerous employers

Meeting with peers to learn about internship experiences is important.

Research

Your own study of applicable resources can be helpful.

- *The Internet*. Many organizations have websites that provide information about their company; an increasing number also have an employment opportunities section on the site. (For example, check out the websites of the organizations mentioned throughout this book.)
- *Professional and trade associations in the hospitality industry*. Many feature employer information and job boards (check out the websites of those included in this book).
- *Trade publications*. Each segment of the hospitality industry has trade magazines that feature articles about current events, prominent organizations, and related information. A review of current magazines may help you to identify organizations worth a second look.
- *Other written information*. Annual reports submitted by organizations, recruitment and other brochures, and class handout information are examples of other written information that can tell you something about prospective employers.

Talking with alums from your school can be very beneficial.

- *Career centers*. Many colleges and universities offer a variety of resources to help students to learn about prospective employers. For example, they may have hard-copy brochures presenting information about employment opportunities and annual reports that describe the company's financial position. Career centers may also compile information about positions accepted by past graduates, which is invaluable in gathering ideas about prospective positions.

OBJECTIVE 3
Cite advantages and disadvantages of working for large and small companies.

LARGE OR SMALL HOSPITALITY ORGANIZATION: WHICH IS BEST?

There are excellent large and small companies within most segments of the hospitality industry. What are the pros and cons of working in both types of organizations?

ALL ABOUT CAREER FAIRS

Many employers participate in career fairs sponsored by higher-education hospitality professional associations and/or state and local employment agencies to promote their opportunities and to prescreen applicants. Career fairs range from small community-sponsored events to giant regional career expositions. Career fairs at educational facilities may be sponsored by a department, college, or the entire college or university.

Most career fairs are attended by recruiters who are human resources personnel and/or other company representatives. For on-campus events, some employers also send recent graduates whom they have employed. Large corporations and some government agencies have staff members who work the career fair circuit nationwide.

The purpose of career fairs is to allow students to network by sharing their résumé and professional history with those with hiring responsibilities. They also enable you to conduct an informational interview to assess whether a company might be a good professional fit for your strengths and interests.

Displays vary widely from a simple table with, perhaps, brochures and business cards and a lone representative to an elaborate multimedia extravaganza with interactive displays, videos, and a team of recruiters.

DRESS FOR SUCCESS

Generally, the appropriate attire for career fair attendees should be business professional. Think of your attendance at a career fair as a dress rehearsal for your real interviews!

Bring copies of your résumé, a few pens and pencils, a folder or portfolio, and some sort of note-taking device (a paper or electronic pad). Keep track of the recruiters with whom you speak and send follow-up notes to those of interest.

STOP, LOOK, AND LISTEN

Keep your eyes and ears open. There is nothing wrong with subtly eavesdropping on the questions asked and answers received by other attendees. You might learn valuable information and witness real-life career search "dos and don'ts."

Be an active participant and not just a browser. Chat with the company representatives and ask meaningful questions. Remember that your goal is to introduce yourself. You should also show your knowledge of the company, express enthusiasm and interest, and relate your background to the company's needs.

YOUR INITIAL GOAL: NOT TO SEEK A JOB BUT TO SEEK INFORMATION

You can use all the information you can discover when you are making an employment decision. An organized approach to gathering and analyzing as much information as possible is much better than the alternative ("applying everywhere and seeing what happens!"). Networking and research will yield useful input to the decision-making process. Take your time, carefully consider what you want to do, and gather as much information as you can to enable you to rationally make this very important professional employment decision.

Much information about potential employers can be learned by studying their websites.

Advantages of Large Companies

Advantages of working for large companies include these:

- Greater opportunities to advance and relocate. When one works for a very large company, it may even be possible to transfer to other locations worldwide.
- Prestige associated with a name. Large organizations are often better known than their smaller counterparts. You may want your name and work associated with these companies.
- Less employment risk. Many people believe there is greater job security within a larger company.
- Compensation and benefits may be greater at larger companies.
- Legal protection. Smaller companies may be exempt from some labor regulations. Employees at large companies will be protected by OSHA and other regulations.
- Training is often more structured and effective in larger companies and enhanced by dollars devoted to technology for training and guest use.

Disadvantages of Large Companies

While there are advantages to working for a large company, there are possible disadvantages:

- Less control over one's work. In larger companies, strategies may be set, and employees may have fewer opportunities to contribute ideas.
- Some people believe that they are just a number in a larger organization. (This is similar to how some persons feel about colleges or universities with large enrollments.)
- Less access to senior executives. If you work for a large organization, you may rarely see the general manager and never see the owners.

Advantages of Small Companies

- Employees are likely to know each other. There is a sense of camaraderie, which may be less common in large companies.
- Employees may have a greater variety of duties. They often have more control over their work and can make a greater contribution to the company's short- and long-term strategies.
- Executives in small companies tend to be approachable and available to all employees.
- Employees may have more responsibility. One is not limited by a job title or job description.
- More company-wide involvement. One is more likely to be involved in the entire organization, rather than in a specific department.
- Less bureaucracy (rules and regulations).
- The best small companies do not stay small. (Some of America's best companies were recently small companies, for example, America Online, Dell Computers, and Home Depot.) Small companies offer the potential of a job that can grow as the company grows and the chance to be part of building a business.

Disadvantages of Small Companies

- Limited benefits. Many small companies do not offer the same benefits as do larger companies.
- Smaller companies often provide less training; structured training programs are relatively rare.
- Fewer opportunities for promotion. There are, by definition, fewer positions in small companies, which limits one's advancement.

In the United States, most new job growth comes from small businesses. The hospitality industry readily lends itself to entrepreneurs beginning a new business and enjoying the success that it brings. (The world of hospitality entrepreneurs is discussed in Chapter 34.)

RISING STAR PROFILE

Lorin Meskin
Senior Operations Integrity Lead
Affiliated Computer Services
Denver, Colorado

Career Change: Hospitality Management to Health Care Administration

Lorin received his university degree in hospitality business. After graduation, he worked as an assistant restaurant manager for the Chicago Marriott Downtown. He then worked as a front-office manager for a Residence Inn in Chicago, and then became a floating manager for Prime Hospitality to train personnel for entry-level positions and managers and supervisors to improve their skills in goal setting, employee and guest problem resolution, and the conduct of internal audits. Lorin ended his hotel career as an assistant general manager of the AmeriSuites Hotel at the Mall of America in Minnesota.

Lorin's most unforgettable moment during his hospitality career actually lasted several weeks or longer when he had to deal with distressed travelers after the terrorist attacks on September 11, 2001.

Lorin used his hospitality business experience by booking conferences and conventions for Auriaria Higher Education Center while completing his master of science degree in health education at the University of Colorado. In his current position, he deals with privacy, security, and safety concerns relating to national healthcare privacy laws as they relate to his company and also special projects. Lorin notes the importance of his hospitality management background because, in his position, he must emphasize profit maximization and associate and customer satisfaction.

Lorin has some good advice for those considering a career in the hospitality industry: "Realize that it takes a lot of hard work, dedication, long hours, and networking to be successful. Sometimes it can be who you know—not what you know—that can benefit you most at a specific point in your career."

Lorin commented on his plans to change careers from hospitality to healthcare: "There are many similarities between the hospitality and healthcare industries. The words *hospitality* and *hospitals* both come from the same root word (hospice), which means to serve and to care. In healthcare, you are serving people in a life-saving business rather than in a travel business. However, they are both businesses. In the U.S. healthcare system, facilities address business goals through the use of business concepts. Both industries rely on huge amounts of human capital. Knowing how to manage human resources is key to success in both environments. One big difference is the science one must know in healthcare, and other factors, such as insurance, Medicare, Medicaid, and government regulations, must be understood by the effective healthcare manager."

EXHIBIT 32.2
Human Resources
Differences in Large
and Small Companies

Large Company	Small Company
Centralized personnel department	No personnel department (personnel issues handled by an operations manager)
Formal recruiting program coordinated by human resources personnel	No full-time recruiters; external recruitment activities are limited
Standardized hiring procedures	No standard hiring procedures
Retains résumés on file for a specified period of time	Usually does not retain résumés for lengthy time periods
Interviews held off-site with recruiters and then on-site with managers and supervisors	Interviews held with owner or immediate supervisor
Company literature available	No printed literature
Employment commitment made long in advance of starting date	Employment needs are more immediate
Formal training programs	On-the-job training
Predetermined job categories and pathways to advancement	Jobs emerge to fit needs
May have profile of successful employees and use personality testing to assess company fit (will not employ if profile is not met)	No profile available or used

Adapted from *Career Passport 2002–2003.* Michigan State University Career Services and Placement, 2002.

OBJECTIVE 4
Learn about factors that are important to employers recruiting job applicants.

Exhibit 32.2 shows some differences that might be important as one considers a position in a large or small company.

Successful employment interviews are critical for attaining your first professional position.

WHAT EMPLOYERS LOOK FOR[1]

Employers are looking for employees who can "think outside the box" and have flexibility in their skill areas. Preferred candidates will possess the following:

- Effective communication skills
- Computer aptitude
- Leadership and organizational traits
- Teamwork abilities
- Interpersonal abilities
- Personal accountability
- Enthusiasm (enthusiastic personality)
- Problem-solving and decision-making skills

Employers typically state their desire for a total package of knowledge, skills, and aptitudes. They mention critical thinking, intelligence, common sense, and a willingness to learn quickly and continuously. Exhibit 32.3 shows a ranking of key candidate characteristics that are important to employers.

[1]Adapted from *Recruiting Trends 2000–2001*, Collegiate Employment Research Institute, Career Services and Placement, Michigan State University, 2002.

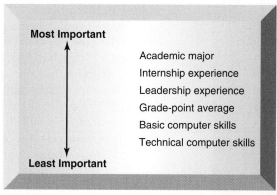

EXHIBIT 32.3
Candidate Characteristics Important to Employers

These characteristics were suggested by employers responding to a generic survey that was not focused directly on hospitality recruiters. Many hospitality industry observers would agree, however, that one's academic major, leadership (effective use of interpersonal and communication skills), and a basic grasp of technology are very important. They would likewise agree that grade-point average (GPA) is not as important as several of the factors just noted.

ALL ABOUT RÉSUMÉS

A **résumé** can be a helpful tool in obtaining **employment interviews.** It can help you to recall the strengths you want potential employers to know about and will help employers differentiate between you and others seeking the same position.

Several steps are helpful in writing a résumé. These are summarized in Exhibit 32.4. Let's look at each of the steps in résumé writing more carefully.

Step 1: *Target Your Position* As a result of the career planning process (see Chapter 31), you have determined the segment of the

OBJECTIVE 5
Learn how to develop an effective résumé.

résumé a summary of a job applicant's education, experiences, and job-related qualifications

employment interview a conference between an organizational representative and a prospective job applicant in which both parties learn information helpful in an employment-related decision

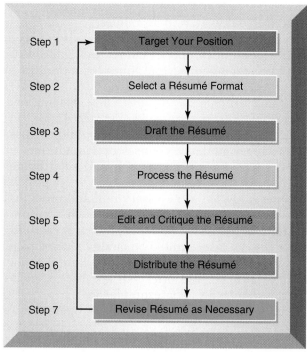

EXHIBIT 32.4
A Recipe for Résumé Development

You may want to work for the organization where you completed an internship or worked for the summer.

hospitality industry in which you wish to begin your career. As a result of research (see earlier sections of this chapter), you have identified potential employers within the segment. Now is the time to think carefully about the position for which you are applying. These decisions will drive the development of your résumé. What can set you apart from others who will apply for this position? Your answers to this question may help you to write your résumé. (Some résumé writers include an objective statement at the beginning of their résumé.)

Step 2: *Select a Résumé Format* A *chronological résumé* lists one's work history in reverse order (present position first, beginning work experience last). A *functional résumé* highlights skill areas applicable to a specific position. This is effective for persons with limited work experience and for those seeking a position in a field that does not match their career experiences. A *combination résumé* uses both chronological and functional formats that allow one to tailor the résumé style to specific employers.

Step 3: *Draft the Résumé* List skills, work experiences, honors, awards, activities, and internship experiences along with other information that you think is relevant to an employer. Place the items from your list into the headings you chose when you selected a résumé format (step 2). Be concise; a résumé for a student graduating with relatively little experience should be generally less than one page. (Do not use full sentences; do not use personal pronouns such as *I* or *my*. Use action words and phraseology to describe your work responsibilities.)

Step 4: *Process the Résumé* Make sure it is easy to read. Highlight or bold section titles, check (and recheck!) all spellings, and proofread the document several times (or more!) to assure that it is error free.

Step 5: *Edit and Critique the Résumé* Once spelling and grammatical errors have been eliminated (see step 4), ask several people to critique the résumé for you. Get opinions from faculty members, career guidance counselors and advisors, employers, and others who have worked with and seen numerous résumés. (Don't just ask student peers; you need professional advice!) After it is revised as necessary, edit and proofread it again (several times or more!). Then, with each revision, reprocess the résumé as necessary. *Be certain that it is error free.* Finally, have your resume laser-printed on quality résumé paper.

When editing your résumé, be careful about making vague claims. Instead, use brief and specific examples that demonstrate your skills. For example, instead of writing "I experienced a fast-paced, busy restaurant operation," say something like, "I served 85 guests on an average shift while working at a casual-service restaurant."

Step 6: *Distribute the Résumé* Some prospective employers may desire or require electronic versions of your résumé. Hard copies should be available for distribution at career fairs and for other occasions where a person to person distribution is acceptable (and preferable).

Step 7: *Revise the Résumé as Necessary.* Exhibit 32.4 suggests that the résumé development process is cyclical; it is, in fact, a tool that will evolve throughout your professional career. The experience section of the document will need to be revised as your job titles and responsibilities change. The receipt of honors and awards, the completion of additional education and training, and the restatement of your career objective as your career evolves are additional examples of opportunities to update your resume.

Exhibit 32.5 shows a sample résumé that might be applicable to one seeking an entry-level professional position within the hospitality industry.

RÉSUMÉ COVER LETTERS

OBJECTIVE 6
Obtain information useful in developing a cover letter.

How are résumés distributed to potential employers? You may personally circulate your résumé at career fairs and give it to guest speakers in classes. Other copies will be given to recruiters during employment interviews. You will likely mail or e-mail others. Recruiters and managers of **employer of choice** organizations receive many such documents; a **cover letter** can make your résumé stand out from others.

Your cover letter should generally include the following information:

* Since companies may have multiple positions to fill, state the position for which you are applying and how you learned about an opening (or why you are contacting the company)
* Special aspects of your background that would help you to be an outstanding match for the position being applied for
* Factors that attracted you to this organization
* What action you desire (such as an interview)
* A statement of appreciation for the reader's consideration of your candidacy and information about how you can be contacted

Exhibit 32.6 presents a sample cover letter.

employer of choice an organization with a reputation of being a desirable place to work and whose recruiting efforts are made easier because of this

cover letter a transmittal letter that accompanies a résumé being sent to a prospective employer; its purpose is to introduce a potential applicant and expresses his or her interest in employment opportunities

---

TIPS FOR AN EFFECTIVE COVER LETTER

Word process it neatly (and error-free) on a single page of stationery matching that of your résumé.

Address the letter to a specific individual (do the research!). Recall that the cover letter is a sample of your writing; be simple and direct.

Edit your letter *carefully;* be sure it contains no misspelled words or inconsistencies in format. Have someone (or, preferably, several people) proofread it.

Retain a copy of each letter you send.

Do what you say you are going to do. (If you are going to "call" or "stop by," then do it!)

EXHIBIT 32.5
Sample Résumé

SANDY J. STUDENT
♦♦♦
e-mail address

School Address:
1234 Academic Street
Anytown, Anystate
Telephone Number

Permanent Address:
4567 Smith Drive
Mytown, Mystate
Telephone Number

♦ OBJECTIVE
To obtain a management position in hospitality that will allow me to use my education, experience, and passion for the industry.

♦ EDUCATION
Bachelor of Arts in Hospitality Business
Expected Graduation, May 2005
3.49/4.0 GPA

Name of University
Department Name
Anytown, Anystate

♦ PROFESSIONAL EXPERIENCE
The Grill, Somewhere, CA
Management Intern   *June 2004-Present*

- Acquired extensive working knowledge of restaurant profit and loss management.
- Rotated throughout kitchen in culinary training
- Implemented operating procedures to improve sanitation
- Rotated through four food production-related positions

The Dining Room, Somewhere Else, AZ
Restaurant Supervisor   *April 2003-May 2004*

- Managed a food and beverage outlet, including 50 full-time and student employees
- Assumed daily restaurant management functions, including floor supervision menu planning, food expediting, weekly scheduling, and constant guest interaction
- Coordinated community promotion events

First Class Restaurant, Midwest, IL
Management Intern   *May 2002-August 2002*

- Rotated through all front-of-house operating positions
- Implemented several procedures to improve daily operations of restaurant

♦ SPECIAL SKILLS

- Certified in "Controlling Alcohol Risks Effectively" (Educational Institute, American Hotel and Lodging Association), 2004
- Experienced with Squirrel and Sable Point of Sale restaurant systems
- Proficient in spoken and written Spanish

♦ ACTIVITIES AND AWARDS

- Treasurer, Hospitality Club   April 2002 to April 2003
- Executive Director, Culinary Club   April 2004 to Present
- First Recipient, Special Endowed Scholarship   April 2003
- Member, Eta Sigma Delta Hospitality Honor Fraternity   October 2003 to Present
- Recipient, Housing and Food Services Scholarship   April 2002

REFERENCES AVAILABLE UPON REQUEST

EXHIBIT 32.6
Sample Cover Letter

Your Name
Address
Telephone Number and E-mail Address

Date
Potential Employer's Name
Potential Employer's Address

Dear Ms. _____,

I really enjoyed learning about (*Name of Company*) when you spoke to our (*Name of Hospitality Management Class*). Your program of orientation and training for new management personnel was especially interesting.

I will be graduating with a degree in hospitality management (*date*). Two internships in restaurant operations along with classwork and student hospitality club activities have convinced me that a career in foodservices will be right for me. I also know that on-job experience after beginning work will be very beneficial, and I want this to happen in a company such as (*Name of Organization*), which emphasizes professional development for all its staff members.

I am enclosing a résumé and would like to learn more about how I can be part of your company's ambitious growth plans.

If additional information is desired, please let me know. I hope it will be appropriate for me to follow up this letter with a telephone call to learn about your interest in further discussing opportunities, and I will do so on Wednesday, November 3.

Thank you sincerely,

(*Your Name*)

EMPLOYMENT INTERVIEWS: THE NEXT STEP

OBJECTIVE 7
Utilize basic principles when participating in employment interviews.

Congratulations! Your résumé with accompanying letter has opened the door for the next step in your job search: the employment interview. Unfortunately, interviewing can be stressful. This is especially so if you really want the job and/or have not had experience participating in interviews. Your interview will be ideally effective if, when it is completed, you have learned information to help you to further evaluate your interest in the company. Conversely, the interviewer will have learned more about you and the potential match you have with the organization.

Since one of your interview goals is to learn as much as you can, here are some sample questions that you can ask to help you to accomplish your goal.

- What would be my most important responsibilities?
- What type of training do you provide for new employees?
- What types of ongoing professional development programs do you provide?
- How will I be evaluated? How often?
- What is the short-term career ladder (five year) for a very effective and successful employee who begins in the position I am being offered?
- What are your company's short- and long-term goals?
- What feedback has your company received from persons recently hired for the position I would assume?

Some college grads start their own business right out of school. This recent grad is a salesperson with a specialty line of foodservice products.

behavior-based questions
an interviewing approach designed to assess how one has behaved in specific situations

Many interviewers ask a combination of direct questions, such as these, and **behavior-based questions.** Using this approach, an interviewer might identify common situations that an employee in a specific position may encounter or ask you to describe situations in which you have worked. These become situational questions that can be asked during an interview. Also, many employers believe that action taken in past situations will predict future performance. They may ask you to describe, for example, times in which you demonstrated a specific leadership skill that they believe to be important. (For example, "Tell me about a situation in which you had to plan and carry out an activity involving lots of people. What happened?")

Behavior-based questions can include these:

- What would you do if you knew a fellow employee was stealing?
- Describe what you might do if a guest complains to you about ineffective service in the organization?
- How would you supervise an employee who does not speak the same language that you do?
- If you were exceptionally busy, how would you establish priorities for work tasks?

Good news! You're hired!

TIPS FOR EFFECTIVE INTERVIEWS

Be on time. (Arrive early!)

Dress professionally. (Don't try to "express yourself.")

Have a positive attitude.

Greet the interviewer with a firm handshake and a smile.

Remember your objective: to gain information and to sell yourself.

Bring a notepad and pen. Résumés and a list of references may be requested, so have them available as well. (Print them on résumé-quality paper with your name and contact information on top.)

Practice, practice, practice before you begin interviewing.

Be sure you know how to spell and pronounce the interviewer's name.

Obtain the interviewer's business card so that you can send a thank-you note after the interview.

Learn as much as possible about the organization *before* the interview. (You will know what you need to ask about, and you will show the interviewer you are sincere because of the research you have conducted.)

Effective interviewers want you to do most of the talking; they want to do most of the listening. Here are some sample questions you may be asked:

Tell me what you know about our organization and the position for which you are applying.

How would you describe your ideal job?

What do you want to be doing in five years?

What are your career goals?

How did you prepare for this interview?

What knowledge and skills do you have that can help you to be successful in our organization?

How will you decide on the organization for which you will work?

How has your experience helped you to prepare for this position?

How has your education helped you?

What do you think will differ the most between what you learned in school and what you will be doing on the job?

What do you like best about your current job? What did you like least about your last job?

What suggestions did you make at your last job?

What were things you liked about the best boss you ever worked for?

Can you tell me about how you handled an upset customer in an earlier work experience?

How would you keep multiple customers happy when you are working on a busy shift?

How do you manage stress in your current job?

What annoys you most about your job?

How did you decide what you would major in?

What subjects have you liked the most? The least? Why?

Do your grades accurately reflect what you have learned?

What are your two or three greatest achievements in school? Out of school?

If you had to do anything differently in your life, what would it be?

WHAT ABOUT COMPENSATION?

Interviewees are obviously interested in the answer to this question. Your preinterview research should have provided a range of salary and the benefits offered by the prospective employer. This will provide you with a benchmark. The time to discuss compensation, including benefits, is during the negotiation process that occurs after a job offer has been made.

OBJECTIVE 8
Learn tactics helpful in postinterview job search activities.

site visit a trip to a business location of a prospective employer that allows a prospective job applicant to learn firsthand information about the potential employer

job shadowing (for permanent placement) a combination employment interview and site visit; prospective applicants can ask questions and, at the same time, follow a position incumbent on the job to gain a realistic overview of the organization

Our list of examples can continue; however, you will do best in answering these questions if you think about potential questions ahead of time by considering the position and organization for which you are interviewing. Practice these questions by attempting to apply the knowledge and skills that a successful position incumbent would bring to the behavioral situation.

AFTER THE INTERVIEW: WHAT'S NEXT?

After the interview is complete, a thank-you letter (on résumé paper) or, increasingly, an e-mail note should be sent. It should be forwarded on a timely basis (within a few days after the interview); most persons suggest that it be word processed, not handwritten. A sample is shown in Exhibit 32.7.

Many hospitality organizations offer a follow-up interview for candidates who performed well in the initial interview. Candidates are often invited to a company location for a **site visit** (an interview or tour, perhaps with **job shadowing,** and an opportunity to meet other company employees). As noted earlier in this chapter, some large companies utilize personality testing (and/or even telephone interviews) to assess whether candidates will mesh with the corporate culture. Those who appear incompetent will not be invited to participate in the next phase of interviews.

When you are offered a position, the terms and conditions of the job offer become very important. Some lucky persons receive more than one job

EXHIBIT 32.7
Sample Thank-You Letter

Your Name
Address
Telephone Number and E-mail Address

Date
Potential Employer's Name
Potential Employer's Address

Dear Ms. _____,

Thank you very sincerely for the time you spent in interviewing me earlier this week. I learned much more about (_Name of Company_), and I really think that working with your company as a management trainee after graduation would be an excellent way to begin the next phase of my hospitality career.

Please contact me if you desire further information. I hope to soon become a member of your professional hospitality team.

Thank you sincerely,

(_Your Name_)

offer. How should you evaluate any (and all) job offers you receive? Exhibit 32.8 lists some of the most important factors that you should evaluate. To begin, learn what other students in your school are receiving for initial compensation and other benefits. Talk directly with your peers and with those in your school's career office, if applicable. Use this information as a benchmark for your own negotiation.

Remember that it is your output (what you will do for the company) rather than your input (the experience and education that you bring to the job) that will be most important to the employer. If, for example, your experience

EXHIBIT 32.8
Checklist for Evaluating Job Offers

FACTOR	IMPORTANCE TO ME			
	SIGNIFICANT	VERY	SOMEWHAT	NONE
General				
Relevance of your education	❏	❏	❏	❏
Location	❏	❏	❏	❏
Physical demands	❏	❏	❏	❏
Your aptitude to do required work	❏	❏	❏	❏
Total compensation	❏	❏	❏	❏
Your interest in doing the work	❏	❏	❏	❏
Future of organization	❏	❏	❏	❏
Daily work hours	❏	❏	❏	❏
Weekly work hours	❏	❏	❏	❏
Workplace environment	❏	❏	❏	❏
Location				
Cost of living	❏	❏	❏	❏
Friends and family	❏	❏	❏	❏
Moving expenses	❏	❏	❏	❏
Recreational opportunities	❏	❏	❏	❏
Travel requirements	❏	❏	❏	❏
Position				
Level of responsibility	❏	❏	❏	❏
Quality of training	❏	❏	❏	❏
Challenges	❏	❏	❏	❏
Mentor available	❏	❏	❏	❏
Advancement	❏	❏	❏	❏
Transfer of knowledge and skills to other positions	❏	❏	❏	❏
Company				
Culture	❏	❏	❏	❏
Reputation	❏	❏	❏	❏
Mission	❏	❏	❏	❏
Job security	❏	❏	❏	❏
Management quality	❏	❏	❏	❏
Support for additional education	❏	❏	❏	❏
Compensation				
Salary	❏	❏	❏	❏
Bonus	❏	❏	❏	❏
Health insurance	❏	❏	❏	❏
Life insurance	❏	❏	❏	❏
Vacations and holidays	❏	❏	❏	❏
Sick leave	❏	❏	❏	❏
Pension	❏	❏	❏	❏
Retirement	❏	❏	❏	❏
Profit sharing	❏	❏	❏	❏
Overtime	❏	❏	❏	❏
Stock options	❏	❏	❏	❏
Pretax accounts (health and childcare)	❏	❏	❏	❏
Relocation expenses	❏	❏	❏	❏

NO JOB OFFER—NOW WHAT?

Not all job interviews are successful. Some organizations routinely interview many (typically hundreds) of potential job applicants, but accept only a relatively few. A letter of rejection only means that one specific company does not believe that you were the best candidate for a specific position at that company at that time. Remember that many other companies can make employment offers that will fit your needs and interests. Your best tactic: learn from the experience. Think about the questions you were asked that may have given you trouble. Learn from that experience so that these and related questions will not pose problems in the future. Continue to interview and seek other options.

Send a letter to your organizational contact. Thank him or her for the opportunity. Ask about feedback, if any, that may help you to plan interviewing strategies in the future. The world of hospitality is small; you may have opportunities to revisit employment opportunities with this organization sometime during your career. As you gain experience and learn additional skills, companies may be willing to reassess your abilities at a later time. Therefore, do not burn bridges, which could prevent this from happening.

and education are significant, this should translate to effective on-job performance. It is the latter (what you do on the job) that will determine your future with the organization.

It is always best to think about your long-term career and what you want to do, rather than your first position (its pay and location, for example), when you make your most important employment decision. Remember that accepting a job offer represents a commitment to work and to do your best for your new employer. If you have multiple job offers (congratulations on your success!), be certain that you make the right decision for you before accepting an offer. When you do, write a thank-you note to the other organizations. Thank your contact for offering you an opportunity and indicate that you have accepted another employment offer.

SUMMARY OF CHAPTER LEARNING OBJECTIVES

1. **Review the process for making decisions about industry segment, company, and position as one plans a career in the hospitality industry.**
   There are three basic approaches: one can consider segment, company, and position sequentially; one can consider the industry segment first and company and position simultaneously; or one can consider industry segment, company, and position simultaneously.

2. **Learn basic ways to secure information about potential employers.**
   Common ways include networking with classmates, faculty members, campus recruiters, school alumni, and family and friends. One can also study applicable resources found on the Internet and in professional and trade publications. Attending career fairs and talking with representatives of potential employers at

every opportunity are additional ways to learn about potential hospitality employers.

3. **Cite advantages and disadvantages of working for large and small companies.**
   Large companies provide greater opportunities to relocate, possible prestige associated with their name, less employment risk, and the potential for greater compensation. There is likely to be greater legal protection and more structured training. Disadvantages include less control over one's work, the concern that an employee is just a number, and less access to senior executives. Advantages of working with smaller companies include the greater likelihood that employees will know each other, have a greater variety of duties, and be more accessible to executives. Likewise, one typically has more responsibility and more organization-wide involvement with less

bureaucracy (rules and regulations). Disadvantages of working for small companies include the potential for fewer benefits, less structured training, and fewer opportunities for promotion.

4. **Learn about factors that are important to employers recruiting job applicants.**
Preferred candidates will possess effective communication skills, computer aptitude, leadership traits, teamwork and interpersonal abilities, personal accountability, and enthusiasm. Recruiters typically favor (in descending order of importance) academic major, internship experience, leadership experience, and grade-point average.

5. **Learn how to develop an effective résumé.**
There are seven steps in a recipe for résumé development: target your position, select a résumé format, draft the résumé, process the résumé, edit and critique the résumé (numerous times), distribute the résumé, and revise the résumé as necessary.

6. **Obtain information useful in developing a cover letter.**
Cover letters are utilized to transmit résumés. They should be word processed neatly and correctly on a single page of stationery matching that of the résumé. The letter should be addressed to a specific individual, edited carefully, and should indicate the following: how you learned about an opening, aspects of your background that will make you an outstanding employee, factors that attracted you to the organization, and the action you desire.

7. **Utilize basic principles when participating in employment interviews.**
Basic principles include the need to be on time, dress professionally, and have a positive attitude. Practice before the interview, know how to spell and pronounce the interviewer's name, and be aware of typical questions that interviewees are likely to be asked. Also, know questions to ask that can help you to learn as much as possible about the prospective employer.

8. **Learn tactics helpful in postinterview job search activities.**
Send a thank-you letter and be prepared to participate in a follow-up interview, which may be at a company location and include a tour and job shadowing. Talk with your peers and with persons in your school's placement office, if applicable, about the initial compensation and other benefits that you should expect. If you have multiple job offers, make the right decision, accept the appropriate offer, and inform other prospective employers about your decision.

MASTERING YOUR KNOWLEDGE

Discuss the following questions.

1. Review Exhibit 32.1. Which of the alternative planning approaches (plan A, B, or C) seems most reasonable to you when trying to narrow down options for companies and positions within the industry segment in which you want to work? Why?
2. What are examples of questions you can ask faculty members, campus recruiters, and school alumni as you attempt to learn information helpful in identifying alternative industry employers?
3. What do you see to be the biggest advantages and disadvantages of working with large and small hospitality industry organizations?
4. If you were a recruiter for a hospitality organization, what would be the most important factors you would be concerned about as you recruited potential applicants? Why?
5. How important do you think an effectively developed résumé is to your job search? What are some simple tactics you can utilize to assure that your résumé is the best that it can be?
6. Which of the questions frequently asked by interviewers noted in this chapter would be the most difficult for you to answer? (Practice them!)
7. What are some questions, in addition to those noted in the chapter, that you would like to ask recruiters in efforts to find out as much as possible about their organization?
8. What are the most important concerns that you will have as you evaluate alternative job offers? Why are these the most important factors to you?

FEEDBACK FROM THE REAL WORLD

Our real-world advice comes from John Lee, Director of College and External Relations, Sodexho Talent Acquisition, Newark, Delaware.

What are some of the most important tactics that hospitality students should use in their job search?

Their research activities should include the following:

- Visit industry-related websites such as applicable associations and, if possible, attend trade shows and national or state conferences, conventions, and other meetings where you can learn about and begin to develop professional networking relationships.
- Read trade journals and industry publications to learn about trends and what organizations are doing to set themselves apart from their competitors.
- Thoroughly review the websites of companies you will interview to learn as much as you can about them.
- Talk to faculty members about companies in the industry segments of interest to you.
- Ask for and accept honest feedback about how you may fit into companies in the segments of the industry in which you wish to work.

What are your suggestions about developing a résumé?

- Indicate all work experience. Hospitality students should be working in the industry and, when possible, they should have a variety of experiences.
- Don't overstate the responsibilities of the positions you have held.
- Don't clutter up your résumé with nonrelevant experience, but do include all of your leadership and supervisory experiences.
- Try, wherever possible, to take on positions of additional responsibility at work and include this information in your résumé.
- Be involved in community or charitable service activities, if possible, and include these experiences in your résumé.

- Be active in campus activities such as honor societies and clubs, and be sure to note these experiences in your résumé.

What are helpful tactics for employment interviews?

- Consider the industry segments in which you want to work. Prioritize these alternatives while recognizing that your first choice may not be available.
- Spend time with your college and university's career services staff to learn how to improve your interviewing skills and to learn about potential employers.
- Read "Dress for Success" or other professional attire materials. Always be sharp, and dress professionally for these important interactions with potential employers.
- Recognize that employers who have significant professional employment needs at the beginning of your education program may have fewer (or no) needs for professional staff at a later time (and vice versa!).
- Be aware of the cyclical impact that the economy has on different segments within the hospitality industry.
- Be sure you know details about the organization and the types of positions it has available before the interview. Excellent sources: the company's website, recruitment information, and employer-sponsored open-house or mixer sessions on campus.
- Disclose any geographic limitations you have. Don't lead employers on wild goose chases, and don't interview with employers who you know cannot place you in a required location.
- Be yourself in an interview. Insincerity comes across quickly!
- Answer questions with actual examples from your own personal experience.
- Be confident and demonstrate a customer focus.

- Follow up the interview with a letter or e-mail. Be reasonable in your follow-up communications; lengthy correspondence is not necessary (and may have a negative impact on those who read it).

What advice can you give to students who have more than one job offer?

- If an offer has been made and you are given a short time frame for response, ask for an extension if you have other options. This is a much better tactic than to burn a bridge by rejecting an offer you have already accepted.

What are some the most important tactics that hospitality students should *avoid* in their job search?

- Don't pigeonhole your career interests; be open to alternatives.
- Don't be overconfident or "cocky."
- Don't oversell yourself; be willing to admit your weaknesses. (Remember, we all have them!).

- Don't be untruthful on your résumé or in your interviews; remember that companies check references.
- Don't criticize your prior experiences, bosses, or companies. If asked, respond constructively.
- Don't be overexuberant; be friendly and outgoing, but be yourself.
- Don't lead recruiters down a path you are not willing to take about jobs, location, or any other personal concerns.
- Don't begin an interview or other job search interactions with salary or other compensation-related discussions.
- A final suggestion: recognize that many recruiters typically travel and maintain very busy schedules. Do follow-up with appropriate letters or e-mails, but recognize the need for a realistic turnaround time for correspondence. Don't make numerous attempts to contact company representatives shortly after an interview.

LEARN FROM THE INTERNET

1. Check out the websites for several hospitality industry employers throughout the text. Read about positions, if any, that are currently available. What are things that you would like or dislike about these positions? What types of knowledge and skills do you currently have that would help you to effectively perform in these positions? What additional knowledge and skills would help you to become better qualified for these positions?

2. Check out websites of additional hospitality employers and review additional positions that they have available. Practice writing position and/or career objective statements to include at the beginning of your résumé that would suggest that these positions are an integral part of your career plans.

3. Check out the websites for the following hospitality industry recruiters:
   - Harper Associates: www.harper-jobs.com

   - Adventures in Hospitality careers: www.hospitalityadventures.com
   - The Boutique Search Firm: www.boutiquesearchfirm.com

   Pretend that you are interested in applying for a position they are advertising. Write a cover letter to transmit your résumé to them. (Be sure to address the specifics of the position being advertised and, if applicable, the information suggested in this chapter to be included with cover letters.)

4. Websites are also available that allow persons to post résumés and /or review position vacancies listed by hospitality employers. To review several of these, go to:
   - Wargo and Associates: www.wargo.hcareers.com
   - Hospitality Link: www.hospitalitylink.com
   - Hoteljobs.com: www.hoteljobs.com

KEY HOSPITALITY TERMS

The following terms were explained in this chapter. Review the definitions of any words with which you are unfamiliar. Begin to utilize them as you expand your vocabulary as a hospitality professional.

networking

career fairs

résumé

employment interview

employer of choice

cover letter

behavior-based questions

site visit

job shadowing (for permanent placement)

Your First Professional Position
Celebrate Success

33

Learning from a mentor can help to assure success in your new position.

CHAPTER LEARNING OBJECTIVES

After studying this chapter you will be able to:

1. Recognize the importance of active participation in an organization's orientation program.
2. Review competencies required for success in a hospitality position.
3. Learn basic tactics helpful during the first few days in a new position.
4. Recognize factors that suggest the need to find a new position.
5. Learn the importance of participating in an ongoing professional development program.
6. Explain procedures useful in planning and implementing an effective and ongoing professional development program.

The authors wish to thank Authella Collins Hawks, Director, Student Industry Resource Center (SIRC), The School of Hospitality Business, Michigan State University, for her assistance with this chapter.

605

FEEDBACK FROM THE REAL WORLD

Students majoring in hospitality management have invested a significant amount of time, money, and enthusiasm in their preparation for the world of work. Most complete their formal studies and feel they are ready for the real world of hospitality management and the challenges it brings. Most do very well in their first position and use it as a springboard to increasingly more responsible positions within the industry. Some, however, have difficulty as they move from an environment of academics to the world of hospitality management.

What are some of the most important characteristics of new managers who are successful in their first position? What are some characteristics that new managers who are less successful in their first position seem to share?

As you read this chapter, think about answers to these questions and then get feedback from the real world at the end of this chapter.

---

professional placement the first full-time position that a student assumes after graduation from college

Your first professional position! The years spent in formal education, the part-time jobs, and the internships are now behind you. Most importantly, you have made important **professional placement** decisions about the segment within the hospitality industry and the organization and position in which you will begin your career.

What's next? The rest of your life—much of which will be spent working. Many hospitality industry leaders profiled throughout this book have emphasized the need to find meaningful and enjoyable work and have suggested that you develop a life-style that allows the right mix of work and nonwork activities. The time to begin thinking about your after-college professional career is now, and the job that should occupy many of your thoughts is your first position. This is the topic of this chapter.

OBJECTIVE 1
Recognize the importance of active participation in an organization's orientation program.

ORIENTATION PROGRAMS ARE IMPORTANT

empathy an appreciation for and an understanding about how someone feels

The research undertaken for your employment after graduation is worthwhile. It will have yielded the decision about your first employer—who it is and how it will help you in the career you have tentatively planned. During

---

REMEMBER YOUR ORIENTATION PROGRAM TOMORROW

In the not too distant future you may be responsible for planning and/or delivering orientation programs for the new employees you supervise. When the time for this responsibility arises, think about your first days on your new job and the orientation that you received. Thinking about how you felt and remembering the good features (which should be repeated) and the poor features (which should not) will be helpful.

There is no need to suggest that you should remember your orientation program because you *will* remember it! Begin building your own leadership qualities the very first day on the job. Start now to develop **empathy** for staff members you will supervise by thinking about how you reacted to your own supervisor.

your first experiences on your new job, you will be looking for affirmation that your employment decision was a good one. Human resources professionals know the importance of effectively planning for a new employee's first days and weeks on the job. Even little things, such as organizing the paper work required for tax, insurance, company records, and other purposes and the friendly attention that managers pay to new staff members, create significant first impressions. A well-organized **orientation** program should be in place to introduce you to your new employer so that you can learn expectations and the way things work within the organization.

Your orientation program will help you to formulate an opinion about long-term opportunities with the company. After all, your goal is to find a rewarding career, and your first job is the first step in that career. Learn about the company's mission, study the company's organizational chart, and discover through words and actions the philosophies of those with whom you work. Then start asking yourself these questions: How well do I fit in? Do I belong here?

Use your experience during orientation to fine-tune the thought processes you initially utilized to select the company and position. Doing well in the job and moving forward in your career will require that you incorporate your experiences into the decision-making process. Remember, your experience begins the first day on the job. Learn from it while working in that job and when considering your future.

orientation the process of providing basic information about a hospitality organization that must be known by all employees

COMPETENCIES FOR SUCCESS

Many hospitality management graduates begin their careers by working in a management training program. The best of these permit them to learn basic management skills as they move between departments (functional areas) according to a preestablished schedule. They also permit the trainee to learn the basics of positions within the department and how they relate to each other and to positions in other departments. The best training programs also allow the trainee to be placed in a specific management area agreed on when the employment offer was made following the interview and selection process. The best training programs identify the **competencies** that should be learned as a result of training, and **job descriptions** will be available that indicate the tasks a trainee must know and be able to do in the position assigned after the training is completed.

Managers in any type of organization, including hospitality, in any position from entry-level supervisor to the highest management level must acquire and effectively use basic on the job competencies. While the specifics vary by position, Exhibit 33.1 identifies some basic management competencies and provides examples of each. The hospitality industry is a people business; note the emphasis on people with competencies relating to interaction with others, effective communication, and understanding organizations (which, of course, are comprised of people). Note as well the emphasis on basic management competencies, including those relating to making decisions, using technology, managing resources, and utilizing information. Finally, a manager must have appropriate personal qualities to be effective. This is increasingly so today and will certainly be true tomorrow as managers lead by facilitation rather than by direction.

Exhibit 33.2 further illustrates the importance of human relations competencies. Note that supervisors require significant technical skills, while their top-level manager counterparts utilize more conceptual skills. However, human relations skills are an integral part of the job of managers at any organizational level.

OBJECTIVE 2
Review competencies required for success in a hospitality position.

competency a requirement that specifies what an individual must know and/or be able to do to be successful in a position

job description a list of tasks that an incumbent in a position must be able to effectively perform

EXHIBIT 33.1
Basic On-Job Management
Competencies

Competency	Example
Interact with others	Facilitate the work of employees; interact with guests
Communicate effectively	Write letters and memos; speak in public; converse with employees, peers, bosses, and guests
Make decisions	Solve problems; think creatively; analyze alternatives
Use technology	Apply technology to collect and analyze information and to communicate with others
Manage resources	Maximize the use of limited resources to attain objectives
Understand organizations	Know and use information about how business, social, and political systems work
Utilize information	Collect, organize, and study necessary data as needed for effective management
Use basic skills	Read, write, speak, listen, and use mathematics and science-related abilities
Demonstrate personal qualities	Integrity, time and self-management, social skills, and respect for oneself and others

RISING STAR PROFILE

**Brian Risch
Human Resources
Manager
Komatsu America
Corporation
Rolling Meadows, Il**

Work Takes a Significant Amount of Time: Enjoy It!

Brian graduated from the university with a major in hospitality business and spent several years working with Hyatt Hotels in human resource positions in three properties. His next move would have been to director of human resources (the number one human resources position) at a hotel. However, he was then offered a position in another industry, and he accepted. (In some respects, this move was not actually a career change because Brian still has responsibilities related to human resources.)

Brian was asked about factors that prompted him to leave the hospitality industry. "My decision was not an easy one. I initially desired a position in human resources to help people and to help my organization strategize ways to move ahead in the industry. By contrast, most of my time was spent dealing with short-term human relations issues, such as staff members who had problems with tardy arrivals and unsatisfactory job performance. As much as I wanted to help employees do better, during my last few months on the job we were terminating several persons weekly. This, by far, was the most undesirable part of my job and made me rethink the role I wanted to have in human resources management.

"At that time in 2000, the 'tech boom' was going strong, and I moved to an organization where I could interact with company executives and have a more meaningful role in planning for the future. The company was a tech start-up, and I basically created a human resources function. I learned a lot in the process. However, that company, along with thousands or more of its counterparts, was not successful. I then began employment with a similar company with better financial backing, but it too was a victim of the downfall of these types of organizations. I then moved to my present position in the more stable insurance industry, and it was an excellent career move for me.

"I would really like to rejoin the hospitality industry because of the challenges it presents; however, I would not make that move unless it was to a strategic position at the corporate level."

With his background in hospitality, technology, the insurance industry, and, currently, the manufacturing industry, Brian is uniquely qualified to talk about common challenges confronting human resource experts in these industries: "I think one of the most common challenges is finding the right people for the job. For example, it would seem easy to find persons for entry-level hospitality positions. It isn't easy, however. One must recognize that these persons, most of whom will be in high-guest-contact positions, consistently represent the organization to the consumer and therefore have significant impact on the employer's success.

"No matter how good or bad the labor force pool is, it is still a most challenging process to find the right match for one's company. Recruiting is an incredibly difficult and important part of human resources.

"Training is another key challenge that faces human resources professionals. There are not many human resources generalists who really excel in training. One person or a small group of persons within the HR function is typically responsible for managing training or directing its outsourcing. Training is very expensive and tends to be one of the first things to be eliminated when there are budget cuts."

Brian has some advice for young persons who are considering career opportunities: "The first advice I can give is to find out what you like to do and then find a position that allows you to do it! For example, I like to help people and I wanted to be part of the hospitality industry. However, I also wanted a quality of life that would help me to provide for a future family. To me, this suggested positions within human resources, accounting, or marketing and sales. I chose human resources and was rewarded with some great experiences in the industry. I still like to help others and have been able to do this in new and different industries.

"Young persons should recognize that, at some point, they may want to reexamine career opportunities. My suggestion: take apart your career; start by examining your résumé. Think about other things you have done in your positions besides what the title suggests. For example, I have worked in the broad discipline of human resources. However, I have also been involved in planning employee compensation and benefits programs. I might parlay that experience into a completely new and different career. I also have a background in hotel operations and might be able to transfer these skills as an operations manager to companies in hospitality or another industry.

"The bottom line is that work takes up a significant amount of time in your life. It is best to like what you do and to get satisfaction from it at the end of the day."

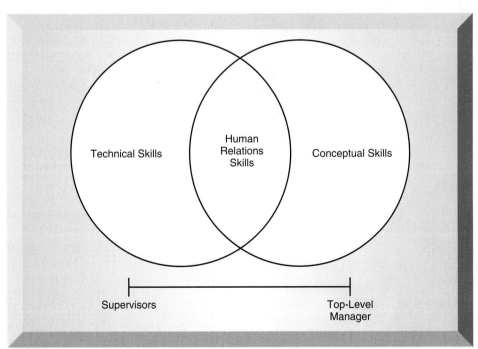

EXHIBIT 33.2
Human Relations Competencies Are Always Important

YOUR FIRST DAYS ON THE JOB

You have been employed to add value to the organization. In other words, what you provide to your company should be worth more to it than what it must pay for your services. Remember also that it is your output (work performance), not your input (education and years of experience), that is most important to your employer.

You can use a wide range of tactics to begin a good relationship with your employer. The good news is that the same tactics should be consistently applied in all positions throughout your entire hospitality career. These include the following:

- Dress the way you are expected to dress. If there is a uniform requirement, for example, comply with it. (Remember that a clean and pressed uniform will help with your professional attitude.) Management positions often require professional business attire (suits) that are not provided by the employer. Begin to invest in appropriate attire so that, over time, you can develop a professional wardrobe.
- Develop a system to remember the names of those to whom you are introduced. You may need to write them down or, perhaps, you can use a system that helps you to relate a name to something else. (For example, "The lady's name is Penny; she is a cashier who takes in dollars.")
- Take careful note of your own supervisor and others who are successful in the company. What do they seem to have in common? What can you learn from them that will help you with your own performance? If it is someone you admire, consider asking him or her to be a mentor to help guide you in your career.
- Use a personal time planner, if applicable. At the end of the day, think about what you need to accomplish tomorrow. Alternatively, at the beginning of the day, think about your plans for that day. (Make an electronic note or just use pen and paper.)
- Be punctual; don't make others wait for you.
- Don't get into a routine; make sure that you are always doing whatever has the highest priority.
- Be friendly; say "Hello; how are you?" because you are genuinely interested in the person to whom you are speaking.
- Listen much more than you talk!
- Be quick to praise others when they have earned your praise.
- Practice conflict resolution to avoid confrontations. (The other person may be your boss tomorrow.)
- Look for solutions rather than for problems. (Remember the old saying: If you are not part of the solution, you are part of the problem!)
- Remember that neither life nor your position is always fair. Over time, however, you are likely to be rewarded according to the extent of your efforts.

A hospitality executive can work in many places besides the office.

- Don't get involved in office politics. Stay away from the **grapevine,** don't complain about your supervisor, and look for opportunities to build, not tear down, your organization.
- Remember that hospitality managers are typically successful because of their teams; be a team player and give the members of your team credit for their accomplishments. Contribute your skills and talents freely to help your team to be successful.
- Solicit feedback. Ask your manager and your peers for advice about your performance. Incorporate, if applicable, the improvement suggestions that you receive.
- Find a **mentor.** Some hospitality organizations have formal mentoring programs. Participate if possible. If a formal program does not exist, try to identify someone, perhaps even in another department, who can give you advice.

Coaching occurs on the job.

- Volunteer for special projects. This will help you to learn more and, at the same time, show your management team that you want to learn as much as possible.
- Recognize that you will likely work extra hours; 50-hour work weeks are not uncommon, especially early in hospitality careers. Long hours and hard work are typical in many entry-level management positions in the hospitality industry.
- Meet persons outside your department. **Networking** can be a very effective tactic in learning about an organization and advancing in one's career.
- Think about the present and the future. Work hard to succeed in your first position, but recognize that it is just the first step in what may be a very long and rewarding career.
- Keep alert to job openings within your company. Even though you have carefully considered your career, positions may become available within your organization that provide educational and professional advancement opportunities for you. In fact, most companies prefer to **promote from within.** Pay attention to the requirements for these positions and carefully evaluate them for growth potential.

grapevine   the informal network of communication within an organization

mentor   a senior employee of the hospitality organization who provides advice and counsel to less experienced staff members about matters relating to the job, organization, and profession

networking   the development of personal relationships for a business-related purpose

promote from within   the concept that a company considers existing employees at a lower organizational level as higher-level positions are filled

Take time for some relaxation in your new job.

A WORD ABOUT WORK ETHICS

The concept of **ethics** refers to a person's perception of what is right and wrong. Ethical behavior is influenced by factors such as one's cultural background, religious views, professional training, and personal moral code.

Hospitality managers in every position, from beginning supervisor to top-level chief executive officer, should be ethical. When considering alternative courses of action, it is helpful to ask these questions:

Is the alternative legal?

Would the alternative hurt anyone?

Is the alternative fair?

Is the alternative the right and honest thing to do?

How would I feel if I was affected by the alternative?

Would I like to publicize my selection of the alternative?

Would the organization be improved if everyone utilized the alternative?

Some hospitality organizations have a **code of ethics** that indicates the acceptable philosophy for ethics and frequently indicates policies that should be utilized to assure that ethical positions are maintained. Always remember that it is not possible to be a professional or an effective hospitality manager without being ethical.

- Have fun at work. Industry leaders quoted throughout this book have noted the importance of enjoying what you do.

ethics a person's perceptions about what is right and wrong

code of ethics a statement adopted by an organization that outlines policies developed to guide the making of ethical decisions

DID YOU KNOW?

Many sons and daughters of successful hospitality operators carry on the tradition of hospitality by getting involved in the family business. Exposure to the business as one grows up is a reason. Sometimes they are encouraged by their parents and other family members. As well, the inheritance of the business is a ready option that can make the "What should I do the rest of my life?" decision a lot easier. Frequently, the building and equipment are already paid for, and few people can begin business without some capital outlay and the risks that are associated with it.

Family members in the hospitality business already know about some of the potential downsides, such as the need to work long hours and on weekends and holidays. Therefore, they are less likely to be discouraged when they learn that this schedule is part of many positions in hospitality.

Other reasons for second- or third-generation hospitality entrepreneurs include family traditions, encouragement, and the offering of help when it is needed. This is especially important during extended transition periods as the business moves from one generation to the next. Then family-owned hospitality businesses can be an easy choice for those entering the business.

OBJECTIVE 4
Recognize factors that suggest the need to find a new position.

MOVING FORWARD IN YOUR CAREER

A successful career contains successively more responsible and/or enjoyable positions. How do you know when you should consider another position?

Here is the simple answer: when you have accomplished the goals you aspired to when you accepted the position. For example, if you decided to take a position to learn as much as possible or to gain experience as part of a longer-term strategy, you will likely know when the time is right for a new job search. Employees in many organizations typically have numerous opportunities to change jobs while remaining in the organization because of company growth, turnover, and/or **diversification** into new businesses.

Some people believe they should only leave a position if they are not going anywhere or if they are fearful of being terminated. These may be reasons to consider a career move; however, there are others, including the following:

- You are in the wrong position (one that does not fit your skills, abilities, or temperament). Ask whether you would like to have your immediate supervisor's position. If the answer is no, a job transfer or reassignment may be in order.
- You are experiencing interpersonal problems with your immediate boss. Even the best people persons may not be able to relate well to each other. If this problem cannot be resolved, consider a career move.
- Your department and/or organization is having difficulty. Technology, for example, may reduce the need for specialists in procurement, and the **outsourcing** of noncommercial self-operated foodservices to a contract management company may signal the need for other employment by an on-site manager of self-operated programs.
- Physical or intellectual reasons. For example, you can become exhausted or bored with a position. These factors typically affect job performance and attitude and provide reasons why a new position should be considered.
- Long-term career advantages. Persons interested in advancing within their careers will recognize that a position change may enhance their careers. They should be alert for this possibility. At the same time, however, many persons become frustrated when they accept too many responsibilities too soon by accepting positions for which they are not ready.

diversification movement into varied businesses and/or industry segments

outsourcing retaining an external supplier to provide a product or service that has traditionally been produced or offered within the organization

> **OBJECTIVE 5**
> Learn the importance of participating in an ongoing professional development program.

professional development activities formal and informal training and education undertaken to provide the additional knowledge, skills, and experience to prepare one for progressively more responsible positions within a career

PROFESSIONAL DEVELOPMENT NEVER ENDS

Exciting initial plans for your career have been developed (see Chapter 31). Your first position represents the first step in your progress toward the career goals that you planned. However, **professional development activities** will likely be necessary to help you as you move along in your career.

Some students graduating from a hospitality management program may think, "My education in hospitality industry is now over; what I need to learn now will come from experience." They are partially correct because experience can be a good teacher. However, in the fast-changing hospitality industry, a mix of additional education along with experience will likely be necessary as one advances up the **career ladder.** Exhibit 33.3 notes common professional development opportunities. Some of these occur on the job, for example, as one gains experience in a specific position. Opportunities also occur during other training activities, which include special training activities (often group training on specific topics), **job rotation,** and **job enlargement.**

A business lunch may be needed to solve problems in a hurry.

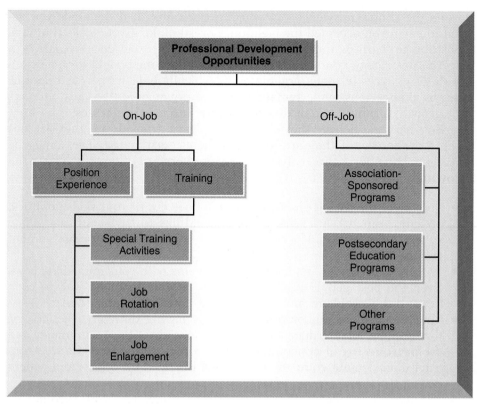

EXHIBIT 33.3
Professional Development Opportunities

career ladder a plan that projects successively more responsible professional positions within an organization or industry; career ladders also allow one to plan and schedule developmental activities judged necessary to assume more responsible positions

job rotation a systematic plan to move employees into (rotating) different positions so that they acquire the knowledge or skill required to be effective in these positions

job enlargement the act of including additional tasks or assignments in one's position to provide more opportunities to learn how the position relates to others

interdisciplinary between disciplines; involving several domains of knowledge; for example, basic business principles can be applied in organizations of all types in all industries

Exhibit 33.3 also illustrates professional development opportunities that arise from off-site job sources:

- *Association-sponsored programs.* Professional associations such as the American Hotel and Lodging Association, National Restaurant Association, and National Automatic Merchandising Association, and many others consider professional development for members to be a high-priority responsibility. Programs are often made available at national and state conferences, through correspondence study, and through resources available for less formal self-study.
- *Postsecondary educational programs.* Educational institutions frequently offer programs on generic topics applicable to managers in hospitality and other organizations. Also, programs specific to the industry may be offered across a regional or other basis or may be developed for a specific hospitality organization. Programs are increasingly available online for anyone at any place at any time. If you would like to advance in your company, additional formal education (MBA in finance, for example) may help you to move into senior leadership and management positions.
- *Other programs.* For-profit companies offer a wide range of applicable programs, as do community-based groups such as local Chambers of Commerce and governmental agencies. Since the practice of hospitality management is **interdisciplinary,** a widely diverse range of subject matter is applicable for study as an element in one's professional development program.

Meetings are part of the day's work for many young hospitality executives.

THE PROFESSIONAL DEVELOPMENT PLAN

Perhaps you already have developed a long-range career plan (see Chapter 31). Regardless, however, most persons have concerns about short-term plans, so professional development activities (which evolve with career plans) can be organized accordingly. Here are some suggestions:

- Think about activities in your present position that you could do better. You will likely know about these and, as well, you may receive formal feedback during performance reviews and informal feedback from your own supervisor's coaching comments.
- If you have a mentor, he or she can be a ready source of professional development alternatives.
- Try to objectively assess your strengths and weaknesses relative to your career plans.
- Think about your likes and dislikes, which will influence your career plans and the activities you will undertake to move toward career goals.
- Establish professional development priorities. You may decide, for example, to first develop knowledge and skills in areas that will help you to be promoted. Alternatively, you may wish to focus on areas of your

OBJECTIVE 6
Explain procedures useful in planning and implementing an effective and ongoing professional development program.

WHY PROFESSIONAL DEVELOPMENT?

Why should you be concerned about ongoing professional development? The answer is simple: to keep up with your current position and to prepare for other, increasingly more responsible positions. Changing guest preferences, increased opportunities to cost effectively use technology, changing business philosophies, and the need to maximize the use of increasingly limited resources are examples of factors that emphasize the need to learn more about ways to be effective in one's profession.

Involvement in professional development activities is almost a must to be considered for promotion. Consider, for example, the person who has already acquired some of the knowledge and skills needed for effective performance in a new position. Consider also his or her counterpart without this foundation of additional knowledge and skills. Who do you think will most likely be promoted?

Attaining a certification designation can be a significant step in career advancement.

strengths (to become stronger) or areas in which you are weak (to bring them up to a par with your other competencies).

Exhibit 33.4 illustrates a process for working your professional development plan and features these objectives:

- Establish your learning goals.
- Identify the supportive activities that will most help you to attain your learning goals.
- Establish a schedule for completing your learning activity, obtain necessary training resources, if any, and complete the training (work your plan!).

Along the way, success is best assured when you remain motivated and remove obstacles that hinder your progress.

You cannot be successful in continuing education activities if you want to do them "when you have the time." Rather, a commitment is necessary, a priority must be established, and time (always a precious resource) must be allocated. Some hospitality employers provide compensated time and/or the financial assistance necessary for staff members to complete relevant training

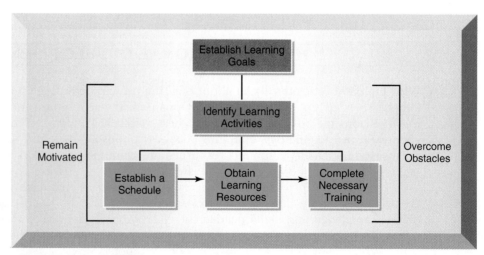

EXHIBIT 33.4
Working Your Professional Development Plan

WHAT ABOUT CERTIFICATION?

Several hospitality industry-related professional associations, including the American Hotel and Lodging Association, National Restaurant Association, National Automatic Merchandising Association, and Club Managers Association of America, offer certification programs to members. Effective certification programs typically have several common elements:

A body of knowledge (competencies) perceived necessary for effective job performance has been identified.

Training and education programs and resources are identified and developed that present information applicable to the competencies.

Factors including qualifications for certification eligibility are established.

A certification exam is utilized.

Persons qualified to sit for the exam and who successfully complete it are certified (recognized) by the association. Certification programs, then, provide an additional incentive (recognition by one's peers) for professional development. Resources developed in support of certification study and the methods made available to deliver applicable education and training provide additional opportunities for persons to participate in ongoing professional development programs.

and education; others do not. Either way, the drive to be better in your position and to move forward in your career is an important first prerequisite in an effective professional development program.

Certification increases your competency in a specific area, which may provide an opportunity for advancement or a salary increase due to the additional knowledge that you have gained. Conversely, if you do not have certification in an area that requires it, this may affect your job performance in this area.

Interacting with professional peers is a critical component of many hospitality managers.

SUMMARY OF CHAPTER LEARNING OBJECTIVES

1. **Recognize the importance of active participation in an organization's orientation program.**
   If properly planned and conducted, the orientation program will provide an excellent overview of the organization in which you have chosen to work. It can also help to reinforce the attitude that orientation is beneficial, and this concern can drive the development of quality orientation programs when you become responsible for them.

2. **Review competencies required for success in a hospitality position.**
   Competencies are requirements that specify what an individual must know and/or be able to do to be successful in a position. Basic on-job management competencies relate to interacting with others, being an effective communicator, making decisions, and using technology. Other competencies include managing resources, understanding organizations, utilizing information, practicing basic skills, and exhibiting appropriate personal qualities.

3. **Learn basic tactics helpful during the first few days in a new position.**
   Basic tactics are helpful in all positions throughout one's hospitality career. These relate to following the rules, being an effective communicator, showing respect for others, being a participating member of the hospitality team, emphasizing an interest in gaining experience, possessing skill and knowledge that will help you in your present and future positions, and assuring that you fully enjoy your work.

4. **Recognize factors that suggest the need to find a new position.**
   Reasons to consider a career move include when you are in the wrong position, when you are experiencing interpersonal problems with an immediate boss, and when your department and/or organization is having difficulty. Other reasons include physical or intellectual issues and long-term career advantages.

5. **Learn the importance of participating in an ongoing professional development program.**
   One must continually learn to keep up with the industry and to move ahead within it. There are on-job opportunities (experience in one's position and training) and off-the-job experiences (association and postsecondary school-sponsored programs, as well as others).

6. **Explain procedures useful in planning and implementing an effective and ongoing professional development program.**
   Procedures for planning a professional development program include thinking about present activities that you could do better, soliciting input from a mentor (if available), and objectively assessing strengths and weaknesses and likes and dislikes. Finally, one must establish professional development priorities. It is also necessary to work your plan by establishing learning goals, identifying appropriate supportive activities, and establishing and adhering to a schedule for completing learning activities.

MASTERING YOUR KNOWLEDGE

Discuss the following questions.

1. Think about orientation programs in which you have participated. What did you like about them? What did you dislike? How, if at all, would you have changed the orientation program if you were the manager in charge of it?

2. What competencies required for success in a hospitality position do you think are the most difficult to acquire? Which do you think are utilized most frequently? Which competencies are the highest priorities in terms of being successful in a hospitality management position? Why?

3. If you were a manager desiring to implement a mentor program in your operation, what kinds of things would mentors need to know and be able to do to be successful? How would you teach or train them to do these things?

4. Assume that you have just completed applicable management training and are assuming

your first management position in a hospitality operation. When would you begin to have an interest in formal professional development activities? How would you find out about the programs available? What assistance do you think they would provide as you are preparing for promotion?

5. How, if at all, can your membership in a local, state, or national association or community group such as the Chamber of Commerce help you in your first position and as you prepare for career advancement?

FEEDBACK FROM THE REAL WORLD

Our real-world advice comes from Jeffrey R. Gillett.

Jeff has served as a senior management recruiter for a national restaurant chain, has coordinated a management internship programs in a restaurant organization, and has served on numerous hospitality management advisory boards.

What are some of the most important characteristics of new managers who are successful in their first position?

Successful new managers share several characteristics:

- They have initiative; they are self-starters. They do not wait to be told what to do, and they effectively manage by taking care of problems as soon as they are noticed.
- They have the courage to make tough decisions when they are the right ones, rather than easy decisions just to avoid conflict. Effective managers can think about a situation and its impact on the restaurant and then do what's best within this context. Managers are successful when they can diffuse potentially disruptive situations, and they do this by thinking about what's right and by defending and justifying the decisions they make.
- They are smart. They know how to operate a restaurant. They are also knowledgeable about the world of business and have the ability to continually grow smarter by learning from their experiences.
- They are mature beyond their years. Maturity means doing what you say you will do, meeting deadlines, and taking responsibility for your actions. Successful managers

can make effective decisions because they carefully think through their goals and the best alternatives for attaining them, and they respect and utilize the opinions of others to facilitate the decision-making process.

- They have a passion for all aspects of the business. They embrace what they do and recognize the importance of quality food and beverage products, service, and the dining environment. Their goal is zero defects (no mistakes), and every step they take toward this goal provides an incentive to do still better.
- They have a drive to get better every day. They are concerned about professional development activities for themselves and their employees. They recognize that there is no such thing as standing still; they recognize that one either gets better or gets worse. They challenge themselves to be the very best they can be and to be better today than yesterday.
- They pay attention to details. Successful managers have identified all the loopholes that can cost the restaurant thousands, hundreds, and tens of dollars and even single dollars. Their current march toward excellence involves looking at how to save pennies!

(continued)

What are some characteristics that new managers who are less successful in their first position seem to share?

New managers who are unsuccessful share these characteristics:

- They lack commitment. These managers consider their employment to be a job or a position, rather than a lifetime vocation. Their professional development planning has been and continues to be more spontaneous and less purposeful. Their concerns address "How many hours a week must I work?" not "What can I accomplish?" While quality of life is important (and good employees are concerned about it), less successful managers are frequently unable to balance their personal and work lives.

- They don't take criticism well. Unsuccessful managers don't seem to understand that an opportunity to do something better is not a personal affront. They often think that their way is the only way and that criticisms are more personal insults than suggested opportunities.

- They lack initiative. The first characteristic for a successful manager noted above was initiative and being a self-starter. The unsuccessful manager often doesn't have the high energy and creativity necessary to get going on addressing problems.

- They have poor follow through. Perhaps, because they are less organized, unsuccessful managers either don't evaluate or do so inadequately. They tend to move off mission and don't follow up to assure that decisions, once implemented, are effective.

- They lack courage. This attitude of courage was noted to be important in successful managers. It follows, then, that their unsuccessful counterparts may not have the conviction and assertiveness to implement what they believe in.

- They have problems with the life-style of the restaurant business. Restaurant managers and their employees must work at times when their families and friends do not. Weekends, holidays, late evenings, and warm spring days are examples of times when restaurant managers will likely be at work. People often note that restaurateurs are in the show business; this is, in fact, true. It is also true that the show must go on, and effective restaurant managers are available to assure that the show is a success.

LEARN FROM THE INTERNET

1. Check out the websites for several organizations in the segment in which you wish to work. What kind of information do they provide about what you can expect when you work for them? What kind of additional questions would you like to have answered that are not addressed on the websites? Which sites are most helpful to persons seeking a first professional position? Why?

2. Check out the websites for several professional associations. What kinds of professional development activities do they have available? How effective are they in selling the need for members and others to participate in these programs?

3. Check out the websites for the following hospitality associations that offer professional certification programs:

- National Restaurant Association Educational Foundation: www.NRAEF.org

- Educational Institute of the American Hotel & Lodging Association: www.ei-ahla.org
- Club Managers Association of America: www.cmaa.org
- American Culinary Federation: www.acfchefs.org
- Meeting Professionals International: www.mpiweb.org
- National Automatic Merchandising Association: www.vending.org

For what employee groups are programs available? What are the requirements? What types of competencies are addressed? What kinds of training activities, if any, are available to help in preparing for the certification exam? What types of resources are available for self-study for the certification exam?

KEY HOSPITALITY TERMS

The following terms were explained in this chapter. Review the definitions of any words with which you are unfamiliar. Begin to utilize them as you expand your vocabulary as a hospitality professional.

professional placement	ethics
empathy	code of ethics
orientation	diversification
competency	outsourcing
job description	professional development activities
grapevine	career ladder
mentor	job rotation
networking	job enlargement
promote from within	interdisciplinary

34 Entrepreneur or Intrapreneur?

The ground-breaking ceremony for a new business location is exciting and is a visible sign of the accomplishment needed to start a business.

CHAPTER LEARNING OBJECTIVES

After studying this chapter you will be able to:

1. Explain the terms *entrepreneur* and *intrapreneur*.
2. Describe four steps involved in the entrepreneurial process.
3. Review the potential risks and rewards that confront entrepreneurs.
4. List common reasons why many new businesses fail.
5. Review principles and practices helpful to intrapreneurs in the hospitality industry.
6. Review differences among traditional managers, entrepreneurs, and intrapreneurs in the hospitality industry.

FEEDBACK FROM THE REAL WORLD

Many hospitality managers working for some-one else want to be their own boss and own their own place someday. By contrast, some managers who do own their own place wish they did not. There are reasons why some indi-viduals want to work for themselves (be self-employed) and why others would rather work for an organization. As a result of careful career planning, by chance alone, or (probably more commonly!) as a result of both planning and chance, many managers in the hospitality in-dustry discover what is best for them and they are, consequently, happy about their careers.

What are some of the most important ad-vantages and disadvantages of being an entrepre-neur? How, if at all, can one realize some of the advantages of being an entrepreneur while still working for someone else? How, if at all, can one realize some of the advantages of being an in-trapreneur while still working for someone else?

As you read this chapter, think about answers to these questions and then get feedback from the real world at the end of the chapter.

The hospitality industry has lots of examples of persons with great ideas who built them into very large and successful businesses. Kemmons Wilson expe-rienced difficulties in finding safe, clean, and inexpensive lodging on a family vacation; his frustrations led him to develop the chain of hotels we now know as Holiday Inns.

Willard Marriott's small diner in Washington, D.C., was the forerunner of today's Marriott Corporation. Ray Kroc discovered a successful ham-burger stand to whom he sold a malted milk machine. He then bought the business, and today's McDonald's Corporation is the result. Colonel Sanders was in his seventies when his "secret seasonings" for fried chicken became popular, and the Kentucky Fried Chicken (now KFC) organization was launched.

Our list of success stories can continue. Unfortunately, there are also sto-ries of persons with many years of hospitality industry experience, of those with small or large fortunes who have invested in the industry, and still others with great ideas who have not been successful and who have lost a life's savings as they pursued their dreams.

> **OBJECTIVE 1**
> Explain the terms *entrepreneur* and *intrapreneur*.

ENTREPRENEUERS AND INTRAPRENEURS

This chapter will explore the world of entrepreneurs and intrapreneurs. Along the way, you will discover that both offer opportunities to those with the atti-tude and background to be successful. The future of the hospitality industry requires people who fulfill both roles. Brief definitions of entrepreneur and intrapreneur follow:

- An **entrepreneur** is a person who assumes the risk of owning and oper-ating a business in exchange for the financial and other rewards that the business may produce; they may be called **independent operators** if they own or operate one or just a few properties.
- An **intrapreneur** is a person employed by an organization whose com-pensation is based, at least in part, on the financial success of the unit for which he or she has responsibility.

The concept of entrepreneurship basically involves a person starting his or her own business. Perhaps, for example, a person has worked in the

entrepreneur a person who assumes the risk of owning and operating a business in exchange for the financial and other rewards that the busi-ness may produce

independent operator an entrepreneur who owns or operates one or a very few hospitality properties

intrapreneur a person em-ployed by an organization whose compensation is based, at least in part, on the financial success of the unit for which he or she has responsibility

RISING STAR PROFILE

Martha Keller
Catering/Convention Services Manager
Sheraton Chicago Hotel and Towers
Chicago, Illinois

Martha received her degree in hospitality business in December 2003. She began work at the Sheraton Chicago Hotel and Towers in February 2004 as a Star Meeting Concierge with responsibilities for assuring that meetings and events were properly implemented. Several months later she transferred as a Hospitality Manager to plan executive events ranging from 10 to 150 people held in guest suites. In June 2005, Martha was promoted to her present position.

"I grew up in a hospitality business family in a small tourist town in Michigan called Frankenmuth. My great-grandparents started Zehnders Restaurant in 1927, and my grandparents started the Bavarian Inn Restaurant in 1950. Currently, my grandmother still runs the kitchen. My grandfather is chairman of the board. My uncle and aunt operate the Bavarian Inn Restaurant. My oldest cousin is the accounting manager at the restaurant. My mother built and operates the Bavarian Inn Lodge. My father does all the marketing for the corporation. You could say, then, that hospitality is in our blood.

"My life has been my work experience. Growing up in a fourth-generation restaurant and hotel family, we are constantly comparing and analyzing other properties wherever we may go. However, I actually began working in our Bavarian Inn kitchen at the age of 11. I filled jam jars and trimmed chicken for sandwich meat. All of us fourth-generation kids started in the kitchen at the Bavarian Inn Restaurant under the guidance of our grandmother. I have worked in every department of our restaurant and hotel. I was referred to as the 'miscellaneous girl': whatever needed to be done, I did. Usually the grandchildren did the jobs no one else wanted to do. Managers loved us since our pay per hour was low, and this improved labor costs.

"My long-term goal is to be the general manager of a hotel. Perhaps in 5 to 10 years, I will return to Frankenmuth and work with my family. I can see myself doing this, but I want to go out on my own first and see what the future holds for me.

"Some of my fondest memories of growing up in a fourth-generation business occurred over the holidays. We work every holiday and that is our family tradition. I remember sitting around a table with my two brothers and my two older cousins trimming turkey on Thanksgiving. What I remember most about it is seeing how proud my grandfather was to have his whole family involved in the business he started. Also, spending time with my grandmother in the kitchen and having her teach me how to prepare the menu items that we serve is something I will never forget.

"My advice for those considering a restaurant career: Be willing to work hard, work long hours, and work most holidays. You must love what you are doing. Also, be able to communicate with others. Public speaking is very important whether you are talking to guests, employees, or colleagues.

"Most importantly, have fun! Whatever you do in life should be enjoyable. You should love to go to work. I have loved all of my jobs and plan to continue working only where I have fun. Otherwise, what is the point?"

Author's Note: Zehnder's of Frankenmuth was ranked 47th in food and beverage sales volume (2004) for U.S. independent restaurants by *Restaurants and Institutions* magazine.

capital relating to the acquisition of land, equipment, buildings, and other fixed assets

hospitality industry for many years. Along with this experience, he or she has accumulated and/or gained access to the **capital** resources needed to buy or lease, equip, and start up a business. Perhaps, alternatively, a person has grown up in an independent restaurant or lodging operation and has the opportunity to take over the family business. Some entrepreneurs are satisfied when the business they own provides for the wants and needs of themselves and their families. Others, however, are challenged to learn whether the success in one or several units can be extended to still more units. Then sustained business growth, rather than maintenance of ongoing operations, becomes a very important goal.

The concept of intrapreneurship, by contrast, is more difficult to understand. Intrapreneurs are persons with entrepreneurial talent who do not want

The bank's loan officer often plays a critical role in raising a business's start-up funds.

to start their own business. They work best in organizations that give them responsibility for a specific and defined part of the business. Consider, for example, a general manager of one unit in a multiunit restaurant organization. The manager may be compensated, in part, by a profit-sharing plan based on the financial success of the unit and/or organization. This is an example of an intrapreneur in the hospitality industry. Within the limitations imposed by the organization's general quality standards (restaurant design, menu, purchase specifications, and standard operating procedures, for example), the general manager can plan and implement tactics to reduce expenses and to increase revenues. In so doing, he or she can share in the profits generated by an increasingly successful business.

As a second example, department heads in a hotel's rooms division or food and beverage department can be given great discretion (they can be empowered!) by their own boss to make decisions and will be compensated, at least in part, based on the results of these decisions.

In the examples cited, intrapreneurs have been involved in revenue-producing activities. However, this is not a necessary prerequisite. Consider, for example, managers responsible for housekeeping, procurement, or security who really enjoy seeing ideas implemented and goals attained. Their decisions might lead to cost reductions without quality sacrifices, and their compensation can, at least in part, be based on this.

THE ENTREPRENEURIAL RECIPE

The entrepreneurial process involves the four steps illustrated in Exhibit 34.1. We will explore each of these steps in this section.

> **OBJECTIVE 2**
> Describe four steps involved in the entrepreneurial process.

DO WHAT YOU LIKE TO DO

Entrepreneurs and intrapreneurs who really enjoy what they do have at least one thing in common: they don't consider their job to be work. The goal of having fun at and looking forward to one's job is one that everyone should strive for. As one thinks about the amount of time spent in a professional career, the old saying, "Life is short; be sure to have fun at work!" becomes meaningful.

It is very important that you enjoy what you do. Entrepreneurial and intrapreneurial positions within the hospitality industry allow this to happen. Positions in the industry become even more meaningful when one considers that, while enjoying work, he or she can provide necessary products and services to the guests of the hospitality operation.

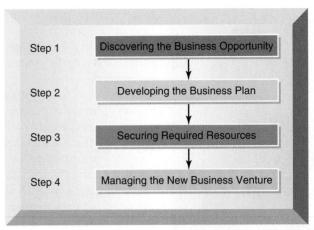

EXHIBIT 34.1
A Recipe for the Entreprenurial Process

Discovering the Business Opportunity

This task is, perhaps, the most challenging because it requires the potential entrepreneur to be uniquely creative. How do you discover products and services that consumers will purchase that are either not currently available or that can be significantly improved on so as to become the preferred product and service?

Consider, for example, today's cutting-edge technology businesses that provide new and better ways for hospitality organizations to serve their guests. An idea about a cost-effective way to do something represents an opportunity that can launch an entrepreneurial venture. These opportunities can be discovered by one who is doing the work, sees a problem, and can grasp a solution. Keeping up with the industry and recognizing its challenges (opportunities) may also yield creative ideas for future entrepreneurs. One may also consider how an idea utilized in one industry can work in another. (For example, the concept of **retina scanning** in the security industry may lead to new ways to control guest-room access in the lodging industry, and it is likely that one or more entrepreneurs are working hard to make this happen.)

Developing the Business Plan

This step involves the careful analysis of a business opportunity and defines how that opportunity can be captured and exploited. The development of a **business plan** requires the potential entrepreneur to define and consider numerous factors, including these:

- Characteristics and size of the potential market
- A market plan: information about the proposed product or service along with its price, distribution (place), and promotional tactics. Also included is an analysis of the market in which the proposed business will operate and the existing competition for the products or services to be offered.
- Production and service requirements
- How the new organization will be organized
- Financial (start-up and **working capital**) requirements. These include a **pro forma budget** of start-up and operating costs, projections of income and expenses and cash flow for the first several years of operation, and financing needs along with potential sources.

retina scanning the use of the retina patterns in one's eye as a unique source of personal identification; retina scanning may replace fingerprinting as the identification of choice

business plan a comprehensive, well-organized written document that defines a company's goals and the strategies to be used to attain these goals

working capital current assets minus current liabilities; the amount of cash (or other resources that can quickly be converted to cash) that can be used to purchase necessary products and services

pro forma budget a budget made in advance of the start of business; a pro forma budget is part of a business plan

Intrepreneurs must know the company's operating procedures.

- Mission, goals, and objectives for the new business
- Background information about the origin of the new business and the characteristics of the industry in which it will operate
- Detailed listing of products and services to be provided
- Background and qualifications of the proposed management team
- Marketing strategy: projection of revenues, market share, strategies to identify and advertise to potential customers, selling price plans, applicable customer services, and proposed advertising tactics (among other information)
- Design and development plans: if applicable, a description of the product to be developed, including costs
- Operating plans: detailed information about the physical facility, equipment, and labor
- Schedule of completion dates for major aspects of the business plan
- Applicable risks, problems, and challenges that need to be addressed and alternatives for addressing them

Securing Required Resources

Money to fund the proposed business venture must be available. These funds can come from the prospective entrepreneur's personal resources and/or from loans from family members, friends, and financial institutions. As more money must be borrowed, **interest** payment obligations increase. Then, after the business begins operation, the amount available to the entrepreneur for other expenses, including personal compensation and profits, is reduced.

interest   the expense incurred to borrow money

Managing the New Business Venture

The goal of the entrepreneur is not to start a business; it is to operate a business successfully. The basic principles of managing the organization do not differ based on whether the organization is owned by someone else or, alternatively, owned and operated by an entrepreneur. These management principles have been explored at length in numerous hospitality-related and general management and business books.[1]

---

[1]See, for example, two books by David Hayes and Jack Ninemeier, *Restaurant Operations Management: Principles and Practices.* Upper Saddle River, NJ: Pearson Education, Inc., 2006, and *Hotel Operations Management,* 2nd ed. Upper Saddle River, NJ: Pearson Education, Inc., 2007.

TAKE THE ENTREPRENEURIAL TEST

Ask yourself the following questions. Their answers may suggest whether you should consider finding an entrepreneurial niche within the hospitality industry.

Question	Answer	
	Yes	No
1. Do you have a passion for the concept of your business?	❑	❑
2. Are you fully committed to doing everything you can to make your business successful?	❑	❑
3. Do you like to be creative?	❑	❑
4. Are you a high-energy person?	❑	❑
5. Do you like to make decisions?	❑	❑
6. Do you understand the risks that you will be taking when you start a new business?	❑	❑
7. Do you know about the consequences of being unsuccessful?	❑	❑
8. Do you have adequate time to build a business from just an idea?	❑	❑
9. Are you willing to work long hours every day and week?	❑	❑
10. Are you flexible and able to adapt to changing business conditions?	❑	❑
11. Have you thought about the impact of your business start-up activities on your family and friends?	❑	❑
12. Do you have the necessary knowledge, experience, and skills required to be successful?	❑	❑
13. Do you have the leadership, management, and organizational skills and talents required to be successful?	❑	❑
14. Is your health able to endure the physical and mental work and the stress and anxiety that may occur as a result of your business start-up efforts?	❑	❑

OBJECTIVE 3
Review the potential risks and rewards that confront entrepreneurs.

RISK VERSUS REWARDS: THE ENTREPRENEURIAL DREAM

No one begins a new business with the thought that it will fail. Unfortunately, however, many new businesses, including those in the hospitality industry, do fail. Some literally close their doors. Others remain open but fall significantly

ENTREPRENEURS AND SMALL BUSINESS VENTURES

Independently owned and operated hotels and restaurants are generally **small businesses.** There are two types of small businesses:

Life-style business: an organization built around the personal and financial needs of the entrepreneur and his or her family.

High-growth venture: a business often run by a team, rather than an individual, whose plan is to expand rapidly by obtaining sufficient investment capital and by introducing new products and services to a large market.

What you learn on a job can be very helpful when you begin to work for yourself.

short of the prospective entrepreneur's dreams and create extensive stress and anxiety because of financial obligations in the process.

There are at least four types of risks involved in starting a new business:

- *Financial risks.* All or most of one's **assets** (something that is owned; home equity and personal savings, for example) can be lost if a business is unsuccessful. Loans, if any, will need to be repaid even if the business is not successful. Consider also that, especially during the initial start-up period (which can last months or even years), the entrepreneur's compensation may be much less than what he or she might earn in a comparble professional position.

- *Career risks.* Some persons looking for a new position after a business failure may be concerned about reputational issues. (If he or she could not do it in a personal business, are they really effective managers?) Others may have been so busy trying to build their business that they were unable to keep up with changes in the industry.

- *Personal risks.* New businesses require lots of time away from home and one's family and friends. (This overwork and exertion may create physical problems and stress. Anxiety, with its own physical and side issues, may also arise.)

- *Psychological risks.* Failing at one's business is an additional source of potential stress and anxiety that can have significant negative impacts on one's psychological well-being.

What about the possible benefits (rewards)? There are at least five, including these:

- The possibility of financial success that yields wealth not otherwise possible.
- Personal and professional satisfaction that comes from a sense of achievement; to "meet or beat" a business plan requiring a significant input of resources can be very pleasurable.
- Community status: Independent businesspersons are frequently active in community civic service organizations and are respected for their social contributions.
- Independence gained from being one's own boss: This psychological reward is a priority incentive that encourages many entrepreneurs to become involved in a business venture.

small business a company that is independently owned or operated, is not dominant in its industry, and that generally has relatively few employees and a low volume of revenue

life-style business an organization built around the personal and financial needs of the entrepreneur and his or her family

high-growth venture a business whose plan is to expand rapidly by obtaining sufficient investment capital and by introducing new products and services to a large market

assets something of value owned by a business or person

Entrepreneurs and intrapreneurs may work 24/7.

A successful entrepreneur may no longer need to dream about "expensive toys", like this classic (and very expensive) sports car.

- Control over one's life: As a business becomes more successful, one may have opportunities to maintain personal and professional schedules that might not otherwise be possible.

<table>
<tr><td>**OBJECTIVE 4**
List common reasons why many new businesses fail.</td><td>## NEW BUSINESSES DO FAIL</td></tr>
</table>

New businesses, both those that are franchised and therefore have brand recognition and access to proven standard operating procedures and those that are developed by entrepreneurs, can and do fail.

THINKING ABOUT DOING IT YOURSELF?

Consider the risks and rewards of owning your own business. Which are the most important to you? Which most influence your interest in doing it yourself?

Possible Advantages	Possible Disadvantages
Ability to make more money	No assured level of compensation
Work when you want to	Need to work very long hours (especially during the period of business start-up)
Make your own decisions	More difficulty in getting objective feedback from others
No bureaucracy	Lack of the financial resources enjoyed by an established organization
Ability to make quick decisions	Possibility of making wrong decisions if they are not well thought out
Can take risks and realize great rewards	Can suffer great personal losses and will need to repay financial losses
Reduced tax liabilities (because of small business deductions)	No corporate benefits and perks
Don't need to report to a boss	Must report to numerous other "bosses," including guests and governmental regulatory agencies
Can be your own boss	Must be responsible to operate the business
Can work when you want	Must be motivated and a self-starter
Will not be bored	Will have a demanding schedule

- Lack of management ability
- Inadequate industry experience
- Lack of financing/funding
- Unrealistic business plans
- Failure to consider realistic goals
- Inability to generate revenues
- Higher-than-necessary costs
- Poor location
- Ineffective operating procedures
- Inability to think creatively

EXHIBIT 34.2
Reasons for New Business Failure

A new business may grow slowly, and an entrepreneur's creative energy is an important element in success.

Common reasons why new businesses fail are identified in Exhibit 34.2. When reviewing this exhibit, note that the reasons for new business failure basically focus on two concerns: lack of management ability and lack of financing and funding. The good manager will likely have industry experience, know how to develop an effective business plan (see our earlier discussion), and develop realistic goals. Financial plans will also be in place for reasonable estimates of revenues and costs, and good managers consider location, develop effective operating procedures, and think creatively. They also recognize that adequate funding is critical. Effective managers do not make the all too common mistake of believing that the operation will be successful immediately and that revenues generated at the onset of operations can be utilized to fund business start-up costs.

An old saying is that "You can't win if you don't play the game." In the context of our present discussion, then, you can't be a successful entrepreneur unless you start your own business. However, the chances of success increase dramatically when a creative idea is translated into an effective business plan that drives the organization toward its goal.

INTRAPRENEURS IN THE HOSPITALITY INDUSTRY

As we have explained, an intrapreneur works within a large organization and takes responsibility to meet specified financial goals. He or she uses a process of risk taking and innovation very similar to that utilized by his or her entrepreneurial counterpart. Some hospitality organizations encourage intrapreneurship, and there are relationships between general managers and **subordinates** in which empowerment allows this to happen. Hospitality organizations that are considered intrapreneurial generally have four traits:

- They have a realistic vision that is widely understood by and shared with their staff members.

OBJECTIVE 5
Review principles and practices helpful to intrapreneurs in the hospitality industry.

subordinates a person whose work is directly overseen by a supervisor or manager

- They have recruited staff members with entrepreneurial talents and abilities.
- They emphasize teamwork.
- They reward success and do not punish persons for creative efforts to improve the organization.

Many managers working for hospitality organizations have opportunities to think and act like an entrepreneur. For example, they typically:

Entrepreneurs and intrapreneurs should pay attention to their health.

- Dream or think about ideas that could improve the operation. Questions such as, "How would I do this if this were my business?" might provide answers that can be implemented. Room-service managers, for example, are likely to have great suggestions about process improvements if only their boss (the food and beverage director) would ask them.
- Obtain ideas from others. Those who perform specific work tasks may have improvement ideas. As these ideas are implemented, feelings of accomplishment enjoyed by entrepreneurs can also be enjoyed by the employees of hospitality organizations.
- Take ownership in ideas. An intrapreneur can explain and defend why something new should be tried. He or she should also be open for feedback about potential challenges that can arise and why modifications of initial ideas should be made.
- Know when they need to obtain approval and when they can experiment with existing procedures.
- Experiment with new ideas. The fact that it was never done before or done yesterday without success doesn't mean that the time is not right today for another attempt, especially if updated techniques are implemented.
- Look for short-term successes. Successful intrapreneurs know the advantage of changing a procedure before they develop a new product!
- Understand the environment and know its expectations and limitations.
- Encourage open discussion with their team members, including peers and others working in other departments within the organization.
- Build a coalition of supporters with similar organizational improvement goals.
- Are persistent; they recognize that success frequently correlates with revisions to procedures that have originally yielded failures.
- Recognize the importance of the team; they work together to create visions of improvement that can involve and inspire others within the organization.
- Keep the boss informed; the best surprise is no surprise. Input from supervisors (who may have access to "big picture" ideas and information) can be helpful as one plans improvement efforts.

SUCCESSFUL INTRAPRENEURS HAVE SOME THINGS IN COMMON

They are driven by a vision for a better way and have the desire to make it happen.

They consider risks and assess ways to manage or reduce them.

They are consistent and recognize that purposeful change often takes time.

They use careful analysis when information is available and use intuition influenced by knowledge and experience when it is not.

They are honest and share good and bad results with others.

They are willing to do any job necessary to further their ideas.

They ask for suggestions before they ask for financial commitment.

They share the credit with the team.

They always keep the best interests of their hospitality organization and its guests in the forefront of the decision-making process.

They stick with their goals, but are realistic about the tactics best used to attain them.

They have a clear vision about what must be done and the specific objectives to be attained.

Is it a surprise that these traits of successful intrapreneurs are very similar to those of entrepreneurs?

Successful hospitality managers often need to manage on the run.

Intrapreneurs often have an interest in doing their own thing. They believe in their own talents and have an interest in creating something of their own. They want responsibility, are motivated by opportunities for individual expression, and desire some freedom in the organization that employs them. Doesn't this sound like a win–win situation for both the individual and the hospitality organization? A basic principle of motivation suggests that both parties benefit when an individual's needs, wants, and desires can be met on the job. An intrapreneur in the right organization exemplifies this principle.

As you have seen, intrapreneurs are driven by ideas; they are creative and innovative, they are persistent, and they recognize the benefits of working as a team. While an intrapreneurial spirit is often desired, it may not be required. Many hospitality organizations reap benefits from mature staff members who consistently work to meet the organization's quality and quantity standards; they do what is expected of them on a timely basis and can be considered exemplary employees for doing so, even if they do not seek additional work-related responsibilities.

CORPORATE CULTURE AND INTRAPRENEURS

Every organization has a **corporate culture.** The traditional organization's culture typically rewards persons who use a conservative decision-making process: one obtains information, makes a rational decision, and uses the information as justification if optimal results do not occur. Other tactics to get along in a traditional organization are following instructions, avoiding mistakes, minimizing initiative, and understanding your territory.

By contrast, tactics used in an intrapreneurial culture typically involve developing visions, goals, and action plans; being rewarded for actions that are taken; and experimenting, creating, developing, and assuming responsibility and ownership. In other words, the organization's culture supports staff members as they attempt to create something that is better.

OBJECTIVE 6
Review differences among traditional managers, entrepreneurs, and intrapreneurs in the hospitality industry.

corporate culture   the shared beliefs, experiences, and norms (ways of doing things) that characterize an organization

MANAGEMENT PROCESSES ARE EVOLVING

Exhibit 34.3 compares some factors that separate traditional managers, entrepreneurs, and intrapreneurs. It serves as a review of the points we have noted throughout this chapter. As seen in the exhibit, traditional managers (employees of an organization who have little stake in an organization other than continued employment) are motivated by promotion and additional corporate rewards. By contrast, entrepreneurs and intrapreneurs are motivated first by independence and then by the opportunity to be creative. Entrepreneurs have a further motive of (in part) making money; intrapreneurs are motivated by the opportunity to move toward both organizational and personal successes. The time focus of traditional managers is typically short term, with

EXHIBIT 34.3
Putting It All Together:
An Evolution in Managerial
Style

Factor	Traditional Manager	Entrepreneur	Intrapreneur
Primary motive	Promotion and traditional corporate rewards	Independence, the chance to be creative, and the opportunity to make more money	Independence, the chance to be creative, and the opportunity to move toward organizational and personal successes
Time focus	Short term (to meet budgets)	Survival and achieving long-term (five plus years) growth	In between traditional managers and entrepreneurs (depending on the need to meet self-imposed deadlines)
Activity	Delegation	Do it oneself	Do it oneself
Amount of risk	Conservative	Extreme	Moderate
Status	Concerned about status	Not concerned about status	Not concerned about status
Failure and mistakes	Minimizes mistakes and surprises	Deals with mistakes and failures	Reduces risky activities until ready
Decisions	Agrees with upper management	Follows a personal dream	Gets the help of others to achieve dreams
Constituencies served	Others (upper management and customers)	Oneself and customers	Oneself, customers, organization

The hospitality industry really is a people business.

intrapreneurs having a longer-time focus and the entrepreneur having the longest-term (survival) goal.

Traditional managers tend to delegate; entrepreneurs and intrapreneurs tend to do things themselves. Traditional managers tend to be conservative risk takers, entrepreneurs are extreme risk takers, and intrapreneurs are moderate risk takers. Entrepreneurs and intrapreneurs have little concern about status, which is a concern of traditional managers. Entrepreneurs deal with mistakes and failures, intrapreneurs try to reduce risky activities until the organization is ready for them, and traditional managers tend to minimize mistakes and surprises.

Traditional managers make decisions in concert with their bosses, entrepreneurs follow their personal dream, and intrapreneurs interact with others to achieve goals. Finally, traditional managers serve upper management and customers. By contrast, entrepreneurs serve themselves and customers, and intrapreneurs work to serve themselves, customers, and the organization that employs them.

DID YOU KNOW?

Thinking about one's career as it first begins is exciting, and it is a wise thing to do. However, with the many options available today and with unknown alternatives available in the future, it is typically possible to make only very tentative rather than definite plans.

Some hospitality intrapreneurs become hospitality entrepreneurs at some point in their career. Consider, for example, unit-level managers and corporate-level executives who "want to have their own place someday." The hospitality industry is one that provides these opportunities more than many other industries. Could a restaurant executive ever own a franchise of one or more units in the same or a different company? Could a hotel manager or executive purchase a bed and breakfast property? Could a family member working in a family restaurant buy out the owner and/or start another property? The answers to all of these questions are "Of course!"

Career flexibility is important, and it is a characteristic of the hospitality industry.

IN CONCLUSION

The purpose of this chapter has been to explore another dimension of the exciting world of hospitality: the opportunity to start and operate one's own business or to act like a business owner within an existing organization. Just as no single segment of the hospitality industry is right for everyone, different persons enjoy working within different organizational cultures. For traditional managers, the approach of working together as a team to achieve goals is desired. For entrepreneurs, the best approach is to start one's own business, with its culture most influenced by the business owner. Intrapreneurs desire to work within a culture where they have opportunities to create (one of the upsides of being an entrepreneur!), while reducing financial, personal, social, and psychological risks (the downside of being an entrepreneur).

RISING STAR PROFILE

Sarah M. Wagner Barnes
Chef-Owner, Barresi's Italian Restaurant
Cincinnati, Ohio

From Bus Person to Proud Owner of the Same Restaurant

Sarah M. Wagner Barnes is the chef–owner of Barresi's Italian Restaurant in Cincinnati, Ohio. She received an associate's degree in applied science–chef technology from Cincinnati State and her bachelor's degree in liberal arts from Xavier University.

What is the most unforgettable moment in your career?

Buying the restaurant where I first started my career as a bus person. Some things certainly do come full circle!

What is the most significant challenge confronting your segment of the industry?

People . . . the everyday challenge of trying to recruit staff members who want to work as hard and as passionately as I do. The restaurant business is said to be a place where wandering souls go. Some people can't cope with "real jobs," and they work in this business because it is relaxing, and it is not difficult to find a job cooking, washing dishes, or waiting on tables. However, these are not the folks I want to attract! I look for persons who are passionate about cooking as an art and for others who take pride in serving our guests with a smile. These are persons who take their jobs seriously because they realize that they can make a good living as they do so.

When job candidates are interviewed, we ask about many things. We also take the time to do background checks and Internet searches to help assure that their responses match up and that their references check out. Cooking and serving can be relatively easy tasks, but people can be very difficult to manage if the right choices are not made as they are hired and trained.

How are your labor-related challenges being addressed?

We do prehire checks, and we conduct very careful training programs. We attempt to make our training sessions flawless and, if our new employees do not successfully complete the program, they are not allowed to work here. This reduces numerous problems that might otherwise occur.

What, if anything, would you do differently in your career?

I would have taken a leadership class at Xavier much sooner had I known how much it would have benefited me. Instead, I took this class eight years after I graduated from culinary school. By then I was 30 years old and had worked in many kitchens, acting like a stereotypical chef: bull-headed and outspoken and less than respectful to many of my fellow employees. As a result of this class, I became much more sensible, and I resigned from a very chaotic food production position. I came to realize that if you can't change the people around you, the best tactic is, literally, to change the people around you.

I wanted to create my own professional atmosphere. Sometimes systems that are not working cannot be changed, because they have been in place too long and because affected persons are afraid of change. This, in turn, creates an unhealthy work environment for everyone. I resolved the problem for myself in an extreme way: I purchased a restaurant. This allowed me to create a healthy work environment with no chaos, but lots of challenging work at a fast pace. (In other words, the way successful restaurants are operated!) Here at Barresi's Italian Restaurant, we interact like a family. We celebrate birthdays together, and we treat each other the way we wish to be treated. I know this sounds blissful . . . and it is.

What is a favorite anecdote about your career in the hospitality industry?

You can check out some articles on the press page of our restaurant's website (www.barresis.com) to learn the history of how I purchased it from the previous owners. I had worked here as a bus person, hostess, server, and

pantry person from when I was 14 years old until I was 19 years of age. Then I enrolled in culinary school at Odessa Barresi's suggestion. I didn't return until after my formal education and chef positions at many private clubs in the Cincinnati area. I came back to Barresi's as the food and beverage director one year prior to the purchase because the "chef in me" needed some front of the house experience.

What is your advice for young people considering a career in the hospitality industry?

Work hard for other people as you begin, and continue in your career regardless of whether you like them or their rules. You never know who could be your boss one day or what restaurant you may be taking over 17 years later. Impressions last a lifetime!

SUMMARY OF CHAPTER LEARNING OBJECTIVES

1. **Explain the terms *entrepreneur* and *intrapreneur*.**
   An entrepreneur assumes the risk of owning and operating a business in exchange for financial and other rewards that the business may produce. By contrast, an intrapreneur is a person employed by an organization whose compensation is based, at least in part, on the financial success of the unit for which he or she has responsibility.

2. **Describe four steps involved in the entrepreneurial process.**
   Four steps involved in the entrepreneurial process are discovering the business opportunity, developing the business plan, securing the required resources, and managing the new business venture.

3. **Review the potential risks and rewards that confront entrepreneurs.**
   The risks involved in starting a new business are of at least four types: financial, career, personal, and psychological. Potential benefits (rewards) are at least fivefold: possibility of financial success, personal and professional satisfaction, community status, independence, and control over one's life.

4. **List common reasons why many new businesses fail.**
   Common reasons why new businesses fail include lack of management ability, inadequate industry experience, lack of financing and

funding, and unrealistic business plans. Additional factors include failure to consider realistic goals, inability to generate revenues, higher than necessary costs, and poor location. Two final reasons include ineffective operating procedures and an inability to think creatively.

5. **Review principles and practices helpful to intrapreneurs in the hospitality industry.**
   Intrapreneurs cannot be successful unless their employer (the hospitality organization) encourages it. Successful intrapreneurs think and act like entrepreneurs within the encouraging corporate culture. They have many of the same success traits found in their entrepreneurial counterparts. They are driven by ideas, are creative and innovative, and are motivated by opportunities for organizations and themselves to be successful.

6. **Review differences among traditional managers, entrepreneurs, and intrapreneurs in the hospitality industry.**
   Traditional managers are motivated by promotion and traditional corporate rewards. Entrepreneurs and intrapreneurs are motivated by independence and the chance to be creative. In addition, entrepreneurs have the opportunity to make more money and intrapreneurs have the opportunity to move toward organizational and personal successes. Other differences between these three types of managers are noted in Exhibit 34.3.

MASTERING YOUR KNOWLEDGE

Discuss the following questions.

1. What risks would be of most concern to you if you were thinking about starting your own business?
2. What do you think are the most important planning considerations involved in developing a business plan? Why?
3. What else is needed to be a successful entrepreneur besides having a good idea?
4. If you were the general manager of a unit in a multiunit operation, what type of profit-sharing (if any) arrangement would you ideally like to have with your organization? (In other words, what percentage of your total salary should be at stake relative to attaining a predetermined profit goal?) How much discretion would you want to have in making decisions under this ideal arrangement?
5. Pretend that you are a department head in an organization that believes in and practices the concept of intrapreneurship. What percentage of your total compensation would ideally be based on your ability to attain predetermined goals? How much discretion would you want in making decisions under this ideal situation?
6. Assume that you want to be an entrepreneur. What would be the advantages and disadvantages of negotiating a contract with a franchisor of an existing hotel or restaurant chain? What would be the advantages and disadvantages of starting your own business without franchise affiliation?

LEARN FROM THE INTERNET

1. Check out the home pages of several companies that connect franchisers with potential franchisees:
   - Franchise Opportunities.com: www.franchiseopportunities.com
   - Franchise Works.com: www.franchiseworks.com
   - Prime Sites USA: www.primesitesusa.com
   - Franchise Gator.com: www.franchisegator.com

   What information do they provide to prospective entrepreneurs (investors)?

2. To view a Franchise Fee Calculator that allows you to undertake a corporative analysis of hotel franchise companies based on the fees they charge, go to HVS International: www.hvs.hotelmotel.com/Intro.asp.

3. The Internet has an extensive listing of articles, research, and other information about intrapreneurs. To view this information, use your favorite search engine and type in the term "intrapreneur."

KEY HOSPITALITY TERMS

The following terms were explained in this chapter. Review the definitions of any words with which you are unfamiliar. Begin to utilize them as you expand your vocabulary as a hospitality professional.

entrepreneur
independent operator
intrapreneur
capital
retina scanning
business plan
working capital
pro forma budget

interest
small business
life-style business
high-growth venture
assets
subordinates
corporate culture

Domestic or Global Hospitality Positions— or Both?

35

Want to work in Paradise?

CHAPTER LEARNING OBJECTIVES

After studying this chapter you will be able to:

1. Cite three important considerations when making a decision about working and living in another country.
2. State several factors that affect whether expatriate managers are successful.
3. Discuss procedures that a hospitality organization might utilize to determine the cross-cultural adaptability of an employee and his or her spouse and family to an international assignment.
4. Review topics that should be included in a transitional training program for expatriate managers and their families.
5. Provide an overview of factors that will influence the success of a global assignment after the expatriate has arrived in the host country.

FEEDBACK FROM THE REAL WORLD

In this chapter you will learn about the numerous potential advantages and disadvantages of accepting a global hospitality management assignment. What are the advantages of working and living in another country? The disadvantages? What are examples of the totally unexpected positive and negative things that can happen in an international assignment? What are the most important things to consider as you decide whether an international assignment is right for you?

As you read this chapter, think about answers to these questions and then get feedback from the real world at the end of the chapter.

Living and working in paradise! Always warm weather; close to the ocean; palm trees and beautiful scenery and a life-style that will be the envy of all your friends and family! Is this what comes to mind when you first think about an island in the North or South Pacific?

Now think about traditional work and a personal life in a city far away in Southeast Asia, South America, or Europe. Each of these locations also offers professional and personal experiences that are vastly different from what one typically experiences at home.

A central theme of this book has been that people from around the world increasingly travel and will require lodging and food services. Since people travel literally everywhere, hospitality organizations need to be everywhere to provide travelers with the required services and products. Employment opportunities in the hospitality industry are available around the world. Positions outside one's country can be especially rewarding and personally enjoyable. However, they can also create professional and personal disaster! A decision to seek employment in the international hospitality marketplace, then, is very important and is the topic of this chapter.

THE HOSPITALITY INDUSTRY IS A GLOBAL INDUSTRY

OBJECTIVE 1
Cite three important considerations when making a decision about working and living in another country.

laypersons persons who are not professionals in or very knowledgeable about a specific subject (such as hospitality management)

expatriate a citizen of one country who is employed in another country; a U.S. citizen working in Asia would be considered an expatriate by his or her Asian counterparts

You have learned that the world of hospitality is much more sophisticated and complex than many **laypersons** believe. Very large U.S. hospitality organizations own and/or operate hospitality properties in the United States and throughout the world. By contrast, large hospitality organizations owned by Asians, Europeans, and persons of other nationalities own and/or operate hospitality properties in the United States and other regions of the world. It is therefore increasingly true that promotions within an organization may involve relocating around the country and even to other parts of the world. Still other professionals desire international positions as they seek employment with international companies. What are the types of things to consider when the decision to become an **expatriate** hospitality manager is made?

MANAGING AND LIVING IN ANOTHER COUNTRY[1]

Persons considering work in a foreign country must take several things into account.

---

[1]This section is adapted from Steven Robbins and Mary Coulter, *Management*, 7th ed. Prentice Hall, Upper Saddle River, NJ, 2002, pp. 97–102.

The Political Environment

The United States is incredibly fortunate to have a stable and long-standing legal and political system. Political changes are relatively slow, and processes leading to them are democratic and well established. This is not, however, the case everywhere. Governmental structures are much less stable in some countries. This can result in societal turmoil; fast-paced changes in leadership, laws, and travel restrictions; and the potential for personal harm. The decision about managing a business and protecting oneself and family in these environments generally creates a fast "Don't go!" for most persons. Fortunately, in many other countries, while the legal and political environment is different from that in the United States, opportunities for professional success and personal enjoyment do exist.

A crowded street in Hong Kong

Economic Issues

The cost of doing business and living in other countries can be of concern. Diverse tax laws have an obvious effect on business decisions. Currency **exchange rates** and **inflation** affect both business and personal decisions. The expatriate hospitality manager has an advantage when, for example, he or she is paid a competitive salary in U.S. dollars and works and lives in a country where the dollar (or its equivalent) purchases significantly more than it would in the United States. As well, living in countries with very high inflation rates (which can be 2000 or more percent annually in some countries!) presents special challenges when purchasing goods and services for business or personal use.

exchange rate   the rate at which money of one country is traded (exchanged) for money of another country

inflation   the economic condition that exists when selling prices increase throughout the economy of a country

Cultural Environment

Persons living in a country share a **national culture** of values and attitudes that influence their behavior and shape their beliefs about what is important. National culture can have a significant impact on how employees

Europe has a lengthy history of hospitality.

national culture   the values and attitudes shared by citizens of a specific country that affect behavior and shape beliefs about what is important

WHAT TIME IS IT ANYWAY?

Americans typically value punctuality. For example, if they have an appointment at 11:00 A.M., most persons make every effort to be where they need to be at 11:00 A.M. By contrast, the concept of "11:00 in the morning" can mean something entirely different to persons in other countries. For example, in some South Pacific Islands, "11:00 in the morning" means anytime during the hour of 11:00 in the morning. Therefore, if a person arrives at an 11:00 meeting at 11:50 A.M. or even 11:59 A.M., attendees will be "on time" for the 11:00 A.M. meeting. (Equally frustrating for the expatriate U.S. manager, the meeting set to convene at 11:00 A.M. may not actually begin until 11:30 A.M., 11:45 A.M., or later!)

CHECK IT OUT!

To view current articles and other information about expatriate hospitality managers, review the following websites (type, "expatriate managers" in each site's search box.):

Hospitality Net:
www.hospitalitynet.org

Hotel News Resource:
www.hotelnewsresource.com

---

culture shock   the feeling of disorientation, confusion, and changes in emotions created when one visits or lives in a different culture

---

OBJECTIVE 2
State several factors that affect whether expatriate managers are successful.

---

view their work and each other. Differences between people from different countries relative to how they treat each other, behave, compete, and value punctuality (being on time for meetings and appointments), for example, are issues that can significantly affect one's attitudes about and ability to work and live in another country.

Expatriates choosing to work in a country with a similar national culture are less likely to suffer from **culture shock** than will their counterparts relocating to a country with a more diverse national culture. For example, those from the United States working and living in Western Europe will likely feel more at home than will those working in Asia or in West Africa.

DO YOU WANT TO BE AN EXPATRIATE MANAGER?

Exhibit 35.1 identifies several key factors that influence whether expatriate managers are successful. Some (but not all) of these factors are easy to assess.

- A person who does not adapt well to change is more likely to have difficulty adjusting to work and living in another culture.
- Persons desiring an expatriate position will be happier than those who take the position only for reasons of, for example, career advancement.
- Expatriates with an understanding of the host country's national culture will know what they are getting into; fewer surprises are likely that may detract from their continued interest in living and working there.
- Persons with the knowledge and skills required for successful job performance will have less stress on the job and with job security than will others who do not.
- Interactions with people on and off the job are likely to be significant factors in whether an expatriate position is successful. Hospitality professionals typically think of themselves as people persons; however, they must be effective when interacting both with persons in their organizations and in the neighborhood where they live while in the host country.
- Managers with previous experience in another country are likely to know what they are getting into, and both their positive attitude and previous professional and personal experiences will be helpful.
- The interest that family members have in relocating and their general support of this decision are very significant concerns that will dramatically affect the success of the global assignment.
- One's motivation to accept an international assignment is important. Consider, for example, the manager who volunteers for reasons of personal and professional growth and adventure versus another manager who is told that it will be good for his or her career.

EXHIBIT 35.1
Checklist of Factors
Important to Expatriate
Success

Check (√) one box for each factor noted below.

Factor	No	Maybe (A Little)	Yes
You are able to adapt to change.	❏	❏	❏
You want to live in another country.	❏	❏	❏
You understand the country's national culture.	❏	❏	❏
You know the country's language.	❏	❏	❏
You have the knowledge and skill needed for successful job performance.	❏	❏	❏
You have the necessary human relations abilities to manage persons with backgrounds significantly different from yours.	❏	❏	❏
You have previous experience(s) working and living in another country.	❏	❏	❏
Your family will support the decision to accept a global assignment and to adapt to life in another country.	❏	❏	❏
You have positive reasons (motivations) which influence your interest in a global assignment.	❏	❏	❏
You have reasonable expectations about the experiences you will have.	❏	❏	❏
You are willing to listen to and try to understand the perspective of others.	❏	❏	❏

- Expectations about a global assignment must be reasonable. Effective transition training (discussed later in this chapter) will help to assure that the manager realizes what is likely to and what is not likely to happen.
- The ability to listen to and attempt to understand the beliefs of others is very important. Expatriate managers are likely to experience ideas expressed by co-workers, employees, and others in the host country that are profoundly different than theirs.

Let's assume that you have answered yes to all or most of the factors noted in Exhibit 35.1 and that you wish to pursue a global assignment. What factors are likely to influence the success of the assignment? Seldom,

There are many hospitality operations in Tokyo, Japan.

An expatriate manager's commute to work can be interesting.

if ever, is a global hospitality management assignment successful by chance alone. More specifically, many factors must be in place for an assignment to be an ideal one. When these factors work against the international assignment, they can, at best, cause strain and stress and, at worst, can yield disastrous professional and/or personal experiences. Exhibit 35.2 reviews factors that influence the success of global assignments. Note that the chart first addresses the candidate himself or herself. The types of personal concerns and factors noted in this exhibit and discussed above are important considerations. We will discuss other factors (the selection process, transitional training, and the expatriate in the new culture) in the remainder of this chapter.

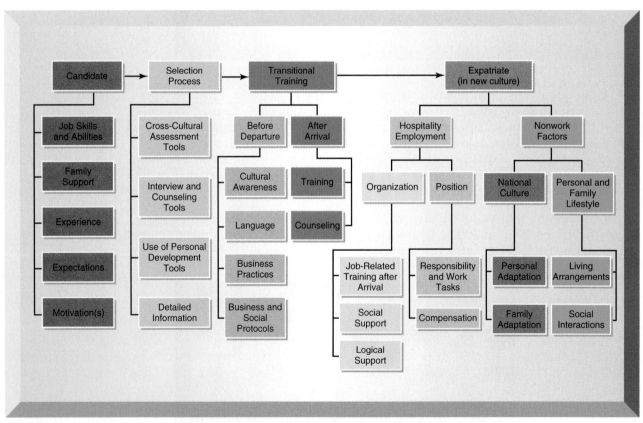

EXHIBIT 35.2
Factors Influencing Success of Global Assignments

Pedro Felix

A Second Career Leads to Foodservices

Pedro's first professional position was with the division of consumer services in New York City. However, he enjoyed foodservices. He reasoned that the hospitality industry as part of the service sector might not be as greatly affected by changes in the economy as would other sectors. Also, statistics said that it was the largest industry in the world, so there should always be employment opportunities! Pedro attended school at night and earned a technical college degree in culinary arts and hospitality management.

Pedro joined ARAMARK in 1995. One major incentive: the opportunity to work abroad. In his first positions with ARAMARK, Pedro learned about retail services, vending, cafeteria management, and catering (how to organize functions and manage their seemingly endless details).

He was offered the chance to work overseas and he took it. Pedro moved to Spain where he managed a healthcare (100-bed hospital) and a petroleum plant account. One of his most interesting opportunities arose when he was assigned to open a quick-service food outlet in the hospital. He started at the beginning by working with the architect on the original design. He helped to determine and select the signage, planned the product (food) mix, and trained the employees. Pedro found it a challenge to manage people in a different culture and to bring what successfully worked in the United States to another country.

His largest career challenge in Spain came when he was transferred to Barcelona as the director of public relations and special events for a large sports and recreational account. There he was responsible for concessions and massive catering events. For example, SAAB Autos hosted a weeklong event with about 15 points of service offered on several levels of the arena. About 700 to 900 dinners were served nightly. Pedro had to develop and implement a Swedish theme into the Spanish environment. He had to interpret and coordinate between the host and Spanish authorities, develop menus and recipes, coordinate with

the executive chef, purchase food, and hire and train more than 200 waiters for the events. All of this and much more had to be done with only two and a half months of lead time!

Pedro then moved back to the United States to manage a $5 million account with Goldman/Sacs, whose business operated out of several buildings in New York City. Administrators with that organization really understood the food-service business and had specific requirements about financial reporting and food standards. Pedro spent two and a half years developing his team, managing the account, and working to stay ahead of other companies competing for the business.

Pedro also served as district manager of business services in the Atlanta market. He managed $8 million worth of business and helped unit (account) managers with client relations and professional development activities. He also worked with his managers to generate new ideas to keep the clients satisfied with his organization.

Pedro's advice to young persons considering the hospitality industry: "You really need to think about what you want to do. What *exactly* are the pros and cons of all alternatives from your own unique perspective? When you make an employment decision, you won't know 100% about everything you wish you could know. It is more likely that your decision will be right when you take college courses, analyze their content, and consider that what you learn will likely relate to a job that you could be doing." His final suggestions: "You must have a passion for your job and your career. Don't let your career take you some place by chance alone. Continue to analyze where you are and where you want to go and what you must do to get there."

When asked what was the most gratifying thing about his work, Pedro responded with a statement that suggests that he has the spirit of hospitality management: "I like the end result that occurs when you successfully understand and meet the needs of your clients and your managers. You don't mind the hours if you enjoy your work. By contrast, only a few hours won't be fun if you don't!"

OBJECTIVE 3
Discuss procedures that a hospitality organization might utilize to determine the cross-cultural adaptability of an employee and his or her spouse and family to an international assignment.

THE EXPATRIATE SELECTION PROCESS

Exhibit 35.2 notes that the selection process is an important event in the success of a global assignment. Until just recently, some hospitality organizations made international assignments by doing little more than asking the question "Who wants to go?" or by making the statement "You really should go!" Today, however, a more focused and formalized selection process is generally utilized.

The success of an international hospitality operation will be influenced by the selection of and placement decisions about the professionals who will manage it. Also, the personal success of an expatriate assignment is more likely to be influenced by cultural adjustments made by the manager and his or her family than by the expatriate's lack of management or technical knowledge and skills. As well, significant financial costs are incurred in the international assignment as expatriate managers are trained, relocated, and compensated or subsidized in the host country. Problems with past global assignments point to the need for a more objective selection process.

cross-cultural adaptability the extent to which one can adjust (adapt to) another culture

Since expatriate assignments often fail because the employee and/or his or her family cannot adjust, the **cross-cultural adaptability** of the employee and spouse or family becomes important to assess. The extent to which one can adapt to a new culture can be determined by the following:

- Administering cross-cultural assessment tools to the employee, spouse, and family. These assessment devices attempt to assess attitudes and attributes judged important for adjustment.
- Interviewing and counseling sessions with the employee and spouse that further explore the potential for cultural adjustment.
- Considering specialized ways in which the employee should plan and implement a personal cross-cultural development tool.
- Providing detailed information to help the staff member to understand the new international assignment and to adapt to daily life within the host country.

The entire family should be counseled about what to expect when a family member accepts a foreign assignment.

REQUIREMENTS FOR EXPATRIATE MANAGEMENT SUCCESS

Successful expatriate hospitality managers have:

Empathy. They try to place themselves in the role of those with whom they interact in their host country.

Respect. They are considerate of and courteous to their employees and neighbors and learn the appropriate ways that respect and courtesy are shown in their new culture.

Interest. They desire to learn about the local cultures that they experience.

Flexibility. They make adjustments for the new culture in which they live.

Tolerance. They make every effort to understand differences between cultures.

Initiative. They have interest in and recognize the need to reach out to persons within their new country.

Self-esteem. They recognize the contributions that they can make to their employer while, at the same time, they understand that they will also learn much in their expatriate management experience.

TRANSITIONAL TRAINING

> **OBJECTIVE 4**
> Review topics that should be included in a transitional training program for expatriate managers and their families.

Exhibit 35.2 indicates that, after personal issues applicable to the candidate are addressed and after the selection process is completed, transitional training becomes important. Persons selected for international assignments will, ideally, receive training before they depart and are relocated. On what topics should training be provided? Examples of subject matter in an ideal curriculum for an international assignment include the following:

- *Cultural awareness*. To allow persons accepted for international assignments to learn how the national culture affects work relations and how teamwork and productivity can be enhanced when working with staff members from that culture.
- *Language training*. Many Americans think that English is (or should be) the world's universal language. In fact, English is widely spoken (at least in the world of business) in many countries. However, expatriates must also live in the community and will likely need to acquire basic language fluency to go about their lives off the job.
- *Business practices*. Changes in basic business practices that will be necessary in the new country, including information about applicable laws, tax issues, and the availability of required resources.
- *Business and social protocols*. Specific dos and don'ts of business and social practices must be learned.

Exhibit 35.2 indicates that a second type of transitional training (after arrival) is also useful. This training can be provided several

A tour of the market can help you to discover new and different types of food in the host country where you live and work.

NICE TO KNOW OR NECESSARY TO KNOW?

There are many necessary (not nice to know) things that one should know about a country before relocating to it. These necessary to know things are generally very basic and include the following:

What is the form of government? Who is the national head of the government? What does the country flag look like?

What role does the government play in business? What taxes do residents pay? Expatriates? Businesses?

What is the prevalent religion? What influence does it have on daily life?

What are the most important social standards? Cultural standards?

What are prevalent attitudes about marriage? Divorce?

What words, gestures, and body language are viewed as profane?

What language is spoken?

What are attitudes and laws applicable to alcoholic beverages?

What kind of literature can be admitted into the country?

What are some laws that one could violate because of ignorance if proper predeparture and postarrival training is not provided?

What are the country's major industries, products, exports, and imports?

What is the size and population of the country?

What is its history?

What are the most important holidays? When and how are they celebrated?

What are favorite recreational activities of the citizens?

What medical facilities are available? When? Where? To what extent can an expatriate utilize them? Where *exactly* does one go for serious medical problems? How does one get there? How, if at all, does medical insurance work in the country? Is air transport to another country generally necessary for serious (or even not so serious) ailments?

What medicinal drugs are available?

What visas are needed to enter or leave the country?

How are drivers' licenses obtained? Who can drive?

What is the normal dress of the country's men? Women?

What are local costs for housing? Food? Utilities? Telephone service and other necessities? Does one's compensation include (or consider) these costs?

What is the availability and quality of schools for expatriate children?

What English-language newspapers and magazines, if any, are readily available?

What is the local currency? The dollar exchange rate? The trend in exchange rates?

When shopping, to what extent should one bargain about the proposed selling prices?

How do people greet each other? (Shake hands? Embrace? Other?)

What are local-language expressions for "Good morning," "Hello," "No," "Yes," and other common terms?

Trips back to see your family and friends may be infrequent.

weeks after the expatriate manager and his or her family arrive in the host country. By this time, they will have had an opportunity to experience the new environment and to interact with local citizens, and they may be seeking answers to numerous questions. Some may be homesick. Their beginning efforts at becoming culturally aware can form the foundation for training and counseling that can make their foreign assignment more enjoyable and rewarding.

A central theme of transition training is the need to help the manager and his or her family to recognize that old methods and ideas will need to be unlearned (or, at least, put aside during the assignment) and that new methods and ideas based on the employees and workplaces within the new culture will often be necessary.

THE EXPATRIATE HAS ARRIVED!

Exhibit 35.2 provides an overview of the factors that will influence the success of a global assignment after the expatriate has arrived in the country.

OBJECTIVE 5
Provide an overview of factors that will influence the success of a global assignment after the expatriate has arrived in the host country.

Hospitality Employment

These factors include the extent that the organization provides job-related training after arrival, social support on and off the job, and logistical support (for example, where are the best schools? the best medical facilities?). Furthermore, the position itself (responsibility and work tasks, for example) and compensation are important. (Compensation for expatriate managers typically includes a salary and normal benefits paid to those working in their own country, but can also include other benefits, such as extended annual leave, travel costs to and from the host country, educational expense reimbursements for family members, costs of moving household belongings to and from the host country, and insurance or reimbursements for emergency travel costs.)

The commerce of Hong Kong drives the hotel business in this vibrant city.

Nonwork Factors

The expatriate and his or her family must be able to adapt to the host country's culture. The personal and family life-style that is enjoyed will dramatically influence the success of the assignment. For example, the expatriate's living arrangements, including transportation to and from work, and the numerous nonwork social interactions will also influence his or her interest in continuing the assignment.

SUMMARY OF CHAPTER LEARNING OBJECTIVES

1. **Cite three important considerations when making a decision about working and living in another country.**
   Three important considerations when making a decision about working and living in another country relate to the political environment, economic issues, and the country's cultural environment.

2. **State several factors that affect whether expatriate managers are successful.**
   Factors that affect whether expatriate managers are successful include their ability to adapt to change, willingness to work in another country, understanding the company's culture, knowledge of the country's language, and having the knowledge and skill needed for success. Additional factors include necessary human relations attitudes, previous experience in other countries, family support, positive reasons for seeking a global assignment, reasonable expectations, and the willingness to understand the perspectives of others.

3. **Discuss procedures that a hospitality organization might utilize to determine the cross-cultural adaptability of an employee and his or her spouse and family to an international assignment.**
   Procedures to determine the cross-cultural adaptability of an employee, spouse, and family for an international assignment include the use of cross-cultural assessment tools, interviewing and counseling sessions, developing and implementing a cross-cultural developmental plan, and providing detailed information so that all aspects of the assignment can be understood.

4. **Review topics that should be included in a transitional training program for expatriate managers and their families.**
   Topics to be included in a transitional training program include cultural awareness, language training, business and social protocols, and changes in basic business practices.

5. **Provide an overview of factors that will influence the success of a global assignment after the expatriate has arrived in the host country.**
   Factors influencing the success of a global assignment after the expatriate has arrived include those relating to hospitality employment (the organization, including job-related training and social and logistical support) and position (including responsibilities and work tasks and compensation). Nonwork factors, including international and family adaptation, and personal and family life-style, including living arrangements and social interactions, are all important.

MASTERING YOUR KNOWLEDGE

Discuss the following questions.

1. What differences, if any, do you think exist in the way that one would manage an American-owned hotel in the United States or a European- or Asian-owned hotel in the United States?

2. What are examples of how the predominate culture in the United States affects the way its hotels are managed and operated?

3. How do you think the national culture of a host country affects the management of hotels in that country?

4. What are examples of ways that the government in the United States affects the management and operation of its hotels?
5. What are differences in the way governments in other countries affect the management and operation of hotels in those countries?
6. What would be some of the biggest challenges in your professional and work lives if you were an expatriate managing a hotel in a country where you were fluent in the country's language? If you were not fluent in that country's predominant language?
7. Would you like to manage a hotel in another country? Why or why not?

FEEDBACK FROM THE REAL WORLD

Our real-world advice comes from Stephen Marquard, Account Manager, American Restaurant Supply Company, Kailua-Kona, Hawaii. Stephen completed a four-year degree in hospitality management and then began his professional culinary career at the Breaker's Hotel in Palm Beach, Florida. He then joined the AAA five-star Maisonette Restaurant in Cincinnati, Ohio. Stephen then became the executive chef at the Outrigger Marshall Islands Resort on Majuro, the capital of the Republic of the Marshall Islands. After a three-year assignment there, he joined the Outrigger Fiji Resort as executive chef. As part of the opening team, Chef Stephen was responsible for hiring, purchasing, and establishing systems and procedures for the new 254-room property on the Coral Coast of Viti Levu (Fiji's main island). Upon completion of his contract, Stephen continued his hospitality career in Hawaii.

What are the advantages of working and living in another country? The disadvantages?

Depending on your career goals, there can be lots of potential professional advantages. Since I was willing to transfer or relocate to a remote island, my opportunities to assume the responsibilities of executive chef were increased. The position in the Marshall Islands was offered to me, and I took it! Another professional advantage of working overseas is that it teaches you new ways to solve problems. Even working within a large organization such as Outrigger, there is much autonomy in a remote location and therefore opportunities to experiment. It is important to know that what works in one location or country does not always work in another. A manager can take many approaches.

There are other professional rewards as well. It was a wonderful experience to work with people who have such a rich culture and traditions. I came from America with a degree in hospitality to train the staff at the hotel. They did learn, but in the process I learned a lot about genuine hospitality. This exchange of knowledge and experiences is perhaps the most rewarding aspect of working on an international level. I was able to learn different languages and to work with different types of people, and I learned an important lesson: to appreciate and utilize diversity wherever you work.

There are also financial advantages to working internationally, including free lodging, meals, telephone and other utilities, and, in effect, full maintenance. Finally, if you are paid in U.S. dollars and live in a country where the exchange rate is beneficial, you can live very inexpensively and bank the rest.

There are some potential disadvantages to international assignments. While it did not affect me, some people have culture shock and get homesick. Access to high-quality healthcare can also be a concern. Even with the Internet, it is still possible to lose touch with the real world. Technology allows one to keep up with current events around the world, but it is still more difficult (time consuming) to keep current. It is also possible to feel isolated, especially when you are off the job.

(continued)

What are examples of the totally unexpected positive and negative things that can happen in an international assignment?

This is an easy question for me. The most positive thing is that I met the woman who would become my wife! On an incredibly trivial scale, you will never know all that one can do with a coconut! (I think that is positive.)

When I moved to the Marshall Islands, I erroneously thought that most of the people with whom I would interact would speak English. This was not correct. Therefore, to be effective on the job I learned the Marshallese language. My efforts to do so earned me respect in the kitchen and the community as well.

Chefs in many parts of the world have much less access to convenience foods. This was good for me because I was able to learn and practice my culinary skills in a way that I would likely have been unable to in a domestic position.

There are a few negative things that I recall. With any job there are trade-offs, and one of the benefits that I missed out on was not being able to stay on the cutting edge of the culinary profession as I might have if I was working in New York, San Francisco, or Miami.

I have had relatively few negative experiences. One happened recently: an attempted coup in Fiji. Citizens had to comply with a curfew at night, there were military checkpoints manned by soldiers with guns during the day, and the international airport was shut down for a while. My employer (Outrigger Hotels) couldn't have been more helpful during this time. Employees were offered the opportunity to go to an outer island (which would be safer) or to fly home at any time and at any cost. In retrospect, this experience was more of an inconvenience than a serious problem. It was short-lived, I kept in touch with the U.S. embassy, and the impact on me personally and professionally was minimal at the most!

What are the most important things to consider as you decide whether an international assignment is right for you?

Many factors are common sense, such as these:

- Get as much information about the location as you can.
- Have an offer in writing from your employer before you leave.
- Talk with others who have "been there and done that."
- Negotiate a trip to the location to look around.
- Remember that a standard contract is two years; you are making a significant professional commitment.

Personal factors are also important. It was an easy decision for me because I have always liked to travel. Living in a country for an extended time is much different than visiting 20 countries in six months. You are not just a tourist passing through; rather, you are a resident working with the locals and indigenous people who can teach you a lot about their country and its society. This is a significant dimension to international assignments; one does not just go for the money and the adventure—you must want to do it for the right reasons.

LEARN FROM THE INTERNET

1. Check out the websites for organizations with hotels in other countries:
   - Mercure Hotels (Accor Hotels): www.mercure.com
   - Mandarin Oriental (Hotel Group): www.mandarinoriental.com
   - Peninsula Hotels: www.peninsula.com

Compare them to the websites of domestic hotel organizations. What similarities do you notice? What are some differences that you notice? Review the employment opportunities information. Do the available positions appeal to you? Why or why not?

2. To review available international hospitality positions, go to:

- Hotel Careers: www.hotel-careers.com
- Caterer Global: www.catererglobal.com
- Intercontinental Hotels Group: www.ichotelsgroup.new-jobs.com

3. Check out the website for Grove Well, LLC (www.grovewell.com). Review the topics of their predeparture expatriate coaching classes. Which of these would be of interest to you? Why?

KEY HOSPITALITY TERMS

The following terms were explained in this chapter. Review the definitions of any words with which you are unfamiliar. Begin to utilize them as you expand your vocabulary as a hospitality professional.

laypersons
expatriate
exchange rate
inflation

national culture
culture shock
cross-cultural adaptability

Glossary

a la carte dining room (restaurant) a foodservice operation in which guests order from a menu featuring individually priced items

a la carte menu a menu in which food items are individually priced

account the contract management company's term for the organization that has retained it to operate the foodservices program; also called *client*

account location a site where a vending company's machines are located; a large account may have banks of vending machines in several (or more) places throughout its location

account retention activities undertaken to ensure that representatives of organizations utilizing the services of a hospitality organization will continue to do business with the organization; contract management companies and vending or office coffee service organizations are examples of hospitality businesses with account retention concerns

accountability an obligation created when a person is delegated duties or responsibilities from higher levels of management

accountability (in vending) the process of matching products loaded onto route trucks with the amount of products returned and vending revenues turned into the money room

accounts payable (AP) the total of all invoices owed by the organization to its vendors for credit purchases made by the property

accounts receivable (AR) money owed to an organization because of sales made on credit

active life-style (senior life-style) a life-style option that attracts retired and near-retirement persons who want to own a place where they will retire

adjusted revenues (sports and recreational foodservices) gross revenues less sales taxes

advancing tours the process by which a production company's technical representative travels ahead of the tour (show) to learn about the performance space and available equipment, meets with theater and facility contacts, and identifies and resolves potential problems in advance of the show's arrival

advertising nonpersonal presentation of products and services offered by the hospitality operation

AGM abbreviation for assistant general manager

allocation the process of distributing revenues earned and/or expenses incurred between departments on a basis that approximates each department's share of the revenues and/or expenses

all-suite hotels lodging properties in which all guest rooms are suites

alternative beverages water and a wide variety of mostly noncarbonated beverages, including juices and teas and a wide range of newly popular flavored drinks

amenities hotel products and services designed to appeal to guests

American burlesque a creative mix of theatrical entertainment with sensual overtones, striptease, double-entendre comedy (jokes or skits with two meanings), and mocking imitations geared to a male audience that was a popular form of entertainment in the United States from about the late 1800s to the 1920s

American Plan the hotel pricing structure in which some (or all) of a guest's meals are included in the basic room rate

Americans with Disabilities Act (ADA) a federal law providing civil rights protection to persons (visitors, guests, and employees); among other provisions, it guarantees equal opportunities for disabled individuals in public accommodations and employment

amusement park a collection of rides and activities located in a central area with no unifying theme and separate admission or ticket requirements for each attraction

appreciation (accounting) an increase in the value of an asset such as real estate

apprenticeship a structured process used to train persons in the skills necessary to be proficient in a trade or profession

assets something of value owned by a business or person

assisted living (senior living and care option) a long-term care option that provides private living accommodations and other services, including dining, housekeeping, laundry, and the management of medications

association an organization with volunteer leadership (and usually a paid staff) that serves persons with a common interest or activity

attrition rate the number of guest rooms in a block of rooms that are not rented

authority the formal power that a manager has to direct the work of employees and to expect that work assignments will be completed

average daily rate (ADR) the average selling price of all guest rooms for a given time period; the formula for ADR is total room revenue ÷ total number of rooms sold = ADR

baccarat a high-stakes table game using playing cards in which the highest (best) hand is nine, and the winner is the player closest to nine. In casinos, this game is played in a formal, separate room; dealers wear tuxedos

backline gear the onstage musical and amplification equipment rented for the performing band (speakers and amps, keyboards, drum kits, and the like)

back catalog show a Broadway show in which the story is based on music that has already been written and released; also called *compilation show*

back-of-house pertaining to employees, positions, and/or departments that have little direct contact with guests

banquet a food and beverage event in which all or most guests are served items on a preselected menu

banquet department the unit within a hotel responsible for producing and serving food and beverages at large meal functions

banquet event order (BEO) a form used by the sales, catering, and food production areas to detail all requirements for a banquet; information provided by the banquet client is summarized on the form, and it becomes the basis for the formal contract between the client and the hotel

banquet manager the person responsible for service of food and beverage products at a group function

banquet service staff employees of the Food and Beverage Department who set tables and serve meals and remove serviceware at the end of a banquet

banquet setup staff employees of the Food and Beverage Department who set up and tear down tables and set and remove chairs and other room furnishings at the conclusion of a banquet

banqueting the process of preparing and delivering a food-related event in a group function room

bar a for-profit business serving alcoholic beverages to guests seated at a counter (bar); limited table service may also be available

bar code lines of information that can be scanned into a computer system; bar code technology is used to update inventory databases and for many other purposes

batch cooking the process of preparing smaller quantities of food several times during a serving period, rather than the total number of portions required at the same time

bed and breakfast (inn) very small (one-to-several guest room) properties owned or managed by persons living on-site; these businesses typically offer at least one meal daily; also called B&B

behavior-based questions an interviewing approach designed to assess how one has behaved in specific situations

benchmark the search for best practices and an understanding about how they are achieved in efforts to determine how well a hospitality organization is doing

big six a carnival-style game in which a large, upright wheel is spun by a dealer and players wager on which number the wheel will stop; the higher the payout, the greater the odds against hitting the number

bingo a game in which players match numbers on cards with randomly drawn numbers

black jack a table game in which the winner is the person closest to 21 without exceeding that number; also called *twenty-one*

block guest rooms reserved for members of a specific group

blood alcohol concentration (BAC) the amount of alcohol in the blood

board plan a payment schedule for meals that is included as part of the charge paid for a residence hall room; schools may offer numerous board plans such as 5, 10, 15, or 20 meals per week at a preestablished charge

board-budgeted deficit (school foodservices) a grant made by the governing unit to the school foodservices program to compensate for losses incurred when revenues do not meet expenses

book a Broadway show term referring to spoken lines in a play or musical

booking (verb) concluding a sale that results in a contract between the hotel and the guest(s)

bottom line a slang term relating to profit; on a budget and income statement, the profit line is the last line of (at the bottom of) the document

boxperson the individual responsible for placing cash waged in a dice game into a drop slot in the dice table, placing waged chips in the rack, and protecting the integrity of the game

brand name of a hotel chain; sometimes referred to as a *flag*

brand loyalty the interest of guests or potential guests in revisiting and/or recommending a hotel or restaurant

brand proliferation oversaturation of the market with different brands

branded food food and/or beverage items manufactured by organizations with, typically, nationally recognized names; examples include Starbucks (coffee) and Pizza Hut (pizza)

breakdown time the time required to return a function room to its original condition after an event; this involves removing tables, chairs, and other fixtures and cleaning the area

breakout room a room used when a large group wishes to temporarily break into smaller groups

budget a financial plan that estimates the amount of revenue to be generated, the expenses to be incurred, and the amount of profit, if any, to be realized from the hospitality operation

budget (or economy) limited-service hotels hotels within the limited-service segment that offer low-priced guest rooms and few, if any, amenities other than a complimentary continental breakfast or coffee service

buffet foodservices in which menu items are selected and generally portioned by guests as they pass along one or more serving counters; in some operations, items such as omelets are made to order and/or other items such as rounds of beef are carved to order

bulk (food portions) a large volume of food that has not been preportioned for individual service

bundled (charges) costs for several (or more) products or services in an all inclusive charge

business and industry foodservices the segment of the noncommercial foodservice industry that provides meals or partial meal components to employees while they are at work; frequently referred to as B&I

business plan a plan of goals and activities that will be addressed within the next 12 months to move the organization toward attainment of its mission

business travelers those who travel primarily for business reasons (often on an expense account to defray the reasonable travel costs incurred)

butler (food serving style) a service style in which food is served to guests who are standing by a food server (butler) who moves among the guests

by laws committee (private club) a committee in a private club that makes recommendations about regulations that govern the club

California-style menu a menu featuring items traditionally available for breakfast, lunch, and dinner that are offered throughout the time the property is open for business

call sheets rehearsal or work call schedules, typically created by the production stage manager, or coordinator, to notify cast and/or stage crew members about show, music, or technical rehearsals

camp and park lodges sleeping accommodations in parks and other nature conservatories owned by government agencies and often operated by for-profit management companies

capital relating to the acquisition of land, equipment, buildings, and other fixed assets

capital improvements remodeling and/or building or facility additions, changes in land use, and other projects requiring substantial sums of money

captain a foodservice management position with responsibility for guest service; for example, the banquet captain is responsible for service to all or some guests in banquets

captive market the relatively rare situation in which consumers have absolutely no choice of product or service alternatives; examples in foodservices include inmates in a correctional institution and naval personnel on long-term sea duty

carafe a glass bottle with a relatively wide mouth used to serve house wines; sizes are usually full- and half-liter

card games games of chance in which customers (players) wager against each other while a casino employee (dealer) deals the cards

career fairs trade show-type events that allow prospective job applicants, moving from booth to booth, to meet recruiters representing numerous employers

career ladder a plan that projects successively more responsible professional positions within an organization or industry; career ladders also allow one to plan and schedule developmental activities judged necessary to assume more responsible positions

cash bar a beverage service alternative where guests desiring beverages during a banquet function pay for them personally

cashless vending technology that allows customers to purchase products from vending machines without using cash (coins or currency)

casino a business operation that offers table and card games along with (usually) slot operations and other games of skill or chance and amenities that are marketed to customers seeking gaming activities and entertainment; many casinos also offer food and beverage services and lodging accommodations for the convenience of their visitors

casino cage the casino's banking center maintained by a cage manager; transactions with casino customers are conducted by casino cashiers at cage windows. The cage is responsible for the property's currency, coins, tokens, and gaming chips; casino pit clerks are an extension of the cage and work in the gaming pits on the casino floor; cage personnel prepare cash banks (for example, for restaurant cashiers) and bank deposits, cash checks for patrons, and place valuable items in safety deposit boxes; currency is also counted in a secure area of the cage

casual-service (midscale) restaurant a moderately priced restaurant offering a full, informal menu often with an ethnic theme or environment; alcoholic beverages are frequently served

caterer a for-profit business that produces food for groups at off-site locations; some caterers have banquet space available for on-site use by groups desiring foodservices

catering (hotel) the process of selling a banquet event and interacting with the banquet client

catering (in-home) off-site catering done in a host's home for a small number of guests

catering (off-site catering) the physical transport of food to an off-site location

catering (sports and recreational foodservices) the production of food and beverages for sale to groups of people

cause-related events events undertaken for reasons of charity (private or public relief for persons in need)

centralized (school foodservices) program a foodservice organization in which general foodservice management duties are coordinated within the school district and a foodservice manager directs the operation of a foodservice program within a single school

chain a multiunit hospitality organization

chain of command the path by which authority flows from one management level to the next within the organization

chained recipe a recipe for an item (such as a sauce) that is, itself, an ingredient in another recipe (such as a casserole)

chapter a group that is a subset of an association; chapters are often formed on the basis of geography (a state association chapter is a subset of a national association)

check average the average amount spent by a restaurant guest: total food and beverage revenue ÷ total number of guests

chef the person responsible for food production

city club a private club within a city's business area or suburban office complex that offers food and beverage services and, often, conference and indoor sports facilities; some offer sleeping rooms

classical brigade a system of kitchen organization established by Auguste Escoffier that was designed for large-volume preparation of complex and extensive menus

classroom style a seating arrangement in which tables and chairs are in rows on each side of a function room; all chairs face the head table and a center aisle separates the rows

client (of contract management company) the organization that negotiates and administers the foodservice contract with the management company

clients (vending) the account decision maker(s) who negotiates and contracts with a vending company

clinical dietitian a food and nutrition expert whose work may involve foodservice management, nutrition therapy (planning special diets, for example), and nutrition education; dietitians working in healthcare foodservices are typically credentialed as a registered dietitian (RD) by the American Dietetic Association (ADA)

closing (timeshare sale) the final meeting in which the buyer and seller (or their representatives) exchange documents, money, and property rights; in most cases, the transfer of title to the property is also registered with the proper state or local authorities at the meeting

club house the club facility used for primary food and beverage production and service, social functions, swimming pool and lockers, and the club's administrative offices, among other purposes

Club Managers Association of America (CMAA) the association that serves the needs of private club managers

co-branding an arrangement in which two or more franchisees of different organizations share common costs, such as building, dining areas, and a parking lot for a stand-alone building

code of ethics a statement adopted by an organization that outlines policies developed to guide the making of ethical decisions

coliseum an indoor recreational facility; also called an *arena*

collective bargaining agreement a contract between an employer and employees who are members of a labor union that establishes the rights and responsibilities of both groups in their employment relationship

collusion secret cooperation between two or more employees for the purpose of committing fraud

combo unit a combination meal in which several menu items are packaged together at a selling price less than the sum of their individual prices

comfort food a familiar menu item prepared in a way that is reminiscent of how it was served during the customer's childhood or how the customer would prepare it at home; also called *homestyle*

commercial foodservice operations foodservices offered in hotels, restaurants, and other organizations whose primary financial goal involves generation of profits from the sale of food and beverage products

commissary a food preparation area (kitchen) utilized to produce food items at least some of which will be transported to and served off-site; also called *central kitchen*

commission a payment made by a contract management company to a client; typically it is based on a percentage of revenues generated from sales at the client's location

commission (booking agent) a fee, based on an agreed-on percentage of an artist's payment for an engagement, that a booking agent receives for securing the engagement

commission rebate a fee typically based on a percentage of revenues generated by a vending machine that is paid by the vending company to the organization in whose location the machine is located

commodities (federally donated) foods purchased by the U.S. Department of Agriculture for distribution to schools and other eligible recipients

competency a requirement that specifies what an individual must know and/or be able to do to be successful in a position

competitive edge the concept that a business does something very well, which encourages persons to purchase products and services from it rather than from its competitors

competitor any business attempting to attract the same guests as one's own business

complete meeting package (CMP) all elements needed to support a successful meeting

concessionaire a for-profit business that has been granted the right to provide agreed-on products and services to the organization's (cruise ship's) passengers (customers)

concierge the individual(s) within a full-service hotel responsible for providing guests with detailed information regarding local dining and attractions, as well as assisting with related guest needs

concierge (contract management companies) an individual responsible for providing specialized personal and professional assistance to organizations and selected staff members within it

condo-hotel a hotel with traditional public spaces and services in which some or all of the guest rooms are purchased by persons who can rent their units as part of the hotel and receive a portion of the unit's rental revenues for doing so

condominium (or condo) a lodging property in which units are individually owned; in some condominium properties, units can be placed into a rental pool with resulting guest fees split between the owner and the company managing the units

conference center a specialized hospitality operation specifically designed for and dedicated to the needs of small- and medium-size meetings of 25 to 75 people

conference center education coordinator the person performing the work of a meeting planner who represents a potential meeting site (conference center) and works with meeting sponsors and planners to plan on-site activities, including educational programs

congregate care (senior living and care option) a long-term care option that provides private living quarters with centralized dining services, shared public areas, and access to social and recreational activities

consulting dietitian a Registered Dietitian who provides technical assistance as a consultant (rather than as an employee) to an organization desiring or requiring this assistance

consumer show an exhibition open to the public (usually for an admission fee)

continental breakfast a morning meal that includes coffee, juices, and pastries. An upscale continental breakfast may include additional items such as fruit and hot and cold cereals with milk and yogurt. Most limited-service hotels offer a complimentary continental breakfast as a guest amenity

continuous quality improvement (CQI) ongoing efforts within a hospitality operation to meet (or exceed) guest expectations and to define ways to perform work using better, less costly, and faster methods

contract management company a for-profit business that contracts with an organization to provide foodservices as specified; the management company may be a chain with many contracts or an independent management company with only one or a few contracts

contribution margin the amount that remains after the product (food) cost of a menu item is subtracted from its selling price

contribution margin (sports and recreational foodservices) total revenue less all chargeable costs; also called *net revenue*

controlling the basic management activity that involves determining the extent to which the organization "keeps on track" for achieving goals

convenience food food or beverage products that have some labor built in that otherwise would need to be added on-site; for example, beef stew can be purchased ready to serve (just heat) and a Bloody Mary mix can be purchased ready to pour

convention a meeting of association members or those working within a profession

Convention and Visitors Bureau (CVB) an organization, generally funded by taxes levied on overnight hotel guests and/or from membership fees paid by members; the purpose is to increase the number of visitors to the areas they represent

convention hotel a lodging property with extensive and flexible meeting and exhibition spaces that markets to associations, corporations, and other groups bringing persons together for meetings

convention sales manager the professional in a convention hotel and conference center who is responsible for booking a continuous flow of desirable group-business

convention services manager the professional in a convention hotel and conference center who helps assure that all groups receive the contracted service negotiated by the convention sales manager

cook–chill system a food production and delivery system in which food is produced in bulk, quickly refrigerated, and then transported to a serving site for later reconstitution and service

cooking applying heat to a food item

coordinating the basic management activity that involves arranging group efforts in an orderly manner

corporate culture the shared beliefs, experiences, and norms (ways of doing things) that characterize an organization

corporate travelers guests who are traveling on business or because of their jobs

cost containment efforts to reduce costs wherever possible while assuring that the quality of products and services being produced are appropriate for their intended use; sometimes called *cost minimization*

cost justifiable relating to the need to assure that the costs incurred are necessary

cost plus a financial agreement in which a contract management company establishes a charge to the sponsoring organization based on actual incurred costs plus a fee for its services

country club a private club with a clubhouse, golf course, and typically other recreation facilities, along with food and beverage outlets, pro shop, locker facilities, and other amenities; also commonly called a *golf club*

cover letter a transmittal letter that accompanies a résumé being sent to a prospective employer; its purpose is to introduce a potential applicant and to express his or her interest in employment opportunities

credits (casino gaming tables) the security task of transporting gaming chips from tables to the casino cage

cross-cultural adaptability the extent to which one can adjust (adapt to) another culture

cross-functional team a group of employees from different departments within the hospitality operation that works together to resolve operating problems

cross-selling messages designed to advertise the availability of other hotel services; for example, a dinner menu may provide information about the hotel's Sunday brunch

cross-training a technique of training persons for more than one position so that they can assist wherever they are needed

cruise ship a passenger vessel designed to provide leisure experiences for persons on vacations

culture shock the feeling of disorientation, confusion, and changes in emotions created when one visits or lives in a different culture

curbside polling the process that allows route drivers using a hand-held terminal (HHT) to determine the current level of products in vending machines while still in their trucks

customers (vending) individuals who purchase products from vending machines

cyberfares low-cost airfares (sometimes packaged with accommodations and rental cars) offered by airlines to increase business during slow travel periods such as weekends, when there is minimal business travel

cyclical menu a menu in which food items rotate according to a planned schedule

data mining using technology to analyze guest- (and other) related data to make better marketing decisions

day-part a segment of the day that represents a change in menu and customer response patterns (for example, time during which breakfast and other menus are offered)

debarkation the process of exiting a cruise ship

decentralized (school foodservices) program a food–service organization in which a manager has independent responsibility for menu planning, purchasing, recipe development, and all other aspects of operating the program within a single school

deeded interest (timeshare) ownership in perpetuity that can be sold or passed on to the owner's heirs

deep pockets a slang expression referring to someone being affluent or an organization having excessive profits, which increases the size of potential lawsuits and judgments against these parties

deficit (or subsidy) the amount of expenses that cannot be paid for with revenues generated by a noncommercial foodservice program; called *loss* in a commercial foodservice operation

delegation the process of assigning authority (power) to subordinates to enable them to do work that a manager at a higher organizational level would otherwise need to do

demand generator an organization, entity, or location that creates a significant need for hotel services; examples include large businesses, tourist sites, sports stadiums, educational facilities, and manufacturing plants

demographic factors factors such as age, marital status, gender, ethnicity, and occupation that can help to describe a person

Destination Marketing Association International (DMAI) a professional association that promotes its member convention and visitor bureaus to meeting planning professionals

dice games table games in which a player wins or loses based on dice rolls; also called *crap games*

diet order the diet (allowable foods and beverages) prescribed by a physician, including detailed nutrient information, extent of consistency modification, and the dates of the diet's initiation and duration

dietary relating to diet (what a person eats and drinks)

dietary manager a professional certified by the Dietary Managers Association who has the education, training, and experience to fulfill applicable responsibilities and who has successfully completed a nationally recognized credentialing exam

dietetic technician a practitioner in food and nutrition who may assist dietitians with medical nutrition therapy, may manage all or part of a foodservice operation and may be involved in nutrition education activities; many

are credentialed as a dietetic technician, registered (DTR) by the American Dietetic Association (ADA)

dietetics the science of food and nutrition as it applies to health and well-being

direct reports persons (or positions) who are supervised by the person in the next highest organizational position

directing the basic management activity that involves supervising the work of staff members

distributor sales representative (DSR) a salesperson representing a product or equipment supplier who sells to the hospitality operation

diversification movement into varied businesses and/or industry segments

downsizing the act of reducing the number of employees, positions, and/or labor hours for cost containment purposes; also called *rightsizing*

dram-shop laws a provision in the U.S. legal code that allows an injured party to seek damages from both the intoxicated person who caused the injury and from the person who provided the alcoholic beverages to the intoxicated person

drop chute in vending, a chute or slot in the door or wall of a money room through which funds collected on routes can be passed without entering the money room

du jour menu a menu in which some or all food items are changed daily

eatertainment (foodservice) the concept that guests desire to enjoy the total dining experience (food and beverage products, service, and the environment, including cleanliness) and may desire pleasurable distractions (television and animatronics, for example) when they visit a foodservice operation

e-commerce (electronic commerce) the buying and selling of products and services on the Internet; also called *e-business*

economy of scale the concept that productivity per unit of input can increase as the volume of output increases

electronic tray ticket (healthcare food and nutrition services) a list of menu items desired by a patient or resident that is generated electronically by a patient, resident, or dietary assistant for electronic transmittal to the kitchen

embarkation the process of boarding a cruise ship

empathy an appreciation for and an understanding about how someone feels

employee assistance program a counseling and/or referral plan sponsored by an organization for its employees with personal problems

employer of choice an organization with a reputation of being a desirable place to work and whose recruiting efforts are made easier because of this

employment interview a conference between an organizational representative and a prospective job applicant in which both parties learn information helpful in an employment-related decision

empowerment the act of granting authority to employees to make key decisions within the employees' areas of responsibility

empty nesters Middle-aged persons whose children are grown and have left their parents' home

entertainment   an activity performed for the enjoyment of others

entrepreneur   a person who assumes the risk of owning and operating a business in exchange for the financial rewards that the business may produce

equity clubs (private clubs)   private clubs owned by their members and governed by an elected board of directors

equity credits (construction loans)   the amount of a developer's equity that a lender will consider as cash; calculated as a percentage of expected construction costs

ethics   a person's perceptions about what is right and wrong

evaluating   the basic management activity that involves determining the extent to which plans are attained

exchange rate   the rate at which money of one country is traded (exchanged) for money of another country

executive committee   short for *executive operating committee;* it consists of members of the hotel's management team (generally department heads) responsible for departmental leadership and overall property administration

exhibition   an industry-specific event that allows suppliers to an industry to interact with, educate, and sell to individuals and businesses that are part of the industry; also called *trade show*

exhibitor   an individual or organization sponsoring a booth at an exhibition

exhibitor's prospectus   marketing information provided to prospective exhibitors with the purpose of encouraging their participation in an exhibition

exhibitor's service kit   a packet of information containing rules of the exhibition sponsor and contracts and promotional pieces offering products and services of the exhibition service contractor(s)

expatriate   a citizen of one country who is employed in another country; a U.S. citizen working in Asia would be considered an expatriate by his or her Asian counterparts

expedite (purchasing)   the act of facilitating a delivery of food and beverage products previously ordered from suppliers

expediter   a person serving as liaison between food production and serving staff during busy shifts

expenses   costs incurred by the hospitality operation to generate its revenue

expiration date   the calendar date at which a product should no longer be available for sale because of a concern that quality deterioration has occurred

extended-stay guest   a hotel guest seeking lodging accommodations in the same property for a period of seven or more days

extended-stay hotel   a midpriced, limited-service hotel marketing to guests desiring accommodations for extended time periods (generally one week or longer)

F&B   abbreviation for food and beverage

family entertainment centers   community-based recreation or entertainment centers with attractions such as miniature golf, go-cart rides, video games, skating centers, bowling allies, movie theaters, and health clubs; also known as *fun centers*

family-service restaurant   a restaurant featuring table (and frequently counter) service and offering a wide range of value-priced menu items that generally does not offer alcoholic beverages

FF&E   abbreviation for furniture, fixtures, and equipment

fills (casino gaming tables)   the security task of transporting gaming chips from the casino cage to the tables

finish kitchen   a food preparation area used to cook or hold menu items preprepared in another food production area; for example, a finish kitchen may be used to cook spaghetti noodles to which a spaghetti sauce prepared in another kitchen is added

finishing   completion of the last step(s) in the recipe for a food or beverage item; for example, preportioned ingredients for a salad (such as Caesar) may be mixed or a preportioned meat item may be cooked with preassembled herbs and spices (steak Diane)

first come, first served (exhibition booth assignment method)   booths are assigned on the basis of the date booth contracts are signed

fixed basis (for timeshares)   access to owned or leased space during one or more specific weeks during the year

flag   the specific brand with which a hotel may affiliate; examples of currently popular flags include brands such as Comfort Inns, Holiday Inn Express, Ramada Inns, Hampton Inns, Residence Inns, Best Western, and Hawthorn Suites; hotels affiliated with a specific flag are sometimes referred to as a *chain*

flatware   guest table-service items, including knives, forks, and spoons

floating basis (for timeshares)   access to owned or leased space during any available week within a certain season of the year

floor plan   a schematic drawing of the exhibition space that indicates all obstructions, entrances, utility ports, and available usage areas

food (menu) items   the food selections that the menu specifies will be available for sale to the guests

food and wine affinity   the recognition that wine, if properly chosen, can complement the foods with which it is served; one should select, for example, the entrée and then consider wines to accompany it

food-borne illness   an illness caused by consuming food that has been contaminated by microorganisms, chemicals, or other substances

food court   an area in which employee- and/or consumer-dispensed foodservices are available

food fad   a relatively short-lived interest in or preference for specific food items

food trend   a longer-lived change in the preference for or interest in specific food items

foodservice liaison   a foodservice management specialist employed by a sponsoring organization to represent its interests in the ongoing administration of the foodservices agreement with a contract management company

formal work group a group of employees who work together in positions or departments as specified by the organization chart

fractional (timeshare) a timeshare product in which no more than 13 owners can own a unit. In other words, on average, each owner has access to the unit for 4 weeks (52 weeks per year /13 possible owners)

fractional ownership persons purchase up to three months of home ownership at a deluxe hotel or resort; also called *private residence club*

franchise an arrangement whereby one party (the brand) allows another (the hotel owners) to use its logo, name, systems, and resources in exchange for a fee

franchisees those who own (or lease) the property and building and buy the right to use the brand name for a fixed period of time and at an agreed-on price; they often pay royalties and contribute to regional and/or national advertising programs

franchiser one who manages the brand and sells the right to use the brand name

freestanding (restaurant) a restaurant that is the sole occupant of a building; freestanding restaurants typically have dedicated parking spaces for their guests

frequent-traveler program a program developed to reward a hotel company's guests with free room nights, frequent flyer airline miles, and/or other awards as an incentive to book rooms at a property within the brand

from scratch the preparation of food on-site with the use of (generally) fresh ingredients; the opposite of convenience foods

front-of-house pertaining to guest-contact employees, positions, and/or departments

full-line distributor a supplier who offers a wide range of products; for example, some suppliers sell thousands (or more) of items, ranging from toothpicks to fresh produce to dishwashing machines; they offer a large variety but not a deep selection of items within a specific category

full-service hotel a hotel that provides guests with extensive food and beverage products and services

function room public space, including meeting rooms, conference areas, and ballrooms (which can frequently be subdivided into smaller spaces), available for banquet, meeting, or other group rental purposes

gaming any activity that involves wagering (betting) something of value on a game or event with an unknown outcome

gastronomy the art of fine dining as enjoyed by a connoisseur (a knowledgeable person) of good food and drink (wines)

gift card (reloadable) a cashless payment system that allows guests to purchase (and repurchase) debit (payment) cards for use at a quick-service restaurant

glass ceiling an expression that describes unofficial or unacknowledged roadblocks for women attempting to advance within an organization

globalization the process by which countries and communities within them throughout the world are becoming increasingly interrelated

grab and go the foodservice option in which a customer selects a prepackaged food item for consumption away from the site

grapevine the informal network of communication within an organization

group a lodging reservation that exceeds 10 rooms per night

group (type of guest) a large number of guests sharing a common characteristic who are staying at a property at the same time; groups may receive special rates, amenities, and/or privileges because of the increased revenue that they generate; also called *tour group*

group function rooms food serving areas (rooms) where guests are served preordered (banquet) menus

guarantee a contractual agreement about the number of meals to be provided at a banquet event; typically, a guarantee must be made several days in advance of the event; at that time, the entity contracting with the hotel for the event agrees to pay for the larger of the actual number of guests served or the number of guests guaranteed

guaranteed reservations an obligation (promise) incurred by a hotel that a guest room will be available on a specific date after a specified time; typically, guaranteed reservations are given upon receipt of a guest's credit card information; the guest-room rental will be charged to the card even if the guest does not use the room

guests per labor hour the number of guests served per each hour of labor incurred by the property; if 10 hours of labor are incurred on a day when 50 guests are served, there are 5 guests per labor hour (50 guests ÷ 10 hours)

hallmark events special events that are repeated because they are significant, sustainable, and revivable

haute cuisine high (fine) food preparation

hawkers (sports and recreational foodservices) employees in the concessions department of a sports and recreational foodservices venue who move through an assigned area of a stadium selling (hawking) their products

hazard analysis critical control points (HACCP) a food safety assurance process that identifies potential sanitation-related problems in food production and service

head table special seating at a banquet reserved for guests of honor

headliner (entertainment) a star (performer) who receives prominent billing for a performance

high-growth venture a business whose plan is to expand rapidly by obtaining sufficient investment capital and by introducing new products and services to a large market

high season (timeshare) period of time when the purchase of a timeshare unit is most costly

high-traffic areas locations adjacent to areas with large numbers of potential customers

holding the task of maintaining food items at proper serving temperature after they are prepared; holding involves keeping hot foods hot and cold foods cold

home meal replacement food purchased away from home for at-home consumption

hospitality industry refers primarily to organizations that provide lodging or accommodations and foodservices for people when they are away from their homes

hospitality suite a private guest room of sufficient size to provide meeting space, food, and/or beverages for a small group of guests

hosted bar a beverage service alternative in which the host of the function pays for beverages during all or part of the banquet; also called an *open bar*

hostel a lodging accommodation, typically available in a dormitory style, that is generally inexpensive and frequented by youthful travelers

hotel a for-profit business that rents sleeping rooms and often provides other amenities such as food and beverage services, swimming pools and exercise rooms, meeting spaces, business centers, and concierge services; also referred to as *motel, motor hotel,* or *motor inn*

hotel occupancy rate the ratio of guest rooms sold (including comps) to guest rooms available for sale in a given time period; always expressed as a percentage, the formula for occupancy rate is number of guest rooms sold ÷ number of guest rooms available

hotel residences units in a mixed-use hotel building that are owned by their residents

house diet a diet that has been adopted (accepted) by the medical director and the foodservice administrator for use at the facility; deviations from these diets are used for special diet needs

independent living (senior life-style) a life-style option for active seniors who are able to live without assistance in a hotel, condominium, apartment, or other facility; accommodations may be modified to include bathroom railings, wide doorways, and emergency alert systems

independent operator an entrepreneur who owns or operates one or a very few hospitality properties

induction the process of providing basic information about the department and position that must be known only by those employees working within the department or position

inflation the economic condition that exists when selling prices increase throughout a country's economy

informal work group a group of employees who are not part of a formal work group, but who still interact with each other on and/or off the job

infrastructure utility systems, roads and sidewalks, land improvements, and other site construction required before building construction begins

ingredients the individual components of a food (menu) item; for example, flour and sugar are two ingredients in bread

in-home catering off-site catering done in a host's home for a small number of guests

interdisciplinary between disciplines; involving several domains of knowledge; for example, basic business principles can be applied in organizations of all types in all industries

interest the expense incurred to borrow money

International Association of Conference Centers (IACC) a professional association of conference centers that focuses on the physical structure of and ability of member facilities to provide specific services

interval ownership a phrase meaning timeshare; also called *vacation ownership*

intoxication legally, the point at which a person's blood alcohol concentration (BAC) rises to a predetermined level; for example, 0.08 in many jurisdictions

intrapreneur a person employed by an organization whose compensation is based, at least in part, on the financial success of the unit for which he or she has responsibility

investor an individual or organization that provides money for a business such as a hospitality operation with the goal of receiving a profitable return

issuing the process of moving products from storage areas to the point of use (place of production)

job description a list of tasks that an incumbent in a position must be able to perform effectively

job enlargement the act of including additional tasks or assignments in one's position to provide more opportunities to learn how the position relates to others

job rotation a systematic plan to move employees into (rotating) different positions so that they acquire the knowledge or skill required to be effective in these positions

job shadowing (for permanent placement) a combination employment interview and site visit; prospective applicants can ask questions and, at the same time, follow a position incumbent on the job to gain a realistic overview of the organization

job specification a list of the personal requirements judged necessary for someone to successfully work within a position

Joint Commission on Accreditation of Healthcare Organizations (JCAHO) a quality oversight board for healthcare organizations in the United States

judicial system the legal system by which persons can make claims and have binding decisions about them made in a court of law

junk foods (school foodservices) foods with little or no nutritional value

keno numbers 1 to 80 are displayed on an electronic board or screen; players mark a keno ticket indicating which 20 numbers they think will be drawn; keno is similar to lottery drawings

kiosk a very small refreshment (concession) stand offering just one or a very few food or beverage products

kiting remote technology that enables vending warehouse staff to learn product refill needs of specific machines; kits containing needed products are assembled, taken to the applicable machine, and loaded into it

labor intensive the need for people rather than for equipment (machinery or technology) to perform required work tasks

laypersons persons who are not professionals in or very knowledgeable about a specific subject (such as hospitality management)

leased interest (timeshare) a right that is limited to a length of time (for example, 10 years); when the lease expires, ownership (access) expires

leisure industry businesses that appeal to the leisure market; these include organizations offering entertainment, recreation, cruises, and gaming

leisure time personal time away from work or other responsibilities to do as one wishes

leisure travelers those who travel primarily for personal reasons; these guests use private funds for travel expenses and are often sensitive to the prices charged

licensed product an item produced under an agreement (license) between the owner of intellectual property (trademark) and another party that permits, for payment of a fee, the latter to use the owner's property; for example, manufacturers of a Spider-Man tee shirt must pay a fee to the owners of the Spider-Man trademark to do so

licensing formal authorization to practice a profession, granted by a governmental agency

life-cycle events activities that celebrate or recognize significant milestones in one's life

life-style business an organization built around the personal and financial needs of the entrepreneur and his or her family

limited-service hotel a lodging property that offers very limited food services or none at all; sometimes a complimentary breakfast is served, but there is no table-service restaurant

line-level employees staff members whose jobs are considered entry-level or non-supervisory; typically positions for which the employee is paid an hourly (rather than salary) compensation; examples include positions such as guest service (front desk) agents, room attendants, and food and beverage servers

line positions those in the chain of command as authority flows from one level of management to the next

lineup meeting a brief informational training session held before the work shift begins

loan-to-cost (construction loans) the percentage of the expected cost of construction that a lender will fund

lobby foodservices food and beverage service offered by limited-service hotels

long-range plan a statement of goals and the activities that will be undertaken to attain them that a hospitality operation will utilize over the next 3 to 5 years in efforts to move toward its mission

long-term care facility a facility offering one or more of a variety of life-style and care alternatives to seniors and other residents who desire or need these services

lottery (exhibition booth assignment method) booths are assigned on the basis of the lowest numbers drawn by exhibitors

lounge a for-profit business serving alcoholic beverages to guests seated at tables; a small counter (bar) may also be available

lounge managers persons responsible for the production and service of alcoholic beverages in the hotel's bars and lounges; they hire, train, and supervise bartenders and the wait staff needed to serve guests

low season (timeshare) period of time when the purchase of a timeshare unit is least costly

luxury full-service hotels lodging properties offering the amenities of upscale full-service hotels and numerous additional features that appeal to discriminating clientele desiring the very best who are willing to pay premium prices

maitre d'hotel the manager in charge of the dining room; sometimes called *head waiter*

make or buy analysis the process of considering quality, costs, and other factors in "scratch" and convenience food alternatives to determine how products should be purchased for the operation

Malcolm Baldrige National Quality Award an award granted to relatively few United States businesses who demonstrate successful quality-related strategies relating to leadership, information and analysis, strategic planning, human resource development and management, process management, business results, and customer focus and satisfaction

managed foodservices foodservices operations that are managed by a contract management company

management the process of planning, organizing, staffing, directing, controlling, and evaluating human, financial, and physical resources for the purpose of achieving organizational goals

management company an organization that operates a hotel(s) for a fee; also sometimes called a *contract company* or *contract management company*

management contract a formal, written agreement that specifies the responsibilities and obligations of both the organization sponsoring the foodservices and the management company that provides them; frequently, the company agrees to assume total responsibility for management of the foodservices operation in return for a management fee and, perhaps, other remuneration; the organization provides the building and equipment and may continue to incur legal and economic liability

manager a staff member who directs the work of supervisors

manager's reception time (typically during early evening) in which registered guests are offered complimentary food and beverages in a central hotel location or dining area

manual foodservices operations in which food and/or beverages are served to consumers by foodservice employees

marker similar to an IOU; casinos do a credit check on customers and extend credit by use of a marker based on their financial background and ability to pay; customers can sign these markers and use the money to gamble

market segmentation efforts to focus on a highly defined (smaller) group of travelers

market share the percentage of a total market (typically in dollars spent) captured by a property

marketing the business from the perspectives of those who consume the products or services provided by the operation

marketing plan a calendar of specific activities designed to meet the operation's revenue goals

master account the folio established by the lodging property that allows certain preapproved charges made by or on behalf of a meeting sponsor to be charged to the meeting sponsor, rather than being the responsibility of the individual incurring the charge

Medicaid a federal and state assistance program that pays covered medical expenses for low-income persons; it is run by state and local governments within federal guidelines

Medicare a federal medical insurance program that primarily serves those over 65 years of age (regardless of income) and younger disabled persons and dialysis patients; medical bills are paid from trust funds into which covered persons have paid

meeting planner a specialist who plans, manages, and follows up on all details of meetings and/or conventions

meeting specification guide a book (binder) containing all information and details applicable to a meeting, including agenda and schedule, contracts, purchase orders for products and services, and applicable communications

megaship a cruise ship that carries 2,000 or more passengers

mentor a senior employee of the hospitality organization who provides advice and counsel to less experienced staff members about matters relating to the job, organization, and profession

menu (alternative choice) a menu that allows consumers to make a selection between food item alternatives

menu (nonselect) a menu that offers no choice of item selections for the consumer

menu engineering the process of menu evaluation that enables menu planners to determine items that are most popular and profitable and to use this information to design menus that emphasize selected items to be sold

menu planning the process of determining the food and beverage items to be offered by the foodservice operation that will most please the guests while attaining acceptable revenue and/or cost objectives

menu rationalization an approach used to maximize the number of menu items that can be prepared using relatively few ingredients

microbrewery a brewery that produces very small quantities of unique beers typically for consumption only on-site and/or for distribution within a small geographic area

micropayment (vending machines) small (several dollars or less) purchases from a vending machine made by credit or debit card

midpriced limited-service hotels hotels within the limited-service segment that offer selected property and within-room upgrade amenities for room rates that are higher than budget (economy) hotels within the segment

midscale full-service hotels lodging properties offering three meals daily, a lounge, pool, and limited meeting and banquet spaces

mini-baccarat a lower-stakes table game similar to baccarat, except the player does not have a turn as the bank and there is one dealer; in casinos, this game is less formal: it is played on the main floor and dealers wear the usual casino uniform

mini-bar a small, in-guest room refrigerator or unrefrigerated cabinet used to store beverages, snacks, and other items the hotel offers for sale to guests

mise en place a French term meaning "everything in its place"; the cooks and bartenders must get ready for production; servers must get ready for service

mission statement a planning tool that broadly identifies what a hospitality operation would like to accomplish and what it plans to do to accomplish it

mom and pop hotels a slang term sometimes used to refer to an independent property (one not affiliated with a brand) that is owned and operated by a single person or family

moments of truth any time that a guest has an opportunity to form an impression about the hospitality organization; moments of truth can be positive or negative

multiplier effect the spin-off financial benefits derived from the operation of a business or industry within a community or other area

name recognition the ability of guests or potential guests to remember and associate with a hotel (or restaurant) name

national culture the values and attitudes shared by citizens of a specific country that affect behavior and shape beliefs about what is important

negative discipline supervision activities designed to correct undesired performance

networking the development of personal relationships for a business-related purpose

niche marketing the process of offering products or services that appeal to a very specific subsegment (niche) of the market; for example, hoteliers may focus on the needs of long-stay business travelers rather than all business travelers, and may provide amenities in lodging accommodations that persons in this subsegment desire

noncommercial foodservices foodservice operations whose financial goal does not involve generating profits from the sale of food and beverage products; also called *institutional foodservices, on-site foodservices,* and *managed food services*

noncommercial foodservices (contract management company-operated) a type of noncommercial foodservice operation in which the program is managed and operated by a for-profit management company

noncommercial foodservices (self-operated) a type of noncommercial foodservice operation in which the program is managed and operated by the organization's employees

nonequity clubs (private clubs) clubs owned by an individual or corporation that are generally not tax exempt; most are corporate- or developer-owned clubs

not-for-profit organization a group of persons working for reasons other than to make profit from their efforts; many nonprofit organizations have charitable objectives

nutrition the science concerned with the study of food and nourishment, especially in humans

nutritional assessment process   the use of information gained from diet history data to make professional conclusions, state goals, and outline recommended approaches to assure that a cost-effective patient or client care plan can be developed

obesity   a physical condition evidenced by excessive body fat

occupancy (hotel)   see hotel occupancy rate

occupancy taxes   money paid by a lodging property to a local taxing authority; the guest-room revenue generated determines the amount paid; also known as *bed tax*

office coffee services (OCS)   a service provided by an external supplier who provides coffee break-related beverages to business and industry and other accounts

off-shoring   the relocation of some business functions, such as production or manufacturing, to a lower-cost location, typically overseas

off-site caterer   a foodservice business that produces food items at a commissary (central kitchen) for transport to remote locations for service; some caterers also offer on-site banquet (dining) areas

on-site foodservice   a contemporary name for noncommercial foodservices operations

open-enrollment program   an educational program developed by a continuing education and professional development conference center on a generic topic that is marketed to attendees from different organizations

operating budget   a financial plan that estimates the amount of revenue to be generated, the expenses to be incurred, and the amount of profit, if any, to be realized

organizing   the basic management activity that involves developing and grouping work tasks

orientation   the process of providing basic information about a hospitality organization that must be known by all employees

outpatient   a person receiving hospital services without being admitted to the facility

outsource   to employ a person or organization to perform activities that would otherwise need to be done in-house

outsourcing   retaining an external supplier to provide a product or service that has traditionally been produced or offered within the organization

overbuilt   the condition that exists when too many hotel guest rooms are available for the number of travelers wanting to rent them

overflow   guest rooms that are part of a larger group booking that cannot be accommodated by a single hotel; the room rates for overflow rooms are often established at a rate similar to that of the hosting hotel

overhead costs   expenses directly related to a specific department and not allocated to it; examples may include utilities, fire insurance, and interest expense

overload (equipment)   the act of requiring equipment to produce more than it is reasonably capable of producing

pai-gow   a game in which four cards or tiles are dealt to players, who must have two hands higher than the dealer's or bank's hand; casinos get a commission on winning hands

pai-gow poker   a combination of Chinese pai-gow and poker using 52 cards and a joker. Seven cards are dealt and the player creates five- and two-card hands; both must be higher than the dealer's hands to win; casinos get a commission on winning hands

pantry (sports and recreational foodservices)   a space used to portion prepared food for later service to customers, for example, preportioned hamburger patties may be heated on a grill in a pantry area

pari-mutuel wagering   betting on horses in which odds based on the amount bet on each horse are established; winners share the total wagers placed in the pool among themselves based on the established odds

pass-throughs (serving line compartments)   hot, refrigerated, or room-temperature units in walls between production and service areas that allow service personnel to quickly obtain food needed to replenish serving lines

patient unit   a section of the hospital that houses patients with specific needs; examples include oncology (for cancer patients), and medical or surgical for persons recovering from surgery

payoff (gaming)   any wager or winnings paid to a casino player; also used to describe the amount of money that will be paid on a wager or jackpot

payroll deduction   an amount withheld from an employee's compensation (paycheck) to pay for taxes, insurance, or other mandatory or voluntary financial obligations

peaks and valleys (business volume)   fluctuating guest counts and revenue volumes; the peaks are business surges, and the valleys are slow business times

per capita   per person, such as the amount of revenue (or expense) per person

per diem   a fixed dollar amount per day that a traveler will be reimbursed for a hotel room and/or meals; the amount is determined by the traveler's employer and may differ by travel destination

per portion   a single serving of food; for example, a portioned hamburger patty

performance appraisal   the evaluation of a staff member's work by his or her supervisor according to preestablished factors

permanent placement   the first full-time position that a student assumes after graduation from college

perpetual inventory   a system that keeps track of all incoming and outgoing products so that one knows, on an ongoing basis, the amount of product that should be available in inventory

personal cheffing   the use of a personal chef to prepare complete meals for each person for several (or more) days at the host's home

petits fours   small (individually portioned, bite-sized) cakes baked in an oven

pilferage   to steal small quantities of some item over a period of time

pit (casino table games)   specific tables in a designated location in the casino

pit clerk   a person reporting to the casino cage shift manager who provides information helpful in generating fill, credit, and marker transactions for a specified number of tables within the casino

planning the basic management activity that involves defining goals, establishing strategies to achieve them, and designing ways to get work done

plate (foodservice) the act of portioning food onto the proper serviceware for service to guests

point-of-sale (POS) terminal a computer system that contains its own input and output components and, perhaps, some memory capacity, but without a central processing unit

points basis (for timeshares) access to owned or leased space based on points determined by factors such as unit size, location, season, and resort demands

positive discipline supervision activities designed to reinforce desired performance

postcon (postconference) meeting a session attended by meeting planners and applicable meeting site personnel to evaluate a meeting that has concluded

postmix the process of mixing carbonated water with syrup for soda (soft drinks) at the time the beverage is served (dispensed)

potentially hazardous foods foods of animal origin or other items high in protein that are most frequently involved in outbreaks of food-borne illness

precon (preconference) session a session attended by meeting planners and applicable hotel personnel to review details and make final decisions about an upcoming meeting

preparing steps involved in getting an ingredient ready for cooking or serving; for example, celery must be cleaned and chopped before being cooked in a stew or cleaned and sliced before use on an appetizer tray

prepreparation the task of getting food ingredients ready for production; for example, frozen shrimp might be thawed, peeled, and deveined to ready them for deep frying when needed; frequently shortened to *preprep*

preregistration the process of registering attendees in advance of a meeting

price sensitive (guest) a person with a great concern about the costs of products and services who makes purchase decisions on the basis of minimizing costs

priority points (exhibition booth assignment method) exhibitors receive points for past exhibits and booth size; those with the most points have the first choice of booth selection

private club a membership organization not open to the public; persons join a club after being accepted by its membership and must typically pay an initiation fee and monthly membership dues; they must also pay for products and services purchased at the club that are not included as part of membership dues

private clubs private membership organizations of numerous types

pro forma budget a budget made in advance of the start of business; a pro forma budget is part of a business plan

pro forma projection estimates of financial performance done in advance of a fiscal period

process revisions changes to work methods in ways that reduce defects and increase opportunities to please the guests

procurement the process of determining the right quality and quantity of all food products and ingredients that should be purchased and of selecting the supplier who can provide these items at the right price and at the right time

product cost percentages the percentage of revenue generated from the sale of a food or beverage product that is required for its purchase

production the process of readying products for consumption

production schedule a management tool that indicates the quantity of each menu item needed, the amount, if any, available, and the quantity to be produced

professional association a group of persons who affiliate to promote common interests (which may or may not include business)

professional development programs a planned series of educational and training activities made available to staff members for the purpose of improving current job skills and knowledge and/or preparing them for other positions

professional placement the first full-time position that a student assumes after graduation from college

professionals persons working in an occupation requiring extensive knowledge and skills

promote from within the concept that a company considers existing employees at a lower organizational level as higher-level positions are filled

proposal response the information sent by a contract management company to an organization that addresses foodservice specification requirements detailed in the organization's request for proposal (RFP)

prospects (timeshares) potential purchasers of timeshares

public cafeteria foodservices in a noncommercial operation that are available to employees of and visitors to the outlet

public relations activities designed to build good relations with a company's numerous constituencies by use of tactics such as press releases, product publicity, corporate communications, and public service

purchase specification a statement (definition) of the quality requirements to be met by purchased products

qualified buyers individuals with purchasing power or who influence purchasing decisions

quality the consistent delivery of products and services according to expected standards

quality (of a food item) suitability for intended use; the closer an item comes to being suitable for its intended use, the more appropriate the product's quality

quick-service restaurant (QSR) an operation that provides a limited menu and limited service (generally self-serve at counters or through vehicle drive-throughs) at low prices; also called *limited menu* or *fast-food restaurant*

race book or **sports book** a casino department that accepts wagers on horse races or professional and collegiate sporting events

racino a race track that has added slot machines to increase revenues

rack rate the price at which a hotel sells its rooms when no discounts of any kind are offered to the guest; often shortened to *rack*

ration the average amount of money that a non-commercial foodservice operation can spend to purchase food for one person for one day; rations are typical budget goals in schools offering board plans, in the military, and in correctional institutions

rebate monies paid to a sponsoring organization by the contract management company; typically based on the profitability of the foodservice operation

receiving the transfer of ownership from a supplier to the foodservice operation that occurs when products are delivered to the operation

recession a period of downturn in the nation's economy

reconstitute to apply heat to a chilled or frozen food item to raise it to the proper serving temperature

recreation activities that revitalize one's mind and body away from work

recreational foodservices industry foodservices offered for persons enjoying recreational pursuits; also called *rec foods*

refresh to clean and restock a meeting room with water, beverages, or other meeting room supplies; this activity often takes place during the meeting's scheduled breaks or meal periods

regimen (diet) a nutrition care plan used to preserve and restore the health of a specific patient or resident

registered dietitian (RD) a member of the American Dietetic Association (ADA) who meets requirements relating to minimum academic and internship experiences; the RD has successfully passed a registration examination and has accrued specified registration maintenance credits by participating in ongoing professional education activities

registration (meeting) the process of gathering all necessary information and fees required for an individual attending a meeting

registration (professional association) acceptance for one to work within a profession that has been granted by (typically) a nongovernmental agency, such as an association

regulars repeat guests or frequent diners

repeat business revenues generated from guests returning to a commercial hospitality operation as a result of positive experiences on previous visits

request for proposal (RFP) a formal document that incorporates the organization's needs for foodservices expressed in the form of detailed specification requirements; the objective of the RFP is to define the required foodservices so clearly that prospective bidders (management companies) can develop accurate costs and other estimates used in their proposal responses

resort a full-service hotel with additional attractions that make it a primary destination for travelers

resort activities director the property manager with responsibility for revenue-generating recreational activities

responsibility the obligation that one has to do the work and to achieve the goals and objectives associated with a specific position

restaurant a for-profit foodservice operation whose primary business involves the sale of food and beverage products to individuals and small groups of guests

résumé a summary of a job applicant's education, experiences, and job-related qualifications

retail store foodservices businesses such as convenience stores, grocery and food markets, and gasoline stations that generate a relatively small percentage of their revenues from the sale of food and beverage products intended for immediate consumption

retina scanning the use of the retina patterns in one's eye as a unique source of personal identification; retina scanning may replace fingerprinting as the identification of choice

return on investment the measure of managerial efficiency that correlates profitability with the investment made to generate the profit

revenue the amount of money generated from the sale of products and services to guests

revenue center a department within an organization that generates revenue; two examples in a casino are the casino operations and hotel operations departments

revpar short for revenue per available room; the average revenue generated by each guest room available during a given time period; the formula for revpar is occupancy % × ADR = revpar

rework to do a task a second time because of defects created the first time the task was done

rider (contract) an amendment attached to a contract to modify it to avoid rewriting or redrafting the entire document; riders to entertainment contracts typically address a performer's equipment, meals and drinks, and general comfort requirements

risk management the process of conserving an organization's assets by reducing the threat of losses that arise from uncontrollable events

room night a single night's use of a guest room; a group using 10 rooms for 5 nights generates 50 room nights; the number is used as an indicator of group size and quantifies the group's importance to the hotel

room service food and beverage products served to guests in their sleeping rooms

roulette a table game in which a large wheel is spun by a dealer who simultaneously spins a small white ball around the inside top rim of the wheel; wagers are placed on a number or color upon which it is hoped the ball will fall

route driver a staff member employed by a vending organization to transport products, resupply products, and retrieve money from vending machines at an account utilizing the vending company's services

route manager the manager within the vending organization who plans delivery routes, supervises route drivers, takes corrective action as necessary based on route revenues and product costs, and provides service to help retain existing accounts

sales mix (menu) the percentage that one menu item sells of the total items served; if one menu item has a known sales mix percent, the number of portions of that item can be calculated: total estimated guests to be served × sales mix percent = estimated units of the menu item to be sold

satellite foodservices a location to which food prepared in a commissary at another location is transported and served; for example, a satellite school serves meals produced in an off-site central commissary

scramble cafeteria system a plan in which specific menu components are available in separate locations of the cafeteria serving area; also called a *modular system*

"scratch" (food preparation) the use of individual ingredients to make items available for sale; for example, a stew may be made on-site with vegetables, meat, and other ingredients, and a Bloody Mary mix can be made on-site with tomato juice and seasonings

seasonal hotel a hotel whose revenues and expenditures vary greatly depending on the time (season) of the year; examples include ski resorts, which are busy in winter months, and northern lake resorts, which are busy in summer months; many seasonal resorts are open for only part of the year

securities laws laws that regulate investments of all types in an organization when there is an expectation that profits will be made through the efforts of other persons

select-service hotel a hotel with one restaurant that is open for service on some basis less than three meals daily for seven days weekly

self-brands food and/or beverage products manufactured by an organization sponsoring or operating foodservices at the site

self-operated foodservices noncommercial programs in which the foodservices management and staff are employees of the organization offering the foodservice

self-supporting (foodservices) noncommercial foodservice program that operates without the need for a subsidy from the sponsoring organization

selling interpersonal activities designed to promote the sale of products and services offered by the hospitality operation

service the process of helping guests by addressing their wants and needs with respect and dignity in a timely manner. Also, the process of transferring food and beverage products from service staff to guests

service bar a bar in which drinks prepared by bartenders are given to personnel who serve them to guests

service charge a mandatory amount added to a guest's bill for services performed by a staff member of the hospitality organization

service contractor (exhibition) a business or individual who provides goods and/or services to exhibition managers and exhibitors that create the environment for an exhibition, including the exhibit floor and its related elements

serving the process of moving the food or beverage items that have been prepared from production staff to service personnel

setup time the time required to modify a function room as required by a client; this involves setting tables and chairs and installing audiovisual equipment and other fixtures

shift leader (quick-service restaurant) a person serving as a supervisor for specific departmentalized activities, such as drive-through, production, and counter service, during a specific work shift

shift log a record of critical information about a work shift completed by its manager for use by the manager of the next shift

short-order food items food products that require only limited production equipment, food ingredients, and cooking experience to produce

shoulder season (timeshare) the period of time (season) between high and low seasons

site visit a trip to a business location of a prospective employer that allows a prospective job applicant to learn firsthand about the potential employer

skilled nursing care (senior living and care option) a long-term care option that provides specialized care for persons with mental or physical disabilities, including those who are bedridden and who are in need of significant assistance with daily activities

sleeping room a lodging alternative of basic sleeping accommodations with or without private restroom facilities

slot drop the collection of slot machine coins taken by casino personnel who transport the coins to the casino cage

small business a company that is independently owned or operated, is not dominant in its industry, and that generally has relatively few employees and a low volume of revenue

SMART the tactic of writing objectives that are specific, measurable, achievable, relevant, and time focused

sommelier a service staff member with extensive knowledge about wine, including its storage and wine–food affinities, who advises guests about wine selection, takes wine orders, and presents and serves selected wines to guests; also called *wine steward*

sous chef the first assistant to the chef

span of control the number of employees supervised by one person; also called *span of management*

special event an activity, program, or occasion that represents a memorable experience that requires an unusual degree of planning and creativity

special events management the profession that plans and manages public assemblies for reasons of celebration, entertainment, and education (among other purposes)

sponsorship money, goods, and/or services rendered by an organization in exchange for a return, including public relations, advertising, and/or charitable tax benefits

sports book a casino department that accepts wagers on professional and collegiate sporting events

stadium an outdoor recreational facility

staff positions technical, advisory specialists who provide advice to, but do not make decisions for, those in the chain of command

staffing the basic management activity that involves finding the right people for the job

staffing grid a matrix that helps managers to plan allowable labor hours for specified positions based on estimated revenues to be generated during hours of operation

standard recipes a written explanation specifying exactly how a food or beverage item should be prepared; a standard recipe lists the quantity of each required ingredient, preparation techniques, portion size and portion tools, and other information required to assure that the item is always prepared the same way

standing committee (private club) a permanent committee that provides advice to the board of directors about matters within the area of their assigned responsibilities

stateroom a guest room on a cruise ship; also called *cabin*

static floor plan a schematic of exhibit space used by a show sponsor each time space in the same facility is utilized

steward an employee responsible for washing pots, pans, and dishes and for cleaning the facility in a food and beverage operation

stock purchase plan an employee benefit that provides low- or no-cost partial ownership (stock) in an organization as an incentive for successful and continuing performance

stockout the condition that arises when a food or beverage item needed for production is not available on-site because it is not in inventory

storing the process of holding products under optimal storage conditions until they are needed for production

straight-line serving line a traditional cafeteria line in which guests move down a serving line, selecting all components of their meal

subcontract a contract under a contract: a person may contract with someone else who, in turn, contracts with a third party to perform part of the contract's obligation

subordinate a person whose work is directly overseen by a supervisor or manager

subsidy funds provided by an organization in support of its foodservice program

suggestive selling the process by which servers indicate menu items to guests that are preferred because of popularity and or profitability factors

suite a hotel guest room in which the living area is separated from the sleeping area

superordinate a person who directs the work of others; one's superordinate is his or her boss

supervisor a staff member who directs the work of line-level employees

support center a nonrevenue-generating department that is necessary to assist (support) revenue centers; two examples in a casino are the human resources and security departments

surplus the amount of revenues that remain after all costs allocated to the noncommercial foodservice program have been paid; called *profit* in commercial foodservices

sustainability the concept that the needs of today's population can be provided for without damaging the ability of future generations to meet their needs

table d'hôte (menu selections) a menu in which food items making up the entire meal are sold at a fixed price

table games games of chance involving wagering between the casino and its customers

table turns the number of times a dining table is used during one dining period

take-out service (foodservice) a dining option in which a guest calls, faxes, or e-mails an order to a restaurant and then goes to the property to pick it up

teleconferencing the conduct of meetings by using audio and visual communication technology to link persons in different locations

temperature danger zone the temperature at which microorganisms causing food-borne illness most quickly multiply (approximately 41°F to 135°F)

terrorism the threat of danger created and harm caused by persons for political or religious reasons

theft to steal all of something at one time

theme park a large recreational destination site that creates an atmosphere and environment of another place and time, enclosed in a central area with an admission price paid at the gate that allows visitors access to all attractions

three-martini lunch a phrase referring to the (sometimes excessive) consumption of alcoholic beverages by business persons during the work day

timeshare a lodging property that sells its rooms to guests for use during a specific time period each year; also called *vacation ownership property*

timeshare properties lodging properties selling a part ownership (for example, one week within a specified time period) in a unit within the property; also called *interval ownership*

timeshare sales manager the condominium manager with responsibility for selling timeshare ownership in the property

trade association a group of persons who affiliate because of common business and/or industry concerns

trade show an industry-specific event that enables suppliers to an industry to interact with, educate, and sell to individuals and businesses that are part of the industry; also called *exhibition*

traffic the guests and/or employees who occupy or move within a specified area

transient (type of hotel guest) a guest who is not part of a group; transient guests can be further subdivided by traveler demographic to gain more detailed information about the type of guests staying at a property

transnational a company with its headquarters in one country but with company operations in several (or more) other countries

travel agent a person or company (travel agency) that sells travel products and services to the public and is compensated for this service by fees charged to the buyer and/or by commissions paid by the travel supplier

travel and tourism industry   refers to all businesses that cater to the needs of the traveling public

tray cards   a card placed on a tray assembly line that indicates for each patient or resident (with room number) food items to be placed on the tray or plate; also called tray *ticket*

turnover rate   a measure of the proportion of a work force that is replaced during a designated time period (for example, month, quarter, year); it can be calculated as number of employees separated ÷ number of employees in the work force = turnover rate

turns   the total number of guests served during a meal period divided by the number of seats in a restaurant; a 150-seat restaurant serving 425 guests during a meal period has a turn of 2.83 (425 ÷ 150)

unit   one property in a multiunit (chain) organization; sometimes called *store* or *outlet*

unity of command   the organizing principle that states that each employee should report to or be accountable to only one boss for a specific activity

universal criteria   guidelines that conference center facilities must meet to receive IACC membership

unscheduled time   time during a meeting when no events or activities are planned; this represents the attendees' personal time

upscale full-service hotel   a lodging property offering the amenities of midscale hotels and additional services, such as a gift shop, concierge, exercise facility, high-speed Internet access, and numerous guest services

upscale limited-service hotel   a hotel within the limited-service segment that offers a wide range of property and within-room amenities designed to provide high levels of comfort, convenience, and elegance to its guests

upscale (high check average) restaurant   a food-service operation that provides very high quality food and beverage products served at a very high standard of service with appropriate tabletop appointments in a tasteful environment; also called *fine dining, white tablecloth restaurant,* or *high-check-average restaurant*

upselling (food server)   information suggested by an order taker (in a room-service operation) or by a server (in an a la carte dining operation) designed to encourage guests to purchase items they might otherwise not have ordered

use-by date   date (time) by which a food product must be removed from inventory and be produced or sold or, alternatively, be discarded

value (menu item)   the guest's perception of the selling price of a menu item relative to the quality of the menu item, service, and dining experience

value (procurement)   the relationship between price paid to a supplier and the quality of product, supplier information, and service received

vaudeville   a theater show with a variety of short acts, including songs, dances, minstrel, actors, stand-up comedy, juggling, and other light entertainment geared to a general audience

vending services   services in which food, beverage, and/or products are dispensed to consumers by vending machines

VIP   short for *very important person* (guest); used to identify guests who should receive special treatment or attention during their visit

vision   an abstract idea about what the hospitality operation would be like if it was ideal

wager   to pledge (promise) something as the result of an event for which the outcome is unknown; also called *bet*

walk guest   a guest with a reservation who is relocated from the hotel where a room reservation was made to another hotel because no room is available

walk-in guest   a guest desiring a room who arrives at the hotel without a reservation

way finding   a term used in the amusement and theme park industry that refers to pedestrian and service, security, and emergency vehicle traffic flow throughout the park

word-of-mouth advertising   informal conversations between persons as they discuss their positive or negative experiences when visiting a hospitality operation

working capital   current assets minus current liabilities; the amount of cash (or other resources that can quickly be converted to cash) that can be used to purchase necessary products and services

"wow" factor   the feeling guests have when they receive or experience an unanticipated extra as they interact with the hospitality operation

yield management   demand forecasting systems designed to maximize revenue by holding rates high during times of high guest room demand and by decreasing room rates when demand is lower

zero defects   a goal of no guest-related complaints that is established when guest service processes are implemented

Index

PHOTO CREDITS

pp. 1, 11 (bottom): Peter Arnold, Inc., Oldrich Karasek photographer
p. 3: Stephen Whitehorn © Dorling Kindersley
p. 5: Linda Whitwam © Dorling Kindersley
p. 8 (top): National Motor Museum Beaulieu, Dorling Kindersley Media Library, Dave King photographer
p. 8 (bottom): Corbis Digital Stock
p. 11 (top): Index Stock Imagery Inc., Ron Strange photographer
p. 12 (top): Getty Images, Inc., Photodisc, Rob Melnychuk photographer
p. 12 (bottom): The Store24 Companies Inc.
p. 13 (top): Getty Images, Inc.-Photodisc, Jack Hollingsworth photographer
p. 13 (bottom): Getty Images-Photodisc, EyeWire Collection
p. 20: PhotoEdit, Jeff Greenberg photographer
p. 22: George Goodwin, Color-Pic, Inc.
p. 24: AP/Wide World Photos
p. 25: Getty Images Inc.-Image Bank, AJA Productions
p. 26: PhotoEdit, Frank Siteman photographer
p. 28: Getty Images-Photodisc, EyeWire Collection
p. 31: Hoechst-Celanese Corp.
p. 33: Gary Ombler © Dorling Kindersley
p. 34: Getty Images Inc.-Image Bank, David de Lossy, Ghislain & Marie
p. 38: Allyn & Bacon, John Coletti photographer
p. 40: Allyn & Bacon, John Coletti photographer
p. 41: PhotoEdit, Tony Freeman, photographer
p. 42: Mike Dunning © Dorling Kindersley
p. 45: Omni-Photo Communications, Inc., Esbin/Anderson
p. 46: Corbis-Stock Market, Rob Lewine photographer
p. 47: Mark Hamilton © Dorling Kindersley
p. 49: David Young-Wolff PhotoEdit
p. 51: Stock Boston, Richard Pasley photographer
p. 52: Pearson Education/PH College, Vincent P. Walter photographer
p. 57, 166: Courtesy of Marriott Bay Point Resort Village
p. 59: Fredrik and Laurence Arvidsson © Dorling Kindersley, Courtesy of Cidade de Goa Beach Resort
p. 64 (top): Getty Images, Inc.-Photodisc, Steve Mason photographer
p. 64 (bottom): Getty Images, Inc.-Photodisc Javier Pierini photographer
p. 66: PhotoEdit, Jeff Greenberg photographer
p. 69: Rob Reichenfeld © Dorling Kindersley
p. 70: Linda Whitwam © Dorling Kindersley
p. 72: Peter Wilson © Dorling Kindersley
p. 73: Michael Moran © Dorling Kindersley
p. 74: PhotoEdit, Deborah Davis photographer
p. 75: Getty Images, Inc.-Photodisc, Jack Hollingsworth photographer
p. 77: Russell MacMasters © Dorling Kindersley, Courtesy of the Bellagio Hotel, Las Vegas
p. 81: Hyatt Corporation
p. 83: Getty Images/Time Life Pictures, Jan Staller photographer
p. 85: © Dorling Kindersley, Courtesy of the Hotel Bellagio, Las Vegas
p. 86: © Dorling Kindersley
p. 88: © Dorling Kindersley
p. 89: Getty Images, Inc.-Photodisc, Rob Melnychuk photographer
p. 91: Stock Boston, Richard Pasley photographer
p. 94: Demetrio Carrasco © Dorling Kindersley
p. 95: PhotoEdit, Michael Newman photographer
p. 102: Quality International
p. 104: Getty Images, Inc.-Photodisc, Ryan McVay photographer

p. 105: Choice Hotels International Inc.
p. 106: Getty Images, Inc.-Photodisc, Janis Christie photographer
p. 107: Nigel Hicks © Dorling Kindersley
p. 108: Pearson Education/PH College, Frank LaBua photographer
p. 110: Getty Images-Photodis, EyeWire Collection
p. 111 (top): John Serafin
p. 111 (bottom): Getty Images-Photodisc, EyeWire Collection
p. 117: Getty Images, Inc.- Photodisc, Rob Melnychuk photographer
p. 119: Reuben Paris © Dorling Kindersley
p. 120: Allyn & Bacon, John Coletti photographer
p. 125: PhotoEdit, Michael Newman photographer
p. 126: Getty Images-Photodisc, EyeWire Collection
p. 128 (top): Getty Images, Inc.-Photodisc, Keith Brofsky
p. 128 (bottom): PhotoEdit, Myrleen Ferguson photographer
p. 132: Alan Keohane © Dorling Kindersley
p. 134: PhotoEdit, A. Ramey, photographer
p. 135: PhotoEdit, Amy Etra photographer
p. 136: Pearson Education Corporate Digital Archive, G. Huntington photographer
p. 139: Scenics of America, PhotoLink, Getty Images, Inc.-Photodisc
p. 141: Demetrio Carrasco © Dorling Kindersley
p. 142: PhotoEdit, Jeff Greenberg photographer
p. 143: Silver Burdett Ginn
p. 144: PhotoEdit, David Young-Wolff photographer
p. 150: Roger de la Harpe © Dorling Kindersley
p. 152: PhotoEdit, Jeff Greenberg photographer
p. 154: Dave King © Dorling Kindersley
p. 157: Alan Keohane © Dorling Kindersley
p. 159: Richard Pasley Photography, Richard Pasley photographer
p. 161: Getty Images Inc.-Stone Allstock, Ken Fisher photographer
p. 165: Getty Images-Photodisc, EyeWire Collection
p. 167: Hammond Indiana Times
p. 168: ImageState/International Stock Photography Ltd., Pictor photographer
pp. 173, 200: Gerald Lopez © Dorling Kindersley
p. 175: PhotoLibrary.com, Roel Loopers photographer
p. 178: Shaen Adey © Dorling Kindersley
p. 180: PhotoEdit Inc., Robert Brenner photographer
p. 181: Getty Images, Inc.-Photodisc, Steve Mason photographer
p. 184: Getty Images, Inc.-Photodisc, Robert Koene photographer
p. 186 (top): Vincent P. Walter, Pearson Education, PH College
p. 186 (bottom): PhotoEdit, Jeff Greenberg photographer
p. 187 (top): Nigel Hicks © Dorling Kindersley
p. 187 (bottom): Getty Images, Inc.-Photodisc
p. 189: Francesca Yorke © Dorling Kindersley. Courtesy of the Coyote Cafe, Santa Fe
p. 194: Stock Boston, Richard Pasley
p. 197: Silver Burdett Ginn
p. 199: Pia Tryde © Dorling Kindersley
p. 202: Getty Images, Inc.-Photodisc, Skip Nall photographer
p. 203 (top): Getty Images, Inc.-Photodisc, Rob Melnychuk photographer
p. 203 (bottom): Getty Images, Inc.-Photodisc, Ryan McVay photographer
p. 205: Getty Images, Inc.-Photodisc, EyeWire Collection
p. 207 (top): Getty Images, Inc.-Photodisc, Rob Melnychuk photographer
p. 207 (bottom): Dorota and Mariusz Jarymowicz © Dorling Kindersley
p. 212: Demetrio Carrasco © Dorling Kindersley
p. 214: Getty Images, Inc.-Photodisc, EyeWire Collection
p. 217: Stephen Hayward © Dorling Kindersley
p. 218: Getty Images, Inc.-Photodisc, Steve Mason photographer

678

p. 219: Lallo Communications, Ed Lallo photographer

p. 220 (top): Aurora & Quanta Productions Inc., Peter Essick photographer

p. 220 (bottom): Max Alexander © Dorling Kindersley

p. 222 (top): Ian O'Leary © Dorling Kindersley

p. 222 (bottom): Corbis/Stock Market, Joe Baraban photographer

p. 226: Stephen Whitehorn © Dorling Kindersley

p. 228: PhotoEdit, Myrleen Ferguson photographer

p. 229: Linda Whitwam © Dorling Kindersley

p. 230 (top): Corbis/Stock Market, Jose Luis Pelaez, Inc.

p. 230 (bottom): Courtesy of Outback Steakhouse, Inc.

p. 232: Pearson Education/PH College, Laima Druskis photographer

p. 234: Getty Images, Inc.-Photodisc, EyeWire Collection

p. 235: Getty Images, Inc.-Photodisc, Rob Melnychuk photographer

p. 237: Index Stock Imagery, Inc., Ken Glaser photographer

p. 241: International House of Pancakes Restaurant

p. 243: PhotoEdit, Michael Newman photographer

p. 244: PhotoEdit, Mary Kate Denny photographer

p. 245: Pearson Education/PH College, Vincent P. Walter photographer

p. 248: PhotoEdit, Mary Kate Denny, photographer

p. 249: Pearson Education/PH College, Vincent P. Walter photographer

p. 250: Getty Images, Inc.-Photodisc, Steve Mason photographer

p. 251: PhotoEdit, Michael Newman photographer

p. 252: Index Stock Imagery, Inc., Stephen Collector photographer

p. 256: Demetrio Carrasco © Dorling Kindersley

p. 261: PhotoEdit, David Young-Wolff photographer

p. 262: Brucker Enterprises, Inc., Franchise of Burger King

p. 263 (top) Getty Images Inc.-Liaison, Tim Wright photographer

p. 263 (bottom): PhotoEdit, Wolfgang Spunbarg photographer

p. 265: PhotoEdit, Spencer Grant photographer

p. 268: Getty Images Inc.-Photodisc, Kim Steele photographer

p. 268: AP/Wide World Photos

p. 274: PhotoEdit, Jeff Greenberg photographer

p. 277: Pearson Education/PH College, Vincent P. Walter photographer

p. 279 (top): Alan Keohane © Dorling Kindersley

p. 279 (bottom): Stephen Hayward © Dorling Kindersley

p. 281: Getty Images, Inc.-Photodisc, Geostock

p. 284: Getty Images, Inc.-Photodisc, Ryan McVay photographer

p. 285: Pearson Education/PH College, Laima Druskis photographer

p. 287: Corbis/Stock Market, Rob Lewine photographer

p. 290: PhotoEdit, Tom McCarthy photographer

p. 291: AP/Wide World Photos

pp. 297 and 330: PhotoEdit, Inc., Richard Hutchings photographer

p. 299: Pearson Education/PH College, Laima Druskis photographer

p. 301: Pearson Education/PH College, Michal Heron photographer

p. 303: Pearson Education/PH College, Michal Heron photographer

p. 304: Getty Images, Inc.-Photodisc, Ryan McVay photographer

p. 306 (top): Pearson Education/PH College

p. 306 (bottom): Pearson Education/PH College, Brady photographer

p. 307: Bruce Forster © Dorling Kindersley

p. 309: Omni-Photo Communications, Inc., Frank Siteman photographer

p. 310: Pearson Education/PH College, Michal Heron photographer

p. 317: Pearson Education/PH College, Laima Druskis photographer

p. 320: PhotoEdit, Mary Kate Denny photographer

p. 322: PhotoEdit, Spencer Grant photographer

p. 323: PhotoEdit, Dennis MacDonald photographer

p. 325: PhotoEdit, Michelle Bridwell photographer

p. 329: Comstock Royalty Free Division

p. 331: Pearson Education/PH College, Laima Druskis photographer

p. 333: Pearson Education/PH College, Vincent P. Walter photographer

p. 338: © Dorling Kindersley Media Library. Courtesy of FSTOP Pte. Ltd., Singapore

p. 341: PhotoEdit, David Kelly Crow photographer

p. 342: Pearson Learning Photo Studio, David Mager photographer

p. 346: PhotoEdit, Michael Newman photographer

p. 348: Pearson Education/PH College, Michal Heron photographer

p. 353: Getty Images, Inc.-Photodisc, Keith Brofsky

p. 354: Pearson Education/PH College, Ron May photographer

p. 358: AP/Wide World Photos

p. 360: Pearson Education/PH College, Marc Anderson

p. 361: Pearson Education/PH College

p. 362: SuperStock, Inc.

p. 366: Getty Images, Inc.-Photodisc, EyeWire Collection

p. 367 (top) Reuters/Yun Suk-Bong, Corbis, Reuters America

p. 367 (bottom): Getty Images Inc.-Image Bank, G & M David de Lossy, photographers

p. 368: PhotoEdit, Michael Newman photographer

p. 370: PhotoEdit, Mark Richards photographer

p. 371: Getty Images, Inc.-Taxi, Chris Salvo photographer

p. 376: © Reuters NewMedia Inc./CORBIS

p. 378: United Parcel Service

p. 379: The Image Works, Sonda Dawes photographer

p. 381: PhotoEdit Inc., Michael Newman photographer

p. 382: Getty Images, Inc.-Photodisc, Ryan McVay photographer

p. 385: PhotoEdit, Jonathan Nourok photographer

p. 387: Lawrence Lim © Dorling Kindersley

p. 397, 477: Michael T. Sedam/Corbis/Bettmann. Used by permission from Disney Enterprises, Inc.

p. 399: Shaen Adey © Dorling Kindersley

p. 400: Guy Drayton © Dorling Kindersley

p. 404: Getty Images, Inc.-Taxi, Ron Chapple, photographer

p. 406 (top): Getty Images, Inc.-Photodisc, EyeWire Collection

p. 406 (bottom): PhotoEdit, Tom McCarthy photographer

p. 408: Art Resource, N.Y., Giraudon photographer

p. 409: Getty Images, Inc.-Photodisc, David Buffington photographer

p. 411: Getty Images, Inc.-Photodisc, Keith Brofsky photographer

p. 412: © Dorling Kindersley, Courtesy of the Desert Inn, Las Vegas

p. 413: Getty Images, Inc.-Stone Allstock, Brian Stablyk photographer

p. 417: Peter Wilson © Dorling Kindersley

p. 419: Rob Reichenfeld © Dorling Kindersley

p. 420: Alan Keohane © Dorling Kindersley

p. 422: Chris Stowers © Dorling Kindersley

p. 424: Getty Images Inc.-Stone Allstock, Jonathan Morgan photographer

p. 425: PhotoEdit, Jeff Greenberg photographer

p. 427: Carnival Cruise Lines

p. 428: Omni-Photo Communications, Inc., Jeff Greenberg photographer

p. 430 (top): Getty Images, Inc.-Photodisc, EyeWire Collection

p. 430 (bottom): Holland America Line

p. 435: Alan Keohane © Dorling Kindersley

p. 437 (top): © Dorling Kindersley, Courtesy of the Las Vegas Hilton

p. 437 (bottom): Alan Keohane © Dorling Kindersley

p. 439: PhotoEdit, Bill Bachmann photographer

p. 441: Russell MacMasters © Dorling Kindersley, Courtesy of the Spa Bellagio, Las Vegas

p. 443: Alan Keohane © Dorling Kindersley

p. 444 (top): Getty Images Inc.-Stone Allstock, Joe Polillio photographer

p. 444 (bottom): Getty Images Inc.-Taxi, Daniel Allan photographer

p. 447: © Dorling Kindersley

p. 449: Demetrio Carrasco © Dorling Kindersley, Courtesy of the Spa Bellagio, Las Vegas

p. 454: AP/Wide World Photos

p. 456: AP/Wide World Photos
p. 457: Corbis/Bettmann, S. Carmona photographer
p. 458: PhotoEdit, Michael Newman photographer
p. 459: Getty Images, Inc.-Photodisc, EyeWire Collection
p. 461: Getty Images, Inc.-Stone Allstock, Patrick Ingrand photographer
p. 462: Garry Bickett, New Orleans, Oklahoma City
p. 463: Getty Images, Inc.-Photodisc, EyeWire Collection
p. 464: Getty Images, Inc.-Photodisc, Steve Mason photographer
p. 470: John M. Greim/Creative Eye/MIRA.com. Disney characters © Disney Enterprises, Inc. Used by permission from Disney Enterprises, Inc.
p. 472 (top): A. Ramey/PhotoEdit, Inc. Disney characters © Disney Enterprises, Inc. Used by permission from Disney Enterprises, Inc.
p. 472 (bottom): Tony Freeman/PhotoEdit, Inc. Used by permission from Disney Enterprises, Inc.
p. 474: Paul L. Ruben
p. 475: Dave King © Dorling Kindersley
p. 476: Brent Stirton/Liaison/Getty Images, Inc – Liaison. Disney characters © Disney Enterprises, Inc. Used by permission from Disney Enterprises, Inc.
p. 477: Michael T. Sedam/Corbis/Bettmann. Used by permission from Disney Enterprises, Inc.
p. 481: PhotoEdit, Robert Brenner photographer
p. 482: © Disney Enterprises, Inc.
p. 486: Tony Souter © Dorling Kindersley
p. 488: Chris Stowers © Dorling Kindersley, courtesy of Croce's Jazz Bar
p. 490: Matthew Ward © Dorling Kindersley
p. 491: Rob Reichenfeld © Dorling Kindersley
p. 496: Peter Wilson © Dorling Kindersley
p. 497: © Dorling Kindersley, Courtesy of Stratosphere, Las Vegas
p. 499: © Dorling Kindersley, Courtesy of EFX, Las Vegas
p. 500: © Dorling Kindersley
pp. 507, 531: PhotoEdit, David Young-Wolff photographer
p. 509: Allyn & Bacon, John Coletti photographer
p. 512: Getty Images, Inc.-Photodisc, EyeWire Collection
p. 513: SuperStock, Inc.
p. 516: Getty Images, Inc.-Image Bank, Larry Dale Gordon photographer
p. 518: Pearson Education/PH College, S. M. Wakefield photographer
p. 519: AP/Wide World Photos
p. 520: Getty Images Inc.-Image Bank, Britt Erlanson photographer
p. 521: Getty Images Inc.-Photodisc, EyeWire Collection
p. 524: Damian Dovarganes, AP/Wide World Photos
p. 529: PhotoEdit Inc., Mark Richards photographer
p. 533: AP/Wide World Photos
p. 534: Demetrio Carrasco © Dorling Kindersley
p. 536 (top): AP/Wide World Photos
p. 536 (bottom): Jeff Greenberg, PhotoEdit
p. 537 (top): Honeywell Aerospace
p. 537 (bottom): PhotoEdit, A. Ramey photographer
p. 540 (top): Richard Leeney © Dorling Kindersley
p. 540 (bottom): Pearson Education/PH College, Laima Druskis photographer
p. 546: PhotoEdit, Robert Ginn photographer
p. 549: Stephen Whitehorn © Dorling Kindersley
p. 550: AP/Wide World Photos

p. 551: PhotoEdit, Mary Kate Denny photographer
p. 552 (top): Getty Images, Inc.-Photodisc, EyeWire Collection
p. 552 (bottom): Scott Pitts © Dorling Kindersley
p. 553 (bottom): Index Stock Imagery, Inc., Spencer Grant photographer
p. 556 (top): PhotoEdit, Bill Aron photographer
p. 556 (bottom): Dave King © Dorling Kindersley
p. 563, 596 (top): Walter Hodges, Getty Images Inc., Stone Allstock
p. 565: Pearson Education/PH College, Laima Druskis photographer
p. 567: Pearson Education/PH College, Laima Druskis photographer
p. 569: Walter Hodges, Getty Images Inc.–Stock Allstock
p. 570: Getty Images, Inc.-Image Bank, Romilly Lockyer photographer
p. 571: PhotoEdit, Gary Conner photographer
p. 572: Getty Images, Inc.-Image Bank, Color Day Production
p. 573: Stock Boston, John Coletti photographer
p. 575: Getty Images, Inc.-Stone Allstock, David Leach photographer
p. 578: Getty Images, Inc.-Photodisc, EyeWire Collection
p. 583: PhotoEdit, Dennis MacDonald photographer
p. 586 (top): PhotoEdit, Robin L. Sachs photographer
p. 586 (bottom): © Dorling Kindersley
p. 588: Pearson Learning Photo Studio, David Mager photographer
p. 590: Pearson Education/PH College, Laima Druskis photographer
p. 592: AP/Wide World Photos
p. 596 (bottom): Mark Hamilton © Dorling Kindersley
p. 605: © Dorling Kindersley
p. 610: Index Stock Imagery, Inc., Michael Paras photographer
p. 611 (top): PhotoEdit, Michael Newman photographer
p. 611 (bottom): Getty Images Inc.-Allsport Photography, Clive Brunskill photographer
p. 613: Keith Brofsky, Getty Images, Inc.–Photodisc
p. 615: PhotoEdit, Michael Newman photographer
p. 616: PhotoEdit, Michael Newman photographer
p. 617: Corbis/Stock Market, David Stoecklein photographer
p. 622: PhotoEdit, Jose Carrillo photographer
p. 625: Getty Images Inc.-Photodisc, EyeWire Collection
p. 627: © Dorling Kindersley
p. 629 (top): Getty Images, Inc.-Photodisc, David Hiller photographer
p. 629 (bottom): Shotgun, Michael Mitchell Photographic Works
p. 630: Linda Whitwam © Dorling Kindersley
p. 631: PhotoEdit, Spencer Grant photographer
p. 632: Getty Images Inc.-Image Bank, Marc Romanelli photographer
p. 633: Getty Images, Inc.-Photodisc, EyeWire Collection
p. 635: Getty Images, Inc.-Photodisc, EyeWire Collection
p. 639: Getty Images, Inc.-Taxi, Ron Chapple photographer
p. 641 (top): Chris Stowers © Dorling Kindersley
p. 641 (bottom): Stephen Whitehorn © Dorling Kindersley
p. 643: Getty Images Inc.-Photodisc, Ken Usami photographer
p. 644: AP/Wide World Photos
p. 646: The Image Works, F. Pedrick, photographer
p. 647: Getty Images Inc.-Image Bank, David W. Hamilton photographer
p. 649 (top): Stephen Whitehorn © Dorling Kindersley
p. 649 (bottom): Getty Images Inc.-Stone Allstock, Doug Armand photographer

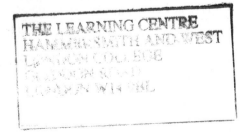